DADI JANKI

A Century of Service

by Liz Hodgkinson

BRAHMA KUMARIS
WORLD SPIRITUAL UNIVERSITY (UK)

BKIS

A Century of Service
By Liz Hodgkinson

Copyright © 2015 BKIS Publications, London

PRINT ISBN   978-1-886872-76-9
KINDLE ISBN   978-1-886872-77-6
EPUB ISBN   978-1-886872-78-3

First published in 2015 by Brahma Kumaris Information Services Ltd,
Global Co-operation House, 65 Pound Lane, London, NW10 2HH

Website: www.inspiredstillness.com
E-mail: hello@inspiredstillness.com

Cover designed by Alex Williams
Layout by Samir Patra
Printed by Imprint Digital Limited

CONTENTS

Dadi Janki being welcomed at the Global Retreat Centre, Oxford 1993

PREFACE

by Sister Jayanti

For more than 30 years, Liz Hodgkinson has had an unusual relationship with Dadi Janki and the Brahma Kumaris. She first came into contact in 1981 with her journalist husband, Neville, while writing an article on Raja Yoga meditation for SHE magazine. Though not attracted by meditation as such, she became interested in the teachings and over the years found benefit in applying many of them in her own life. She has also written several books with spiritually oriented themes, including *Peace and Purity*, a history of the BKs.

Neville and Liz separated after their sons, Tom and Will, had grown up and while Liz continued working as a highly successful author and journalist, in 1994 Neville left full-time journalism to live and work at the BK retreat centre near Oxford.

Liz's continuing engagement with worldly matters has made her the ideal author of this biography of Dadi

Janki. It focuses on Dadi's extraordinary achievement in carrying the BK teachings outside India, to establish the Brahma Kumaris as a significant global movement. This is not an official biography, but an affectionate and personal account based on a 30-year friendship. Liz particularly resonates with Dadi's strength of purpose and will, and her passion for women's empowerment. The book also illuminates Dadi's capacity to bring out specialities and qualities in others that they do not even know they have in themselves.

Liz draws on the stories of many BKs who have worked and studied closely with Dadi - including myself - to give a highly readable account of a remarkable soul.

INTRODUCTION

If an elderly Indian lady who can't speak English, and who has no money, no home and no education, can acquire an English stately home – well, anything is possible.

DADI JANKI

It was in this stately home, now a Brahma Kumaris residential retreat centre just outside Oxford, that I last met Dadi Janki, on 21st May 2015.

A number of delegates were there for a dialogue known as Call of the Time, where people from all over the world gather to discuss matters of current world concern from a spiritual perspective. Dadi Janki was expected at around 1pm to head up this two-day meeting, and there was great excitement and anticipation of her arrival.

Would she make it? For Dadi is always in great demand and although she tries to fulfill those demands, at the age of 99 and a half, her poor old body is constantly in danger of packing up completely.

Not that she lets that stop her. She had flown into London from India about a week previously to begin a packed schedule of events, which included flying to the US, as well as travelling round the UK. I had driven to the retreat centre in the hope of having what might be one final glimpse, although it was not likely with so many people clamouring for her attention, that she would make any special time for me.

I was wrong. A few minutes after she arrived from London, there came the message: she wants to see Liz.

Dadi is not one to be disobeyed so I hurried from the dining room where I was just finishing lunch, to the reception area which was full of white-clad yogis sitting on the floor. Dadi, hunched up in a chair, was also swathed in white and was smiling benignly at the assembled throng.

Already – and she had only been there a few minutes – a potent aura of peace, love and calm had been created. I crept in at the back and she complained that she couldn't see me. 'Here I am, Dadi!' I said, moving nearer to her.

After receiving a holy sweet known as *toli*, from Dadi, the group dispersed and I learned that I was to have a private audience with her. She rose up with great difficulty, helped by her two full-time carers and made her way to her own room which was again, all white.

When Dadi stands up, it is revealed just how tiny and frail she is. She can hardly walk and has to be taken everywhere by her carers. However, her mind is as sharp as ever and during the hour of our meeting, we talked about the book I had been writing about her.

'Are you finding it easy?' she asked.

'No, Dadi, I am not,' I replied. 'I am having to try and describe how you have achieved so much, and it has not been a simple job.'

She looked astonished. 'But I have done nothing,' she said.

'You've only started a major spiritual movement in the West from scratch,' I reminded her.

She pointed upwards. 'It was God who did everything. I was only the instrument.'

As we chatted, Dadi said that she had never been like other girls, as from the age of about two, she had experienced a powerful connection with God. Nearly a century later, that connection is as strong as ever and has enabled her, she would say, to achieve the impossible.

I have known Dadi for more than 30 years but this time, I experienced a new, even physical, intimacy and closeness as we hugged each other. In the past, I have to say, I have been much in awe of her but this time, any remaining barriers were broken down completely. Dadi has a unique ability to make everybody who comes in front of her feel special, and this time I felt I truly connected with her.

For I, you might say, was chosen as the 'instrument' to write the definitive book about her, and that meant I had to establish a close rapport with my subject. Nearing the end of my task, I finally felt that I had done so.

Perhaps, for her part, she has sprinkled the book with some gold dust. I can only hope so, and also hope that I have been able to do her justice.

For this little old lady who can now hardly walk or talk has been responsible for starting a major spiritual movement in the Western world, for persuading hundreds of thousands of people to study and take up the unusual practice she introduced to the West, of Raja Yoga.

Dadi even captured my own husband, which makes my relationship to her even more poignant. I often tell people that he left me for a woman thirty years older.

And our son Will has written a book, *The House is Full of Yogis*, which tells the story of how his father gradually became an adherent to the teachings of an austere, uncompromising Indian spiritual movement led by women. The rest of the family did not become BKs, although we are all close, and lost in admiration of what Dadi Janki has achieved.

There is no doubt that I was sitting in front of a very unusual woman, somebody who has had a profound effect on my own family, and who can be considered one of the great spiritual leaders of our time. Yet for all her success in foreign lands, she remains largely incognito. Dadi, who herself lives a life of extreme discipline and asceticism, has inspired many thousands of Westerners to relinquish their creature comforts, take up their beds, as it were, and follow her example.

When you meet her or come in front of her, Dadi Janki seems serene and happy, always smiling and pressing gifts into your hand. But it has not been easy to introduce the secular and cynical West to this movement.

In answer to the question as to what she felt she has achieved, she said that the message she had to impart was so important that it had to be heard all over the world and not just confined to India. But would any Westerners be interested in what she had to say? That, she said, was her major challenge.

Crossing the cultural and religious barriers was by no means straightforward, but she persisted and gradually gained adherents. When I asked how she had chosen her first Western disciples, she said she had to ask herself whether they were able to live the simple life. 'When people understand the difference between the material world and the spiritual world, they become interested in the message,' she said. 'I had faith that the early Westerners who came to classes and meditation sessions could understand the teachings and as such, could be instruments to share them with others.

'When the heart is honest,' Dadi said, 'the Lord helps.'

She was right. The first Westerners to come and hear Dadi's message in a tiny little flat in London had the courage, faith and inspiration to take the teachings into all parts of the world, so that there are now BK centres in over 120 countries and in just about every major city. 'I saw them as God's children,' Dadi said, 'rather than Westerners, or even as men or women. But I did wonder at first how it might be possible for people of all faiths and backgrounds to accept these teachings.'

Exactly what these teachings were, who precisely Dadi Janki is and how she achieved what might be considered the impossible, will be examined in this book. One true miracle is that I was able to meet her at all, as she had been quite literally on death's door in India, where she has been based since 2005, when she became worldwide head of the BKs at the age of 91.

Her doctors there had not expected her to survive her latest bout of severe illness and at times, this most stoical of humans had been screaming out in pain. She had to be airlifted to hospital, was for a time on an intravenous drip and as a result, almost hourly bulletins were circulated to all the world's centres, so that they could prepare themselves for what seemed inevitable.

And yet, against all the odds, she rallied round and survived, reviving enough to take two arduous flights to Heathrow, one in January 2015 and the next in May. These days, Dadi travels first-class, her fare paid for by a benefactor, but she still has to get to and from the airport and on and off the plane.

Among the people pleased to meet her in London was His Royal Highness The Prince of Wales and at very short notice, a meeting was arranged at Clarence House. It was not an easy task, not only because The Prince himself has such a busy schedule, worked out months in advance and with back-to-back meetings, but also because Dadi can hardly walk and might collapse at any moment. So the logistics of getting the two together needed, as Dadi might put it, much help from Him up above.

Him up above obliged and the meeting took place. The Prince himself is not without courage, and Dadi has long admired the way he has stood up to criticism and battled on. Although born into a royal family and often treated with courtly deference wherever he goes, he has also had to face many adverse and even vicious comments on what he has tried to achieve. His strong beliefs have always resonated with Dadi and this was their third meeting, a true meeting of minds and hearts.

As for me, I was left with the daunting task to trying to get to the heart of the mystery that is Dadi Janki. ✲

Dadi Janki addressing the Plenary at the UN Conference on Habitat 1 Earth Summit 1996 Istanbul

CHAPTER ONE

Dadi Janki comes in London

In April 1974, a 58-year-old Indian lady arrived in London with a seemingly simple message: to impart the true word of God to the West. She was under five foot tall, uneducated, spoke no English, had nowhere to live and no money. She had never been out of India before and in addition, she was in very poor health, with a lifelong history of serious illness.

She slipped in almost without being noticed, and yet there was something in the timing of her coming which meant that the way had been prepared, as it were, by a wave of Indian gurus who arrived in the West during the 1960s and 70s imparting ancient Eastern wisdom, and who had already made a huge impact on Western thinking.

Dadi Janki came to England at a time when Westerners were just getting used to Indian gurus teaching the previously unknown disciplines of meditation and yoga, and the equally strange concepts – to Western minds – of karma and reincarnation.

This was the era of the 'me' generation, a time when hordes of young people, disillusioned with traditional religion and political systems, were in search of mind-altering experiences, personal growth, new ways of raising consciousness, and of reaching their own potential. These new Indian gurus offered an attractive assemblage of the spirituality and wisdom of the mystic East, often carefully packaged to appeal to cynical and educated – and impressionable - young Westerners. It all tied in with the human potential movement gaining ground in California, and by 1974, many Indian gurus had established firm bases in the West and some were by now attracting huge crowds to their ashrams, retreat centres and temples.

The whole thing had started some 10 years earlier, when Indian gurus – many self-styled but how were Westerners to know the difference? – first started arriving in the West and began imparting a very different kind of spirituality to that of traditional Christianity. The emphasis now was on achieving blissful out- of-the-body experiences through meditation, yoga and chanting. These new Indian teachings were given a huge initial push by the Beatles, arguably the most famous pop group the world had ever known, when they became followers of the Maharishi Mahesh Yogi and began practising the form of meditation he popularised, known as TM, or Transcendental Meditation.

TM was a simplified, secular form of Hinduism which quickly caught on and before long, large numbers of people were meditating for 20 minutes twice a day while repeating their special mantra. Meditation was beginning to replace old-fashioned, and as people were increasingly feeling, largely ineffectual, prayer. Also, as it seemed, this new-fangled meditation was getting results and enabling people to turn inwards, become peaceful, release long-held stress and gain new and startling insights without the use of drugs.

At the same time as the Maharishi was becoming influential in the West, another guru, Swami A.C. Bhaktivedanta Prabhupada, arrived in New York. His teacher in India had instructed him to carry the message of Krishna to the West, and he duly arrived to do so in 1965. He began chanting Hare Krishna, Hare Krishna, in Tompkins Square Park, to anybody who would listen and many who would not. But before long, he had raised enough money to open a storefront temple which became known as the International Society for Krishna Consciousness (ISKON).

Once again, the movement quickly grew and hordes of young Western seekers began worshipping at the Krishna temples. This movement was very different from TM in that it included song, dance, incense and flowers rather than the strictly practical, no-nonsense type of meditation developed by the Maharishi. The Krishna movement soon crossed the Atlantic and Londoners became used to seeing groups of devotees walking down Oxford Street in London in their orange robes and with shaven heads, chanting Hare Krishna. Krishna temples also offered free vegetarian meals – and introduced a whole generation to vegetarian cuisine.

ISKON was from the start one of the more 'showbizzy' Eastern movements, and attracted many Hollywood stars. It based its teachings on the Bhagavad-Gita, the most famous of all Hindu scriptures. The movement encouraged members to be continent sexually, to be vegetarian and to abstain from alcohol. Communion with the Supreme Spirit was seen as the whole point of yoga and the Society, seeing itself as Godly and spiritual, looked askance on the fast-growing popularity of physical, or, Hatha, Yoga as just another form of keep fit.

By this time, an organisation known as the School of Economic Science – nothing to do with the London School of Economics – had adopted many of the ideas of Maharishi Mahesh Yogi and was holding courses based on traditional Hinduism in London. The founder of the school, Leon McLaren, first met the Maharishi in 1959 when he was in London promoting TM. McLaren was mightily impressed and went to India to meet the Maharishi's own guru, Shantananda Saraswati. He then devised a philosophy which he called 'unity in diversity' – a merger of Eastern philosophy and Western wisdom.

Since the 1960s, the SES has been teaching advaita vedanta, an Indian concept of 'pure consciousness' which is the non-material essence of every being. Obviously some of these teachings and concepts are very complicated and require a different mindset from standard Western thinking to be appreciated and understood. Many Eastern explanations of our origins and purpose in the world fly in the face of both traditional ideas of creation and also the newer theories of evolution. As such, they are easy to dismiss as cranky, and many of the Indian gurus of the 1960s and 70s were dismissed as charlatans and fakes.

Some of course, were. Journalist Ellen Jameson writes in her memoir *Making God Laugh* about the guru whose 'Knowledge' she sought:

> *'He was undoubtedly a self-promoter who persuaded followers to hand over their life savings to his religious order while he enjoyed a life of fabulous wealth in the United States. There he was chauffeured around in a Rolls-Royce, wearing priceless jewellery and was venerated by the poor, trusting disciples to whom he had promised spiritual enlightenment.'*

Even so, the influx continued, and their influence steadily grew. Others arrived, such as the boy wonder, Guru Maharaj Ji, who came to America in 1971 with his Divine Light Mission. His meteoric rise was followed by a similarly meteoric crash and huge debts but even so, he became world famous, and familiarised people yet further with the basic concepts of Indian spirituality.

Another guru who attracted many Westerners, some of extremely high standing, was Bhagwan Shree Rajneesh. His movement fell into disarray when the ashram moved from Pune, India, leaving unpaid debts, and set up camp at Antelope, Oregon, where members proceeded to try and poison the townsfolk with salmonella in order to gain votes on the local council. The discredited guru, once worshipped by many followers, renamed himself Osho, Japanese for friend. The movement continues today, though in a vastly lower key from its heyday, and very many people believe that Osho, in spite of all his faults, ego and greed, had startling insights which remain relevant today.

There is no doubt that Osho, who died in 1990, was a remarkable man. A former lecturer in philosophy, he set himself up as a religious leader in Mumbai in the late 1960s, when students began to flock round him to hear what he had to say. In the early days all his followers were Indians but before long he began to attract many Westerners as well.

His message was certainly revolutionary for the time, especially for young Indians, as he was telling them to go out and enjoy sex with as many partners as possible. He also preached that true spirituality could come through the orgasm, echoing the work of Wilhelm Reich, a pupil of Freud. Osho was very well read in the Californian human potential movement, and felt that ancient spirituality and modern psychology could come together in a worldwide movement of sexual freedom, peace, love and enlightenment such as the world had previously never seen.

Although Osho came from a poor family he was a tremendously erudite and learned man who could speed-read up to 16 books a day. His teachings attracted many celebrities of the time. One of his beliefs was that women were burdened and enslaved, rather than liberated, by pregnancy and childrearing and that a large majority of men and women were completely unfit to be parents.

He was also a highly charismatic and beguiling speaker, with huge liquid eyes that held his followers spellbound.

Many of his ideas were new and revolutionary at the time and they acclimatised Westerners still further with elements of ancient Eastern philosophy while giving them a modern twist. One of the most important aspects of Bhagwan's teaching, and one that finds an echo in Dadi Janki's messages, is that women are the absolute equal of men.

This was a complete departure from traditional Indian thinking, which often gave the impression that women were not just inferior to men, they were hardly human beings at all.

Swami Muktananda was another guru who became world famous. He arrived in America in 1970 to launch the Siddha Yoga Dham Movement and by 1976, Siddha Yoga had eighty meditation centres and five ashrams in the US, from where it proceeded to infiltrate the UK. Once again, it soon became highly popular all over the Western world.

Although full-time adherents of Siddha Yoga are celibate, vegetarian, teetotal and rise at dawn to spend an hour in silent meditation, most people who have become interested in Siddha Yoga practise it on a much lighter basis and do not take on board the more ascetic aspects.

Siddha Yoga is based on the teachings of the ancient Siddhis, who were considered to possess supernatural powers, and in many ways the teachings are very traditional Hinduism. Siddha Yoga teaches reincarnation and the transmigration of souls, and there is considerable emphasis on the ability of meditation to reduce stress and become more effective generally. In common with Krishna Consciousness, Siddha Yoga has been derided as a 'Hollywood yoga' and has attracted many stars and celebrities. It can provide a little extra spiritual frisson in life without disturbing the status quo too much.

There were other gurus, too, from Swami Sivananda, to Sri Aurobindo, to Sai Baba, who also became famous in the West at around the same time. All attracted Western followers although not all established ashrams out of India.

By 1974, then, it no longer seemed so peculiar to chant and meditate or to practise the bodily contortions of Hatha Yoga, originally a discipline to enable men (and men only) to connect to God by overcoming the limitations of the physical body. Indian words such as *ashram* and *darshan* became common currency and before long, hippy Western people were greeting each other with Om Shanti or Namaste, rather than Hello or How are you?

In place of prayer came meditation, the ability to still our minds and turn inwards. In place of dark-robed priests, vicars and ministers, came colourful gurus, with their chants, their mantras, their incense and their message of universal peace and love. For those who wanted an Eastern flavour to their spirituality and who were bored or disillusioned with traditional Western religions, these exotic bearded gurus and their teachings held a powerful appeal.

By the time Dadi Janki came to London, these ideas, many of which were integral to her own message, had taken hold, at least among the avant-garde and the seekers after truth of the time.

But all these previous gurus and teachers disseminating aspects of Eastern philosophy and wisdom, were men. The human potential movement itself, in common with established religions, was also almost totally masculine. One thinks of people such as Richard Alpert, who took the name Ram Dass, under which he wrote his 1971 groundbreaking book, *Be Here Now*. This book, which first introduced many Westerners to the Eastern concepts of yoga, meditation and spirituality, has sold over two million copies, and has never gone out of print.

So what chance did an elderly Indian lady have against all this charismatic and utterly male competition?

What did she have to offer that was any different from these other gurus? Who would listen to a mere female preaching ancient wisdom – especially one who couldn't even speak English?

And where would she get without any money to establish centres and expand? For while many of the other Indian teachers had become extremely rich through the high fees they charged, Dadi Janki established a firm policy of never charging anything for courses or programmes.

No wonder, some might say, that she was living in a dingy ground floor flat and sleeping on a door (she could not even afford a bed), at the same time as many other gurus were swanning around in chauffeur-driven limousines, wearing expensive robes and living in mansions.

And then the Brahma Kumaris, as the movement – which was by this time quite well established in India – was known, was run by women, not men. From the first founder of the movement, known as Brahma Baba, had put the women in charge, against all the prevailing wisdom of the time which said that only men were fit to disseminate spiritual knowledge and understanding.

Dadi Janki had an uphill struggle even to establish the Brahma Kumaris in the West and for a long time, it all seemed hopeless. Yet she never gave up and by her example and inspiration, she gradually gathered around her a group of loyal lieutenants, rather as Christ gathered around him his twelve disciples. The difference is that most of these early disciples were women, not men. Their task was to take her message of truth and goodness into all corners of the world outside India.

Which, as we shall see, they did, with spectacular success.

And while many of those early Indian-based movements have faded away or been largely forgotten, the movement that Dadi Janki started in such a small and modest way has grown and grown. The Brahma Kumaris World Spiritual University is now a prosperous, confident, global organisation which has strong links with the United Nations and which regularly holds large conferences that are attended by delegates of high international standing such as politicians, heads of state, decision makers and tycoons. No longer does the organisation operate out of two damp ground floor rooms in a grim part of London, but has specially-built halls and conference centres to which thousands of people flock annually.

The only aspect that has not changed is that unlike other gurus, Dadi Janki has continued to live as simply as she began. Although she no longer sleeps on a door, her bedroom is as simple and clean as a nun's cell, with absolutely nothing in it apart from a bed, a chair and a cupboard. You will not see one single personal possession in her room.

Dadi has never remotely become grand and yet, thanks to her, the organisation is considered by Frank Whaling, Professor Emeritus in the Study of Religion,

Edinburgh University, to have met the criteria for a new religion. In his 2012 book *Understanding the Brahma Kumaris*, part of an academic series for students of comparative religion, he describes the BKs as 'a new spiritual tradition.' The blurb goes on to say, 'As with all spiritual traditions, the Brahma Kumaris are different, bewildering and fascinating in their newness and in their complexity.'

One of the main ways the BKs remain so different is that they are still the only spiritual movement of any size or impact to be run by women. They have also continued to refuse to charge for their events and programmes.

So how has she done it? Because Dadi, at 99 (in 2015), is now too old and frail to be interviewed at length, this book takes the form of a series of portraits of her by those who have been close to her for many years. The personal stories are interspersed with her own words of wisdom and inspiration, and together, I hope, these will add up to a portrait of a very retiring woman who is nevertheless one of the most unusual and intriguing figures of our time.

Not for Dadi Janki any pomp or circumstance. She still wears a cheap cotton gown, she owns no possessions and has no actual home of her own. One of her special qualities, perhaps, is that even when she, and the organisation, had nothing, she always projected the feeling that nothing was lacking in her life. She never yearned for any worldly possessions and because in a sense she rose above them, there was always something royal and stately about her.

Like the Queen, she does not carry money and indeed, has never had any money of her own. Whatever is given to her, she straightaway gives away. Her life remains simple and dedicated. She has never sought celebrity or wished for any special treatment for herself.

Retaining this simplicity while operating on the world stage and inspiring a worldwide movement means that Dadi Janki remains enigmatic and difficult to assess. As such, opinions and impressions of her differ widely.

Some see her as a gentle saint, smiling benignly on all as she hands out gifts, while others maintain that she acts like a ruthless dictator, regularly pushing her staff to their limits and beyond.

Some people see her as gently feminine and motherly, while others believe she does not have a feminine bone in her body, and is the most masculine person they have ever met. Many have felt she is the hardest taskmistress ever and it is true that she will never accept the second rate or second best from anybody.

Whatever feelings one has when meeting Dadi Janki, one thing is certain: you cannot be unaffected by her. She has a presence and exudes a magnetic force that cannot be ignored. Some may be repelled and feel like running away screaming, fearing being drawn into her power, while others want nothing more than to sit in her presence and soak up the magic that they sense emanating from her.

Many hard-headed people have softened and become putty in Dadi Janki's hands, including the author's own husband, who gave up a glittering Fleet Street career, a family and a home, to surrender to the movement. His involvement with the Brahma Kumaris is, without doubt, the longest-lasting love affair of his life and shows no end. Neville is in no doubt that it has been Dadi Janki who has inspired him and kept him going. Sometimes, though, it has seemed as though she acts to make his dark moments darker.

She always expects more and more and more of him and sometimes, he has writhed under the mental lash.

Yet for all these strong reactions and the fact that she has changed many people's lives, Dadi Janki will not allow any worship or devotion. If she is anything, she will tell you, she is a companion of God and any power she seems to possess comes directly from Him. Because she communes with God all the time, she can impart such wisdom as is given to few. And because she herself lives such an austere life, she can demand it of others.

Dadi Janki, who began life as Janki Samtani, was born in India in 1916 into a traditional Hindu family. From the age of two, she experienced a strong connection with God and her only wish in life was to serve him. This in itself was unusual as women were not only considered second-class citizens, it was questionable whether they even had souls. It was certainly unthinkable that a woman could ever be a religious leader. No, a woman's only role in those days was to be married at the earliest age possible, have children, serve her husband who was considered to be her guru, and then fade away into the background.

Although Dadi Janki was different and never wanted such a life for herself, she was even so, forced to succumb to the conventional pattern when she was married off, much against her will, at the age of 19, and had a child, again, much against her will. She caused a storm by running away from her arranged marriage to join the Om Mandli, the forerunner of the Brahma Kumaris, and then a burgeoning movement started by Dada Lekhraj, a former businessman who became known as Brahma Baba and who in his late fifties decided to dedicate his life to God. He gathered round him a group of followers, most of whom were young women. From the start, Brahma Baba put women in charge and this was unique at the time as, although there has always been a tradition in Christianity of women dedicating their lives to God by becoming nuns and prioresses, there has never been any such tradition in Hinduism.

Only men, it was thought, were capable of connecting directly to God.

Dadi was 21 when she joined the Om Mandli, never to leave, and never to wish for any other sort of life. She never wanted, or sought, a personal relationship with anybody and has always maintained that her only connection is with God and that He alone is her companion. For many years, Dadi Janki served with the Brahma Kumaris in India but it was always the intention that one day, the message must go out to the whole world.

The full story of the Brahma Kumaris' origins and difficult establishment is told in the author's previous book *Peace and Purity* so this is just a short précis to put Dadi Janki into perspective.

As we have said, she arrived in London at a time when Indian spirituality was no longer quite so new and strange, but the Brahma Kumaris were something else again. Most of the Indian gurus who came to the West had adapted their message and teachings to appeal to a non-Hindu audience and although some were stricter than others, most had compromised to quite a large extent to accommodate Western practices, beliefs and culture.

From the start, Dadi Janki was nothing if not uncompromising. She insisted that all the female adherents, Indian or not, wore a simple white sari and a plait down their back. They were to rise at four in the morning for meditation, followed by a class, or sermon, and were also to follow the strictest vegetarian diet, cutting out onions, garlic and eggs as well as fish or meat.

In addition they were to remain, or become, celibate – even the married ones. They were not supposed to go to the cinema or theatre, read novels or indeed, do anything that might prove a distraction or weaken their connection to God. They had to observe silence at various points during the day. That was just the practical side. The spiritual side, which will be explained later, was equally tough and a far cry from that of most of the other Indian teachers, who watered down their principles considerably to make them more appealing to hedonistic Westerners.

On the face of it, the daily life of a Brahma Kumari sounded distinctly unappealing, as ascetic as that of an enclosed Catholic nun. Yet gradually, as Dadi Janki held court in the dingy little flat that she and her few then all-Indian followers had managed to rent, she began to attract – and retain – Westerners so entranced by her message that before long, the prospect of any other kind of life fell away. From the start, she also had the help and support of a young woman who, although Indian, had been brought up and educated in London, and who was to be Dadi's translator, interpreter and second-in-command. This young woman was Sister Jayanti, who became a BK at the age of 19 and who has been by Dadi's side ever since.

Whether Dadi could have got going without Jayanti or whether Jayanti could have got going without Dadi, is questionable. But there is no doubt that together they made a formidable team, and one that increasingly, young Westerners were finding irresistible.

Since those small beginnings the Brahma Kumaris has grown to become one of the top 200 charities in the UK. It now has a large centre in London with two halls seating 500 and 200, residential retreat centres in Nuneham Courtenay, Oxford, and Worthing, West Sussex and six Inner Space high street shops.

The BKs now hold courses and events in over 50 sites across the UK and have stayed true to their initial promise of never charging for any of their programmes, however large. The BKs, thanks to Dadi's example and admonition, work entirely through volunteers as Dadi believes strongly that those who have benefited will wish to give something back.

Although when you meet Dadi she always seems calm and peaceful, sitting on a chair dressed in white and radiating an atmosphere of serenity, she has actually been very busy in the UK with a huge number of projects, not all of which are of a spiritual origin or have any direct association with the BKs.

For instance, she has been involved with many organisations supporting and encouraging young people; she is a Patron of the World Congress of Faiths; and in 2003 she was one of the religious leaders supporting Respect: It's About Time, launched by Prince Charles and the Chief Rabbi. Prince Charles stated in his message for the opening of the BKs' second large London centre, Diamond House, in 2003:

"The Brahma Kumaris World Spiritual University has become a strong ally of one of my principal charities, The Prince's Trust, working with them to encourage understanding between the UK's faith communities."

Dadi is also the president of the Janki Foundation for Spirituality in Healthcare. Launched at the Royal College of Physicians in 1997, it supports healthcare professionals in the UK through values-based dialogue and training, CDs, books and lectures. It also gives financial support to a largely BK-run hospital in Rajasthan which has combined modern medical technology with spirituality and complementary medicine.

Dadi has worked closely with UK prison staff at all levels including governors, prison officers, educators, probation officers and those delivering drug rehabilitation programmes. To date, hundreds of prison staff have attended BK training programmes and seminars and Tim Newell, former Governor of HMP Grendon and Springhill, has said:

> "The work of prison staff involves relating in ways that respect the humanity of others and particularly those who are vulnerable and who have been damaging in their behaviour. This calls for reserves of spiritual awareness involving a search for meaning, purpose, relationships, hope and commitment. The involvement of the Brahma Kumaris in working with prison staff has enabled this dimension of prison life to be developed in a unique manner of mutual respect."

Thanks also to Dadi Janki's inspiration and commitment to outreach, the BKs hold regular seminars and retreats for social workers, social work managers and those in the caring professions. In 1986, the Peace Bus toured around the UK in honour of the United Nations International Year of Peace, promoting the largest non-fundraising project for the year. People were asked to donate their prayers, meditations or positive thoughts for peace.

In 1988-1991, a United Nations Peace Messenger initiative co-ordinated from the London BK office asked people to describe their vision of a better world, and also create practical projects to realise their vision. During those years, many people helped clean up local areas, help their neighbours, and looked after the physically challenged, or disabled.

In such ways, Dadi has brought spirituality and an example of peace and love to many practical projects and initiatives. She has been tireless in her efforts to reach out to those who she feels need some upliftment in their lives, while not forcing the BK theology or strict lifestyle on those she helps.

Thanks to Dadi Janki, the Brahma Kumaris has never been an inward-looking organisation, but from the start has reached out to those of other faiths, from other walks of life, and of different nationalities, and has embraced purely secular organisations as well. This again is radically different from the attitude of many Indian gurus who have wanted to draw people into their movement, rather than reaching out to those who may not even be interested in their form of spirituality.

As always, Dadi believes her inspiration, courage and ability to engage with people from all walks of life, from royalty and Heads of State to drug addicts and down-and-outs, never seeing the 'costume' or outward appearance but penetrating through to the soul, come directly from God. Without that continuous source of spiritual sustenance, she is certain, none of this would have been possible.

Although the BKs now have a worldwide presence, much of what has happened outside of India emanated from London.

It is unusual for an Indian woman to emerge as a world spiritual leader, but it is not quite unique, and nor is it confined to members of the Brahma Kumaris. Another Indian woman, Mata Amritanandamayi, known as Amma (mother) has made a huge impact worldwide with her hugging, or physical embraces. It is estimated that she has hugged over 30 million people since her mission began, and people will queue for hours to receive one of her magic hugs.

Born in 1953 in Kerala, South India, Mata, like Dadi Janki, spent much of her childhood in profound meditation. She came from a family of fishermen, and when she was nine years old, her mother became very ill and she was pulled out of school to help look after the household and her many siblings – estimates vary between six and seven.

As she went from door to door gathering scraps of food for her family and their small herd of cows, she was struck by the enormous poverty and suffering of those around her – and determined to do something about it. Whenever she could spare it, she brought poverty-stricken families food and clothing and also, shockingly, embraced them.

This was strictly forbidden in her Hindu culture, as teenage girls – she was 14 at the time – must never touch a man (except for their husband once they are married). She defied this tradition and also, unlike Dadi Janki, rejected her parents' attempts to force her into an arranged marriage. She had more important work to do, as she saw it. As well as her daily practice of deep meditation, Amma also started composing devotional songs. Gradually, she gathered around her devotees and followers.

Her impact was such that in 1981 a worldwide foundation was started and Amma, who also wears white like the BKs, began a global network whereby she now tours many countries, always hugging and embracing the people she meets. Her belief is that her embrace actually cures and heals people. Whether or not this is true, Amma has become universally popular and is widely regarded as a saint. She does not teach or preach any particular religion or set of doctrines, but by her lifelong practice of meditation and her many spiritual songs, has come to be worshipped by many thousands of people all over the world.

This is not the place to compare and contrast Amma with Dadi Janki; only to say that it's wonderful for India to have produced two such inspirational women who have made a profound impact on Westerners. Amma is, perhaps, more high profile than Dadi Janki, who is less demonstrative in style, but her meditation practice and her love for humanity are of a similar strength.

It is interesting that both Dadi Janki and Amma see themselves as universal mothers, rather than as great leaders and of course India itself is often known as Mother India. ❧

Dadi Janki at the acquisition ceremony of the land for Global Co-operation House, 1989 London

The first BK Centre outside India, 98 Tennyson Road, Kilburn, London

CHAPTER TWO

The story of Jayanti Kirpalani, a dedicated BK since 1968

∽

Sister Jayanti, now the European Director of the Brahma Kumaris, was born in India in 1949 and her family is distantly related to Dadi Janki's.

At the age of eight, Jayanti met Brahma Baba who told her that she was going to be a great spiritual leader in the world. Her mother became a BK at around the same time. This pronouncement of future greatness did not mean very much to the little girl although she now says she can remember a feeling of profound love coming from him.

Her father, Murli, a successful businessman, was not altogether pleased at this turn of events and in order to get his family away from the influence of the BKs, moved them to London in 1957. The family first lived in Golders Green and then moved to a flat in Clarendon Court, Willesden, North-West London, in 1959. Jayanti's mother Rajni, who had been married at 16 according to Indian custom, continued to live the BK lifestyle, but there was no outreach at all and the practices were confined to the family circle.

Jayanti, who had a younger brother, Haresh, grew up as an English schoolgirl and went to English schools where, until the sixth form, she was the only Indian girl there.

She says that under her mother's influence, she regularly meditated until the age of 12, but after that became a typical English teenager. It was the swinging sixties, after all, and she wanted to be modern. She had hoped to qualify as a doctor but despite achieving top grades, could not gain admission to any of the London medical schools, which in those days had a quota of 25 per cent for women students. The fact that she was Indian might also have made a difference but in the event, she decided to train as a pharmacist, then as now a popular choice of profession for Indians.

She had almost completed one term at university, when it happened; an event that was to change her life completely.

She takes up her story: 'Before going to university in 1967 I had been back to India several times on holiday and to see relatives. While I was there I would make a connection with the BKs but after coming back to London, it would fade. I was always very clear that I wanted to be financially independent and have a profession, and definitely did not want to lead a traditional Indian life. I had been exposed to a much freer way of life in London, particularly for girls, compared to the India of the time.

'That was my aim until one day I was in a lecture theatre watching the professor write some chemical formulae on the board. I was sitting at the back when completely unexpectedly, I had an out-of-the-body experience. Instead of sitting in my chair I was up there above, observing the scene. After a few minutes, or a few seconds, I came back into my body again. Of course I did not literally go up above, but somehow my soul, or spirit, had separated from my body for that short time.

'The experience I had made me feel that what I was now doing was irrelevant, and that I had to do something else. As I had not yet completed one term at university, and had not got very far into the course, I felt I could take a sabbatical and go to India to try and discover what the country was really all about.

'The first thing was that I discovered India to be an immense civilisation of beauty and culture. It was as if I was seeing it in depth for the first time. I knew that I needed space to stay and understand what it was all about. I also felt a powerful sense of the religious passion of India. I was going back to my roots in a sense, I suppose, but there was more to it than that.

'I would see a poor person offering bananas up at a shrine and it made me think: what makes them feel there is something higher? Why are they offering fruit to images and idols instead of eating it for themselves?'

This revelation, says Jayanti, led to her feeling that her present life had no substance and that she wanted to delve deeper and study spirituality. 'And of course, the BKs were right there.' At the time she was wearing Western clothes, jeans and mini skirts, and had no immediate thoughts of becoming a surrendered sister but in the event, things moved fast.

'I met Dadi Janki, who was then running teacher training programmes, and she talked about spiritual matters. For the first time I started understanding the teachings and began to meditate again.' At the time, says Jayanti, all the BK literature was in Hindi and she was no longer fluent in the language.

'It was heavy duty stuff,' she says, 'not easy to understand, but I had powerful meditation experiences and soon made the decision that I wanted to be a BK.

'Brahma Baba, who was then in the last year of his physical life, sent me a telegram saying: Come and discuss your decision. I went with my mother, grandmother and Dadi Janki to Mount Abu in June 1968 and had the most amazing experience looking into his eyes. I was carried to another dimension and the possibility of any other life fell away. I knew there would be challenges ahead, but I was so clear that it was the right decision for me.'

Jayanti now says that in order to become a BK – or indeed a pioneer member of any other religion or faith – it is essential to have at least some taste of visionary or other-worldly experience. 'This makes you aware of another world and enables you to withstand all the hardships that such a life might entail.'

After living in London, in a house with all mod cons, for most of her life, Jayanti found it hard to adjust to the still-primitive conditions of India. 'In those days it was still third world,' she said, 'and I knew it would be tough. In the Mount Abu headquarters, for instance, there was only one place you could get hot water. Otherwise you had to manage with cold water.'

Then she had to deal with her father, who emphatically did not want the Brahma Kumaris life for his only daughter. 'He was shocked and thought that I would one day come to my senses,' she says. 'But nothing was going to stop me. The really significant moment came for me on 18 January 1969 when Brahma Baba died. A few months later, Dadi Janki came to Mount Abu and she told me I should go back to London.

'I was terrified at the prospect, especially as there was absolutely no BK set-up in the West at that time. In India, I had a strong support system. The BKs were already well established there and had many centres. They were also a well-respected spiritual organisation, even if they were considered somewhat odd for being run by women.

'While in India, I had been given a big platform and although still very young, was feted everywhere I went. Once, I was asked to address an audience of 500 in Kanpur, including the state governor. When I stood up it was as though some button was pressed inside me, and the talk just flowed.

'I very much wanted to stay in India. But Dadi Janki was adamant. She told me that I had to return to London. I now see her as being like a mother eagle, forcing the young ones out of the nest. When force is applied, they realise they have wings and can fly. It was much the same with me although I knew there would be no support structure in London. But having got used to doors opening for me in India, I thought the same would happen back in London.

'I was sorely mistaken. They all banged shut and I could not get anything going. Nobody was remotely interested in the BKs and I did not even have a sheet of paper to give anybody to explain what it was all about. It was hopeless. I was living at home with my parents, trying to get the movement going in London, and came across total indifference everywhere.

'In 1971, a delegation of BKs came from India to London to try and get things going in the West. This delegation did not manage to entice any Westerners. However, following their visit, the first centre outside India was established, in Tennyson Road, Kilburn, London.'

Then Dadi Janki arrived in 1974. 'Now things began to change,' Jayanti says. 'Almost from the start, Dadi's intellect and wisdom began to touch the hearts and minds of people in the West. I arranged exhibitions in various venues, such as the London Tea Centre, and the first Westerners came along. Some were intrigued enough to come to our little centre to listen to classes, learn meditation and get to know Dadi. I felt that these small beginnings were my reward for four years' intense meditation.'

From 1969 to 1973 Jayanti could not return to India as her father prevented it, still hoping that she would change her mind and give up the idea of being a BK. Most girls in their early twenties, even in those days, would probably not take any notice of a father's strictures, but for an Indian girl it was different. 'We had respect for our elders and I obeyed my father.'

But once Dadi Janki came to London, and was herself unable to return to India for four years because of visa difficulties, things began to move quickly. Jayanti was invaluable as without her, it would be hard to see how the BKs could have even started in the UK as none of them spoke English. Jayanti is what used to be called 'well-spoken' in that she has a very clear English voice with no trace of an Indian accent, and she was able to translate for Dadi Janki and also talk to the early Westerners in their own language. Without any doubt, it was Jayanti's beautiful speaking voice that started to attract Westerners and she also came across very well on the radio.

Jayanti herself dismisses the value of her voice, saying only that everybody had their different skills and attributes, and that everybody contributed in their own way.

Dadi Janki spoke no English when she arrived, and even after more than 40 years in the West still speaks very little, although she understands more than she lets on. Sister Sudesh, who also came from India at about the same time, did not speak English either, but she has a gift for languages, and soon picked it up.

And so the triumvirate (or should it be 'triumfeminate'?) of Jayanti, Dadi Janki and Sudesh gradually attracted young Westerners to the movement, and to the teachings.

Jayanti has great respect for Dadi Janki and they have worked closely together for over 40 years, but is there anything Jayanti doesn't like about Dadi, or has found difficult to take on board?

'Yes,' she says candidly. 'Dadi absolutely refuses, and always has refused, to see any fault in anybody. I have argued and argued with her in the past, that she is simply not being realistic and that she has to admit that this person is not reliable, that another one is a gossip, and so on. But Dadi always says the same thing: whatever you say, you are saying – not me.

'She has always focused on the positive and believes that deep down, everybody and every soul, is full of virtues, even people generally assumed to be wicked. Dadi simply refused to give any attention to a person's weak points on the understanding that if you give attention to their failings, you multiply this negative energy.'

In this, as in so many other aspects, Dadi knew what she was doing. There is a principle in leadership circles that if you want to get the very best out of people, and drive them to perform beyond what might be considered their limits, you concentrate on their virtues and ignore their failings.

Although Jayanti was introduced, exposed, you might say, to the BKs from a very early age, this would not necessarily have endeared her to the movement in adult life, especially as she had been brought up in the far more secular and cynical West.

What has made her stay with them for all of her adult life? 'Over the years,' she says, 'I have had the most incredible exposure to many different spiritual and religious paths and have had the opportunity to compare them with Raja Yoga, the system of meditation taught by the BKs. What appealed at the outset and has continued to appeal, is that it is, above all, a journey of deep study and exploration which gives clear answers to the most fundamental questions about life.

'I have not come across another path with such clear guidelines. I was getting answers to questions about the self and the concept of God that I have never found in any other religion.'

There was also, for Jayanti, the crucial part that women played in the organisation. 'This was where my exposure to Dadi Janki was so important. In no other religious or spiritual organisation were women playing such central roles.' It was not particularly a feminist decision to become a BK, she insists, but as time went on, she began to realise that a woman-led organisation was very different from one headed by men.

'Having women in charge makes a great difference to the structure and feel of a spiritual movement,' she says. 'For one thing we are above all a family-oriented organisation. In fact, we would not say we were a movement or an organisation so much as that we are a big family – and one that is getting bigger all the time.

'Today Dadi Janki heads a worldwide organisation but her relationship with every member remains personal. Where people are deprived of the warmth of a family, they have often come to us and are attracted because of that family feeling.'

Jayanti does not have a minute's regret that she decided to dedicate her life to the BKs before she had really experienced any other life. 'There is nothing, absolutely nothing, that I feel I have missed out on,' she says. 'I would never have had such an interesting life any other way. At times, yes, it has been an uphill journey but at such times I say to myself: I didn't choose this. Destiny chose me.

'It's a popular misconception that if you opt out of a conventional life such as marriage, family, career, running a home, you are also opting out of all the stresses and challenges that such a life can bring. But you get just as many challenges in the spiritual life.

'Human life is basically all about relationships and there can be severe clashes with others on the same spiritual journey. We do not always see eye to eye by any means. We still also have to deal with planes being late, traffic jams, plumbing not working, no money for essential repairs and maintenance, people not coming up to expectations or letting you down at the last minute. The difference is that regular meditation helps me to manage myself and therefore, become better able to deal with all the problems that come my way.'

And would the BK movement ever have got going in the West without Dadi Janki? Jayanti is adamant: no way. ❧

Dadi Janki at the House of Lords with Lord Ennals at the launch of The UN Initiative, Global Co-operation for a Better World 1988, London

CHAPTER THREE

The basic teachings

At this point, it might be asked: what are the Brahma Kumaris all about? What are their basic teachings and what do they have to offer to the West that is different from any other religion or faith?

When you meet them they seem charming, kind, friendly and positive – as indeed they are. They are immensely busy and practical, organising non-stop intensely varied programmes of events and retreats, and their centres are all havens of peace, tranquillity, cleanliness and order.

The members are ever-smiling and gracious and welcome all visitors as honoured guests. They offer meals, snacks, gifts, all free of charge and they wear white, looking like angels, even if some of them are rather portly angels, given the importance they place on food.

Yet behind all this is a mystical, other-worldly, and some might say fantastical belief system that many Westerners have found difficult to take on board, while others have enthusiastically welcomed it as a truth they never heard before and which makes perfect sense.

It is essential to understand at least the basic building blocks of the belief system to appreciate where Dadi Janki is coming from. Although Dadi undoubtedly speaks a lot of wisdom, this wisdom comes from a deep conviction that she holds the secrets of the universe, or at least, that these secrets have been imparted to her through her lifelong connection with God, and also with Brahma Baba, the founder of the movement.

Dadi Janki's sincere belief is that Brahma Baba was chosen by God himself as His instrument and that he and he alone was to usher in a new world order. To this end, he trained an army of young women who would go out into the rest of India and eventually the world and spread the message.

Some of the beliefs hark back to traditional Hinduism, and some are either new or profound adaptations of ancient beliefs. In common with other Eastern religions or faiths, BKs believe in karma and reincarnation. Put simply, this means that whatever actions we perform in this lifetime, may have dramatic consequences in our next incarnation. The fact that we have no conscious memory of our actions in a past life does not mean that the belief has no substance. After all, say the BKs, can you recall what happened thirty, forty years ago in your life? Can you remember what happened to you as a baby? No – but that does not mean it didn't happen.

Some people have maintained that they can remember past lives. One of the most famous of these was writer Joan Grant, who wrote many historical novels relying on her 'far memory'. She would go into a trance and write about her own life in Ancient Egypt, medieval Rome and so on. These novels, telling the dramatic stories of long-ago heroines, became best-sellers in their day. The late Professor Ian Stevenson carried out much research into the apparent past lives of children and although his conclusions are tentative, they are not so easy to dismiss.

In more recent years, past-life therapy has become very popular in certain circles, and people have been healed of long-standing phobias and conditions by being taken back to a previous incarnation, where the trauma was supposed to have taken place. Under hypnosis, patients have 'remembered' being burned at the stake, killed in battle or been the lover of Charles II, for instance.

However, none of this can constitute proof and sceptics who believe there is nothing to human beings apart from matter, are not convinced. Most Indians, however, accept the reality of past lives without ever really thinking about it, as it is a strong belief embedded in their culture.

Karma and reincarnation are inextricably linked, and it all comes down to: as we sow so shall we reap; if not in this incarnation, then in a future one. It is as if a big book is being kept up there somewhere in which all our deeds, good and bad, are written, and they are not forgotten. This 'big book' is known in past-life circles as the Akashic records.

According to this belief, nothing that happens is ever quite wiped out but leaves imprints, or in Hindi, sanskaras, on the soul that will affect subsequent births. Dadi Janki profoundly believes this. Well, it's not so much that she believes it as that she accepts it as a hundred per cent fact.

She has based her entire life on the principle that you must not set in motion bad karma, as this will rebound on you in like form, at some stage. Keep your heart and your thoughts clean and pure, she says, so that no bad karma enters your soul. Even to think bad thoughts of another, she would say, creates bad karma.

To a professional atheist or rationalist, all this may sound like so much nonsense although since Eastern religions began making inroads into the West, the concepts are not as strange as they would have seemed a century ago. We are fond of saying these days, what goes around, comes around, and that is a glib way of saying that there are consequences from actions. If you believe that whatever you do has an inevitable consequence, this can only have a positive effect on your behaviour and the actions you set in motion.

In order to take on board the possibility of past lives, you have to believe that there is some non-material aspect to life that nevertheless influences behaviour and personality, something more than genetics and environment. For those who have no belief in a soul or some eternal aspect, these ideas are so much nonsense and there is no point in trying to convince them otherwise. Every single religion and faith, it has to be said, since the beginning of time, has believed that human beings, and perhaps animals as well, in some traditions at least, have a soul; something non-material that cannot be seen and which is eternal. It is the basis upon which all religions are founded, although opinions differ as to what that soul actually is.

But there is more. At the very heart of the BK philosophy is the notion that time is circular rather than linear and that this endless circling of time explains the universe and the nature of eternity. It may seem simplistic to a Stephen Hawking, but it is complicated enough for most non-cosmologists.

So here goes with the theology and cosmology underpinning the BK lifestyle and outlook:

The BKs do not believe that we evolved from simple creatures through billions of years by a series of chance events. Instead, they maintain that time moves around an endless loop with each circuit lasting a total of 5000 years. When the 5000 years is up, the world as we know it finishes and a new cycle begins afresh. Thus there is ultimately no beginning and no end and as such, no time when God created matter out of nothing.

Until souls take human bodies – and the BKs believe, in contrast with some other Eastern religions, that we never take the bodies of non-human species – they reside in a non-material state which is outside of space and time. This is known as the Home, where God also resides. God, known as the Supreme Soul, is the reference point for all that is highest in human endeavour – love, peace, joy, wisdom, power. Dadi Janki believes, and teaches, that when we can connect with this Supreme Spirit, we will renew those qualities in ourselves.

All souls start off pure and viceless but with successive incarnations, they become tarnished and full of wickedness. It is only by connecting with God in yoga that the tarnish can be cleaned off and we are stripped back to our original natures, which are all goodness.

There are four basic ages to planet Earth, each lasting 1,250 years. The BKs are very clear as to exact numbers. First of all comes the Golden Age, often spoken of and referred to by poets and also a powerful concept in Ancient Greek philosophy. During the Golden Age, everything is pure and good and everybody is happy. Geographically, the Golden Age takes place in Bharat, the land of plenty and now known as India. The population at this time is small and there is peace and harmony everywhere.

After this comes the Silver Age, which has become slightly tarnished, but there is still peace and abundance. The population begins to increase.

Thirdly is the Copper Age. This is the time when the great religions such as Judaism, Christianity, Buddhism and Islam become established, along with their honoured prophets. The world now becomes divided, evil begins to stalk and the great prophets of these important religions – Abraham, Buddha, Jesus and Mohammed – remind people of the higher values once embraced without effort. All the major prophets basically preach the same thing: that in order to return to our original state, we must be honest, upright, pure in thought, word and deed, not cheat or lie and live a simple life.

The population increases even more as, according to the BKs, new souls keep coming down to inhabit new bodies.

Fourthly is the Iron Age, our own age, characterised by wars, poverty, overpopulation, greed and sin and vice of all kinds. The 5000 year cycle is characterised by successive change and decay.

When life in the Iron Age finally becomes unsustainable, the Supreme Soul intervenes in order to plant the seed of world renewal. As the cycle first started in India, so it is that in India, a new inspired teacher comes to lead the world back to goodness and love. This person was Brahma Baba, the Indian merchant whose apocalyptic visions in the 1930s led him to believe he was the one chosen to usher in a new world order and a change of consciousness. Once more, the simple life was extolled and the new element here was that Brahma Baba put women in charge. Such a thing had never happened before. All the previous prophets had been men, and every single theologian of importance in the world had also been a man.

Even today, it is not fully appreciated just how revolutionary this was, especially in India, where women had no individual status at all.

The period of preparation for the new world order is known as the Confluence Age, which is seen as lasting for about a hundred years. When enough people have learned how to connect their minds to the Supreme and abandon their previous vicious lives, all souls return to the home to begin the cycle again.

This is often known as the end of the world, except that the world does not end but renews itself and begins again.

At the time of the Iron Age, the pull of matter has become extreme, to such an extent that more people than ever before are completely materialistic, not believing in any kind of God and refusing to accept that there is anything beyond matter. At this time, the very existence of the soul is denied by scientists, and the world becomes ever more atheistic and violent.

BKs believe that Brahma Baba, founder of the spiritual university in the 1930s, is an instrument through which God enables the world to return to its pure state and that by the time he died he had himself achieved a condition of such purity that he did not reincarnate but 'sat at the right hand of God' in Christian terminology. Brahma Baba believed that he had taken 84 births, the maximum any soul can experience in the 5000-year cycle and that his task was to show people how to lessen the pull of material things and to separate themselves from violence, addictions and lust of all kinds, including sexual lust.

When he died, he ascended into the 'subtle regions', a metaphysical region seen to exist between the physical world and the Home, which is not a physical region at all.

Towards retirement age, Brahma Baba received a series of visions that led him to believe God was speaking directly through him. By the time he died in 1969, the Brahma Kumaris was already well established in India and Dadi Janki, then aged 53, had been a key player in the organisation for many years.

It will be seen that this is a poetical, mystical interpretation of life on earth and whether it has any foundation in science or cosmology, is open to question. In her book *The Case for God*, religious writer Karen Armstrong makes the point that in our present scientific age, the importance or reality of myth has fallen into disrepute. Myth, she says, helped people to live creatively in a confusing world. She adds that the truth of religion is acquired not by probing into scientific minutiae, but by practical action. Some things can only be learned by constant dedicated practice, and religion is a practical discipline that teaches us to discover new capacities of the mind and heart.

Armstrong goes on to say that science has achieved such spectacular results that myth has been discredited, and the scientific method is now considered the only means of attaining truth.

We can never prove or disprove the truth or otherwise of the 5000-year cycle, the reality of the Supreme Spirit or that Brahma Baba continued in some non-material dimension when he left the physical body. All we can say is that by taking on these beliefs as truth, life is changed – and others are inspired and influenced.

Dadi Janki took on board as literal truth everything Brahma Baba had said or revealed and for the whole of her life has regarded him as her guide, philosopher and friend, and the fount of all wisdom as to how to conduct one's life. Her absolute conviction is what has sustained her during difficult years in the West, and while meeting and overcoming many challenges.

When Brahma Baba died, the messages and knowledge did not die. Even today (2015), one of the founding sisters enters a state of trance in front of thousands of people at the BK headquarters in Rajasthan, whereby she acts as a medium to channel messages and revealed truths to the assembled gathering. These messages are held to come from an entity known as 'Bapdada', the combined form of Brahma Baba and the Supreme, much as Jesus is understood by Christians to have combined with God after his earthly life was over. Jesus now sits at the 'right hand' of God, in Christian understanding, although there is also the Holy Ghost, forming the Trinity, or Three in One, which does not have an exact correlation in the BK theology.

In addition, sermons and homilies known as Murlis, spoken by Brahma Baba during the last five years of his life, are read out to classes the world over, every morning.

Perhaps the most contentious aspect of the BK teachings is their belief that the end of the world is nigh. For this, they have been labeled a 'doomsday' or 'millenarian' cult. Brahma Baba certainly taught that the world as we know it is soon to end and will usher in the golden age. Critics of the BKs have pointed out that it was widely predicted within the movement that the world was going to end in 1976. That did not happen and other predicted dates came and went. Some felt that these ever-shifting dates discredited the entire BK teachings.

As against this, it has to be said that very many religions have prophesied the end of the world, including Christianity. The 'end of the world is nigh' warnings go back to the Bible and were certainly widespread in the Middle Ages. Many medieval texts warn of the wickedness of the people, which will certainly bring about a huge destruction. Christians awaited the Second Coming, while Jews are still waiting for the true Messiah.

According to this belief, a strand in many religions, current society is corrupt, unjust, unsustainable and has to be destroyed by some dramatic and unstoppable force before the new age can begin. Most millenarian groups believe that a small group of the devout and Godly, 'God's elect', will survive the forthcoming apocalypse and usher in the new Golden Age.

In an entry on Wikipedia, the Brahma Kumaris are named as a millenarian movement, along with the Branch Davidians, Jehovah's Witnesses, Mormons, Shakers, Plymouth Brethren, Rastafarians and several Jewish movements awaiting the Messiah.

Dadi Janki's own take on this is that we should not be 'date-conscious' but should act with the certain knowledge that the world as it is will certainly end at some point, and we should use the remaining time to strip away all wickedness from our souls in order to become pure and hence able to be close to God. As the Christian hymn has it, 'Blest are the pure in heart, for they shall see our God.' Nobody knows for sure when the end of the world, as we know it, will come, or whether it will come, but there is no doubt that our present age is characterised by greed, corruption and violence on a scale never known before.

This in essence is Dadi Janki's spiritual background and she uses it to give credence to what she is saying. In some ways, the BK teachings hark back to the Old Testament, where the children of Israel are given harsh strictures on how to live their lives. In fact, all millenarian religious sects and movements place great emphasis on austere lifestyles, a plain and simple appearance, and rejection of hedonism and self-indulgence.

The lifestyle recommended by the BKs has much in common with that lived in monasteries, nunneries and ashrams, in that it is highly disciplined and regulated, with daily rituals and observances which must be practised to the letter in order to attain the purity of heart which enables connection with God. It is a lifestyle that Dadi herself has never wavered from for eight decades.

These daily practices include getting up at four in the morning to meditate, attending a class at 6.30 for an hour, more meditation, then breakfast and 'karma yoga' or tasks to be performed throughout the day, which may include washing and ironing, vacuuming, cleaning, gardening, preparing food. The BK day is punctuated with 'traffic control' – a couple of minutes of silence to reflect and reconnect. In the evening there will be more meditation, and perhaps a programme of events for the general public.

Everybody, at least in the ashrams or centres, wears white and once again, this harks back to traditional monasteries or nunneries, where everybody wears the same clothes.

In this ordered and simple way, professed or surrendered BKs conduct their lives.

The movement is very Indian and as such, it was a big ask, as we might say today, for Dadi Janki to come to the West and start from scratch, especially with such a raggle-taggle bunch of Westerners as she first attracted. She had probably never seen mini skirts and hot pants before or encountered young women smoking in the streets and drinking in bars.

She experienced a culture shock indeed but she was sustained by her unshakeable belief both in God and that she had been chosen to communicate a message of truth that the world needed to hear. The fact that in the early 1970s she was addressing young Westerners from a very different culture and outlook from her own, did not faze her because, as she says:

'By practising Raja Yoga (connection with God) I can be co-operative with everybody. When you have God in your thoughts there need be no worry. When I first came to Baba I had no thought that I would have any connection or friendship with people from the West. But because I am Baba's friend and also my own friend, I became friendly with all these Europeans.

'I will never defame anybody or look at their bad side as that will disturb my own karma and connection with God. I never lose hope in anybody or allow myself to become disheartened with anyone. I try never to get upset by anybody at all and in this way I remain happy and content.'

Nowadays, Indians, Westerners and indeed, people from all races, cultures and backgrounds happily mingle together. My own ex-husband, a BK for nearly 35 years, has lived since 1994 in a retreat centre which houses a kind of mini rainbow nation, where BKs of every hue, every age group and many distinct backgrounds, live in harmony as a community.

So we have to ask: was it Dadi or was it God who was responsible for the global expansion after the mid 1970s? Was it God or was it Dadi who attracted so many Westerners because after all, a belief in a God was not so very strange. Most of us had been brought up as Christians, or perhaps Jews or Muslims, and even if we consciously rejected these faiths in later life, they were in the main too deeply embedded to be rooted out altogether.

So, we all had a concept of what God was, and even if it differed from that taught by the BKs, at least we knew that 'He' was a non-material, eternal being who never changed and who kept a watch from up there on all our doings. And even in our secular, avowedly atheistic age, a popular expression is OMG – Oh My God.

One truth that gave Dadi her unshakeable conviction that she would be able to take her message into every corner of the world is that she firmly believes there is but one God. There is not a different God for Hindus, Christians, Jews and so on, but just the one entity. That is why she was able to cut through the dogmas and rituals of other religions to penetrate to the essence of whom or what God is.

What we were not prepared for was Dadi Janki's unusual vision of God as having made himself known through Brahma Baba or the fact that she saw God as her intimate friend and companion, rather than somebody 'up there' eternally distant and unknowable. Her sense of urgency and dedication draws on her conviction that God is actually showing the way to the Home beyond, and to heaven on earth at this time.

It has to be borne in mind that not all BK beliefs and teachings are unique to the BKs. Hinduism and Sikhism both believe in reincarnation or, should we say, accept it as an absolute fact, and the law of karma is part and parcel of this belief.

Sikhs also believe in the four ages and acknowledge that we are now in kaliyuga, the iron age, where everything is degenerate and getting worse all the time. Where the BKs differ from traditional Hinduism is their firm belief that 'God has come' to take all souls home in this age of confluence between the end of the old cycle and the beginning of the new one; and in having women at their head.

This is, for many, the movement's USP, or unique selling point. ✤

CHAPTER FOUR

The first Westerners to become BKs

∞

The very first Westerners to become BKs were Denise Lawrence and John Kane, in 1975. Denise has remained a BK whereas John Kane later left the movement although he remains sympathetic to its ideals. And then came along three young men who became absolutely central to the development and expansion of the Brahma Kumaris outside India. They were Charlie Hogg, Ken O'Donnell and Balwant Patel.

Charlie Hogg now runs centres across Australia.

He says that his nickname as a schoolboy was 'Swami' as he always seemed interested in religion and, particularly, Eastern religion. However, at first he intended a conventional career for himself and embarked on an architecture degree in his home town of Melbourne, Australia. Architecture is perhaps the longest and most arduous of all university courses and after a time, Charlie deferred his course and decided to see the world instead.

At the time, 1974, certain areas of London were flooded with young Australian backpackers and Charlie was one of them.

In the event, it took Charlie eight months to travel from Australia to London and he took in India along the way, living in religious communities. 'When I arrived in London, I made ends meet by working backstage at the Royal Shakespeare Company and doing other odd jobs. I was living in a squat in Baker Street at the time, so was living very cheaply indeed and in this way, could extend my stay almost indefinitely.'

He came across the BKs in June 1975 when he went along to a meeting of the Spiritual Association of Great Britain, in Belgrave Square. 'Dadi Janki and Jayanti were there, giving a talk. I had no idea what it was all about but as Jayanti was talking, Dadi Janki sat there and I can remember how expressive her face was.

'After the talk, Jayanti invited me back to their tiny flat in Tennyson Road, North West London, which was at the time their world headquarters outside India. I was immediately struck by something although I didn't really know what, and I started going to the morning class by train. I went there for a few months and the more I heard, the more I liked what I was hearing. I moved closer to the centre and got to know them properly.'

Looking back, Charlie says that when he first met Dadi Janki and Jayanti, he was struck by how familiar they seemed and how they didn't seem at all strange to him. 'It was a familiarity I could understand, somehow, and from the start, Dadi Janki had an incredibly powerful impact on me.' Aged just 22 at the time, Charlie had progressed from being a teenage 'swami' to an out-and-out atheist and this was gradually being replaced by agnosticism.

> 'Yet although I did not believe in God at the time, from the start the BK ideas sounded logical, and I now think that Dadi Janki taught me how to get to know God and how to love God. She did not do this in a religious way, but she somehow took me out of a devotional attitude and made God very real. This was, from the start, the strongest impression she made on me.'

But at the same time, Charlie felt that there was something shy and nervous about this woman. 'She once said she was so nervous and anxious that she would jump just when a dog barked. And yet at the same time, she had so much courage and fearlessness. I admired this. She was so small, quiet and unassuming and yet she had enormous, I would say, total, conviction in what she was saying.

'She was born in a country where women were very much second rate and when I met her, she was certainly not used to Western men, particularly big young Aussies such as myself. Yet when I was renting a house in Kilburn, right near the centre, she asked if she could come and see it.

'Naturally I said yes, and she turned up but when she did my landlord got very angry at this little old Indian lady dressed in a white sari being there. You have to remember that there was a lot of prejudice and racism towards Indians in England at the time, and he didn't like her being there at all. Whatever was she doing, he wondered? But I noticed the way that Dadi Janki responded to him. She was very respectful, very cool and calm and there was no response of fear. Dadi had lived a very sheltered life and here she was walking into an unknown flat, confronting an irate landlord without any fear or nervousness and of course he immediately lost all his anger and was entranced with her.'

Charlie says that he did not become a fully-fledged BK right away, even though he was increasingly becoming attracted to the then tiny movement. 'I explored other Indian movements and also the Philadelphia Association, which was founded by RD Laing to challenge accepted ways of understanding and treating mental and emotional suffering. I listened to Krishnamurti and was interested in all this.

'Yet one of the things that attracted me most to the BKs was that I wanted to transform belief into actual experience. I didn't just want something theoretical. Before long, it was clear that Dadi Janki herself had experienced something beyond the intellect or mere belief, and I wanted a taste of it for myself.

'Right from the start I had the strong feeling that I was hearing the truth, perhaps for the very first time. I remember one Saturday night in Tennyson Road that Dadi Janki took a small group of us deep into ideas and this stimulated me into thinking deeply myself. She took us into the idea of reincarnation and that the soul takes many different births on its journey. This in itself opened up new dimensions in thinking for me.'

And then it happened for Charlie. 'I began to have a powerful relationship with God and a sensation of love that began to flood over me. It had such a powerful impact that I have never looked back and from that moment, decided to give my life to the BKs. All my friends were living a very different lifestyle, graduating from their university courses, getting jobs, getting married, embarking on families, buying houses but now I knew I wanted none of that for myself.

'Because of Dadi Janki and my growing involvement with the BKs, I stayed in London until 1977, by which time things were beginning to take off in Sydney. Dr Nirmala, an Indian BK, had arrived in 1975 to spearhead the Australian operation and a fellow Australian, Ken O'Donnell (whose story is told on pages 76 to 82), was involved in a BK centre there.'

After Charlie arrived back in Sydney he started running a centre there and has been running centres there ever since.

'We now have huge centres all over Australia and most of this success is down to Dadi Janki. She seems to have the ability to create a personalised relationship with you and she always gives you her undivided attention. She wants to know about your spiritual journey and encourages you to talk about it – always with an interpreter of course, as she has only ever spoken Hindi herself. It's amazing how Dadi, being so Indian herself, can immediately connect with so many people from all cultures, races and backgrounds.'

The thing is, Charlie adds, that Dadi is always open to learn and from the start, has been fascinated to delve into how Westerners think. 'She feels that by and large, we are honest and straightforward whereas in comparison, Indians tend to be tricky and not like that. Dadi has from the start been open to work with people who have different perspectives, a different take on life, and this has helped her grow as well. She has never been narrow, and is willing to embrace all cultures and religions because she feels that at heart, everybody wants the same things in life – peace, love and harmony – even if often it does not seem like that.'

The fact that Dadi is female was also an important aspect for Charlie. 'Wherever she goes, Dadi creates an atmosphere of love and belonging which to me, is more an aspect of female than male nature. This is of course very important for all BKs coming from different cultures. There are 70 or 80 different nationalities now in the Australian centres and we all come together. This is thanks in large part, I would say, to Dadi Janki and her ability to focus directly on the soul and not the body, or physical costume, which she sees before her.'

Dadi's unique speciality, believes Charlie, is her breadth of vision. 'Although she always sees the big picture in terms of BK expansion, she also has the ability to fix her gaze on you and see your potential. She is never affected by any doubts that you may have. Also her face always radiates peace and calm. You never see her any other way. I have met many powerful and successful people and there is no peace in their faces.

'Dadi in particular always pushes boundaries. She is always pushing, pushing, pushing for you to do better, to open another centre, to run a massive programme when there is no money to do it, and to push you, the individual, to ever greater levels of perfection.

'She always had a big vision as to how things could be in the West and this vision was of something that would touch all cultures.' Charlie believes that in 2015 this vision has largely come true.

'We have three big residential centres now in Australia and, true to Dadi's original principles, we have never charged for any of our programmes or retreats. We have a box for donations and I would say that 90 per cent of people never give more than the minimum, but that a significant few give more, much more. One guy for instance who ran a lightbulb company gave us enough bulbs to last at least 10 years. This is the kind of thing that happens when you don't charge fees. Another guy came to our retreat in the Blue Mountains and it was freezing cold, so he paid for underfloor heating. That made a huge difference to our comfort levels, but we would never have asked for the money for this.

'One chap who came to one of our centres was running an advertising agency and he said his staff never worked anything like as hard as we did. I think that people get a lot of satisfaction from voluntary work and put in more hours than those on a set wage.'

Charlie is certain that not charging gives the BKs a high profile and also makes them different from many other spiritual organisations which charge high prices for their events and particularly, their residential retreats. 'Dadi Janki has such generosity of spirit. She wants to give all the time and giving love and respect to everybody she meets has enabled people to support the organisation financially. We just about balance the books every year but unlike some charities, we never accumulate in Swiss banks, for example. Everything that comes in goes straight out again in some form of service.

'We are, I believe, the only spiritual organisation which doesn't charge and which has remained true to its original principles. Dadi Janki embedded in us all the principles of money and integrity and for this reason, our values have remained high.'

Does Charlie think that the massive growth in the West since 1974 could have happened without Dadi Janki? He is adamant that it would not. 'Dadi's greatest talent as I see it is her ability to impart wisdom. She also invests so much faith in you and sees your potential. Then she works with that. She has a rare ability to connect with people and this is why so many of us have remained loyal and loving and watched the organisation grow while so many other Indian-based movements have fizzled out.

'Dadi's own relationship is and always has been directly with God and this is the most significant aspect. She instilled into me how to love God and make him real in my life. This is the greatest gift she has given me and it continues to this day.'

Because of this, Charlie says, he has never had any regrets about not following a conventional life and that being a pioneer BK, eventually responsible for centres all over Australia, has given him perfect fulfillment.

And all from that one chance encounter – or was it chance? – at the Spiritualist Association of Great Britain.

Ken O'Donnell. Originally from Australia, Ken now oversees BK centres in South America.

Like many young Australians of the time, Ken came to London in the 1970s in search of fun, adventure and perhaps the meaning of life. He found all three, as he explains:

'I was studying to be an industrial chemist in Sydney when I decided to take time off from my studies to travel and see the world. I was a fully paid up – or perhaps not paid-up – member of the hippy generation and I was living in a squat in Regents' Park. I was making just about enough money to live on as a musician, busking in the streets and playing in pubs. I had already spent five months in silence in Morocco, meditating, and so was definitely leaning towards the spiritual and the introspective. And I already felt that I wanted to dedicate my life to others, and to help people.

'I arrived in London in August 1975 and one of the first things I did was to look up Charlie, who I had already known in Sydney. I was astonished to learn that he was getting up early to go and meditate, and decided to go along with him. That was my first contact with the BKs.

'I did not do the introductory course as Dadi and Jayanti were not there, but were up in the North somewhere. Sister Sudesh was taking classes and I got stuck straight into the meditation and early morning classes. There was instantly something which attracted me but when I met Dadi, everything changed.

'Here I was, this hairy critter in my Moroccan clothes – the only ones I had at the time – and I wondered what Dadi would make of me. I remember my first meeting with her, down a narrow staircase in Tennyson Road. She looked at me, gave me long drishti, and said, "You will do service in the whole world."

'I had no such plans and had no idea what 'service' meant, but that was it. I was touched, and very affected by the vibrations that I sensed were emanating from Dadi.'

At the time, says Ken, he didn't understand anything about the BKs' system of beliefs or have any real idea what they were about. 'My five months of silence in Morocco had been spent trying to understand what life was all about and I had been travelling a long time and seen a lot. Because of this perhaps, one thing I understood immediately about the BKs was that they practised purity. They were honest and straightforward and they practised what they preached.

> 'Dadi, it seemed to me, was holding things together with her power of inner peace. She didn't speak any English, Jayanti was very young and Sudesh didn't speak much English either, so it was hardly an organisation that had got off the ground. Dadi Janki would read the Murli – the daily sermon – to us in Hindi, and Jayanti would write out the translation in longhand. There were only half a dozen of us meeting in the early mornings and it so it was very intimate, but also very amateurish. I had absolutely no thought of doing service and after three months I returned to Australia.'

At the time, says Ken, Dadi was taking a very keen interest in all the Westerners who were coming to the early morning classes and meditation sessions and before long, it seemed she had big plans for all of them. 'Dadi was very concerned that I should go back to Australia and so I obeyed her. But I did not become a BK right away. As soon as I completed my studies, I went to work at Max Factor, the cosmetics company. But inside, the idea grew and grew that I should do service, as they called it, for the BKs.

'Dr Nirmala, an Indian sister who had originally come to Australia to start the BK movement there, had had to return to India as her visa ran out, and the centre had closed down. Everything folded and so it was just me there, trying to get service going on my own. I held outdoor meetings in parks, and soon people were coming for meditation.'

In early 1976, Ken found an apartment in Sydney that he thought would be suitable for holding meditation sessions and classes, and he began advertising Raja Yoga meditation. 'We were a band of transformed hippies,' he says, 'Charlie stayed on for another year or 18 months in London while I was trying to get a BK centre going in Sydney. I was the first Westerner to get things going in Australia but for a long time wondered how on earth I was going to get the movement to take off.

'So I did the sensible thing and asked Dadi Janki. From the start, I felt she had such confidence in me. Dadi said that I was essential to the West and she had such faith in my ability; far more than I had myself, I must admit. She has a long-term vision of people and she can see things in you that may not be apparent to others.

'First of all, she has faith in the soul. I would certainly often have felt alone but for her subtle back-up and confidence in me.' From the start, Ken says, he loved the self-discipline of the yoga lifestyle, the ascetic aspects and the fact that so much time was spent in silence. 'Not speaking, remaining silent, was always very attractive to me.'

Before long, Ken felt he wanted to do more than just run centres. The idea was that he should write books explaining Raja Yoga to a Western audience. At the time, the only literature was Indian material translated into more or less unintelligible English. 'Dadi was my inspiration for books,' he says.

> 'She asked me to speak to Jagdish, the Indian brother who had so far written all the BK literature in existence, in Hindi. I promised Dadi that I would not go ahead with writing unless Jagdish gave me the go-ahead. He did. He was a very deep thinker himself and gave me a boost of confidence to start writing. So I started to write books in English, Spanish and Portuguese.'

After Charlie Hogg returned to Australia and started setting up BK centres there Ken felt it was time for him to expand his reach and he went to South America, where he has been co-ordinating BK work since the early 1980s.

'Writing books and explaining the BK wisdom has made me feel useful,' he says, and at 62 years old (at the time of writing) he is as committed as when a young man. Since meeting Dadi Janki, he has had no wish for any other life.

'From the start I could see that Dadi had wisdom and intelligence and she knows how to spot the truth in somebody. She can pick out the genuine people, the ones who are going to be an asset to the BKs. I had a high IQ and was sent to a special school for bright kids, and so I had a lot of arrogance about intelligence, but Dadi was something else. She was beyond intelligence but there was something else that drew me in.

'When I first met her, I had a very strong sense of déjà vu, that I had been here before. But it was the vibrations that pulled me in and kept me hooked. It seems to me now that Dadi had such a strong role to play with each person. There is nobody else in the BKs with her drive, her personality or her vision. She is unique and I feel highly privileged to be one of the first Westerners to meet her.'

Ken says that he has never wanted to get married or have children. 'I felt it wouldn't be fair if I brought up a family while I was on the road so much, and my BK life has been so very busy that a family would have been a distraction. I am still travelling around non-stop and am always organising retreats, programmes and events.'

Now, looking back on his life, Ken feels he has enabled thousands to take at least one step towards something better. As his name suggests, he comes from an Irish Catholic background which, he says, was particularly staunch on his mother's side. But like many lapsed Catholics, he was never happy with the rituals or the hierarchy, and from the beginning, the utter simplicity of the BK lifestyle spoke to his heart.

He never had any problem either, he said, with the BKs being female-led, in contrast with all other religions and Indian spiritual movements. 'That never made any difference. Before I came across the BKs, I had a girlfriend who was a strong feminist, so I was used to women being in charge.'

Balwant Patel

Like Charlie Hogg, Balwant Patel was studying architecture when he came across Dadi Janki and, also like Charlie, he never finished his studies.

The impact of meeting Dadi for both of these young men was so strong that it blotted out any prospect of a conventional life.

Balwant is from a Hindu background but was born and grew up in Nairobi, not India. He first came across Dadi Janki in Leicester, where in the 1970s there was already a big Indian community.

He was 21 years old. Now 60, Balwant says: 'From the moment I met Dadi Janki, thoughts of any other life, or a big career, faded away. It was all down to Dadi, and because of her I left my studies and never qualified. I also never married, which again was very unusual for an Indian.

> 'There was an instant attraction to Dadi. She had that look of attraction that made me want to hang on her every word. I came to London, where I worked for a year in the city, doing office work. But I knew by now that my real calling was to be a BK, and at Dadi's command.
>
> 'When I became a BK there was nobody to look after the property or maintenance, and that became my job. I was also Dadi's driver, a job I held for 36 years.'

As an Indian, Balwant was used to gurus. But they were all men and the idea that a woman could take that role, or be in charge of a spiritual community, was not only unusual, but it was actually shocking. 'When I told my sister that God can come into female bodies, she was stunned and would not believe me. We had all grown up thinking that only men could be in charge, whether this was in charge of the home, the finances, or spirituality.'

What is Dadi's attraction, does he think, looking back? 'From the start, Dadi Janki had the courage of renunciation. It didn't bother her that she was living in two small rooms and sharing a bathroom with the other tenants, when she came to London. She never wanted anything grand for herself, and as the organisation has grown, she has remained as simple in her needs and wants as she was then.

> 'Dadi has never worried about what kind of car
> she's got and in the early days some of them were
> rustbuckets indeed. Nor did Dadi ever see her
> driver as being beneath her. In her view, they were
> equal. Nor has Dadi ever had anything in her
> name. She would never spend anything on herself
> and never even say: this is my car.'

This is in complete contrast, says Balwant, to many
other Indian gurus who put themselves first and expect
to be worshipped by their followers. They have to be on
top, and see their followers as being less than themselves.
Dadi Janki would never allow any worship of herself
and has always treated everybody she meets as an equal.
Even the new students are seen as equals.

> 'Dadi has always practised what she preaches
> and has retained the virtues of simplicity and
> cleanliness. I think this is what attracts people; that
> those in charge live as simply as the new recruits.'

Balwant believes that this simplicity, and Dadi's ability
to treat everybody as equals, is what has allowed the
movement to grow. 'It was very unusual to have women
in charge,' he says, 'but being run by women makes
the BKs very different from other spiritual movements.
Possibly because of being run by women, the BKs have

this quality of openness and of giving. Dadi hates any sort of fuss, ceremony or ritual, and this again is very unlike many other Indian gurus.'

His family, initially, were not at all happy that he wanted to be a BK rather than a professional architect, or that he never wanted to get married. 'My family tried so hard to get me married, introducing me to lots of girls they thought were suitable, but I never succumbed. For me, being married would have been the end of being a BK.'

It is true that the BKs do discourage marriage, possibly because their roots were in arranged, or sometimes, forced marriages, to people they hardly knew and it was impossible thereafter to separate or divorce. Dadi Janki certainly never wanted to be legally tied to another human being and she prefers other BKs to remain single and not complicate their lives with wives, husbands or children. In this, the BKs operate much like Catholic monks, nuns and priests, whose vows (at the moment at least) require them to remain single and celibate.

Again much like Catholic priests, nuns and monks, the BKs believe that if you want to live a truly spiritual life, you must dedicate to God and not try at the same time to bring up a family, or have binding attachments to other people. Buddhist monks and nuns must also embrace celibacy and singleness.

But then, there is a long tradition in both Catholicism and Buddhism of celibacy for both men and women who wish to follow God. In Hinduism there is no such tradition. And although men are allowed to be sannyasis, holy people whose only allegiance is to God, this has never been an option for women.

So, celibacy and singleness has always been one of the most controversial aspects of the Brahma Kumaris, and remains so. One of the big problems with the BKs in the past was that they were accused to breaking up families. 'Celibacy has never been a problem in other religions,' Balwant says, 'but in India, everybody has to be married and celibacy seems very odd. It is one of the major things people have got against the movement and it was certainly the main problem in the early days.'

But once again, he says, the movement could not have taken off in the West in such a big way if adherents had been encouraged to marry and have families. These responsibilities would have seriously weakened the level of service that dedicated members of the movement have been able to offer.

But now we come on to two English people who actually were married – to each other – when they became BKs. ❦

CHAPTER FIVE

Maureen and David Goodman

The first Western married couple to join the organization, they have both been surrendered BKs since 1976.

Maureen and David were a young Jewish couple, newly married, when they came across the BKs. They were immediately attracted but had no idea how dramatically their lives would change as a result of this encounter. At the time, they were both in their early twenties. David had recently qualified as a dentist and Maureen as a speech therapist.

They became BKs together and, 40 years later, remain among the few Western couples to have embraced the teachings and the life so wholeheartedly – and to have remained married to each other.

Once they came into contact with Dadi Janki, the cosy yet ordinary family life they had envisaged for themselves was turned on its head forever. Today, David runs a thriving centre in Leeds and Maureen is the BKs' programme director in London. Both have travelled all over the world, held and organised events, conferences and programmes in a vast number of venues, and given many public talks.

Maureen was once so shy she could not envisage speaking to a crowd of five, never mind five thousand. Today, she is a pillar of the BK community in the West, fully committed and surrendered, as is David.

And, they say, it is all down to Dadi Janki seeing a potential that, at the time, neither they nor anybody else saw.

In 2015, Maureen and David celebrated their 40th wedding anniversary, yet for most of their marriage they have never lived together. They have remained celibate and have never had any children, but they believe their unusual union is happier, and certainly longer-lasting, than most.

Maureen, a petite, dark-haired woman who is often mistaken for an Indian, says:

'I can remember the exact date and time that David and I first came across the BKs. It was on 23rd August, 1976 at 7pm. David and I had been married for 18 months and had already spent a lot of time meditating and searching for something. We were in Edinburgh on holiday and intending to go up to Findhorn, the alternative community in Forres, Scotland. I would say that even at this young age – I was only 21 – we were both seekers, and looking for something more. It wasn't that we were unhappy, but we felt there must be something more to life than what we had experienced so far.

"We were married when I was 19 and David was 22. Nowadays that seems incredibly young but we were in love, we had already known each other for several years and we felt we wanted to make life's journey together.'

At the time, the BKs had only had a presence in the West for a couple of years and there was no centre in Scotland but an early BK who was Scottish had organised an exhibition, and a group had come up from London.

'The exhibition was full of odd pictures illustrating various aspects of Raja Yoga teaching. They were the sort of gaudy, very Indian pictures that you would never see today and we didn't know what to make of it. The BKs had not got going in the UK at this time and there were just a few Indians holding the thing together, without any proper premises or any real idea how they were going to establish the organisation.

'We came to the exhibition through being handed a leaflet on the street by a young Indian woman. Well,' says Maureen, 'that leaflet changed our lives. We heard a lecture given by Sister Sudesh and met her afterwards.'

The talk was not crowded and only around 10 to 15 people were there. 'Both David and I instantly felt a strong attraction towards this group,' Maureen says, 'and we wanted to know more. So instead of going to Findhorn, we stayed in Edinburgh and took the BK course. It was the long hot summer of 1976 and we went every day to meditate and hear the classes. For both of us, something clicked. For me, it was as if I had always been hearing the teachings and they didn't sound at all strange.

'Sudesh then invited us for lunch at somebody's house. We were already vegetarian, so the food did not seem all that strange. It was simple Indian food and although everything was extremely low key, I felt as if I was in Heaven. It all felt so wonderful that Sudesh then said: come to London for a week.

'I already felt as if this was going to take me over. David got a job as a dentist in Bradford and I had just qualified as a speech therapist. We decided to go to London and meet the BKs properly. We both felt that it was our destiny and that, really, we had no choice. Both of us were equally keen on the BK teachings and we stayed in a flat belonging to the BKs. We meditated every morning and were totally immersed. By the end of the week, it all seemed to make sense. Then we met Dadi Janki. That was it, really.'

But there was a lot to sort out. David had now started working as a dentist in Bradford and Maureen started work as a speech therapist in Leeds. 'We were so enraptured by the BKs that we became overzealous and could not get enough of it. Almost at once, we started to teach courses ourselves, in our little flat and we also organised the first event for Dadi Janki and Jayanti in Leeds.'

Things moved faster and faster. By December that same year, David and Maureen travelled to India where they had time to get to know Dadi Janki properly. 'She was an awesome personality,' says Maureen, 'and I was totally in awe. She seemed strong and wise although I wasn't sure what to make of her. Don't forget that I was still only 21. Jayanti and Sudesh seemed more accessible than Dadi, who was completely on another level. I felt that I was coming in front of a great being, and yet she was very simple. She had no airs and graces, and seemed to connect directly with you.

> 'In India, at Mount Abu, I felt it was all completely genuine. There was total recognition. We met Baba, who the BKs see as the combined form of Brahma Baba and the Supreme, channeled through Dadi Gulzar. He said to us that we would be examples for the rest of the world. I felt immediately that this is what I wanted life to be.
>
> 'After coming back from India, we went every weekend to London, where we would sit on a little plastic mat on the floor in Tennyson Road. In those

days, Dadi Janki did the cooking and she seemed an unlikely combination of being awesome and at the same time being a mother. She was like nobody I had ever met before and yet as I got to know her, I felt we tuned into each other perfectly. Not only was I strongly attracted, I quite definitely felt I was hearing the truth. This was IT and I felt I did not need to search any more.'

Both Maureen and David had been to other gatherings and although they were interested by what they heard – the Kabbala, other meditation methods – there was nothing they felt they wanted to give their lives to. 'But this felt safe and right. We did not have to look any further. Dadi Janki of course had a lot to do with it but as well as filling me with these truth vibrations, she saw in me something I didn't see in myself.

'For me, Dadi Janki was the true example of what spirituality was all about.'

Yet they soon hit a major problem. Before long, Jayanti revealed to them the uncomfortable truth that if they wanted to be dedicated BKs, they had to be celibate. Now, this may not be such a big deal for a couple who have been married for 30 years and had their family but for Maureen and David, at 21 and 24 respectively, not long married, and without any children as yet, it was a shocking blow.

'I cried and cried because I wanted children,' remembers Maureen. 'David was happy with celibacy right away and we agreed to give it a try for a two-month trial period. For a couple only just embarking on married life it was a lot to ask and I had to accept at a young age that if I wanted to be a BK I would never have sex again and would never have children. Instead, I was going to have to give myself to a life of service to God.

'But then, it became more important to be surrendered to this life. So after my initial shock, I realised I could not fight it and there was simply no choice. David and I were lucky because we were both equally committed and for most couples, this is not the case. One will be committed and the other will not – and when that happens, serious problems occur.'

By 1978, David and Maureen were working towards establishing a permanent centre in Leeds. David was still working full time but Maureen had gone part time as she decided she wanted to be a full time BK. The projected centre in Leeds took some time to get going but by now there was a centre in Edinburgh. Sister Sudesh was running it and Maureen went there to help out. 'I stayed there for 18 months, going backwards and forwards from Edinburgh to Leeds. Then, in January 1982, Dadi Janki invited me to London for six weeks to look after the office there while another British BK,

Waddy, (as Veronica McHugh, whose story is told on pages 104 to 112, was known) was away. They were still in Tennyson Road although by now had bought the house next door.

'After my six weeks were up I went back to Leeds and in October, an invitation came for Waddy to go to Tampa, Florida. Once again I was invited to go to London for six weeks to help out there.'

Those six weeks, says Maureen wryly, have so far turned into 33 years. Reflecting on that decision now, she says: 'From the moment she came to London, Dadi Janki had a gift for picking the right people, for finding key instruments. Of course in the early days she had to rely on people who turned up, interested in the meditation and the teachings, and they may not have been suitable instruments at all. But many of us who took the course in London became early pioneers.

'Dadi was keen to send people out to Australia, America and so on, and set down BK roots in every part of the Western world.' Charlie Hogg went back to Australia, Waddy to Florida, Denise Lawrence to San Francisco and Ken O'Donnell to Brazil. Meanwhile, Maureen remained based in London.

'From the start, Dadi would know who were the right people for the job. She had that leadership gift of picking the key people, and to see in which ways they would best serve the organisation.'

Don't forget, Maureen says, that she was still in her early twenties and had hardly been anywhere or done anything. But before long, she was plunged into the very hectic BK lifestyle that she has followed ever since. 'I had never seen myself holding conferences, speaking in public or addressing important people. I was far too shy and nervous. But in 1985, I went to see Lord Ennals, who had been a cabinet minister, at a peace conference. I had to pluck up courage to go and speak to him. I worried that I would not be able to utter a word, but I found the confidence to talk to him. It was as if Baba was pushing me out there and I had to keep facing these challenges.'

Maureen was brought up in a religious, although not ultra-orthodox, Jewish household and she sees the BKs and Judaism sitting together comfortably enough. She has also kept a good connection with the Jewish community and that again was another strength that Dadi Janki foresaw. And also before long, Maureen abandoned her Western clothes and adopted the white sari full time.

She says that one reason the sari did not seem all that strange to her was because her parents got married in Calcutta and her mother was brought up in Rangoon, Burma. 'So for me, the Eastern influence was already there, even though like David I was brought up in

Liverpool. In the BKs, we've kept the white sari as a tradition for full-time BKs and I like wearing it as it identifies me as a BK.'

Does she have any regrets that at such an early age she abandoned all hopes of a family and what most people would consider a normal married life to become a fully surrendered BK? After all, she and David have remained married.

She says quite categorically: 'None at all. Once I met the BKs, thoughts of any other life fell right away. On any level, I would not have done half the things I have done without the BKs. I have travelled all over the world, met a host of interesting people including world leaders, have hosted and spoken at any number of conferences, devised programmes and played a central part of the organisation's expansion. I can't now remember how many times I've been to India.

'It seems to me, looking back, that I have been the recipient of amazing fortune.' The greatest gift that Dadi Janki gave her, Maureen says, is that she believed in her.

'And she continues to believe in me and care for me. She always understood just how far she could push me and quite honestly, I would never have imagined half the things she has pushed me into.'

Now it's David's turn to give his side of the story.

'Maureen and I had gone to Findhorn quite a few times and in fact had our honeymoon there, so we were gradually getting immersed in spirituality and another way of looking at things. As Maureen has said, we were both spiritual seekers from an early age and preferred this journey to the fun and games that other young people of our age were having in those days.'

This may be the place to say a few words about Findhorn, once a bleak caravan park on the coast of Scotland and now one of the biggest 'alternative' communities in the world. It began life in 1962 when Peter and Eileen Caddy and their friend Dorothy Maclean were sacked from their job at the Cluny Hotel near Findhorn. They had no money and nowhere to live and ended up in a caravan at Findhorn village.

All three of them had for a long time been interested in spiritual matters and at the caravan park things changed for them forever. Eileen Caddy began to meditate on one of the public lavatories, having nowhere else to go, and there she heard a voice saying, 'Be Still and Know that I am God.' Eileen began to listen and the 'voice' told her to plant a wonderful vegetable garden. Now, Findhorn is famous for the fact that nothing will grow there but Eileen heeded the words, bought some seeds from their dole money, and planted them.

Before long a wonderful garden began to grow where the vegetables were twice their normal size. Or at least, we have to take their word for it as no pictures are extant. But the word spread and people came to see this wonder of nature. Meanwhile, Dorothy Maclean was in touch with vegetable fairies or 'devas' as they were known.

By 1972 a community had grown up and Peter and Eileen were able to buy the hotel from which they had been ignominiously sacked. When David and Maureen travelled to Findhorn in the mid-1970s, it had become a well-established residential centre offering meditation, lectures and spiritual experiences, and was world famous.

Although the Goodmans were attracted to Findhorn and the then very new experiences the centre was offering, they did not feel that it was their final spiritual home.

> 'From a young age, Maureen and I both had the desire to explore spirituality, although I cannot say that I was at all religious,' David says. 'My own Jewish background was less religious than Maureen's and although I had done my Bar Mitzvah, and gone to the synagogue regularly as a teenager, by my early twenties I had become an atheist. I could no longer take on board what the rabbi was saying about God being a jealous God or a vengeful God.
>
> 'What I did know was that I liked kindness, honesty, authenticity and knew that all these were spiritual qualities, but it seemed I was not finding them in established religion.

'I was a fanatical sports person, both playing and watching and from that perspective had become very confident in my abilities. I was also quite clever and the youngest person in my year at dental school. But I was not used to dealing with people and at dental school we were only taught technical skills. There were no classes or courses on how to deal with patients, or how to handle people who had dental phobia – very common indeed, in both adults and children.

'So initially, I was looking for spiritual answers as to how to deal with stress, how to reduce it in myself and also in my patients. Once I qualified, I started working with young children and in particular, working with children who other dentists couldn't treat as they were so nervous. My young patients were mainly from rough working class estates and from dysfunctional families. Many had come originally from Indian villages. They had often come straight from their village to a reception centre in Bradford where I was then working and of course their parents couldn't speak any English.

'As a young dentist of 22, I was expected to be able to deal with these people. I was seeing 25 to 30 terrified kids a day.'

When David met the BKs he had, he says, 'a garage full of spiritual books' and he knew he needed to be calm and peaceful at work. The spiritual books he read were not really working for him and he soon realised he needed something other than books, some genuine introduction to the spiritual dimension.

His initial attraction to the BKs came about because he felt they embodied deep spirituality with practicality. 'I hadn't seen that in other movements,' he says. 'In those days Dadi Janki did the cooking and she was filling the food with vibrations that helped the mind to become peaceful. It seemed a strange idea at the time, that food could have vibrations, but now of course there is scientific evidence to show that the mood in which food is cooked, does make a difference.

> 'But of course, Dadi was not just cooking. She was also giving classes and talking about spirituality and my God she packed a punch. She was able to talk about deep spiritual matters and make them accessible to everybody. Don't forget,' David adds, 'that a lot of Westerners coming in the early days were intelligent, educated people who were not going to put up with a lot of stuff that didn't make sense.'

> 'Added to that was her vibrational energy. She was sensible and clear and at the same time, lived the life she was recommending. She definitely, as we would say today, walked her talk.'

In his previous searches, David had found talk about spirituality, and particularly Indian spirituality, waffly and vague. 'I didn't understand why spirituality couldn't be clear but here was a clear explanation about who I am. I had never before heard anybody say: I am a soul.

The clarity was there right from the start and that for me was one of the main attractions. Plus, the vibrations emanating from Dadi were hard to ignore. No, let me rephrase that: they were impossible to ignore, and that was what kept Maureen and myself coming back time and again for more.

'I also liked the way Dadi talked about God, as a close intimate companion. She brought home to me what God was really all about. There was no mystery to it.

'Once, Dadi was talking about God with a French monk. He was saying that God was a mystery, and Dadi said, he's not a mystery to me. She added that she spoke with God every day and they understood each other perfectly. That was what I wanted to hear. The Jewish idea of God being vengeful and jealous didn't make sense and now I was hearing that God was the source of every good quality and that through constant connection we could access those qualities for ourselves.

'I saw that Dadi Janki was both spiritually high level, and grounded, and soon realised this was the path for me. For instance, when I went to their little centre in Tennyson Road, Dadi would say: cook something for David. She was never up in the clouds, but she looked after my bodily needs as well as imparting the highest level of spirituality I had ever come across.'

David and Maureen soon understood they were seriously fast-tracking with the BKs and they found some of the cultural practices strange. 'For instance, men and women sat on different sides of the room and did not sit together when they ate, either. I realised that this was probably more of a cultural than a spiritual thing, but I went along with it.'

The next hurdle was the insistence on celibacy. As a very young, newly married couple, David and Maureen did not expect to have a celibate marriage. But when it was mentioned, David instantly realised the value of it. 'Dadi said quite early on that if people wanted to get the maximum out of spirituality, they had to be celibate. It would not have occurred to me on my own but once it was mentioned, my soul immediately understood that this had to be the case.

'Maureen was so upset because she wanted children but she agreed to give celibacy a try and of course, it hastened our stage of progress. So before long, we embarked on a celibate marriage, which ruled out children, but I have never minded about that. The vibrations and the body of knowledge that was being imparted was so irresistible that it blotted out every consideration of what most people consider a normal married life.

'But then, what would you call a normal family life? There are many marriages where partners don't see much of each other. Our marriage is different, yes, but it works for us. It didn't happen by design but just evolved. I don't see any loss in our relationship. There are certainly no regrets for the way things turned out.'

David is keen to point out that he is fond of children, and the fact he never had any of his own doesn't mean he is anti kids. 'I have always worked with children and enjoyed working with them. It didn't happen that we had any of our own, but for us that is OK.

'Celibacy felt natural to me and once Maureen got over her thing about having kids, she was happy with it too. We are still married after 40 years and if one of us had felt strongly that we wanted children, or that celibacy was a hard struggle, we would have separated and sought other partners. But we are happy with how things are and I would say we are deeply and equally spiritual. Many people say they have never seen a marriage like it but I've still got a wife, we are still good friends, and I see Maureen as my line manager.

'She is a warm, special person and very kind but more than that, I have seen how she has developed as a person. Dad Janki instantly saw that Maureen had a huge amount of potential and she has been able to fulfill that. I certainly was not going to stand in her way. Being Jewish, Maureen has a good sense of humour and she is also a good joke teller. This has also stood her in good stead with the BKs, who have a strong sense of humour themselves. When once I asked Dadi Janki whether angels had a sense of humour, she said: you bet!'

Some years ago, David was diagnosed with cancer and this led him to take early retirement from his job and concentrate on running a BK centre full time. 'If I had not had that grounding in spiritual practice, it would have made things so much worse,' he says.

Whether God played a part in David's recovery from cancer can never be known, but after extensive treatment he was given the all-clear.

Veronica McHugh also became a BK in 1976.

Veronica, always known as Waddy, came from a large family of traditional Irish Catholics. She left Ireland with her brother in early 1968 with no idea that the discontent that had been tamped down in Northern Ireland for so long was about to erupt and that the Derry march in October would mark the beginning of it all.

Although she had left Ireland just before what has since been known as 'the troubles' began in earnest, it was fortuitous that she was no longer there when the civil rights march in Londonderry happened, owing to what followed.

The peaceful march, which has gone down in history, was brutally broken up by police using water cannon and batons, and many people, including MP Gerard Fitt, were injured. Beaten by the Royal Ulster Constabulary, Fitt was taken to hospital where he received several stitches to the head. Considered to be the start of the Troubles, the march was held in protest at what many saw as discrimination against the mainly Catholic population by the minority Protestant local authority.

'I felt I could no longer remain in Ireland,' she said, and she went to England where, at the time, she had no thoughts of joining an Indian spiritual movement. For one thing, she was too strongly Catholic. 'When I was 15 and on holiday, I missed Mass for the very first time in my life, and thought that the sky would fall in. I was a true dyed in the wool Catholic, where the belief is that God and Christ are the same, and with the Holy Spirit, the three in one. Yet something in me yearned for mystical experiences of my own. Once I left Ireland, I began to travel the world in search of experiences, although at the time I did not know exactly what.

'Whenever I had saved up enough money from my job as a civil servant, I would go travelling. I had always had a deep longing to travel, and was now satisfying my wanderlust at every opportunity. At the age of 26, much like Charlie and Ken, I was a backpacker in search of adventure. As I travelled, I came in contact with a wider world than that of Northern Ireland and the dreadful political situation there, and realised that I was looking for something beyond Catholicism, beyond ritual and prayer.

'Back in London in 1974, I started looking for meditation courses and one of my brothers sent me an article from the Guardian about Hatha Yoga, then very new. Very few people had heard of Hatha Yoga in those days and this article stimulated my interest. I signed up for it, with an Indian teacher, but I really wanted to learn meditation. Transcendental Meditation was just getting going in London then and I checked it out but was horrified by the prices being charged. I felt very strongly that they were charging for something that should be freely available.

'Then by accident, I heard Jayanti speaking on the radio. This was the long hot summer of 1976 and I was entranced by her voice. She was promoting an exhibition at Kensington Town Hall, and mentioned meditation. I was captivated by her clear English accent, and decided to go along.'

It was a typical BK – or should we say typically Indian – exhibition, with gaudy pictures of the Knowledge and gods and goddesses of the Indian religion. Waddy now says she cannot remember much about the exhibition, but something made her sign up for the seven-day course, which was being held at the little flat in Tennyson Road.

'At the time, I did not have any inclination to join a group and when I filled in the form for the course I put my name down as Waddy, rather than Veronica, and refused to give my phone number as I didn't want them calling me.

'I went along to the centre and was not very impressed. The flat was a tenement house and had gaudy Indian decorations all over it. It was abysmal and this was at a time when many other Indian spiritual teachers were living in splendour in mansions or expensive flats.

'But at my very first session I met Dadi Janki, and that was an amazing experience. She was sitting on a big white stool, known as a gaddi, and her hair was out, not in a plait. There was a group of about 10 to 15 Westerners in this tiny room and they were going up to Dadi to have a badge pinned on them. I'm sitting there thinking, there is no way she is going to pin a badge on me.

'Sister Sudesh kept beckoning to me to go up, thinking I was holding back because I was shy, and I kept shaking my head. Then Dadi picked up the vibe, looked at me and said: you don't have to do anything you don't want to do.

'At that very point, I felt that Dadi Janki 'got' me, that she understood. She immediately seemed to know something about me and sensed that I was reluctant to go up for this little ceremony. I was not immediately overwhelmed by the BKs and yet something kept puling me back. I loved the classes, although the Murli – the sermon supposedly channeled directly from God – didn't make a lot of sense to me.'

Eventually, Waddy felt she had to check the organisation out at its source and later that year, went to Mount Abu where she stayed for several months. 'I had been wearing a sari in India and when it came time to go back, I found I could no longer get into my jeans. So I headed back to England in a sari, taking a huge amount of *toli* (sweets) back with me for the Tennyson Road centre.

'When I got back and gave the toli to Dadi, she asked me where I was staying. It was with one of my brothers in Harlesden, in the London borough of Brent, North-West London, which was quite a deprived area at the time. It was a big deal to get on the bus every day to go Tennyson Road, particularly on a Sunday, when the schedule was different and the classes were longer than on weekdays.

'So Dadi said, why don't you stay here for a few days? At the time there were three Indian sisters living at the centre: Dadi, Sudesh and Jayanti. By now I was running out of money, and went back to work. I didn't like the idea of being on the dole or living off charity and I wanted to get my own flat. However, before long I had decided to throw my lot in with the BKs and I did not work again.'

Waddy soon became a surrendered BK and, forty years later, is still as convinced as ever that this organisation is speaking the truth. Now running a centre in Miami, Waddy believes that it was Dadi Janki who worked the magic.

'Everybody remembers the first time they met Dadi,' she says. 'When I first came to the centre there was nobody to tell me anything. The organisation was so new in the UK and had hardly got going. But from the first, I felt, I really like this woman. She seemed to have a quality of being able to look into your heart. Another BK of the time said to me, Dadi knows, but she doesn't know she knows. It's all through intuition. Whatever it was, she gave me something that turned the whole thing round for me. I kept thinking to myself: why do I have so much love for her?

'It seems as though she embodies everything I want in my life. I knew from an early age that my life was not going to be about marriage and kids, although I never had a calling to become a

Catholic nun. Rather, I saw myself as this freaky old lady, a kind of benevolent aunt, but not a mother or a wife. And because of my forty-year involvement with the BKs, I do not feel that I have missed out on a thing. I would not have wanted any other life.'

Waddy says she soon realised that this path mapped out by the BKs was the highest she had ever come across, higher than Catholicism and as all Catholics will agree, their roots go very deep and are difficult to dig out. But there was another aspect which held a great appeal for Waddy and this was that women were in charge and women were running the show, in contrast to every other religion or spiritual movement, new or old. 'I had never come across it before and it was a major attraction for me.'

Waddy has lived in America since 1982, firstly in Tampa, Florida and then in Miami, where she has been in charge of operations since 1985. And although a dedicated BK for nearly forty years, she still feels that she is being subtly influenced by Dadi. 'I seem to have a special relationship with her and there is and always has been, a feeling of equality between us. Dadi never puts any distance between you and her and I like to make her laugh. She has a great sense of humour in addition to all her other special qualities.

'Once I asked her whether she still loved me and she asked me whether I thought I could manage if she didn't. For me, she is the personification of what the BKs are all about.'

Although Dadi Janki has suffered from many serious illnesses in her life, she keeps going because she always feels she has more to give, Waddy believes. 'As soon as she gets some energy, she is up and about again. I have seen some of the other elderly sisters become permanently incapacitated, but not Dadi Janki.'

Summing up what she believes Dadi Janki is all about, Waddy says: 'You never see her taking anything for herself. She doesn't hold onto anything and as soon as any money or resources come into the organisation, she thinks about what to do with them immediately. Dadi has also, in common with many tycoons, always thought big. Even when she was living in that tiny two-roomed flat, she was thinking beyond it, thinking about how to get big centres going, how to hold major programmes and how to attract Westerners to the movement which was, I have to say, totally Indian in the early days. But although Dadi Janki always had a big vision, she also saw ways of making it happen. It was never pie in the sky, but always practical and down to earth.'

It's the same with people, Waddy adds. 'She always sees beyond what you are doing at the moment and takes you beyond what you thought was your ultimate capacity. I never saw myself running a centre in Miami, of all places, in the early days, but that is what Dadi saw for me.' One of Waddy's achievements was to bring

Bee Gee Robin Gibb and his wife Dwina (who came from the same part of Ireland as Waddy) close to the movement and for a time, programmes and events were held in their sumptuous house on Miami beach.

Back in the UK, Dwina and Robin also held events for the BKs at their home in Thame, Oxfordshire, a 13th century former abbey.

In 2006, Robin Gibb composed a song especially for Dadi Janki which he called Mother of Love and when Robin died in 2012, there were many BKs at his funeral.

If you are a woman, making the decision to be a surrendered BK means you have to strip away every aspect of personal vanity and also take on an alien costume, at least, a form of dress alien to Westerners. This has never been a problem for Waddy. She has worn a sari, or sometimes kurta pyjamas, since 1976 and sees this outfit as her 'hair shirt'. 'I had widened out while in India in 1976 so I wore a sari and have worn one ever since. It was part of what I knew I had to do if I wanted to dedicate to the movement and people often say I look like an angel. It is a basic aspect of surrender, like being a nun.' ❧

The Importance of Celibacy

Now that we have met the first (Western) married couple to dedicate their lives, jointly and separately, to the BK organisation, this seems an appropriate point to discuss what is perhaps the most controversial aspect of the teachings, which is the insistence on celibacy, not just for those living in centres and ashrams, but for everybody who wishes to follow the precepts and live the BK lifestyle.

This especially applies to the inner circle of course, but even casual, occasional members are introduced to the idea of celibacy, or chastity, as a goal to aim at. Chastity is intimately associated with purity, cleanliness and self-denying ordinances, all practices associated with religious belief. It is one of Dadi Janki's most profound beliefs, that anybody who wants to come close to God and to connect constantly with God, cannot at the same time be having a sexual relationship with another human being.

Several religions, or faiths, embrace celibacy and all have strictures, or guidelines at the very least, as to how sexual behaviour should be conducted or regulated. Catholic priests and nuns, and also Buddhist monks and nuns, are supposed to be celibate and indeed, must take a vow of celibacy when they enter the monastery. As we know, not all are able or willing to adhere to that vow, but it is a counsel of perfection that men and women who have dedicated their lives to God, must eschew all intimate human relationships.

Where the BKs differ is that they say everybody who aspires to know God intimately and deeply, must practise celibacy. This includes married members and those in an intimate partnership. This is in direct contrast with the Catholic church which encourages married members to 'increase and multiply'. Which, it must be said, many of them have done with enthusiasm. One BK, from a Catholic family in Switzerland, has 13 brothers and sisters. Fourteen kids! She herself is avowedly celibate.

In order to understand the insistence on celibacy for everybody, one has to go back to the origins of the Brahma Kumaris, then known as the Om Mandli. When Dada Lekhraj, later known as Brahma Baba, began having his visions, young women, both married and single, flocked to the fledgling organisation. In doing so, they were not only rebelling, but betraying their allotted fate, which was to marry at an early age and have as many children as possible, preferably boys, although in the days before so-called wrong-sex abortion, this could not be guaranteed. Even nowadays, it is said that although many Indian villages do not have clean water, they all have amniocentesis, the process by which the gender of an unborn child can be determined.

There was no possibility in Dadi Janki's day that any woman would be able to escape the fate of enforced marriage and enforced sex. No woman in the India of the time dare refuse her husband as she belonged to him, body and soul.

The refusal of the married women to return to their husbands brought about an important court case where the English judges of the day handed down the verdict that a woman over the age of 18 could choose for herself whether to marry and whether to have sexual intercourse. It was a radical decision that, more than anything else, enabled the Brahma Kumaris to flourish and expand, while being led by women.

Such a thing had never been known in India before and it gave a new and unprecedented freedom to women. If they had been forced back into their homes and forced into marriages, such expansion would never have happened and the BKs would have simply died out.

For Dadi Janki, the insistence on celibacy was even more meaningful than for the other young women who made up the Om Mandli. Although she had always wanted to dedicate her life to God – but saw no way of doing so until the Om Mandli came into existence – she was forced into an unwilling marriage with a young man she did not know at all.

Although this was common practice in the India of the time – and still is in many cases – it was not what Dadi wanted for herself. Things became even more desperate for her when she became pregnant and had a child. It seemed as though her dreams of dedicating her life to God were over, and that she would have to live an unhappy life as an unwilling wife and mother, with no power and no freedom.

As is told in the author's book *Peace and Purity*, Dadi engineered her escape, not without considerable difficulty, and achieved her ambition. It was possibly her own experience of unwilling and unwanted marriage, sex and children, that made her particularly determined that all BKs should become celibate, whether they were Indians or Westerners.

Dadi was certain that the insistence on celibacy would enable the message to be heard all over the world. It would mean that all races and cultures would be able to benefit, as members and adherents would have the freedom to travel the world, to dedicate their lives to God, and not be troubled by the limited attachments of a husband or wife and children.

In this she has been proved correct. The early Westerners who heard and understood the message, did become celibate – even the newly-married couple Maureen and David Goodman – and they did go out into the world and establish centres everywhere. None of this could have happened without this insistence.

Although Dadi Janki was the first Indian woman to come to the West and preach celibacy as a requirement for the spiritual life, she was not the first woman to found an influential movement based on absolute celibacy.

Most people nowadays have heard of the Shakers, if only in terms of furniture on clean, simple lines. The Shakers, originally known as the Shaking Quakers, were an offshoot of Christianity that flourished in the eighteenth century in Britain and America. In 1758 a woman, Ann Lee, became the head of the organisation after a series of visions and revelations whereby she foresaw the end of the world, and she prophesied that a new world order was about to come, and that the Shakers were to usher it in.

This new world order was based on celibacy, pacifism and complete equality between men and women. In particular, members were to renounce all lustful gratifications. In the days before effective contraception, there was no way that married women could avoid yearly childbirth, and this effectively prevented them from doing anything else.

But the Shaker women were different. In 1774 Ann Lee and her followers left England for America where they became extremely successful, particularly for their architecture and furniture, both of which were of a plain, durable style based on elegance and practicality. During their heyday, they had productive farms, orderly communities and were dedicated to hard work and perfection.

Their simple architecture, very different from the ornate styles at the time, had a lasting influence on American buildings. Because of their absolute insistence on celibacy, numbers naturally dwindled and the movement came to an end. But one wonders, how much of its success was due to celibacy and the consequent equality of women in the movement?

In many other religions and faiths, the lack of insistence on celibacy has been one of the main reasons for women's low position in society. One thinks of women in countries like Saudi Arabia, where men can have more than one wife, where women have no power or influence and the only thing they can do, really, is to have dozens of children. In Palestine, women routinely have 14 children and Orthodox Jews to this day have arranged marriages where women are expected to have as many children as possible. There are even ultra-orthodox girls' schools in London where girls are taught not to have a career of their own but to subjugate themselves to a husband. Nine children per family is not an unusual amount among the ultra-orthodox community in London.

Dadi Janki believes that it is impossible for women to be equal unless they are celibate. Many other Indian-based movements, such as Siddha Yoga and Sivananda Yoga, also place importance on celibacy, known as 'brahmacharya' in Hindi, but none are as strict as the

BKs. Perhaps again because of this high aim, the BKs have won great respect in leading religious and political circles.

Nor do women play such a central role in other spiritual movements, for all that Siddha Yoga now has a woman, known as Gurumayi, at its head.

There is absolutely no doubt that the Brahma Kumaris would not have expanded in the way it has without the insistence on celibacy. That is also why their centres can flourish and grow without ever charging for services, events or programmes. If members had families to keep, such expansion would have been unthinkable.

In much the same way, Catholic nuns and monks would not have been able to achieve their autonomy and influence without taking a vow of celibacy.

Some BKs maintain that celibacy is the organisation's greatest strength and also its greatest weakness, because it is easy to scoff and deride a movement which disallows an activity many people believe is as essential to being a human as food and drink. The author's book, *Sex is not Compulsory*, published in 1986, outlines many of the arguments in favour of a celibate lifestyle and one has to say that in recent years the results of unbridled lust have been easy to see.

One thinks of the recent cases against celebrities such as Jimmy Savile, Rolf Harris, Bill Cosby and Gary Glitter, to name but a few. All were accused of sexual activity with children and people were suitably horrified. In recent years also, there have been many cases brought against schoolteachers, heads of children's homes and others in positions of influence for engaging in sexual activity with minors. There were the disgraceful cases of vulnerable girls in children's homes being groomed for sex. The internet is full of pornographic images that anybody can download. Daily newspapers have their 'sidebars of shame' where bikini-clad women parade daily.

We have the spectacle of old men becoming fathers in their fifties, sixties and even seventies. It is never too late for sexual activity, it seems. Yet even in India, where women are forced to marry, it has long been the norm that men at least can go off and be sannyasis, holy men, when their reproductive days are over.

In the height of the sexual revolution, where women were being 'liberated' by a new ability to have sex with multiple partners without paying the price of pregnancy, Dadi Janki was encouraging these same young women to do without sex, not just for a brief period, but for a lifetime.

For some early adherents this was too much. They left the movement, got married, had families and disappeared, never to be seen or heard of again. The celibate members, men and women, meanwhile, went on to establish flourishing centres in many parts of the world.

Some BKs and ex-BKs have made the point that when they feel they are connecting directly to God, celibacy is easy. But if that connection is lost – and maintaining it throughout a lifetime does not happen for everybody – one of the first desires is to try and establish an intimate relationship with another human being. In my long association with the BKs, I have met former adherents who have proudly introduced me to their girlfriends, boyfriends, spouses or children.

Others can feel lonely and as if they have missed out by not having a human relationship and these people too, will usually leave the organisation. For Dadi Janki, the strong connection she feels with God has never been lost and some detractors feel that she is too harsh on them by insisting on celibacy, even if it wrecks a marriage.

For Dadi, there has never been any compromise or backsliding possible; the message is too important for that. Also, some who have writhed under Dadi's harsh strictures have pointed out that many of the other Dadis, who reside in India, have never been as strict as Dadi Janki. No, one might say, but on the other hand, they have not been responsible for inspiring and growing a global empire outside their home country.

It was the celibate army that went out into the world and established centres in just about every country outside India. Maureen Goodman has said that she cannot now count the number of times she has been to India. Would that or any of the other countless forms of service Maureen has been involved in have been possible if she had been bringing up the four children she originally wanted? For the BKs, instead of giving birth to children, you are enabled to give birth to yourself. ❧

Dadi Janki with Dadi Prakashmani, previous Head of Brahma Kumaris

CHAPTER SEVEN

Feminism

Hand in hand with celibacy, goes Dadi's stand on feminism.

Very quietly, without any obvious fuss, stridency or shouting but with total conviction, Dadi Janki is, and has been all her life, a radical feminist.

This is mainly because she believes that God is first and foremost the Mother, rather than the Father, and this has led her, throughout her life, to put the mothers first. By 'mother' she does not necessarily mean one who has given birth to a child, but one who mothers, who nurtures and who sets an example of how to behave.

This strikes a chord with the Catholic faith, where nuns are often called 'Mother' or 'Mother Superior' even when they have never been actual mothers.

On a more mundane level, Dadi's feminism also springs from rebellion against her restrictive childhood in India, where women were not only given no status at all, but were not considered capable of becoming religious leaders.

Although Dadi felt a strong connection with God from her earliest years and wanted to serve Him, there would have been no way she could have achieved this aim without the founding of the Brahma Kumaris in the 1930s which, for the first time in Indian history, put women to the fore.

This movement gave not only Dadi, but all the other young women who joined the organisation, a power, confidence and self-sufficiency that Indian women had never before possessed. They were now enabled by the sheer force of their convictions to venture out, firstly in India and secondly into the rest of the world, to start centres and to usher in a completely new kind of spiritual knowledge and wisdom.

Inwardly Dadi had never felt there was any reason why a woman could not lead but both in the East and in the West, it was not easy in a society where women always took their status from the men in their lives. What was it the poet Milton said in Paradise Lost: 'He for God only; she for God in him.' The idea that a woman was a weaker vessel, and in many cases a very weak vessel, was a universal concept, not confined to India.

Given the weight of society, custom and also women's own generally low opinion of themselves, Dadi knew she would not have an easy task showing that women were the spiritual equal of men, if not their superior, in either India or the West. She might have assumed that women had more freedom in the West as indeed they did, but when she arrived in the 1970s she would soon discover that women had not even started to make inroads as religious leaders.

They were forbidden by law to be ordained priests or vicars in the Church of England and there were certainly no women priests in the Catholic faith. There were no female rabbis either until 1975 and although women were allowed to become ministers in non-conformist churches, the prejudice was so great that their numbers remained insignificant.

During her time in the West, Dadi has seen things change dramatically as gradually, the bulwarks were broken down and women began to be religious leaders, first as a trickle and later as a flood. The whole thing took years and was the result of a huge and relentless campaign by women, who were hardly aided and abetted by male religious leaders on the whole, it has to be said.

As long ago as 1975, the General Synod, the Church of England's governing body, passed a motion saying there were 'no fundamental objections' to women being ordained. Yet for years it did not happen. In 1981, women were allowed to be deacons; one step down from an actual ordained priest. In 1984 the Synod voted for legislation to 'permit the ordination of women to the priesthood' to be prepared. In 1988, approval was given to the draft legislation, and in 1993, the measure finally received Royal Assent and became law. The first 32 women priests were ordained at Bristol Cathedral on 12 March 1994 - a historic day. It was to be another 20 years before the first woman bishop, the Rev Libby Lane, was appointed – amid much male, and some female, opposition.

In Judaism, women were officially allowed to become rabbis in the Reformed synagogue in 1987, and in 2014, Rachel Kohl Finegold, 33, was allowed to become, if not an actual rabbi, then the next thing down in the Orthodox Jewish faith in America.

Nowadays, at least at the lower levels, there are probably more practising women priests and rabbis than men, and one wonders what all the long drawn out fuss was about. Even the most traditional of church and synagogue goers have accepted that a woman can take the service and for most, it now seems perfectly normal to have a woman in charge of a place of worship.

But one has to remember that Dadi Janki was there first, holding court and gathering groups around her when it seemed that women would never be allowed to become full vicars, priests or rabbis. So you could say that she blazed a trail for women being spiritual leaders and not having to take their lead from men. She was the first female Indian spiritual leader to arrive in the West and if it was with less pomp and circumstance than the male gurus, at least she has lasted and gathered strength over the years.

Because she believed so fervently that women were naturally more attuned to the spiritual than men, she was able from the first to move forward with utter conviction.

There were other ways, too, in which Dadi Janki was a pioneer in a strange land. There was never any suggestion that the nascent Brahma Kumaris would be financially beholden to a man. Rather, they would raise their own finances and handle their own money. When she arrived in London in 1974, Western women were still widely expected to be kept by a man, to take his name on marriage and to follow where he led. Of course, that was also the norm in India, but Dadi was surprised to find it so prevalent in the West where women had by now claimed many freedoms for themselves still denied most women in India.

For instance, as late as the 1970s, it was difficult for women to secure an education or follow a profession in India, and divorce, even from the most dreadful husband, was considered a disgrace and reflected badly on the woman, whatever the actual circumstances. Women were still kept very sheltered and expected to enter into an arranged marriage at a young age. It was also still the situation in India that the birth of a boy was considered an occasion for rejoicing yet the birth of a girl, an occasion for sorrow and commiseration. Better luck next time!

Things were not all that different in the West, although change was in the air. Even though she was Indian and from a very traditional background, Dadi Janki played her part in empowering Western women to take charge of their own lives, to reject conventional marriage and being kept by a man, and to claim their inheritance as people and spiritual leaders in their own right.

From the start, Dadi Janki would not allow even the smallest suggestion that women were inferior to men or had to kow tow to them in every little aspect. She knew, though, that she would have an uphill struggle and so it proved to be. The two small damp rooms where classes and meditation sessions were originally held, were not likely to attract the rich and the powerful; and on top of that, Dadi and her two loyal assistants, Sister Jayanti and Sister Sudesh, had a double, if not quadruple, whammy against them.

For one thing they were all Indian, and there was still much racial prejudice against Indians in the 1970s. The charismatic male gurus were allowed special dispensation as they were exotic and mysterious, but three small women in cheap white saris were hardly a major draw. They were Indian (and very Indian); they were women; they were all extremely small in size and the fourth whammy was that they had pledged never to charge for any of their programmes or events.

Between them, they had a lot to overcome. Plus, they had no powerful or influential Western supporters. In the early days the only Westerners they attracted were very young seekers of no influence themselves.

So what kept the BKs afloat in the beginning? One has to say, it was the vibrations that emanated from Dadi, not just because of her connection to God, but also because of her total conviction that she was herself sent by God to proclaim a powerful message and one that could not be ignored.

When Dadi arrived in 1974, she was granted only a visitor's visa. She kept extending this visa but in 1976 applied for a permanent visa and was given indefinite leave to stay. As Dadi remembers it, she told the authorities: 'I have not come here to make money, but for service. I have come as a mother. I want all of God's children to stay happy.' Possibly because the authorities had never heard such a reason before, she was granted the visa.

By this time, the BKs had been accorded charitable status in the UK.

Her view is that people often believe they cannot do anything without money or position, but she had neither of those when she arrived, and yet she still managed to pack a powerful punch.

From the start, she had a simple message for women who wanted equality: claim your inheritance from God, trust in Him, connect with Him, and then courage and valour will be yours.

She would say that she had a powerful ally on her side – God himself – and by making Him her companion, she could accomplish things that would have been impossible otherwise.

One of these was to champion female independence and emancipate women from their centuries-old dependence on men, and empower them to shake off feelings of inferiority and lack of self-confidence.

Women, she said, have largely lost their self-respect and this is because external opinions have been imposed on them until they have come to believe them themselves. The traditional view, in both East and West, is that women do not have strong intellects and are easily swayed by others' opinions until they become hopelessly reliant on others, in particular, men. 'Frailty, thy name is woman' has echoed down the ages until many people, including women, have believed it. They have acquiesced in their own weakness and internalised it.

Another Shakespeare quote, 'Men were deceivers ever' (from Much Ado About Nothing) found resonance with Dadi, who maintained that women had been deceived throughout the ages by males everywhere: husbands, children, politicians, doctors, lawyers, teachers, even religious leaders. As a result of this, they have lost confidence in themselves and this lack of confidence and sense of powerlessness has been handed down from mother to daughter. In fact, mothers very often – perhaps unconsciously – imbue their daughters with a sense of inferiority right from the start.

Dadi was putting out a different message: instead of putting your trust in deceitful people who will always try to do you down, turn directly to God, where you will find all the answers you seek.

Once women become aware of God's love, says Dadi, they will be uplifted and will be able to break free of the centuries-old shackles that have held them down. God alone, Dadi promised, knows about women's greatness, and once a woman puts her faith in God, she can uplift not only herself but the whole world. She can become the universal mother.

Because of this, a woman does not need a male guru, priest or rabbi to show her the way. When connecting with God, she will find everything she needs to gain wisdom. Traditionally, women have depended on men, in all societies. But in order to remain strong and independent, as Dadi saw it, women can benefit even more than men from daily meditation. This allows them to make and sustain the connection, enabling them to transform the weaker vessel into the stronger vessel.

Dadi strongly believes that the feminine principle, which is all about virtue, is more needed than ever in today's world. She says: 'I have never believed that this is a man's world and that we as women cannot succeed. However, attaining such success in this wicked world requires courage and honesty.' Have faith, she says, in yourself. 'Go inwards, understand that you do have a solution to all of life's problems and by constant connection with God, you will know what has to be done.

> 'Most of all, you must never let yourself be influenced by what others are thinking because you can access all the wisdom you need inside yourself.' She says that we are never without the

solutions to our problems. It's just that sometimes we may have to wait a little and in the waiting time, learn to remain peaceful and patient. Then the solutions will definitely come.'

Whereas many women have had the aim of getting married, having a family, setting up home and these days, following a fulfilling, high-paid career, none of these has ever appealed to Dadi Janki.

She says, 'I have always had the thought that my life should serve as an example to the rest of the world. I never had any intention of wasting my time on ordinary things, but wanted a life filled with unique purpose and meaning. I never wanted to be a leader who leads through a lot of external show, but a true leader leading through the power of truth, honesty and purity.'

Dadi also says that 'in these times of darkness and sorrow', a woman's role becomes very powerful indeed. There are three qualities, she believes, that come quite easily to a woman: tolerance, mercy and truth. Mind, men can have these qualities too but Dadi believes they come more naturally to women. The curse of ego is firmly embedded in the male psyche, and this prevents their spiritual growth. Women can exhibit ego too, but this vice is far more prevalent in men and also more difficult to extricate as it has many subtleties and non-obvious ways of showing itself. Men can take pride in their appearance, sporting prowess, earning power, ability to attract a beautiful woman, drive a wonderful car, in their intellect or academic achievements and so can strut around, in novelist Tom Wolfe's words, as self-styled Masters of the Universe.

Women are much less likely to parade their achievements and so can move forward quickly once they realise the source of their strength: God within and without.

On marriage, Dadi Janki is very clear: you must never, she says, become attached to another person and in particular, you should never seek to own another person with rings or gifts. This, perhaps Dadi's most radical belief, does not go down well in all quarters where even today, marriage is seen as some sort of ultimate achievement. Indeed, it has now extended to gay couples and been given the blessing of law. Gay couples such as Elton John and David Furnish have made a great show of their marriage to each other, as have Stephen Fry and Elliot Spencer. When gay women form civil partnerships or marry, they are much less likely to make a huge song and dance about it; highlighting once again a major difference between men and women.

But marriage, or any kind of permanent coupling, can so easily become a trap whereby you become dependent on the other person and credit them with your success, or blame them for your failure. How often have husbands and wives blamed each other for things that go wrong in their lives? How often does love turn to indifference, if not hate, in a marriage?

People often believe that marriage, or hooking up with a life partner, will bring them happiness but how often does that actually happen, Dadi Janki asks. No, the time has come for each of us to become independent, to love our fellow men and women, yes, but not to seek a binding attachment to any of them. If we have God, we do not need an intimate human being in our lives.

Since Dadi Janki arrived in the West, marriage has come to be a show of wealth and pride in how much money you can spend, more than at any other time in history. Yet many such marriages are a complete sham.

It is often said nowadays that the more glittering and expensive the wedding, the shorter the actual marriage and for Dadi, this is horribly self-indulgent and a complete waste of money. Indeed, she would probably go so far as to say that nowadays, it is not actually possible to find happiness with another human being either within or outside marriage. In time, the relationship will almost always become one of dependency and attachment – and by concentrating on another human being so closely, the essential connection with God will be lost.

To Dadi, a wedding ring is not so much a symbol of love and commitment as a sign of ownership and dependency. Marriage itself, as many feminists have pointed out, has historically never been an equal contract between men and women. Nowadays, there is much more equality but by marrying somebody, you are still buying into an institution that has for centuries had its roots in the subjection of women.

Avoid marriage and definitely avoid children if you want to be a woman of God!

Dadi Janki has many times been accused of breaking up my own marriage and no matter how many times or how loudly I say that it would have broken up anyway, and that the BK understanding enabled us to part as friends rather than enemies, nobody wants to listen. The prevailing idea among some circles is that the BKs' main aim is to break up marriages and Dadi and other BKs have had to live with this. This is perhaps the fifth whammy that Dadi has had to combat over the years, but she remains adamant that family life and children are incompatible with a life dedicated to God.

The naysayers have some ammunition on their side and Dadi's stance on marriage and intimate, interdependent relationships has caused her to come in for a lot of strong criticism. She has for instance, separated couples by sending them to different parts of the country, or of the world, and it is rare when this happens, that the marriage has survived. For most people faced with this situation, something has to go: either the husband or wife, or the BK lifestyle.

Dadi of course, has always discouraged having children as a distraction from the connection with God, which she sees as top priority at this time in history. Her lack of interest in family life is total and she prefers everybody to be individuals following their own path and not being dragged down, as she sees it, by others.

Even Maureen and David Goodman, who celebrated their 40th wedding anniversary in January 2015, have not lived together for many years and nor have they had children. True, they are not divorced or estranged but they are hardly your normal married couple.

Dadi's defiant position on marriage, family and sex has led to strong criticism and to some people blogging on anti-BK websites, often very nastily. The anti-BK websites have caused the movement much hurt but even so, Dadi stands firm.

Some people have argued that Dadi's own bitter experience with marriage and motherhood – both against her will – have made her such a strong opponent of family life for those who want to connect with God, and there may be some truth in this – who knows? – but against that it has to be said that for nuns and monks in the Catholic and Buddhist faiths there is the same attitude. For thousands of years they have maintained that full, daily connection with God necessarily involves separation from your family of origin.

A close schoolfriend of mine became a Carmelite nun, possibly the strictest enclosed Catholic order for women. As such, she was not allowed to leave the convent to attend her own father's funeral, and she accepted this as the price she paid for dedicating her life to God.

Jesus Christ said much the same thing to his disciples: give up your family life and follow me. Separate yourself from what has gone before!

Dadi believes that at this particular time, all souls must reunite with God, with their own original natures, and that this has to be a personal, not a joint quest. You cannot connect with God in conjunction with another person. All our journeys must be made individually. Interact with God and not with another flawed human being, she says.

Dadi's feminist (some may say, anti-male) stance goes even further. A vital aspect of female empowerment, she believes, is not to be seduced by the vast amount of products on offer which purport to make women beautiful, to prolong youth or to enable them to be fashionable. Dadi's own unvarying outfit has always been a white sari, and this is what she tries to persuade all the surrendered sisters to wear. No show, no perfume, no make-up, no visits to the hairdresser. When connecting to God, these things all become completely unnecessary because you are no longer concerned with showing or making an impression on others. Well, only an impression of genuine goodness, virtue and purity, she would say.

Most of the BK sisters look like nuns, with hair scraped back, dressed in simple white and with no jewellery or rings except perhaps a ring or badge with the BK symbol on it. Dadi believes that today's women are totally taken in by fashion and consumerism, spending their money on trinkets and expensive clothes that take a lot of earning power to afford.

You can live much more simply than this, if you want to be a true feminist. For many women, giving up every aspect of vanity is hard indeed but it has to be said that generally speaking, the BK sisters look much younger than they are, without the help of cosmetic aids. If they have discovered the secret of eternal youth, it lies in meditation rather than the latest skincare product, a conviction that you are an independent operator, and in constant connection with God.

In India, the beauty industry is huge, and Dadi, for all her years in the West, remains very Indian in outlook and attitude. Injunctions from religious people against the use of beauty aids is not new of course, and has been an aspect of just about every religious movement since time began.

It is never going to be the case that every woman follows Dadi's injunctions to the letter or becomes a surrendered sister. She teaches, and practises, a counsel of perfection that, by its nature, only a few will ever fully follow. But the example of one poor, elderly woman coming to London, one of the richest and toughest cities in the world, and establishing a worldwide movement with impressive centres and residential retreats in many cities, cannot be easily dismissed.

Dadi would say, if I can do it with no cards in my hand, so can you. That may not be entirely true, but there is truth in it. It is a strong form of feminism that more women should think about taking on board.

A personal note: when my husband and I separated in the 1980s, I had never before lived on my own and although I had a highly paid career in journalism, I had no particular individual survival skills. Thirty years later, I am still living on my own, I have a lovely home, enough money in the bank and am still working. Never have I been dependent on a man, or indeed, any other person and looking back I wonder whether I would have been able to make it, whether I would have had the strength to branch out and remain on my own, to buy houses and cars all by myself and handle my own finances, without Dadi's input.

Somehow, I doubt it. Dadi showed me that it could be done and while I have no wish to wear a white sari or expunge all vanity from my life, the feeling of being strong and independent instead of weak, dependent and fearful, owes a lot to her example.

Doubt and sorrow do creep in from time to time but the ability to survive for 30 years on my own has given me a lot of self-confidence.

There is another aspect to all this, and one that more than any other, exemplifies Dadi Janki's powers of leadership. In leadership circles there is a concept known as the big D, or Distraction. This means that if you genuinely want to be a great leader, you must never allow distractions to get in your way, or to dilute your focus. Whenever you admit a distraction in your life, your attention is turned away from your goal and this means your powers of leadership decline.

For Dadi, sex, marriage, children, partners, families, are all big Ds. Although her strictures may seem harsh to some, in her view they are absolutely necessary to establish the Kingdom of God on earth and show by example that one can lead a fulfilling life without any of the trappings that many might consider necessary. ❧

Dadi Janki with Mother Teresa at the Women's Conference in Nairobi, 1996

CHAPTER EIGHT

Two Hindu women
who became BKs in 1978:
Jaymini Patel and
Gayatri Naraine

Jaymini and Gayatri are both of Indian descent but were born and brought up outside of India.

Jaymini is now in charge of the literature and publishing department at the BK London headquarters, Global Co-operation House.

(She is no relation to Balwant Patel. Patel is the commonest Indian surname; 'worse than Smith' say those saddled with it.)

Although born into a Hindu family, Jaymini had not come across the BKs until she started picking up her little seven-year old sister from an after-school dancing club in London and discovered that the woman running the club was a BK herself.

Jaymini was born in Tanzania as was her father, and she spent five years in India from the age of 10, living with relatives, but did not hear about the BKs while living there.

She says that she was always a seeker, and from an early age was drawn to the spiritual. 'Nothing attracted me in the world,' she says. 'When I came back to London, I took O levels and A levels and went to work in a bank. My father's idea was that I would work my way up to a prominent position in the bank and be a modern career girl but in the event, the BKs intervened and showed me the way to a quite different life.'

In a way, her introduction to the BKs happened by accident. 'I used to pick up my little sister from this club and went to the house on Saturday mornings to see them dancing. The Indian lady who ran the club was a BK, and something about her attracted me although I didn't really know what. There was a calm, peaceful atmosphere about this lady's house and this was pulling me, but at the time it was all very vague.

> 'Then she invited my sister and myself to a dance event in Trafalgar Square. Dadi Janki was there and also Sudesh and Jayanti. 'There was a peace march, which I joined, and I then thought about meditation for myself.

'The lady who ran the dance club also used to hold early morning meditation sessions at her house and I wanted to go along. I asked my Dad for permission to go and he said: 'You can go if you can get up in the morning.' He knew I was not a natural early riser and always had problems getting out of bed in the morning. But I got up at three o'clock to go along to these sessions and I absolutely loved them.

'This lady started reading the Murli and instantly, something happened. I felt complete detachment from the body and was so drawn to the knowledge and beliefs that were being revealed. It was a wonderful feeling, but before long I knew I wanted more. So one day this lady said, you must go along to the main centre. This was Tennyson Road, where Dadi Janki was still living. I went one morning and the class was packed, in this tiny house. I sat on the staircase and it truly touched my heart. I felt so drawn to Dadi and the knowledge that I was hearing from the Murli. My family were religious Hindus and observed many spiritual practices but they were not BKs, and this was very different from anything I had heard before.

'I didn't know anybody at the Tennyson Road centre at the time but I was instantly drawn to God's knowledge, as it seemed to be. I felt I was hearing Truth and I couldn't get enough of it. What drew me further was the practical application of this knowledge in Dadi Janki. She was always talking about having love for humanity, for the whole world, not just a narrow group. From the very first, my focus was always Dadi.'

In the BK movement, as with many others, both spiritual and secular, many are called but not all last. Many early BKs faded away, so what kept Jaymini going? 'What I saw in Dadi Janki was the deep love in her heart she had for God. From the age of two she was in search of God. I was searching too and soon I felt I had found what I was looking for in the BKs.'

Dadi's main quality, says Jaymini – and this has been noticed by many others – was her ability to focus on each person before her individually, and immediately see their strengths. 'She found in all of us a quality that nobody else saw. She was always looking for something unique in each person she met and had the ability to guide them in that direction without them knowing they were headed in that direction.

'One of the first things she said to me was: you have to become free from bondage and take it one step at a time.'

This was not so easy for an Indian girl from a traditional Hindu family, where the Biblical injunction to honour thy father and mother is taken much more literally than it ever has been in Christianity. 'When I said to my family that I would like to dedicate my life to being a BK, my father was dead against it. Dad hit the roof. He had seen me as a career girl but over and above that he wanted me to get married and have children.

'He was matchmaking like mad and kept introducing me to young men who might be suitable. If I had got married, it would have been an arranged marriage and by this time I knew I did not want this life for myself. Then Dad said, you could have had degrees, you could have had an important position at the bank, and you are throwing it all away to follow this old woman.'

But then, says Jaymini, he met Dadi Janki himself and everything changed. 'After this he was happy for me. He stopped matchmaking, stopped saying I could have had a big career. His heart was completely melted by Dadi.

'In everything, Dadi guided me. She told me to take it one step at a time and I did everything she said. I saw her quite literally as being next to God.' And for Jaymini, the fact that Dadi was female was absolutely crucial. She would not have wanted to take spiritual instruction from a male guru and never wanted to have a traditional guru in her life.

'Dadi was an upfront radical feminist and this was very new to me. In our culture women are always considered secondary and certainly not able to take the lead in religious or spiritual matters. This was another way Dadi was unique and although quiet and peaceful, some of her ideas, particularly concerning women, were startling to me.

'She was saying that we should not become attached to another human being, that we should have love only for God, but love our fellow human beings as souls on a journey. For many Indian women, especially in those days, their entire life was centred around their husband and family and she was saying, no, there is another life you can have. I loved all these ideas and she gave me the courage to defy my family and become a BK.'

Before long Jaymini left the bank, dedicated herself to the burgeoning BK movement, and adopted the white sari, which she has worn unvaryingly ever since.

Jaymini is particularly interested in how Dadi always seems to overcome illness. She was already over 60 when Jaymini first met her and even 40 years ago was often laid low with serious illness. Yet always she recovered. 'Dadi has been constantly ill ever since I have known her,' Jaymini says. 'And then she wakes up, as if from a sleep. She has nearly died so many times but because she believes God is using her as an instrument and that her work has nowhere near finished, she recovers. Because I have lived closely with Dadi for so many years, I have often seen her get up from death's door.

'People say to her, you can't do this programme, you can't travel to that country, you can't meet these people, you are too ill. But she never takes any notice. Anybody else would have been dead long ago. It's as if God wants her to be around.'

Jaymini has a theory as to why Dadi always seems to recover from even the most debilitating illness. 'Her policy is never to speak about illness, not to let it take over her life or to give it houseroom. She believes that the more you talk about illness and dwell on it, the more you bring it into being. I think that is very true and it's an ancient belief.

'When she was younger, Dadi nursed others and said that was the way you became free of pain, to concentrate on other people rather than your own state of health. I am certain that is why she is still around at nearly 100.'

Gayatri Naraine

Gayatri is one of the six children of Shiv Sahai (Steve) and Betty Naraine. Their forefathers were originally from India, who settled in Guyana in the 1830s when it was under British rule. Steve trained as a civil engineer, attending London University and Delft University in the Netherlands, and later served as Vice President of Guyana. He was appointed Guyana's High Commissioner to India, Sri Lanka and Bangladesh in 1983. He stayed in this post until 1990 and then returned to engineering, setting up a consultancy, SRKN engineering, with his two sons. He and Betty retired to Canada, where he died in July 2013, aged 89.

Uncle Steve, as he was known, first came across the BKs in December 1975 when Jayanti made a visit to the country and stayed in the Naraine household for a month. During that time Uncle Steve became a student of Raya Yoga and with his family, helped to set up the country's first Brahma Kumaris centre in Georgetown. He believed that the practice of Raja Yoga helped him to withstand two operations for open-heart surgery without anxiety.

Although not all of his children became dedicated BKs, the message was heard and understood by the whole family and it was Gayatri who decided to dedicate fully in 1978.

Since then, she has run the BK office for the United Nations in New York, and for many years has worked closely with various UN programmes to further spiritual understanding in the secular world.

She takes up the story: 'Although we were Hindus, my parents were not acquainted with the BKs before Jayanti came to Guyana, and the teachings were very new for us. From the start, my parents had deep love for Jayanti and the teachings she was imparting.

'I was moved by the yoga, by the direct connection with God and definitely felt a presence as I sat in meditation. I had been to a Catholic school and religion as a whole made no sense to me at all in terms of implications for daily living.'

At this time Gayatri had not met Dadi Janki. But another of the Dadis, Gulzar, invited the family to Mount Abu, where their knowledge of the teachings developed.

'We came back via London, and one evening, tired and jetlagged, we were told that Dadi Janki was outside in her car and had come to see us. She was supposed to be the senior sister of the BKs, so of course we were keen to meet her. When I went out, there was this little old lady sitting in the car and I felt at that moment, through her presence, that here was a great being.

'Dadi immediately put others first and this was the first time I had an experience of deep love being expressed with gentle humility, which is one of Dadi's great qualities.'

Does she think the BKs would have got going in the West without Dadi Janki being there? She says yes, they would have got going, but without Dadi there would not have been the same level of unity and harmony. 'She is above all a unifying force, and that was very noticeable even at first sight. It was clear that she had genuine qualities of God's power.'

Gayatri was 25 when she went to New York in 1978, and was one of the first people to become a surrendered BK in America. 'I was attracted to the idea of serving others while developing my own spirituality.' Since those days, Gayatri has overseen not just the expansion of outreach in America but also a deepening connection with the United Nations, where the BKs are one of the few spiritual movements admitted to its various councils. As such, the BKs work together with branches of the UN – that Hydra-headed organisation – on joint peace projects.

Gayatri has also worked for many years with Sister Mohini, an Indian-born BK who was sent over – or sent herself – to conquer the New World for the BKs. In her capacity of Regional Coordinator of the Americas and the Caribbean, Sister Mohini's role required her to work in close consultation with Dadi Janki, and at the same time find distinctive ways of working appropriate to the other side of the Atlantic.

When Dadi, at 99, flew to the USA from the UK in 2015, the visit was marked by an atmosphere of enormous love and mutual respect, bearing witness to a long-standing and successful "special relationship" between the two women.

Gayatri says that in observing the spiritual dynamic between them, she has identified certain feminine principles that she highly values. These include, for both of them, an extraordinary capacity for multi-tasking, and an unusual ability to align everyday actions to a constant awareness of the eternal. This means that neither will seek short-term solutions to problems or challenges at the expense of losing spiritual direction and power.

By constantly checking as to whether a particular action has the right spiritual principles at its heart, both Dadi Janki and Sister Mohini have successfully worked together, on either side of the Atlantic.

For Gayatri, a potent attraction to the organization was the fact that it was run by women and that women were at its head. She says: 'This was one of the main factors for me. I first came across the BKs in 1975, which was the United Nations' International Year of Women, and for me, the two things were auspicious. This is our time, the time for women to take charge and make a difference in the old world.

> 'So far as Dadi Janki is concerned, she upholds standards and is completely fearless. Nothing has stopped her from doing what she wanted, and she did it her way. She has been inspired by God all along and has awakened the potential of courage in all of us.
>
> 'She took us out of our boundaries and we could go as far as we wanted. Either she saw the potential in us, or we looked at her and saw our own potential. Whichever way it happened, Dadi helped to make us blossom.'

Now in her 60s, Gayatri says she is as enthusiastic as ever and has never for one minute doubted that the spiritual path she has chosen speaks the truth.

Does she think that Dadi Janki is a great leader? 'Dadi said once that the world doesn't need leaders so much as mothers. By that she meant that the world needs leaders with motherly qualities, and women are more likely than men to have those, whether or not they are actual mothers. But at the same time, yes, I would say that she is a great leader – perhaps the greatest! ᛉ

CHAPTER NINE

Meditation

We have already spoken of the importance of meditation; now is the time to examine exactly what it is, or, at least, what the BKs understand by meditation.

The practice of meditation is probably as old as humanity but it was introduced into the West as a new concept by the many Indian gurus who arrived in the 1960s and 70s and persuaded many thousands of people to sit in silence, turn their minds inwards, and experience a state of altered consciousness.

Dadi Janki has made regular meditation a major cornerstone of her life and when people ask her how many hours a day she spends meditating, her favourite reply is: 'It would be easier to ask me how many hours I don't spend meditating!'

When Dadi says she spends many hours a day

meditating, this doesn't mean that she sits in a blissful reverie all day and every day. That would hardly get anything done. What she means is that she is always in a meditative state, that she is always connecting with God and that she refuses to let anything break that connection.

At the same time, if you come before Dadi or ask her a question or advice, she always gives you 100 per cent attention, so it's not as though she is in another realm or away with the fairies.

The kind of meditation that she introduced into the West was quite different from any other kind of stilling your mind technique brought over from India. Known as Raja Yoga, the BK form of meditation unashamedly and uncompromisingly asks you to connect with God. It does not ask you to chant, sit in special postures, writhe around, stare at flickering candles or burn an incense stick. Nor do you have to repeat a secret mantra.

On the face of it, Raja Yoga meditation seems simple enough. You focus your gaze on the yogi in front of you and with open eyes, gradually turn your mind inwards, listening for the sounds of silence and shutting out the external world.

But of course, there is more to it than seems apparent, as connecting with God, or the Supreme Spirit, is not as easy as it sounds. It takes concentration, effort and practice and for many, it is just too difficult.

The rewards, though, say practitioners, are great indeed as gradually, through regular meditation, you turn into a different person, one who is more loving, calmer, more peaceful and serene than before. Regular meditation, Dadi Janki would say, enables you to get in touch with your true self, and to strip away the impurities that have accumulated over the years. And while to outward appearances, nothing much may be going on, inside great changes are being made.

In contrast, for example, Transcendental Meditation is a secularized, simplified form of sitting still and turning inwards, and as such, it appeals to sophisticated Westerners who feel they have long outgrown a belief in God but want some calming techniques to help them cope with their busy, stressful lives.

Transcendental Meditation and the newer practice of Mindfulness have been shown to be highly effective ways of calming the mind and reducing stress, but they do not depend on a belief in a God or connection to a higher power to work. You are, if you like, your own higher power.

TM, which has been going in the West for half a century now, remains popular and is now practised by many celebrities, including the subversive and outspoken comedian Russell Brand. It has been the subject of much scientific and medical research over the years and has been proven to have the power to alleviate stress-related conditions. It induces an altered state of consciousness without the use of drugs, and is an active process that must be practised for a lifetime. As anybody who does it regularly will tell you, TM is hard work and emphatically not the same as daydreaming or going off into a reverie.

You are supposed to sit in silence and turn your mind inwards for 20 minutes, twice a day, while you repeat your individual mantra. The point about repeating the mantra is that it drives out all other thoughts – or at least, that is the idea – and allows you to concentrate on stilling the mind and preventing intrusive mental interruptions, such whether you left the gas on, from disturbing the process.

Although it may sound simple, TM is trickier than it seems and the intense tedium many people feel when attempting it means that few keep it up for any length of time. It was developed as a purely practical form of meditation not overlaid with mysticism, and was – and is – taught one-to-one by an experienced meditator.

Other forms of Indian meditation which became popular in the West involved chanting, swaying and special types of breathing (pranayama) sometimes accompanied by postural yoga. For most people, these forms of meditation are an optional adjunct to life, rather than being life-changing in themselves. The idea is that they help you to cope with life's stresses but they do not demand dramatic lifestyle changes in order to be effective.

Because TM has to be taught, either one to one or in a group, there is usually a charge attached. Its courses are expensive. In some cases the costs are graduated according to household income but even the 'affordable' courses and sessions cost several hundred pounds.

So far as I am aware, Raja Yoga meditation as taught by the BKs, is unique in that it is free to all.

As the Supreme Source to which – theoretically at least - you connect in meditation is in itself unlimited and available to all, how could anybody, Dadi Janki reasoned, make a monetary charge?

But there are some important aspects to Raja Yoga meditation which have to be appreciated for it to work properly, and basic to all these is the belief that at heart, we are pure, peaceful souls and that it is by connecting with God that we can retrieve this purity and peace.

According to Dadi Janki every human being has peace, wisdom, joy and purity as original traits and when a person begins each day with meditation, positive thoughts and forms of behaviour are gradually reinforced and power is received from God.

This power, rather like plugging into a permanently strong battery, enables spiritual transformation as it moves consciousness away from the body into an awareness of the soul. This does not happen immediately for most, although many people who came into Raja Yoga in the early days did experience intense bliss and joy and a sensation of peace and calm, particularly when sitting in front of Dadi Janki.

But as with any battery-operated device, the charge has to be daily renewed. And you will never imbibe enough power or peace to stop the daily practice of meditation.

Meditation is for the mind what going to the gym is for the body. As any gym enthusiast knows, if you don't go for a couple of weeks, your fitness levels decline. It is exactly the same with meditation. Let it go, and the power and calmness will go as well. As with anything else, it is a case of use it or lose it. You must keep it up for a lifetime.

Even at the age of nearly 100 and having spent her life meditating, Dadi Janki still observes the discipline every day, particularly in the early morning. She does this however ill she may be or however busy her schedule. Meditation always comes first in her life. Early morning meditation is known as Amrit Vela, or the early hours of nectar. It entails getting up in the middle of the night and being ready for four o'clock meditation. This may be done in a class setting, at least for people who are living in a centre, or at home for those who are not.

Obviously it is easier to get up at four in the morning if you are in a centre with no other distractions, and a holy quiet space is created every day. There is also the fact that meditation, much like going to an exercise class at the gym, is more powerful and effective when done in a like-minded group.

Although many people find it hard to be ready for 4am meditation every morning, even when living in a centre and the bell tolls to call the faithful, there is no doubt that something special happens at this time, when everything is still, the world has not yet woken up and the concentrated power of a roomful of people meditating does definitely alter consciousness, and for the better.

But for the BKs, meditation is not just a part-time activity but a whole philosophy and has much theology behind it. It is a profound practice which can bring about deep and lasting change, once you understand what it is all about.

Luckily, Dadi Janki is very clear about what Raja Yoga meditation means, and she can explain it. Whether or not the meditator can take on board the whole edifice, is another matter.

When meditating, according to Dadi Janki, we do not merge with God but retain our separate identity. And gradually, through long practice, the spiritual dimension comes back into our lives. 'When we lose sight of the spiritual dimension, everyday activities become burdensome and we lose our creativity,' says Jayanti in her book on meditation, *God's Healing Power*.

Raja Yoga is a discipline allowing an individual to dwell on truth, and it brings clarity into everyday actions. It enables us to see other people in a positive light rather than riddled with faults, and helps to keep us free from negativity. The more we meditate, at least according to the theory, the more we gain creative energy to break free from all negative and destructive habits.

When Raja Yoga speaks of God, there is the understanding that God is both the Mother and the Father, with the emphasis on Mother. Jayanti again: 'This follows the biological pattern, where the child first bonds with the mother. The Father comes later.' And although most religions speak of God as the Father, or at least in the masculine gender, the understanding in Raja Yoga is that God is the Mother first.

Again, this is a radical departure from the understanding and language of other major religions.

When new people come to her, Dadi Janki often asks whether they believe in God and of course the answer is often, no. Very many people who have been attracted to the BKs come as atheists and although they may feel Dadi Janki's vibrations, they have no intention of changing their beliefs or unbeliefs.

But if they persist, in many cases they will eventually come to believe in God. I have seen this happen with quite a few people including my own former husband. When he first met the BKs he was a fervent atheist. Now, more than three decades later, he too believes in the supernatural structure on which, eventually, the whole Brahma Kumaris philosophy depends.

He has experienced what Dadi promises, that through intense daily meditation people will begin to feel the connection that Dadi Janki says she herself never loses. If they never start to feel this connection, they will probably fade away and realise that Raja Yoga meditation is not for them. Unless the connection is made somewhere along the line, meditation becomes boring and starts to feel a waste of time.

But it is worth persisting, say the BKs, as through meditation it is possible to clear away all negative traits and become free to move on to the future. In particular, the regular practice of meditation enables people to perform miracles on themselves, improving their ability to learn; their power to face up to things; their power to decide and discern; and the power to co-operate with one another.

Gradually, through the daily practice, we will attain freedom from ego, the ability to realise the mistakes of the past and not to repeat them, and the power of forgiveness. This happens because after a time – or possibly immediately – we will start to feel a flow of calming, fulfilling energy from this connection with the Supreme.

At the same time there will be increased concentration, relaxation and a better ability to focus on the things that matter.

You may think that a lot is being claimed for meditation, but as a lifelong meditator, Dadi Janki is her own best example of what it can achieve.

'Meditation,' says Jayanti, 'opens the door to taking one's inheritance from God. Yoga power is actually pure consciousness accumulated from loving remembrance of God.'

What does this mean?

According to Dadi Janki, regular, daily meditation is the only way to become a companion of God and once you make that connection, everything falls into place and you are bathed in a constant ocean of bliss, joy, love and peace.

Meditation also has great practical value, in that it is a method of being able to make big plans and have major visions for the future.

Because although when you meet Dadi Janki she always seems smiling and peaceful and benign (which she is), underneath all the peace and calm, a very busy mind is always at work. It is the regular connection with God, she believes, which has enabled her to see the potential of people who come before her – and in some cases, this potential might have been hard to spot – and also to envisage and bring about expansionist plans for the future.

Because Dadi Janki has such faith that the BKs hold the key to the truth, she can work on future plans with perfect confidence and with no doubts in her mind that she is doing the right thing.

On the matter of seeing potential where it may be hidden from others, there is the story of one Indian BK who was very shy and reserved and seemed to have little personality or vitality. She was working in a pharmacy and but for Dadi would probably have continued in that career. But what Dadi saw in her was a shining quality of honesty. Accordingly, Dadi persuaded her to take over the BK accounts. The result is that this same person is now running the financial side of the BK organisation, without any formal accountancy qualifications or training.

This ability to see the potential of others – which often they do not see themselves - comes from a regular, deep connection with God, Dadi Janki would say. Daily meditation enables her to see through negativity, shyness, lack of confidence and nervousness, to the shining qualities of the soul. Dadi believes these qualities are there in the first place, but they need help and encouragement to be brought out. Maureen Goodman is convinced that from the start, Dadi saw qualities in her that she did not see herself, and her vision of this potential has enabled Maureen to achieve things she would never have thought possible. For many years Maureen has been a key person in the running and organization of the London end of the BK movement, and she happily moves in the highest circles, mingling with heads of state, peers of the realm, royalty and leading politicians.

If you had asked Maureen at the age of 21 whether she would be travelling all over the world meeting VIPs she would have shuddered in disbelief and bewilderment. In order to achieve meetings with the highest in the land, and introduce them to Raja Yoga, Maureen does much meditation herself. She, like Dadi Janki, would say that it was essential to enable her to remain in a calm, anxiety-free state of mind.

Dadi from the start has simply refused to see the downsides of other people and she argues that if you just concentrate on their best points, you can enable them to perform miracles. Even when people criticise Dadi and the BKs – and some criticism has been truly defamatory and vicious – she still strives to send out good wishes to those perpetrators. Her view is that, at the very least, you can learn from such people and their negativity.

And perhaps they might have a point, and help you to improve yourself. Meditation, she would say, helps you to see the good in every situation and in every person.

This is how meditation works, according to Dadi:

As a first step, you must imagine what it must be like to experience your self in its highest form and see the soul in its original, pure state. It is definitely possible to create such an experience and this is what meditation is all about.

Meditation has the ability to shift you from one consciousness to another, from the limited, worldly consciousness, to the unlimited one we know as soul consciousness.

When you experience soul consciousness, the soul feels distinct and separate from the body. You are entering another realm and you start to feel enlightened and free. In this state, you begin to experience peace, love, power and bliss. Keep up the practice and you will never again find yourself saying things like, 'I am upset, I am angry, I am unhappy.' That is because your internal world changes completely.

Meditation enables you, in the words of Elizabethan poet Sir Philip Sidney, 'to grow rich in that which never taketh rust.' The constant renewal of the connection with God makes this possible. Dadi is fond of using precious metals and stones to drive home her point, and says that in time, meditation will make you as pure as a many-faceted, flawless diamond. It is no accident that the later addition to the BK London headquarters is called Diamond House.

Dadi often chooses the names for new centres and buildings and they are always called something inspiring, like Lighthouse, Global Cooperation House, Peace Village, Global Harmony House. Every retreat centre is a powerhouse of meditation and every centre follows the same pattern of meditating in the early morning, punctuated by shorter meditation periods, known as traffic control, throughout the day. There is often a meditation session in the evening as well, and frequent 'bhattis' or hour-long meditation sessions are part of the routine.

All cooking is done in a spirit of meditation, ensuring that good vibrations go into the food.

Dadi Janki maintains that meditation enables you to see the things of the world as they really are, and to become aware that possessions, fame, lovers, health, can all be taken away from you. But once you enter the soul world, you will access attributes that cannot be taken away. Instead of having the awareness that you own material possessions, you will learn to see see yourself as a trustee – a trustee of your body, your home, your job, your children – because all, at the end of the day, are temporary.

Meditation enables the switch from consciousness of the things of the world, to the things of the spirit.

Once this state is reached, Dadi says, you will start to see your problems clearly and gain the strength to overcome them. You will be able to keep your mind free from worry (this is something Dadi returns to again and again, knowing how much people worry in today's world, often unnecessarily) and you will not harbour resentment, grudges or anger against other people as although this may not affect them, it will certainly affect you and your peace of mind.

But along with meditation, go other disciplines. In order to attain your highest state, a highly ascetic lifestyle of the utmost simplicity is required. Dadi has lived like this for most of her life and once again, it is too much for some people, however much they may like the idea of the BKs.

For example, you have to eat what the Indians call a 'sattvic' diet, which means it must consist of the purest ingredients and be home-cooked. BKs do not eat out in restaurants and the strictest will not even eat food prepared by a non-BK in case it contains negative vibrations. Some will even take their own saucepans when visiting non-BK relatives, in case the relatives' saucepans are contaminated by meat or onions and garlic, emphatically not allowed. In order to keep your mind stable, you are not supposed to watch violent films or TV programmes, and of course alcohol is totally forbidden as are recreational drugs and cigarettes.

It all makes entertaining or catering for a BK very hard work and for this reason, they tend not to go into other people's homes. All BK centres offer food and refreshments and although they will gladly cook for visitors, they will rarely accept a non-BK's invitation to dinner.

Many other religious groups follow dietary guidelines although in recent years they have tended to lighten up on the foods they will allow. Even the Dalai Lama, supposed to be a vegetarian, has admitted that he eats meat on occasion. But the BKs remain super-strict, thanks to Dadi Janki's example and strength of will. For her, there can never be any letting up. Although Dadi smiles and greets all, whatever their faith or beliefs, she insists that those who consider themselves BKs should not deviate from the core practices she introduced into the West.

Some people have remarked that the BKs, in modern society, are by far the strictest Indian-based movement, as they have hardly compromised since arriving in the West. Rather than diluting their message, practices and disciplines to appeal to cynical Westerners, they have made the Westerners shape up to their disciplines.

When the outside observer sees a group of BKs, all in white, sitting in blissful meditation, it is possible to feel like an outsider, not admitted to this holy circle. In fact, everybody is welcome but meditation itself is hard work and the blissful state is evanescent and can easily be lost. Some BKs do start to lose this connection and can start to feel angry with Dadi Janki for insisting on an unattainable perfection.

As one BK put it: 'Once I asked Dadi: "Has it ever occurred to you that by showing people something higher, and in pushing them to go for that, you could be creating sorrow if they should fail?" She snapped back, "What are you saying - that I shouldn't try?"'

Many BKs have their struggles in trying to live up to Dadi's ideals but her conviction is that if she lets

high standards slip even a tiny bit, the power of the BK
organisation will be lost. ❦

The Importance of Decluttering: Dadi was there first

When you go into a BK centre, wherever in the world it may be, you will notice that it is remarkably clean, free from clutter and utterly neat and tidy. There is a potent atmosphere of calm and orderliness and this is brought about in large part by the fact that there is not a trace of mess or 'stuff' in the place.

This is the case however large the centre may be, and once again, is one of Dadi's abiding principles: no mess or extraneous objects must come between her and her connection with God. Mess and clutter, she would say, detracts from this connection. It weighs on the mind, and is an indication of a messy, cluttered-up mind. It is also a clear example of laziness and Dadi hates any kind of laziness.

If you stay in a BK retreat centre or even go for lunch, you will notice that everything is cleared away immediately after use. No dirty plates, crumbs or litter are allowed to remain for any longer than necessary, and all leaflets, flyers, books or other material is neatly stacked.

Nothing is too small to escape Dadi's attention and she insists that all kitchens, dining rooms, reception rooms and bedrooms must be clean and clear at all times.

If they are not, she will notice and order the place to be cleaned at once. In this, Dadi Janki is in line with the latest thinking on the subject, that if we want to live harmoniously, we must make sure that our exterior environment is as clean and free of clutter as our minds and thoughts must be. Over the past 10 to 15 years, there have been many books and television programmes on decluttering your home, your office and your car, and indeed, you can now hire a professional declutterer to do the job for you – at a cost.

But Dadi was there first, ruthlessly decluttering before anybody had thought of making money from it.

Since being in the west, Dadi has become aware of the steady accumulation of goods in people's homes, and notes how much they clutter up the mind and prevent us from thinking clearly. According to a new book, *Stuffocation*, a sociological survey of the way in which people's lives have gradually been overtaken by clutter, the average man now has over 30 pairs of socks and the average woman buys 58 different items of clothing a year.

As a society, we are cluttered up with more goods than at any other time in history, and, it seems, we keep wanting more. A popular punishment for children used to be to send them to their rooms. There is a cartoon doing the rounds on the internet showing the results of this punishment in 1950 and 2015. In the 1950 cartoon, the child is sitting in a dark corner, on the floor of a bare room, looking abjectly miserable. In the 2015 cartoon, the child is in his room surrounded by computers, Playstations, mobile phones, a state of the art desk, hundreds of books, CDs and DVDs. Instead of looking miserable, a smile is on his face. His room contains everything he wants and it is no longer a punishment to be sent there.

You will not find any of that in Dadi Janki's own personal room. Indeed, she will not even allow a spare hanky to be there and everything must be ruthlessly 'edited' as we might say today. Her room is bare and simple. She does not even own 58 items of clothing; six dresses, she says, are all she needs. And why have more than one pair of slippers? 'Am I going to wear them one on top of the other?' she asks.

For Dadi, clutter is a sign of a disordered mind and if you cannot keep the externals clean and tidy, what must your mind be like? Her room must always be kept ready to receive visitors, whether they are Heads of State or just ordinary people coming to say hello. You will never hear Dadi say, excuse the mess – because there never is any mess. She does not like dark colours, either. She herself always wears white, and all BK centres are white, or based on white.

This again is in tune with the times. How often do homes and interiors magazines have a 'white' issue? Once a year at least, and in the UK, The White Company has high street shops containing white, or predominantly white, goods. Plain, simple, clean, white – these are Dadi's watchwords for her appearance and her home.

Although Indian décor is often associated with the ornate and the exotic, a 'maximalist' rather than a minimalist look, this is emphatically not Dadi's style.

Yet again, Dadi was there before anybody else. In 1974, when she came to London, she insisted that the rooms in the tiny flat were painted white. One day a neighbour from over the road came to the newly-created centre and was so impressed with the white walls that she went home and painted all her own walls white. And this was in the days of 1970s decor when dark brown and orange profusion, with geometric patterns everywhere, was the order of the day.

This simplicity and insistence on utter cleanliness and neatness not only gives a good first impression, but in a subtle sense, it means that the rooms in a BK centre are anybody's. They are utterly devoid of anything personal, such as family photographs, and this is deliberate. It does mean that no dedicated BK can ever make a 'home' for herself as we understand it, with no personal possessions around the place, but once again, this cleanliness and simplicity is in keeping with all monastic orders throughout the ages. A present day nun's cell is as bare and stripped of ornament as it would have been 500 years ago.

The difference with Dadi is that she insists on it or at least recommends it, as a lifestyle choice for everybody and not just those who live in centres or retreats.

This lack of personalization, Dadi would say, makes visitors feel welcome. If a room is full of clutter, ornaments and photos, visitors feel crowded out.

As the many television programmes on messy homes have shown, you go into some people's houses and immediately feel awkward because of the amount of clutter and mess in the place. Dadi Janki would be appalled at the state of writer Redmond O'Hanlon's study as described in a profile in The Guardian:

> 'O'Hanlon's house in Oxfordshire is notoriously messy and chaotic, with tilting piles of books and drifts of magazines: his attempts to tidy it up bring on panic attacks. When he moved to the house, he felt it necessary exactly to reproduce the look of his previous study; otherwise he felt unsafe. He likes to stack up around himself everything he has ever valued, as if he fears it'll all be taken away: stuffed animals, skulls, a giant pelican, a mummified frog, hundreds of photographs of pygmies, a pair of buffalo horns and lots of cabinets – for beetles, butterflies, birds' eggs and an alarming spider.'

For this reason, and because Dadi wants everybody who comes to a BK centre to feel welcome, there are not only no stuffed animals or stags' heads, there is an absolute minimum of ornaments and pictures. There is always a big picture of Brahma Baba of course and this in itself puts some people off – my son Will's memoir The House is Full of Yogis mentions his distaste when such Indian pictures, seen by some as idolatrous, began to invade our own home – but nowadays, as Westerners don't tend to like bad-art Indian pictures, even these are kept to a minimum.

The standard advice for anybody wanting to sell their house is always declutter; remove family photos, ornaments, anything highly personal, and make the space as clean and clear as you can. There has been research showing that houses that are clean and smart sell more quickly than those which are untidy, dirty and full of mess. This is not surprising, perhaps, but Dadi would argue that you should never allow mess to build up, but must return the house to its pristine state daily. As with meditation, you have to make drudgery divine and clean the rooms every day. It is an essential aspect of the BK's life; there must be no slackness ever, in any area of life.

One BK brother said to me: 'When I've finished work in the evening I'm too tired to clear up, and next morning, I'm too busy. So mess piles up.' When Dadi Janki saw his room she ordered him to clear away the mess and empty the waste paper basket instantly. She is almost mortally offended by mess, even when it is not her own.

Yes, it takes attention and work, but that is what Dadi is all about: never slacken off in the slightest, in any degree. Clean the windows! Polish the floor! Get rid of that pile of newspapers!

But there is also a spiritual side to decluttering. One of the earliest books on the subject was, *Creating Sacred Space with Feng Shui*. This bestselling book, first published in 1995, spoke of the vital importance of decluttering when almost nobody had heard of the concept. In the book, author Karen Kingston explains how energy either flows or is blocked in the home, and how clutter creates stuck energy and means that you are unable to move on in your life.

Feng Shui, as most people will know by now, is the ancient Chinese art of arranging objects and positioning rooms so that the energy will flow, and that 'poison arrows' cannot enter and detract from your health, wealth or happiness. Of course many people have derided Feng Shui as nonsense but anybody who enters a Feng Shui'd home will immediately be aware of a calm and harmonious atmosphere, not to say an almost tangible vibration of peace within.

I know that I would far rather be entertained in a clean, tidy room that has some Feng Shui touches than one which is full of tottering piles of papers, crowded with ornaments and has trailing wires everywhere.

Dadi herself has this to say about accumulating, or hoarding, possessions: 'People have a habit of holding onto old things. They might buy lots of new things but still they hang onto the old things as well. They never want to part with these old possessions. Sometimes, they are not even of any use – they may have broken or stopped working. But still they won't throw them away or donate them to charity. 'Why on earth,' Dadi asked, 'are we holding onto those old things that are of no use to us?'

Meditation, she adds, is a way of clearing out all the mental rubbish we have accumulated within us. As is the external, so is the internal. If we don't hold onto physical possessions, she argues, we are less likely to hold onto bad habits. In every way, both inside and out, we should consciously strip away from our lives everything we are holding onto which is not of any benefit or use. This is what makes it easy to connect to God.

Dadi herself has never accumulated any personal possessions. She would never have more than half a dozen saris, saying that any more would constitute clutter, and she has never had a personal car of her own. Nor does she ever keep a car for her own sole use. Whenever she goes anywhere by car, she always takes passengers. This is not only because she believes it is wasteful to use more cars than absolutely necessary on a journey, but also because it gives her a chance to converse with her passengers, thus not wasting a minute. During car journeys, Dadi will discuss future plans, get to know people, and devise future projects.

One reason Dadi has never stored up personal possessions is that in a sense, she has never had a home. She has always been nomadic, travelling to many countries, dividing her time between India and London, and always having only one room for her own use, never a whole house or even her own kitchen. 'Travelling light' she would say, 'enables you to go anywhere at a moment's notice and never be dragged down by ownership or bricks and mortar.'

Some wags have pointed out that whereas we have 'Greenwich Mean Time', Dadi proceeds by 'Indian Generous Time.' This can also mean that she is not as strictly bound by the clock as perhaps she might be, when she feels there are important matters to attend to. Once again, this is Indian rather than Western, and it can be difficult for Westerners, used to absolute punctuality, to get their heads round.

In the same way that Dadi has no personal possessions, she has no money of her own. She is fond of saying, 'You won't find even one rupee in my purse.' This may not be literally true, but what she means is that no money ever stays in her purse. Emphatically not a hoarder, she ensures that whenever money comes into the organisation, it straightaway goes out again, on improving the services offered.

This emphasis on not accumulating can sometimes cause problems, such as when a large sum is needed for a major repair of a centre, and there is not enough in the bank to pay for it. But Dadi has the Biblical attitude of not taking thought for the morrow and letting the future look after itself. It is an attitude which has enabled the BKs to purchase or construct beautiful buildings, so who is to say it's wrong?

When the Icelandic banks crashed, it was found that many British charities, even quite small ones, had millions of pounds stashed away in them, hoping of course for better rates of interest than other banks provided. In some cases, the charities lost a lot of money. Dadi would never allow this. Although the BK organisation obviously has bank accounts, nothing is ever accumulated to no particular purpose or for some vague future use.

In her book *First Hand Experiences with a Great Yogi*, BK Hansa, who has been looking after Dadi for many years, and is her constant companion (apart from God of course) says that whenever money comes to Dadi, she immediately gives it to the organisation, even if the donor says it is for her personal use. She will never accept it for herself.

Dadi also insists however that whenever money comes into the organisation for a specific purpose, it must be used for that purpose and no other. For instance, if there is a donation for the hospital, it must go to the hospital – even if other areas are crying out for funds. Also, if somebody donates money for vegetables, fruit or flowers, once again, it must be used for this purpose and no other.

The understanding behind this is that whenever anybody gives money to the organisation, they give it with love and it must be used in the same spirit. There is a Hindi word for this, bhavna, which means, pure feelings of love. Nothing must ever break this bhavna.

On the money issue, some leadership experts have interesting thoughts on the matter of charging for events. They say that if an organisation charges for its services, then you will pay the amount asked, but never any more. If, for instance, a retreat centre charges £500 for a residential weekend, you will pay that amount, but you wouldn't pay £750 because you felt it was better than expected. You have paid your dues and that's it.

But in the case of the BKs, where all services are given free (but donations are invited) some people may give £1000, or even £2000 for a weekend. Of course many people will give nothing at all because the word 'free' has attracted them in the first place, but where there is no set charge, very often attendees feel moved to give more.

There is a downside to this, in that where no fees are charged, there is less commitment on the part of potential attendees. BK centres find that when they advertise a programme or a retreat, many people will not show up, even though they have booked. Very often, they will not even let the organisers know, and this can be a particularly difficult problem when it comes to catering. The cooks may cater for 100 people to find that only 60 arrive, and this has been a recurring problem with BK events.

When you have to pay, and there is no refund for no-shows, such as with the theatre, this is much less likely to happen, and it is something BKs increasingly feel they must address.

But by and large, the principle of not charging works, and it endears people to the organisation. There is an interesting parallel here with Findhorn, the spiritual community mentioned in the chapter on Maureen and David Goodman. Findhorn is famous – or notorious – for charging high fees for its residential retreats. Yet a few years ago it copied the BKs and decided to charge nothing for one of its courses. When the community fell into financial difficulties, in spite of charging high fees, the free centre was the only one in the black. Once again, people were invited to donate, and often they gave more than they would have been charged.

The same principle is at work with guided tours in Oxford, where I live. Most of them make a charge, but some are free. Once again, you are invited, although not compelled, to give a tip. The guides conducting the 'free' tours find they make more money than those who charge.

This outlook may not work with all businesses but it seems to have its advantages and of course the BKs, in common with any other organisation, has to remain solvent and the books have to be balanced each year. But it has long been a guiding principle of spiritual organisations that money is not hoarded but must be spent to the greater glory of God or to further the work. It must never stay in the pockets of those at the top. Is there a lesson here for bankers? Many people in the banking industry earning huge amounts are not even keen on spending. It is money, and the accumulation of money, that interests them, rather than what they can buy with it.

In the BK world, nothing is ever hoarded, whether money or possessions. But there is more to it than that. In so many ways, Dadi has been forward-thinking and she has always said what is only just coming home to people more generally: more money, more possessions, more goods, don't make you happy. Indeed, just the opposite. They lead to what has become known as Status Anxiety, where you are always nervous that your friend or neighbour has more than you – a better house, better car, more expensive clothes, a better-paying job.

There used to be a saying, 'much wants more' and that has become all too true today, with stuff endlessly pushed at us from every quarter, with advertisements on television, on the internet, in magazines and newspapers and on all social media. Our lives are increasingly cluttered up, one might say, with ads telling us to buy, buy, buy or offering us 'phenomenal' bargains. You cannot open Facebook without seeing streams of ads and if you even look up a crossword clue, for instance, on the internet, you will see numerous ads claiming your time and attention. Charity websites are also often plastered with ads and it seems as if we cannot escape consumerism, wherever we look.

Dadi of course takes no notice of any of it and according to the book *Stuffocation*, there are signs that we, too, are now tiring of having too much stuff, too many material possessions in our lives. Author James Wallman points to many examples where people are decluttering, downsizing and deciding to live more simply. It is even starting to become fashionable to boast about how few things you have, rather than how many.

When you stop accumulating stuff, says Wellman, you can concentrate more on meaningful experiences, and Dadi would concur with that. Because at the end of the day, there is no end to accumulation, and acquiring things can become an addiction in itself. Wellman analyses the differences between being a collector and a hoarder, but is there really all that much difference? Both types of people are surrounding themselves with possessions as a form of security. But as we know, possessions never do offer any security.

I am reminded of the story of two friends, a married couple, who bought an old rectory and gradually did it up beautifully. They spent years lovingly restoring the house and hunting down objects and artefacts that would enhance it. The house had a billiard room, a games room and several antique four-poster beds in the bedrooms. There was also a valuable collection of paintings, china and Victorian kitchen utensils, to name just a few.

One evening, they went out to dinner to celebrate their wedding anniversary and returned to find the house surrounded by fire engines. While they were out, a fire started – to this day nobody knows how – and it was the water hoses, rather than the fire, which destroyed most of the goods they had carefully collected over 25 years.

For the wife, this was the turning point. She decided to downsize drastically, ditching the husband as well as much of the material clutter in her life. The couple separated, she went to live in a tiny cottage and resolved never to accumulate stuff again. Instead, she turned her attention towards nurturing herself spiritually.

Something similar happened to me, years ago. I went out with my son Tom, then aged about 13, for half an hour or so and came back to find the house had been burgled and all my jewellery had been taken. Once I recovered from the shock, I decided never to buy any 'real' jewellery again. To this day, I have never owned any jewellery of any value and have not missed it for a minute. Because of this I never have to worry about it being lost or stolen.

I have taken my cue from Dadi Janki in other ways, too, in that I only ever have a small selection of clothes in my wardrobe. I have learned not to accumulate stuff either, although I have to say this does not apply to my book collection, which grows all the time. I'm not sure what Dadi would make of my 3000 or so books but my excuse is that my library contains much wisdom and I can imbibe some of this wisdom from taking down a book from the shelves. But I never crave designer clothes, expensive handbags or smart shoes and never miss them at all.

This is just one other important way in which Dadi Janki is showing by her own example how little we actually need to live well. It has to be remembered too that Dadi comes from the mercantile Bhaibund community, where the emphasis was above all on ostentation and showing off wealth. These were business people who delighted in showing friends and family how rich and splendid their houses were. They also had vast collections of valuable jewellery, so it's not as if Dadi has never known the appeal of wealth and possessions.

But the insistence on simplicity should not be taken to mean that we should all live miserable lives in hovels. Far from it. Since those early days in two little rooms, the BKs, guided by Dadi, have expanded mightily, now owning a former stately home in Oxford and many impressive, well-appointed centres all over the world. They have a 350-acre estate, Peace Village, in the Catskill Mountains, New York State. The headquarters in India are also enormous, with vast meeting rooms and accommodation houses for the hundreds of thousands of visitors they host each year.

Dadi likes to make sure that visitors are comfortable, have comfortable beds and rooms, are fed well and have a good experience of meditation while they are in residence. This is part of her hospitality approach; you look after your visitors, even when they are complete strangers, before attending to your own needs.

Nowadays, the only concession Dadi makes to her age and infirmity is to fly business or first class, rather than steerage. Even then, she had to be persuaded and it went much against the grain for her to have a better, more expensive seat than the other BK travellers. But this concession is once again purely practical as even at her advanced age, Dadi often gets straight off the plane to speak at a conference or attend a meeting, so needs to be as well rested as possible.

One concession she absolutely refuses to make to old age, though, is to use a walking stick. Although getting about is not so easy for her now, she acts and conducts herself as much as she can as a young and healthy person. To Dadi, even at 100 years old, a walking stick is more than just another piece of clutter she does not need. It says 'old' and that is a message she will resist as long as she lives. ❧

Dadi Janki inaugurating a BK centre in Accra, Ghana, 2004

CHAPTER ELEVEN

The role of illness

Dadi Janki, much like theoretical physicist Stephen Hawking, is a medical mystery. When Stephen Hawking was diagnosed with motor neurone disease at the age of 21, he was expected to live two to three years. He is now 73 (in 2015) and working as hard as ever.

Dadi Janki, too, has defied medical prognoses. Constantly ill from childhood with serious debilitating conditions, she has continually bounced back to live another day.

When asked the secret of his long life – with virtually no organs still working – Stephen Hawking replied, as he entered his 74th year, in the robotic voice for which he has become world-famous, that it was down to two factors: doing a job he loved, and excellent care all his life.

Dadi Janki could probably say the same. Her long life has been spent doing a job she loves and she too has had excellent care from people who love her. I think that perhaps we could add a third factor to the long lives of both these exceptional people, and that is love and adulation from large numbers of people. Also, both Hawking and Dadi Janki are extremely feisty, rarely refusing an invitation to speak or to appear at a public event, however difficult the journey for them. Hawking was at the premiere of the film of his life, *The Theory of Everything*, dressed up in his wheelchair in black tie.

Stephen Hawking's illness was diagnosed at an early stage, and followed the expected progression – apart from the expected early death. But nobody knows exactly what has been wrong with Dadi. She has had heart and digestive problems for many years. She had TB as a child and for many years was plagued by a persistent severe cough. In the early 1960s her left side became paralysed.

In 1982 she was out of action for a year from a thyroid deficiency that doctors in London failed to recognise. She spent virtually the whole of that year in isolation, only seeing people for very short spells. Aged 80, during a severe winter in Mount Abu, she had double pneumonia and almost died. She counted her recovery from this, in January 1991, as a new birth.

Since then she has had two stents inserted to improve her coronary circulation. Even today, as the aftermath of three falls, she has chronic pain from spinal fractures and also gastric pain from diverticulitis and a hernia.

And although she recovers from her bouts of serious illness, there is always a possibility that she will become ill again and on death's door.

What we can say about both Dadi and Hawking is that they could not have achieved more if they had been in robust health all their lives – and may even have achieved less. But in Dadi's case at least we can ask: why is she so often ill and do her frequent illnesses serve any wider purpose? Dadi maintains that illness has the benefit of bringing about the blessing of solitude.

Part of the reason for her illnesses must also be that she sets herself such a punishing schedule. She is the yogi, the guru, who never sleeps – or hardly ever. And then her constant travelling to distant parts of the world must take its toll.

But maybe there is more to the story. Perhaps for Dadi, illness itself has played an important part in her ability to achieve what some people might consider the impossible.

In order to get a clue, we can take a look at the long life of another great reformer, Florence Nightingale. After she came back from the Crimean War, Florence more or less went to bed for 50 years with an illness never really identified. From her sickbed she proceeded to invent the modern nursing profession and established nursing as a proper career. She also enacted many social reforms, particularly where women were concerned.

And both women were convinced from an early age that they received calls from God to do His work and as such, would not let anything stand in their way.

Like Dadi Janki, Florence Nightingale heard calls urging her to devote her life to the service of others. She came from a rich, well-connected family where women were not expected to work for a living. Indeed, most of the men never worked either. Florence's father William never did a day's work in his life although he did educate his daughter at home.

Also like Dadi, Florence did not want to marry as she felt marriage would hinder her ability to dedicate her life to nursing. Before she became the most famous nurse in history, nursing the sick was something undertaken by the lowest in society. Dickens' Sarah Gamp is perhaps a caricature, but nurses were generally seen as drunken, uneducated women who undertook work no decent woman would consider. Florence Nightingale changed all that and put nursing on a proper footing whereby it became an honourable job and indeed, was considered a vocation.

But in order to achieve her reforms, Florence Nightingale could not cope with any distractions. Illness served to isolate her from the world, and from the world's demands.

Dadi Janki of course in spite of her unwillingness to enter into the marital state, did have an arranged marriage, until she managed to escape it a short time later. Florence Nighingale did not find it so easy to escape marriage, either. She was courted for nine long years by Richard Monckton Milnes, a politician and poet. She kept him hanging on a string and hoping, but never had any serious intention of marrying him.

Florence Nightingale also had other influential suitors and admirers, among them Sidney Herbert, another politician, and religious reformer Benjamin Jowett. Her strong calling to God, as she saw it, meant that she used her suitors and admirers ruthlessly, making them work hard in her service and in some cases, nearly killing them. The poet Arthur Hugh Clough, author of the poem *Say Not the Struggle Naught Availeth*, was kept occupied tying up paper parcels for Florence. Indeed, he expended enormous energy working as her unpaid secretarial assistant and maybe it was not surprising that he died at the early age of 42. Such was Florence's charisma and drive. She did not spare herself and she did not spare others.

Sounds familiar? Dadi Janki, too, has attracted many loyal lieutenants, who she has kept hard at work in her service, or – the service of God. There is no suggestion that any of them died in her service but all attest to her slave-driving propensities – and for the same reason. There was no time to waste; what both women were doing was too important for ordinary considerations of rest and social life to be entertained.

A busy chronic invalid indeed, Florence Nightingale was above all a statistician and wrote many books on nursing, social reform, hygiene and public health. Much of the military-style nature of the nursing profession, which she introduced, along with recognisable uniforms, is still in place.

Nobody ever knew quite what was wrong with Nightingale during her bedridden years, but being ill and prostrate in bed gave her many advantages that she would not have had if she had been up and about.

For one thing it enabled her to go into silence, not to have any visitors if she didn't feel up to it, and not to do anything she didn't want to do, because she always had the pretext of illness.

One also thinks of that other professional Victorian invalid, Elizabeth Barrett Browning. Again, nobody knew exactly what was wrong with her, but her continuing illness meant she never had to get out of bed or attend to any duties that might be expected of a Victorian lady of her class. Her father had ordered her, along with his other eleven children, never to get married and for a time, that suited Elizabeth, or Baba as she was called, extremely well. It did not seem as though she would ever be well enough to get married. When romance happened, it changed her life forever. Her fervent admirer, fellow poet Robert Browning, six years her junior, came to visit her. Visitors were allowed when she felt up to it but it has to be remembered that at the age of 40, she had never even done her own hair. She could not cook or undertake any domestic tasks and she had never appeared in public. Nevertheless, her growing fame – and mystery – intrigued many writers of the day and after he got to know her, Robert Browning uttered these famous words: 'I love your verses with all my heart my dear Miss Barrett – and I love you too.'

These words enabled Elizabeth Barrett to rise from her sickbed and with her faithful servant Wilson, get married in secret to Robert Browning and elope with him to Italy. She was already past 40 and would go on to have a son, known as Pen, while her former servant Wilson married an Italian and set up a guesthouse. Elizabeth Barrett's furious father disinherited her, as he had threatened all his children if they married, but the love she felt for Robert Browning was stronger than any father's inheritance.

It is true that the Victorians made a big thing of illness and up to a point, indulged it. Even so, we might ask: what do Florence Nightingale, Elizabeth Barrett Browning and Dadi Janki have in common?

All are or were, remarkably talented and single-minded women who used illness, whether consciously or unconsciously, to retain an air of mystery and remoteness that nevertheless enabled them to do great things. It is worth pointing out that Dadi still receives and uplifts people, even on her sickbed.

That great genius Virginia Woolf, herself a victim of many illnesses including serious mental illness, wrote an essay in 1925, *On Being Ill*, where she asked:

> 'Considering how common illness is, how tremendous the spiritual change that it brings, how astonishing, when the lights of health go down, the undiscovered countries that are then disclosed, what wastes and deserts of the soul a slight attack

of influenza brings to light...it becomes strange indeed that illness has not taken its place with love, battle, and jealousy among the prime themes of literature.'

In this same essay, Woolf wrote that 'great oaks are uprooted in us by the act of being ill'.

Such insights into illness have rarely been bettered and it is interesting that Woolf speaks of the spiritual insights that can come with illness. At the time Woolf wrote, influenza, or flu, could be a serious illness resulting in death.

To put it more prosaically, illness can give time to think, time away from the cares of the world and the demands of other people, in order to have peace and space to further one's work. Even though all the women mentioned here were constantly ill, at least two of them – Florence Nightingale and Dadi Janki – lived on into their nineties, still madly working right up to the end. Virginia Woolf, as we know, committed suicide during one of her mental breakdowns, but she is generally regarded as one of the greatest writers of the twentieth century, a true literary giant.

There is also a value in illness when it gives you time out of your ordinary cares and concerns to bring about – possibly – world transformation. Another example is Nelson Mandela. Although so far as we know he did not suffer from serious illness, his 27 years in prison gave him time to think, to read and reflect, so that by the time of his release, he had become a very wise man. Many gifted people have done their best work in prison or when removed, either by choice or by force, from everyday life, and enabled to be solitary.

Mandela's nearly three decades in prison made him compassionate and determined not to prolong the conditions in South Africa where one race was seen as superior to another. Instead of revenge, he wanted reconciliation and to this day, South Africans see his ability to forgive and forget as some kind of miracle. His coming to power could so easily have ended in bloodshed.

You might say that Mandela's years in prison were a kind of enforced meditation. He could not escape physically but in his mind he was free.

So it has been with Dadi Janki. Her periods of illness have also given her time out, as it were, to think and plan and meditate and connect with God even more. Retreating into illness can give the time out from ordinary life to formulate and then enact great visions.

While writing this book, some non-BKs have asked me whether I think that the big centres and worldwide expansion of the movement would have happened without Dadi Janki and my answer to that is, most probably no. Without Dadi, it is entirely possible the BKs would still be a tiny Indian organisation operating out of the two-roomed flat in Tennyson Road. Throughout her time in the West, Dadi has come up with one extraordinary vision after another, and has then set about bringing them into reality.

And then, once that has been achieved, it is immediately onto the next thing. Dadi has never been one to rest on her laurels.

Yet although major transformation is often the inspiration of one person, Dadi Janki has at the same time never been alone. In much the same way as many other significant people struck down by recurrent illness, Dadi Janki has always had loyal people to look after her. This has undoubtedly prolonged her life as there is strong evidence to show that nursing care and devotion helps patients to survive and live another day. Dadi is much loved by many people around the world, and this, as much as anything, has undoubtedly given her the strength to carry on.

For many years, BK Hansa has been Dadi's carer, going everywhere with her, sleeping in the same room and devoting her life to Dadi's wellbeing. Hansa feels privileged to undertake this task, and herself receives many blessings for the quality of care she has bestowed on Dadi.

And Jayanti's father, Murli, now in his nineties and in a wheelchair, also receives constant, devoted care at the Oxford Retreat Centre, as a reward for enabling the BKs to gain a foothold in the West, via Jayanti and her mother Rajni.

Of course, suffering from so much illness all her life, from a very young age, Dadi has thought a lot about recurrent sickness and what it means.

First of all, she says, there is the role of karma, or what you bring with you from a previous birth, or births. Although this is not a doctrine that everybody accepts, we know that babies are often born very ill or suffering from handicaps when we might ask, what have they done to deserve it? In Dadi's view, those who do not have a good start in life will have brought some baggage with them from a former incarnation. There is not a lot you can do about illness that is related to activity or behaviour in a past life, apart from accept it, and learn from the special circumstances and challenges it brings.

The BKs do not delve into past lives, as some therapists and parapsychologists have done, in order to explain the present. It is enough for them to believe that whatever happens to you in this incarnation is in some sense related to what went before. Illness can be a kind of karmic account, according to this belief.

By the same token, those who have always enjoyed robust health, may be seen to have brought some good karma with them from a previous life.

In modern times, genetics has often been blamed for certain illness, such as some cancers and heart conditions. But although genetic inheritance undoubtedly plays a part, it can only ever be a partial answer, as many people have suffered a lifetime of illness when nobody else in the family has ever had that particular complaint.

Illness in this life does not only come about as a result of actions carried out in a previous incarnation. We have to take full responsibility for our own health and there are two other major factors that Dadi Janki believes cause illness. These are: laziness, or carelessness; and addictions.

Carelessness means the inability, or perhaps wilful refusal, to look after yourself properly. This of course at a simple level includes not getting proper rest, not eating properly, eating and drinking the wrong things, and succumbing to health-destroying habits such as drinking or drug-taking.

It might also mean not wrapping up warm when going out in winter or deliberately harming yourself in ways to cause illness. Such psychological or psychiatric conditions as anorexia or other eating disorders and obsessive-compulsive disorder are all conditions that can lead to serious physical illness and in extreme cases, even early death.

The BKs insist on a healthy, home-cooked diet prepared with natural, fresh ingredients. In common with many other religions, visitors are always offered food and refreshment. It tastes delicious and many people believe this is directly caused by the spiritual vibrations that have entered into it by the act of 'offering up' food to God before it is eaten.

In such ways, the BKs try to take care of themselves. One thing many have let slip in their lives, though, is lack of physical exercise. The yoga they practice does not include hatha, or postural yoga and although the founder Brahma Baba insisted that all the early BKs did regular exercise to keep fit, this is no longer part of the daily routine as, in my view, it ought to be.

These days, many BKs become overweight and as a result, suffer from diabetes and other conditions associated with obesity and lack of exercise. Carelessness? Or is it that they consider they don't have time for exercise?

When it comes to addictions, we now know that these can lead to serious illness and early death. The connection between smoking and illness is now well established, as are the links between many recreational drugs and illness, and alcohol dependency and illness. Such activities often start off by being enjoyable, they give a lift; and then before long, we find they have taken hold and we are in thrall to them.

An important aspect of the BK lifestyle is separating oneself from addictions. We all know that this can be hard, but over the years, many drug addicts, alcoholics and people with eating disorders have found themselves able to recover their health through the BK practices of meditation, eating pure food and living a simple, pure lifestyle.

As part of the BKs' commitment to healthcare, Dadi Janki has overseen the development of courses and events aimed at helping people suffering from addictions and dependencies. This is yet another way that the BKs are continually reaching out to those who need help and spiritual sustenance.

Dadi also believes that much chronic illness comes about from negativity, stress and wrong ways of thinking which in themselves can become hard-to-break habits and thus develop into addictions. It is not always an outside substance that causes an addiction. Some people are addicted to anger, for instance, and it is now well known that being perpetually angry can lead to heart and digestive conditions that then have to be treated by pills. Research has also shown that long-held resentments can lead to illness. The BKs understand this and hold anger management and positive thinking courses all over the world.

The best way to deal with addictions, whether they result from substance abuse or wrong ways of thinking, is, once again, meditation. This, Dadi Janki believes, can in itself heal a lot of illnesses and bring about recovery without medical intervention. Meditation can work to bring the mind and body into harmony and so overcome many physical conditions.

These days, Dadi also has access to the best medical attention that can be provided and no expense is spared to make sure she has the best doctors, attends the best hospitals, and receives whatever state of the art care is available for her condition.

Her frequent illnesses have also served the purpose of turning her attention to healthcare and, under her guidance, The Janki Foundation for Global Healthcare, later renamed The Janki Foundation for Spirituality in Healthcare, was inaugurated in 1997 at the Royal College of Physicians in London. It is a UK-based charity supporting research into the links between health and spirituality.

The Foundation publishes leaflets, books and CDs and holds annual lectures exploring the spiritual dimension of health care. From small beginnings, the Janki Foundation now extends its reach into over 30 countries. It also supports the work of the Global Hospital in Mount Abu, India, where cutting-edge mainstream medical treatment is aided and abetted by meditation and complementary treatments where considered appropriate.

As President of the Janki Foundation, Dadi said:

'Today, there is a lot of research in medicine and science but we have forgotten to research inner peace. I have experienced a lot of illnesses throughout my life. I have also nursed others during my service in a spiritual community for many years. I found patients' recovery was helped when I served with love, and that "blessings" and love from others contribute greatly to healing. I came to the conclusion that to understand the patient and give with compassion is what is truly needed. I would encourage all health professionals to work with compassion and peace.'

Throughout her life, Dadi has also given great attention to healthcare workers; from nurses and doctors to administrators and anybody professionally concerned with dispensing health. Dadi was also herself designated a nurse during the early years of the BKs, when they spent 14 years in seclusion and isolation.

She is a great believer, too, in the importance of the role of the carer, and at the Global Retreat Centre in Oxford, regular weekends are organised for those in the caring professions, such as social workers, nurses, doctors, prison workers, teachers and probation officers. Dadi is aware that members of these professions suffer a lot from stress, and that they themselves need help as much as those they are trying to care for.

Many years ago the Bristol Cancer Help Centre, later known as Penny Brohn Cancer Care, pioneered residential weeks and weekends for cancer patients and their carers, with the carers being given as much attention as the actual patients. The BKs now also do this and at some of their centres, hold special retreats for cancer patients and their carers.

The main difference between the Bristol sessions and the BK retreats is that the Bristol weeks are very expensive, whereas the BK retreats are free. Cancer patients and their carers are often unable to work, and so may not have much spare money. These cancer retreats are highly popular, and provide yet another example of the many ways that the BKs support the wider community, as well as those within the BK organisation.

There is more, far more to Dadi Janki than just sitting in meditation! ❧

CHAPTER TWELVE

The 1980s

As the BKs expanded, so did the numbers of Westerners dedicating and surrendering. Centres were opening all over Europe and at the same time, Dadi Janki and Jayanti were travelling to remote parts, spreading the word. Large conferences were being held in London and at the main centre there, numbers for early morning class grew so large that the house in St Gabriel's Road, North West London, was no longer big enough and the sessions had to move to a community centre in Dudden Hill.

During this time, the BKs forged strong links with local councils and began to expand the scope of their classes and courses. But Dadi Janki, always restless, was never content.

At the same time as she was looking to expand, she was also inspiring ever more people to become BKs.

I came across the BKs in 1981. My then husband, Neville, had got to hear about them and mentioned them to me, as I was becoming increasingly feminist and although not particularly interested in spirituality or meditation, was intrigued by this Indian meditation group run by women.

We both heard the course, and began attending meditation classes at a small house in Kew, near Richmond, which was then owned by Jayanti. There we met Sister Sudesh, Jayanti, and finally, Dadi Janki. Although beset with many initial doubts and fears, before long, Neville was living the BK lifestyle and observing all the recommended practices, including celibacy and vegetarianism. Although he did not finally surrender until 1994, he became ever closer until there was really no other option for him.

Of course, as with any group, not all who were initially beguiled stayed the course. For some, the lifestyle was too austere, for others, it felt too Indian and alien and yet others decided that they would rather lead a conventional lifestyle of marriage, children, career and home. But an ever-increasing number heard the call and realised that no other life was possible for them. Whatever the price, they had no choice but to try and lead the life of pure spirituality exemplified by Dadi Janki.

Here are inspiring stories of three people from very different backgrounds who dedicated in the early 1980s.

Luciana Ferraz, a BK since 1980 and now National Co-ordinator for Brazil.

Luciana was 23 and working as a Hatha Yoga teacher as well as finishing her last year studying Social Science at university, when she met Brother Ken, one of the original Western BKs who had gone out to South America to start service there.

She says:

'In January 1981 I was going to Mount Abu for the first time and had a stopover in London. Some of the sisters met me at the airport and took me to the house in North West London which they then shared. In the morning, I was taken to the house in St Gabriel's Road, Willesden, where Dadi Janki, Jayanti and Sudesh were living, for early morning meditation and class.

'I had always been interested in spirituality and had been fascinated by the BKs ever since Ken was invited to give a talk at the Hatha Yoga centre where I was teaching. But I was very shy in London, partly because I did not speak very good English at the time, so sat at the back of the room where I hoped I would not be noticed. I had not met Dadi Janki before, but when she came into the room, she came straight up to me and embraced me, saying that we were not strangers but had been together in a previous birth.'

From that moment, says Luciana, 'I felt so much love and care and as if I belonged immediately. I was the first person from South America to become a BK and instantly, Dadi and I seemed to establish a close and loving relationship. She gave me so much attention and was never hard or firm with me, although I have heard her be quite harsh with others. She seems to sense what you need and gives it to you.

'I felt that she was like a mother to me but what struck me most forcibly was her intensity. She is always extreme, and never compromises. Dadi is intelligent and perceptive but balanced at the same time, although you would rarely find that level of intensity in a – shall we say – ordinary person.

'The best way I can describe this intensity is that she is somebody who never gives up and is never swayed by other people's opinions. And although she seems loving and sweet and gentle, I know that she has another side.

'When I brought my father once to Oxford, Dadi invited us into her sitting room. The phone went and she answered it, getting up from her chair. She was talking sternly and pointing her finger and although we could not understand what she was saying as she was speaking in Hindi, we got the gist from the tone of her voice. My father turned to me and said, "She's really a general."'

Luciana also sees Dadi as a businesswoman. 'Yes, she has a sweet nature but she is at the same time firm in her aims and goals and does not lightly change her views or opinions. When once a group of brothers was trying to persuade her to do something against her will, she said, "I have a lot of love and respect for all of you but I'm not going to change my views".'

In common with many BKs outside of India, Luciana does not believe the organisation would ever have got going without Dadi Janki. It certainly would not have been so big or successful, she feels, partly because in non-Indian countries, people want proof and are not usually willing to just believe – at least when the religion or spiritual path they are offered is dramatically outside their own culture. 'To be able to surmount all these different cultures and belief systems without speaking English – well that is some achievement,' she says.

'The reason for this, in my view, is that Dadi completely fulfills the values of the BKs and has never watered down her beliefs or way of life. She is the living embodiment of what she preaches, and as an example of this, will never agree to charging for anything. This was a fundamental principle of the BK philosophy from the start and although it was a rare way of going about things to Western eyes, it has worked.

'Very many times, when facing money difficulties, other BKs have asked, maybe we could charge for this, or that, but Dadi would never allow it. And while she is alive, the BKs never will charge. Her values are so strong and are much more than just a belief.

'She has been without a doubt the best person for service outside India and one reason for this is that she has always made herself available. She has never created any barriers between herself and those who come in front of her, either with staff, grand rooms, grand clothes or rituals and observances that acolytes must perform when they meet her. There is no kissing of rings, no genuflecting, or anything that would put you in awe of her. Anyone can come into her room, from the highest to the lowest, from VIPs and Heads of State to tramps off the road.

'She is always there, always travelling to meet people and will always arrange a translator. This makes all of us very close, one big family, even though she doesn't speak English. Even that does not create the barrier that one might expect.

'Dadi Janki is the face of the BKs outside India; there is no doubt about that and she lives a hundred per cent by her values. Once when we were in the beautiful stately home in Oxford and having a conversation, or chit-chat as she calls it, she said that the Oxford centre came about because of her.'

Yet there was no arrogance about it, said Luciana. 'She was just reminding us that if this little elderly Indian lady could acquire an English stately home, any of us could do the same. She added that we all had that much power, and could achieve wonderful things with enough concentration, focus and self-respect. If she could be an instrument for such a grand building, she said, any of us could achieve the same.'

A present-day version of log cabin to White House. This was the story of Abraham Lincoln, who rose from a humble childhood to become President of the United States. That is the sort of thing that great leaders achieve but whether 'anyone' can achieve it, is perhaps debatable.

Luciana, one of three sisters, was originally intended for an international career. Her parents divorced when she was 14 and her father, a civil engineer by profession and also a highly successful businessman, was hoping that at least one of his daughters would carve out a big career for herself. Luciana's two sisters had married very early and so all career hopes were centred on Luciana. 'He saw me working at the United Nations building in New York,' she said. 'He never wanted me to get married and have children.

'When I became a BK, he soon understood that in a sense, I was embarking on that international career, and so it has proved. I have travelled all over the world on BK business, and have been a

BK for 35 years.' Luciana's father also provided practical help by donating some land and money to build a big BK retreat centre in Sao Paulo.

The BKs have had a presence in Brazil since 1979, and expanded rapidly in South America during the 1980s, with Luciana at the head, and Ken O'Donnell in charge of the whole of South America.

Jacqueline Berg

Jacqueline, a Dutch journalist, became a BK in 1982.

She says: "I was leading a very busy life as a journalist, and I was looking for some peace of mind in the midst of my hectic schedule. I had started doing a Zen meditation course in Amsterdam and came across some lamas from Tibet. But somehow, it never felt right for me.

'Then I was about to leave for the Canary Islands for a fashion photoshoot for my magazine, and was collecting up clothes and shoes for this shoot when I met a man who asked if I was interested in meditation. He told me he was a member of the Brahma Kumaris, who at the time I had never heard of.'

Jacqueline's interest was immediately aroused when he told her the organisation was run by women, as she was active in the feminist movement at the time. 'That was a major attraction,' she said.

'I was not interested in male gurus, and I arranged to meet this man – who is now dead – in a coffee shop in Amsterdam. He told me that the BKs had a tiny centre in the city and I made up my mind to go after I returned from my photoshoot.'

At the time, said Jacqueline, she was very fashionable, into interior design, and hardly saw herself adapting to a little-known, austere Indian cult. 'But in any case, I went along to this little centre, which I did not like at all. It was run by a Dutch woman who had become a BK, and she had no money, which was why the centre looked so poverty-stricken. This was in July 1981.

'We could not have made a greater contrast. This sister was wearing white, her home was bare and impersonal and I was wearing leather and lots of make-up. Yet, immediately, something touched me. This sister was very simple, pure and peaceful and I liked the vibrations that were emanating from her. She was aged 26, I was 24, and I felt that she was genuinely spiritual. I decided to take the course from her and when she spoke about God, she showed me a picture of a universal point of light.

'Instantly,' says Jacqueline, 'there was a recognition that she was speaking the truth.' And gradually, Jacqueline's life began to change. She carried on with her job but the BK knowledge and experience started to pull her ever more. At the end of 1982, she decided to go to Madhuban, the Indian headquarters.

Although only 24, Jacqueline had already packed a lot in. She was divorced from her husband and had another boyfriend. He liked the idea of the BKs as well, and went with Jacqueline to India. 'We were backpacking,' she says, 'and I liked Madhuban so much I took a sabbatical from my job and stayed there for four months.'

It was while she was in Madhuban in 1982 that she met Dadi Janki for the first time. 'She did not influence me to become a BK, because I was pretty much there already, but she certainly inspired me. When I came back to Amsterdam, I helped the sister who had introduced me to Raja Yoga run the centre. She then left and I was there on my own.

'By this time I had a new job, with the magazines of the Telegraph Company, and worked there for another decade while also being a BK.'

One big attraction for her was the insistence on purity, or celibacy. 'This was actually an attraction before I even met the BKs,' she says. 'The last two years of my marriage were celibate, and that was OK with my husband. I had started reading feminist books and did not want sex. Instead, I wanted space to find myself, as we might say today.'

These days, Jacqueline is a full-time BK in Holland, and is the National Co-ordinator, in overall charge of eleven main centres and three sub-centres. In Holland, the majority of BKs are of Dutch origin and there are no Indians, in contrast with the set up in the UK.

Looking back at how the BKs in Holland have expanded from one tiny centre in Amsterdam to eleven big and thriving centres all over the country, Jacqueline says it could not have happened without Dadi Janki. 'The whole thing has worked purely because of her spiritual power. As a leader, she has a wonderful balance between love and power. She has been to our centres eight or 10 times and inspired all the brothers and sisters here.'

Jacqueline does not even consider the BKs an Indian organization. 'So far as I'm concerned, although the BKs originate from India, the spiritual message is universal and has just as much relevance to the West as to the East.'

And in Holland at least, the BKs have modernised themselves. 'Although we adhere to all the principles, we don't wear white and certainly don't all wear our hair in long pigtails down our backs. We are much more modern, whereas the movement remains traditional in the UK.'

Nowadays, it is not just Jacqueline who is a full-time BK, but also her ex-husband Wolter, and her mother and brother. 'My ex is such a good spiritual friend,' she says, 'and my relationship with him now is so much better than when we were married.'

On Dadi Janki, Jacqueline has this to say: 'Just being in her company is a transformative experience. I have met Dadi many times and she has guided me, supported me, empowered me, joked with me, played with me, pulled me up short in either a light or serious way, and saved me from many mistakes or misunderstandings. Being with her is like riding the waves of her tranquil and serene mind and her warm and compassionate heart. Being with this magical soul has always given me hope, courage and stamina on my spiritual journey.'

Jacqueline has, over the years, noted down every single word or sentence that Dadi has spoken to her. 'I consider these a treasure of truth, coming from a most elevated yet so approachable human being. She is definitely an instrument of the Divine, a spiritual leader par excellence. She is a true and eternal friend.'

You can't get a much higher accolade than that.

Francois Becher, from France, became a BK in 1979 and is now the National Co-Ordinator for France.

After doing Army service, Francois started working for France Telecom as an electrical engineer, but ever since 1969, when the first (and so far only) men landed on the moon, he has been fascinated by what human beings could achieve.

To him, that walk on the moon was a magical moment. And at the age of 24, he was no longer satisfied with his routine job at Telecom and decided to take extended leave while he travelled the world in search of truth. As it turned out, he spent six years on the road with his rucksack looking for wisdom. Some of those wanderings were interspersed with temporary jobs to keep him going and perhaps inevitably, eventually he came across the BKs.

He says: 'Everywhere I went I was meeting interesting people and it came home to me how intimately the culture of a country was shaped by its religion and religious values. Yet I was not impressed by any of the religions I came across. It was while I was in Melbourne that I met my first BKs, and then later, in Sydney, I was given the seven-day Raja Yoga course by Michael and Joe, twins who had surrendered together. I was delighted by what I was hearing. I loved the knowledge but try as I might, I did not get God.

'I wondered what God had to do with it all. I liked the concept of seeing the soul as a point of energy, and it seemed that something spoke to me for the first time. I was initially surprised that the BKs had so many direct answers to difficult questions. Every morning it seemed I was hearing about a new aspect of the truth.'

Francois did not become a BK at that point but in later in 1979 he went to Auckland, New Zealand, where he stayed for five months, renting a flat near a newly-established BK centre there. 'I started to feel I was hearing truth such as I had never heard before. I still didn't like God and wondered why He had to come into it, but every other aspect delighted me.

> 'At the time I never thought I would actually become a BK, but a sister in Wellington, New Zealand, told me to write a letter to Nirwair, one of the senior BK brothers in India. Very few Westerners were BKs at this time, and this sister thought Nirwair could provide me with answers to the questions I still had. I did write to Nirwair, saying "I don't know if I am a BK".
>
> 'The concept of God grew slowly in my awareness, due to numerous experiences, and the gentle feelings I could get during my meditations.'

Francois went back to Paris and in May 1980 helped start the first centre in France, together with other brothers who had taken BK teachings in the UK and India. Sister Sudesh, along with some BKs from Germany, advised on setting up the centre.

> Then he met Dadi Janki in Madhuban. He says: 'Long before meeting her of course I knew who she was and that she had been instrumental in starting service outside India. I was inspired by her classes as it seemed she was bringing spirituality into practical terms that I could understand and

appreciate. It was a new spiritual language for me, but it all made sense.

'Dadi gave me a new angle from which to understand spirituality and through her classes I came to appreciate what God meant. Dadi Janki is a wise teacher, the number one, I would say. At first, her classes came by letter, through the post and later, by fax.

'Dadi has undoubted charisma and it was clear to me that she took her example directly from Brahma Baba. Dadi practises what she preaches and is a powerful example of an Indian spiritual person who never stepped out of the Indian culture.'

This aspect, that Dadi never stepped out of what was essentially an alien culture, especially in France which unlike the UK had never had close links with India, started to worry at Francois and eventually led to what he calls a "sweet and subtle" quarrel with Dadi. 'Although I loved the teachings, the knowledge, the explanations of who we are and why we are here, the total Indianness of the BKs was a major concern. Although I love Dadi, that gap gave me the feeling that I was not fully her friend.'

It was of concern not just to Francois, but also to the French government. As the BKs expanded in France they began to be seen as a dangerous cult.

Francois explains: 'It makes sense to me to say that Raja Yoga is a spiritual path, because it's God's teaching. Spirituality is universal and is responding to the needs of all mankind, beyond cultures and belief systems.

'Spirituality is the science of the soul, helping us to understand all laws and divine laws. As such, Raja Yoga should not be dominated by Indian culture and tradition.

'Yes, spirituality can adopt white as the universal colour which contains all colours. But white can be expressed in all cultures, it doesn't have to mean Indian pyjamas and sari. Dadi insisted on imposing an Indian flavour in external matters like clothes and hair, and this was a hot area between us.

'A dark-skinned person can wear a white sari in France with no problem, but it would not be the same for a white-skinned person. That could legitimately be understood as proselytising, because a white sari has a religious connotation. France is a secular country, so one could expect heavy reactions from that kind of behaviour.

'Also, people would see it as being under some kind of conditioning, which would mean losing your freedom. That is big for a country of " liberté".

'It's a paradox: God is teaching us to go beyond name, fame, and appearances – and we BKs get stuck in outside appearances?

'There has been confusion among us for a long time as to what is a religion, and what is a spiritual path.

'There are a variety of differences between the two. Religion, in an organised sense, tends to encourage the individual to attach to and identify with a packaged set of externally prescribed beliefs and rituals, thereby sustaining an "egoic" state of consciousness. Spirituality on the other hand tends to encourage detachment from all beliefs and the use of a meditative and reflective practice to realise, reveal and "see" what is true for oneself. From a spiritual point of view this is only fully possible when the ego dies and the authentic self is realised.

'One of the original meanings of religion is to reconnect, to bind together. Religion however tends to connect people with an institution and its ideas and beliefs, whereas spirituality seeks to help the individual restore their awareness of their true selves, their true nature, which is peaceful and loving, directly with the Source.

'Even today,' says Francois, 'we are considered a dangerous cult in France and it is not easy to be a BK here. We are not allowed to go into hospitals or schools to teach meditation and we are not allowed to advertise in newspapers and magazines. We are allowed to exist – just – but we have been nailed as a black cult. Yet that has never stopped us. In a democracy we could not be outlawed. But we do have to be careful.'

Francois himself is as dedicated as ever but says he has had to translate the BK message into Western terms and scour out any trace of Indianness. 'For instance, we have very few Indian pictures or images in our centres and there are few Indian BKs in France. In order to make things easy for people to continue, we have had to become totally Western.'

When Francois says that Dadi Janki is not fully his friend, what he means is that in his view, her Indianness has been too uncompromising and she has not been prepared, or able, to become as Western as the French authorities would prefer. He adds, however: 'One must say after all these years, Dadi has given us full rights to adapt and organise ourselves in our respected countries.'

The more Western the BKs become in France, the less chance there is of them being demonised as a dangerous cult.

'We have had to be very discreet and it has not been easy,' he says. 'Yet if you take away the worst of the Indian trappings, it is still the case that the BKs are speaking the truth one hundred per cent. I am still totally convinced of this and it has kept me going all these years.

'When I met Dadi in March 2015 in India, she took me in her arms. Although I was not her close, docile follower, we have so much respect and gratitude for each other. We don't always have the same vision of things but love is indestructible.'

The continuing 'Indianness' of the BKs is an aspect which attracts some and repels others. In the 1970s, it was seen as exotic, hippy and new-age to embrace an Indian spiritual movement and many hippies of the time wore the tilak (red dot) on their foreheads and gave themselves Indian names. Many also went on the hippy trail to the East, seeking truth.

Most of those former hippies settled down to jobs and families, leading conventional lives thereafter, but for some, like Francois, there eventually came no other choice but to embrace an Indian movement. No other religion or faith seemed to hold the answers.

Many have asked: do Western BKs really have to wear white saris? After all, it has never been a Western form of dress. Some hold Dadi Janki responsible for making the sisters all look like Indians and have argued that the white sari gives a continuing cultish appearance at BK centres.

But gradually, as the organisation matured, the white sari was being abandoned, at least in Europe, and giving way to a less conspicuous kind of dress. Ever since the early 1970s it has been a matter of much argument as to what surrendered BKs should wear. Dadi adhered to the traditional simple dress as the sari is both modest and cheap. It also means that the sisters do not have to adapt themselves to the vagaries of commercial fashion. Also, it has to be said, it was the form of dress that Dadi was used to, had grown up with and felt comfortable with, even in a cold country such as the UK.

It has always been easier to decide what the brothers should wear. In India, they wear the traditional white pyjamas or, for looking smart, a Nehru suit. But out of India, they pretty much blend in and wear jeans, tracksuits, hoodies and T-shirts, much like other men these days. You would hardly know they were BKs, although most wear a little badge or a ring, which is discreet but serves to remind them of who they are.

Where the brothers are concerned, Dadi still puts forward her forthright views on what they should wear and how they should conduct themselves in public. She does not like beards, moustaches or indeed any facial hair as she says these hide expressions and furthermore she does not like them to wear shorts. Like the sisters, they must look modest and not try to draw attention to themselves.

In all religions, the matter of dress and hair has been seen as important. Some religions do not allow women to cut their hair, some do not allow men to cut their hair and others, such as Orthodox Judaism, make the men wear ringlets and the women wear wigs. Christian monks have often had to shave their heads or wear their hair in a tonsure. Similarly, the BKs have rules, or at least guidelines, in the matter of hairstyles, although as time goes on, they are becoming less strict about these matters.

It has to be remembered that Dadi Janki spent 14 years in isolation and seclusion, during which the BK philosophy and way of life was being finalised, and then when she and others took the message out to the rest of India, they adhered to the simple dress they had worn while in the yagya, as it was known. Dadi's own take on this is that dress and appearance should be the simplest possible, so that no time or energy is taken up wondering what to wear or how to do one's hair. There should be no thought given to these worldly aspects at all.

Yet when those strictures come from an alien culture, they are going to be questioned and ever since the BKs began expanding in the West, questions have been asked about how the movement will appear to the outside world. As I write in 2015, these matters have not been finally resolved though while Dadi remains alive, it is expected that the BKs will largely adhere to the traditions she introduced. ❦

Peace Bus beginning its tour of the UK for the Million Minutes of Peace Appeal, 1986 London

CHAPTER THIRTEEN

The Nineties and Noughties

If the 1980s saw much consolidation of the Brahma Kumaris in the West, the nineties can be seen as the decade when the really big expansion took place, and when, for the first time, large centres began to be built or acquired. Once again, it was the courage and inspiration of Dadi Janki that was responsible for this.

Manda Patel, director of the Global Retreat Centre in Nuneham Courtenay, just outside Oxford, and a BK herself since 1981, explains how it came about.

'Towards the end of the 1980s, we were expanding fast, and had nowhere big enough to accommodate everybody who wanted to come to classes or meditation sessions. We had by this time bought some detached houses, but they were quite small and in any case, we were not allowed by the council to hold large gatherings in them. For the past nine years we had been meeting in Dudden Hill Lane Community Centre, but that did not have the right atmosphere and was by no means ideal.

'We had to recreate a peaceful atmosphere every single morning as often, the night before, there had been a drunken party and the vibrations were not conducive to calm meditation.

'However,' says Manda, 'there was a serious problem about constructing a purpose-built centre as we had absolutely no money. We had found a suitable site in Pound Lane, North-West London, which at the time was an abandoned warehouse, but we did not even have enough money to draw up plans, so what should we do?

'The message that came from India, via the trance messenger, was that we were to go ahead and instead of adapting the warehouse, we had to build three floors from scratch. This was in late 1989. We managed to secure planning permission for the new building, but how were we to raise the money actually to build it?'

It was entirely Dadi Janki's hard work that made it possible, says Manda. 'She inspired people from all over the world to help us. Our contractor, naturally enough, had to know that we had enough money, or could raise it, to complete the project but we did not even have two per cent of the cost.

'We managed to get a £1 million loan facility from the bank, but that again posed a serious dilemma. It was an absolute cornerstone of BK philosophy that we should never borrow or lend money. Dadi did not want us to take a loan but the contractors would not start work otherwise. But all the time she had the determined thought that we should never use the loan, especially as we would have had to pay it back with interest.

'She inspired people to contribute, and the magical thing was that whenever another tranche of the cost had to be paid, we just had the money to pay it. This went on for 18 months and we never once had to call on that bank loan.'

Manda puts this all down to Dadi's faith in God. 'She always thinks big, and the thought in all this was to bring benefit to others. She never worries about anything and had no qualms in asking people for money when it was never for herself, but for others. Dadi has never been grand for herself, but has always thought big, much like other great leaders.'

We are often told that faith can move mountains, but it can also work in modern times, to achieve the apparently impossible. 'All through the construction of this building, which came to be called Global Co-Operation House in recognition of the co-operation of everybody around the world, Dadi was thinking of helping others, and bringing the message to all people at their own level. Don't forget,' adds Manda, 'that Dadi was by now in her late seventies, an age when many people have long retired.

'But she, far from taking a back seat, took an active interest in everything. We had to give exact specifications to the builders, and for this, we had to look for tiles, curtain fabric, lighting and so on. We went round theatres to look at seating, as we were constructing a theatre-like auditorium and we also went round big London department stores.

'Dadi always came along with us. She had never been to a department store before and had no idea what to expect. But when she walked through the ground floor, and saw all the expensive perfumes and cosmetics on display, she commented: "Now I see what my girls are exposed to, every day". Dadi was completely hands-on and gave her thoughts on everything, from flooring to radiators and heating systems.'

Her brief, as always, was, nothing too ostentatious, nothing too cheap. The correct term would probably be mid-range, and this was deliberate. The idea was that everybody, from the highest to the lowest, who came to the new centre would feel comfortable. It had to look welcoming to everybody, whatever his or her status in the outside world.

And there was never any temptation to cut corners, however tight the money was, or however impossible it seemed at times to afford everything. 'As an example,' says Manda, 'when the building was in the middle of construction, we discovered that the radiators were going across the windows. I thought to myself that we couldn't have that, as it would look awful. The builders said that the only way round it was to have an air conditioning unit that could be both hot and cold but said it would be extremely expensive.

> 'Dadi was in no doubt. She said that people all over the world had given their heart and soul for this building to be the best it could be and we were not cutting corners at this stage. She changed the spec, and the AC units went ahead.'

The building was completed in 1991 and cost a total of £4 million. But it was not designated a residential building, and they were only allowed to construct a caretaker's flat. It soon became clear that a visitors' facility was also needed as the growing numbers had nowhere to stay. They either had to crash down with other BKs or find a nearby hotel, neither of which was satisfactory.

> 'Global Co-Operation House was the first purpose-built facility outside India, but it created another need – that of a residential retreat centre. So,' said

Manda, 'we started looking.

'I was part of the team that was searching for a suitable house, and we must have looked at 40 places, none of which seemed quite right. Then a firm of accountants working for the building company who constructed GCH told us about a stately home outside Oxford that was in receivership. It had been empty for four years, while a hotel group drew up plans to turn it into a five-star hotel, but they had gone bust.

'Before the hotel group came along, the house had been owned by Rothman's, the cigarette company, and run as a conference centre.'

The house was a Palladian mansion set in 50 acres of landscaped gardens. Once owned by the Harcourt family, it had over the years been put to many and varied uses, including a teacher training college, and had been requisitioned by the RAF during World War 2. Now it was a white elephant, too small really to be a viable hotel, too large to be a family home, too far out of Oxford to serve as a college or residential facility. Plus it was a listed building, so there were severe restrictions on what could be done with it. The place and land was now owned by Oxford University, who had no real idea what to do with it.

The BKs must have seemed a godsend. They found they could acquire the 125 -year lease for £1.2 million – a fraction of its true value – but having just finished GCH, did not have anything like that amount of money.

Between 1991 and 1993 Dadi quietly put the word out about the amount of money needed, to buy the lease plus an extra £600,000 required for renovation. And once again, it arrived on time and no loan was needed. Just another miracle, one might say.

> Manda says that when she first saw the place, she felt she had been there before. 'It felt familiar from day one. We were lucky that it was in reasonable condition, and all the rooms were ensuite. The bathrooms were in place and the house was usable. There was also some furniture already there, including a hundred dining chairs. So we did not have to spend much on renovation or furnishing. For the first six months, volunteers came in from all over the world to turn it into a retreat centre, and in 1993 we opened for business, as it were.'

The stately home changed its name once again and became the Global Retreat Centre, the BKs' first residential centre outside of India, and was imposing indeed. The idea was that a small number of BKs would live there permanently, and the new centre would hold day and residential retreats where the full BK experience would be on offer.

Dadi's speciality, believes Manda, is that she applies spiritual principles to make practical, worldly things work. And here was another new departure. In all religious houses, of which this was undoubtedly one, or soon would be, men and women have lived separately, as monks in monasteries or nuns in nunneries and convents. Although in both Buddhism and Christianity, there have been religious houses for both men and women, the sexes have always been kept separate. Dadi's break from tradition was to have men and women living under the same roof, chastely, as bothers and sisters.

One of the reasons for religious men and women living separately is, obviously, so that they don't fall in love, reproduce, have children and create complications for the Order. It is also a facet of the religious life, at least in traditional religions, that monks and nuns living in monasteries should only have a relationship with God, and what are called 'particular friendships' between surrendered brothers and sisters are discouraged.

One's only connection must be with God and for this reason, it would seem foolish to put carnal temptation in the way by having men and women living and working together.

Dadi's take on this was different, and she thought that men and women ought to be able to live together in a religious house observing celibacy and connecting with God rather than with each other. But it was still a major, and somewhat risky, experiment to have both sexes under the same roof, even if it was a particularly large roof.

Also, it was a brand new idea. Both Buddhism and Christianity have had several centuries to get their act together and neither religion has ever sanctioned a co-ed religious house. Out of India, it was a big departure as well, and a radical experiment.

Ways had to be worked out whereby men and women could live and work together, and yet observe all the BK principles. To this end it was decided that brothers and sisters should eat separately, at separate tables. So in this sense there was also segregation. Another matter that might seem trivial was in the matter of washing intimate garments.

Male and female underwear had to be washed separately and kept separate, in separate baskets and allowed to dry in separate airing cupboards.

After more than 20 years it has to be said that the experiment has worked pretty well, although there was one incident of a brother and sister at the Global Retreat Centre falling in love, getting married and leaving the organisation. But then, this happens in traditional religious houses from time to time as well. It is impossible to set up an institution where this is guaranteed never to happen, human nature being what it is.

> 'Yes, it was an experiment,' says Manda, known by inmates as 'The Commanda'. 'The good thing about a residential retreat centre is that we have the daily practice of collective meditation. We revive ourselves every day and the key thing is that the people in the Centre have love for God above all. They are here because they like the lifestyle. They like chastity, the vegetarian diet, the safety, the simplicity.'

The author's own former husband, Neville, has been a resident at the Retreat Centre since 1994, surrendering every aspect of his previous life to live as a BK. As with every religious house, all inhabitants have to bring with them, or at least acquire, a skill to help run the place. Neville has no gardening, cooking or building expertise, so what does he contribute, I asked Manda?

> She quickly replied: 'Neville is exceptionally good with people, at meeting and greeting. Not everybody has this gift.' As a professional journalist on national newspapers for many years, he can bring much-needed writing skills to the organisation. Also, he has become a renowned public speaker. Not all the skills that people bring have to be strictly practical ones. Everybody brings something different, but each person has to contribute in some significant way, in order to allow the centre to run efficiently, as it is a huge building with 52 bathrooms and has extensive rolling grounds that take a great deal of daily maintenance.

It took just 20 years for the BKs to progress from three people in two small rooms to become a significant organisation owning a major English stately home, but Dadi still was not satisfied. There now had to be a residential facility by the sea. In 2005, a row of houses in the seaside town of Worthing was bought, and this became a smaller version of GRC, where BKs would live together and hold retreats, both residential and day, plus meditation courses and other events, for both BKs and non-BKs. Thus the BKs widened out into the south of England, and with their network of smaller centres, now cover most of the country.

GRC now attracts more than 20,000 people a year to its retreats and other events. It can take a total of 65 residential guests at a time. Twenty five people live there permanently and eight BKs live permanently in Worthing. In both cases, the presence of the centres has attracted both BKs and those sympathetic to the teachings, to move to the area and buy or rent homes nearby.

In both centres, strong links have been forged with the local community as the BKs are never content to remain inward-looking.

Also, it seems that wherever the BKs have established a large centre, the surrounding district comes up in the world. When they first built Global Co-Operation House, Pound Lane was pretty much a wasteland. Now it has smart apartment buildings, several of them inhabited by BKs.

With the Worthing centre, there was initially much opposition to having a facility right in the town, but Dadi would not let go. 'When she first saw the house she loved it and said yes, we must establish a centre here,' Manda says. 'Dadi was determined to have a centre by the sea and we had been looking at Hastings. But that was much further from London, considerably more difficult to get to, and so Worthing seemed an ideal location.'

Before long, Global Co-Operation House itself was no longer large enough. A house with residential facilities had to be built next door and so Diamond House came into being, also built from scratch and with a dozen bedrooms on one floor, each with an ensuite shower room.

After that a large centre was constructed in Leicester, this time from an existing warehouse. This was a mini-Global Co-Operation House.

High street shops, known as Inner Space, are also proving popular as 'drop in' centres for meditation and courses in spiritual understanding. The first was in Covent Garden, London, and gradually others were set up. There is one in each of England's ancient university cities of Oxford and Cambridge, and four others dotted around the country. The idea here is that people can come off the street, ask questions about the Brahma Kumaris, buy books and CDs, attend a meditation session or other event, all without making a huge commitment. The Inner Space shops give a flavour of the BK life for those who might be casually interested or curious. They raise awareness, as one might say, and there is then the opportunity to take the search further, if it is so desired.

The 50 acres of the Global Retreat Centre had to be put to use as well, and so Peace in the Park was initiated; a summer event taking place over a weekend where visitors can – free of charge as ever – wander round the grounds, attend cookery demonstrations, theatrical productions and performances, listen to musical recitals and concerts, join in games and fun and generally have a wonderful time. This annual event attracts between 10 and 12,000 visitors and grows every year.

Oh, and did I mention the publishing company, Brahma Kumaris Information Services, headed and developed by Sister Jaymini? When Dadi arrived in London, there was absolutely no BK literature in English. Now the BKs have a professional book publishing company, and also produce CDs, videos and other spiritually-oriented material to a high English (not Indian) standard. Dadi herself is the author of several books containing her wisdom and pithy sayings.

So far, we have just been speaking about expansion in the UK, but once Dadi Janki had given the lead, other countries also began acquiring or building large centres. 'She supported other places to get going,' says Manda, 'and before long, other countries were establishing residential retreat centres as well. We have a large residential centre in the Catskill Mountains in America, and in Australia we have three large centres. There are also retreat centres in San Francisco, the Philippines and Brazil – all emanating from Dadi's inspiration.'

Would any of these centres outside the UK have sprung up without Dadi? Manda has no doubt. 'Not at all. None of this would have happened without her. Although she was not directly instrumental in establishing the retreat centres in other countries, they would not have happened without her support. '

One of the reasons these centres have become possible to establish and maintain is that most of the work is done by volunteers, in-house. 'We have plumbers, electrical engineers, carpenters, decorators and builders living in the houses. We also have cooks, cleaners and gardeners, so we don't have to pay any for any labour,' says Manda.

In this, the BK retreat centres work pretty much like traditional religious houses, where between them, the monks and nuns brought or learned all the skills necessary to run the place and also to do outreach work. Obviously some very large jobs have to be contracted out and it is always a matter of discussion as to how these should best be tackled. At the time of writing, the Global Retreat Centre needs a huge sum of money spending on plumbing work and this is far too highly specialised to be carried out by volunteers. As ever, how they will raise the money for the work, and to what extent such work should be carried out in a building of which they do not own the freehold, is not an easy one to resolve.

It is all the more remarkable when you consider that Dadi Janki arrived in London in 1974 with no real idea of how she could possibly make the Brahma Kumaris work outside India, how she would attract students, or how she would find suitable premises.

Within just two decades, much of this had been achieved.

Gopi, who also lived at the Global Retreat Centre for several years and is now based in London, became a surrendered BK in 1995, after training to be a barrister.

She has this to say about Dadi Janki: 'Her style of leadership is so different from that of other great leaders, in that with other leaders, it's all about outcomes. Dadi has no thought about outcomes.

'Her speciality is the practice of soul consciousness and constant linking with the Supreme. Once somebody had written a critical letter to me and I was very upset. I showed it to Dadi, sat down and waited for her feedback. She read the letter, took off her specs and said, if you keep any of that in your mind, you will be holding onto it. Whatever you have received from God is not getting to that person. It was a powerful lesson for me and I realised that for Dadi, everything is referenced to what gets in the way between you and God.

'When once I asked Dadi, what was my weakness, she said, "You don't need me to tell you. Your weakness is whatever keeps you distant from God".'

Reflecting on the way Dadi Janki established the Brahma Kumaris outside of India from nothing, Gopi says: 'It takes incredible energy to create something from nothing so you have to ask: where does that energy come from? It is Dadi's constant connection with God which enabled something to be created that did not exist before. Our movement has sustained itself with the practice of yoga and direct connection with God. God is the massive transmitter.

'Dadi's job has always been to keep things spiritually clean. She gives a hundred per cent energy to the task in hand and never gets distracted. It's when you lose connection with God that you get seduced by outside things, lose concentration and distraction happens. But Dadi constantly monitors herself to make sure this doesn't happen. Dadi sees all problems at the level of the spiritual, not the emotional.'

One of the reasons the BKs have moved forward so fast, according to Gopi, is that while holding firmly to the spiritual principles established in the early days, Dadi has never been tied down to tradition but has always listened to Westerners and thought about what might be right for non-Indians. She is also extremely interested in technology and just as the monks of old saw the value of printing, Dadi has been quick to see the value of mobile phones, the internet, and other modern methods of communication.

She holds Skype conference calls and is often on her iPad. 'Dadi is not attached to tradition,' said Gopi, 'and has always been very techy. You might not expect it of an old lady but she has always been fascinated by new technology.'

Gopi also paid tribute to Jayanti's input. 'As I see it, Dadi is legitimised by Jayanti. Without the second person, the first cannot be legitimised. Jayanti has never been in a subordinate partnership with

Dadi, but the two have worked together. Although great, Dadi is not superhuman, and she needed somebody like Jayanti to facilitate the expansion of the movement in the West.'

On Dadi's attitude to money, Gopi has this to say: 'She has always kept the money flowing while adhering to her principles of never charging for sharing spiritual knowledge. She is generous-hearted yet always economical. Everything has to be done for a good reason and she epitomises the principle that when you connect with God, your energy doubles overnight. That is how Dadi sees it and that is the main message she has been imparting all these years.'

As the years went by, the BKs started to attract older, professional people to their ranks. In the early days, all the non-Indians attracted to the Brahma Kumaris, and many of the Indians as well, were either young or very young. Denise Lawrence and Waddy were in their mid-twenties, Maureen and David Goodman were in their early twenties, and none of them had embarked on family life or become firmly established in their careers.

As the organisation matured, so did the incoming students. Two people who surrendered in later life are Rosemary Turberville-Smith and Judy Rodgers. Here are their stories.

Rosemary Turberville-Smith

Rosemary, born in 1944, was in her fifties before she became a BK. Now a fully-surrendered sister, she lives near Global Co-operation House in a flat of her own. This, she says, gives her the best of both worlds: a place to escape to, and yet she is near enough to do service with the organisation.

Rosemary grew up in Beirut where her father worked for the British Council. She attended a boarding school in England and later worked in India for the British Council. 'I have always loved dance, and originally wanted to be a ballet dancer,' she says. 'Instead, I did what so many girls of that era did and took a secretarial course. After qualifying, I lived and worked in the US for four years, so at an early age, had been exposed to a number of different cultures.'

She then married and had two children. In her forties, she divorced and remarried, this time to a widower with three children. Now with five children, two of her own and three stepchildren to bring up, Rosemary did not have much time for spiritual study. In her spare time, she played competitive golf and was otherwise leading the life of a leisured housewife.

Then everything changed. Her second husband's company went bust and she had to go out to work again at the age of 49. She got a good job working for a famous (or notorious) British MP, David Mellor. Mellor had been a cabinet minister but came unstuck when he was discovered to be having an affair with a glamorous model, Antonia da Sancha. The story became a media sensation and Mellor, at the time still married and with two young children, had no choice but to resign.

A QC and very clever man, Mellor established several businesses and Rosemary ran his private office. She did this successfully for five years and says it gave her a huge burst of confidence, having been a housewife for so many years.

Meanwhile, she left her second husband although they did not divorce. 'I got another job, and then my husband unexpectedly died. Everything collapsed around me and I was not sure how to move forward. As it happened, I was already in touch with the BKs and had been to some of their lectures in Kensington. Then I took the seven-day course. I was looking for links as to why certain things had happened in my life, and the course provided them.'

At about this time, Rosemary met Dadi Janki for the first time. 'She had a big influence on me and saw something in me that I did not see myself. She saw what I might call greatness and told me that God had a task for me. Since 2000 I have been a surrendered BK, thanks to her.'

By the time she surrendered, she felt she had done everything. 'I'd had a family, a career, a home, two marriages and because I had done all this, I had no yearning to do it again. I felt I now had a higher purpose in life and Dadi Janki saw that I had the ability to surrender. It was also true that I now had the freedom to become a BK, with family responsibilities over. So for me the timing was perfect.'

There was another good outcome for Rosemary in that, because she had never divorced her husband, she was entitled to half of his pension when he died. 'That gave me enough to live on. I had also sold two properties at a good profit, so I am comfortably off as well as being surrendered, which is not the case for everybody.

'For me,' says Rosemary, 'the BKs and Dadi Janki go together. Dadi is completely non-judgmental and it took me a while to realise that she was looking beyond "Rosemary". Because of her foresight, she can see what is about to happen, and who is the right person at the right time. As the BKs matured, they needed more mature people coming into the organisation, people who could relate to others who had had an outside career and a family.

'I have always been treated with respect and never felt I had to bow down to Dadi in any way. She inspired me to embark on my spiritual quest as at the time I was not in the very closest coterie, but the next circle, as you might say. For me, Dadi inspires Westerners through her undoubted spiritual power. She is a conduit from God but at the same time she is lighthearted. She is always giggling and laughing.'

Looking back, Rosemary says she feels just as committed after 15 years and is definitely experiencing her longest-lasting and most intimate love affair – with God. 'Dadi Janki has brought me closer to God. Her connection with the Supreme Being is so strong that she enables you to see beyond ordinary things and glimpse the divine. I used to love the cinema, theatre, restaurants, but not any more.

'I believe it is part of God's plan for me to resonate with people in the world, and as I have experienced just about everything that life can throw at me, including a brother committing suicide, I can appreciate where people are coming from. We are a family here, all voluntary workers and at the age of 70, I am so busy. You do have to be quite strong to work in an environment where everybody is on a spiritual path, and be careful they don't drive you round the bend, because those on a spiritual quest can be very intense and dogmatic.

'My task now is to organise events. I travel a lot and am involved with media work. The great thing is that I never have to retire. I feel I have the best of all worlds as I am surrendered but yet have my own flat away from the centre. There is no time to be lonely and quite honestly, I am having the time of my life at an age when many people have nothing whatever to do.'

Judy Rodgers

Judy is an American woman who, like Rosemary Turberville-Smith, became a BK after having a big career and a family. She now says that she would not have become a BK but for Dadi Janki.

She was working for 20th Century Fox in their newly-created home video department in Chicago when one day she went to a Sindhi conference. 'There were a million Indians in Chicago and somebody asked if I would like to go to this event. I was by now becoming interested in spirituality and I later went to a meeting in somebody's home. This would be in 1995.

'There were about 50 people at this meeting, all BKs dressed in white. I stood out as I was wearing black. From the start I picked up that something unusual was going on and I met Jayanti for the first time. I felt such love for her right from the start. There were some American BKs there; Waddy, and Bradley Arkin, if I remember. I knew by the time I went to that meeting that I was looking for the truth.

'We sat in a circle and introduced ourselves. Dadi Janki was there and she was certain she had met me before. I had the same feeling, so much so that I forgot she was speaking in Hindi and was being translated. It was as if I understood every word she was saying and the language barrier did not seem an obstacle. By the end of the talk I felt such a strong connection and Dadi said to me, why don't you come to a morning class? The address where the class was being held was only 10 minutes from where I lived and so I went the very next day, on a Sunday at 7am.

'I got there a few minutes early and discovered it was the day of Raksha Bandhan, where sisters tie a sacred thread around your wrist. This is not specifically a BK ceremony, but is a traditional Hindu occasion where the chaste bond of love is celebrated between brothers and sisters – not necessarily related by blood.

'As a new kid on the block, I had no real idea what was expected of me. There were about 100 people in the room, and I was watching, sitting at the back. I was told that we had to go up to Dadi Janki and she would tie this thread. Eventually somebody motioned me to go up, and as Dadi looked at me my heart started to thump. It seemed like a physical thing and I thought I would break a rib. Such feelings of love were pouring out from me but at the same time it was a scary experience.

'I was like this for maybe 20 seconds and when I stood up, it all stopped. What it was I don't know to this day. What was it all about? Because the ceremony was so Indian, the cultural gap might have made things difficult, but the feeling I had was so profound it overcame all those potential obstacles. It was also totally unexpected.

'Then I was asked if I would like to take the seven-day course, which I duly did. Dadi and Jayanti flew off to India, and I went to India myself the following February. Dadi was there and she said that God was blowing the rubbish out of my heart and that was the reason for the thumping experience.'

In 1997, Judy moved from Chicago to Boston. Her company sold out to Rupert Murdoch and Judy received 14 months' redundancy money which came in handy as she was coming ever closer to the BKs. She rented a house in order to be nearer to the BK centre and in 1998 went to Oxford to create what came to be called The Call of the Time, a dialogue involving personal sovereignty and world transformation – two very profound topics, one might imagine.

> 'By now I was a fully-fledged BK and it was completely Dadi Janki who achieved this feat. I totally trusted her and she smoothed the way for me, in a practical sense as well as a spiritual sense.
> 'In 2003 I accepted a job to open a business centre. This meant I had to sell my house in Boston, but it was January and the house would not sell. I said to Dadi, "I have a real problem. I have to move for my new job but I cannot sell my house." I had to sell it in order to get the money. She said: don't make specific plans to sell the house but just imagine what it feels like to be liberated.

'I did just that and within two weeks the house had sold. Now, I often use this technique. I know now that the universe supports what we are inviting into our lives. If I had not been able to sell the house I would have had to rent it out but I wanted to turn my whole attention to my new life and not be pulled back by something I wanted to leave behind. Dadi will give a spiritual response to a practical question, and it almost always works.'

Judy, who has been a fully-fledged BK since 2006, now lives in Peace Village in the Catskill Mountains. She says she does not think she could have become a BK at the age of 20, but like Rosemary, by the time she surrendered she had done everything in the worldly sense that she had wanted to do. 'I'd had big jobs, brought up a family, driven fancy cars, lived in lovely houses. It seemed as if I had done enough in the outside world and there was nothing left on my bucket list. I had already started to look round for something more, and with the BKs I found it. I had come home.'

'I did look at other spiritual groups, but nothing really clicked. For a time I was in love with the search, and after coming across the BKs, did not feel I needed to look any further.'

Many people view a life of dedication to the BKs, or indeed, any other spiritual group, as being one of deprivation, of giving everything up. Judy sees it differently. She says, 'When you first turn away from the regular world, the inner world seems a very small place and you start to miss the things that had previously given you pleasure or meaning, such as your job, your home, your family or your social life.

'The spiritual life is very demanding and at first can seem dry and bleak. But as time goes on, a transformation occurs. The more you meditate and study, the larger the inner world becomes and the outer world starts to shrink. You start to access different domains and different experiences, and eventually the inner world becomes huge, shutting out the other one. You start to pick up new currents, understand new layers.

'Of course the other world is still there, but the inner one becomes ever more compelling. William James puts it well in his book *Varieties of Religious Experience*, where he says that things which previously were dry and cool become warm and juicy and things that were warm and juicy before, become dry and cool. Your inner world becomes jammed, and everything looks different when you go deeper and deeper.

'You can move around in this new inner world,' Judy says. 'You look inside and can see old memories, images of people, old disappointments. You can move them around and it gets ever more interesting. This world becomes so fascinating that you now ask yourself whether you really want that glass of wine any more.

The BK disciplines, she adds, are all necessary as they support this introverted state of mind. 'You now no longer want distractions as they are not helping you in this big search. It's like running a marathon – you have to train hard. You have to have the right nutrition, the right surroundings.

> 'So it is with the spiritual life, and once you get a taste of it, the outer world fades right away.' As the 13th century Italian poet Bianca da Siena put it, earthly passions turn to dust and ashes and are consumed in the fire of divine love.
> 'This inner world,' says Judy, 'is never static, but ever-changing as you move into different states. You start to see states of mind as almost physical things; the energy of anger, for instance.
> 'I would never have these insights without the BKs. I now understand how thought processes work, how awareness works. Once you get into this inner space, you will do whatever it takes to remain there and the other world is no longer interesting to you.'

You have to feel the soul as a living essence and make a link with the Supreme. This, says Judy, keeps your mind tireless as it is a constant current coming into you and refreshing you. It's much like drinking water when you are parched, or getting fed when you are starving.

'If this is not happening, you would run out of steam in the spiritual life. You have to make that connection and Dadi Janki led me to it.' ❦

Dadi Janki reading her emails, 2013

CHAPTER FOURTEEN

The Middle East

When Dadi Janki arrived in London, her mission was to take the message into all corners of the world outside India. She knew, however, that serving in the Middle East would not be easy. These were countries, after all, where women often had limited freedom of expression and movement and where, in any case, it might not even be possible in strict male-dominated Muslim strongholds to impart her spiritual message.

However, this did not stop Dadi in her desire that people all over the world should benefit from the 'treasures' as she sees them, as imparted by the Brahma Kumaris. At the time of writing the BKs have a presence in Kuwait, United Arab Emirates, Egypt, Turkey, Oman, Bahrain, Qatar, Israel and the Maghreb countries.

Dadi has never differentiated between religions, races or cultures. So far as she is concerned, everyone is a soul and one of her favourite sayings is that whatever our race, colour or background, our blood is the same, our tears are the same, and our smiles are the same. Everywhere in the world, the smile is the most universally recognised facial expression, and the BKs always stress the importance of smiling.

A smile conveys welcome and friendship in every single culture, and Dadi is always keen to draw attention to the similarities, rather than the differences, of the human race. That is why she does not see the Middle East as being any different from anywhere else in the world. They are all people, all souls and similar underneath. It is because of this awareness that Dadi Janki has been able to attract people from all races and all walks of life. Nobody is excluded because of race, colour or position in the world.

Here are some stories of BKs who were inspired – and sometimes simply "ordered" – by Dadi Janki to go to the Middle East to teach the importance of meditation and positive thinking.

Aruna Ladva, a BK since the age of 14, has been running the Kuwait centre since 2007.

The youngest of seven children, Aruna was born in Kenya but moved to London in 1973 with her parents aged seven. A year later, her parents came across a leaflet about Raja Yoga and all nine family members took the course. Her parents continued to be BKs and Aruna first met Dadi Janki at the age of eight or nine.

She says: 'Even at that age, Dadi Janki struck me as being somebody very special. She was cute, short, chubby and like an Indian grandma but initially I bonded more with Sister Jayanti.

'It was in 1983 when I was 14 that I had a wake-up call of my own and I told my parents that I wanted to go to the morning class. I knew by then without any doubt that I wanted to lead a spiritual life, and did not want anything else for myself. When I was 16, I stayed in Tennyson Road for the whole of the summer holidays and I did not want to go back to school, but Sister Jayanti felt I should get more education!

'The following year I went to Madhuban and that was where Dadi got hold of me. She said, stay here for one month, then two and then three months. And my ticket got extended every month.

'As it is, I have lived in BK centres since the age of 17 and I ended up in Turkey in 1997. Then I went to Bahrain, eventually running the Kuwait centre. At the time Kuwait didn't have a proper centre and this did not get going until 2005.

'We enhance the personality of the person through meditation,' says Aruna, 'and there are many people who are attracted to meditation. So we concentrate on building harmonious relationships with people based on the precepts of peace and love. This is a universal message which can be understood by anybody.'

Aruna does not believe she would have gone to the Middle East in the first place, and certainly not have stayed there, had it not been for for Dadi Janki. 'When Dadi Gulzar was about to visit Bahrain, Dadi Janki instructed me to go as I had a British passport and therefore, it would be easier to get visas.

'I was reluctant as I was happily settled in Istanbul at the time, but Dadi kept insisting and so I stayed. To make it easier for me, Dadi said I had to phone her every day for one minute for guidance. Initially, I said to Dadi that the Gulf area needed an English person as although there are lots of Indians working in the Gulf, most are manual workers, whereas the white collar professional jobs are mainly held by westerners. Therefore, I felt that they might respect a white person more, but Dadi insisted and kept on insisting.'

As with many other BKs, Aruna does not believe the movement would have got going outside India without Dadi. 'I know what it's taken her,' she says. 'Her dedication, discipline, the fact that she never gives up and that she has this amazing talent for picking the right people for the job – even if it's the wrong person.

'With somebody who seems wrong, Dadi will work on them until they become the right person. I've seen this happen so many times. She is called a magician, a grandmaster chess player. Dadi will also always have the right taste, even when it comes to choosing a carpet. Everything has to be appropriate, and this is one reason why she has been so successful. Nothing is too small to escape her attention.

'By the time the BKs came to the Middle East, most of the world had been served. Yet doing service in Kuwait has not been easy, not just because it is a Muslim country, but because through its newly found vast riches, the black gold – oil – it has become a materialistic society.

'The Kuwaitis don't have a need to attract people to the country through tourism,' Aruna says. 'They are rich enough without it. It's just oil, oil, oil. For instance, almost everyone has a flash car. You hardly ever see an old car there. All Kuwaitis are taken care of by their Government.

'At our centre, which now has four sisters and two brothers, we teach meditation and self-development. The emphasis is on making yourself a better person, and we now have 60 to 70 people coming to our weekly seminars.'

Sona is a married BK sister living in Abu Dhabi with her husband, an engineer. She says: 'Ever since I can remember I have thought of God. As a child I always used to ask: Why is there so much suffering and sorrow in the world?'

Sona's parents became BKs but for a time she rebelled, went to university to study Japanese and wore fashionable clothes. She met her husband Mohit at university in New Delhi and they married when she was 22. It was a love match, not an arranged marriage. 'The only problem was,' she said, 'that however hard I tried to run away, God kept coming back.'

Sona's father had been an engineer and during her childhood the family moved around a lot, living in Hong Kong, Italy and South America as well as India.

When Sona married, the idea was that she and her husband would emigrate to Australia. Fatefully, she met Dadi Janki in Sydney.

'I had heard of her, of course, but up to this time had never met her. It seemed to me right from the start that her power was incredible. I took the BK course there in Sydney and my husband came along with me. Well, that was it. We both became BKs hook, line and sinker. There had always been this void inside me and now, it was filled. It felt as though I was living in heaven and that I had come home.

'While we were still living in Australia, we went on a European tour for three months and we were in Italy when it was announced Dadi Janki was coming. This was 1997 at the centre in Rome being run by an English sister, Wendy.

'Dadi did not like pasta so they asked me to cook an Indian meal for her. I wasn't a good chef by any standards but I cooked some simple Indian-type food, which she liked, and she asked me: did you cook this? I said yes and she gave me her special drishti. Her appreciation of me cooking her a special meal left a deep impression.

'One incident stands out. We had to pick Dadi up from the Rome airport in this little Renault Clio car. It was pouring with rain and we had forgotten to take an umbrella. Dadi Janki was in a wheelchair, accompanied by Sister Jayanti, and we had to get her to the car. We had no umbrella and were wondering how to wheel Dadi to the car without her getting wet when suddenly, out of nowhere, this Italian boy came up with a massive umbrella and offered it to us. Dadi smiled and said, typically, "I have God's canopy of protection wherever I go." I thought that having such protection from God was magical.

'In 2008 I was running a retreat centre in Australia and Mohit was suddenly offered a lucrative job in Abu Dhabi. I have never been fond of hot weather and I was not keen to go. We had been in Australia all these years and were well settled there.

'So we wrote to Dadi Janki to ask her what we should do. Sister Jayanti replied saying that she thought it was a good idea for us to go. At the time, there was no centre offering the BK teachings in Abu Dhabi although there was a large centre in Dubai.'

So – naturally – they went. 'Being in Abu Dhabi has made me re-evaluate the BKs,' says Sona. 'Because we are in a Muslim country, we have to ask ourselves what is the basic knowledge that everybody will accept, whatever their religion, or none. You have to remember as well that around 85 per cent of people in the United Arab Emirates are expats, and that about 70 per cent of these are Indians – mostly Muslim Indians.

'We have an Inner Space shop and we teach meditation and self development, as do the other Middle East centres. We have been here since 2008 and I would never have gone, not in a million years, without Dadi Janki's support and encouragement.

'She gave us instructions as to what we had to do. We had to set up a house that was not too rich, not too poor, and we had to take special care that we were not seen as an Indian cult. Although many Western BKs wear a sari, this would be completely inappropriate in the UAE. Dadi said we had to dress correctly for the country we were in. As non-Muslims, we don't have to wear a headscarf but we wear standard Western clothes so that we don't stand out as being any different from the rest of the population.

'Dadi always helped us to feel at ease and the fact that we are a married couple makes us legitimate and gives our centre a family feel.'

When **Carol Lipthorpe** worked as a design manager for a flooring company based near Nottingham, she had no idea that one day she would be serving as a BK in Cairo. 'In fact,' she says, 'I had no inkling until I was at a class in London one Sunday morning and Dadi Janki announced: "Carol's going to Cairo!"'

What?

For Carol, her BK journey began at the end of 1990 when she saw an advertisement in a local paper for meditation classes in Nottingham, the Midland town where she was then living. 'I felt I was very stressed with my job and needed some relaxation. What I didn't admit to myself at the time was that inside of me, something seemed to be missing, even though I had a very good life. I appeared to be successful, I had a good salary, I travelled a lot, and had a lively social life.

> 'I was rather suspicious at first. I remember questioning the teacher on the phone before I went to the first lesson – I wanted to make sure that wasn't getting caught up in a weird cult or a religion.
>
> 'I had already tried many things – self-development courses, Neuro-Linguistic Programming, which was very new then – but nothing seemed to give me any real answers or fill the void I was feeling. Yet

from the moment I attended the BK meditation course, it all felt familiar and somehow, right. In the second lesson I almost headed for the door as soon as the teacher told me that we would be talking about God, but I am glad I stayed because the lesson blew away for me all the old and negative concepts I was holding about this 'Being', and my perspective changed completely from that moment. The BK concept of God felt very natural and right to me.'

In March 1993 she went to Madhuban for the first time. 'I was by now following all the principles,' she says. 'I found that the desire to eat meat just dropped away. I also stopped drinking alcohol, again quite naturally, but also surprisingly, as it had been a big part of my life until then. The biggest problem was giving up smoking but even here, I woke up one day and realised with amazement that I hadn't even thought about cigarettes for some days. It seemed to me that something was happening, that another force was at work. Yet I was happier than I had been for as long as I could remember.'

The first time Carol saw Dadi Janki was also a revelation. 'I was at the main centre in London. The minute Dadi walked onto the stage, I felt overwhelmed and tears emerged. It was like meeting a long lost, close friend.'

Carol, in her thirties, carried on happily with her job for the next six years. Then came the crossroads.

She says: 'I had started to have the feeling that carpets may not be the be-all and end-all of life! I was already teaching classes in Raja Yoga, but I wanted to serve society in a more meaningful way. I knew that Raja Yoga could change many people's lives for the better.

'At just about the same time I was called by a headhunting agency who were recruiting for a design manager. I went for two interviews and sailed through them. Was this a signal? Perhaps this was what I was meant to do instead? I was confused. I told Dadi about this job and she told me, no. My ego protested, and I decided to pursue it anyway, I could not let this opportunity go by.

'I was in a huge dilemma because this new job would be a major step-up for me, leading to a directorship, and yet at the same time I knew it was not the direction that I wanted my life to go in. Dadi was wise enough to see what I really needed.

'Eventually the decision was taken away from me, as the recruitment was halted, so I will never know whether they would have offered me the job or not. But I breathed a big sigh of relief, and was later able to resign my job without any regrets when another surprising opportunity came my way.

'I was driving Dadi Janki to a meeting one day when she announced that they needed somebody to run a new centre in Hounslow, Middlesex. "We thought of you," Dadi said. I was stopped in my tracks. Somehow this was not the service I had envisaged, I wanted to do things my way! But by this time I had the feeling that Dadi knew best. She had a vision for me that I could not have for myself, and she knew what the soul needed in order to grow. So I left my career and moved to Hounslow where I stayed for 11 years, doing some enjoyable part-time work as well as sharing in the co-ordination of the centre.'

The last thing Carol did before leaving her job was to create a range of carpets, keeping the dining hall of the Global Retreat Centre in Nuneham Park in mind. The carpets were installed, and 17 years later are still there, going strong after hundreds, maybe thousands, of feet have walked on them.

The Cairo assignment came about like this. At class in London she and another sister were asked to offer bhog, the refreshments provided after Sunday class and which are offered up to God first. She got onto the stage to hear Jayanti announce: 'Catherine is going to Pakistan – and Carol is going to Cairo.'

'There had been no previous discussion, so it was completely out of the blue. No-one had remembered to tell me about it. Yet I didn't even have a thought about it, I just said yes immediately. Instinctively it felt like the right next step for me even though I had never been to Egypt. This was 2009.'

By now, though, Carol trusted Dadi completely and knew that she was ready for this challenge. 'I went two weeks later,' she recalls. 'This was in the pre-revolution days and I knew nothing about modern-day Egypt. It has been the most testing time of my life without a doubt, but also immensely rewarding.

'I had worked a lot previously with people of many different faith backgrounds, which gave me an appreciation for the Islamic culture. Ten percent of the population in Egypt is Christian, mostly Coptic, but I wholeheartedly feel we are there to serve the whole community. Egyptians have lost a lot of self-esteem over the last few decades, and we see our role as being there for everyone. Many take aspects of the Raja Yoga course, the self-development talks and workshops, and apply these in their lives or their own religious practices, and it does help them. We see a lot of people looking for self-empowerment as they have had so much taken away from them.

'Dadi Janki said that there are many "jewels" in Egypt, and it certainly is an old land with a rich and diverse cultural and spiritual legacy. Dadi genuinely is a world server, and she is concerned to serve people in every last corner of the world. I feel privileged that I have been sent here even though it's something I would never have dreamed of.

'All along I have felt that Dadi had a vision for me that I could not have had for myself, and she held that vision. She saw something in me that I did not see in myself. She holds her faith in you and you rise up to the challenge.

'Dadi always sees qualities in people that are maybe not evident to others. In a way, she pushes people beyond their own limitations, a little bit like a mother bird pushing her chicks out of the nest so that they realise they can fly.'

Background note: Although BK service in Cairo has only been in existence since 2009, the BKs' connection with Egypt goes back much further than that. In February 1984, Jehan Sadat, the attractive second wife of former President Anwar Sadat, was a guest of the BKs in Madhuban. I (Liz Hodgkinson) was in Madhuban at the same time, and got to know Jehan quite well.

Her husband had been assassinated in 1981 and so she was no longer the first lady, having ceded that role to Suzanne Mubarak. The half-English Jehan was now in her late forties, having married Anwar at the age of 15 (!) and the mother of four children. She was already a prominent spokeswoman giving many lectures on world peace from a variety of platforms. While in India, she also managed the difficult task of climbing a mountain in Charles Jourdan stilettos.

After the conference in Madhuban was over, Jehan Sadat invited Jayanti to her home in Cairo, where

Jayanti spent some time giving classes in meditation. Later, Jehan moved to America, where she established the Anwar Sadat Chair for Peace and Development at the University of Maryland. Aged 82 in 2015, Mrs Sadat is still active on the lecture circuit campaigning as ever, for peace – particularly in the Middle East.

A Muslim woman who prefers not to be named is also now running a centre in the Middle East. She says: 'At the centre I run, we don't mention the BKs, but like the other centres in the region, teach meditation and self-development skills.

'Dadi Janki has inspired me and given me courage to do this,' she says. 'She is not like any woman I have ever met before. You've heard of the One-Minute Manager? Well, she is the one-minute leader. She always has time for everybody and one of her priorities is to motivate people.

'She hasn't studied leadership but she has it naturally. She remembers everybody by name and her work is all the more remarkable when you think how often she has been seriously ill. She does things that most people would say were impossible with her state of health but somehow, she is always up and meditating by four in the morning.

'One thing about Dadi is that she is flexible. She will change her plans at a minute's notice if circumstances alter, and take a quite different direction.'

It is not easy for a Muslim woman to be a BK and it has to be kept slightly secret; hence the need for anonymity. But the success, against all odds, of the centres in the Middle East show how hungry people in those troubled regions are for peace and stability. Dadi Janki does not involve herself in politics or take sides, but gives to all her universal message of peace and hope.

Israel

Many of us may think of Israel as being very different from the other countries in the Middle East in that it is predominately Jewish, being carved out as a homeland for the Jews in 1947, but Dadi does not. In her view, people in the Middle East, and the rest of the world come to that, are all one – even if they may not see it that way – and that it is only with God's power that the current powder-keg region will be united. We are all part of the human family and must see each other as brothers and sisters.

Sharona Stillerman, born in 1952, is of Jewish heritage and originally from America. Since 1998 she has been in overall charge of BK centres in Israel.
She says:

> 'I was brought up in the American mid-west in a traditional middle-class family. Although we were Jewish, we were not at all strict, so I did not have a

strong religious background. It might have seemed to outsiders that I had everything and yet I was always dissatisfied. There was a feeling of emptiness and great longing which I ultimately came to understand as a longing for truth and love I could trust.'

Sharona trained as a dancer and was fully intending to make that her profession but at the same time, she was engaged in a spiritual search. She went to Israel at the age of 17 to live on a kibbutz. 'I felt that the kibbutzim as they were in those days, offered the kind of life I wanted, where we were all one family, and where everything, including the children, was held in common.

'I stayed there for two years and felt that I was three-quarters satisfied but there was a quarter of me that was still searching. I did find the kibbutz way of life stimulating and fulfilling and loved how the aim of the kibbutzim – in those days at least – was to create a society that was not capable of going to war, because of the feeling of all belonging to one family. I loved the idealism of it and yet, something was missing. I found out what, later.'

After two years on the kibbutz, Sharona went to France where she intended to pursue her dancing career. But then fate intervened. 'I had a massive accident which was actually caused by a birth defect. For many years, the muscle strength that I gained through dancing had disguised the fact that the bones in my legs were not holding together properly, and I had to have extensive knee surgery. That put an end to my dancing days and, as the problem had not been spotted by my dance teachers, who could have prevented a lot of the problem in advance if they had known about it, I thought I would train as a doctor for dancers.'

It was while Sharona was pursuing her studies in France that she came across some interesting brain research, which showed how you could learn complicated things in your sleep. 'Sleeplearning was very new then and I found it fascinating. It also opened up doors to new studies of the brain, and it was through these that I first came across the term Raja Yoga. I completed my studies and began working in education. I did not meet any of the BKs during that time but a little while later I travelled to India as part of a volunteer work force and the atmosphere of India touched me beyond words. I was particularly moved by the eyes of the Indians and I wanted to investigate yogis and eyes – the gaze that so often holds you.'

On her return to France, she saw an advertisement for a BK meditation course in Paris, where she was living, and decided to go along.

> 'Almost at once I was certain I was hearing the truth,' she said. 'I loved the BK knowledge, and knew this was what I had been looking for. The final pieces of the jigsaw started coming together.
> 'I feel now that if I had stayed in the kibbutz,

my feeling of being three-quarters full would have diminished. The kibbutz was a great experience but in hindsight, I know that they did not have any practical knowledge of the inner spiritual resources that make lasting harmony and unity possible. This knowledge, so abundant in the teachings of the Brahma Kumaris, was what I was really looking for. As this all important spiritual power was missing, it only would have been a matter of time before the longing would have taken me over once again.

'I studied with the BKs for three months, in France, before being invited to attend a "weekend intensive" for new students, in London. There I had the most astonishing experience of Godly, spiritual love, and knew there was no turning back. For me it was clear: this was my path and destiny.

'I first went to Madhuban in February 1984 and it was there that I met Dadi Janki. She struck me as the wisest, most knowledgeable person I had met in my entire life and it was very exciting to be with her. Dadi took all this BK information and knowledge and turned it into love...the kind of true love that I'd always been seeking but could never find. She was filled with it.

'This was my first experience with a truly wise person, yet she was never like a guru. She was more like your colleague in a great and elevated task, such was her respect for each and every one of us and her passion for sharing her experiences. She was more like a guardian angel, with an absolute commitment, at every moment, to your well being. She was like a loyal friend, always believing in you and ready to bolster your spirits. She was like a doting grandma, always ready with a sweet, and a hanky to wipe away any tears.

'After my first meeting with Baba, the combined form of Brahma Baba and the Supreme (channeled through another senior sister, Dadi Gulzar, in trance), I talked with Dadi about my hopes for the future.

'I told Dadi that I wanted my life to be on service to God and the world. The way Dadi looked at me as I spoke made me feel that she knew me from the inside, out. There was such a feeling of belonging, rejoicing and strength in her eyes. I felt degrees of love and trust for Dadi that I had never felt for anyone before. I knew with all my heart that whatever she wanted for me was exactly what I wanted, too. I had never felt I'd met anyone who I could rely on for guidance, but in that first conversation, it was as if that pact was sealed and she became a most all-knowing, ever-compassionate guide. She invited me to leave France and come to live with her in London by way of deepening my spiritual studies, undertaking some teacher training and figuring out best next steps.

'I followed all her advice very enthusiastically

and returned to France to close down all my affairs. I moved to London and after a few months, Dadi invited me to open a centre in Boston, where I remained for 15 years. Then in 1998 I got a call from Jayanti inviting me to start a centre in Israel.'

There were already some BKs in Israel but they were scattered and there was no co-ordination. 'So I went as national co-ordinator in Tel Aviv, where I have been ever since.'

Sharona says that Dadi's relentless passion for truth, for benevolent self transformation and world transformation, endeared her to Dadi. 'Dadi embodies the feelings I had in that amazing experience of pure, spiritual love the first time I went to London.'

On Dadi and the Middle East, Sharona has this to say: 'The peoples of the Middle East are old souls and because of this, a good proportion of the different populations there are searching for the truth. All people, no matter their background, whether they are Jews, Christians or Muslims, can relate to the BKs, as we work with the universal, spiritual experience of all belonging to the One God, one Family. Where many of us are still struggling to identify our prejudices and stereotypes, let alone dismantle them, Dadi has a living, equal vision of everybody in the Middle East and in this way provides us with a very inspiring example.'

'She is a universal, global citizen and sees everybody in front of her as an equal soul. That is why she had been able to attract people of so many different cultures and religions.'

Sharona relates a story that illustrates this. 'We had a programme in London which a Muslim dignitary attended. After the formal programme ended, he was invited to meet Dadi privately in a small room at the back of the stage. Dadi greeted him warmly and invited him into a few minutes of silence. After a few minutes of gentle quiet, the dignitary said that he

The World Council of Religious Leaders at the Millenium World Peace Summit, United Nations, New York, August 28-31, 2000

was very happy to be with Dadi because up to then he had never had the opportunity to sit in the same room as a Hindu lady.

'Dadi remained in that silence, looking at him with a lot of love and peace. Then she said: "You're still not sitting with a Hindu lady, because I am not a Hindu and you are not a Muslim. I am a soul, and you, too, are a soul. We are both the children of the one, same God, and so you are my brother. And I am your sister." He was moved to tears by the feelings with which Dadi shared this remark. She truly sees everyone with the feelings of belonging

and the experience of this is life transforming.

'The thing about Dadi,' says Sharona, 'is that she breaks down barriers wherever she goes and whoever she meets. She has nothing but respect for the many different faiths in the world, but at the same time, she sees us all as one family. There is one God and He is the same God everywhere, whatever your particular religion.

'To me, Dadi's example is proof that God is at work. She acts like a magnet on all those who, like her, want to give heart and soul to the task of world betterment, drawing them closer to God so that they can receive the support and strength to carry on. A right hand for God, herself, she serves to pulls you even deeper into His reality and once you experience it, you know without a shadow of a doubt that this is the truth.' ❧

Epilogue

꧁

We are now coming to the end of our exploration of who and what Dadi Janki is, although we will probably never completely understand the mystery of how she has achieved so much, and goes on achieving.

Dadi herself would point upwards and indicate that it was all God's doing but there are many people who profess a strong and intimate connection with God without matching anything like Dadi's achievements.

For me, Dadi is more than a remarkable person; she is, in her own way, a genius. Here, to sum up, are what I believe are her strongest qualities:

She has the ability to give to whoever is in front of her, her undivided attention. It's as if you are the only person in the world who matters to her at that moment; a rare skill in itself. At the same time, she never enters into particular friendships or relationships, preferring one person to another. To Dadi, everybody she meets is God's child, and she gives them all due respect and time. All who come in front of her are given gifts and sweets and made to feel special.

There is always care taken to bestow drishti, or the level eye gaze, on all who meet her. For some, this feels uncomfortable or strange but for most, this steady eye contact is a gift in itself, some sort of transfer of energy, peace and calm.

Perhaps because she is a woman, she has managed to create and retain a family atmosphere among the BKs. This intimate atmosphere has remained, however large the organisation has grown. Dadi has a particular gift for making even the largest gatherings seem intimate. It is this family atmosphere that undoubtedly attracts many people to the Brahma Kumaris, and one of the main aspects that differentiates the BKs from many other Indian-based spiritual movements, where you are expected to bow down to and worship the guru, and maintain a respectful distance between him, the Master, and you, the lowly supplicant.

Since arriving in the 'decadent' West, Dadi has never compromised her principles or way of life. In order to remain strong and courageous, she has herself led the BK lifestyle to the max, rising at four am every morning, reading or hearing the morning class, meditating throughout the day, eating a pure vegetarian diet and wearing a simple cotton sari or gown.

At the same time, she pays close attention to detail. Nothing is too small to escape Dadi's attention and although her mind is always on higher things, she will happily discuss what kind of diaries or notebooks might be best, or which curtain fabric offers the best value.

Dadi has terrific courage. That is plain for anybody to see. It must have taken amazing bravery in the first place to come to London at the age of nearly 60, when she had never been outside India before or come into contact with foreigners. She would say that God gave her the strength, but by no means all BKs have had this level of dedication to go where nobody had gone before. Additionally, Dadi has said that when she was young, she was frightened of Christians and here she was, coming to a land that was teeming with them, at least theoretically.

Would they, in a reverse of their own early treatment, throw her, metaphorically speaking, to the lions? Well, some people have, or have tried to, but she presses on regardless, shaking off any naysayers as a mere bagatelle.

Although very simple in her lifestyle and tastes, Dadi has always thought big. She has never been content to live on past glories but is always moving onto the next major project, whether this is for the acquisition of new centres, or for global programmes. As soon as Global Co-Operation House in London was completed, she started looking for a residential retreat centre, even though there was no money for such a scheme. She has never remained in her comfort zone; perhaps she has never even had a comfort zone.

Dadi could teach the secular world a lot about money. While concerned never to waste a penny, she is not afraid to spend large sums on magnificent projects.

On the money pages of newspapers, famous people are often asked whether they are a spender or a saver. Dadi is neither. She spends when appropriate and never ever hoards. Whatever comes in goes straight out again. Moreover, everything has been achieved without ever formally fundraising.

The principle that one should never charge for imparting or sharing spiritual knowledge has been strictly adhered to. No fees or charges are ever made for events and programmes and although people are invited to donate, there is no compulsion for them to do so. And somehow, the books are balanced. Nobody has to pay to spend a weekend in a residential retreat centre, even though these places cost a lot of money to run. Dadi has always believed that if people feel they have received benefit, they will want to contribute to the further work of the organisation and largely, she has been proved right in this.

The policy of not charging has led to a lack of commitment by some, and it is not uncommon for people to book an event and then not turn up, without contacting the organisers and letting them know. And inevitably, there may be people who take advantage and spend a residential weekend in one of the retreats without considering giving a donation. Yet there are some who make up for this by donating a lot, whether in cash or services.

By her example, Dadi has shown how it is possible to live on very little money, once you have no desires or wishes of anything for yourself. It is amazing how one can cut down on expenditure when applying Dadi's principles. It is by all BKs living simply that the organisation has been able to expand.

Dadi also has a keen sense of what is appropriate. When the BKs acquired Nuneham Park, just outside Oxford, she decreed that the curtains and furnishings had to be grand enough to grace a stately home. There could be no cheapskating in such a place. Dadi has always paid great attention to interior design, on the grounds that all BK centres must be welcoming to those from all backgrounds and from all sections of society. Therefore, simplicity goes with quality.

She is, in her own way, a radical feminist. She believes the time has come when women must lead and not follow. In this she is continuing the teachings of the founder, Brahma Baba, who decreed that women must always be in charge of the movement. This was in itself a big step to take, especially in the India of the time. Nowadays, the Brahma Kumaris is probably the biggest organisation in the world, whether spiritual or secular, to be run by women. It just shows what women can do when given a chance.

Although Dadi always appears serene and calm, she has also faced tremendous challenges and opposition, both in India and outside. Some who fall in love with the organisation, later fall out of love with it and have done all they can to discredit it. Much mud has been slung, both at Dadi Janki and the BK movement generally, but Dadi never takes any notice, admonishing all the BKs to send the detractors good wishes all the time. She has also suffered severe illness all her life and it is a true miracle that she has defied medical science by staying alive for almost a century. Once again, she would say that she has a lot to live for and much work still to do, and that her love for God has kept her going.

Perhaps Dadi's greatest strength has been her unwaveringness. Not for a minute, even from early childhood, has she once weakened in her resolve or her connection with God. Many other BKs have had nights of doubt and sorrow but not Dadi. She believes that worries and problems come in when the Godly connection is lost or not maintained.

Does all this prove that there is a God and that He moves in a way much less mysterious than has been thought, enabling this little Indian lady to inspire so many people? No, because this never can be proved, but Dadi would probably echo what an elderly nun said on her deathbed: 'If when I go, I discover there is no God, the journey has still been wonderful, and if there is a God, I've hit the jackpot.'

Without doubt, Dadi Janki has enabled many people to have a glimpse of heaven, a priceless experience of peace and bliss. For those who have glimpsed it, this vision is worth all the trials and tribulations that may beset them.

Dadi and all the BKs look forward to the time that is summed up in the closing verse of a once-popular Victorian hymn:

When knowledge, hand in hand with peace,
Shall walk the earth abroad –
The day of perfect righteousness,
The promised day of God.

The hymn expresses a Christian sentiment but also embodies Dadi's abiding message that at their heart, all religions and faiths are basically saying the same thing.

Throughout her long life, Dadi has always emphasised that love and peace must go hand in hand with knowledge. Without the backbone of the knowledge, love and peace will be empty words.

It seems fitting to finish with her favourite words: Om Shanti, Om Shanti, Om Shanti. These words have to be said three times to triple their power.

TIMELINE

In order to give some idea of what Dadi has achieved, here are some important dates in the growth of the Brahma Kumaris in the West.

1957: Sister Jayanti and her parents, Murli and Rajni, came from India to London, to settle. Rajni maintained a BK lifestyle and household but there were no centres, no meetings and no programmes held.

June 1971: A delegation of five BKs travelled from India to London with the idea of establishing a centre in London. They stayed with Jayanti's family in Willesden, North West London. The Tennyson Road Centre, the first outside India, was opened. Dr Nirmala stayed there for less than a year, followed by Dadi Ratan Mohini. However, they returned to India and during their time in London, did not manage to attract any Westerners.

24 April 1974: Dadi Janki arrived in London with Jayanti, soon followed by Sister Sudesh. In December that year, a house in Tennyson Road was purchased, next door to the original rented flat.

1974: Sister Denise and John Kane were the first Western students.

July 1975: The BKs were legally registered in the UK as The World Renewal Spiritual Trust – the same as the official name used in India.

July 1977: The BKs organised their first major event in London, the World Renewal Festival, attended by senior sister Dadi Prakashmani.

1978: A large suburban house was purchased in St Gabriel's Road, Willesden, and it became the second main centre. In May 1979 Jayanti and Dadi Janki moved from Tennyson Road to St Gabriel's Road to live. The Tennyson Road centre was retained.

1982: The St Gabriel's Road centre was now too small to hold the numbers of people coming to morning class, and so it moved to the Dudden Hill Lane Community Centre, Willesden.

September 1991: Global Co-Operation House, in Pound Lane, London NW10, was inaugurated by

Dadi Prakashmani and was the BK's first purpose-built centre outside India.

January 1993: A stately home in Oxfordshire was purchased and renovated and became the Global Retreat Centre. This was the first residential retreat centre outside India.

1995: The first Inner Space High Street shop was opened in Regent Street, London, later moving to Covent Garden. This shop paved the way for many more Inner Space shops to be opened in major cities.

2004: Diamond House, an extension of Global House, was inaugurated, once again by Dadi Prakashmani, with a message of support from Prince Charles.

August 2007: Dadi Prakashmani died and Dadi Janki was asked by the management committee to become the administrative head of the organisation, moving back to India. This meant that her active involvement with BK expansion outside India came to an end, but she had set enough in motion for the organisation to progress under its own steam or, rather, under the steam of those early lieutenants. ❧

Acknowledgements

ᜧᜧᜧ

The author is grateful to the BKs who gave their time and thought to talking about the importance of Dadi Janki in their lives. So, huge thanks to all those mentioned in the book who helped to make the story so interesting. Thanks are also due to the author's ex-husband Neville Hodgkinson who edited the text and to Jaymini Patel who was responsible for overseeing publication. The text was copy-edited by Jane Kay.

Further Reading

⌀⌀⌀

The Brahma Kumaris has almost become part of the Hodgkinson
family's publishing industry, and between them they have written
the following books:

Peace and Purity, The Story of the Brahma Kumaris
A Spiritual Revolution, by Liz Hodgkinson. HCI, 1991

The House is Full of Yogis
The story of a childhood turned upside down
by Will Hodgkinson, Borough Press, 2015

I Know How to Live, I Know How to Die
The Teachings of Dadi Janki, by Neville Hodgkinson,
Mantra Books, 2015

The following also shed more light on Dadi Janki's
teachings:

Inside Out
A better way of living, learning and loving, by Dadi
Janki, Brahma Kumaris, 2003

Something Beyond Greatness
Conversations with a Man of Science and a Woman of
God, by Judy Rodgers and Gayatri Naraine, HCI 2009

Feeling Great
How to change your life for the better, by Dadi Janki,
BKIS 2010

God's Healing Power
By BK Jayanti, Sterling, 2010

Is There Another Way?
By Dadi Janki, Sterling Ethos 2010

Understanding the Brahma Kumaris
By Professor Frank Whaling,
Dunedin Academic Press, 2013

Om Shanti, Om Shanti, Om Shanti
The Essence of Truth and Love
By Dadi Janki, BKIS, 2014

First Hand Experiences with a Great Yogi
By BK Hansa, BKIS, 2014

These relevant books are also mentioned in the text:

The Case for God: What Religion Really Means
By Karen Armstrong, Vintage 2010

Stuffocation: Living More with Less
by James Wallman, Penguin 2015

ABOUT THE BRAHMA KUMARIS

The Brahma Kumaris is a network of organisations in over 100 countries, with its spiritual headquarters in Mt Abu, India. The University works at all levels of society for positive change.

Acknowledging the intrinsic worth and goodness of the inner self, the University teaches a practical method of meditation that helps people to cultivate their inner strengths and values.

The University also offers courses and seminars in such topics as positive thinking, overcoming anger, stress relief and self-esteem, encouraging spirituality in daily life. This spiritual approach is also brought into healthcare, social work, education, prisons and other community settings.

The University's Academy in Mount Abu, Rajasthan, India, offers individuals from all backgrounds a variety of life-long learning opportunities to help them recognise their inherent qualities and abilities in order to make the most of their lives.

All courses and activities are offered free of charge.

For more information: brahmakumaris.org
For Brahma Kumaris Publications: inspiredstillness.com

SPIRITUAL HEADQUARTERS

PO Box No 2, Mount Abu
307501, Rajasthan, India
T: (+91) 2974-238261 to 68
F: (+91) 2974-238883
E: abu@bkivv.org

www.brahmakumaris.org

International Co-ordinating Office & Regional Office for Europe and The Middle East

Global Co-operation House,
65-69 Pound Lane,
London, NW10 2HH, UK
T: (+44) 20-8727-3350
F: (+44) 20-8727-3351
E: london@brahmakumaris.org

....

REGIONAL OFFICES

AFRICA

Global Museum for a Better
World, Maua Close,
Off Parklands Road, Westlands,
PO Box 123, Sarit Centre, Nairobi,
Kenya
Tel: (+254) 20-374-3572
Fax: (+254) 20-374-3885
E: nairobi@brahmakumaris.org

THE AMERICAS AND THE CARIBBEAN

Global Harmony House, 46 S.
Middle Neck Road,
Great Neck, NY 11021, USA
Tel: (+1) 516-773-0971
Fax: (+1) 516-773-0976
E: newyork@brahmakumaris.org

AUSTRALIA AND SOUTH EAST ASIA

181 First Ave, Five Dock,
Sydney, 2046
Australia
Tel: (+61) 2 9716-7066
E: ashfield@au.brahmakumaris.org

RUSSIA, CIS AND THE BALTIC COUNTRIES

2, Lobachika, Bldg. No. 2
Moscow – 107140, Russia
Tel: (+7): +7499 2646276
Fax: (+7) 495-261-3224
E: moscow@brahmakumaris.org

WILD HIMALAYA

WILD HIMALAYA

A NATURAL HISTORY
OF THE GREATEST
MOUNTAIN RANGE ON EARTH

STEPHEN ALTER

ALEPH

ALEPH

ALEPH BOOK COMPANY
An independent publishing firm
promoted by *Rupa Publications India*

First published in India in 2019
by Aleph Book Company
7/16 Ansari Road, Daryaganj
New Delhi 110 002

ISBN: 978-93-88292-77-1

6 7 9 10 8 5

Printed at Saurabh Printers Pvt. Ltd, India.

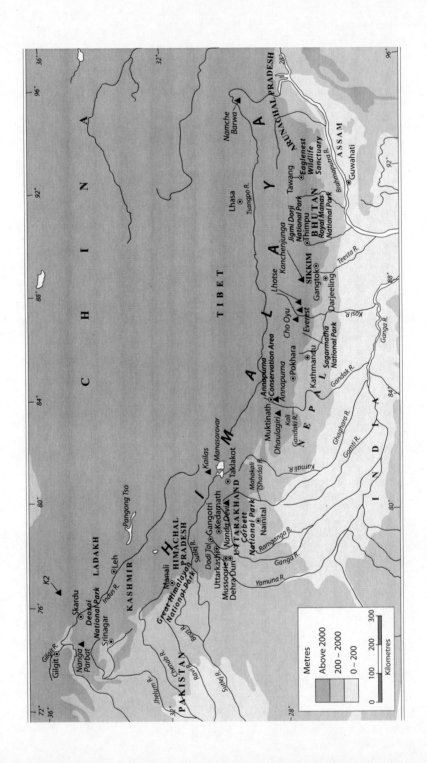

Long ago, before the earth or the sky was made, Zongma, who is the greatest of all, had two sons, Nipu and Nili.

Nipu and Nili were without form; they were not human beings, they were not animals, nor were they like the rocks. Many ages passed and then Nili made the earth and Nipu made the sky. When it was ready the earth was very big and Nipu put the sky like a lid above it. But the lid was too small and Nipu said, 'Brother, make the earth smaller so that the sky will fit it.' So Nili pushed and pulled the soil together until the sky and earth were the same size, and as a result parts of the world stood up as mountains.

—Bugun creation story, Arunachal Pradesh
From *Myths of the North-East Frontier of India* by Verrier Elwin

CONTENTS

AUTHOR'S NOTE

In previous books, I have used the spelling 'Himalayas' because my editors insisted on popular usage, rather than 'Himalaya' which is a traditional and more accurate transliteration of the Sanskrit proper noun. This may seem a small matter, and many readers will not even notice, but as most of the sources I quote use 'Himalaya', in deference to linguistic precedent, I have deleted the 's', which might save a few millilitres of ink.

Prologue

OAKVILLE

Being at home in the Lower Himalaya, I often feel like an endemic species. Born in Landour, part of the larger town of Mussoorie, I continue to live here at 2,250 metres above sea level. Oakville, our family property, is where I sit and write—my benchmark and point of view. Living in the mountains shapes a person's perspective, gazing out across the valley below or back into the interior ranges, observing both the familiar and the unknown from the vantage point of home.

Situated on a spur at the eastern end of a forested ridge, Oakville almost seems part of the hill. Its corrugated sheet-metal roof, painted an earthen red, slopes upward to a peaked summit guarded by four stout chimneys. Chequered windows mirror a dense arcade of surrounding trees—oaks, cedars, maples and rhododendrons. While the building was designed by a nineteenth-century military engineer it seems to reflect a blueprint of nature, an organic structure that rises out of the ground like some sort of geological formation or, perhaps, a giant anthill.

Between interlacing branches of deodar trees, the Gangetic plain is visible to the south, 2,000 metres below the elevation of the house. Ascending steeply to the west, the top of the hill rises 300 metres higher up. Just over a shoulder of the ridge, a panorama of Himalayan massifs, capped with snow and ice, appears along the northern horizon. Eastward lies a layered expanse of lower ranges, unfolding like the bellows on a vintage camera that might have been used to photograph this scene a century ago.

Whenever I am asked about Oakville's history, I like to say the house was built in 1840, though there is no certainty to this date. Many of the earliest houses in Mussoorie and Landour came up around that time, when St. Paul's Church was consecrated. The first permanent construction was a 'shooting box' built in 1825 by Captain Frederick Young, who settled here after fighting in the Gurkha War. A number of East India Company officials followed on his heels, visiting Mussoorie for leisure and sport when summer temperatures rose in the plains. In the 1830s a sanatorium and British military hospital for tropical diseases was established in Landour. The man who built Oakville was probably the garrison engineer, responsible for constructing the hospital and other cantonment facilities.

The original house burned down in October 1836. This story comes to us through John Pollock's *Way to Glory*, a biography of Major General Henry Havelock, KCB, 'the hero of Lucknow'. Memorialized with a statue in Trafalgar Square, he has cities and towns named in his honour from New Zealand to the Andaman Islands. Havelock's wife, Hannah Marshman, was the daughter of Baptist missionaries in Serampore. During the spring of 1836, she came up to Landour with her three young children, a maid named Lucy, an ayah and several other servants. They rented Oakville for the summer season, while Havelock, a brevet captain at the time, was posted in Karnal. Hannah homeschooled her sons and took them for picnics on Pepperpot Hill. She also amused herself by collecting birds that she skinned and stuffed.

In those days, the Oakville roof would have been made of thatch gathered from grass-covered cliffs nearby. As the weather turned cold at the end of autumn, Havelock's family must have kept the fireplaces burning all day. One night, after they had gone to sleep, the thatch roof ignited with Hannah and her children trapped inside. The maid, Lucy, and the ayah both died, while the baby was fatally injured by a falling beam that fractured her skull. Plunging through flames and smoke, Hannah was able to rescue her two boys, though she was badly burned.

When news reached Havelock in Karnal, he immediately set off on horseback for Landour. Ten days after the fire, he arrived to find his wife alive, though their infant daughter had just died. In a mournful letter, he describes how they 'buried the child on the north side of the hill, in the valley of the wolf and the leopard'. Hannah was badly disfigured from the burns and for a while it seemed she would lose the use of her hands and feet. 'I trust I should not have loved her less if it had been,' Havelock wrote. Fortunately, she recovered and the couple went on to have ten children altogether, of whom seven survived. Fighting in the Afghan campaign, Havelock quickly rose to the rank of major general without having to buy his promotions, but it was during the Sepoy Rebellion of 1857 that he became a celebrated colonial hero. Having led a column of loyal troops that recaptured Kanpur (or Cawnpore, as it was known at the time) he went on to secure the relief of Lucknow, where he died of dysentery several days later. A devout Christian soldier, Havelock is also known for distributing Bibles and promoting temperance amongst troops of the East India Company army, both of which would seem to have been lost causes.

Hannah and Henry Havelock's tragedy at Oakville didn't deter future residents and the man who rebuilt the house was another major general, William Henry Jamieson. A plaque at St. Paul's Church is dedicated to his memory. Other important residents of Mussoorie at the time included Sir George Everest, the Surveyor General of India, who lived on the opposite side of town at Park Estate, where he oversaw the mapping of the Himalaya, between 1832 and 1843.

While the old houses in Mussoorie preserve a colonial legacy they are also part of the natural history of the region, each an ecosystem of its own. Oakville was constructed with materials that came out of the earth and the forests nearby. The masonry walls, more than half a metre thick, were made of rocks excavated from the hillside on which it stands. These are held in place with lime mortar, mined from the surrounding hills. This strata of marine sediments extends across the Central Himalaya, formed out of fossilized remains of molluscs and coral from a primordial ocean that existed long before the mountains rose up. Ruined kilns, once used for processing the limestone, can still be seen near Mullingar Hill in Landour. Lime was also used to plaster and paint the walls.

The masons who built Oakville must have come from the plains where they constructed similar bungalows in places like Meerut, Delhi or Lucknow. Years later, in the 1980s, when my father was digging vents for a solar heating system, he discovered a grid of channels under the floor filled with charcoal to absorb moisture and keep the house dry. He also unearthed two wooden trowels buried in the foundations. These simple, hand-carved implements provide a direct link to the origins of our house. The trowels were probably used to fashion the ornate moulding that decorates the walls.

Lime mortar, plaster and whitewash are versatile and durable materials.

Unlike reinforced concrete, which can deteriorate over time, composites of calcium carbonate become stronger the older they get. The floors of the house were covered in a form of lime plaster that takes a glossy polish and looks like marble. Architecturally, the main house is modelled on plains bungalows from the mid-nineteenth century, with high ceilings and broad verandahs that help a building stay cool in hot weather. Here in the mountains, however, these features make the house virtually impossible to heat in winter when the floors turn cold as ice.

The ceilings at Oakville are supported by giant beams of sal wood (*Shorea robusta*). Sal trees do not grow at this altitude and the nearest forests would have been 14 kilometres away and 1,500 metres lower down the hill near Rajpur. This means the lumber had to be hauled up the mountain by teams of men, manoeuvring along narrow, winding trails. Each beam is 6 metres long and would have weighed half a tonne. Sal is the strongest, most resilient timber in India, though it does not lend itself to carpentry for it is almost as hard as metal and has a rough grain. Nevertheless, it survives dampness better than any other wood and the beams at Oakville are in excellent condition, even after 178 monsoons, with only a few minor cracks and no warping at all.

The door and window frames are also made of sal but the rest of the woodwork is shisham (*Dalbergia sissoo*), which also came up from the Doon Valley. Shisham, sometimes called North Indian rosewood, has a fine grain and a rich, red lustre. In Saharanpur, which would have been the largest town nearby when Oakville was built, woodcarvers create delicately ornamented screens and other furniture out of shisham. Saharanpur was also the site of one of the first botanical gardens in India, planted by the British in the 1750s to explore the potential of forest resources and other crops. Two eminent Victorian naturalists served as superintendents of this garden, John Forbes Royle and Hugh Falconer.

The reason local timber wasn't used at Oakville is because there wouldn't have been much around in 1840. Etchings from that period show that these hills, particularly the southern slopes, were covered mostly in grass with only scattered trees. The deodars (*Cedrus deodara*) that now grow throughout Landour were introduced by the British from higher altitudes and take half a century or more to mature. Oakville gets its name from banj oaks (*Quercus leucotrichophora*), the most common indigenous species of tree. Though tough and long-lasting, most Himalayan oaks grow into crooked shapes, full of knots that cannot be sawed into planks. A common Garhwali saying compares this tree to a cantankerous old man. Those few oaks that stood on the property would have been used for firewood. In the mid-nineteenth century, when the first brewery opened in Mussoorie, many oaks were lopped or felled to make charcoal that fuelled the process of brewing beer.

Though Oakville lies within the municipal limits of Mussoorie, the property has an enduring connection to the mountain habitat that existed long before human beings settled here. Among the first wild flowers to bloom in Landour is a bright yellow species known in Garhwal as 'phyunli'. The scientific name is *Reinwardtia indica*. A hardy plant with a stiff, woody stem, it grows throughout the Himalaya from Kashmir to Eastern Tibet and beyond. After the cold, dry months of winter, its showy yellow petals appear before any other colours emerge.

This flower occupies a popular place in Garhwali folklore. Several stories are told about phyunli, which is seen as a harbinger of spring, appearing in Chaitra, the first month of the Hindu calendar. Chandramohan Raturi, a Garhwali author, has written a book-length poem about phyunli. The most popular version of this folk tale describes Phyunli as the daughter of a saintly ascetic who lived in the Himalaya. A child of nature, the girl grew up innocent and unworldly, in the company of birds and animals. One day, a shadow fell across her path and she saw a young man standing in front of her, a bow and arrows in his hands. She asked him who he was and he replied that he was a prince from the plains who had come to the mountains on a hunting expedition. After persuading the prince not to kill the animals near her home, Phyunli fell in love with him. The royal hunter was overcome by her beauty and took her away to his palace in the plains and made her his bride.

Though the prince gave Phyunli everything she might desire and provided a life of luxury, the girl soon grew homesick for the mountains. She missed the forests where she was raised, pining away in the plains. There was nothing the prince could do, as slowly she grew weaker and weaker. On her deathbed, Phyunli made the prince promise to carry her body back to the mountains and cremate her on a hilltop near her father's home. He fulfilled this last wish. The following spring, at the place where her final rites were performed, the yellow flowers appeared in profusion, blooming out of the ashes.

Oakville's gardens are full of foreign flowers like dahlias, hydrangeas, banksia roses, cornflowers, poppies and peonies. A few of these, like irises and delphiniums, were developed by European horticulturalists from seeds and bulbs of wild Himalayan plants that travelled to Europe and then returned in hybrid form. At one time Oakville was known as 'bagichawalli kothi' or the 'garden house' because of terraced vegetable plots on the southern face of the hill. Remains of the gardens can still be seen though these are hidden beneath a canopy of oaks and other trees. Before piped water reached the estate, mules were used to carry it up in goatskin waterbags from a spring on the north side of the ridge. A large cistern for storing water was built at the same time as the house. Soon after my parents bought the property in 1981, my father incorporated the cistern into a rainwater harvesting system that he installed, using Oakville's roof as a collector. The same roof is part of his solar heating system in which warm air from the attic is drawn into the house.

When Ameeta and I moved back to Oakville in 2004, after my parents retired to the United States, one of our objectives was to restore the house, as much as possible, to its original form. Previous owners had divided Oakville into four apartments, adding a number of rooms and enclosing most of the verandahs, turning it into a warren of cramped, claustrophobic spaces. The original kitchen was an adjacent building, converted into a cottage where my cousin's family live.

Ameeta gradually transformed the building over a period of twelve years during which floors and walls were repaired, woodwork stripped and restored. Layers of limewash were scraped off to reveal stone fireplaces and ornamental moulding that had been hidden for decades. The main entry hall of the house was designed with a conscious sense of grandeur as well as whimsical touches, reflecting a lush orientalist fantasy. At the centre of the hall is a scalloped arch that radiates upward from a niche between two doors, opening into the drawing and dining rooms. The shape of the arch is reminiscent of sea creatures out of which the limestone was formed. Surrounding this arch are ornate Mughal jali patterns, similar to decorative elements in Lucknow's palaces, an artful tangle of vines and tendrils forming arabesques. At the centre of the arch, above the niche, is a floral medallion on which two plaster parakeets are perched. A pair of Corinthian pillars adds a Greek touch to the muddle of Tudor roses, fleur-de-lis and Mughal motifs.

While in many ways this bungalow may seem out of place in the mountains, it has accommodated itself to its surroundings, as well as the wildlife that thrives about us. Leopards prowl near the garden gate hoping to feed on our Tibetan mastiffs who, in turn, have set their unrequited appetites on rhesus macaques and langurs that raid the gardens. The pashm or furry undercoat that gets combed off the dogs, is collected by black-throated tits to line their nests. From the edge of the yard, I've seen barking deer, kalij pheasant and foxes, as well as nocturnal visitors like wild pigs, porcupines and flying squirrels that leap from branch to branch before gliding off into the night.

Some creatures have even ventured indoors. Spiders and scorpions inhabit the bathrooms, particularly during the monsoon. One year my nephews collected scorpions in glass jars, the mothers carrying their brood of tiny, translucent offspring clinging to their backs. Bats squeeze in through cracks in the windows and fly about like manic shadows. Many of the doors have been gnawed at the base by rats and mice that have occupied Oakville over the years. For a while, a pair of yellow-throated martens took up residence in the roof of the cottage. They were interested, mostly, in feeding on honey from a beehive under the rafters.

We used to have hunting trophies on the walls, left behind by a friend and distant relative, John Coapman, who was a professional shikari—a leopard skin and the head of a chital stag with branching horns, as well as a couple of urial, a species of wild sheep, and a pair of goral, which are goat-antelopes. Fifteen years ago, I took the trophies down and stashed them away in the attic but recently, because there were no documents to prove that these were legally shot, I followed the advice of a senior forest department official and burned them using 20 litres of kerosene. Watching the trophies consumed by flames and smoke, I felt a strange sense of remorse, not because I regretted their loss but because a few years earlier I had scattered John's ashes in the nearby hills where he and I once hunted together.

Of all the wildlife that has taken up residence at Oakville in our time, the most persistent were a family of jackals that made their home in one of the ventilation channels under the house. A musky stench alerted us to the fact that a litter of jackal pups had been born beneath our dining room floor. Early mornings and at dusk, the parents emerged and set off hunting and scavenging. Eventually, as the four pups grew older they crept out into the yard. We would watch them from a glassed-in porch, as they tumbled about in the grass, chasing each others' tails. But once they started tearing up the rose trellis and other plantings, the gardener in our family insisted they had to be evicted. This wasn't an easy task, for the pups were too quick for me, darting into their burrow before I could barricade it with a piece of plyboard. Finally, however, I was able to seal off the entrance when all of them were outside. For a week or so, the jackals moved into a covered drain nearby and then disappeared into the forest.

Living in close proximity to wildlife is one of the privileges we enjoy.

Our home in the Himalaya is enlivened by the birds that come to call—
plum-headed parakeets that feed on deodar cones, green pigeons attracted
to mansura berries, crested serpent-eagles that hunt within the branches
of the oaks and white-throated laughingthrushes that splash about in the
birdbath. If none of these visitors came around, I would feel bereft, even
more than if we had no human company at all.

My study lies at the south-east corner of the house, with a bay window
overlooking the Tehri Hills, where the sun rises above blue ridgelines that
stretch from Garhwal to Kumaon. As I settle down to write at my desk, a
grey-winged blackbird improvises a song while barbets in the valley below
provide a wailing chorus. Moths and beetles cling to the windowpanes as
langur monkeys perform acrobatics in the limbs of deodar trees. Looking
around me, on the bookcase to my right, I can see a framed photograph
of my grandparents who first came to Landour in 1916, just over a century
ago. Another picture is of my parents who were married here in November
1948. Ameeta and I began living at Oakville in 1978, right after we were
married. Our son and daughter grew up here, as did a flock of nieces,
nephews and cousins. My two brothers and their families come to stay at
Oakville every year.

By now, I can hear the familiar call of a common hill partridge
somewhere down the ridge. These birds, well camouflaged with olive, grey
and rust-coloured feathers, make a single plaintive whistle as well as a two-
note breeding call from which they get the onomatopoeic name 'pyura' in
Garhwali. The folklore of this partridge, as recounted by Tara Dutt Gairola
and E. S. Oakley, serves as an ornithological fable and a subtle allegory
about our use of forest resources.

Long ago, before the British came to India, when these mountains
were divided into feudal kingdoms, a pyura was going about its business,
foraging for seeds and insects in the litter of dead leaves on the forest
floor. By chance, the bird found a small copper coin. Delighted with its
discovery the pyura picked up the coin in its beak and began to cry out:
'I am wealthier than the king!' As the persistent song continued, word
reached the palace and the raja demanded that his forest guards confiscate
the pyura's wealth. After searching through the jungle, the guards located the
bird and snatched the coin from its beak but the pyura was unperturbed. It
now began to sing: 'The king is rich because of my wealth!' Once again,
the song of the partridge was relayed to the palace. Wanting to silence the
bird, the raja ordered his guards to go back and return the pyura's money.
Happily taking the coin in its beak again, the partridge now began to sing

even louder: 'I gave the king so much wealth, he couldn't spend it all!'

Parables like this are an essential part of the natural heritage of the Himalaya, interpreting the life story of these mountains and the creatures they contain, including our own species. Oakville isn't just our family home but a part of something much larger, a habitat for hundreds of thousands of life forms—microbes, plants, trees, insects, arachnids, reptiles, birds and mammals. The natural history of the Himalaya includes myths, legends and lore as well as scientific narratives of exploration and discovery that explain and imagine unique taxa, geographical and environmental phenomena, as well as our shared memories and dreams of origins, evolution and the intersection between biological and metaphysical realms. The simple act of retelling these stories becomes an affirmation of nature's diversity and an argument against extinction.

I

OROGENESIS
The Persistent Memory of Stones

chapter 1

UNCERTAIN ALTITUDES

Mountains are often defined by their height, though the summit of a peak is nothing more than the point where it ends, giving way to clouds and sky. The true substance and structure of a mountain rests beneath, amidst the cliffs and crags that fall away into fluted snowfields and sun-sculpted ice. More than elevation, other elements of a mountain help establish its presence—the contours of its ridges, the angle of its slopes, the solidity and depths of its foundations as well as the meadows and forests that grow at its feet. When we measure and calculate the complex geometry of a mountain, all its various dimensions must be taken into account, including where it stands in relation to other peaks.

The Himalaya may be the tallest mountain range on earth but to focus on altitude alone limits our perspective and lessens their significance. The splendour of these mountains exists as much in their valleys as it does on the steepest inclines. The inspiring presence of Himalayan massifs has less to do with magnitude than the subtle nuances of nature out of which they rise: the trickle of a glacial stream flowing through channels of ice; translucent crystals of quartz embedded in a granite boulder; a twisted juniper root clutching loose moraine; or a herd of wild sheep silhouetted on a distant pass.

As we approach the Himalaya and observe their physical features, our eyes trace each fretted profile, where sunlight dazzles off the snow and casts uneven shadows on the rocks. At times, these mountains seem almost alive for they are always changing. The clatter of falling stones echoes the process of erosion or the scrambling hooves of an ibex gaining purchase on a precipitous ledge. The boom and thunder of an avalanche disperses clouds of white particles that float like mist yet settle and harden as firmly as concrete, burying whatever lies beneath. The Himalaya contain places of terrifying beauty, vertiginous terrain and extremes of weather that inspire both awe and fear. With their immense grandeur they appear to have been around in perpetuity despite the fact that these are among the youngest mountains on earth and continue rising several millimetres every year. Constantly pushing upward, they have formed a series of arcs that stretch from the arid borderlands of Baltistan to the tropical jungles of Arunachal Pradesh.

The Himalaya span a distance of roughly 2,500 kilometres in length and between 350 and 150 kilometres in breadth, rising to a maximum height of almost 9 kilometres above the level of the sea. Altogether, fourteen of the world's tallest summits exceed 8,000 metres and ten of these are located in the Himalaya. The other four are in the neighbouring Karakoram. More than half of the fifty highest peaks on earth lie along the Himalayan chain. Five nations—China, Bhutan, India, Nepal and Pakistan—include a portion of the Himalaya within their borders, though many of these boundaries are in dispute and the exiled government of Tibet still lays claim to much of the territory occupied by China.

Just as the spelling and pronunciation of the Himalaya has been debated for centuries, ever since the Sanskrit name was first transliterated into English, geographers have struggled to define these mountains with any coherence or consistency. While most writers, like myself, limit the Himalaya to the mountains that stand between the river Tsang Po or Brahmaputra in the east and the Indus in the west, others allow for a more flexible definition, often including parts of the Karakoram and Hindu Kush as well as some of the mountains further eastward. Regardless of these discrepancies, the two giant peaks that bookend the Himalaya are Namche Barwa in south-eastern Tibet and Nanga Parbat at the north-western edge of Kashmir. An equally difficult question is where to draw a line for the northern and southern limits of this range. For example, Mount Kailas, the most sacred mountain of all, sometimes called the 'keystone' of the Himalaya, is technically situated in the trans-Himalayan region to the north. On the other hand, the Shivalik foothills to the south are considered a separate range, though they merge with the Himalaya at many points. Similarly, the Duar Range, the 'doorway' to higher mountains in north-eastern India, is virtually contiguous with the Himalaya. Both the Bhabar and Terai, consisting of grasslands and jungle, below an altitude of 500 metres, that skirt the central foothills, are an integral part of the Himalaya, as are the upper margins of the Tibetan Plateau, where the northern slopes of the mountains level out at 4,000 metres. Nevertheless, whatever ambiguities are found on maps, these mountains rise above the contentious and confusing boundaries of cartography and politics that divide them.

'In a thousand ages of the gods, I cannot tell you all the glories of the Himalaya,' exclaimed a Vedic sage, while another wrote: 'As the sun dries the morning dew, so does the mere sight of the Himalaya dissipate the sins of man.' However remote and ineffable the mountains may seem, nothing on earth exists in isolation and it is our story as much as theirs—whatever we choose to tell of these high places and our place amongst them.

Origin myths from different regions of the Himalaya seek to explain the formation of the mountains. According to Verrier Elwin's *Myths of the North-East Frontier of India,* the Hruso tribe (also known as the Aka) in Arunachal Pradesh believe that the world was created out of two eggs. When these hatched, one produced the sky, which was male, and the other the earth, which was female. When the sky tried to copulate with the earth, he discovered that she was too large for him to take her in his arms, so he asked his terrestial lover to make herself smaller. As she did, her pliable body was drawn together and folded into hills, mountains and valleys. 'When the Sky made love to the Earth, every kind of tree and grass and all living creatures came into being.'

In another story that Elwin collected, the Nocte tribe of Tirap district recount how the earth was first covered in water. 'Deep down in the water there lived a snake called Pu.' Gradually, over time, the all-encompassing ocean receded and areas of land began to appear. 'At first, everything was mud and when the snake moved over it, there was a long winding track which became a valley through which the rivers could flow. When the mud dried up, part of the earth became flat and part turned into hills.'

At the opposite end of the Himalaya, where the Indus circles Nanga Parbat, another folk tale recounts how the world was once submerged beneath a primordial sea. Ghulam Muhammad, who recorded this story in 1905, explains how certain areas of water were frozen and a race of giants, called Yaths, lived on this desolate ice cap. To make their kingdom more habitable, they decided to dredge soil from the seabed and place it above the water. Accordingly, the ruler of the giants and his council sent a messenger to 'a wolf called Bojare Shal who lived at a place named Milgamok (old ice) and who, owing to his great genius, would be able to perform this work.' The wolf was initially reluctant but he was finally persuaded and told the Yaths to summon a bird named Gorai Pattan, as well as a mouse that lived nearby. Then the wolf told the king of the giants to lift the bird on his shoulders where it spread its wings while the mouse was instructed to dig a hole in the ice. 'The orders were obeyed and the wings of the bird covered all the water, while the mouse brought out all the soil which was beneath the water.' The earth was then spread on Gorai Pattan's wings and in this way the land and mountains were formed.

The scientific view of Himalayan origins, put forward by twentieth-century geologists, suggests that the Himalaya were conceived beneath the surface of the Tethys Sea. Their gestation and birth is one of the greatest creation stories of all time, as complex and awe-inspiring as tribal folk tales or myths from the Mahabharata and the Ramayana. This formative epic was composed and written upon the land long before the earliest ancestors of man evolved, long before language and thought, long before life itself.

When the Himalaya began to emerge from the earth's womb, the first contractions started somewhere around a hundred million years ago, as the primordial landmass of Pangaea started to cool and break apart. The earth's crust fissured and sagged into a deepening trough, which was filled by the Tethys Sea. Known as a geosyncline, this depression gradually sank and widened. Meanwhile, fast-flowing rivers fed by violent storms drained into the trench, depositing tonnes upon tonnes of sediment every day over millions of years. The silt and debris of these ancient, unnamed streams are what form the bedrock or basement of the Himalaya. As the weight and pressure of those vast alluvial beds grew heavier, the birth pangs intensified. Volcanic eruptions shot through the planet's crust and molten magma cooled to form igneous layers. Crushing forces that generated intense heat served as a crucible for granites and gneisses. Much later, veins of limestone accretions, from the remains of aquatic creatures, were added to the matrix.

Over the gradual passage of geological time, the protracted ebb and flow of the earth's surfaces reassembled areas of land and water. Eventually, when the subcontinent of India collided with the rest of Asia, perhaps fifty million years ago, a series of three major thrusts occurred. Giant slabs that geologists call 'nappes' buckled upward out of the ocean and closed the trench. Those lines where the collision occurred and the continents fused together are known as 'sutures'. One is the Indus Valley and another, the Tsang Po or Brahmaputra Valley. These great rivers serve as the parenthetical limits of the Himalaya. The ongoing process of mountain building is called 'orogeny,' from the Greek words 'oro' for mountains and 'genesis' for beginnings.

Traces of early upheavals are still evident throughout the Himalaya, older and younger zones of rock that lie in recumbent folds. Instead of pushing upward in sequential order, one layer of the earth's crust is often thrust beneath another through a process of subduction. In this way, overlapping strata from different eras are shuffled like a pack of cards. The friction created by these monumental forces can change the rocks themselves. Loose debris is compressed into conglomerate stone while the heat and pressure of collision creates metamorphic rocks. Ultimately, erosion cuts away cross-sections of strata, exhuming ancient timelines of geological history. Through the gradual chiselling of rain and wind, the birthmarks of the mountains are exposed for all to see, crumpled striations that are like convoluted puzzles sandwiched in stone.

Today, we accept the idea that mountains are like rafts of rock and soil, frosted with ice and snow, floating upon a molten sea. Plate tectonics is the key to understanding the formation of the Himalaya. Though the German meteorologist and geophysicist Alfred Wegener first proposed the theory of continental drift in 1912, this fundamental concept regarding the earth's evolution was only accepted in the mid-1960s. Until then, most geologists were debunking the idea of continental drift and calling it a fantasy. In an essay, 'The Validation of Continental Drift', Stephen Jay Gould explains how attacks on plate tectonics were biased by the way in which geologists perceived the problem. He writes that virtually every scientist rejected the idea of continental drift, though the empirical evidence was indisputable. 'It was dismissed because no one had devised a physical mechanism that would permit continents to plow through an apparently solid oceanic floor. In the absence of a plausible mechanism, the idea of continental drift was rejected as absurd.'

Gould argues that science depends on 'creative thought' to propel knowledge forward and it was only through a leap of imagination that such a theory could emerge. John McPhee, in his Pulitzer-winning *Annals of the Former World*, confirms this view, explaining how, until 1963, editors at *Nature* were still rejecting articles on plate tectonics because this emerging theory was considered far-fetched while their colleagues at *The Journal of Geophysical Research* suggested that discourse on continental drift was more suited to cocktail party conversation. He goes on to explain that the proof for this theory was found not on mountain heights or exposed surfaces of the earth but in the depths of oceans where the technology of naval warfare helped unlock these submerged secrets. McPhee writes: 'The Second World War was a technological piñata, and, with their new fathometers and proton-precession magnetometers, oceanographers of the nineteen-fifties—most notably Bruce Heezen and Marie Tharp at Columbia University—mapped the seafloor in such extraordinary detail that in a sense they were seeing it for the first time.' He goes on to say that though these naval charts of the ocean floor were kept secret to protect the location of submarines, they revealed deep trenches and mountain ranges beneath the surface of every ocean around the globe—the wrinkles and stretch marks of continental drift.

Essentially, the proof of plate tectonics and Himalayan orogeny was unveiled by US naval officers hunting for enemy U-boats. These discoveries were further reinforced by seismographic data collected by military scientists who were busy monitoring nuclear tests in the 1950s and 1960s. McPhee asserts that the, 'by-product of the Cold War was seismological data on a scale unapproached before. The whole of plate tectonics, a story of steady-state violence along boundaries, was being brought to light largely as a result of the development of instruments of war.'

The rumpled contours of the ocean floor as well as volcanic and seismic activity along the edges of submerged plates, allowed oceanographers to confirm that as continents drift apart, the resulting ruptures are filled with molten magma that bubbles up out of the earth's interior and cools to form scabs and scars beneath the sea. McPhee describes the Himalaya as 'the crowning achievement of the Indo-Australian Plate', which collided with Tibet and levered up fractured sections of the earth's crust until they protruded more than 8,000 metres above sea level. As he points out, when Tenzing and Hilary reached the top of Mount Everest in 1953, they were actually setting foot on the fossilized remnants of aquatic creatures that once lived in the Tethys Sea.

As with any creation story, whether scientific or mythological, many fundamental questions remain unresolved. Amongst contemporary geologists, no clear consensus has been reached as to when the Himalaya were formed. While plate tectonics continues to provide the broad narrative arc and offers a variety of possible scenarios, there is considerable disagreement as to how long ago this process actually began and whether it was a gradual uplift or a sequence of relatively sudden and violent events. Scientists from different disciplines, including glaciologists, climatologists and botanists have examined the evidence in their respective fields and contributed competing hypotheses on the geomorphology of the Himalaya. Carbon dating of tooth enamel from jawbones of ancient herbivores, pollen samples preserved in peat and computer-generated models of river systems or paleoclimates, are all part of the data being studied. Old theories, which were once graven in stone, have now been disassembled or deconstructed while new pieces of the puzzle have yet to be fitted together into a coherent and integrated whole. The more we learn about the origins of the Himalaya the less we seem to agree. Like any epic, it is possible to read this story on many levels and interpret each episode according to conflicting priorities, prejudices and perspectives.

Some theories suggest that Himalayan–Tibetan orogeny occurred between 100 to 45 million years in the past but there are others that argue it is much more recent and happened closer to 25 million years ago. A few geologists have proposed that instead of a single event the mountains were formed in two stages, first with a collision between the Indian subcontinent and an archipelago of islands off the coast of Eurasia. This lifted the Himalaya up to nearly their current height before they finally rammed into the Tibetan Plateau. In recent years, a bewildering variety of time frames and tectonic reconstructions have been postulated.

Regardless of the shifting sands of science, most of which is the result of faster and faster computers that have outpaced the human mind, we can still effectively imagine the genesis of these mountains in primordial slow motion. Born out of rock and water, the mountains continue to be shaped by these elements—the corrosive energy of flowing streams, their freezing and melting. A succession of ice ages, beginning 2.5 million years ago, abraded the features of the Himalaya, as glaciers carved out broad cirques, leaving lateral trails of moraine. On the surface, this process represents a perpetual conflict between fluids and solids, minerals and moisture, precipitation and accretion—the blood and bones of the mountains.

At the same time as the monumental engineering of orogenesis was occurring in the Himalaya, the smallest forms of life, single-celled organisms and other microbes, began to emerge in wetlands amidst rocks and soil, incubated by sunlight, nourished by minerals and germinated by water. The earliest alpine plants were ancestors of lichens, liverworts, mosses and, eventually, ferns. Fossils of these paleontological specimens are impressed upon rocks, their delicate death masks preserved in hardened sludge.

As the mountains rose up over millions of years, they hosted more and more plants and grasses, as well as insects, birds, reptiles and mammals such as rodents, wild sheep and goats, along with predators like wolves and *Panthera blytheae*, the ancestor of snow leopards and other big cats. The presence of human beings in the upper Himalaya is a relatively recent intrusion, dating back to somewhere between 10,000 to 7,000 years ago, during the Neolithic Age when the first nomadic hunters crossed over high passes in search of meat.

chapter 2

ROCK ART

On an eroded shelf a hundred metres above the Zanskar River in Ladakh stands a snow leopard, profiled against the bronzed patina of a polished boulder. The stylized form of its body is instantly recognizable, as is the pattern of spots on its coat and the long tail that curves behind. Crouching, I study the ancient artistry of this figure that has remained unchanged for thousands of years, a timeless image baked by the sun and buffed by wind. Harsh winters and the fast-flowing streams and rivers of Ladakh have scarred the mountains all around us, but the snow leopard (*Panthera uncia*) remains unscathed. He watches me with a stony demeanour, alert to danger yet equally attentive to the presence of prey.

On another cluster of rocks nearby, a herd of ibex with long, arching horns and fleet hooves escape the arrows from a hunter's bow. They seem to race across the burnished, undulating surface. The animals on display exhibit a primitive beauty that underscores their antiquity. Himalayan petroglyphs are found throughout Ladakh, extending from Lahaul–Spiti in the east and westward into the Karakoram and beyond, as far as Mongolia in the north and across the Pamir in Central Asia. Just as the formation of the mountains is chronicled in stone, so is the migration of Stone Age hunters. Their rock art is an eloquent record of arrival and discovery, of man's successes and failures, as well as the host of creatures with whom we share these perilous heights.

Petroglyphs are the first field guides for Himalayan wildlife. Each species is carefully delineated. Wild yaks (*Bos mutus*) are hunted down by men on horseback, accompanied by packs of dogs that drive the shaggy cattle within range of an archer's bow. A large bird with open wings appears to be an eagle or a vulture, perhaps a Himalayan griffon (*Gyps himalayensis*). The artists who etched these images understood the taxonomy of wild goats and sheep, classifying and cataloguing them on the rocks surrounding their campsites.

Admiring the petroglyphs, I wonder what purpose they served. Were these meant to signal the presence of particular animals at specific sites? Or were they boastful illustrations for heroic yarns of hunting prowess told around a campfire? I can imagine the glimmering light of smouldering dung kindled with juniper twigs. Silhouettes of the hunters' hands provide a shadow puppetry of gestures describing the chase. Or were these ritual figures carved as prayers to ensure success and survival? The images evoke the chanting of shamans calling upon animal spirits for guidance and protection.

Petroglyphs are precursors of mane stones, the Buddhist engravings of prayers like *Om Mane Padme Om* (Hail the sacred jewel in the lotus) inscribed on rocks throughout the Himalaya and piled up in walls or cairns along pilgrimage routes. Tsewang Rigzen, my guide and companion in Ladakh, runs his fingers over the outline of a bharal, or blue sheep, tracing the double arch of its horns. A few centimetres away a spiral sunburst suggests a solar deity, or maybe it simply signifies another dawn. On some of the rocks are handprints, where the anonymous artists signed their work with impressions of an open palm.

Ladakh is where the prow of India ran aground on the beachhead of Central Asia. It is a land of stark contrasts and vacant spaces, where frozen lakes like Pangong Tso reflect the vastness of the sky while the sparse grasslands, desiccated earth and skeletal shapes of barren ridges convey a sense of deathly solitude. Walking across these high altitude deserts, I can feel the inner chill of loneliness that must have accompanied those Stone Age hunters who came here seven to ten millennia ago and scratched images of animals on the rocks. The landscape has changed little since then—dry, boulder-strewn wastes and sprawling glaciers out of which flow streams of meltwater that carve the earth into grooves and channels. The cartography of erosion defines the land more decisively than survey maps, creating natural boundaries and lines in the sand. The loose, friable soil is like unformed, unfired clay. Here at the western limits of the Himalaya, it feels as if the mountains are still taking shape, on the cusp of creation, as if Ladakh were a huge, primeval construction site.

Driving through the arid landscape along the Indus, a startling strip of bright green fields suddenly comes into view, bordered by a stand of poplars. Where a stream flows out of a gorge, someone has planted a crop of barley. Yet, it seems like a flash of spontaneous generation, the first brushstroke of life on a blank, brown canvas. On ahead, rounding another bend in the road, the opposite slope also seems to be clad in green, but a much darker iridescent shade. Again, it looks as if life were springing abruptly from the sterile soil but this time it is minerals that give the ridge its illusory colour. What appeared, at first glance, to be a fertile hillside is nothing more than bare green rock, devoid of life.

In another valley, more than 100 kilometres east of the Zanskar River, flows the Khyamar Chu, a small tributary that joins the Indus at Upshi. A short distance upstream from the confluence, Rigzen leads me across a flimsy bridge of willow boughs and along the opposite bank. A covey of chukar partridge scuttle up the slope and into the sheltering rocks above. We clamber over loose talus and stop to eat orange buckthorn berries ripening in the autumn sun. The sharp, acidic flavour catches at the back of my throat.

Earlier, from the motor road, on the opposite bank of the river, Rigzen had pointed out a single petroglyph, the shape of a lizard about 15 centimetres long. One of its descendants now crosses our path and darts into a crevice beneath a rock. A few steps ahead I see the lizard emerge again, watching us with a cold-blooded gaze. When we finally reach the petroglyph, the reptilian image is etched on the stone like a man-made fossil. All around us are the smooth shapes of dark boulders that rock artists favoured. The coppery hue is like a ceramicist's glaze, vitrified in the furnace of Ladakh's harsh climate and tinted by chemical reactions on the surface of the rock.

Scrambling down to get a closer look, I can see familiar shapes and figures. A dog has grabbed a wounded yak by the throat. Ibex scatter as a hunter shoots an arrow tipped with stone. Human figures surround a dying sheep. A series of symmetrical dots, like a spiral ellipsis, radiate from a scalloped depression on another boulder. Next to this is an image of an antelope fleeing a hunter on horseback, its legs like calipers with symmetrical horns converging above its head. The arrested movement in these images transcends the stillness of stone.

Petroglyphs convey ancient stories but there is no linear narrative or spatial perspective. Instead, the natural contours of the rock dictate the arrangement of shapes and forms. Trying to recognize a cluster of obscure figures, I ask Rigzen what these are and he directs me to the other side of the boulder, where I finally make out a herd of yak. No language appears on the rocks and only a few abstract symbols. A pentagon with what looks like a star at the centre appears to be a random scrawl—graffiti that bears no meaning beyond its own whimsical design.

Farther upstream, near a village called Lato, Rigzen stops at another site. Climbing up to a telltale outcropping of dark rocks, we find more petroglyphs. As I identify images of wild sheep, a pebble tumbles down the slope from above. Looking up, we see two animals crossing a landslide. It is an urial ewe and her lamb, their wool a dull cream colour against the brown slope—the same species that appears on the rock. In Ladakhi, the males are known as shapo and the females are called shamo. The two animals stop and look at me, just as I look up at them. We observe each other as if in a timeless frieze.

A short while later, I spot the rest of the herd grazing in a narrow valley above the Khyamar Chu. Hardly any grass grows on the bare slopes but there are a few sparse bushes on which the urial browse. Getting down from our vehicle, I approach them slowly, taking cover in a trench carved by run-off from a rare cloudburst years ago. Moving cautiously, I stalk the urial to within bowshot range, about 30 metres. They seem oblivious of my presence as I stand up slowly and focus my camera. In my mind's eye, I picture myself as a Stone Age hunter, slotting an arrow and taking aim. At the barely audible whine of the zoom, one of the wild sheep raises her head and I can see small horns between her ears. After taking a dozen photographs, I turn my back on the urial. Immediately they spot me, dashing out of sight into the surrounding cliffs above.

chapter 3

A SCHOLAR OF STONES

In 1906, a young geologist accepted a position as a lecturer at the Prince of Wales College in Jammu, teaching both science and English. Beyond the windows of his classroom, he could see a line of mountains rising out of the flatlands of the Punjab. In the foreground, pleated folds of dusty hills were covered with scrub jungle and scored by dozens of dry riverbeds. The geologist began to explore this puzzling terrain, where the Shivalik Hills converge with the Dhauladhar and Pir Panjal ranges of the Western Himalaya.

As he wandered through valleys and across crumbling ridgelines, the scholar discovered seasonal watercourses filled with stones, which had been smoothed and rounded by monsoon floods. The variety of colours and textures caught his eye. He came upon creamy quartzite, pink limestone and purple shale. Some rocks were the size of pigeon's eggs, others larger than footballs. A few boulders were as big as oxen. Compared to the mountains that rose above them, the river rocks were like granules of sand. Washed down from higher elevations, out of the core of the Himalaya, these were the crushed debris of forgotten epochs filtering through an hourglass, each grain composed of minerals containing vital secrets of the earth's creation.

Most of the riverbed rocks were distinctly different from the composition of the Shivalik Hills. This wild and rugged foreland consisted mostly of loose conglomerates and reddish clays. The stones in the riverbeds came from drastically different eras. As the geologist began to record his observations and investigate the research done by others, his curiosity was fired by the mysteries he confronted.

In the college library, he read accounts of early British scientists such as the *Paleontological Memoirs and Notes of the Late Hugh Falconer.* A contemporary of Charles Darwin who explored the Western Himalaya, Falconer served as superintendent of the botanical gardens in Saharanpur, 450 kilometres east of Jammu. In the 1830s, he discovered a trove of fossils in the Shivaliks, including *Stegodon ganesa,* an elephant ancestor with fourteen-foot tusks, prehistoric hippos, and *Sivatherium giganteum,* an extinct giraffe from 2.5 million years ago, with antlers like a stag. The clayey soil of the Shivaliks also offered up the bones of *Sivapithecus,* an early hominid, who walked across these hills between twelve to seven million years ago. This distant predecessor of man resembled an orangutan and stood 4 feet tall.

As summer temperatures in Jammu began to rise above 40° Celsius, the geologist must have counted the days until the end of term, when he could escape into the mountains and make his way to the alpine vistas and cooler climes of Kashmir. In those days, the traditional route to Srinagar lay farther north along the Jhelum River beyond Rawalpindi and Murree. But from Jammu, the geologist could ascend directly into the Pir Panjal, on the other side of which lay Kashmir. The Panjal Thrust of the Himalaya tilts above the Shivaliks in a densely wooded concertina of ridges and valleys.

The geologist Darashaw Nosherwan Wadia was born at sea level in the coastal town of Surat at the western edge of Gujarat. He came from a Zoroastrian family, whose ancestors were exiled from Iran to India, sometime between the ninth and tenth centuries. The Wadias were shipbuilders by tradition, though they diversified into other trades ranging from textiles to film-making. D. N. Wadia came from a humble branch of the family tree. He was the son of a railway stationmaster. After receiving his primary education in Surat, he went on to high school in Baroda, where his interest in science flourished. He studied botany and zoology, as well as geology, receiving both his BSc and MSc degrees. From Baroda, he took up the teaching post in Jammu, which would expose him to the Himalaya for the first time.

Wadia was an independent and resourceful man. Finding no suitable textbook for teaching earth sciences, he set out to write one himself. His *Geology of India,* first published in 1916, has gone through multiple editions and was assigned in Indian colleges for almost a century. Unlike most other publications on this topic, the book is marked by clear, coherent prose that makes the subject accessible to students of all ages. Wadia believed that geology was not an arcane discipline to be studied by a privileged few but a story that everyone should understand and appreciate, for it reveals a rational, scientific explanation of the earth's formation.

As soon as his summer holidays began, D. N. Wadia set out from Jammu for Kashmir. His route, on foot and horseback, eventually took him over the western syntaxis of the Himalaya, a 'deep knee bend', where the strike of the ridges suddenly turns at right angles from east-west to north-south. This massive hinge fastens Kashmir to the rest of Asia, forming the dividing line between the main Himalayan range and the Hindu Kush to the west and the Karakoram to the north.

Walking from Jammu to Srinagar would have taken two weeks at least, climbing over ridges and descending into valleys along winding paths. Most of the altitude gained in a morning's ascent was lost again by evening, though gradually Wadia moved farther and farther into the mountains. The rocks he encountered changed from sedimentary bands of siltstones to metamorphic layers of schist. In the course of a single day's hike, the geologist set foot upon several epochs, from the Precambrian to the Eocene. The winding route took him along narrow goat trails and across landslides, up near-perpendicular slopes that left him gasping for breath. Yet, for Wadia the mountains were not an onerous obstacle but a fascinating sequence of ridgelines and riverbeds that compressed geological time into folded contours. Each rucked-up slab was like a chapter of a book, revealing new episodes in the chronicles of stone.

He moved slowly, in short stages, stopping often to observe the different features along his path. From time to time, Wadia scrambled up a slope to collect rock samples. Slight of build, bespectacled with pince-nez glasses and dressed in professorial coat and tie, he was obviously not a mountaineer. But curiosity overcame a fear of heights. Clutching tufts of grass and stone, he carried his geologist's hammer as resolutely as an ice axe. The notebook in his pocket was damp and stained with sweat. He jotted down his observations, noting the different strata and drawing the profiles of ridges. Each evening, camped along the margins of a stream or on a highland meadow, he reviewed his notes and made corrections, labelled samples and reflected on what he had seen.

With precise, evocative vocabulary, Wadia narrates the ancient stories that lay beneath his feet: 'The Dogra slates pass upward into imperfectly cleaved and foliated clays, arenaceous beds, greywackes, with a few lenticular limestones.' These rippled rocks contained traces of early life. His journeys through the Pir Panjal revealed evidence from almost every period of Palaeozoic history. In Cambrian layers, he discovered trilobites and brachiopods. Silurian strata divulged corrals. In the Lower Carboniferous, he took note of 'Syringothyris limestone', named after a prehistoric species of clam, *Syringothyris cuspidata*. Resting on this were Middle-Carboniferous Fenestella-shale beds, containing crystals of feldspar and quartz.

Crossing the Banihal Pass at 2,832 metres above sea level, Wadia finally got his first view of the Kashmir Valley. Rather than echoing the romantic hyperbole that so many others have spouted on seeing this fertile dale, he surveyed the landscape with a studious and critical eye, remarking how the Pir Panjal Range, which he had just traversed, '…generally present a steep escarpment towards the plains and a long gentle slope towards Kashmir. Such mountains are spoken of as having an "orthoclinal" structure with a "writing desk shape".'

This precocious son of a Parsi stationmaster was not only a scientist but a teacher of English literature too. He could just as easily discuss the poems of Thomas Moore as he might give a lecture on Himalayan stratigraphy, tracing the main thrust of the Lower Himalaya as deftly as scanning lines of verse.

Who has not heard of the Vale of Cashmere,
With its roses the brightest that earth ever gave,
Its temples, and grottoes, and fountains as clear
As the love-lighted eyes that hang over their wave?

As his summer journeys through Kashmir took him to different parts of the valley, Wadia appreciated the poetics of rock. For him the picturesque panoramas of the Lidder Valley leading up to Kolahoi peak and glacier became all the more dramatic and enticing when he saw, 'a thin but continuous band of Silurian strata', which he described as 'sandy shales and shaly sandstones'. Higher up were Permian deposits known as the 'Zewan beds', and finally those granite spires that form the high points of the Western Himalaya, towering pillars of silence where little or no evidence of life can be found.

Few people have studied Kashmir with as careful and appreciative eyes. D. N. Wadia devotes a whole chapter of *Geology of India* to this region, with diagrams and illustrations executed in his own hand.

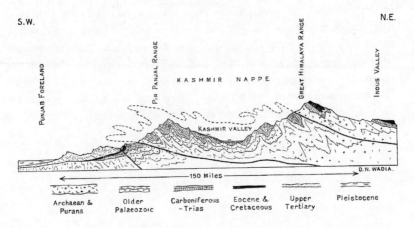

Diagrammatic section across the Kashmir Himalaya, showing the broad tectonic features.

Wadia's mastery of his subject evokes a lyrical voice, as if the 'writing desk' of the Pir Panjal, on which he recorded his geological observations, also inspired literary metaphors and allegories. In one passage, he reveals the motives of a storyteller, who recounts a seminal narrative of the earth's creation. Wadia argues that geology is much more than a dry catalogue of data about fossils and minerals but a compelling tale of a dynamic process. 'A sand-grain or a pebble of the rocks,' he writes, 'is not a mere particle of inanimate matter, but a *word* or *phrase* in the history of the earth, and has much to tell of a long chain of natural operations which were concerned in its formation.'

Considered the founding father of Indian geology, D. N. Wadia received many honours. The Wadia Institute of Himalayan Geology in Dehradun is named after him. The institute maintains a small museum, which contains a variety of rock specimens collected by Wadia and others. The stones are of all shapes and textures, with ripples, rills and waves. Samples of rock salt from Tibet are exhibited alongside 'sinus-crested sandstone', mica schist and porphyritic granite out of which he compiled a chronology of creation.

Some of Wadia's personal effects are also on display, donated by his wife Meher, who accompanied him on many of his expeditions to Kashmir. His briefcase and spectacles, a compass and his geologist's hammer can be seen in the museum. Brass buckles bearing the crest of the Geological Survey of India are placed amongst an assortment of medals presented to Wadia in his later years. In 1984, a one-rupee postage stamp in his honour was posthumously released. But the most interesting items in the exhibit are his notebooks in which Wadia recorded observations in the field. The handwriting is neat but cramped, no pages wasted. The letters and numerals are as tightly knotted as the cursive patterns in gneisses. Most entries are brief and cryptic, little more than dates, place names and classifications of different strata, accompanied by pencil sketches of ridgelines. These were his first impressions of the landscape, conveying an intimate appreciation for mountainous terrain and the narratives hidden beneath its surface.

chapter 4

EQUILIBRIUM AND UPHEAVAL

While we often assign metaphorical attributes of strength and fortitude to mountains as well as longevity and even divine immortality, they are, in fact, more fragile and less resilient than they appear. As D. N. Wadia and others have observed, the paradox of mountains is that they represent 'weaker belts of the earth's crust' which are more susceptible to seismic activity. Recurring earthquakes have shown how unstable the Himalaya can be, as their moorings shift and buckle. Seemingly solid rock is shaken or rises and subsides along fractured fault lines. But almost as dramatic as these periodic and violent tremors are other, more subtle, distortions and anomalies that reveal the impermanence of the mountains and raise larger, fundamental questions about the origins of the Himalaya.

In 1802, when the Great Trigonometrical Survey of India was launched, East India Company surveyors began the laborious task of measuring and mapping the subcontinent, through a process of triangulation. Historian John Keay, in his book *The Great Arc: The Dramatic Tale of How India was Mapped and Everest was Named*, describes how this feat of cartography was accomplished. With theodolites, perambulators, spirit levels, measuring rods and plane tables, the surveyors established benchmarks and wove an intricate web of measured lines and angles, stretching from the southernmost tip of India to the summits of the Himalaya. While these 'compass-wallahs', as they were known in Anglo-Indian slang, worked their way up the peninsula, they soon discovered that the pull of gravity exhibited puzzling inconsistencies, which set their calculations awry and made them question the laws of physics. Surprisingly, it was a man of faith rather than science who came up with the answer. In 1854, Reverend J. H. Pratt, the archdeacon of Calcutta, put forward the idea of 'mountain compensation'. In essence, he proposed that the enormous mass of a mountain range generates gravitational deviations.

As Keay explains, the Survey of India tested Pratt's hypothesis at its headquarters in Dehradun, which lies at the foot of the Central Himalaya and at the northern end of the Great Arc. They conducted a variety of experiments with plummet lines and pendulums to determine the gravitational deflection caused by the presence of the mountains. Not all the results confirmed the Archdeacon's prophetic pronouncements. Occasionally, even in the absence of mountains, the readings from the surveyor's instruments were skewed and when the mass of the Himalaya was computed, the projected angle of 'topographic deflection' did not correspond to their apparent size and stature. But as the surveyors soon realized, the mountains we see, like the tips of icebergs, are only the visible portions of a much larger mass suspended below. Out of Pratt's hypothesis came the concept of isostasy, the state of equilibrium that exists in the earth's crust, both the protruding peaks overhead and the deep substratum that extends beneath. Subsequent geodesic surveys have shown that the imposing magnitude of the Himalayan chain sits atop immense foundations of both solid and molten rock of varying densities.

Another anomaly that confounded geologists and surveyors was that certain rock formations sometimes cause a compass needle to deviate from pointing north. At first, this was blamed on lightning strikes, which can alter the surface magnetism in stones. But the explanation did not satisfy most scientists who gradually realized that some stones retain an indelible 'memory' of their creation, specifically the position they once held in relation to the polarity of the earth. This means that as the earth's crust shifted and plates rearranged themselves, each layer of rock preserved an innate sense of direction according to its origins.

Palaeomagnetism became a serious field of study in the early nineteenth century, initiated primarily by the German scientist Alexander von Humboldt, who persuaded the British East India Company to sponsor a Magnetic Survey of India alongside the ongoing Great Trigonometrical Survey. The Schlagintweit Brothers, Robert, Hermann and Adolph, were dispatched on this mission. Much of their exploration took place in the Himalaya, all the way from Kanchenjunga in Sikkim to Nanga Parbat in Kashmir. From the nineteenth into the twentieth century, scientists continued to puzzle over the magnetism of rocks, which ultimately supported the theory of plate tectonics. It was only in 1906 that Motonori Matuyama and Bernard Brunhes demonstrated that the earth's polarity had been reversed less than 800,000 years ago. The fact that different generations of rocks held onto their original orientation relative to the shifting surfaces of the globe, allowed geologists to compile a more accurate timeline of the earth's formation. Using new tools like magnetometers, geologists were able to calculate the age of different strata in the Himalaya, which had been shuffled through tectonic upheaval.

The unsettling idea that various layers of Himalayan rock are pointing us in opposite directions proves that these mountains are not as permanent or immutable as they might seem, but formed out of geological migration. The stratified fragments of the earth's crust that make up these tiered ranges have wandered here from disparate parts of the globe and from different epochs. The provenance of those tectonic journeys is locked into the magnetic memory of stones, each of them a compass that directs us towards continents that no longer exist.

chapter 5

THE POETICS OF ROCK

Formed of a living god, Himalaya, supreme
Raja of the Mountains, rises in the north
and bathing in the western and eastern oceans
stretches out like a rod that could measure the earth.

The opening stanza of Kalidasa's verse narrative, *Kumarasambhavam*, deifies the mountains even as it maps out their geography. By comparing the Himalaya to a measuring rod, the poet suggests not only their height and breadth but their mythical and spiritual pre-eminence too. *Kumarasambhavam* is one of the earliest Sanskrit poems telling the story of Parvati, daughter of the Himalaya, and Lord Shiva, the supreme creator and destroyer of the universe who sits in meditation on Mount Kailas. The poem, which exists only as fragments, recounts the birth of their son, Kartikeya, the war god. In Hank Heifetz's modern translation it is a timeless narrative with contemporary resonance.

Little or nothing is known of Kalidasa, though he was likely to have been a court poet in the fourth–fifth century CE. His patron was probably a king of the Gupta dynasty, possibly Vikramaditya, who ruled over much of North and Central India. Whether Kalidasa ever saw the Himalaya himself, it is hard to say, though the mountains make appearances in most of his other works like *Meghaduta—The Cloud Messenger*. His vision of the Himalaya is of an idyllic, supremely beautiful world of high snow peaks overlooking verdant forests full of magical and medicinal herbs while beneath the soil lie veins of gold and precious jewels.

Kumarasambhavam is full of erotic imagery suggesting the fertility and innocent lusts of Himalayan inhabitants, all of which underscores the seductive devotion of Parvati for Shiva. Passion and piety go hand in hand, as the beautiful daughter of the Himalaya approaches the Divine Creator with adoration and desire. In Kalidasa's romantic imagination, the people of the high mountains live in a wildly primitive yet perfect world. Beautiful women write love letters on birchbark using ink made from red minerals dug out of the soil while a mythical herb, which glows in the dark, illuminates hidden caves where amorous couples make love.

Himavata himself, both the god and the mountain range, rules over this highland kingdom, which is rich in natural resources. In an obvious tribute to his own royal patron, Kalidasa praises the Himalaya for their protective nature as well as their grandeur and munificence.

> With their tails from which human kings
> make chowries, the yaks do him honour as truly
> Raja of the Mountains while they fan him with elegant
> gestures waving white as moonlight through the air.

The reference to chowries or royal flywhisks made from yak tails would have been a familiar image in the court, as these were one of the luxuries imported from Tibet, centuries ago. Mixing metaphors and myths, Kalidasa praises Parvati, the daughter of the Himalaya. She is a reincarnation of Lord Shiva's first wife, Uma, who immolated herself. The goddess assumes a new form in Parvati and, against her parents' warnings, approaches her lord and master, the wild ascetic on Mount Kailas. With a sense of duty and self-abnegation, she submits to Shiva's austerities and accepts the harsh existence of her consort's home.

The opening stanzas of *Kumarasambhavam* are, in essence, an invocation to the Himalaya, a statement of desire and an acknowledgement of the mysteries the mountains contain. Kalidasa's verses blend religious lore and legends with keen observations of Himalayan landscapes, celebrating a fecund, life-giving world in which the poet's imagination roams freely between the heavenly realm of gods and goddesses, as well as the equally enchanting forests and meadows on earth. Mingling the exotic with the familiar, Kalidasa eulogizes the natural beauty of the mountains, which are the source of life-giving rivers like the Ganga.

A translator of Sanskrit is like a geologist teasing the meaning out of fossilized remains, resuscitating an ancient language in which the grammar and syntax has been garbled and all the punctuation marks removed. At places the ink has dissolved, forming new patterns on the page. A good geologist or a good poet, inspired by his or her 'stone muse', is able to recount those ancient tales engraved on the earth or on a strip of birch bark, so that we can understand what happened years ago, and realize that our human existence is little more than a comma within nature's voluminous archives.

In his exhaustive account of geological history, John McPhee writes about the mechanics of continental drift and mountain formation but he also brings to light the idea of 'geopoetics', by which he suggests the intangible mysteries of the earth are explored and elucidated. Just as poets express the transience of life and death, geologists write passionately of past upheavals and the relic remains of vanished continents, fossilized shells and skeletons of creatures that became extinct millions of years ago, by which they date the strata of the mountains, their slow movements and folded features. The Himalaya are often described as being a 'young' range of mountains, compared to the Aravalli and Satpura ranges, which have eroded into insignificance. Yet, in their youthfulness, the Himalaya preserve the wrinkled features of the earth's aged crust, potshards of primordial tectonics and the detritus of seismic activity.

THE MOUNTAINS OF INSTEAD

John Bicknell Auden, elder brother of the poet W. H. Auden, was another
pioneer of Himalayan geology. He was based in Calcutta and employed
by the Geological Survey of India from 1926 until 1953. As a young man,
freshly arrived in India, Auden became fascinated by the Himalaya during
summer visits to hill stations like Shimla, Mussoorie and Darjeeling. He was
a founding member of the Mountain Club of India, which merged with
the Himalayan Club in 1928. Auden was one of the first Europeans to visit
Nepal in 1934, following a devastating earthquake that flattened parts of
the Kathmandu Valley. Accompanying D. N. Wadia, who was twenty years
his senior, Auden participated in the first geological survey of Nepal at the
invitation of the Rana rulers. He was able to approach Mount Everest and,
despite the summer haze, took the first photograph of its southern face.

Auden's primary contribution to our understanding of the Himalaya
comes from his surveys in Garhwal that focused on stratification and
glaciers. He identified the Krol Belt of limestone, named after a hill near
Shimla, an important feature that extends throughout much of the Lower
Himalaya. In 1935, at the end of September, instead of taking his furlough
in England, John Auden set off with a friend, D. G. Macdonald, to explore
the headwaters of the Ganga. They trekked with three Sherpas enlisted from
Darjeeling, Da Tondrup, Ang Tsering, and Pasang Angju and twenty-five

Garhwali porters. Though their primary objective was to conduct a cursory geological survey, they also hoped to climb some of the nearby peaks, particularly the Satopanth group to the south-east of Gangotri. Neither Auden nor Macdonald was an experienced mountaineer and after a few tentative attempts, they wisely decided to turn back.

The Gangotri Valley and Bhaironghati Gorge are among the most dramatic phenomena in the Central Himalaya, where the Bhagirathi tributary of the Ganga gouges a path directly through the main thrust of the mountains. Leucogranite formations at Gangotri are sculpted into surrealistic shapes by the glacier-fed stream. Hindu myths of Ganga's descent from heaven amplify the natural mysteries with sacred lore and Gangotri attracts pilgrims from all across India.

On a side excursion near Gangotri, Auden ascended the Rudragaira Valley, hoping to climb one of the summits above Kedarnath, which he describes with a geologist's eye: 'To the north of the bedded metamorphic rocks that form the southern line of peaks of the main Himalayan range lies a zone of granite. This granite weathers along major joint planes into appalling precipices, such as that on the north-west face of Satopanth and those bounding the lower part of the Kedarnath glacier.'

Deborah Baker, in her book *The Last Englishmen: Love, War, and the End of Empire*, describes J. B. Auden's infatuation with the Himalaya and the many-layered relationships within his circle that converged and collided as the British empire fell apart. After his first visit to Garhwal, Auden and Michael Spender, brother of another celebrated poet, Stephen Spender, joined an expedition to the Karakoram led by Eric Shipton and Bill Tilman. While their siblings were reshaping the contours of modern English verse, J. B. Auden and Michael Spender were surveying and charting Himalayan terrain. They drew some of the first maps of this region, measuring massifs and glaciers near K2.

Back in London, W. H. Auden and Christopher Isherwood had written a play inspired in part by John Auden's mountaineering adventures, titled *The Ascent of F6: A Tragedy in Two Acts*. The protagonist, Michael Ransom, is a troubled colonial hero, modelled on Lawrence of Arabia. His efforts to climb F6, a fictitious mountain haunted by a demon with Freudian undertones, conveys the ambivalence both Audens felt towards England and the empire. In his poem 'Autumn Song' Wystan seems to speak wistfully of the Himalaya:

Clear, unscalable, ahead
Rise the Mountains of Instead,

From whose cold, cascading streams
None may drink except in dreams.

In the summer of 1939, as Hitler prepared to invade Poland, J. B. Auden returned to Garhwal, equipped with better maps and determined to complete his survey of the region. This time he travelled only in the company of his porters. Much of his time was spent in the upper reaches of the Jadh Ganga Valley, near the Nelang Pass into Tibet. His account includes an anecdote of rescuing a wolf cub that had been picked up by an eagle and dropped near their camp. Auden adopted the cub. 'During the nights it slept with me somewhat incontinently in my sleeping bag.' He also writes evocatively of the remains of extinct glaciers: 'Old moraines, oxidized and crumbling like rotten slag heaps, flanked the oppressive gorge, and we arrived with relief at the top of one of the glacial steps formed during the Pleistocene Ice Age, camping in the rain at 14,800 feet just west of Tirdhara.'

One of the places Auden revisited was the Rudragaira Valley above Gangotri, where in 1935 he had spotted a remote pass that led directly over the bulwark of the Himalaya from the Bhagirathi Valley into the Bhilangana watershed. J. B. Auden crossed over this pass with his porters and descended to the Khatling Glacier. At the end of his journey, conscious of the clouds of war gathering over Europe, he adds a sombre postscript to his report, wondering how he can explain to the people of the Jadh Ganga Valley about 'war in peace, of Blubo-empires, bombs and concentration camps'. He suggests that though the inhabitants of this region live a harsh and difficult life they are blessed by their isolation from the horrors of Hitler's fascist ambitions. Auden's words remind us of his brother, who was, at that same moment, self-exiled in New York City, 'sitting in one of the dives on Fifty-Second Street', composing his famous poem, 'September 1, 1939', written on the eve of global conflict.

Though he was part of the British Raj, John Auden had little time for colonial hierarchies and the rules of empire. He understood the fault lines, false summits and tectonic clash of egos that accompanied India's struggle for independence. As Deborah Baker explains, in her essay, 'From the Summits of Empire', John Auden rejected the jingoism that accompanied the waning years of the Raj and shared his brother Wystan's anxiety and depression over the outbreak of World War II.

Following his brother's lead in opting for imprudent love over martyrdom in war, John braved the 'studied insolence' of his compatriots in Calcutta, 'as violently opposed to contamination as any Nazi bourgeois', and married a Bengali. His new wife, Sheila Bonnerjee, was a painter and a granddaughter of W. C. Bonnerjee, the founder and first president of the Indian National Congress. John resigned without regret from both the Saturday and Tollygunge clubs because his wife wasn't allowed entry.

After Independence, Auden 'stayed on' with his family in India, the last Englishman to step down from the Geological Survey of India. He and Sheila continued to maintain homes in both Calcutta and London. One of their two daughters, Rita, wrote his obituary in the *Himalayan Journal*. 'Dr Auden passed away at London on 21 January 1991, aged eighty-seven years. He was cremated on the 29th after a Mass at Westminster Cathedral. As per his wishes, the ashes will be immersed in the waters of the Ganges at Rishikesh on 14 December 1991.'

A hundred and fifty kilometres upstream from Rishikesh, above Gangotri, lies the pass that connects the Rudragaira Valley with the watershed of the Bhilangana. In a fitting tribute to a man who deciphered the garbled and cryptic stories embedded in rocks, this pass now bears his name. Auden's Col stands at an altitude of 5,490 metres, directly upon the ramparts of the Himalaya.

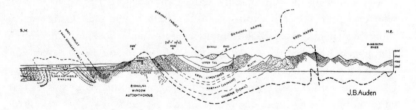

Diagrammatic representation of the nappe structure of Garhwal Himalayas.

chapter 7

BREAKING STONES

One of the traditions of trans-Himalayan trade, up until the early part of the twentieth century, was to seal a partnership by splitting a stone. As E. T. Atkinson's *The Himalayan Gazetteer*, published in 1886, recounts, each Bhotia trader, from opposite sides of the mountains, kept half of the broken stone as a simple means of confirming his identity and acknowledging transactions. When a shipment was dispatched, one piece of the stone went with it and upon delivery the two halves were fitted together and returned, providing proof of receipt. In this way the stones guaranteed debts and symbolized a connection between two sides of the mountains, an unwritten trust amongst merchants but also a larger, more enduring covenant with the land.

There is a cynical saying in Uttarakhand: 'Patthar todogey toh patthar hi milengey.' 'If you break a stone you only get more stones.' Yet the consequences of human activity in the Himalaya have been almost as profound as plate tectonics. The changes that human beings have wrought on these ranges amount to far greater environmental degradation than thousands of years of erosion and seismic upheaval.

Before the modern era, the most obvious evidence of human habitation was terraced fields, which can still be seen throughout the lower and middle Himalaya. Using stones excavated from hillsides, farmers continue to build retaining walls that shore up their land and provide level ground for crops. These pushtas help protect the soil from erosion and keep precious rainwater from flowing away. In certain places, entire slopes and ridgelines have been reshaped into a vertical mosaic, extending hundreds of metres up and down. Terraces in the valleys tend to be broader, where the land is relatively flat. As the slope gets steeper, the fields grow narrower, sometimes no more than the width of a single furrow. Often, the terraces appear to replicate the lines on contour maps, as if each level were a measured rise in elevation.

Rocks are the primary building material in Himalayan villages. Homes are made with masonry walls and slate roofs. Stones are fashioned into hearths, thresholds, pillars, steps and balconies. Slate-lined canals redirect a stream for irrigation. Cobblestones cover the path to keep it from being washed away or mired in mud. A drinking trough for cattle and mules is carved out of a limestone boulder while the hardest rocks are used to sharpen sickles and axes. Flagstones pave village courtyards where grain is threshed. Granite millstones grind the wheat, barley and millet, driven by the power of falling water, the same force that shaped and pulverized the rocks long before the first farmers came here.

Stones are also used to construct temples, cut and carved into sacred shapes and symbols. Hindus and Buddhists worship idols made of rock, investing them with sacred powers. Often the ritual image is little more than a weathered shard, with unusual contours that devotees interpret according to their spiritual imagination. In other instances, rocks are fashioned into the likeness of a deity, the mother goddess riding on a tiger or the coital symbol of a phallus placed within a vaginal groove that represents the regenerative powers of Shiva and Parvati.

With the rapid spread of recent development, transport and industry, man's intrusive effect on the mountains has escalated, dominating the landscape. The building of roads destabilizes fragile terrain and landslides scar the slopes. Trees are cut for firewood and fodder, their roots no longer anchoring the soil. Riverbeds are dug up for stone and sand, increasing the impact of erosion. Concrete or earth-filled dams block rivers, creating huge reservoirs to produce electricity and regulate the flow of water. Strip mining gouges the face of ridges, exposing belts of limestone and gravel that are quarried to build more homes. Miners tunnel for veins of phosphate and other precious ore, deep within the heart of the mountains.

Only the highest peaks and passes remain inviolate, far above the limits of human habitation. But even here, man leaves his mark. At almost every crossing in the Himalaya stand cairns of rock that recall the passing presence of human travellers—migrants, pilgrims, traders and explorers. Each person who follows these paths instinctively picks up a stone and places it upon another, building a crude structure to represent our common dreams, desires, fears and fortunes.

Just beyond the north-western limits of the Himalaya, near the village of Hinzil, there is a large pile of rocks that evokes a legend. This story is recorded in Ghulam Muhammad's *Festivals and Folklore of Gilgit*. He recounts that many years earlier a huge army was marching from Skardu against the forces of Chitral. The princes who were leading this campaign decided 'to order their men to throw stones together in a heap at one stone per man, and to take out one stone from the same heap on their return in order that by this means they might be able to deduct the casualties'.

Whatever their purpose, cairns are a primal gesture, acknowledging the vast scale and elevation of the Himalaya, while reducing them to human dimensions. By constructing a simple stack of stones we seek to replicate those giant slabs of rock, thrust skyward by the collision of ancient continents. Each piece of a cairn holds within it the memory of an individual who crossed the mountains, surrendering herself or himself to the collective anonymity of stones. Fragments of schist and granite, slate and mica signify our wandering journeys even as they retain evidence of their own migrations. Certain stones are poems etched by time. Others are stories, without beginning or end. Some may be prayers, silent orisons resting one upon another, personal statements of veneration or requests for blessing, guidance and forgiveness.

Mangalesh Dabral, a distinguished poet of Garhwal, has composed a brief elegy to the Himalaya, titled in Hindi 'Abhi Bhi Aag Hai', which translates as 'A Fire Still Burns'. In nine short lines, he speaks of origins, loss and memory, survival and defiance.

> In these stones
> a fire still burns
> and history too
> a house will be built from them
> a retaining wall for fields
> one more battle
> will be fought
> soon
> with these stones.

II

THE THIRD POLE
Of Glaciers, Rivers and Clouds

chapter 8

HIMALAYAN WARMING

A wave of rain and hail bursts through the deodar branches and onto the verandah of our house like a tidal surge breaking over a sea wall. Spray hits me in the face and drenches my shirt as a deafening cannonade bombards the sheet-metal roof accompanied by rolling thunder and blasts of wind in the trees. Pellets of ice lash the wisteria vines and hydrangea bushes—our garden planted for gentler days. Rain gutters overflow with hailstones that cover the lawn like an avalanche of mothballs. A bolt of lightning strikes one of the tall trees nearby with a phosphorescent flash followed by a sharp explosion, as if the sky has split in half.

Each year, when the monsoon arrives in the Himalaya it carries with it the momentum of a deluge that has travelled more than 2,000 kilometres from the Malabar Coast, overflying the burning expanse of the Deccan Plateau and Gangetic Plain. India is shaped like a funnel with water on either side. This tapered wedge of land, stretching from 8 degrees above the equator at Kanyakumari to the 34th parallel north in Ladakh, is heated in summer to temperatures as high as 50° Celsius, siphoning moisture from the sea. Arranged across the top of the subcontinent is the arc of the Himalaya that forms a meteorological dike. While the lower slopes of the mountains absorb the summer heat, at the uppermost elevations temperatures remain below freezing year round.

On the other side of the Himalaya, as days grow longer, the vast expanse of the Tibetan Plateau thaws out, creating thermal suction and wind patterns that help draw the monsoon inland. Through this annual confluence of elements, the evaporated waters of the Indian Ocean flood the sky, moving northward as a torrent of clouds until they wash up against the mountains. Armadas of moisture, travelling as fast as 30 knots—the velocity of an aircraft carrier heading into battle—collide with the Himalayan headlands.

Storms like this are nothing new. Similar squalls have battered these mountains for millennia, even before the earth began to gradually grow warmer, following the last period of glaciation, which ended roughly 10,000 years ago. Tumultuous weather reminds us of our tenuous ancestry. In the extended timeline of creation, human history is nothing more than a brief episode, bracketed between the last ice age and whatever future awaits our descendants. Yet in the short span of 150 years of industrialization, we have altered the pace of climate change, accelerating the warming of our planet to a critical tipping point.

In virtually every religious tradition the story of a devastating flood is an enduring myth (and an indictment of mankind) that describes the end of the world, or at least the end of terrestrial life as we know it. For anyone who lives at sea level today, the realities of a watery demise are anything but mythological. Here in the mountains, 2 kilometres above the highest tide, rising oceans aren't an immediate concern. However, in recent years, we have seen catastrophic cloudbursts, prolonged droughts, widespread forest fires, flash floods and other extreme events that suggest unsettling, inauspicious trends in the atmosphere.

◆

If we trace the latitude of Mount Everest, which coincides with the 28th parallel north, and follow that line around the world, it leads us westward through Nepal and North India into the deserts of Rajasthan and Sindh, beyond the Persian Gulf to the Arabian Peninsula. After dividing the Red Sea, the line passes over Egypt and the Sahara, all the way across North Africa to Morocco, keeping well below the southern coast of the Mediterranean. In the Atlantic Ocean the 28th parallel north grazes the Canary Islands before making landfall in Florida and continuing on through the badlands of Texas, into Mexico's Baja Peninsula. From there it crosses the Pacific, just north of Hawaii, and carries on to the Yellow Sea, after which it penetrates southern China and stretches into Burma, before completing its global circuit through Arunachal Pradesh, Bhutan, Sikkim and finally, the north-eastern corner of Nepal.

The Himalaya are sometimes referred to as the 'Third Pole' because they represent the largest accumulation of ice, after Antarctica and the Arctic. However, as our mental circumnavigation of the globe illustrates, one of the coldest places on earth shares the same latitude as many of the warmest, driest spots on our planet. Compared to Saudi Arabia, Libya or southern Texas, the Himalaya are considerably wetter and retain frozen reservoirs that irrigate South and Southeast Asia. For this reason they are also called the 'water towers of Asia'. One of the reasons they are especially vulnerable to climate change is because of their latitude. If Himalayan glaciers dry up and disappear, as some scientists suggest they might, this entire region would then begin to look like the sandy wastes of the Sahara. While the North and South Poles are experiencing rising temperatures, the Himalaya are subject to even greater warming because of their proximity to the equator.

Throughout their existence, the Himalaya have endured the effects of climate change. Palaeobotanical studies of floral variations over thousands of years demonstrate that meteorological trends have shifted back and forth from centuries of moist and temperate weather to extended periods of arid cold. Vegetation profiles based on pollen data from soil samples, as well as fossil evidence, show that during different eras the dominant tree species alternated from pines and other conifers to broad-leaved oaks and alders. Expansion and retreat of forests and grasslands have mirrored climate shifts throughout the region.

To appreciate the changeable nature of Himalayan weather and its contrasts, we can compare the climate on high passes at varying times of year and in different regions of the mountains. At the eastern end of the Himalaya, in Sikkim, lies Goecha La (4,940 metres) at the foot of Kanchenjunga. Setting off from the roadhead at Yuksam in May, we climb 3,000 metres in three days, ascending from humid, semi-tropical conditions into dense bands of cloud forest, enveloped in mist and drizzle. Our final camp lies above the timberline, where 10 centimetres of snow falls on our tents that night. Later in the year, in Central Nepal, at the beginning of December, we cross Thorung La (5,416 metres) between the Marsyangdi and Kali Gandaki watersheds. Though the sky is cloudless, most streams and rivulets are frozen and the glare off the snow is blinding. Night temperatures drop to fifteen degrees below zero. A thousand kilometres to the west, in Ladakh, during August, traversing Shingo La (5,091 metres) the high-altitude desert of the Zanskar Valley is so hot and dry that we become dehydrated and the sun scorches our skin.

If such dramatic extremes exist in the Himalaya, then why should we be concerned about an average increase of a degree or two over the past hundred years? Perhaps because, unlike previous climate change, the current shifts are a direct result of human consumption and waste. Seemingly insignificant variations in temperature have dire consequences—glacial lakes bursting fragile ice dams, mudslides that bury villages, unpredictable monsoons, disappearing species and disrupted migration patterns.

Ladakh, which has an average annual rainfall of 100 millimetres, experienced a catastrophic cloudburst in 2010, with some areas receiving as much as 250 millimetres in the space of a few hours. This caused severe flash floods, mudslides and debris flows that destroyed sections of the capital, Leh. According to official reports 234 people were killed and nearly 9,000 were displaced. However, when I visited several years later I was told, 'The number of victims will never be known. The local people who died, we know who they were, but the labourers from Nepal and elsewhere, there is no record of them.' Contractors will never disclose their names or numbers, because it would make them accountable for their deaths. Rigzen, my driver and guide, explained that there are many other consequences of climate change. He said that in Dha Hanu, a north-western district of Ladakh, 'the apricots were all destroyed by worms because the birds that eat the worms never came—their migration was disturbed'. He also told me how his parents and grandparents used to speak of three seasons in Ladakh—four months of winter (when nobody does anything), four months of wind and four months of warmth. 'Now it has all changed. The wind continues into July and we have warm days in November.'

In the current debate over climate change both sides accuse each other of manipulating science but amidst the polarized rhetoric there is a failure to recognize that science itself is not a rigid absolute. Whether it be the origin of species or plate tectonics, the truth remains that science is changeable and constantly corrects itself. 'Facts do not "speak for themselves",' Stephen Jay Gould writes, 'they are read in the light of theory. Creative thought, in science as much as in the arts, is the motor of changing opinion. Science is a quintessentially human activity, not a mechanized, robot-like accumulation of objective information, leading by laws of logic to an inescapable interpretation.'

Today, climate change or global warming, whatever we may call it, has been 'accepted' by the vast majority of scientists, becoming a new orthodoxy of environmental discourse. Most of those who debunk and debate its efficacy subscribe to other, older orthodoxies that emerged from the industrial revolution, presenting human development, enterprise and ingenuity as being the internal combustion engines of civilization and modernity.

Just as the theory of continental drift provides a convincing explanation for the formation of the Himalaya and helps us understand their geological history, global warming offers persuasive answers to meteorological events and trends. While maintaining a healthy level of scepticism, as Gould suggests, it is difficult to ignore the mounting evidence, both empirical and anecdotal. Over the past decade a number of mountaineers have commented on the differences they find on Himalayan peaks as snow packs melt and glaciers recede. In some cases, it seems as if they are climbing a different mountain altogether, where slabs of rock, once corniced with ice, are now exposed. Established routes no longer hold the same obstacles or challenges, while others have become even more treacherous than before. The lost remains of climbers like George Leigh Mallory, who vanished almost a century ago, are no longer entombed in snow. All these observations, along with statistical data on annual temperatures, rainfall and wind velocities, as well as the depth and breadth of glaciers, point towards the validity of climate change and its attendant consequences.

In addition to annual weather patterns, innumerable microclimates exist in the Himalaya caused by altitude and terrain. Some slopes and valleys lie in rain shadows while other areas attract excessive precipitation. In the foothills of the Central Himalaya, where I live, the northern face of a ridge is generally moist and densely forested while the southern exposure is drier and covered in grass. At higher elevations this pattern is reversed and the northern slopes receive less precipitation. Anyone who has followed the course of a river like the Ganga knows that its waters pass through distinctly different belts of forest as it twists its way between the ranges, from silver birch (*Betula utilis*) and deodar (*Cedrus deodara*) at upper altitudes to *Bauhinia* creepers and cactus-like *Euphorbia royleana* lower down. Vegetation and wildlife vary according to temperature and humidity. Human habitation too seeks out the most advantageous climate for growing crops and accessing pastures.

Weather is both cause and consequence in the Himalaya. Colonial migration to the hills is the reason my home town exists because the first British residents came here to escape searing temperatures, oppressive humidity and virulent fevers on the plains. In May and June, when the heat in Delhi climbs to 45° Celsius, our thermometers seldom rise above 30°. Landour, Mussoorie, Murree, Dalhousie, Shimla, Nainital and

Darjeeling continue to be summer resorts, where tourists migrate each year because of intense heat at lower elevations.

Climate affects everything in the Himalaya, from biology and glaciology to mountaineering and philosophy. On the highest peaks, almost as many climbing deaths are linked to bad weather and storms as they are to altitude sickness, avalanches or fatal falls put together. Most Himalayan agriculture depends entirely on seasonal rainfall from rice paddies in the valleys to buckwheat above the treeline. The composition of Himalayan forests serves as a natural hydrometer, signalling levels of humidity in the air and moisture in the soil. Epiphytic species, such as ferns or orchids that take root in the saturated branches of a cloud forest, rely on mist as much as rain.

Governments have fallen as a result of weak monsoons and wars have begun and ended as temperatures climbed and dropped. Artists and poets have been inspired by the monsoon. Pahari miniature paintings illustrate approaching storms as metaphors of desire—a young woman standing on a balcony, ardently awaiting the arrival of her beloved as thunderheads darken and swell. Religious faiths teach lessons based on climate from the stoic asceticism of monastic retreats in barren highlands to the voluptuous divinity of mother goddesses, whose fecund blessings enrich the soil. Indra, the god of storms, hurls thunderbolts from heaven and Lord Shiva catches the monsoon torrents in his matted dreadlocks. White clouds symbolize purity and transience for Buddhist teachers just as rainbows serve as archways to paradise.

Migration is governed by the seasons. Rosefinches and black-necked cranes fly south or north as winds change direction and temperatures rise or fall. Nomadic shepherds time their departures and arrivals according to weather patterns, reaching high meadows with their herds soon after the monsoon brings forth an abundance of grass and herbaceous plants. Fish, ferns and fungi flourish in this wet season while erosion shapes the ridges, carving ravines and uprooting trees, while washing away the detritus of glaciers. Even the deities and their devotees move up and down the valleys from winter sanctuaries below the snow line to summer temples near the sources of rivers. In Garhwal and Kumaon, biannual pilgrimages transport gods and goddesses from lower to upper elevations in the spring, then back again in the fall. These ritual journeys are often compared to a bride departing her parental home or returning from her husband's abode, suggesting the displacement of marriage as well as the reproductive process of conception, gestation and birth. Perhaps it is only natural in a landscape fostering seasonal journeys that human beings would believe in the transmigration of the soul.

Climate change in the Himalaya is everyone's problem. The causes often lie far away, sometimes in distant corners of the globe. In 1991, during the First Gulf War, when Kuwait's oil wells were set on fire, a pall of smoke drifted thousands of kilometres eastward. Flying home to India that year, I remember seeing a shadowy black smear stretching towards the horizon. When I reached Mussoorie, the oak leaves were covered with an oily film, the residue of fossil fuels set alight by war. This greasy soot also settled on snow peaks and glaciers leaving a stain that not only sullied the face of the Himalaya but accelerated their melting. Seasonal winds carry various kinds of particulate matter from sand and dust to vehicular pollutants. In his book *Life in the Himalaya: An Ecosystem at Risk,* botanist and environmental scientist Maharaj K. Pandit links the darkening of the surface of glaciers and ice fields to both local and global pollution. 'A number of recent studies have shown that the deposition of mineral dust and black carbon has contributed to the darkening of the western Himalayan snow cover, which accelerates the seasonal snowmelt and the regional snow albedo feedback producing more warming and higher glacial ablations.'

Calculating the human cost of Himalayan warming would be a staggering exercise. These high ranges separate the two largest populations on earth, with China (1.418 billion) to the north and India (1.363 billion) to the south. While the upper regions are sparsely populated, particularly above 2,500 metres, they provide a vital source of fresh water for those who live on either side. The roof of Asia is sharply pitched, collecting snow and draining moisture into the valleys. Both on a local and global scale the diminishing ice cap could quickly deplete some of the most important river systems upon which billions of people rely—not just the Brahmaputra, Ganga and Indus but also the Salween and Irrawaddy in Myanmar, the Yellow River and the Mekong in China and Southeast Asia. If these giant waterways, all of which have tributaries in the Himalaya, were to diminish or disappear, the effects downstream would be devastating and irreversible.

Himalayan folklore acknowledges the vital importance of water for sustaining life on earth, with stories about the origins of rivers that recall a time when water was scarce or nonexistent. In a tale from the Dobang (Gallong) tribe, who live along the Siang or Brahmaputra, we can see how people for whom water has always been plentiful still understand that it is an invaluable, finite resource:

Now whilst gods and men were living together on the earth, there was much distress because there was no water, and gods and men alike

were lean and thin. But it was noticed with a good deal of wonder
that the rat was always fat and sleek. So one day a man followed the
rat and tracked it to a big stone in which it found water to drink.
Then the man came back and told what he had seen. But when the
men came to break the stone and get the water out for themselves
they found that the stone was very hard, so hard that it broke the tools
they brought with them. So the god Debo-Kombu took his bow and
shot at the stone with an arrow and a trickle of water—the stream of
the arrow—came welling out of the rock. And so Debo-Kombu is
worshipped with his bow and arrow to this day. But only a tiny flow
of water ran out of the stone. Then the god Nurupur took an axe, and
broke the stone and the water gushed out freely over the thirsty earth.
And he too is worshipped for ever in the water he gave to gods and
men.

This story was recorded by Captain G. D. S. Dunbar, a British military
officer who was dispatched to quell uprisings amongst the tribes of the
North-East Frontier Agency (NEFA), though he developed a fascination for
their culture. Another folk tale collected by Verrier Elwin from the Hruso
(Aka) tribe also tells of a time before water when men and animals suffered
greatly. A bird named Horsi-Basam knew that beyond the horizon where
the sun rose each day there was a giant serpent that held 'a great lake in
his coils'. The bird set out to release the water but when it saw the snake
it became afraid and waited until nightfall, when the serpent fell asleep.
Creeping forward, 'the bird pecked out both its eyes and in its pain the snake
uncoiled itself and let the water escape and it poured down as a great river.
Ever since then the bird Horsi-Basam has lived on the banks of rivers.'

chapter 9

RIVER OF MILK

Chomolungma, mother of all mountains, commonly known as Everest, stands amidst an arena of peaks in the sub-range of the Mahalangur Himal, which harbours the watershed of the Dudh Kosi River. Aside from being the highest point on earth, the Everest region is an enormous assemblage of ice. Glaciers with multiple arms wrap around the ridges at altitudes between 4,500–7,000 metres above sea level. Directly beneath the south-west face of Everest, and bounded by Nuptse on the opposite side, lies the Western Cwm, an oval basin of frozen moisture hundreds of metres deep.

Cwm is a Welsh word for a glacial trough, known in the French Alps as a cirque, and in Scotland, a corrie. Essentially, the Western Cwm is an enormous stone vessel that stores and decants an annual accumulation of precipitation from Everest, Lhotse and Nuptse. Avalanches slough off the steep slopes of these mountains and the compacted snow and ice feeds the glacier. Appropriately, cwm rhymes with womb, for this frozen source of life lies deep within the belly of Chomolungma, and the Khumbu Icefall is her birth canal.

Though clearly visible in satellite imagery and on survey maps, the Western Cwm remains hidden from sight as we walk up the Dudh Kosi Valley. The first European mountaineers to approach Everest from this angle were Bill Tilman and Charles Houston, in 1950. Tilman was puzzled by the obscure access point to the cwm, which he described as the 'merest slit, not more than three hundred yards across, filled by a broken icefall that falls steeply to the Khumbu glacier…'

Today, thousands of trekkers ascend this valley each year, especially in October and November, for an opportunity to stand at the shifting site of Everest Base Camp, which lies on the glacier. From here the summit of Chomolungma itself is hidden and only the threshold of the icefall is visible, spilling through the narrow cleft that Tilman identified. Below this spreads a ghostly procession of frozen pinnacles descending for a couple of kilometres, like the bleached bones and cartilage of a mythological beast, a stark white contrast to the grey debris that covers most of the Khumbu Glacier. As Tilman and Houston discovered, a better view of Everest can be obtained by climbing a rocky outlook, known as Kala Patthar. From there the structure of the mountains becomes evident as the South-West face of Everest reveals itself, leaning away from Nuptse in the foreground. The South Col and a corner of Lhotse also come into view and it is possible to make out a ring of rock walls enclosing the cwm.

Dudh Kosi means river of milk. The swift current is a creamy colour that churns and curdles as it descends. Like most glacier-fed streams, particularly in summer when ice melts rapidly, the meltwater is a viscous fluid saturated with the powdery remains of pulverized rock. Stirred up by the torrent, these minuscule particles of silt, known as glacial rock flour, take more than a day to settle in a water bottle and quickly clog a microfilter.

While the Khumbu Glacier is a tributary of the Dudh Kosi, the river's primary source lies to the west, in the Ngozumba Glacier that descends from Cho Oyu (8,188 metres). Unlike Everest, this Himalayan giant does not hide behind her neighbours but stands unabashed at the head of the valley displaying her southern exposure. Despite Cho Oyu's height, her profile isn't as dramatic as the lesser summits of Ama Dablam, Kangtega or Thamserku, which rear up in grand and grotesque shapes. A conventional-looking mountain, Cho Oyu exhibits a stolid silhouette that gradually tapers to a squat, unprepossessing summit.

The name, Cho Oyu, translates as 'the turquoise mountain' though its predominant colour is white. Nevertheless, a chalky blue-green can be seen in the chain of Gokyo lakes that extend from its base along one side of the Ngozumba. These wetlands look like a turquoise necklace shaped and polished by the lapidary action of the glacier. Separated from the main current of ice by a steep scarp of moraine, the five lakes drain from one to the next, laced together by a clear, swift stream. Though their surfaces freeze in winter the lakes are now independent of the glacier and provide a gentle contrast to the harsh features of the Ngozumba, bounded on both sides by high walls of marginal debris. When glaciologists speak of retreating ice, we usually think of a glacier's length but a true measure must also include its width and, more importantly, its depth.

The length and breadth of Himalayan glaciers cannot match the enormous scale of the Baltoro and Siachen glaciers in the Karakoram, which stretch over 50 kilometres each and cover areas as large as 700 square kilometres. Monitoring glaciers is not a simple matter, partly because of their scale and irregular shapes, but also because most of the frozen mass is hidden from view. While glaciers in other parts of the world, such as Alaska, Greenland and the Alps, have been studied extensively, the terrain and seasonal temperatures are radically different and comparisons are difficult. In the Himalaya, scientists have begun to record glacial dimensions and study core samples of ice in Ladakh and Nepal, yet these vital reservoirs remain enigmatic. They are a crucial piece of the climate change puzzle but few reliable benchmarks exist beyond anecdotal records of nineteenth and twentieth century explorers and early photographs. While many Himalayan glaciers are receding, it is difficult to predict the rate of decay without accurate timelines of data.

Raikot Glacier, which flows off the north face of Nanga Parbat, is one of the few that is currently advancing. Susanne Schmidt and Marcus Nüsser of Heidelberg University's South Asia Institute have compared photographs dating back to the 1930s, when the first German mountaineering expeditions approached Nanga Parbat. Through a chronological sequence of images and with other corresponding data they have been able to demonstrate that the length and breadth of the Raikot Glacier has fluctuated considerably over a period of more than seventy-five years.

Crossing the Ngozumba is like threading a path through a tumultuous labyrinth that contains unexpected twists and turns, as well as plenty of dead ends. This obstacle course shifts from week to week. A clear passage one day suddenly opens into a crevasse the next, or is blocked by an uplifted slab of ice. A few helpfully placed cairns assist trekkers traversing the glacier. The indistinct trail detours around shallow ponds and icy grottoes. Fissured chunks of frozen mud calve off and splash into murky shallows, while a steady dribble of gravel and sand accompanies trickling streams of meltwater. Like most Himalayan glaciers, the Ngozumba is covered with a crust of rocks and soil that helps insulate it from the sun and hides the inner core of ice migrating towards its snout. Generally, the central portion of a glacier is extruded at a faster pace than the peripheral ice.

The Ngozumba appears virtually lifeless, though at a few places moss has sprouted on the rocks and grasses have taken root in the surface soil, at least for a season or two. A pika, or mouse hare, scoots out of its burrow as we pass by, though there seems to be little for the animal to feed on. A young golden eagle drifts overhead, displaying white coverts under each wing, but quickly turns towards the cliffs beyond, where it is more likely to find prey or carrion.

Shapes in a glacier mirror the uplift of mountains on either side, as if the ridges of ice have modelled themselves on the surrounding topography. The dimensions and structure of a glacier are dictated by the terrain it passes through, even as it sculpts the rocks in its path. Geological and glacial time progress in parallel but each at its own pace. The process of orogeny is infinitely slower than the relatively swift transit of ice. We often speak of the 'glacial pace of change', but in comparison to the tectonic forces that thrust the Mahalangur Himal to its current heights, the Ngozumba and Khumbu are like refrigerated express trains, relentlessly ploughing their way forward.

By human measures, however, the movement is imperceptibly slow, though on occasion, glaciers accelerate with remarkable speed and devastating force. One of the results of thinning ice, brought about by rising temperatures, are glacial lake outburst floods, which have caused immense destruction in many parts of the Himalaya. Melting glaciers harbour ice-rimmed ponds held back by fragile dams of unstable moraine, which pose a potential threat to all forms of life in the valleys below including human habitation. Unlike the Gokyo lakes, which have established themselves over centuries and are relatively secure, many glacial ponds are ready to burst their banks. Ice dams quickly reach a point where they can no longer hold back the water they restrain. A sudden monsoon downpour, such as the cloudburst that occurred in 2013 at Kedarnath, unleashed a wave of freezing water, mud and rock that obliterated most of the temple town. Similarly, entire settlements in Nepal have been decimated by glacial lake outbursts. In 2015, the village of Langtang was completely destroyed by mudslides and flash floods triggered by an earthquake.

After crossing Cho La between the Ngozumba and Khumbu glaciers, we come upon Chola Tso, a glacial lake at least 2 kilometres in length and blocked at one end by the Chola Glacier. Observed from above, it is a picturesque scene with turquoise waters set amidst steep, corrugated cliffs. But as we descend it becomes apparent that the only thing holding the lake back is a finger of rubble and ice that descends off Cholatse and Taboche peaks. The town of Pheriche lies a few kilometres downstream, at the edge of an open, unprotected valley. On the other side of Pheriche, the Imja Khola tributary descends from another glacial lake, roughly the same size as the Chola Tso. As the hydrologists Marcus and Nadine Konz and their colleagues have written in Georg Miehe and Colin Pendry's *Nepal: An Introduction to the Natural History, Ecology and Human Environment of the Himalayas*:

> Most glaciers in Nepal are characterized by retreating ice fronts and down-wasting processes as a result of global warming... Glacier shrinkage can lead to depressions in lower ablation areas, which in turn can develop into glacier lakes. A well-known example is the Imja Glacier, a large debris-covered glacier with ice supplied from vigorous upper tributaries. The glacier shows a pronounced loss of thickness and retreat, accompanying the formation of the proglacial Imja Lake...

By their estimates, if either of these water bodies above Pheriche were to burst, roughly 50 billion litres of water would be discharged at a rate of 30,000 cubic metres per second, all of which would surge into the narrow confines of the Dudh Kosi Valley, destroying everything in its path.

chapter 10

CATCHMENTS AND WATERSHEDS

Water is one of the most changeable elements on earth, which gives it an elusive, transient quality. In his lyrical travelogue, *From Heaven Lake*, Vikram Seth describes the numerous streams and waterfalls flowing off the face of the mountains as he crosses from Tibet into Nepal. Seth's words succinctly capture the poetic essence of Himalayan hydrology:

> ...against the grey verticality of a cliff a thin strand of water...vanishes into a mist or smoke atomized by the wind, to reappear, reconstituted from, it seems, the air itself into a liquid skein of light. There is enchantment in flowing water: I sit hypnotized by its beauty—water, the most unifying of the elements, that ties land and sea and air in one living ring.

Following a river to its source is like tracing a fluid timeline that delineates the history of the valleys and mountains through which it flows. Two hundred kilometres to the west of Everest, in Central Nepal, lies the Marsyangdi River, which drains from the northern slopes of Annapurna. Before being absorbed into its confluence with the Trishuli, the Marsyangdi passes between margins of jungle and terraced farmland. Mango and citrus trees grow along its banks, as well as ficus, silk cotton and bamboo. As we drive upriver, men are selling fish at the side of the road, strung on poles like bunches of bananas. At this point, the river lies deep within the valley, with feathered rapids and long pools reflecting verdant shadows rather than the opaque blue of the sky.

Farther upstream a large hydroelectric project is being built by the Chinese, who are assisting Nepal in harnessing the power of falling water with penstocks and turbines. After millions of years of carving its course through the Himalaya, the Marsyangdi is being tamed by armies of men in hard hats, constructing reinforced concrete dams and spillways. A sign, in English, warns the Nepali labourers: 'Don't Come to Work in a Drunken State'. Constricted gorges, through which the river descends, lend themselves to hydropower technology, though the reservoirs are already filling up with silt. By diverting and stalling the current, the Chinese engineers have rerouted the river but also arrested erosion. The myriad particles of sand and soil that flow down from the mountains will eventually choke the turbines, unless these channels are regularly dredged.

Rivers are much more than just water—they contain a constant stream of mineral and vegetable matter, as well as microbial and other aquatic life. At several places along the drive, we pass fish farms, where trout are being hatched and raised. The fingerlings look like schools of semicolons punctuating the streams. Like the recently harvested rice fields, these trout farms thrive on the unpolluted currents that carry nutrients from their source. Human beings have redirected Himalayan streams for centuries, using the force of flowing water to irrigate their crops and grind grain but never before on the scale of giant hydroelectric projects.

Nepal is as much a birthplace of rivers as it is the home of mountains. In their *Illustrated Atlas of the Himalaya,* David Zurick and Julsun Pacheco calculate that more than 6,000 separate streams have their sources in these highlands, flowing into a network of waterways that weave between the ridges. They estimate that Nepal's potential for hydropower is sufficient to supply all of its own electricity needs as well the combined demands of India, Pakistan and Bangladesh. Of course, the investment required and the environmental consequences are forbidding, but these numbers demonstrate the enormous quantity of water that the Himalaya capture and release. Annually, more than 200,000 million cubic metres (200 trillion litres) of water runs off the mountains and into the plains of North India. At least one-third of the Ganga's flow comes from Nepal and more than half of this water is discharged during the monsoon from June to September.

Beyond Besisahar, where the paved road ends, a newly excavated jeep track runs parallel to the Marsyangdi, so rough at places that 4 x 4 vehicles move no more than 5 kilometres per hour, grinding their way over boulders, landslides and waterfalls. Our progress is far slower than the river itself, which tumbles in the opposite direction over rocks and crashes down natural sluices and cataracts. The drive from Besisahar to Chame, where we finally start walking, feels like a violent earthquake that lasts for twelve hours.

Approaching the end of the motor road we encounter evergreen forests of fir, hemlock and yew. The claustrophobic depths of the Marsyangdi gorge give way to our first views of snow peaks like Phungi Himal to the east and Lamjung Himal to the west. Annapurna II, the second highest peak of the massif, appears above Chame. At 7,937 metres it is only 154 metres shy of the main summit. Equally impressive is an enormous concave slab of rock on the opposite side of the valley near Dhikur Pokhari, the dove pond. This giant tsunami of stone, at least 500 metres high, stretches for a couple of kilometres and seems about to break over us like a tectonic tide.

The Annapurna Circuit has been a popular trekking route for backpackers from the 1960s onward. Originally, this route took a minimum of three weeks to hike, though now it has been shortened by the ingress of motor roads and airfields. Largely through the vision and persistence of two conservationists, Mingma Norbu Sherpa and Chandra Gurung, the Annapurna Conservation Area Project (ACAP) was launched in 1986. Since then ACAP has evolved into an ambitious, multifaceted development effort sponsored by Nepal's National Trust for Nature Conservation (formerly the King Mahendra Trust for Nature Conservation).

Chandra Gurung came from a village called Siklis, overlooking the Marsyangdi Valley. Unlike many of his family and friends who joined the Gurkha regiments, Gurung chose to become a scholar and environmental activist. He was a charismatic leader who went on to direct the WWF's Kathmandu office before he died in a helicopter crash in eastern Nepal, where he and his colleagues were starting another conservation project near Kanchenjunga. According to his biographer, Manjushree Thapa, Chandra Gurung was committed to handing over responsibility for protecting and preserving the natural heritage of the mountains to local communities. ACAP remains the controlling agency for the Annapurna region, with offices and checkpoints at major halts along the trek. Though the original model has changed over time and the Maoist insurgency between 1996 and 2006 halted many ACAP initiatives, the project continues to engage and assist villagers in preserving their environment. Among its many activities, ACAP helps train teahouse owners on everything from basic hygiene to breakfast menus. It also empowers the people of the mountains to manage their demands on forest resources and employ responsible ecological strategies like micro-hydel and solar power generation.

Annapurna, the Hindu deity after whom the mountain is named, is an avatar of Parvati, daughter of Himavata and consort of Lord Shiva. A goddess of fertility, she is the purveyor of plentiful harvests. One of the myths celebrating Annapurna's sustaining powers is a story in which Shiva arrogantly declares that everything is illusion, even the food we eat. Annoyed by this dismissive pronouncement, Parvati sets out to prove him wrong and immediately makes herself vanish. In the absence of the mother goddess, the world suddenly becomes barren. Forests die and rivers cease to flow, while crops wither and animals starve. As hunger spreads throughout the land, Shiva quickly realizes his mistake. Meanwhile, Parvati cannot bear to see the world consumed by drought and famine, so she assumes the guise of Annapurna and descends from the mountains to the banks of the Ganga, where she begins to feed the hungry. Chastened, Shiva finally approaches her with his begging bowl and asks for forgiveness, after which the goddess feeds him with her own hands. He then builds a temple for her at Kashi and fertility returns to the land.

While most of the people living along the lower reaches of the Marsyangdi River are Hindus, further upstream in Manang the population is almost entirely Buddhist. Elaborate mane walls appear along the trail, with tiny painted frescoes of bodhisattvas framed in niches amidst piles of slate that are carved with Tibetan prayers. Sprigs of juniper adorn these shrines. Elsewhere, at the top of a climb overlooking the valley, dozens of miniature cairns have been piled up like stacks of coins. There are plenty of chortens too, almost always arranged in groups of three and painted different colours—red for wisdom, white for compassion and black for power. The skulls and horns of wild sheep decorate these sacred sites.

Trekking through the Marsyangdi Valley, the main summit of Annapurna is hidden from view though Annapurna II, III and IV make impressive appearances. The most prominent peak, however, is Gangapurna, a 7,455-metre mountain that looms above the town of Manang. One of the primary sources of the Marsyangdi, Gangapurna's uppermost slopes are shaped like the cupped palms of two hands held open to receive the snow.

The Annapurna catchment area extends over the entire length of the massif, which is almost 90 kilometres from end to end and includes dozens of glaciers, snowfields and wetlands. Tilicho Lake, immediately to the north of Annapurna, at an elevation of 4,919 metres, is one of the highest waterbodies in the world, 4 kilometres in length and more than a

kilometre in width. To the south, on the other side of the range, beside
the town of Pokhara, lies Phewa Lake, only slightly larger than Tilicho
but at a much lower altitude of 742 metres. All the streams and rivers in
this region drain into the Gandaki River, a major tributary of the Ganga.

At Manang, we spend a day acclimatizing in preparation for crossing
Thorung La. The town feels abandoned and the trekking lodges, overcrowded
earlier in the year, are mostly empty. There are a few shops and a bakery
selling apple pie and brownies, as well as Lavazza coffee. Anantha Rai,
my guide, tells me that the Manangis have a reputation for being shrewd
businessmen who cater to homesick and hungry trekkers from around the
world. The window of a restaurant advertising yak burgers and pizzas is
plastered with stickers from international travel agencies in every language
from Japanese to German.

Farther down the main street is a Projector Hall that also advertises
shoe repair and laundry services. The two movie titles, written in chalk
on a blackboard outside, are *Into Thin Air* and *Seven Years in Tibet*. The
scheduled showtime is 5–7 p.m. but without any other patrons around, the
owner is happy to screen a DVD for us whenever we wish. With plenty
of time to kill, as our bodies adjust to the altitude, Anantha, our porter
Dawa, and I, settle into the seats, which are covered with yak hides. Small
electric heaters are provided at our feet for the cinema is freezing cold.
The power in Manang is generated by a micro-hydel project and is much
more reliable than in Kathmandu.

We choose to watch *Seven Years in Tibet*, which I've already seen, though
I'd forgotten what an unconvincing film it is. Both the story and the setting
are contrived. Brad Pitt plays an airbrushed version of Heinrich Harrer, the
Austrian mountaineer who was a member of the Nazi SS. The script glosses
over this part of his resume and presents Harrer in an entirely sympathetic
light, as he becomes a prisoner of war in British India, escaping into the
Himalaya and finally ending up in Lhasa where he works as a tutor for
the young Dalai Lama.

Shot mostly in Argentina, with the Andes substituting for the Himalaya,
very few of the locations appear authentic. The internment camp in
Dehradun, where Harrer was a prisoner, looks like some place in North
Africa and as they cross the mountains, even with a film editor's sleight
of hand, it is virtually impossible to suspend disbelief. When the DVD
finally ends I am relieved to step outside and see that the real Himalaya
are still around us.

It is early December and no rain has fallen for more than two months.

The snow line has receded high above the valley floor, which is brown and bare. The Marsyangdi is running clear, only a hint of silt in its current. Short, bright days are one of the pleasures of trekking in winter, offset by long, dark nights when everything freezes from the contents of water bottles to the faecal slurry in a communal latrine. Except in the lower reaches of the valley, we see no clouds for over a week.

Climbing a lateral ridge above Manang, I watch spindrift blowing off the scalloped rim of Gangapurna, a fleece of frozen vapours carried on the wind like shreds of cirrus dispersing in the dry, winter air. A few minutes later, the silence is broken by a muffled thump as an avalanche shears off, sending up a plume of snow. From every angle Gangapurna seems designed to collect the snow that coats her slopes, scooped ridges that curve into a deep bowl, their lips corniced with ice.

Gangapurna's glacier emerges from beneath a pristine mantle of snow near the summit. Groomed by the wind like a gentle ski slope, it abruptly tapers into a gnarled and fractured icefall, full of seracs and crevasses. Lower down, the glacier fills the valley with a mangled cascade of ice. Three thousand metres below the summit lies the snout, where two ridges of fluted moraine fan out to form a broad basin of rubble and rocks. As we climb up one side of this moraine our path skirts the crumbling edge, where the slope falls away to the shallow waters of Gangapurna Tal. At one time, this lake was covered by ice but all that remains is a cirque of debris. A sequence of photographs taken by the veteran Swiss geologist, Toni Hagen, who first visited the Marsyangdi Valley in 1952, illustrates how the glacier has rapidly receded to its present limits. A little more than half a century ago, almost the entire valley and lakebed were covered, though now the ice has withdrawn several kilometres upstream.

More vertical than horizontal, the hanging glacier bulges with seracs suspended high upon the face of the mountain, as if defying gravity. These frozen cataracts accumulate over hundreds of years and gradually release their burden through avalanches. Unlike the Ngozumba and Khumbu glaciers near Cho Oyu and Everest, which stretch out into the valleys, Gangapurna's icefall has very little debris on the surface to serve as insulation. Being on the north face of the mountain it is partially shielded from the sun, but less moisture is deposited here and it is likely to be depleted sooner than south-facing glaciers.

Whatever their shape or size these solid currents of moisture are historical reminders of past ages of glaciation, when most of the Himalaya were covered by an extensive ice cap. What remains are relics of much larger reservoirs that have long since melted and drained away.

While some of the consequences of climate change are slow-moving, others arrive with unexpected swiftness. On 14 October 2014, the worst tourism disaster in Nepal's history occurred on Thorung La. Forty-three people died and more than 300 had to be rescued after a sudden blizzard dumped almost 2 metres of snow in the space of twelve hours. Twenty-one of the fatalities were foreigners who had come to Nepal to undertake the Annapurna Circuit Trek. The rest of the dead were Nepali guides, porters, villagers and herdsmen. October is the peak trekking season and an estimated 100,000 trekkers pass over Thorung La every year. As Sam Moulton and Grayson Schaffer reported in an article in *Outside Online*, the storm was not unexpected nor was it unique but the warning signs were ignored. A severe cyclone off the eastern coast of India had moved steadily inland and northward, over the course of two days, striking the Himalaya with greater intensity than most monsoon storms. Many of those who died were poorly equipped and unprepared for this fierce blizzard that trapped them at altitudes above 5,000 metres. Those who survived suffered frostbite, dehydration, hypothermia and altitude sickness.

Two years later, crossing Thorung La in December 2016, it is hard to believe that this was the scene of a catastrophe, though it is easy enough to imagine how the disaster must have unfolded. The pass, which connects the Marsyangdi Valley with Mustang, is slightly higher than Everest Base Camp but much more exposed, with a steeper ascent from both east and west, which makes acclimatization difficult. Though Thorung La itself is a broad, undulating saddle situated between two 6,000 metre peaks, the path on either side drops steeply down near-vertical slopes. This means that under whiteout conditions, with the trails and cairn markers hidden beneath snow, the trekkers had no exit. Moulton and Schaffer describe how avalanches poured down from either side while strong winds and plummeting temperatures made it difficult to survive. Because of heavy cloud cover and high winds it took rescue teams and helicopters two days before they could reach the site. They discovered frozen bodies scattered in all directions, where people had floundered about in a desperate struggle to find shelter or escape.

Meteorologists strongly suspect that this event was the result of climate change. Post-monsoon storms can be severe but usually by the middle of October most of the unsettled weather has ended and clouds disperse. Abnormally warm temperatures in the Bay of Bengal created a tropical depression that made the Category 4 hurricane spin out of control.

Hindsight is always a dubious perspective but setting out to climb Thorung La in the aftermath of the blizzard, each of us has the tragedy in mind. On the advice of lodge owners and guides, we depart in the dark, an hour before dawn, our wavering queue of headlamps inching up the shadowy ridgelines under a canopy of stars. The air is absolutely motionless and the silhouette of Thorung peak stands above us like a giant fossil ribbed with ice. The calmness of the hour and the clear sky are reassuring though it must have been very different setting off with snow beginning to fall and the freezing wind gaining force with every step.

We reach the crest of the pass at sunrise but the bright rays of light streaming over the ridges offer little warmth at these frigid heights. A rag heap of prayer flags decorates a cairn where a sign, erected by ACAP, welcomes and congratulates us. The lone tea shop is closed for winter and the pass has a deserted, desolate feeling, bereft of life. When I remove my gloves for a few seconds to take a photograph, my fingers ache from the cold.

Atmospheric conditions at this altitude are less predictable than lower down. Yet in the stillness of a winter dawn, I am aware of the absence of wind and clouds, as well as minimal oxygen in the air. While my breath condenses when I exhale there is virtually no humidity. It is almost like being in a vacuum though the sky is open above us and I can sense what it must be like to stand at the edge of space. The earth is lifeless here, a frozen desert curving upward. Later in the morning, a breeze will start to ruffle the prayer flags and blow dust across the pass, whistling as it sends particles spiralling through the air. But right now, the only thing that moves are shadows retreating down the ridge as the sun climbs higher. The empty sky is charged with light, a harsh, unfiltered glare that crystallizes on scabs of snow and ice, as if the vacant atmosphere around us were an infinite, ethereal prism.

chapter 11

SACRED HYDROLOGY

After crossing Thorung La, our trail descends sharply to Muktinath Temple, one of the most sacred and remote destinations for Hindu pilgrims. Mukti means salvation, or a release from the cycle of suffering and rebirth. Devotees believe that they can visit all the holy sites in the Himalaya but until they have been to Muktinath, their sins will never be completely washed clean.

A small, three-tiered shrine with a pagoda-style roof stands within a walled compound of poplar and willow trees. These are the first signs of life we encounter after crossing the pass. In early December only a few brown leaves cling to the trees and the grass has been scorched by frost. Dhaulagiri (8,167 metres), the seventh highest mountain in the world, rises directly from the riverbed below. We have now entered the northern end of the Kali Gandaki Gorge, the deepest valley in the world, connecting Tibet and Mustang with the central highlands of Nepal. Only a trickle of pilgrims visit at this time of year, though Muktinath remains open throughout winter for prayers and propitiation. Because of the dry climate snow seldom falls on these slopes. A mendicant, his skin smeared with ash, sits cross-legged near the gate, lost in cosmic contemplation as he soaks in the afternoon sunshine.

The sacred waters at Muktinath emerge as a spring from the barren slope above. This perennial stream is channelled into a trough out of which a hundred and eight water spouts spill into a drain that encircles the temple and fills a rectangular tank before irrigating the trees and garden. The entire design of the complex is dictated by the course of flowing water. A hundred and eight is a sacred number—signifying the 108 names of god. The brass spouts are each shaped like the head of a cow with its mouth open to convey the stream. At either end are slightly larger spouts designed to look like makaras, an aquatic monster, part crocodile and part elephant. Makaras are the divine vehicle of the Ganga and are associated with the mythology of Vishnu, the presiding deity at Muktinath.

The main sanctuary is dedicated to Vishnu, who is worshipped as the preserver and sustainer of life. Water is the element that transforms this raw and desolate region. Unlike the glacial streams that flow directly out of the ice, the sacred source at Muktinath springs from an aquifer buried beneath rocks and earth. At this time of year, where the spring emerges, strings of faded prayer flags are tied in a pinwheel pattern on the hillside above, like a tattered mandala.

The temple complex at Muktinath contains a number of shrines, including a Shiva temple and a Buddhist gompa. To one side, just beyond the compound wall, an enormous Buddha statue is being constructed, out of scale with the older structures. Giant idols like this suggest religious chauvinism that undermines the unique blend of faiths at Muktinath. As I enter the main temple, a Hindu priest anoints my forehead with a vermilion tilak but when I approach the inner sanctum, a young Buddhist monk in ochre robes is lighting incense in front of Hindu idols. The caretakers of both religions seem to share ritual duties without compromising or contesting each other's beliefs.

Inside the sanctuary at Muktinath, along with images of Vishnu and dozens of other sacred objects and votive offerings, are several large saligrams. These fossilized ammonites are an extinct species of predatory mollusc that died out at the end of the Cretaceous period, more than 65 million years ago. Their closest living relative today is the nautilus, which has a shell that exhibits the same spiral shape as a ram's horn from which ammonites get their name. Coincidentally, Argali (*Ovis ammon*), a wild species of sheep, live in Upper Mustang and share the same taxonomic root.

Found in many parts of the world, ammonites are imbued with myth and lore. In Europe they are called 'snake stones' and here at Muktinath, Hindu mythology associates them with the coils of the celestial serpent on which Lord Vishnu sleeps. Finding these ancient marine creatures 5,000 metres above sea level and 2,000 kilometres from the nearest ocean only adds to their mystery, as does the prevailing theory that they were wiped out in a mass extinction, along with the dinosaurs and most other forms of life, when a giant asteroid struck the earth, kicking up a dense cloud of dust and debris that blocked sunlight and smothered the earth.

Those who worship the saligrams at Muktinath do not question or confirm the scientific narratives that explain their existence. Instead, they see mysterious patterns embedded in stone that can only make sense within the logic of faith. At Muktinath, saligrams are venerated as symbols of Vishnu, the preserving deity of the Hindu triad, who keeps the world in balance, a divine conservationist in whose serpentine dreams we exist for only a fleeting fraction of eternity. These fossils from the Himalaya have been carried to temples all across India, as far away as Orissa and Tamil Nadu, where saligrams are placed alongside idols and invested with spiritual powers that drive our innermost fears and desires.

The Buddhist temple is less than 50 metres from the main shrine at Muktinath. A mud brick building with a whitewashed facade, it has a chorten in the courtyard painted a rusty hue. A channel of water has been diverted into this section of the compound and spills out of the mouth of a gilded cow wrapped in Tibetan katha scarves. The flowing stream is also used to turn a prayer wheel. Wooden paddles rotate this ritual mechanism like a watermill or micro-hydel turbine. Human ingenuity and engineering harness a force of nature to invoke the supernatural.

Inside the temple, the dimly lit walls are covered with murals of bodhisattvas, Manjushri (representing insight) and Chenrezig (representing compassion), as well as Buddhist goddesses, both the green and white Taras. However, the primary object of worship is an eternal flame that burns in a sacred hearth, where natural gas emerges from a tiny crevice in the rocks. In the shadowy interior of the gompa, the air has a sulphurous smell though the fire burns without smoke. It looks like a pilot light in an oven, a guttering blue and yellow spark. Like the water that flows out of the earth, the fire emerges at Muktinath from a hidden source deep within the mountain. All five primary elements are here, including the wind that whips through the poplar trees outside and an ethereal sunset reflecting off Dhaulagiri. This enormous peak, with its concave eastern face, dominates the valley, catching the first and last rays of light while the rest of the mountains lie in darkness.

The next morning, when I revisit the temple, soon after dawn, the rising sun reflects off a frozen pond below the town. Water is still flowing from most of the cows' mouths, though 108 icicles hang below them and the flagstones are slick and treacherous. Most pilgrims circumambulate the temple, sprinkling their heads with a few drops of water from each of the spouts, but at this hour I can only reach the first one without slipping on the ice and my fingers recoil from the cold as I hurriedly baptize myself.

From the courtyard of Muktinath Temple, the massive pyramid of Dhaulagiri dominates the skyline, one of the most beautiful, imposing giants of the Himalaya. Its slopes, gilded by the sunrise, descend directly into the Kali Gandaki Gorge. The Austrian mountaineer Kurt Diemberger, who was on the first successful summit team to climb Dhaulagiri, writes about the 'alpine geometry' of mountains, recalling how, as a schoolboy, he learned about cylinders, cones and pyramids; then later, as a climber, appreciated the same shapes in the Himalaya. 'He knows the thrill, the unique inexplicable tension, which the regular shapes of the mountain world awake in him: huge pyramids, enormous rectangular slabs, piled-up triangles of rock, white circles, immense squares—the thrill of simplicity of shape and outline (and the excitement of mastering them, to an unbelievable extent, by his own efforts, his own power), the thrill of the straight line upwards...'

Years later, Diemberger, who also made a first ascent of Broad Peak with Hermann Buhl, wrote about a horrific tragedy on K2 in which his climbing partner, Julie Tullis, and twelve other mountaineers died in a monster storm. Diemberger himself was fortunate to escape. Telling the story, he uses the metaphor of an endless knot, a geometric design of interwoven lines. One of the eight auspicious symbols of Tibetan iconography, its maze-like pattern represents a continuum of time and space, the eternal path of existence and suffering. In his own mystical imagination, Diemberger equates the endless knot with the motives that drive him to climb a peak like Dhaulagiri or K2 as well as the figure eights and double bowlines he ties in his rope. Looking at the morning light and shadows on the great white mountain, the geometry of its slopes is easily apparent, an elevated symmetry of lines and shapes.

Later in the morning, I buy a saligram as a souvenir from a street vendor in Muktinath. A black pebble, the size of a walnut, it breaks neatly in two, revealing the spiral shape of the fossil inside. The ribbed whorl of a sea creature that no longer exists serves as a totem of Himalayan evolution. Encased in mud and through a slow gestation, this prehistoric sea creature has been transformed into stone. Nothing of the original life form survives. What we discover after splitting the stone is not what remains but evidence of something no longer there. Like the rocks that Himalayan traders once broke in half and then fitted together to seal commercial partnerships, these are emblems of intangible truths and a historical trust with the land.

Each saligram coils in upon itself, a perpetuum mobile. The tiny chakras rotate on an invisible axis, signifying the cyclical nature of life and death, resilience and renewal. A natural motif of intrinsic motion, the saligram maps out the cosmos, the movement of galaxies and planets, the orbit of our earth spinning in the void. Tibetan monks form an endless knot, or phelbe, by interlacing their fingers in meditation. Like the saligram this sacred geometry leads us into a peaceful, eternal existence where suffering and sacrifice do not exist. Here is the elemental pattern, the coiled spring at the base of our spine, the eternal wheel of energy and creation.

chapter 12

CURRENTS OF LIFE

Tucked away inside one of the pigeonholes of my rolltop desk, which I inherited from my mother, is a small jar of water that I collected at Lake Manasarovar. The same compartment contains a handful of pebbles from the bottom of the lake that I carried back with me after visiting Tibet, ten years ago. Though I am an atheist and don't believe in the dogmas and dictates of any religion, I can still appreciate the sanctity and spiritual significance of natural phenomena that are imbued with mythical attributes by different faiths. Manasarovar or Mapham Tso, as it is known in Tibet, is one of the highest and holiest lakes in the world, situated at the apex of the Himalayan watershed.

Arriving on the shore around noon, after four dusty days of driving across western sections of the Tibetan Plateau, I was eager to plunge into the lake. A group of Hindu pilgrims, with whom I travelled, congregated at the water's edge and conducted a puja, burning incense and reciting prayers before they took a cleansing dip. Walking a discreet distance away from the others, I stripped down to my shorts and waded out into the shallows. While the sun on my back was burning hot, the water retained the icy chill of Himalayan glaciers that feed Manasarovar. Gurla Mandhata, a huge wave-like mountain to the south, swelled against the skyline, while Mount Kailas, to the north, was hidden behind a bank of clouds.

Entering the water, I was immediately aware of the lake's transparency even as its surface reflected the turquoise blue of the sky. It was like stepping into a fluid mirror, seeing the shingle and sand at my feet as well as the passing shapes of clouds drifting overhead. Each of the elements seemed to merge together—gusts of air, the heat of the sun, the cold water and solid earth. A few rust-coloured brahminy ducks huddled some distance away along the shore and a flock of terns were preening on a sandbar further out, occasionally taking flight on knife-like wings. The water came up to my knees and I had to walk out 20 metres or more before I was able to submerge myself. It almost felt as if I could have waded across Manasarovar, though the opposite shore seemed an infinite distance away. As I lowered myself into the lake, different layers of perception seemed to melt together so that the shrill calls of the terns, the temperature of the water and time of day, my errant thoughts and suppressed tears, were all one in the same. Sinking below the rippled meniscus, I opened my eyes underwater and could see the blurred white shapes of my limbs and the intricate mosaic of pebbles on the bottom. While I knew there were fish in the lake, I saw none, though I could imagine them slipping through the passing shadow of a cloud as it covered the sun. Instantly, the lake felt colder than before and when I raised my head to take a breath, I shivered unconsciously, reminded of the altitude and the ice-covered peaks surrounding the lake. We were more than 4 kilometres above sea level, on the north side of the Himalaya. As the sun emerged again from behind the clouds, I stood up to soak in its warmth. Cupping my hands, I drank deeply from the lake, swallowing its pure, cold essence.

One of the most diligent geographers to explore this part of the Himalaya was Swami Pranavananda, a Hindu ascetic originally from Andhra Pradesh. In his book, *Kailas-Manasarovar*, an early edition of which was kindly gifted to me by Bill Aitken, Pranavananda writes that followers of every religion, including the 'wandering minds' of atheists and agnostics, can feel 'vibrations' that emanate from this sacred landscape, just as 'particles of iron' are attracted to a magnet. While I have never felt any psychic sensations that might have been generated by supernatural forces, it is true that bathing in the clear waters of Manasarovar and circumambulating Mount Kailas, are among the most memorable experiences in my life.

The lengthy, poetic descriptions in Pranavananda's book reflect a combination of his spiritual and scientific sensibilities for he was fascinated by both the sacred resonance and physical nature of the landscape. Hindus believe that Manasarovar was created in the mind of Brahma, a divine dream that became a reality. Immediately to the west of this sacred lake is Rakshas Tal, named for demons, as if the geography of this region were divided between the opposing forces of good and evil.

As the swami writes, 'Tirtha-sthanas', or places of pilgrimage like Manasarovar and Kailas, 'are said to be sanctified by the great efficacy of earth, water, and fire and by the fact that munis or sages have lived here.' From 1928 until 1949, Pranavananda undertook the 386-kilometre pilgrimage every year by foot from Almora to Manasarovar. On two occasions he stayed through the winter at Thugolho monastery on the southern shore, in the company of Buddhist monks. Meditating on Manasarovar for more than two decades, he carefully mapped and measured the lake, which has a circumference of 87 kilometres. Pranavananda completed the parikrama, or circumambulation of the lake, a total of twenty-five times and even took an inflatable rubber dinghy out on the water to make soundings of its depths. (He also hauled the dinghy up to Gauri Kund, a small pond on the northeastern side of Mount Kailas, at 5,630 metres.) Later, he brought a galvanized steel boat from India with an outboard motor to continue his research.

But perhaps the most transcendent moment of all was at dawn on 28 December 1936, when Pranavananda emerged from his meditation room in the monastery and witnessed the lake freezing over as a sheet of 'milk-white ice' that spread from the shores to the centre of Manasarovar, solidifying like 'the mythological ocean of curds'. Later that winter, he recounts how the ice cracked with long, irregular fissures as the water level dropped beneath the frozen surface. And then, a few months later in spring, he watched it break up and melt away. Describing the freezing and melting of Manasarovar Lake, he employs a variety of colourful metaphors: 'The white ice-garment on the Holy Lake presents a fine and beautiful spectacle of a huge Bengali sari with broad blue borders at the edges.'

As Pranavananda points out, this region is the point of origin for four great rivers that define the Himalaya—the Indus and the Tsang Po, which becomes the Brahmaputra, as well as the Sutlej and the Karnali. Travelling through Western Tibet, much of which is arid steppes, I became aware of the presence of water in a way that I had never fully understood before. Wherever there was a small stream or marshy patch, the colours changed from dusty browns to shades of green and bright-hued flowers. Herds of kiang (wild asses), pairs of gazelle, marmots and birds that had migrated here for the summer—black-necked cranes, eagles and bar-headed geese—were all drawn to the water just as we had been. It was almost as if the accumulation of moisture from melting snow not only fostered diverse and vibrant forms of life but also sustained the mountains themselves, cladding their slopes with ice, polishing their eroded features and irrigating their foundations. The natural history of the Himalaya is as much a legacy of water as it is of rock. In concert with sunlight and air these lifeless elements nurture a vast array of living species.

◆

While the Indus and the Brahmaputra provide the parenthetical limits of the Himalaya, dozens of other major rivers channel through the mountains. In the west are the great arteries of the Punjab—the Chenab, Ravi, Sutlej and Beas—all of which join the Indus before draining into the Arabian Sea. The Yamuna and its tributary, the Tons, mark the divide where waters flow eastward into the Ganga and on to the Bay of Bengal. Most Himalayan rivers have their sources on the southern face of high ranges but a few, like the Karnali and the Sutlej, originate to the north in Tibet and penetrate the main thrust of the mountains. Many emerge out of glaciers while others descend from high altitude lakes or wetlands and a few are fed by perennial springs. But ultimately, wherever their source, all of these waterways depend on the monsoon flowing out of the clouds.

In Himalayan legends and lore the crossing of rivers is a momentous event, a passage from one region to another, or from one life into the next. When the Macedonian invader Alexander entered India in 326 BCE he successfully crossed the Indus, Chenab and Ravi but when he came to the Beas (which he called Hyphasis) his army refused to go any further. Alexander built altars and performed sacrifices on the riverside but he could not persuade his men from turning back and ultimately the army retreated before reaching the Ganga. According to Alice Albinia in her book, *Empires of the Indus: The Story of a River*, the Kalash tribe in Chitral, who trace their ancestry to Alexander's army, still perform animal sacrifices beside rivers and pray for safe crossings and protection from floods. Albinia also quotes the Chinese pilgrim Xuanzang in 645 CE who wrote: 'The River Sin-tu [Indus] is pure and clear as a mirror... Poisonous dragons and dangerous spirits live beneath its waters. If a man tries to cross the river carrying valuable gems, rare flowers and fruits, or above all, relics of the Buddha, the boat is engulfed by waves.'

Before modern bridges were built, river crossings were always dangerous and fraught with anxiety. Fording Himalayan streams can be a terrifying experience and rustic bridges made of logs, twigs, ropes and vines don't make it any easier. Anyone who has been ferried across rivers that flow out of the mountains can't help but be aware of the risks involved. At the same time, most Hindus and Buddhists realize that these flowing waters will ultimately carry away their mortal remains. Despite the sanctity of rivers, the swift currents evoke a sense of existential dread. More than monsters and serpents that may swim in their depths it is an awareness of the fluid divide between life and death that arouses primal fears.

Rivers serve as natural boundaries that divide the land into distinct ecological, political, cultural, linguistic and ethnic areas. For the most part, Himalayan rivers flow north to south, while the arc of the mountains runs south-east to north-west. This provides a rough grid that helps map out different regions, with unique altitudinal bands that support different species of plants and wildlife, ranging from semi-tropical forests and grasslands along the foothills to temperate and alpine zones. Each river changes as it descends from swift, turbulent rapids and waterfalls to languid currents and pools.

Moving from east to west, the Himalaya curve from lower to higher latitudes, which affects everything from the distribution of moths and butterflies to the size of glaciers. Though birds have little respect for borders, ornithologists have determined certain dividing lines for avian species. Robert L. Fleming, Sr. and Jr., the father and son team who published the landmark *Birds of Nepal* in 1976, have observed:

> The Kali Gandaki River in central Nepal emerges as a very distinct breaking point in bird distributions. Eastern birds including the Brown Parrotbill, Golden-Breasted Tit Babbler, Rufous-bellied Shrike Babbler and the Blood Pheasant extend only as far west as the Annapurnas. Conversely, western birds that reach Dhaulagiri and apparently no further east are the Simla Black Tit, Spot-Winged Black Tit, White Throated Tit, Missel Thrush, White-cheeked Nuthatch and the Eurasian Nuthatch. Thus, virtually in the center of Nepal, and also in the center of the 2557 kilometer (1,600 mi.) Himalayan arc, we find a fairly narrow region of considerable species change.

Himalayan streams support many different forms of life, from fish and other aquatic creatures to birds and insects, amphibians, reptiles and mammals. These riverine species are as much a part of the streams themselves as the submerged boulders that shape the current or the vegetation that takes root at the water's edge.

Crested kingfishers with pied plumage frequent Himalayan rivers, hovering over a ruffled current before plunging after a minnow beneath the surface. Spotted forktails dart through dappled light, drawn to the moist shadows and still pools of forest streams. Their long, bifurcated tails wag up and down as they perch on rocks. As restless as the forktails are white-capped redstarts that flit from stone to branch and back again, flying low over the water in short, swift forays. Their white Gandhi caps and a red flash on the rump are a vivid contrast to the drab feathers of a brown dipper that skims the water and dives beneath the surface in search of nymphs and other insects. Its bullet-shaped body is designed to plunge into rapids and its feathers are particularly dense to keep it dry. Similar to the American water ouzel, it has an extra, transparent eyelid that allows it to see underwater. Dippers seem impervious to cold, alighting on ice-covered stones near the snout of a glacier and disappearing into freezing meltwater.

Different species of fish populate the rivers at various elevations. Slower-moving bottom feeders like kalabans and goonch lie upon the riverbed and lurk in deeper pools. Sometimes mistakenly described as 'fresh-water sharks' because of their menacing features and sharp teeth, goonch (*Bagarius yarrelli*) are a giant catfish and grow as large as 100 kilograms. A muddy green colour they appear to have no scales, and their brutish faces are whiskered with barbels. Heavy-bodied, with short, flimsy tails, goonch can negotiate rapids but are more at home in sluggish water, feeding on smaller fish and frogs. Because of their weight and an ability to wedge themselves beneath submerged rocks, goonch are disdained by anglers who often cut the line if they hook a goonch rather than try to play the fish. Fatty, yellow flesh with a greasy texture makes them almost inedible. Unlike goonch, kalabans (*Bangana dero*) won't strike at a lure or baited hook and are never caught with fly or spinning tackle, except when foul-hooked. Village fishermen catch them with nets, or strings of horsehair nooses cast across the current.

Trout are not a native species, though many Himalayan streams and lakes have been stocked with both brown and rainbow trout brought in from Europe and America. The so-called Indian trout is not a salmonid but *Barilius bola*. It has the same tapered shape and speckled pattern as a trout, and takes a fly or spinner without hesitation. I remember fishing on the Song River as a boy, when a swarm of these fish suddenly started to bite in a feeding frenzy. Within ten minutes two of us had landed a dozen each. The snow trout (*Schizothorax richardsonii*) is also a trout only in name. Found in Kashmir's high rivers it is now a threatened species, mostly because it has been eaten by exotic salmonids, introduced from abroad.

But among sport fishermen in India only one species really matters— the mahseer (*Barbus tor*). Powerful and aggressive, the mahseer has a bulky head, thick lips and large scales that vary in colour from dull green to bright gold. Several subspecies are found in different parts of India. The largest mahseer ever caught weighed in at 43 kilograms in the southern waters of the Kabini, near Mysore. Himalayan fish tend to be smaller but can exceed 30 kilograms in the Ganga and other large rivers. Anglers have celebrated the mahseer as a piscatorial prizefighter and champion of Indian rivers. As Henry Sullivan Thomas, author of *The Rod in India,* wrote: 'I venture to say from experience that an energetic Mahseer telegraphs such an enlivening thrill of pleasurable excitement up the line, down the rod, and through the wrist and arm, to the very heart of the man who has got well fixed, that it makes his pulse beat quicker, and is altogether as good as a tonic to him.'

◆

In a lifetime of journeys up and down Himalayan rivers, I have bathed in the freezing source of the Pindar, below its glacier in Kumaon, and soaked in hot springs along the Parbati in Kullu. As a boy of eight, I almost drowned in the Ganga, before I learned how to swim. Later, I went on to fish those same waters. While fording innumerable streams, some rose only to my ankles, while others threatened to wash me away. During a monsoon trek to Gaumukh, one of the streams we crossed was so shallow that I could step from stone to stone, without getting my feet wet. By the next day, when we returned, the water flowed above our waists and we could hear boulders thundering beneath the surface, swept down by its swollen current. I have drunk from the Indus, Tsang Po, Kali, Sutlej, Yamuna, Bhagirathi, Mandakini, Alakananda and the Dudh Kosi, as well as countless unnamed springs that join these waters. Most of the pollution in Himalayan rivers occurs downstream, after they debouch onto the plains, where raw sewage and industrial effluents from cities and towns are pumped directly into the current. Nevertheless, with growing settlements in the mountains and tourist or pilgrim traffic, even the headwaters of these rivers are now tainted with poisons and filth.

Flowing water is an object of worship in most parts of the Himalaya and there are many ceremonies and rites associated with Himalayan rivers. Hindus perform pind pujas or daans to ensure that their ancestors, whose ashes have been swept away by the current, are not tormented in the afterlife. Devotees bathe at sacred confluences, especially during auspicious festivals like Makar Sankranti and the twelve-year cycle of the Kumbh Mela.

One of the most unusual river rituals occurs in Jaunpur every summer, an annual fishing festival called the Maun Mela. Just before the monsoon arrives in June, men from villages on both sides of the Aglar River gather in an open field 6 kilometres upstream from its confluence with the Yamuna. Surendra Pundeer, a historian and folklorist from the region, explains that the tradition goes back to the time of the maharajas of Tehri Garhwal who gave the people of Jaunpur a special dispensation to fish without permits one day of each year.

As with most festivals in the hills, drummers gather crowds as a throbbing tempo echoes between the ridges. Different villages are assigned to collect the leaves and bark of timru (*Zanthoxylum armatum*), also known as tejbal, a thorny shrub that grows in the Lower Himalaya and is used as a medicine and spice. Timru has anaesthetic properties and numbs a person's mouth in the case of toothache. For the Maun Mela, timru is dried and crushed into a powder then stored in gunnysacks. Men dance to the rhythm of the drums and get ready for the festivities by stripping down to their shorts and equipping themselves with mesh bags to hold fish. Each of the participants has his own get-up and gear, some carrying nets and other devices to snag the fish. Most are barefoot though a few wear canvas shoes.

After half an hour the dancing becomes increasingly frenzied as the drums beat louder until suddenly the villagers rip open the bags of timru powder and throw these into the Aglar. A cloud of green dust fills the air. Being the dry season, the river is less than a metre deep and only 4 to 5 metres wide, forming long pools that descend into rapids. The timru powder quickly turns the clear water the colour of tea. Between 200–300 men dash downstream, some plunging into the river while others race further on to take up position, reaching under submerged boulders and logs, anywhere a fish might hide.

The timru powder stuns all forms of life in the water and as the toxic infusion works its way downriver hordes of villagers follow in its wake, collecting fish that float to the surface. Most of these are no more than 15 centimetres long and many are fingerlings. Frogs, crabs, snakes, snails and other small creatures are all affected as the chemical numbs their senses. In the clamour and confusion it is difficult to identify species but many of the fish are tiny mahseer, as well as a number of bottom feeders such as loaches. With a mouth like a tiny suction cup, the loach attaches itself to rocks to keep from being swept away by the river. A few struggle and slip out of the men's hands but most are unconscious. To keep up with the discoloured current, the men scramble over each other, wading frantically or leaping from rock to rock.

The Maun Mela ends about 5 kilometres downstream, close to the Yamuna confluence. Here the women are waiting, gathered together in groups on a terraced expanse of fallow fields. As the men arrive, splashing downriver and picking up the last few fish, their mothers, sisters, wives and daughters have already lit fires and are cooking rice. Stumbling ashore, the men are soaking wet and out of breath. The festival concludes with a feast during which the fishermen compare the number and size of their catch along with the bruises they've earned.

Traditions like this raise contentious questions about culture and conservation. The wholesale poisoning of fish in a river, particularly minnows and fry that aren't even eaten, destroys a whole generation of aquatic creatures, though the fishermen insist that timru only stuns them and those that escape will revive. Other fish from upstream and down will repopulate this stretch of the Aglar during the monsoon, but there is no question that a large number are wiped out in the space of two or three hours. It isn't clear what long-term effects timru may have on the river but they aren't likely to be beneficial. Other methods of killing fish, such as dynamite, are illegal and occasionally prosecuted by the forest department but as a part of Jaunpur's culture, the Maun Mela continues without sanctions though some voices have been raised in protest to stop this aquatic sacrifice.

While the fishing festival on the Aglar is unique, at other places, such as temple ghats along the Ganga in Rishikesh and Hardwar or Renuka Lake in Himachal Pradesh, fish are protected and revered. Pilgrims feed them in a ritual of devotion, recognizing both the transience and constancy of water, a sacred environment containing and supporting many forms of life.

chapter 13

RAM GANGA

Two rivers that remain in my memory from childhood are the Lidder in Kashmir with willows draped over its banks and the Parbati in Kullu overshadowed by groves of deodar trees. But of all the Himalayan streams I've known, the most beautiful is the Ram Ganga, which flows through Corbett National Park. Near the forest rest house at Gairal, it leaves the foothills of Kumaon and empties into the Patlidun, a relatively open valley that lies between the Shivalik Hills and the first range of the Himalaya. In the late 1960s a dam was built at Kalagarh and the Ram Ganga backs up into a broad reservoir, flooding a large area of the Patlidun, drastically reducing open grasslands that once supported a wide variety of wildlife ranging from hog deer and elephants to tiger.

Upstream from the park headquarters at Dhikala, the Ram Ganga remains much as it was when I was a boy. In winter, our family often booked a rest house for a fortnight and camped along its banks, the water so clear that the rocks and pebbles beneath its surface seemed magnified. So were the fish, particularly schools of mahseer that faced upstream like tapered shadows. One of my early memories is of witnessing the chilwa run on the Ram Ganga, a shimmering ribbon of tiny fish like a stream of quicksilver flowing against the current, as far upstream and down as the eye could see. The migration of chilwa (*Chela cachius*) was once a common sight in North Indian rivers but with the building of dams and irrigation channels as well as other disruptions, it has become a rare occurrence.

Without the river, the foothills of Corbett Park could not support its diversity of species and without the surrounding forests the Ram Ganga would not have its pristine character. Named after Jim Corbett, the British hunter-naturalist and author of the bestseller, *Man-Eaters of Kumaon*, who was born nearby in Nainital, the park protects one of the few unspoiled stretches of Bhabar and Terai that girdle the lowest elevations of the Himalaya. Until the beginning of the twentieth century, this belt of jungle remained uninhabited, largely because of the prevalence of malaria. Only certain tribal communities, like the Tharus of Nepal, were immune to mosquito-born fevers that made this region treacherous, particularly in summer. Corbett's family owned a farm to the east of the park and most of his books were set in this terrain, along the lower margins of the mountains. He fished in the Ram Ganga and many other streams that flow through the foothills of Kumaon. As an interlude to his man-eater adventures, Corbett included a chapter, 'Fish of My Dreams', in which he describes a day on an unnamed river, very likely the Ram Ganga. With evocative detail, he recounts how he caught a large mahseer, estimated at 22 kilograms but as he reflects:

> The weight of the fish is immaterial, for weights are soon forgotten. Not so forgotten are the surroundings in which the sport is indulged in. The steel blue of the fern-fringed pool where the water rests a little before cascading over rock and shingle to draw breath again in another pool more beautiful than the one just left—the flash of a gaily coloured kingfisher as he breaks the surface of the water, shedding a shower of diamonds from his wings as he rises with a chirp of delight, a silver minnow held firmly in his vermilion bill—the belling of a sambhar and the clear tuneful call of the chital apprising the jungle folk that the tiger, whose pugmarks show wet on the sand where a few minutes before he crossed the river, is out in search of his dinner. These are things that will not be forgotten and will live in my memory, the lodestone to draw me back to that beautiful valley, as yet unspoiled by man.

Growing up in the Himalaya, I enjoyed a privileged childhood but of all the natural wonders we experienced, our visits to Corbett Park were among the most memorable. Staying at Gairal or Sarapduli forest rest houses, the river was our playground. Today, the park authorities forbid swimming in the Ram Ganga and after a British birdwatcher was killed by a tiger in 1985, tourists are not permitted to venture out on foot and are only allowed to tour the park by jeep. Fishing too has been banned.

We had none of these restrictions and during our visits to Corbett Park my brothers and I spent most of our time in the water, riding air mattresses and inner tubes down the rapids and diving off rocks into deep pools. The only animals that worried us were elephants but, for the most part, they kept their distance. In the early mornings or late afternoons, we would drive out to see what deer and other wildlife could be spotted but the rest of the day was centred on the river. After dark, we retreated into the rest house and ate dinner by the light of candles and kerosene lanterns, hearing the night sounds of the forest, the sawing of leopards, the ticking of nightjars and the eerie cries of jackals.

The river was full of life, not only fish, but crocodiles too that sunned themselves on the sand. These prehistoric beasts were shy and never threatened us. Most of them were muggers, which grow more than 4 metres in length, with broad reptilian heads. There were gharial too, a larger species with long, narrow jaws and a bulbous nose. Smaller, but more like dragons, were monitor lizards that grew up to a metre long. The river is also home to pythons and other reptiles or amphibians, large and small.

Along the banks of the Ram Ganga, particularly near deep pools where the water was still and dark, we would find skeletons of fish, mostly goonch with heavy wedge-shaped skulls. These had been killed by otters and dragged out onto the shore where other scavengers helped pick the bones clean. Often, I watched otters playing in the shallows, their sleek, graceful bodies and long tails moving with an undulating swiftness both in the current and on land, though they seemed most at home in water. Their webbed feet marked the sand, along with so many other animal prints—the heart-shaped hooves of chital, or axis deer, the larger sambar and smaller barking deer, or the clustered cloven prints of a sounder of wild boar. We kept a sharp lookout for the round disc-like impressions of wild elephants' feet, where they crossed the Ram Ganga.

Over the years, I absorbed the river's lore with stories of places like 'Champion's Pool', a favourite fishing spot near Sarapduli, named after F. W. Champion, a contemporary of Corbett and one of the first photographers to take pictures of Indian wildlife in the jungle. One evening, returning to Gairal bungalow after fishing until dusk, I made my way along the river in the dark, guided by memory and hearing the shrill alarm calls of chital all around. Whether they were spooked by me or some other predator, I couldn't be sure, but I was glad to see the amber glow of the kerosene lantern and hear the screen doors of the rest house clap shut behind me.

In the spring of 1980, I made one of my last visits to Corbett Park before the rules were changed. Early one morning, I had gone upstream from Gairal to fish a stretch of water above the crocodile pool. The winter sun had yet to penetrate the valley and a thin gauze of mist lay over the water like muslin. Birds were calling from either shore, the high-pitched crowing of red junglefowl, and gaggles of 'seven sisters' babblers all speaking at once, as well as raucous treepies and the shrill shrieks of woodpeckers both pied and flame-backed.

The rest of our group was still asleep as I slipped out of the rest house. Wading through dew-soaked grass, vaulting over a fallen tree and crossing the sandy shoulder of the river where it turned at right angles, ripples pleating its surface, I saw a tawny fish-owl take flight from a dead branch but there was no other movement, besides the flowing water. Shadows draped the jungle and while the sky had brightened to the point where the last stars were fading, it was still too early to peer into the dark current, which slid past me as the night drained away with the dawn. Though alert and attentive, I wasn't afraid. Daybreak in the forest is always reassuring. My plan was to reach a pool half an hour's walk upstream, where a couple of days before I had seen a huge mahseer basking near the foot of a cliff at a bend in the river.

By the time I got within sight of the cliff, sunlight was striking the ridges above and the dappled grey shadows of the jungle had turned into a kaleidoscope of greens from bright bamboo and haldu trees to the darker foliage of lantana and sal. In one hand, I was carrying my spinning rod. A box of lures rattled in the pocket of my shorts. Tempted to try a few casts, I stopped to study the water. Suddenly, I noticed something in the middle of the river, a round object 50 metres away, coming at an angle downstream in my direction. It took me several seconds to realize that a tiger was swimming across the Ram Ganga towards me, leaving a V-shaped wake.

My immediate impulse was to run for cover but the closest trees were 100 metres away. Along the riverbank lay several huge rocks, half-buried in the sand. I wasn't sure if the tiger had seen me, though he probably had, but rather than try to dash downriver and escape, I crouched behind a boulder. Moments later, the enormous cat emerged from the Ram Ganga, roughly 10 metres from where I was hiding. Peering around the rock, I could see him take a few steps forward then shake himself vigorously, spraying water in all directions. Ignoring me, the tiger strode on up the riverbank, eventually vanishing into the trees. When I finally stood up, after several breathless minutes, I crept forward and examined his pugmarks in the sand, the damp impressions of massive paws. I also noticed that the boulder, which had given me shelter, was spattered with drops of water the tiger had shaken off his fur. Mixed with the flood of terror was a sense of exhilaration at having been so close to this wild and beautiful creature, at home in the jungles surrounding the Ram Ganga.

chapter 14

A LOST RIVER

As we consider the future of the Himalaya and the ever-changing features of these mountains, it is important to remember that one of the great rivers of the past has vanished. In ancient texts there are references to the Ganga as well as the Indus and its tributaries. The Brahmaputra too is identified in scripture and sacred lore. But another Himalayan river called the Saraswati is also mentioned, which has puzzled scholars and geographers because it no longer exists. This elusive stream flows through the pages of Indian literature and mythology without beginning or end. The goddess Saraswati, who embodies its waters, is the patron deity of learning, knowledge and literature. She is listed as one of India's seven sacred rivers, each of which is associated with a female deity.

The Rig Veda contains a hymn to Saraswati, translated by Wendy Doniger, that invokes her maternal blessings as a life-giving source: 'Your inexhaustible breast, Sarasvati, that flows with the food of life, that you use to nourish all that one could wish for, freely giving treasure and wealth and beautiful gifts—bring that here for me to suck.'

In his *Secret of the Veda,* Sri Aurobindo writes, 'Saraswati means, "she of the stream, the flowing movement", and is therefore a natural name both for a river and the goddess of inspiration.' In Max Müeller's translation of the Vedic hymn Saraswati 'goes on pure from the mountains as far as the sea'. But in other accounts her waters fall from the Himalaya and are 'lost in the sands of the desert'. Echoing this, the Mahabharata contains a story of the Brahmin sage Utathya, whose wife is carried away by Varuna, god of the sky, oceans and rivers. Utathya becomes so enraged with Varuna, he curses the river: 'Saraswati, disappear into the deserts, and let this land, deserted by thee, become impure.'

A number of interpretations and explanations have been offered for the disappearance of the Saraswati including the most popular theory that it went underground and is now a subterranean stream that joins the Ganga and Yamuna at Allahabad. The meeting of their waters is often referred to as 'triveni', meaning the confluence of three rivers. Some scholars have assumed that the Saraswati is a purely metaphorical stream, a poetic evocation of sacred geography in which her waters represent an inner current that inspires and cleanses our souls even as we submerge ourselves in the Ganga to wash away our mortal sins.

Geographical quests for the Saraswati have led many to believe that this river may have originally flowed through what is now Haryana, Rajasthan and Gujarat, parts of which are arid wasteland. In Pehowa village, near Kurukshetra, there is a Saraswati temple with a stagnant tank of water, where the Pandavas are believed to have worshipped their ancestors. Looking at a map of India, it would appear that the Rann of Kutch, a broad delta of desert and salt marshes that extends into the Arabian Sea, could once have been the mouth of a river that flowed 200 kilometres south-east of the Indus. This hypothesis remained in the realm of speculation until scientists began to look down on the earth from space.

Satellite imagery has revealed evidence of a 'palaeochannel' flowing out of the Himalaya, where an extinct river clearly entered the plains of North India. The location is east of Chandigarh near the foothills of Sirmur, below the royal capital of Nahan. The remnants of the lost river match the course of two seasonal streams called the Ghaggar and Markanda that pass through the Shivalik Hills. Coincidentally, the Markanda is the site of important archeological excavations near the village of Suketi, where fossils of prehistoric beasts like Stegodons and an ancestor of man, *Sivapithecus,* were unearthed.

While the evidence is convincing that a substantial river once flowed out of the mountains, its origins remain unclear. The most plausible explanation is that the Sutlej and the Yamuna once followed a very different course than they do today. Instead of veering off in opposite directions they came together after leaving the Himalaya and their combined currents cut through the Shivalik Hills and carried on across north-western India to the Arabian Sea. Driving through the Sirmur region, the landscape can be disorienting because the streams and dry riverbeds that flood in the monsoon diverge in opposite directions.

Historically, it was not unusual for Himalayan rivers to change course once they left the mountains, particularly in the days before dams and canals regulated their flow. For instance, the Kosi, which emerges from central Nepal into the plains of Bihar, has shifted westward almost a 150 kilometres over a period of less than three centuries. This was caused by flooding and siltation during heavy monsoons. Several theories have been advanced for the Sutlej and Yamuna's change of direction, including the gradual elevation of the Himalaya, earthquakes, and climate change. More than likely, it could be a combination of all three.

Whether the Saraswati is an extinct river or an ongoing myth, her stories remind us of the fickle, fragile nature of Himalayan watersheds. A benevolent goddess who takes the form of a celestial stream, she comes down from the mountains in seasonal torrents, bearing a rich mother lode of silt. Yet, on a more immediate level, the disappearance of the Saraswati is an ominous warning to those who believe that rivers are eternal. As glaciers and wetlands disappear and weather patterns change, how many other Himalayan streams may vanish?

III

FLORA HIMALENSIS
The Power of Vegetation

chapter 15

EXILED BY ICE

Of all the Himalayan migrations, surely the most persistent and pervasive must be the march of plants, shrubs and trees, advancing and retreating over hundreds of millennia, with the ebb and flow of glaciers. Since the end of the last ice age, coniferous and deciduous forests have gradually climbed the slopes they abandoned millions of years ago, pushing back to reclaim territory once buried under snowfields and glaciers. While a number of species were wiped out by successive tides of ice, others simply withdrew to lower altitudes until climatic conditions rebounded.

When warmer temperatures returned and the snow line ascended, these species reestablished themselves at higher and higher elevations, populating distinct botanical bands that we recognize today from sub-tropical jungles to temperate forests and on up to sub-alpine and alpine zones, where meadows of herbaceous plants extend beyond the treeline. Above these distinct strata of foliage lies the 'dead zone' of ice and rock, a stark reminder of the age of glaciation.

The common perception of an ice age is a continuous period of sub-zero temperatures that buries the land under snow and ice. In fact, the Pleistocene was an unsettled era of more than 2.5 million years during which Himalayan glaciers advanced and retreated, while the monsoon grew stronger and weaker. Scientists generally agree that the glacial maximum ended 10–11,000 years ago. What followed has been a gradual period of global warming during which the Himalaya emerged from a deep freeze. Even after the Pleistocene, there have been several sustained dips in temperature that led to the advance of Himalayan glaciers though nothing on the scale of the earlier period, when a vast carapace of ice extended from Namche Barwa to Nanga Parbat and the dead zone lay 2,000 metres lower than its present elevation.

Seeing the mountains as they are today, covered by an abundance of life forms and diverse communities of plants and trees, the immediate question arises: How did Himalayan flora regenerate after thousands of centuries of glaciation that would have killed off previous generations of plants? Field biologists like Georg Miehe have spent their entire careers searching for answers, gathering everything from ancient pollen samples to the charred remains of prehistoric forest fires. Miehe's *Flora of Nepal* and *Nepal: An Introduction to the Natural History, Ecology and Human Impact of the Himalayas,* co-edited with Colin Pendry, are the most comprehensive botanical and environmental studies of the Himalaya conducted in recent years. By studying recent flash floods or other natural disasters and the species of plants that quickly take root on barren, unstable surfaces, Miehe and his colleagues are able to hypothesize about environmental changes long ago, connecting geomorphology to species distribution. 'Giant rockslides are another feature of the Himalayan disequilibrium,' he writes. 'Their locally devastating impacts on biodiversity are obvious, but it is possible that they may explain disjuncts of poorly dispersing species found on both sides of deep antecedent gorges.'

The first species to return, after the mountains were scoured of life, would have been lichens, liverworts and mosses, similar to those that appear on the rocks today with the onset of the monsoon. This spreading mantle of green that covers stonewalls and cliffs as soon as the summer rains begin, makes it easy to imagine how life regained a roothold on sterile moraine, as temperatures rose and the Himalaya came out of their frigid hibernation.

The monsoon, which stretches from June through September, elicits greenery out of the hardest, least fertile surfaces. Where winter cold and summer heat have left the rocks barren, rain and mist revive tiny spores that are carried by the wind and lie like fine dust in crevices and declivities. These primitive plants have shallow roots with filaments thinner than the finest hairs, clinging to rough surfaces. In most cases, they draw moisture from the air rather than soil. Yet within a few weeks of the monsoon's arrival mosses and other bryophytes form a plush carpet, several millimetres thick, that hides the rocks beneath. Sometimes it seems as if the minerals themselves have turned into moss.

These are the earliest botanical taxa that started to appear on earth 470 million years ago, long before the Himalaya came into being. The shape and form of liverworts and mosses is often too minuscule for observation by the human eye. Species are often identified using microscopes and dyes that reveal their intricate structure. Ferns followed mosses, just as they do in the monsoon season, equally adept at finding somewhere to grow on a vertical plane and quickly covering the most unyielding ground in verdant profusion. While only a limited number of fossilized mosses remain, ferns have a more rigid structure and lend themselves to transferring botanical shapes to stone. Stencilled by time on sedimentary layers of hardened mud and silt their unfurled fronds leave neat impressions, as if preserved between the pages of a collector's album.

The highest plants in the Himalaya offer clues regarding the first flowering species to colonize these mountains. According to Oleg Polunin and Adam Stainton's *Flowers of the Himalaya,* both *Stellaria decumbens,* a variety of stitchwort and *Arenaria bryophylla,* a sandwort, are found as high as 6,100 metres. These plants look like mosses, with small, tightly packed leaves that form compact cushions growing close to the ground. They survive for months beneath layers of snow.

To understand the process of botanical regeneration that followed the last ice age, it is important to remember that the Himalaya form an arc from east to west that also curves northward from roughly 29 degrees latitude at Namche Barwa to just over 35 degrees at Nanga Parbat. During the Pleistocene the impact and extent of glaciation would have been much more severe and prolonged in the Western Himalaya than in the east, where a number of species could have survived in relatively warmer foothills and valleys.

Even today, change is constantly occurring in plants as they adapt to evolving environmental conditions. Though it may take thousands of years for a split to occur and a new botanical species to emerge, plants continually adjust to climate, soil conditions and other forms of life around them. Botanist Maharaj Pandit explains how plants have transitioned over time: 'The biological diversity, established during the Miocene-Pliocene epochs, was subsequently reshuffled during Pleistocene glaciation. A period of prolonged glaciation ensued, which forced the displacement of several plant taxa to lower elevations and common habitats, facilitating genetic exchanges, among hitherto isolated plant populations.'

Ascending Himalayan valleys and ridges, we often think of birches as the 'last' trees standing before the snow takes over, like resolute sentries guarding the timberline, but from another perspective these are the 'first' trees, because they represent the uppermost reaches of the forest. For this reason birches are often referred to as a 'pioneer species' because they go before others and establish their presence at the outer limits of climate change. Unfortunately, in places like Bhojbasa (birch camp) in the Bhagirathi Valley near Gaumukh, where a grove of birches once flourished a few hundred metres from the snout of the glacier, these inveterate pioneers have been destroyed by religious tourism, cut and burned to warm pilgrims and ascetics.

Bhojpatra, the Hindi name for birches, comes from a legend about Raja Bhoj, the young heir to a Himalayan throne, whose uncle was trying to usurp his kingdom. The prince wrote a poignant letter on birchbark, pleading his case so persuasively that the uncle and his soldiers changed their minds and allowed Raja Bhoj to ascend the throne. Traditionally, the papery bark has been used for manuscripts including copies of the Upanishads penned in Kashmir. It is also used to make parasols that pilgrims carry during the Raj Jat Yatra pilgrimage of Nanda Devi. On a more prosaic level, herdsmen and villagers construct the inner ceilings of thatch huts out of birchbark. It is also used to line pits for storing potatoes and other root vegetables in winter. In northern Pakistan, a traditional delicacy is prepared by wrapping packets of butter in birchbark, which are then buried underground for several years. Dug up on special occasions like weddings, the strong cheese produced is sprinkled on food as a flavouring. The usefulness of birchbark is reflected in its Latin name, Betula utilis. Unfortunately its utility has also led to over-exploitation. As ice falls back, foliage advances, unless it is hacked and burned by man, which has been the case in many areas on both sides of the Himalayan chain. Soil testing on the Tibetan Plateau has revealed that large areas of birch, rhododendron and conifer forests once covered parts of this region but were burned to the ground years ago, probably by herdsmen who hoped to extend pastures.

On an evolutionary time scale, ten or eleven thousand years is a very short span of natural history, yet the current Holocene age represents a sustained and rapid expansion of life in the Himalaya. Plants, insects, birds and animals, all of which had been pushed out of higher elevations by glaciers into lower refugia were suddenly on the move again as climatic conditions improved, ascending not just from the east but from the south and north as well.

Among the fascinating puzzles of India's natural heritage are relict species of Himalayan plants and wildlife found in the Nilgiri Mountains near the southern tip of the subcontinent. Separated from their northern counterparts by more than 2,000 kilometres, barberry bushes, whistling thrushes and thar, a species of wild goat, continue to flourish in isolation. A number of theories have been put forward to explain this phenomenon. For years, scientists have debated the 'Satpura hypothesis', which suggests that an ancient range of hills in Central India served as a land bridge for species that sought warmer temperatures and more welcoming pastures during periods of glaciation. Some have argued that these relics were essentially exiled or left behind in their South Indian refugium, following the end of the Pleistocene when the Satpura ranges and the Deccan Plateau became hotter and drier.

Travelling from east to west along the Himalayan arc, the total number of species gradually diminishes. Arunachal Pradesh, where the Brahmaputra emerges from the mountains in eastern India, is one of the world's most fertile biodiversity hotspots. On the other hand, northwestern Pakistan, where the Indus separates the Himalaya from the Karakoram and Hindu Kush, has far fewer varieties of plants and wildlife. Much of that region comprises high altitude grasslands and desert.

Life along the two major rivers that border the Himalaya offers a clear contrast in botanical diversity. Both the Brahmaputra and Indus have their sources in the trans-Himalayan region, roughly 50 kilometres apart on either side of Mount Kailas. Flowing westward before turning south through Ladakh and along the edge of Kashmir, the Indus supports narrow margins of greenery on either side. Most of its course passes through areas of rain shadow. In Ladakh the river is fringed by essentially two species of trees—willows and poplars—mostly planted by man. Spring and summer bring about a dramatic flowering of plants and the banks of the Indus are carpeted with an array of alpine herbs but these are short-lived. For eight months of the year, the valley remains as dry and desolate as the barren hills above. Even when it flows out of the mountains near Attock and crosses the plains of Sindh, on its way to the sea, the Indus does not support a substantial variety of flora or fauna, flowing mostly through arid terrain.

Meanwhile, the Tsang Po begins its journey in much the same way, as it crosses trans-Himalayan steppes, but the moment this great river bends south and carves a passage through Eastern Tibet, it enters some of the densest jungles in Asia. Where its gorges penetrate the main thrust of the Himalaya it is so wild and inaccessible that for years geographers failed to connect the Tsang Po to the Brahmaputra, which emerges on the other side. This 'missing link' lay obscured beneath a canopy of foliage so intensely varied and tangled, few travellers could cut their way through.

chapter 16

THE CURIOUS QUESTS OF PLANT HUNTERS

On 29 November 1847, Joseph Dalton Hooker, a thirty-year-old naturalist with dusty brown hair, side whiskers and unruly eyebrows bristling over an inquisitive gaze, stood at the upper end of the Yangma Valley in Sikkim and looked out upon a seemingly barren scene of timeless devastation. The treeline was well below him and most of the botanical specimens he was searching for had all but disappeared except for a few lichens and hardy high-altitude plants sprouting from the shallow soil between the rocks. Hooker's tent was a makeshift patchwork of rough woollen blankets draped over bamboo struts. His bed was made up on a fragrant pallet of juniper boughs. Seven years earlier, Hooker had observed the glaciers of Antarctica from the deck of the HMS *Erebus* and her sister ship the HMS *Terror* but this was the first glacial terrain he had encountered in the Himalaya. What seems to have struck him first was not so much what he could see but that which no longer existed.

> A superb view opened from the top, revealing its nature to be a vast moraine, far below the influence of any existing glaciers, but which at some antecedent period had been thrown across by a glacier descending to 10,000 feet, from a lateral valley on the east flank... I descended to my camp, full of anxious anticipations for the morrow; while the novelty of the scene and its striking character,

the complexity of the phenomena, the lake-bed, the stupendous ice-deposited moraine, and its remoteness from any existing ice, the broad valley and open character of the country, were all marked out as so many problems suddenly conjured up for my unaided solution, and kept me awake for many hours.

Liminal terrain like snow lines has always fascinated botanists because it represents the upper boundaries of life. In these extreme conditions the plants that emerge hold clues to what might have been the first species to colonize the earth. As Hooker noted, the high valleys in Sikkim contained specimens that survived brutal temperatures and a scarcity of water.

In the afternoon, I botanized amongst the moraines, which were very numerous and had been thrown down at right angles to the main valley, which being here very narrow, and bounded by lofty precipices, must have stopped the parent glaciers, and effected the heaping of some of these moraines to at least 1,000 feet above the river... Betweeen the moraines, near my tent, the soil was perfectly level, and consisted of little lake-beds strewn with gigantic boulders and covered with hard turf of grass and sedge, and little bushes of dwarf rhododendron and prostrate juniper, as trim as if they had been clipped. Altogether these formed the most picturesque little nooks it was possible to conceive; and they exhibited the withered remains of so many kinds of primrose, gentian, anemone, potentilla, orchis, saxifrage, parnassia, ampanula, and pedicularis, that in summer they must be perfect gardens of wild flowers.

Hooker was not the first plant hunter to scour the Himalaya for new species. Several others preceded him including William Moorcroft who arrived in India in 1808 as a veterinary surgeon but went on to become one of the earliest Himalayan explorers. He was also known for testing the limits of English syntax. On his first visit to Kashmir, Moorcroft noted:

The horses are small and indifferent; the sheep are plentiful and the mutton is well flavoured; the fat is particularly white. Whether this is owing to any peculiarity in the feed, I shall not undertake to determine; but although it would be very possible to prepare an ample sufficiency of hay for winter fodder, the preference is given to the leaves of certain trees—as the walnut, willow, mulberry, elm, and several others, which are considered much more warming and nutritious than hay, especially for sheep.

With irrepressible curiosity and a scientist's obsession for detail, he goes on to catalogue various forms of forage available in Kashmir and the mountains beyond. One species in particular caught his attention, *Prangos pabularia*, a tall plant with yellow flowers that is dried and kept as fodder. He writes, 'Healthy sheep fed upon Prangos hay are said to become fat in twenty days, and that if fully fed with it for two months, their fatness approaches to suffocation.' He proposed transplanting prangos to Britain where it would convert 'her heaths, and downs, and highlands, into storehouses for the supply of innumerable flocks'. Sadly, Moorcroft's dream died with him. Following his mysterious disappearance and reported death in northern Afghanistan, later contributors to the *Asiatic Journal* added a footnote: 'The seeds sent home by Mr Moorcroft in 1822 lost their vegetating power...'

Hooker's motives in hunting for plants were less practical or commercially driven than Moorcroft's search for fodder. Though he collected quantities of seeds that were shipped back to England and successfully germinated in the nursery beds and hothouses of Kew Gardens, the purpose of Hooker's quest was more to cultivate botanical knowledge and extend the reach of taxonomy.

Not only was Hooker interested in plants; he was fascinated by the Lepchas who are the original inhabitants of Sikkim, an animistic community of mountain dwellers who settled in this region long before the arrival of Buddhists and Hindus. As hunters and gatherers, their indigenous knowledge of botany helped inform Hooker's research and his journals include descriptions of their appearance and customs. Despite his admiration for Lepchas, who served as porters and plant collectors, Hooker's notes are tainted by the patronizing prejudices of the times. 'The Lepcha is the aboriginal inhabitant of Sikkim, and a prominent character in Dorjiling...,' he writes, 'the race to which he belongs is a very singular one; markedly Mongolian in features, and a good deal too, by imitation, in habit; though he differs from his Tibetan prototype, though not so decidedly as from the Nepalese and Bhotanese, between whom he is hemmed into a narrow tract of mountain country, barely 60 miles in breadth.'

A mezzotint of Hooker, surrounded by a party of Lepchas gathering flowers for him to identify and collect, offers a beguiling picture of the naturalist at work. Snowy mountains rise above him, offset by lower ranges and framed by shadowy firs and hemlocks. This image, an etching by William Walker based on a painting by Frank Stone, was obviously drawn from the imaginations of British artists and is a mythological tableau. It depicts a mountainous Eden in which knowledge takes the form of a European gentleman in frock coat and tie, with an oriental turban on his head. The 'native' Lepchas are gentle, half-naked people, dressed in unstitched robes, intently plucking flowers from wild shrubs and trees. Altogether it is a visual parable of botanical science through which floral mysteries are revealed. Hooker sits like an oracle amidst a jungle of Himalayan rhododendrons, which became a horticultural craze in nineteenth century English gardens. This mezzotint would have illustrated the distant origins of those exotic blooms.

Having identified thirty-six species of rhododendrons in Sikkim, twenty-four of which were new to science, Hooker paid tribute to his friends and mentors by naming many of the flowers after them. *Rhododendron Falconeri* honours Hugh Falconer, one of the pre-eminent naturalists of his time. He was superintendent of the Botanical Gardens in Calcutta and hosted Hooker on his arrival in India. Another rhododendron was named after Dr Nathaniel Wallich, a Jewish botanist from Denmark employed by the East India Company, who was the first curator of the Indian Museum in Calcutta and introduced *Rhododendron arboreum* into England. *R. Wallichii* is 'a very distinct and handsome species, worthy to bear the name of one who may justly be called, "*Botanicorum Indicorum facile princeps*",' Hooker writes and of *R. Thomsoni*, 'To this species I give the name of Dr Thomas Thomson, surgeon, H. E. I. C. S. late of the Thibetian mission, son of the learned professor of chemistry of Glasgow University, my earliest friend and companion during my College life and now my travelling companion in the Eastern Himalaya.' Perhaps the most prolific and eye-catching species was named *R. Hodgsoni*. 'Such are the characteristics of this Rhododendron, which I desire to dedicate to my excellent friend and generous host, B. H. Hodgson, Esq. formerly the Hon. East India Company's Resident at the Court of Nepal; a gentleman whose researches in the physical geography, the natural history, especially the zoology, the ethnology, the literature of the people, &c. &c., of the Eastern Himalaya, are beyond all praise.'

Aside from Hooker's *Himalayan Journals* his monumental work was the seven volume *Flora of British India* and the large-format series, lavishly illustrated, *Rhododendrons of Sikkim-Himalaya*. After his sojourn in India, Hooker settled in England and took over the directorship of the Royal Botanic Gardens in Kew from his father, who was also an eminent botanist. Joseph Dalton Hooker married twice. With his first wife, Frances Harriet Henslow, he had five children. Following her death, he married Lady Hyacinth Jardine, with whom he had two sons. Portraits from his later years reveal a sombre, cragged face framed by sideburns as tangled and hoary as the bearded lichens (*Usnea longissima*) that hang from trees in Sikkim. However, a daguerreotype from 1852, the year after he returned from India, shows clean-shaven, pensive features and brooding eyes. Hooker lived a full and varied life, of which only two years were spent in the Himalaya. He was later knighted and received the Founder's Gold Medal from the Royal Geographical Society, among numerous honours. His closest friend and colleague was Charles Darwin, to whom he dedicated the publication of his *Himalayan Journals*. Even in later life, Hooker continued to travel, making journeys to Palestine, Morocco and North America, in search of far-flung botanical specimens.

Above all else, Hooker was an inveterate observer who noted down virtually everything he saw. By his own admission, this was his purpose in life. 'In making excursions as this, it is above all things desirable to seize and book every object worth noticing on the way out: I always carried my note-book and pencil tied to my jacket pocket, and generally walked with them in my hand. It is impossible to begin observing too soon, or to observe too much…'

chapter 17

ARBOREAL COMMUNITIES

Following in Hooker's footsteps, we set off from Yuksam at eight in the morning and pass a stream of schoolchildren heading in the opposite direction, on their way to class. The students' faces register amusement and curiosity as they watch us striding off into the mountains while they prepare to study mathematics, science, Hindi, English, history and geography. Their uniforms—white shirts and ties, tomato-red jumpers and the girls' pleated skirts—are crisply ironed and neatly buttoned. Our paths cross briefly as they amble towards a rapidly evolving future while we venture into a landscape that has scarcely changed over the past millennia.

Accompanying me is my friend and neighbour, Bhrigu Singh, with whom I've shared several Himalayan journeys. We have a common interest in the outdoors and tend to walk at the same pace, which is a good measure of compatibility. Bhrigu's maternal grandmother was the daughter of a Rana ruler of Nepal, Dev Shumsher Jang Bahadur. He occupied the throne for only 144 days and was known as a reformer who abolished debt slavery before escaping into self-exile in 1901 and settling in Mussoorie. On many occasions, particularly in Sikkim, I've been grateful for Bhrigu's company and knowledge of the Nepali language, which I do not speak.

Yuksam is the original capital of Sikkim, where the first Chogyal or Buddhist king received the blessings of three lamas after whom the town is named. The coronation throne is maintained as a shrine inside a sacred grove called Norbugang. Carved out of granite slab, this rustic seat of power is situated beneath an ancient cypress, believed to have sprouted from the walking stick of one of the lamas. Directly opposite the throne stands a chorten containing soil from different parts of Sikkim, a spiritual and political monument that recalls the sovereignty of this mountain kingdom, annexed by India in 1975.

On a hillock above Yuksam lies Dubdi Gompa, the oldest monastery in Sikkim. Damaged by an earthquake in 2011, the main building is under repair when we visit. Stonemasons are chipping away at blocks of granite while artists repaint colourful murals. Sheltered beneath a colonnade of giant cypress trees, with stray dogs asleep on the lawns, Dubdi evokes a peaceful atmosphere of sanctity that many gompas have relinquished to flocks of devotees and tourists. More than the man-made structures, dating back to 1701, the place itself conveys a spiritual aura, as shafts of sunlight pierce a dark canopy of cloud. Beneath a leafy tunnel of oaks and rhododendrons, the cobbled paths are cushioned with moss, leading us into a natural sanctuary where monks escape the material demands of the world and the relentless progress of time. In a nearby shed, young acolytes with shaved heads and maroon robes, instead of school uniforms, learn to recite Tibetan prayers rather than scientific formulae, English grammar and mathematical equations.

Leaving Yuksam we enter Kanchenjunga National Park, trekking along the eastern slope of the valley. In 1849, Hooker followed this route on one of several expeditions. His descriptions of the terrain and diverse botany of this region still serve as an accurate account of the mountains and forests that exist today. The trail from Yuksam to Dzongri, and from there across Kang La into Nepal, has been used for centuries. This is also the path followed by early mountaineering expeditions to Kanchenjunga. As one of the first Europeans to travel this route, Hooker wondered why more people didn't traverse the direct and easily accessible Singalila Ridge. Later, he learned that the valley above Yuksam had been popularized by smugglers who surreptitiously carried loads of rock salt from Tibet over Kang La, to avoid taxation. Instead of being transported by yaks or horses, the contraband was carried by porters, stooping under the weight of 50-kilogram sacks. It seems the remote highlands and dense jungles near Dzongri were not patrolled by the Chogyal's revenue agents.

We are here in the first week of May and the lower stretches are warm and humid, though the higher we climb the cooler it gets. Hooker camped the first night at Bakhim, a small settlement that still exists, though it is nothing more than a few seasonal shacks. The Himalayan Mountaineering Institute in Darjeeling, which conducts climbing and adventure courses nearby, built a lodge at Bakhim but it is now uninhabitable because of huge cracks caused by the same earthquake that damaged Dubdi Gompa. While the region has been closed to permanent settlements since the Kanchenjunga Biosphere Reserve was established in 1977, it has become one of the most popular trekking routes in Western Sikkim.

Justin Lepcha, our guide, was leading a group up to Dzongri when the earthquake, measuring 6.9 on the Richter Scale, struck on 18 September 2011. Returning to Bakhim, he and his clients discovered the path to Yuksam had been swept away in a landslide. Six years later, the scar is still visible though a new trail has been constructed up and over a broad gash of mud and exposed rock that stretches for several hundred metres down to the river. 'One of the men from Bakhim agreed to guide us but we had to cut our way through the jungle,' Justin recalls. 'It was monsoon and leeches were everywhere. It took us ten hours to reach Yuksam.'

Soft-spoken and almost diffident, but with a quiet sense of humour, Justin is proud of his Lepcha heritage though he and his family, who live in Kalimpong, are now Roman Catholics. 'Originally Lepchas had no religion,' he says, though one of the stories Justin tells us is a creation myth in which the first man and woman were formed out of snow, high up on Kanchenjunga. 'It is almost the same as the story of Adam and Eve,' he continues, conflating Lepcha folklore with Christian myths. 'The man and woman lived together in the forest but one day they ate a forbidden fruit and after that…' he gestures vaguely to suggest a sexual encounter. 'They had a son but were afraid that God would punish them for their sin, so they cast the child into the forest.' Later, when God asked them what had happened they denied they had slept together, telling the first lie. The child they abandoned grew up to be a demon. After this the couple went on to have other offspring who became the first generation of Lepchas. Meanwhile, the demon began to torment people until God sent a new god, Tamsang Thing Rum, 'like Jesus Christ, to save the world'. Tamsang Thing Rum came down from the mountains and fought with the demon and killed him, after which the Lepchas cut the demon into tiny pieces, which were scattered throughout the mountains. Each of these fragments turned into mosquitoes, ticks and leeches that still torment the people of Sikkim.

Lepcha folklore assigns gender to everything, including mountains and rivers. One of the most unusual stories, recorded by the anthropologist Geoffrey Gorer, asserts that women originally had genitals on their foreheads like the petals of a flower. However, menstruation made this inconvenient and birds, particularly the red-vented bulbul, known as Mongklyok, were enlisted to help relocate women's vaginas. In recognition of this service, the bulbul has a bright red patch beneath its tail and is permitted to eat freely from the first crops of the year.

Intriguingly, the philosopher George Santayana in his essay, 'The Philosophy of Travel', makes a similar case for the way in which human anatomy, particularly our sexual organs, evolved from plant forms.

The shift from the vegetable to the animal is the most complete of revolutions; it literally turns everything upside down. The upper branches, bending over and touching the ground, become fingers and toes; the roots are pulled up and gathered together into a snout, with its tongue and nostrils protruding outwards in search of food... Meantime the organs of fertility, which were flowers, sunning themselves wide open and lolling in delicious innocence, are now tucked away obscurely in the hindquarters, to be seen and thought of as little as possible.

Altitude and climate dictate reproductive cycles in the mountains as the annual regeneration of plants moves gradually upward in an escalating tide of multi-coloured flowers. The blooming of rhododendrons is like a moveable orgy as the blossoms open labial petals and thrust ardent stamens and pistils, to attract insects or birds that serve as pollinators. The fragrance and nectar that entice an insect into the erogenous depths of a flower is part of nature's seductive stratagems. A rhododendron forest in full bloom possesses a rampant carnality, cloaked in diaphanous mist and layers of shadowy foliage. Even the entwined, flesh-coloured limbs of rhododendrons suggest a passionate embrace, knotted together in orgiastic contortions.

Himalayan forests are complex communities that compete, collaborate and coexist in much the same manner as human society. Even the most casual observer can see how the different strata of foliage function in a hierarchical manner, from violets and primulas at the roots of an oak to the understorey of larger plants such as wild ginger and bamboo. Above this lies a mezzanine level of shorter trees like laurel and cinnamon, then further up are the trunks and branches of forest giants—oaks and conifers, each of which provide scaffoldings for elaborate ecosystems of vines, fungi, mosses, ferns, polypods and orchids. Epiphytic species like *Rhododendron dalhousiae* take root 20 to 30 metres above the ground, drawing nutrients and moisture not from the earth but from a nurturing cradle of branches and soft interstices within decaying bark. Only after ascending through each of these tiers of foliage do we come to the domed canopy of the forest, its leafy crowns arching toward the sun.

On a mountain, most trees grow straight upward regardless of the angle or contours of the ridge. They align themselves with rays of sunlight that fuel photosynthesis. Only when a tree is bent in a storm, or when its roots are dislodged by a landslide or earthquake, does it follow a different trajectory, leaning outward or inward and often falling to the ground. Because level land is scarce in the Himalaya, trees must grow in precarious places, balancing their weight according to the pitch of the slope. As their limbs extend upward and outward in acrobatic manoeuvres, they distribute their weight to compensate for the force of gravity as well as the buffeting of wind and the burden of snow.

Were the Himalaya to be flattened out in the same way we take a crumpled sheet of paper and smooth its wrinkles and folds, the land's surface would spread over more than twice the space these mountains occupy on a map. If all the nappes and geosynclines, subduction zones and recumbent folds were ironed out, the total surface area would extend from the Tibetan Plateau to the outer limits of the Gangetic Plain. For this reason, the density of the forest on a slope is greater than on level ground because the foliage is stacked in order to absorb as much of the sun's energy as possible.

Just as skyscrapers in a city accommodate a larger number of occupants per square metre of plinth area compared to a single-storey suburban home, Sikkim's forests house many more individual plants and trees per acre, tucking and crowding them into ravines and hollows, spurs and saddles. Because everything grows close together, various species must share resources. Most ferns and ground orchids, for instance, die off or become dormant in winter when days are shorter and less sunlight is available. Four to six months later, upon reappearing, they follow a kind of forest etiquette, queuing up as they take their assigned places within the dappled light and shade. Some species of trees, like magnolias and maples, shed their leaves in the fall, allowing shrubs and plants beneath to receive light and warmth during their dormancy. On the other hand, oaks cast off their foliage only as they bud and form new leaves, though in those brief few weeks between loss and renewal, smaller saplings and creepers receive a concentrated dose of sunshine to help them compete. In many ways, forest canopies are like venetian blinds that open or close with the seasons, rationing energy and allowing each species to survive. This also regulates and disperses precipitation and guards against soil erosion. Vital to the well-being of a Himalayan forest are clouds and mist, which ascend and descend from valleys to ridgelines with changing temperatures and wind patterns during the course of a day. These humid vapours penetrate the densest jungles, providing moisture for moss and other aerial species that have no access to water from the earth.

Decay and degradation are as much a part of a vertical ecosystem as the procreation and life cycles of trees and plants. The dead foliage and humus underfoot, along with a multitude of microscopic organisms that feed upon them and break them down into particles of soil, are an essential element in every biome. In 1930, when the British mountaineer, Frank Smythe, accompanied G. O. Dyhrenfurth's international Kanchenjunga expedition, he found the jungles above Yuksam melancholy and unnerving.

> Passing through this magnificent primaeval forest cloaking the Upper Rangit Valley one can forgive the path its vagaries. None of us had ever seen an Amazonian forest, but it can scarcely be finer than the forests that line the trench-like valleys of the Himalaya. Yet, to one who finds pleasure in tramping the windy moors, fells and bens of the North Country, there is something indescribably depressing about such a forest. The dense walls of vegetation on either side of the narrow straggling track and the interlacing canopy of vegetation far above the head shut out the health-giving sunlight and breezes. An awed silence seems somehow to hold in its arms a breathless suspense. There exists undefined menace, suggested perhaps by the dank odours of rotting vegetation. I experienced a feeling of being imprisoned in a vault, and longed to escape into more open places, to breathe air untainted by the miasmal odours of decay.

This was Smythe's initiation into Himalayan climbing, though he would go on to become one of the most successful mountaineers of that era between the two world wars. He had obviously read his Hooker, which later inspired him to write *The Valley of Flowers*, a book in which he describes plant collecting in the Bhyundar Valley of Garhwal.

Sitting at the side of the path below Bakhim, where both Hooker and Smythe must have rested, a century apart from each other, Bhrigu and I look back down the valley towards Yuksam, where the slopes are covered with mixed, broad-leaved forest. From where we sit, several firs and hemlocks are visible, as well as monstrous oaks, each of which have been colonized by dozens of species. Pristine white orchids with fleshy leaves are draped from an elbow on the branch overhead. Bracket mushrooms, like miniature pagodas, have fixed themselves inside a hollow bole. A thick creeper trails up the trunk as if it were an alpinist's rope, offering a leafy belay through the crux of the tree. At the roots of the oak, which are gnarled and exposed, a pair of gold-naped finches search for fallen seeds, the male with a gilded chapeau and the female a ruddy brown. A hoary-bellied squirrel, the colour of dead leaves, scuttles about, its tail bristling in agitation, alongside a plain-backed thrush, whose mottled plumage provides perfect camouflage within the flecked shadows and leaves. Further up the trunk, a hunting party of nuthatches and tits are feeding on insects and seeds while a woodpecker drills beetle larvae out of the trunk with the determination of a dentist performing a root canal. Altogether, this scene is a living reminder that no species survives alone and here at 2,000 metres above sea level in the Eastern Himalaya the checks and balances of life are fully functioning just as they must have been two centuries ago or two millennia before that.

Rhododendrons are by far the most prolific botanical genera in this part of Sikkim, except perhaps for primulas. Trekking in early May, we encounter a profusion of rhododendrons of every size and colour. Below 2,000 metres most of the blooms have withered and gone to seed but as we ascend it feels as if every hundred metres we come upon a different species. Tubular petals of white and cream with delicate freckles give way to yellows and pinks of darker and lighter shades. Scarlet and crimson varieties appear at alternating altitudes, some with drooping blossoms like temple bells and others opening outward like a bouquet of trumpets. The diversity and abundance of flowers continue upward for another 1,200 metres until we reach the top end of the bloom where the pale purple buds of *Rhododendron campanulatum* have yet to open.

Almost as remarkable as the flowers are the interwoven trunks and limbs of the trees, which form natural barricades that make it impossible for large animals, including human beings, to penetrate the jungle. Yaks and ponies along this route are forced to stay on the trail while squirrels and foxes, martens and other small mammals such as musk deer can penetrate these labyrinths with ease. Birds too find sanctuary under shingled parasols of leaves. As we climb to Phedang flocks of nutcrackers and black-capped laughingthrushes appear and disappear around us. Above 3,000 metres much of this region is covered in snow for several months of the year. Rhododendrons are perfectly suited to the seasons for they bend like springs under the weight of the snow. While taller, less compliant species like conifers and birches may lose their branches in a heavy snowfall, rhododendrons suffer little damage, even in a blizzard.

Lepcha folklorist, Lyangson Tamsang, recounts a story about the hierarchy of trees. Originally, the rhododendron was king of the forest, the tallest and most imposing tree with beautiful, regal flowers. This rhododendron king was known as Aetok Koong and his trusted adviser was the silver fir, Daong Shying Koong. Yet, like most Himalayan courtiers, the fir tree conspired to dethrone the rhododendron through trickery and guile. Eventually, Aetok Koong lost his position of power and was reduced to grovelling on the ground, his branches bent and twisted, while the fir rose high above him to become the tallest and straightest of all. Seeing how he had been betrayed by his devious minister, the rhododendron cursed the fir tree, saying that though Daong Shying now reigned over the Himalayan forests, his trunk would always be hollow.

In a groundbreaking study published in the journal *Nature*, Dr Suzanne Simard of the University of British Columbia discovered communication networks in stands of Douglas firs, which she dubbed the 'Wood Wide Web', suggesting the connectivity of trees. This research has been popularized by German naturalist Peter Wohlleben in his bestseller *The Hidden Life of Trees*. He describes how oaks and beeches share information using microscopic fungal filaments, comparing these to fibre-optic Internet cables. 'One teaspoon of forest soil contains many miles of these "hyphae". Over centuries a single fungus can cover many square kilometres and network an entire forest. The fungal connections transmit signals from one tree to the next, helping them exchange news about insects, drought, and other dangers.'

If the forests of Canada and Germany are hard-wired with underground fibres, it is likely that Himalayan forests operate on a similar principle, though it must be far more complex because of the greater diversity of species. Evidence shows that not only trees communicate but plants, shrubs and grasses too. One can hardly imagine the level of silent 'chatter' that pervades a Himalayan jungle. Trekking through a multi-storied forest in Sikkim we appreciate the profound silence and stillness of nature though all around us are wild yet inaudible conversations. As we climb above the treeline onto the high meadows at Dzongri, the chorus of voices changes along with the vegetation. Another community of species takes over, with the fragrant *Rhododendron anthopogon* and *R. setosum*, both stunted shrubs that flower in late summer, along with junipers and cotoneaster, all of which hug the ground.

The lamas of Pemayangtse Monastery in Pelling believe that under the surface of a landscape lies another world of even greater beauty and spiritual significance. They consider the high meadows of Dzongri a beyul or hidden paradise, like Shambala. Every monsoon, around the full moon in August, they hold sacred ceremonies in the monastery's temple to worship the mountain deity, Kanchenjunga. Simultaneously, a delegation of monks are dispatched to Dzongri, where they sit in meditation. One of the lamas told us they were guided by a wild yak. Synchronized to the seasons these auspicious rites are perfumed with the fragrant smoke of burning juniper and rhododendrons. In all their colourful fertility, the meadows reveal a landscape of eternal, organic bliss. The austerities and penance of the monks aspire to visions of this celestial realm and as the lamas sit in meditation, their consciousness opens like the petals of rhododendrons blooming in the mist.

Atop the ridge above Dzongri stand four stone chortens, three of which memorialize the ancient lamas of Yuksam, while the fourth commemorates the first Chogyal of Sikkim. Silhouetted against the mist they look more like a line of boulders than man-made shrines. Higher up, when the clouds separate, the forbidding cliffs of a nearby mountain called Black Kabru rise above the meadows and guard the white-capped ranges beyond, including Kanchenjunga. Here is a landscape full of symbols that pollinate a spiritual imagination. Like an invisible network of fungal fibres, through which a forest or meadow communicates, hidden layers of reality connect us to a secret web of floral dreams.

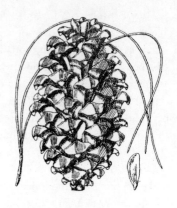

chapter 18

SEEING THE FOREST FOR THE TREES

The cross-section of a massive deodar tree measures close to 3 metres in diameter, as broad as a banquet table. Time has stopped in its rings, a sequence of centuries locked within circular layers of wood. Until 1919, this giant cedar towered above the Tons Valley, in Jaunsar. According to a timeline painted on its trunk, the tree lived for 704 years. When the Qutab Minar was built in Delhi, in 1192, this deodar would have been a sapling.

The Timber Museum at the Forest Research Institute (FRI) in Dehradun also contains splinters of wood from ancient palaces, 2,000 years old, alongside a display on the modern process of pencil-making. All variety of wooden objects can be found here, from household furniture to toys and spindles, demonstrating the versatility of wood and its potential for manufacturing a wide range of products. The museum is testimony to the commercial exploitation of India's forests. The main gallery is panelled with planks of wood from 126 different species of Indian trees ranging in colour and texture from the velvet lustre of Kashmiri walnut to the resolute grain of Burma teak. These are arranged in alphabetical order, beginning with *Abies spectabilis,* an East Himalayan fir and concluding with *Xylocarpus moluccensis,* a species of mangrove found in the tidal flats of the Bay of Bengal. With high, arched ceilings and rows of glass cases containing relics of ancient jungles felled in the name of progress, the museum feels like a mausoleum built for India's forests.

In 1923, the Imperial Forest Service acquired a thousand-acre estate on the outskirts of Dehradun, and constructed a grand edifice to match the magnitude of its dominions. Built on the scale of a maharaja's palace, its main building occupies a plinth area of 6 acres. Among the largest brick structures in the world, it has a neo-Georgian facade of Grecian columns and peaked roofs that front a maze of arched corridors, opening onto a series of inner courtyards and arcades. The lawns in front of the institute stretch for almost a kilometre to the south. To the north rise the foothills of the Himalaya. Both the architecture and the landscaping represent a deliberate statement of expansive, omnipotent power and absolute authority.

The original purpose of the Forest Research Institute (FRI) was to establish scientific methods for planting, protecting and harvesting timber, as well as other forest products. Over the years, that mission has evolved to meet changing priorities, though the FRI remains a remnant of old growth policies imprisoned in a magnificent but moribund structure. Several museums are housed here, including one for silviculture and others for forest pathology, entomology, non-wood forest products, and social forestry. The last of these is a relatively recent concession to engaging local communities in forest management but the message in each of the galleries is the same: the forest department controls and cultivates its lands, protecting them from indiscriminate use by indigenous populations.

On one wall are three large paintings labelled: 'The Evils of Deforestation', 'The Evils of Forest Fires', and 'The Evils of Uncontrolled Grazing'. Each painting crudely illustrates the moralistic dictates of forest management, showing the land denuded and destroyed by forest dwellers and nomadic communities. In the same room dioramas depict the 'correct' methods of felling trees. Prominently displayed on one wall, like an arsenal of medieval weapons, are axes, saws and choppers.

Swarms of bored-looking schoolchildren are herded by their teachers through each of the galleries. The only exhibit that seems to catch their attention is a stuffed tiger, its glass eyes gazing into a shadowy void. Most of the displays are outdated and many exhibits have deteriorated over time, often to a point where they are unrecognizable. In a cabinet devoted to 'drugs and spices' the yellowed label on one specimen indicates that it was 'used in native medicine'. A withered specimen of *Punica granatum*, a common pomegranate, donated a century ago by the divisional forest officer of Rawalpindi West, now part of Pakistan, is captioned by the following text: 'a decoction of the bark is most efficacious for the expulsion of tape-worms'.

Many of the exhibits at the FRI are devoted to diseases and infestations that damage a tree and render it worthless as timber. The pathology museum is full of examples of wood rot and fungal infections. From the perspective of foresters, insects are pests and entomology is limited to the study of insidious species like woodborers that destroy healthy trees by drilling into their trunks. A giant model of a termite, twenty times its normal size, looks like an alien monster. Given the countless species of beetles and other insect larvae that burrow under the bark and feed on the sweet outer rings of a living tree, it seems a losing battle. One display case even contains an old forest department ledger eaten through by termites, the paper crumbling into dust.

Most conservationists today and a few enlightened forest officials recognize the fundamental flaw in the colonial model of forest management that promulgates the wholesale annexation of forest lands and the exclusion of village and nomadic communities. By creating an adversarial relationship between the state forest departments and those people who have been using forest resources for generations, British authorities set in motion a cycle of conflict that continues today.

Commercial deforestation in the Central Himalaya began in the mid-nineteenth century, when Frederick 'Pahari' Wilson made a fortune felling stands of timber in the upper reaches of the Ganga watershed and floating it down the river. A renegade army deserter, Wilson persuaded the Maharaja of Tehri Garhwal, Sudarshan Shah, to grant him a logging concession along the Bhagirathi above Uttarkashi. Having already explored this region, Wilson co-authored a book titled *A Summer Ramble in the Himalayas*. Using the pseudonym 'Mountaineer', he wrote an account of an extended shikar expedition that spanned the Central Himalaya. Referring to himself in the third person he writes, 'It was considered a good morning's work to meet with three or four (musk deer), now that the forests have been thinned; but when Wilson first commenced hunting here he sometimes met with more than a dozen.' During one shikar trek of seventeen days, he killed eleven bharal, eighteen musk deer, two bears and a snow leopard.

After establishing his personal fiefdom at Harsil, near the headwaters of the Ganga, he became known as Raja Wilson and even minted his own coins. He also had a habit of taking the law into his own hands. In one instance, Wilson personally flogged the maharaja's revenue officers for detaining one of his men. After setting up a timber depot near Hardwar, Wilson floated logs down the newly built Upper Ganges Canal. By the time of his death in 1883, this timber baron had become one of the wealthiest

Europeans in North India.

Most of Wilson's fortune came from a single species, *Cedrus deodara*. Its vernacular name, deodar, translates as 'tree of the gods'. Wilson showed little concern for divine associations though he described this species with a combination of awe and greed.

> Its favourite habitat is between 6,000 and 9,000 feet, and here only extensive forests of which are found. It seems to thrive best in a dry rocky soil, and it is wonderful to see the places where some trees take root. In the perpendicular face of a smooth granite rock is a little crevice, into this a seed in some manner finds its way, vegetates, and becomes a large tree, flourishing perhaps for centuries where to appearance there is not a particle of soil, deriving sustenance probably from the rock itself. The cedar grows to a great size, some having been measured with trunks upwards of thirty feet in circumference... The highest cedars attain a height of a hundred feet. The wood is everywhere in the greatest esteem for building purposes, as it is easily worked, almost imperishable, and splits easily into planks, an indispensable requisite in a country where saws are unknown.

Without any concern for sustainable forestry, 'Pahari' Wilson clear-felled stands of virgin deodar near Harsil, where he built himself a palatial home. European travellers at the time remarked with dismay on the wholesale destruction of forests along the Bhagirathi. At the same time, Wilson's approach to indigenous communities in the Himalaya was much more accommodating than the dismissive attitude of forest officers. In fact, Wilson's hunting for musk glands and animal pelts was accomplished in close collaboration with local hunters who were members of the Bajgi community, temple drummers from the village of Mukhba near Harsil. According to his biographer, D. C. Kala, Wilson ended up marrying the sister of one of his shikaris, a woman named Sangrami, who bore him three children and later converted to Christianity, changing her name to Ruth. (Kala dismisses the popular belief that her name was 'Gulabi'.) Wilson also had a longstanding liaison with Sangrami's niece, Raimta, all of which scandalized Anglo-Indian society, though the 'Mountaineer' seems to have been indifferent to colonial mores and propriety.

Surprisingly, despite its 'dominion over palm and pine', Britain did not have a professional forestry service until the second half of the nineteenth century. When colonial authorities in India realized that they needed to scientifically and effectively manage India's timber resources, partly as a result of depredations by freebooters like Wilson, they turned to the Germans. Dietrich Brandis, a lecturer in botany from the University of Bonn, was appointed head of the forest service in Burma in 1856 and went on to spend thirty years in the Imperial Forest Service, ultimately serving as inspector general of forests in India from 1864–1883. Brandis recruited two other senior German foresters, Dr William Schlich and Berthold Ribbentrop. These men brought a systematic, Prussian style of management to the Indian jungles.

According to Madhav Gadgil and Ramachandra Guha in *This Fissured Land: An Ecological History of India,* Brandis and his team began drafting policies that ultimately formed the basis of the Indian Forest Act, 1878, establishing the 'absolute proprietary right of the state' over all uncultivated lands. This meant that the forest department essentially became the largest landholder in India. In one of the most audacious land-grabs ever, the British asserted control over both man and nature, with an equal disregard for both. Colonial authorities were quick to annex forest land for the state and declare graziers, hunters and gatherers to be recalcitrant interlopers or poachers rather than stewards of the forest. Following Independence, when the former princely states relinquished sovereignty to the republic, extensive tracts of jungle within their kingdoms also devolved to provincial forest departments. Consequently, indigenous, forest-based communities such as hunter-gatherers and migrant shepherds lost most of their hereditary rights to natural resources and became dependent on forest officers for access and permits. Traditional methods of conservation were set aside in preference for government-approved 'working plans' that encouraged the felling of indigenous species and the planting of more commercially attractive timber.

Unlike his British superiors, Brandis seems to have had some appreciation for the conservation and utilization methods of forest dwellers in India. Brandis noted the simple strategies of traditional foresters, who maintained sacred groves and limited felling and lopping in a sustainable manner. However, the agriculture secretary admonished Brandis for proposing that forest dwellers could be given even limited freedom in the management of the forests, suggesting his 'views as to rights of aboriginal tribes, forest villages, etc. are to my mind clearly in advance of my own, and a fortiori of those of the government of India'.

The emphasis on commercial forestry from the 1850s onward was initially fuelled by the Indian Railways, which had an insatiable appetite for timber. As thousands of kilometres of tracks were being laid across North India, forests of deodar and sal from the Himalaya provided wooden sleepers on which the steel rails were laid. Roughly 400 trees had to be felled for every kilometre of track. During the middle of the nineteenth century, steam engines burned wooden billets rather than coal, adding to the demand for wood. Similarly, the British Navy placed huge orders for teak from India and Burma to construct their battleships. Later on, during World War I, many of the trenches of Europe were bolstered by timber from Indian jungles, as the forests of France were decimated in the conflict. Mesopotamia and the Middle East also swallowed up India's forest resources throughout the war. During 1917, in one year alone, Gadgil and Guha calculate that '228,076 tonnes of timber (excluding railway sleepers) were supplied by the specially created "timber branch" of the munitions branch, 50,000 tonnes of fodder grass exported to help military operations in Egypt and Iraq'.

The persistent focus on commercial forestry remains a colonial hangover in the forest departments of Indian states, where officers look upon the lands they manage primarily as a source of revenue. This has led to destructive practices that have altered the ecological balance of forests throughout the subcontinent, most significantly in the Himalaya. Throughout the foothills of Kumaon and Garhwal, the chir pine (*Pinus longifolia*) has been a favourite species for the forest department, not only because it shoots up rapidly and provides usable timber within twenty to thirty years, but also because it can be tapped for resin.

During the twentieth century, both before and after Independence, large swathes of chir pines replaced indigenous species such as oaks that foresters like Brandis disdained because they had 'much too slow a rate of growth to justify their maintenance, as component parts of the high forest'. Monoculture has been blamed for a variety of unwelcome consequences from the prevalence of wildfires to the extinction of many shrubs and plants that once made up the forest understorey.

An equally dramatic ecological change, not often noted, has been the widespread disappearance of Himalayan grasslands. While focusing on trees, many environmentalists have failed to register this significant factor. If we look at photographs of Himalayan hill stations like Mussoorie or Shimla, from a century ago, the changes are immediately apparent. Most of the southern slopes of the mountains up to 2,500 metres, were once covered in grass, plants like sorrel (*Rumex hastatus*) or shrubs like mansura (*Coriaria nepalensis*) and kingod (*Berberis vulgaris*).

Grasses have played a significant role in traditional Himalayan economies, providing fodder for animals, thatch for roofs, and materials for making ropes, shoes and other products. Covering much of the Terai, where the Shivalik

Hills and the first range of the Himalaya form duns or broad valleys, there were once extensive grasslands that supported a variety of wildlife such as rhinoceros and buffalo, which today are found only in small pockets of Nepal and Assam. Part of the reason for their endangered status, along with poaching, is the disappearance of grasslands.

Harvesting grass remains an important part of the daily routine in many Himalayan villages. Both women and men set out in the morning with sickles and return home carrying enormous loads of grass that are stored as fodder for cattle or used as thatch. Grasses grow faster than trees and do not require decades to mature, but it is important to view these 'gregarious communities' not just as seasonal pastures but as longstanding constituents of a larger biome. Their shallow network of roots has been knitted together over centuries. In the same way that thatch roofs shed water, this living carpet of fibres keeps the monsoon rains from washing away the soil. And when a landslide occurs, their roots and rhizomes are quick to suture and bandage the mountain's wounds.

More than trees, grasses shape themselves to the contours of the mountain to gather the sun's energy efficiently. The photosynthesis that occurs gives them their nutrient value and attracts mountain mammals and other creatures. The loss of Himalayan grasslands has affected wildlife distribution for the simple reason that ungulates like deer and goats can't climb trees. Species of birds like the chir pheasant and chukar partridge also depend on grasslands, feeding on this wild granary and using it as cover to protect themselves from raptors and other predators. The near mythical Himalayan quail, *Ophrysia superciliosa,* now considered extinct, was last found on grass slopes near Mussoorie and Nainital in 1876. It would seem reasonable to suggest that the disappearance of grass cover may have contributed to the loss of this bird. A large assortment of skinks, millipedes, ground beetles, spiders and ants, not to mention invisible mites and microbes, also depend on grasslands to survive and propagate their species amongst the matted roots. These tiny life forms may seem insignificant compared to the enormous scale of Himalayan landscapes but as we look out upon the vast panoramas of peaks and forested ridgelines we must also appreciate the diversity of species that exist at our feet.

chapter 19

STALKING THE CARNIVOROUS SUNDEW

A number of bloodthirsty creatures inhabit Jabarkhet Nature Reserve (JNR), near our home in Landour. Not the least of these are leeches, during the monsoon. There are also yellow-throated martens, leopard cats, foxes, jackals and panthers but the only animals that really worry me are bears. Unlike the other predators that can sense our approach and slip away into the leafy shadows, Himalayan black bears (*Ursus thibetanus*) are less attentive and short-tempered. In winter, particularly, there's always a chance of stumbling upon one at dawn or dusk, though they usually move about after dark, mauling the oaks for acorns.

Today, however, we are going in search of another predator, *Drosera peltata*. This patient hunter lies in wait on grassy, sunlit slopes and traps its unsuspecting victims when they touch its deadly tendrils. A fine coating of sticky mucous helps the killer grip its struggling prey. Sundew is an insectivorous plant genus, of which there are almost 200 different species worldwide. It feeds on tiny gnats and midges for whom it must be a terrifying monster with dozens of limbs and ferocious jaws. Even worse, it begins digesting its victims before they are dead.

Leading our expedition is Dr Gopal Rawat, one of the foremost authorities on Himalayan plants. As dean of the Wildlife Institute of India (WII) in Dehradun, Rawat doesn't get out in the field as much as he'd like but is always happy to trade his coat and tie for a bush shirt and binoculars, leaving behind the stacks of files and reports on his desk. A walking encyclopedia, Dr Rawat makes an ordinary landscape come to life with facts and stories. Being from the Himalaya himself, he has an intimate connection to the land. His ancestral village is near Munsiyari in the north-east corner of Kumaon.

At the entrance to JNR, Rawat points out a tree, about 5 metres high, *Euonymus tingens,* with numerous branches and dense, glossy foliage. Known in the hills as kum kum it has medicinal properties and is used both as a purgative and for curing eye infections. The inner bark, Rawat explains, is a yellow colour and is used for dyeing textiles and, in parts of Kumaon, as a substitute for chandan tika applied on the forehead as a part of worship. Another species he identifies is *Daphne papyracea,* a sturdy shrub with long, tapered leaves. This plant was traditionally used for making paper. Its fibrous inner bark, or bast, is collected and soaked then beaten into a pulp, after which it is spread out in sheets to dry. Though *Daphne* paper is seldom made any more, it was once used for important documents and ledgers, as well as janampatris or birth charts and horoscopes. Today, it is still produced in Bhutan, at the Jungshi Handmade Paper Company in Thimphu, where traditional methods are employed. Yet, here in Uttarakhand, *Daphne* serves a more immediate, practical purpose for grass cutters, who strip away the strong, supple bark and use it to tie up bundles of fodder.

Rawat is an expert on the relationship between flora and fauna, studying the kinds of alpine grasses and plants that support different species of birds and animals from leaf warblers to high-altitude ungulates. While his colleagues and students at WII are busy putting radio collars on snow leopards or camera-trapping tigers, Rawat focuses on critical links further down the food chain. His primary interests lie in those plants that are consumed by herbivores though the object of our quest today is a form of Himalayan flora that is uniquely non-vegetarian.

Much of Rawat's research has focused on bugiyals, or alpine meadows, which are seasonal pastures for herds of sheep, goats and buffaloes. 'Bugh or Bughi, means fodder plant or grass,' he explains. 'And each of these bughis form profuse herbaceous meadows that the shepherds identify by distinct names. There is dudh bughi, dhaniya bughi, sun bughi but the best plant for grazing animals is known as bas bughi. The shepherds say that if their flocks feed on bas bughi for three weeks, it is equivalent to eating other plants for three months.'

Further on we come to a swathe of yellow and pink balsam, which has just finished blooming, though it still adds colour to the hillside. The seedpods are tiny bean-like capsules that explode when touched, which is why they have the generic name *Impatiens*.

'Shepherds warn you to stay away from balsam patches when the seeds are ripe because the bears are attracted to them,' Rawat recounts. 'They'll sit in the middle of a patch and use their arms and paws to burst the pods.' He gestures with both hands as if shovelling the popping seeds into his mouth.

Jabarkhet Nature Reserve is a hundred acres of private land adjoining a large tract of government forest. It consists mostly of the south-west face of a protruding ridge known as Flag Hill. The predominant trees in this forest are *Quercus leucotrichophora*, *Rhododendron arboreum* and *Lyonia ovalifolia*. In Garhwali these are known as banj, burans and anyar. From Western Nepal, through Kumaon, Garhwal and Himachal Pradesh, these three species dominate this crucial band of foliage in the elevation between 1,800 and 2,500 metres, which corresponds with the highest year-round settlements in the Central Himalaya. Though herders take their animals much further up in summer, few permanent villages and towns are situated above 2,500 metres, except for religious sites and trading posts on the way to Tibet.

Running a hand over the soft, spongy surface of a rhododendron trunk, Rawat shows us charred sections from a forest fire several years ago, explaining that the bark is a natural flame retardant that protects and insulates the tree. On the slope nearby is a species of wild gerbera (*Gerbera gossypina*), known as kapas in Garhwali. The underside of the leaves has a thin, white membrane that can be peeled off like sunburnt skin. In the past this was collected and dried for use as tinder, because it ignites easily from a spark of flint.

As in other parts of the Lower Himalaya, several exotic or invasive species have taken root on Flag Hill, partly because of an old 'working plan' that the owners employed under the supervision of the forest department. These arboreal interlopers are mostly conifers—blue pine (*Pinus wallichiana*), chir pine (*Pinus longifolia*), and a few exotic cypresses (*Cupressus arizonica* and *C. lusitanica*) all of which were planted less than a hundred years ago and have spread through self-seeding. In addition to these, JNR has plenty of horse chestnuts, dogwoods, wild cherries and wild pears, all of which make it a healthy mixed forest. But the most aggressive alien species is *Eupatorium adenophorum*, a waist-high weed native to Mexico and Central America. Nobody is entirely sure how *Eupatorium* arrived in India, though it has infiltrated almost every part of the Lower Himalaya. Rawat suggests that the plant's seeds probably came here by accident in a shipment, years ago, to ports in Burma or Bengal from where it spread rapidly into the mountains. In Garhwal *Eupatorium* is known as kala ghaas, or black grass, because of its dark stems. In many places, including parts of JNR, it has covered hillsides and choked out indigenous species. Neither wild nor domesticated animals eat its leaves and after a forest fire, kala ghaas is one of the first species to recover.

Along our path, we find leopard scat, as well as pellets of barking deer dung that look like dry dog food and the droppings of a yellow-throated marten, containing fragments of bone, eggshells and hair, evidence of its eclectic diet. Martens are some of the most opportunistic predators, constantly hunting through trees and hillsides for bird nests, rodents and reptiles. By comparison, *Drosera peltata* is a finicky eater.

Drosera means 'dew of the sun', and it gets this name because the mucilage on its leaves is similar to tiny drops of dew. This saliva-like substance not only traps insects but also contains acids that work as digestive juices. After a victim is captured, the leaf closes around it and consumes the insect, drawing nutrients from its prey rather than the soil.

Charles Darwin wrote an entire book on *Drosera*, titled *Insectivorous Plants*, in which he focuses on a common species of sundew found in England. During the summer of 1860, Darwin conducted a variety of experiments on a heath in Sussex to determine how the plant reacted to different stimuli as well as testing the chemistry of its deadly secretions. He writes:

> When an insect alights on the central disk (of the leaf), it is instantly entangled by the viscid secretion, and the surrounding tentacles after a time begin to bend, and ultimately clasp it on all sides... It is surprising how minute an insect suffices to cause this action: for instance, I have seen one of the smallest species of gnats (Culex), which had just settled with its excessively delicate feet on the glands of the outermost tentacles, and these were already beginning to curve inwards, though not a single gland had as yet touched the body of the insect... Whether insects alight on the leaves by mere chance, as a resting place, or are attracted by the odour of the secretion I know not. I suspect from the number of insects caught by the English species of Drosera, and from what I have observed with some exotic species kept in my greenhouse, that the odour is attractive. In this latter case the leaves may be compared with a baited trap; in the former case with a trap laid in a run frequented by game, but without any bait.

Darwin tested the plant's reflexes by exposing it to both heat and cold as well as a number of substances including morsels of meat, cork, human hairs, splinters of glass and even gluten (to which the plant seems to have been allergic, for its leaves quickly withered and turned black). What fascinated Darwin most of all was the way in which the plant sent signals through the tendrils on its leaves. 'Some influence does travel up to the glands, causing them to secrete more copiously, and the secretion to become acid. This latter fact is, I believe, quite new in the physiology of plants; it has indeed only recently been established that in the animal kingdom an influence can be transmitted along the nerves to glands, modifying their power of secretion...'

Towards the end of his career Darwin also wrote a book titled *The Power of Movement in Plants*. As he tested his theories of evolution and natural selection, he recognized that *Drosera* was unique. Rather than being an insentient species, it operates through botanical impulses, similar to the reflexes of other predators, that allow it to catch and feed upon its prey. Rawat suggests that the plant probably emits some kind of pheromones that attract flies, though he feels that the glistening beads of mucous on the leaves could also lure insects.

'*Drosera* grows in nitrogen-poor soil and usually in an open area where insects pass through,' he explains. 'There are only a few insectivorous plants in India, including a species of pitcher plant in Meghalaya. Aside from *Drosera*, in the Himalaya, there is a species of bladderwort, *Utricularia brachiate,* and a butterwort *Pinguicula alpina*, both of which are carnivorous.'

As we make our way along the overgrown path through the nature reserve, I repeatedly check my ankles for leeches though the monsoon has almost ended and the clouds have disappeared overhead. Rawat leads us up a steep ridge fringed with bracken, the trail covered with slippery needles of blue pines. Eventually, we reach a lone oak at the edge of a clearing on the crest of the ridge. A few tiny gnats are circling in the sunlight and we can hear a chorus of cicadas.

Stepping cautiously forward, Rawat scans the open expanse of grass and weeds as if searching for pugmarks or a blood trail. Pausing, he beckons us forward and points at the ground. There, growing out of the rocky soil, amidst a dozen other species of plants, is a thin stem, twisting upward and branching off in several directions. The tiny white flowers are unassuming but the leaves fringed with fine hairs have a menacing appearance. Crouching, I can just make out the miniscule droplets of mucous. Two insects have been trapped by *Drosera*, one of which is nothing but a dry husk, several days old, though still ensnared in the predator's green grasp. The other is a translucent fly the size of a pinhead. Struggling in the death grip of a salivating leaf that slowly clenches around it, this helpless creature succumbs to the botanical appetite of a ravenous sundew.

chapter 20

PLACE OF THE SACRED THUNDERBOLT

As we sit down to breakfast on the verandah, Sudhir Prakash insists I take a chair facing the mountains. 'A guest should always be given the best view,' he says, though the clouds have closed in and there is no sign of Kanchenjunga or the nearer ranges that descend to the confluence of the Rangeet and Rung Dung rivers. To the south-west, I can just make out the rooftops of Darjeeling on a ridge above us, girdled in clouds. A rumpled counterpane of mist is draped across the foot of the tea gardens and the pleated contours of surrounding ridges.

Almost 175 years ago, Joseph Dalton Hooker described this same scene, having fallen under the spell of these mountains:

> …As the sun's rays dart into the many valleys which lie between the snow mountains and Darjeeling, the stagnant air contained in the low recesses becomes quickly heated: heavy masses of vapour, dense, white, and keenly defined, arise from the hollows, meet over the crests of the hills, cling to the forests on their summits, enlarge, unite, and ascend rapidly to the rarefied regions above—a phenomenon so suddenly developed, that the consequent withdrawal from the spectator's gaze of the stupendous scenery beyond, looks like the work of magic.

Glenburn Tea Estate was founded in 1859 by Scottish planters and its gardens have been producing fine teas for more than a century and a half. At breakfast, we are served a first flush, picked and processed less than a month ago, around the beginning of April. Poured into Wedgwood china, it has a pale saffron colour with a delicate but distinctive aroma and flavour described by connoisseurs as 'luscious undertones of flowers and peach'. The terminology of tea tasting is as mysterious and full of garbled adjectives as a vintner's vocabulary. Glenburn is not only a tea garden but also a boutique heritage resort for visitors who want to relive the romance and nostalgia of Darjeeling's colonial past.

While Sudhir appreciates the history and lore of tea gardening and enjoys recounting stories of the eccentric Scotsmen who first cultivated Glenburn estate, he is more interested in the day to day practicalities of the business. 'I keep saying I'm going to retire,' he tells me. 'But every time I come up here there's so much to do.' Producing tea isn't easy and a great deal depends on the vagaries of climate that influence the subtle flavours in a cup.

'The perfect weather for growing tea is sun all day and rain all night,' he says, after looking askance at the overcast sky. A Doon School graduate with a mildly cynical manner and a love of good cigars, Sudhir looks more like a philosophy professor than a tea planter.

In the wild, *Camellia sinensis* is actually a tree not a bush and grows as tall as 5 or 6 metres. But in tea gardens it is heavily pruned, stunted to the height of a metre so that pickers can easily reach the new leaves as they sprout. Though tea bushes can live for more than a century, they usually have to be replanted every twenty or thirty years, on a rotational basis, to ensure the best results.

Being a labour-intensive industry, tea planting also requires a large workforce. Teams of pickers are deployed over hundreds of acres of land and the harvest must be carefully choreographed so that leaves are plucked at exactly the right moment. Excess rain or drought, as well as humidity and varying hours of sunlight affect the timing and quality of new sprouts.

'As soon as tea is picked, it begins to deteriorate and decay,' Sudhir explains, 'and it must be processed immediately. That's why every estate has its own factory on the premises.' Within twenty-four hours, the leaves are withered, fermented, rolled and dried. This process removes moisture while enhancing and preserving the natural flavours. Three or four hours of fermentation and oxidation gives tea its dark colour and brings out the taste. The standard method of processing—crush, tear and curl (CTC)—is done by large automated machines though most of the sorting and other factory work is completed by hand. Crushing and rolling helps release flavour and compacts the leaf. Finally, drying in an oven helps preserve the tea, reducing moisture to no more than three per cent.

Alongside its standard black teas, Glenburn also produces partially fermented oolong, and unfermented green and white teas, as well as limited batches like 'silver needle', made only from the bud. Illustrating the time-consuming and painstaking nature of picking and processing tea, Jeff Koehler, in his book, *Darjeeling: The Colorful History and Precarious Fate of the World's Greatest Tea*, tells us, '…it takes a staggering *twenty-two thousand* selectively hand-picked shoots—just the tender first two leaves and a still-curled bud— to produce a single kilo of Darjeeling tea.'

After production, the tea is tasted, graded and packaged then shipped to Kolkata, to be auctioned by brokers. Each of Darjeeling's estates is well known by reputation and the distinctive flavour of its tea. Makaibari, Castleton, Runglee Rungliot and Lopchu, as well as dozens of other gardens, feature different grades of tea identified by a confusing array of acronyms—FP (flowery pekoe), BOP (broken orange pekoe), GFBOP (golden flowery broken orange pekoe) and top of the line, FTGFOP (finest tippy golden flowery orange pekoe). In 2014, the average wholesale price of Darjeeling tea was Rs 150 per kilogram, though a special lot of Makaibari second flush set a record as bidding reached Rs 1,000,000 per kilogram. Another indication of the enduring value of Darjeeling tea is the fact that many spurious varieties, grown elsewhere and falsely labelled, are sold in the market to keep up with worldwide demand.

After breakfast, I head off on a short trek to the Rangeet River at the bottom of the hill. My guide is Neetu Mangrati, one of the staff at Glenburn, a petite, self-confident young woman in her twenties. Four generations of her family have worked on the tea gardens. Neetu's great-grandparents came from Nepal and settled here at the beginning of the twentieth century. She tells me that though her family speaks Nepali at home, she has never been back across the border. While some of her relatives still work in the tea gardens, 'Many have moved away and got jobs in Delhi or Dubai.' The pattern of migration that brought her great-grandparents here in search of employment continues as people from the Himalaya travel farther and farther away from their roots in order to seek a better life.

Neetu was educated in Darjeeling and is fluent in Nepali, English and Hindi. She also speaks some Bengali. As we walk down a path between hedgerows of tea, she stops to show me the characteristic two leaves and a bud, which is plucked. On the hill above us a dozen women are working their way up the ridge, filling conical bamboo baskets on their backs. When I ask why the pickers are all women, Neetu replies, 'Women are more careful. It's delicate work. Men are hired mostly as labourers or supervisors.'

'Are there any women supervisors?'

'A few,' she answers, then goes on to say that some of the older women are hired to take care of young children while their mothers are at work. Glenburn has established crèches and schools as well as medical facilities for its workers. Neetu continues: 'It's not an easy job but an experienced woman at this time of year can pick fifty to sixty kilos a day. During the monsoon, even more, and they get paid bonuses according to the weight they pick.'

As we pass a cluster of sheds, Neetu greets a group of pickers who are resting in the shade of a concrete pavilion. All of them live in one of three villages on the estate. Their morning's harvest is being weighed and will be transported to the factory by jeep. Each of the pickers has on a sturdy pair of rubber gumboots.

'Because of the mud, when it rains, but also to protect them from snakes,' Neetu explains. The women wear broad-brimmed hats and carry umbrellas that shade them from the sun and protect them from rain. With shifting clouds, the weather can change from one minute to the next.

A few of the tea bushes are in bloom, small white flowers with bright yellow centres that look like tiny fried eggs. I ask Neetu what kind of tea she prefers and, without hesitation, she says, 'Moonshine,' a rare, white tea. All the employees at Glenburn receive a monthly ration from the factory, mostly lower-grade broken leaf, fannings or dust. Neetu admits, 'At home we drink masala chai.'

She picks the leaves of a plant growing by the side of the path. *Artemisia vulgaris*, known in Hindi as nagadona or nagadamni, is commonly called mugwort in English. Crushing the leaves between my fingers, I inhale its sweet pungency. Neetu lists nagadona's medicinal qualities, saying it is used for everything from nosebleeds to stomach ailments. She also identifies a tall semal or silk cotton tree, which is shedding tufts of white kapok that carry its seeds on the wind like miniature clouds. Further down the hill, we see the lurid pink and yellow flowers of wild turmeric sprouting from the forest floor.

Neetu confesses to being a fan of Bollywood films, many of which have been shot in Darjeeling, with picturesque panoramas of the tea gardens. She mentions that actor Ranbir Kapoor is currently in town, shooting a new romantic comedy. Countless dramatic scenes and song sequences, from Raj Kapoor's *Barsaat* in 1949 to 'Mere Sapno ki Rani' in 1969, have featured Darjeeling's scenery. Satyajit Ray's film, *Kanchenjungha,* was shot here too. Though many Indian film-makers, seeking mountain vistas, have shifted to foreign locations like Switzerland, the Himalaya still serve as a popular cinematic backdrop.

Descending into the Rangeet Valley, I can feel the temperature rising as we enter a dry teak forest, with large saucer-shaped leaves cast about on the ground. At the foot of the hill, Glenburn maintains a cottage and campsite on the southern bank of the Rangeet River. We are now less than a thousand metres above sea level, well below the ideal altitude for tea. The foliage and bird life is noticeably different. Noisy jungle mynas bicker loudly in the trees replacing the silent presence of furtive thrushes. Across the river lies Sikkim, where a motor road connects the state's western districts with the capital, Gangtok. Both upstream and downstream hydroelectric projects interrupt the flow of the Rangeet but here the river tumbles between margins of rounded boulders. When I make my way to the water's edge, the current is swift and brown with silt, the colour of masala chai.

◆

A living legacy, tea carries with it a fragrance of fortune, a mercantile flavour and the bitter aftertaste of empire. Jeff Koehler explains that by the first decade of the nineteenth century, England was importing more than 12,000 tonnes of tea from China, which amounted to sales of roughly £3.5 million. For the East India Company, tea was by far the largest and most lucrative commodity. This British addiction led to an alarming trade deficit that drained the exchequer's silver reserves. A growing demand for tea extended to America as well and fleets of merchant vessels were ferrying 'black gold' from Chinese ports to the Company's agents in London, Liverpool and Boston. The economics were unsustainable but the shrewd merchants of Leadenhall Street and their nabobs in India came up with a botanical solution, as ingenious as it was immoral.

In order to balance the trade deficit, caused by their growing dependence on tea, the British began to export an even more addictive commodity—opium. The East India Company's Crest features two rampant lions and a pair of Union Jacks but it would have been far more appropriate if it had been decorated with the camellia and the poppy. The cynical strategy of encouraging the use of opium in China to create an insatiable demand and then using that monopoly to counterbalance the trade in tea ultimately led to the Opium Wars.

Following the Treaty of Nanking, in 1842, efforts began in earnest to propagate tea in India. Until now, the Chinese had jealously guarded their crops but an enterprising Scotsman, Robert Fortune, smuggled close to 20,000 tea plants from China into India. According to Koehler, when the seedlings arrived in Calcutta, in portable greenhouses balled Wardian cases, they were transferred to the Company's botanical gardens and then introduced to hilly tracts along the foot of the Himalaya. Some of the first Indian tea was planted in Kumaon and Garhwal and cultivation extended as far west as the Kangra Valley, where a few gardens still remain today. Meanwhile, another Scottish plant hunter named Charles Alexander Bruce had discovered wild tea trees in Assam and brought these to the attention of Nathaniel Wallich, superintendent of the Calcutta gardens. Though judged inferior to Chinese leaf, this indigenous species was well suited to lower altitudes along the banks of the Brahmaputra.

Darjeeling was first established as a hill station around 1835. The broad ridge on which the town stands was originally the site of a Buddhist monastery known as Dorje Ling, meaning place of the sacred thunderbolt, from which the current spelling has evolved. For more than 300 years, these foothills have been contested territory. In the 1780s, Gurkha armies from Nepal crossed over the Singalila Ridge and conquered much of this region from the Chogyal of Sikkim. Only after the Anglo-Nepalese War ended in 1816, were the mountains to the west of the Teesta River returned to the rulers of Sikkim by the East India Company. But the British soon had second thoughts and decided to set up a sanatorium and summer retreat so that Europeans in Bengal could escape the heat and diseases of the plains. The Chogyal was persuaded to hand over 138 square miles of foothills, from the Rangeet southward. As Koehler writes: 'In exchange, the rajah received one rifle, one double-barreled shotgun, twenty yards of broadcloth and two pairs of shawls, one of superior quality, the other inferior.'

This lopsided lease of territory soon became a contentious source of dispute, as Darjeeling quickly developed into a prosperous town. Eventually, an annual payment of Rs. 3,000 was negotiated. This was later raised to Rs. 6,000 but it did not quell resentment in Gangtok. At the same time, the British authorities began playing politics in the mountains. Sikkim was seen as a buffer between the hostile kingdoms of Nepal and Bhutan. It also provided relatively easy access to Tibet, across Nathu La and through the Chumbi Valley. Later, in the 1920s, this would be the route followed by early Everest expeditions to their base camp on the Rongbuk Glacier.

When the British acquired Darjeeling, tea had yet to be introduced, though by the early 1840s, Dr Archibald Campbell, medical superintendent in Darjeeling, began experimenting with growing tea in his private garden, using both Chinese and Assamese seeds. Campbell had earlier been posted as surgeon to the British mission in Kathmandu, serving under the resident, Brian Houghton, who later retired to Darjeeling and wrote up his voluminous account of the natural history of Nepal.

Dr Campbell's tea plants showed more resilience than many of his patients who are buried in Darjeeling's cemeteries. It soon became evident that this part of the Himalaya had the perfect climate and soil for tea. Today it is hard to imagine the prescient vision of colonial planters, who looked down upon dense, vertiginous jungles and foresaw the cultivation of *Camellia sinensis*. By the middle of the nineteenth century the rush to grow tea in Darjeeling had begun. Ironically, though the British decried the traditional Lepcha approach to agriculture, known as jhum cultivation, planters used the same slash and burn method to clear the forests. The denudation of native species, replaced by exotic tea plants, dramatically changed the composition and character of Darjeeling's ecology.

Over time, the town has acquired an exclusive appellation, similar to the wine-growing regions of Champagne or Chianti. According to Koehler this relatively small Himalayan hill tract currently contains eighty-seven tea estates, covering approximately 48,000 acres of steeply contoured land. Images of quilted green bushes lost in drifting shoals of clouds evoke romantic visions of an idyllic, manicured Eden but, in fact, the tea gardens with their single, cultivated crop, decimated the natural diversity of Darjeeling's forests.

Tea also altered the social make-up of the region. An influx of labour required for picking and processing attracted a large number of immigrants from Nepal, whose descendants now form the majority population in Darjeeling. The indigenous Lepchas, as well as Bhotias from Tibet and Sikkim, were soon outnumbered. Though some Lepchas found work in the tea gardens, Nepalis were more willing to do manual labour and the British were quick to hire them, allowing entire families to settle in villages established on each estate.

The Nepali language and culture now dominate Darjeeling. The political consequences can be seen today in the ongoing Gorkhaland agitation, where leaders from the predominant Nepali community have been agitating for a separate hill state, independent from West Bengal. Much of their power and influence stems from labour unions organized on tea estates.

In addition to being employed in the gardens, Nepalis found work as rickshaw pullers, porters and day labourers, particularly in the summer months when the British moved up to the hills. In the 1920s, when Darjeeling became the point of departure for mountaineering expeditions to Everest and Kanchenjunga, it was labourers from Eastern Nepal, especially from the Solu Khumbu region, who were hired to haul tonnes of gear to base camp and beyond. When General Charles Granville Bruce sent out word that as many as 500 porters were required to transport equipment and supplies to the Rongbuk Glacier, the migrant network of Sherpas and other Nepalis produced those numbers. In this way, the cultivation of tea in Darjeeling contributed to the conquest of Everest.

chapter 21

IN SEARCH OF THE BLUE POPPY

The last of the great plant hunters was Frank Kingdon Ward, who came to the Himalaya almost a century after Hooker and explored some of the most remote corners of the mountains at the eastern edge of the range. He too was drawn to the upper limits of life.

> Of all the devices which so beautifully trim the fabric of a mountain chain—meadows, and bog, and cliff, and moor, the most barren, the most grim, the most harsh are the screes.
>
> Screes are the mountain's rubbish heap, the chips and splinters left over from the carving of the earth; the dust and litter, from the impact of weather—wind and rain, ice and snow, heat and cold, on rock; the waste and ruin of battle after combined attack by horse, foot, and guns. They are peculiarly the product of a land of fierce contrasts, of ruthless oppositions; hard and proud and cruel—cruel as hell…
>
> But the high alpine screes are home to some of the finest flowers imaginable. On the granite screes are flaring Rhododendrons, and on the limestone screes, blue poppies, primulas, and best of all, species of cyananthus, with flowers of a soft lavender blue.

Kingdon Ward first visited the Himalaya in 1911 and his last expedition ended in 1953. On twenty-four visits to the Eastern Himalaya, he collected the seeds, roots, corms and bulbs of thousands of species of flowering plants that were then propagated by British horticulturalists. The flower most often associated with his name is the blue poppy, which he collected in the highlands of Tibet. This species created a sensation when it first bloomed in London.

Not only was Kingdon Ward a celebrated botanist but he was a writer with a poetic gift for describing the mountains in ways that immediately carry us aloft to the high rock gardens of the Himalaya. He published twenty-five books including *The Land of the Blue Poppy* (1913), *The Romance of Plant Hunting* (1924), and *A Plant Hunter in Tibet* (1934). While other Englishmen were shooting tigers and stalking Marco Polo sheep, Kingdon Ward was hunting more delicate prey like slipper orchids, *Myosotis Hookeri,* named after his predecessor. In order to identify plants and gather the seeds, his expeditions followed a circuitous route, locating the blooms on his way in, then doubling back a few weeks later to collect seeds on his way out.

Unlike most English explorers, Kingdon Ward approached the Himalaya from the north-east, out of China. Many of his journeys, on foot and horseback, took him to places where no other Europeans had been. His books record the wonder and delight he experienced on finding rare species but also the hardships and adventures. He was one of the first men to enter the thundering gorges of the Tsang Po and help solve its riddle, proving this was the same river that flowed into Assam as the Brahmaputra. He survived knife-wielding bandits, rock avalanches and an earthquake that measured 8.4 on the Richter Scale. After feeling the ground heaving beneath his tent like a storm-tossed sea, he found that his campsite had risen 200 feet.

By all accounts, Frank Kingdon Ward was a difficult man. He usually travelled only in the company of servants and staff. Those few friends who joined him on his journeys complained that he walked too slowly, stooping down every few steps to inspect each plant that caught his eye. Evidently, he also had an explosive temper and was often moody, lapsing into brooding silences that could last for days. But on the page, he is an exuberant writer, full of anecdotes and observations that bring his experiences to life, almost a century after they occurred.

Though Kingdon Ward's legacy can still be seen in the bucolic gardens of country estates in England, he was happiest in the harsh highlands of Tibet and writes with nostalgic regret upon leaving those remote passes and mountains.

There comes a day in the life of every Tibetan traveller when he stands on the crest of the last range, and gazes across the foot hills to the plains below. It is evening. The sun is wallowing in a lake of gilded mist, and fiery tongues are licking up the last wads of cloud. Behind him rise in awful and paralyzing grandeur the most desperate mountains in the world. Below him rise spirals of blue smoke from the hearths of men; and as he looks, and dusk slinks down the sky, he sees as it were men and the children of men, and families gathered into villages, and villages into towns, and towns into cities; and hears the dull roar of transport and industry, as man tries to inhabit the whole earth. But behind the mountains lies the garden of God.

IV

WINGED MIGRANTS
Creatures of the Air

chapter 22

PAINTED COURTESANS AND CHESTNUT TIGERS

Entering his house, Peter Smetacek points out a torn screen on the wire mesh door. 'That's where a leopard got in last month and took our mastiff,' he says, gesturing towards a chair nearby where the dog was sleeping when it was attacked and carried off. He also mentions how a group of students came to visit a few days after the incident and the leopard began calling on the front lawn while they were having dinner on the verandah. The students were so terrified they rushed inside and locked themselves in their room. It took a lot of persuasion to bring them out to finish their dinner.

'The Retreat', Smetacek's home, is an old planter's bungalow on a wooded ridge above Bhimtal Lake. It also houses his Butterfly Research Centre and the sitting room contains an extensive collection of butterflies and moths. Most of the specimens were caught here in the gardens and surrounding forests of the family estate. Glass cases on the walls are full of swallowtails, skippers, sailers, sergeants, tigers, jesters and jezebels. There is a common leopard (*Phalanta phalantha*) too, its wings a rusty gold with distinct black spots. But this leopard feeds on nectar rather than dogs.

Peter Smetacek knows more about Himalayan butterflies and moths than almost anyone alive. He has authored a number of articles and field guides including *A Naturalist's Guide to the Butterflies of India*. His memoir, *Butterflies on the Roof of the World*, recounts his family's preoccupation with Lepidoptera.

In 1939, Peter's father escaped from Nazi-occupied Czechoslovakia after he took part in a failed attempt to assassinate Adolf Hitler. The intention was to blow up a railway tunnel through which the Führer's train was supposed to pass. Dodging the Gestapo, who were hard on his heels, Frederick Smetacek made his way to Hamburg and got himself hired on a cargo ship that sailed for India. Though he had been hoping to emigrate to South America, his plans abruptly changed on 30 August 1939 after the vessel docked in Calcutta harbour. Noting that secretive preparations were underway to leave India in a hurry, Frederick realized that war was about to be declared and jumped ship. For a while he worked for the Bata Shoe Company and then set himself up in business, manufacturing everything from flight suits to parachute silk brassieres. A couple of years later, he met Shaheda Ahad with whom he fell in love. After they persuaded her family to let them marry, the Smetaceks moved to Kumaon and settled on the shores of Naukuchiatal, the nine-cornered lake. They had five sons, whom Frederick was determined to raise with an appreciation for the outdoors. As Peter writes:

> Father had been brought up amidst the rolling forested hills of Sudeten Silesia, with forests and forestry in his blood. Naturally, he wanted the same sylvan surroundings for his children, especially now that he could afford it. After the war, it was clear that he could never return to Czechoslovakia, which was still under occupation by the Red Army. The rest of Europe was in shambles, so he decided to settle in India, in a place as similar as possible to the Central European hills he had known.

Soon after the war ended, Frederick persuaded his own father to visit India and this re-ignited their shared passion for butterfly collecting. The senior Smetaceks assembled a large collection of Himalayan butterflies and moths, including rare species like the painted courtesan (*Euripus consimilis*). Moon moths (*Actias selene*), with a wingspan of 15 centimetres and a luminous green colour, were among their prized specimens. While Czechoslovakia has 163 species of butterflies, India has more than 1,300 and in Bhimtal alone there are 243. Peter's grandfather, who had been a forester by profession, was delighted to escape war-torn Europe and enjoyed the relative peace and rich diversity of Himalayan jungles. In 1949, however, he died suddenly of typhoid fever and is buried in the military cemetery below Nainital.

Peter was born sixteen years after his grandfather's death but he quickly inherited the family passion. As a young boy he learned how to wield a butterfly net almost as soon as he could walk. By this time, his parents had sold their property at Naukuchiatal and bought a portion of the Jones Estate overlooking Bhimtal, where he now lives. The land their family owns was once a tea estate, started in the 1860s.

'The reason the British planted tea in Kumaon was for trade with Tibet,' Peter explains. 'The tea bushes on this estate were cultivated to make brick tea, which Tibetans prefer.' A strong, coarse variety, both leaves and twigs were plucked and processed, then formed into bricks to be transported across the Himalaya on pack animals like sheep and goats, as well as ponies and yaks. Opening a copy he shows me a passage describing the trans-Himalayan tea trade and the Bharatpore Tea Estate, which later became Jones Estate.

On a slope below The Retreat rows of tea bushes with dark green leaves still survive, though they have gone wild and a dense oak forest has grown over them. Tucked inside the centre of this abandoned tea garden is the family cemetery, where Peter's parents and two of his brothers are buried.

Sitting in the yard next to a buddleia bush in full bloom, with cascades of white flowers, we spend the better part of a day watching and photographing butterflies. 'This is what I call research,' Peter says with a contented smile. We are joined by Rajashree Bhuyan, a postgraduate student from Assam, who is doing fieldwork for her PhD under Peter's supervision.

Glassy and chestnut tigers, cabbage whites and bluebottles swarm the buddleia, proving why this shrub is popularly known as a 'butterfly bush'. Spring has just arrived in Kumaon and these are some of the first species to appear. In a flowerbed at the other side of the yard, Peter points out a pair of brimstones performing a courtship ritual. The female is white and the male bright yellow with orange flecks. 'She's not being receptive,' Peter remarks. 'You can see how the female raises her abdomen, so he won't be able to connect with her.' The male keeps flitting about like an anxious suitor while his prospective mate remains on the ground refusing to yield to his advances. 'Brimstones live for ten months, longer than most butterflies. They are one of the few species that hibernate in winter. Sometimes they sit snugly in a hollow under the snow and emerge again in the spring. You can see from the damaged condition of their wings that these two are near the end of their lives.'

Some butterflies live for only a few weeks and remain within a confined radius, while others enjoy a longer lifespan of several months and travel great distances. When asked about the migration of Himalayan butterflies, Peter shakes his head. 'Not enough studies have been done,' he says. 'With most species we really don't know where they come from, or where they go.' Throughout the spring, an itinerant procession of butterflies stops over at Jones Estate.

'I've counted more than three hundred pea blues passing through this yard in less than forty-five minutes,' Peter recalls.

He explains that it's likely some butterflies travel from Bhimtal, at 1,500 metres above sea level, all the way up to altitudes of 4,000 metres or more. 'We know that a species called the painted lady (*Vanessa cardui*), which is also found in Europe, flies from Spain to the Scottish Highlands. If it migrates that far over there, we can assume it does the same here.' The common emigrant is another strong flier that travels great distances, which is how it gets its name. Peter has found specimens high in the Himalaya near Badrinath, as well as in Ladakh. 'They use air currents to migrate, blown back and forth across the mountains by the wind.'

The fact that these insects travel so far during such a short lifespan underscores the transient nature of their existence. Like the Smetacek family many species that exist in the Silesian hills of the Czech Republic are also found in the mountains of Kumaon.

Peter has studied how changes in temperature and humidity influence the distribution of butterflies. He has convincingly demonstrated that Lepidoptera can serve as bio-indicators of climate change. His research on hawkmoths, for example, proves that over the past century they have gradually moved westward in the Himalaya, as conditions became more conducive for breeding. The journeys of butterflies are also linked to the plants on which they feed. This relationship is twofold. While the adults nourish themselves on sugars of a buddleia bush they will lay their eggs on specific food plants, so their larvae, after hatching, can gorge on the leaves. Common emigrant caterpillars feed on cassia plants that grow at lower altitudes but as adults they sip nectar from a wide variety of flowers higher up. Through this reciprocal process they serve as pollinators, helping plants and trees multiply while, at the same time, propagating their own kind. Throughout the Himalaya this cycle of reproduction carries on year after year, as millions of insects contribute to the larger community of nature.

Butterflies often use mimicry to ensure their survival. As we sit drinking tea on the lawn of The Retreat, Peter points out a pair of butterflies drifting over the flowers in a seemingly listless flight. Though they appear identical, these are actually two separate species. One is a chestnut tiger (*Parantica sita*), its white wings broadly striped with a ruddy patch at the bottom of the lower wing. The other is a circe (*Hestinalis nama*), named after the sorceress in Greek mythology whose magical powers include transmutation. As Peter explains, the chestnut tiger is poisonous and birds will not touch it, while the circe is perfectly eatable. Yet, by mimicking the appearance of a tiger, the circe protects itself. This defensive strategy includes imitating the slow, awkward flight, which is characteristic of a poisonous butterfly. In fact, like other non-poisonous species, circes are perfectly capable of flying much faster in order to escape from predators.

Some years ago, Peter conducted an experiment with butterflies that mimic each other. His wife, Rajni, had set up a bird feeder in the yard outside their house, which attracted flocks of white-crested and white-throated laughingthrushes. Catching a variety of butterflies, Peter added these as a garnish to the daily ration of birdseed. In this way, he investigated which were palatable and which were not. Certain species, like swallowtails, are poisonous because their caterpillars ingest toxins from the plants they eat and these chemicals remain in their bodies throughout each stage of metamorphosis. Others manufacture poisons in their bodies to make themselves distasteful.

By observing the laughingthrushes it was easy for Peter to discover the butterflies they relished and those they rejected. As he explains, the colours, patterns and shapes of a butterfly's wings are like menu cards for birds, from which they select what they wish to eat. Yet mimetic associations between species are not always as simple as a tasty butterfly pretending to be toxic. In some cases, one poisonous species mimics another. The purpose behind this behaviour, as Peter describes it, 'reduces the price of advertising the fact that they are poisonous'.

Mimicry in butterflies takes many forms. One of the largest and most spectacular Himalayan species is the orange oakleaf (*Kallima inachus*). The inside of its wings are a colourful palette of saffron and indigo but the outside is a dull, dusty brown. When its wings are folded this butterfly looks exactly like a dead leaf, so that when it sits on the ground, or on a branch, it becomes virtually invisible.

Orange oakleafs are distinct from the butterflies that swarm around the buddleia bush. While chestnut tigers, circes, common bluebottles (*Graphium sarpedon*) and brimstones (*Gonepteryx rhamni*) sip nectar through a thin proboscis inserted into the flower, oakleafs and certain other butterflies feed on rotting fruit. Because the sugar content in fruit is much higher than it is in nectar, which contains only 20–30 per cent glucose, these butterflies must wait for the fruit to ferment so their proboscises don't get clogged with fructose syrup. As a result, butterflies and moths that feed on rotting fruit often become inebriated. Fortunately for an orange oakleaf, if it falls down drunk in the forest it can safely sleep off its stupor while camouflaged amongst the dead leaves.

Sitting in a Himalayan garden, watching butterflies all day is an idyllic, intoxicating pastime, as each delicate imago appears before us, fluttering through sunlight and shadow. Vladimir Nabokov, who was both a novelist and a lepidopterist once mused, 'Literature and butterflies are the two sweetest passions known to man.' He also wrote, 'Our imagination flies—we are its shadows on the earth.'

As we sit outdoors, other creatures interrupt our reverie, including troops of rhesus and langur monkeys that stop by to drink from a tub of water Peter has set out on the lawn. He has a love-hate relationship with his primate neighbours who have vandalized his property, tearing apart the netting he erected for a butterfly breeding centre and snapping the pipes on his solar water heater. A less destructive visitor is a barking deer that calls below the yard but darts off into the tea bushes as soon as we peer over the edge. Plenty of birds come and go as well, from tits and warblers to parakeets. A pair of yellow-naped woodpeckers keep up a persistent piping from a nest they have built in a hollow tree along the bridle path to Sat Tal.

As the day wears on, more and more butterflies visit the buddleia. Peter identifies common peacocks (*Papilio bianor*) with iridescent wings, blue crows, and a red pierrot (*Talicada nyseus*), whose upper wings are black while the lower parts are a brilliant orange. All along the edges is black and white embroidery that looks like a hand-stitched hem. Until 2002 this species had not been recorded in the Himalaya and was confined to southern parts of India but it has gradually extended its range until it is now relatively common in Kumaon. During his research on palatable and unpalatable species, Peter discovered that the laughingthrushes rejected the red pierrot proving that in the butterfly world, 'beauty can be dangerous'. Another dramatic species we observe is a common map (*Cyrestis thyodamas*), its ivory colour similar to the buddleia blossoms. When this butterfly opens its wings, it resembles a Mercator projection of the globe, with a tracery of thin markings that look like lines of latitude and longitude.

Suddenly, late in the afternoon, both Peter and Rajashree grab their cameras and jump to their feet. When I follow to find out what is happening, all I can see is a drab-looking butterfly perched on a spray of buddleia blossoms. In a whisper, Peter tells me it is an evening brown (*Melanitis leda*), a common species that appears around dusk. His excitement, however, comes from the fact that it is feeding on nectar. Ordinarily, like the oakleaf, evening browns subsist on rotten fruit or tree sap. Rajashree takes more than a dozen pictures, zooming in on the tiny proboscis that is clearly sucking sustenance from the flower. 'We haven't seen this behaviour before,' Peter continues, under his breath. 'It must be desperate for food.' The evening brown seems untroubled by all of this attention and after drinking its fill it flies off in search of more potent brew.

As shadows spread from the deodar trees at the corners of the yard and twilight settles over the garden we too retire for the day. By now it is cold outside and Peter lights a fire in the fireplace of the Butterfly Research Centre. Surrounded by winged specimens in glass cases, we pour ourselves generous measures of rum and raise a glass in honour of the anomalous evening brown.

chapter 23

THE BIRDMAN OF PALI HILL

May 1945. Three days' march beyond Taklakot, a small party of men and pack animals approach Thugolho Gompa on the shores of Lake Manasarovar. The water is a darker shade of blue than the sky and in the distance, to the north, Mount Kailas appears above the lower ranges, its striated, snow-covered slopes like the tiered chortens surrounding the monastery. Leading the party and walking ahead of the horses and yaks, is a diminutive, bearded man with a broad-brimmed khaki hat on his head and a pair of field glasses dangling from his sunburned neck. As the travellers arrive at Thugolho, a lone figure emerges from the monastery dressed in saffron robes with long black hair. Recognizing each other as fellow Indians, they exchange greetings, speaking a combination of English and Hindustani.

Salim Ali, India's greatest ornithologist, had travelled by foot up the pilgrimage route to Mount Kailas, from Kumaon into Tibet. Arriving at the monastery, he was welcomed by Swami Pranavananda, 'a rational and science-oriented holy man with long experience of exploration in that region,' as Salim Ali described him. 'We took to each other immediately and had a long and interesting conversation on a purely physical plane—therefore in a language I could understand.' These two men, a Hindu ascetic and a Muslim ornithologist brought together by coincidence, shared notes on their Himalayan observations. As mentioned earlier, Pranavananda carefully measured Manasarovar's dimensions and catalogued scientific data on climate and altitude as well as the physical features of the region, from minerals to plants and animals of Tibet. For his part, Salim Ali shared his knowledge of the birds that congregated on the shores of the lake, particularly bar-headed geese and brahminy ducks (ruddy shelducks).

Pranavananda later published two books, *Kailas-Manasarovar* and *Exploration in Tibet*. The former served for many years as a standard guidebook for Indian pilgrims visiting the holy sites. Though he doesn't mention his meeting with Salim Ali, the swami does explain that the mythical Rajahansa or Royal Swans that are said to swim on Manasarovar are actually bar-headed geese and he reassures the faithful that these birds subsist on a vegetarian diet of acquatic weeds. Pranavananda also notes that the Dogra general, Zorawar Singh, who died in Taklakot in 1841, is buried nearby though one of his testicles is kept in a Tibetan monastery as an auspicious relic. Much of the guidebook is full of spiritual and practical advice as well as scientific data that Salim Ali would have appreciated.

Three decades after these two explorers crossed paths in Tibet, they met again at Rashtrapati Bhavan in New Delhi, when the President of India honoured Swami Pranavanada with a Padma Bhushan and Salim Ali with a Padma Vibhushan.

In his autobiography, *The Fall of a Sparrow*, Salim Ali devotes an entire chapter to his 'ornithological pilgrimage'. In amusing detail he writes about everything along the way from yaks feeding on the dry dung of kiang or wild asses to the morose company of his travelling partner, a young man named Pritam, who fell into a deep depression and spent his whole time reading a book of Hindi verses by Mahadevi Verma, even while walking along the steep and narrow trails. Eventually, after completing a circumambulation of Mount Kailas, Salim Ali had to cut his trip short because of his sullen companion, though he himself seems to have maintained a sense of humour throughout. After instructing his guide, Khem Singh, to make biscuits out of gur and tsampa, he writes, 'Result: the hardest and most waterproof type of reinforced concrete ever heard of in the toffee line... Chewed a block like supari for over half an hour then gave it up. Would do well as catapult ammunition!'

Before crossing into Tibet, the party experienced a severe earthquake that he describes in his journal, '(It) resulted in numerous landslides and avalanches. Thick clouds of dust on steep hillsides, as after a cannon bombardment, all around, accompanied by rattle of stones and loosened boulders—some as large as a double-storeyed house—bounding down.'

Throughout the journey, Salim Ali kept notes on the fauna and flora he encountered including two species of snow finches (red-necked and Tibetan) sharing a burrow with a mouse hare, 'apparently liv(ing) together on friendly terms'. Along the north-east shore of Manasarovar, he discovered a large number of nesting birds in the marshy wetlands bordering the lake. He comments on the dangerous quicksands along the shore and takes note of a number of breeding birds, including great crested grebes, brown-headed gulls and fifteen pairs of black-necked cranes, performing their breeding dance. After having subsisted on a diet of dal and rice for several weeks, he admits to pilfering one of the cranes' eggs, which he scrambled for breakfast and declared 'delicious'.

Though he seems to have enjoyed Tibetan yak butter tea ('not at all bad!') Salim Ali expressed disappointment with the monasteries, which contained 'a curious haphazard collection of "jari-purana" bric-a brac' that included badly stuffed and moth-eaten bears, leopards, wild yak and even a badly deteriorated specimen of a Schomburghk's deer. These were all jumbled together with an assortment of prayer wheels and other ritual objects. In his journal he declared: 'Afraid I am very little impressed, rather depressed, at all this weird mumbo-jumbo that goes for religion, and at the blind faith that mankind has developed in things we imagine (why?) will bring salvation in the hereafter.'

A self-described 'materialist' Salim Ali had little time for the mysticism, rituals and superstitions of any faith. His expedition to Kailas and Manasarovar almost ended in a tragedy that would have deprived us of the many popular bird books and articles on natural history that he wrote in later life. Negotiating a narrow trail up to Lipu Lekh Pass, with a straight drop of 100 metres into the swollen rapids of the Kali River below, he spotted a yellow-naped yuhina. Grabbing his field glasses, he took a step backward to get a better view of the tiny bird. Hearing the sound of a pebble slipping from under his boot and rolling down into the gorge below, he realized that he himself had almost tumbled over 'the very edge of beyond—two incles more and I would have followed that rollicking pebble. The great leap forward I made at that instant would have done credit to Mao's reforming zeal.'

Born in Bombay in 1896, Salim Ali grew up in what is now known as Mumbai, long before it became the megalopolis or 'Maximum City' it is today. He spent his childhood in a middle-class neighbourhood of Khetwadi and holidayed with his family in Chembur. After studying science at St. Xavier's College, he tried his hand at business and travelled to Burma before returning home and deciding to pursue a career in ornithology. As a young boy, he had brought a yellow-throated sparrow (which he later described as having a 'curry stain' under its neck) to the Bombay Natural History Society (BNHS), where the curator identified it for him. Years later, he would become president of BNHS and one of the most respected and influential naturalists in India. For much of his adult life, Salim Ali and his wife Tehmina shared a spacious bungalow in Pali Hill, with his brother Hamid. This forested suburb later became a favourite haunt of film stars and remains one of the most exclusive addresses in the city. It was from their house, 46 Pali Hill, at the top of Zig Zag Road, overlooking the Arabian Sea at an altitude of no more than 100 metres, that he set out on scientific expeditions throughout the subcontinent.

Salim Ali had a particular fascination for the Himalaya and he conducted bird surveys in Afghanistan, Kashmir and Garhwal, as well as Sikkim, Bhutan and the North-East Frontier Agency (NEFA). Both the Chogyal of Sikkim and the king of Bhutan, Jigme Dorje Wangchuk, sponsored his expeditions. He worked closely with a number of eminent naturalists like Hugh Whistler, Colonel R. Meinertzhagen, S. Dillon Ripley, Loke Wan Tho and E. P. Gee.

Salim Ali's exploration of NEFA, what is now Arunachal Pradesh, was particularly important. He was one of the first ornithologists to do research in this region, at a time when there were very few roads and travel was extremely difficult. Nevertheless, he recorded extensive data, particularly migration patterns of birds and the comparative distribution of species. In an article, 'The Himalaya in Indian Ornithlogy' he writes: 'The Oriental element in the avifauna is richly represented in the eastern Himalaya and gradually diminishes westward until in Kashmir and far west it ceases to be a significant constituent, its place being taken by Palaearctic forms.' As an avid trekker Salim Ali had an acute awareness of the effects of altitude on plant and animal life. He comments on the noticeable differences in 'life zones' at different elevations, where changes in temperature, humidity and other factors create easily recognizable bands of flora and fauna by which an experienced naturalist like himself could estimate the height above sea level 'without the aid of an aneroid'.

Belonging to an earlier generation of naturalists, Salim Ali saw no contradiction in being both a hunter and a conservationist. In fact, he credited his interest in birds and wildlife to a youthful fascination with shikar. Nevertheless, he decried the wholesale slaughter of birds that occurred under royal patronage and British rule at places like Bharatpur, where the viceroys and their entourages shot thousands of ducks. Salim Ali was instrumental in creating a sanctuary for waterbirds in Bharatpur, now the Keoladeo National Park, where hundreds of thousands of seasonal visitors from across the Himalaya migrate during winter.

Shooting, skinning and stuffing birds were all part of the process of research, though he began to use mist nets as soon as they became available and avoided killing specimens indiscriminately. As he explains, his love of birds 'is not of the sentimental variety' and the pragmatic requirements of science forced him to kill and collect a large number of species. Though he did feel an occasional 'prick of conscience' he argues that it was essential to collect and preserve bird skins for taxonomical purposes. But he goes on to say, 'However, I believe a stage has now been reached when the *ad hoc* collecting of Indian bird specimens is no longer essential, except for special studies...'

The influence of Salim Ali's bird books on several generations of wildlife enthusiasts is immeasurable. His *Indian Hill Birds,* first published in 1949, is one of the most beautiful field guides ever produced, with exquisite full colour plates by G. M. Henry accompanied by a lyrical yet informative text. Though a number of new, updated bird books have been published in recent years, with fresh illustrations, there will always be an appreciation for the voluminous research Salim Ali conducted and his evocative style of writing. Few naturalists can match his succinct eloquence and precision when describing a species such as *Ithaginis cruentus*:

> The blood pheasant is a large, gaudily coloured partridge-shaped bird, chiefly grey and apple-green, with a mop like crest, black forehead and crimson throat. A black-bordered bright red naked patch surrounds the eye. The upper breast is splashed with crimson, like fresh bloodstains, and there are similar splashes also on the shoulders and the tail. The female—bright rufous brown with ashy-grey crest and nape—is so startlingly different in looks that initially it was even described as a different species from the cock. Successive observers have remarked upon the 'stupidity' of members of a covey coming out in trustful inquisitiveness to a companion fluttering in its death throes, and thus being killed one by one by the hunter—a shameful commentary on the vileness of man rather than on the bird's stupidity!

Today we understand and appreciate the natural history of the Himalaya far better and in greater detail because of the work of those like Salim Ali, who explored the mountains and forests with a clear and critical eye, as well as a poetic sensibility that found beauty in wild things without resorting to sentimentality.

chapter 24

BLOOD PHEASANTS OF KANCHENJUNGA

Snow has fallen during the night and the roof of my tent bulges under its soft weight. Punching the synthetic membrane, I try to shake it off. The sharp cry of a fox awakened me a few minutes ago—a vulpine alarm. When I unzip the tent's outer fly and peer into the darkness beyond, everything is white. A crystalline stillness envelops the valley. Squirming out of my sleeping bag and struggling to get dressed, I grapple with the frozen laces on my boots. Finally, when I emerge, the clouds have vanished and stars fill the sky, like hoar frost in the heavens.

My companions are still asleep but when I call his name, Bhrigu switches on a headlamp and his tent lights up like a glowing igloo. Justin, our guide, and the porters are sleeping in the cook tent, which has shrunk to half its width beneath a sagging layer of snow. I can hear them moving about and cursing under their breath but within fifteen minutes we are ready to go.

Crossing the Thangsing Valley our breath condenses in feathery plumes. We don't need our headlamps for the starlight is bright enough, reflecting off the snow. The path is buried and rhododendrons block our route, weighed down with burdens of fresh snow. After Justin locates the trail, we start up the narrow ridge. Climbing steadily but losing our way several times, we make slow progress. After half an hour, I come upon the tracks of a fox crossing our path, a solitary line of dimpled footprints in the snow. Finally, at about 4,500 metres, we reach a cairn overlooking the valley, draped with frosted prayer flags.

The sky is already brighter and the silhouettes of Pandim (6,811 metres) and Narsing (5,825 metres) rise directly above us to the east while the broad white furrow of the valley stretches northward to the foot of Kanchenjunga, still cloaked with blue shadows. In the semi-darkness, we hear the shrill call of a snow partridge somewhere ahead of us. Scanning the slopes, I can just make out the indistinct shape of a bird working its way up a parallel ridge. A second partridge follows its mate, moving slowly over the blank surface of the mountain as if searching for something it has lost. The pied striations on its back and wings, as well as the ruddy breast and pink beak are not visible, only a dark, blurred shape. From this distance it could be almost any bird, except for its scratchy cries that squeak like an unoiled hinge.

Partridges are members of the Phasianidae family that includes pheasants, francolins and quail, as well as peacocks, junglefowl and chickens. They are part of the larger order of Galliformes, bulky, terrestrial birds that usually stay on the ground unless forced to fly. A variety of these wildfowl occupy different elevations of the Himalaya and some of them, like the snow partridge, live at the uppermost limits of life along the snow line. Older than the Himalaya, Galliformes have been around since the Oligocene, 30 million years ago.

As I watch the partridges cross the ridge above us, the first rays of sunlight strike the eastern profile of Kanchenjunga. Unlike the famous panorama seen from Darjeeling, where a broad massif with five summits floats above the lower ranges, here on our southern approach the mountain has a distinctly different profile, tapering sharply to a single, rugged spike above a chaotic foreground of seracs and glaciers, knife-edged arêtes and saddles of ice. At 8,586 metres above sea level this is the third highest mountain in the world. Earlier, in the darkness, Kanchenjunga's summit looked unimposing, overshadowed by nearer peaks but now the rising sun heightens contrasts on the snow-plastered slopes that make the mountain stand out with greater prominence, as if it were elevated by light. Almost as soon as the first rays pick out its hidden features, we can see snow spume unfurling on the wind and the mountain is soon wreathed in frozen vapours.

Kangchendzönga is transliterated with a number of spellings, none of which accurately conveys the correct pronunciation of its name. In Tibetan, Kang means snow-covered mountain and Chen means 'great' or 'lofty' and dzong denotes 'treasure house' or a fort. Lepchas and Buddhists regard Kanchenjunga as a sacred mountain. Its name is often translated as 'the five treasures of the great snow', referring to the five summits, each of which is believed to house sacred elements such as gold, turquoise, salt and other precious minerals.

Lepcha and Bhotia folklore asserts that the mountain is guarded by demons who personify the dangers that await those who climb its slopes. When Douglas Freshfield reconnoitred the approaches to Kanchenjunga in 1899, he declared that the mountain was protected by the 'demon of inaccessibility'. As Harish Kapadia relates in his *Into the Untravelled Himalaya*, the first expedition was launched in 1905, led by Aleister Crowley. It ended in disaster when three porters and one European climber, Alexis Pache, were buried under an avalanche. This naive and reckless foray was one of the most ill-advised and acrimonious climbs in history. Crowley was not a serious mountaineer. Though he was co-leader of an earlier attempt to climb K2, he had exhibited erratic behaviour including pulling a pistol on one of his teammates.

The first attempt on Kanchenjunga was marked by Crowley's cruel indifference to the porters, most of whom climbed barefoot on the snow. He showed almost equal disdain for his teammates, who ultimately mutinied and set off down the mountain without him. The accident occurred on their descent. After hearing that his companions had been buried under tonnes of snow, Crowley made no effort to rescue them, but instead brewed himself a cup of tea and wrote in his journal: 'A mountain accident of this sort is one of the things for which I have no sympathy whatever... Tomorrow I hope to go down and find out how things stand...the doctor is old enough to rescue himself, and nobody would want to rescue de Righi.' Alcesti C. Rigo de Righi, a hotel manager in Darjeeling, survived and unsuccessfully tried to dig the victims out from under the snow with his bare hands. Crowley has been widely vilified for his role in the disaster and gave up climbing after this. Better known as a scandalous libertine, he later founded his own occult sect under the pseudonym 'Beast 666'. Some called him the wickedest man on earth because he indulged in satanic rituals and wrote sado-masochistic pornography. Kanchenjunga is said to have its own demons, including yetis that prowl its slopes, but none of these creatures could match the abominable behaviour of Aleister Crowley.

With gloved fingers, Justin points out Kabru North and Kabru South, as well as Kabru Dome. Each of these imposing mountains stands at least 1,500 metres lower than Kanchenjunga. Talung and Goecha peaks, at the head of the valley, directly beneath the summit, are now dwarfed by the magnitude of the holiest mountain in Sikkim, what the Lepchas call

Kingtshoomzaongboo—the bright auspicious forehead, the sacred guardian, where ancient deities reside and from whose pristine snow the first man and woman were formed.

Lephchas believe in a terrestrial paradise, similar to the Tibetan idea of a beyul, though they call their promised land Mayel Lyang—'ma' is the word for hidden, 'yel' means eternal and 'lyang' is land. This is where the mother goddess, Na-zong-nyo, makes her home, somewhere in the upper regions surrounding Kanchenjunga. When migratory birds pass through Sikkim, the Lepchas believe they go to Mayel Lyang where they build their nests and hatch their young. By some accounts, this hidden paradise is synonymous with Sikkim itself, suggesting the idea of a lost, ancestral homeland of fertility and peace.

In one of many stories about Mayel Lyang, recorded by Vanya and Ajeya Jha in their *Ethno-Ornithology of the Lepchas of Sikkim*, a fisherman travels upriver into the mountains and suddenly finds himself in an idyllic valley. Arriving at a house, he meets an elderly couple who welcome him, offering food and shelter. The next morning, when he wakes up, the fisherman discovers two children playing outside. Puzzled, he asks them where the elderly couple have gone. The children laugh and tell him that it is them; they are the same pair he met the night before. All the inhabitants of this valley pass through a lifetime every day; from infancy at daybreak and childhood until noon, they continue ageing until midnight. With each new day the cycle begins again and in this way they never die.

According to the Jhas, virtually every bird in the Eastern Himalaya has a Lepcha name. Some are onomatopoeic like kunnyong, the great barbet that wails incessantly from the tops of trees. Other birds are identified according to their distribution. If a name begins with 'dang', which means hot, this indicates a lowland species, such as dang rabchil pho, a silver-eared mesia, and dang sagvyet, the black-throated sunbird, both of which are found in subtropical forests below 1,500 metres. Birds whose names begin with 'lho', which means cold, are found at higher elevations such as lho peu-rentiep, the snow pigeon, or lho towa, the nutcracker. In other cases the names are derived from the colour of the bird's plumage. Fat nok kyok is a large brown thrush, one of several possible species—'fat' being the word for earth and the colour brown. 'Chap' means green, as in chap-fong-pho, the green magpie. Some bird names have stories attached like the female white-capped redstart, which is known as cee-bee-pho. 'Cee-bee' means, 'where are you?' This bird is said to be hunting for its mate, who drowned in a flash flood.

Lepchas believe that birds can tell time like the hornbill that flies back and forth from its nest at dawn and dusk. The whistling thrush, chamong pho, is also known for its punctuality. The first bird to call before daybreak, it is seen as a harbinger of dawn. Believed to be divine, the whistling thrush was chosen by the goddess and sent from Mayel Lyang to clean her sacred lakes by carrying away the leaves and twigs that fall in the water from surrounding trees.

But the most auspicious bird of all is the blood pheasant, sumong pho, which lives in high alpine forests above 3,000 metres. It is the state bird of Sikkim and regarded as the saviour of the Lepcha people. Sumong pho's story begins with a great flood, when the rivers Rangeet and Teesta quarreled and their waters rose up in the valleys, inundating the forests, fields and villages. The goddess, Na-zong-nyo, sent the blood pheasant from Mayel Lyang to protect and guide her people to safety on Mount Tendong, the only peak that was not submerged by the flood. Sumong pho then drank up all the floodwaters and restored the mountains and valleys so the Lepchas could return to their homes. For this reason, the blood pheasant is never killed by tribal hunters and worshipped as a protected species. The high altitude forests where it lives along the treeline are preserved as sacred groves.

In another myth, the blood pheasant is also said to have guided the Rangeet River along its course as it flowed down from the southern face of Kanchenjunga. Following the pheasant, the Rangeet finally reached its confluence with the Teesta, which was guided by a snake from the northern slopes of the sacred mountain. According to Lepcha lore, the rivers Rangeet and Teesta are lovers, who unite in the confluence. Their offspring are the first Lepcha people.

After our early morning climb to view Kanchenjunga, we return to camp at Thangsing for breakfast and then set off for Goecha La. By now the valley is flooded with sunlight and the snow is melting quickly. After an hour's walk we pass Lamunay, the last camp on this route and head on up to Sungmoteng Lake. Along the way are several cairns, one of which is topped by a rounded stone the size and shape of an ostrich egg. By now the clouds have swept in and Kanchenjunga is veiled in mist, though the sharp prow-like cliffs of Pandim keep appearing and disappearing above us. As we pass beneath its hidden seracs and hanging glaciers, we can hear avalanches crashing down, as the mountain shrugs off its fresh mantle of snow. There are no trees at this altitude and only a few low shrubs like junipers and *Rhododendron anthopogon*, which emits a cloying fragrance as the snow melts off its rust-coloured leaves. Flocks of snow pigeons circle above us, their white wings like scraps of white paper printed with prayers that monks cast into the wind.

A number of birds keep us company along this stretch of the trail, the brightest of which are grandalas, the size of a small thrush, their plumage the colour of blue ink. With short, nervous flights, they seem to lead us up the trail. Sungmoteng Lake is wedged between walls of moraine that form a rocky barrier separating the valley floor from the higher mountains above. The water of the lake is a chalky blue in contrast to the vivid indigo of the grandala that flits along its shore. A ruddy shelduck takes off and circles overhead, as we avoid the muddy edges of the lake and scramble over scree and talus to follow the grandalas.

By now the valley has narrowed and another half an hour brings us to the threshold of the pass. Somewhere above us stands Kanchenjunga, hidden from view. Surrounded by clouds and patches of snow, the terrain seems lifeless until I see what appears to be a boulder changing shape. Two bharal rams with heavy horns are standing above the trail. Through the mist, I watch them move slowly away from us. Their mottled coats of mineral colours match the moraine. The grandalas have dropped behind and we now follow a robin accentor, slightly larger than a sparrow, its ruddy feathers blending into the russet and grey stones. The bird is unafraid of us and comes within inches of our fingers as we offer it biscuit crumbs. Other than this solitary creature Goecha La is deserted, cold crosscurrents of wind wrapping us in clouds.

As we return down the valley past Sungmoteng Lake, I hear a loud cackle and see a large bird darting up the slope. For a moment, I think it might be a blood pheasant. But as I reach for my binoculars, I realize that these are Tibetan snowcocks, another species of Phasianidae with grey plumage and distinct black rings around the neck. Dark vertical stripes mark their breasts and their wings are trimmed with white. Like the snow partridges we saw earlier in the morning, they do not take flight, but scurry along the ground, stopping occasionally to lift their heads and look down their beaks at us. There are two species of snowcocks, Himalayan and Tibetan, the former being somewhat larger and with slight colour variations.

Further down the valley, we come upon more herds of bharal, mostly ewes and lambs, grazing on the meagre grasses of the valley. The presence of wildlife and birds at high altitudes relieves our sense of isolation. In this harsh environment, these creatures must adapt to the scarcity of food, freezing temperatures and limited shelter. The upper reaches of the valley lie above the range of blood pheasants, though every movement stirs in me an expectation of seeing the sacred sumong pho.

After a second night at Thangsing, Bhrigu and I pack up early to head down the valley. Leaving Justin and the others to load the tents and gear onto horses, the two of us descend into a birch and rhododendron forest, draped with bearded lichens the Lepchas compare to 'old women's hair'. No more than a hundred metres into the trees, we are startled by two bulky birds crossing our path. This time, there is no mistaking a male and female blood pheasant. Alarmed by our approach they dart up a mossy slope, stopping for only a second or two, before disappearing into the tangle of limbs and leaves beyond. My binoculars and camera are buried in my backpack, so I focus on the pheasant with my eyes alone and recognize the streaked silver plumage of the male, flecked with splashes of red. The hen is a grey-green colour and slightly smaller.

Elated, we carry on, and soon another covey of six blood pheasants appears ahead of us. They are less shy, loitering by the trail, amidst fallen birches and moss-covered moraine, as if intentionally posing to be photographed. For at least five minutes we watch the birds from a distance of 10 metres. Their eyes are upon us, alert and attentive, but without apparent fear. The pheasants have a natural elegance, each feather perfectly groomed and heads held high, seemingly aware of their sacred status. Like our view of Kanchenjunga this morning, these birds convey a memorable, mysterious beauty. Simply by their presence they seem to lead us towards an earthly paradise.

chapter 25

A CONVOCATION OF EAGLES

The stench of rotting flesh lingers in the winter air like a foetid perfume. Hundreds of birds of prey have congregated in the trees or are circling overhead—mostly Himalayan griffon vultures and pariah kites, as well as fifty or more steppe eagles. Almost as large as vultures, with leaner profiles, they look strangely human, perched on the bare branches of silk cotton trees. Like wrestlers hunkering down before a bout, the steppe eagles flex their wings and twist their necks from side to side. Even at rest, they have a powerful, aggressive stance and their eyes dart about, ever watchful and aware of their surroundings.

Aquila nipalensis is one of the largest Himalayan raptors with a wingspan that can exceed 2 metres. Adult birds are a dark brown colour with a coppery tinge at the nape of the neck. They are not quite as pale as tawny eagles and do not have the distinct markings of a spotted eagle, though the three species are often confused with each other. As with many raptors, juvenile steppe eagles exhibit distinctly different plumage from their parents, with white coverts under the wings and varying shades of tan that gradually darken with each successive moult. According to Rishad Naoroji, author of the definitive *Birds of Prey of the Indian Subcontinent*, steppe eagles can be distinguished from similar species by their oval nostrils (which are round in other eagles). The cere, or rear portion of the beak, is bright yellow and extends below the eye, giving the bird the appearance of smiling. A steppe eagle's black beak is a lethal instrument, sharply hooked like a steel barb.

Birds of prey, observed on the wing, are difficult to identify. Seen with the naked eye, circling several hundred metres overhead, the silhouette and kink of the wings are recognizable features, as are the length and shape of the tail. Nevertheless, it is often impossible to be absolutely sure. Experienced bird watchers speak of the 'jizz' of certain species, an intangible element that helps them instinctively tell the difference between similar birds. (Also spelled GISS, the acronym for 'general impression, shape and size'.) Even while listing the scientific details and field characteristics—the colour and shape of scapulars, tertials and tarsus—experts like Naoroji refer to a bird's jizz with a note of clairvoyance. Unlike weight and size, or the calls and nesting habits, jizz is something that cannot be measured or described with any specificity, yet it serves as a means of identification for those who understand its subtle nuances and distinctions, even if these can't be put into words.

For several years now, I have watched an annual convocation of steppe eagles on the outskirts of Raipur village in the Dehradun Valley. These birds are drawn to a garbage dump at the side of the highway, where dead animals and waste from nearby slaughterhouses are discarded. Chicken feathers and goat entrails are tossed into the lantana bushes along with road kills and other carcasses, far enough away from any buildings, so the decomposing odours can only be smelled by those driving past. In addition to the rotting remains, plastic bags and foil wrappers are strewn about, as well as used packing materials and other trash. The scene is a depressing reminder of India's failure to cope with waste.

Watching these birds roosting on the branches, waiting for free handouts, I feel an unsettling ambivalence about their presence. Aside from carrion, the raptors are also drawn to rodents that inhabit the garbage dump. Giant bandicoot rats are a favourite prey of steppe eagles, an unappetizing relative of the marmots and picas they feed on in Tibet and Mongolia.

As I watch, a kite is mobbed by half a dozen crows that try to harass it into releasing a scrap of meat from its talons. A flurry of black wings is accompanied by frenzied cawing. Within moments a larger shadow materializes out of the air as a steppe eagle swoops into their midst, sending the crows racing for cover. The kite manoeuvres a couple metres off the ground, desperately trying to gain altitude but the two birds collide in a cartwheel of wings and are nearly hit by a passing truck. As they separate, just in time to avoid the speeding vehicle, the kite makes good its escape.

While this encounter ends peacefully, there are accounts of steppe eagles snapping kites' wings or killing them in the process of stealing their prey.

Collective nouns for birds are based on human judgements and imagination—a murder of crows, a wake of vultures, a kettle of hawks. The phrase, 'a convocation of eagles' invests these birds with nobility and gravitas. As they circle overhead their flight is orchestrated by invisible wind patterns in the sky. Soaring and gliding, eagles inspire us with their majestic detachment from the earth, a separation that seems almost divine. In Hindu mythology the vehicle of Vishnu is Garuda, part man, part raptor, who sports a hooked beak and wings. Stories of eagles travel as far as these birds migrate and Mongolian folklore recounts that Genghis Khan's hunting eagle was named Girid, very likely a rendition of Garuda.

The shamanistic Bon tradition in Tibet incorporates a number of winged deities in its pantheon, among which the most powerful and prevalent is the horned eagle depicted in ceremonial masks and thangka paintings. These fierce-looking creatures are mountain gods, inspired by the steppe eagle and other birds of prey like the imperial and golden eagles. In their rituals, Bon shamans employ bird wings and feathers as fetish objects that contain mystical energies by which they practise divination and map out the hidden contours of sacred geography.

Direct human contact with eagles is rare, except in Mongolia and Kazakhstan, where they are trained for hunting. Most eagles exist outside our reach, which imbues them with a mythic aura. We yearn to travel in their company beyond the mountains, above the clouds. They are creatures that connect the sky to the earth, stitching the horizon with their wings.

Steppe eagles are transients in the Himalaya. They do not make their home in the mountains but pass through twice a year, often without touching down. A number of other raptors are resident species, such as crested serpent-eagles, mountain hawk-eagles and lammergeiers, or bearded vultures that can be found at different elevations, from the foothills to higher alpine zones. Their presence along the southern exposure of the Himalaya is closely tied to the forests and terrain, as well as small mammals, birds and reptiles on which they prey. Steppe eagles and other migrants who pass over the mountains amidst the clouds have little contact with the ground below. Yet the flight of these birds is an intrinsic part of the Himalayan story, occupying the heavens instead of the earth.

To cross the Himalaya requires an innate knowledge of geography and climate, as well as an ability to predict changes in the atmosphere. As winter ends, the steppe eagles wait at the base of the mountains while the foothills grow warmer. Their initial sorties are a means of testing the air, which rises along with the earth's temperature. The return flight across the Himalaya is more challenging than their autumn migration for instead of starting at altitudes of 4,000 metres on the Tibetan plateau and crossing over at 6–7,000 metres, the spring journey commences 3,000 metres lower down but still reaches the same altitude.

While the end points of a steppe eagle's migration may be roughly north and south, their flight paths don't always follow a straight line. Studies have shown that tens of thousands of these birds cross over from Tibet at various places and then follow the arc of the Himalaya, in a northwesterly direction before heading to lower latitudes. This route is reversed in spring, stretching from as far west as Afghanistan and Pakistan, across North India, Nepal, Sikkim and Bhutan where they breach the mountains at different points. These lateral flight lines allow the birds to use air currents along the lower ranges to position themselves for high altitude crossings. Timing their migration with instinctual precision, they gauge weather and wind patterns, until the moment arrives when they can feel sufficient lift beneath their wings to propel them northward.

Moving back and forth across the mountains, steppe eagles occupy a vital niche on either side of the Himalaya, helping to maintain a balance of creatures in two very different eco-systems. As sky-borne predators, *Aquila nipalensis* are opportunistic by necessity for the open grasslands of the Tibetan Plateau and Central Asia are not the easiest hunting grounds. Though powerful killers that can bring down a young gazelle, steppe eagles are just as content to scavenge off a kiang carcass left by wolves or the corpse of a Buddhist monk consigned to a sky burial. In Bharatpur Bird Sanctuary, Naoroji reports that steppe eagles have been observed feeding on the remains of both a python and a jungle cat. They have also been reported killing a mongoose and attacking herons and storks. Hunting is often done at night, by moonlight, when semi-darkness provides them with cover.

The death of other creatures is vital to their survival yet they are an integral part of the life cycle of the mountains and open plains. Their wintering grounds range from Rajasthan and Gujarat to the Deccan Plateau. Vagrants have been identified as far south as Kanyakumari, at the tip of India. In summer they settle and breed throughout Central Asia, from Tibet, across the Chang Tang to the northern reaches of Mongolia. Occasional stragglers stay in Nepal year round.

The coming and going of eagles match a pendulum of seasons. Their arrival and departure is part of the synchronized patterns of nature. Aerial predators disturb the complacent lives of certain species that might otherwise overbreed. Whether it is rats and palm squirrels in India or picas and hares in Tibet, the rodent population is controlled by eagles and other raptors. In the cold calculus of natural selection, weaker, unhealthy individuals are eliminated while stronger, more agile members of a species survive. There is no cruelty in this equation, simply a constant winnowing of the gene pool that eagles help perpetuate and strengthen through their predation.

Meanwhile, the Himalaya themselves play an important role in regulating the population of eagles. The mountains ensure that only the strongest fliers will be able to cross over. Diseased, injured or ageing birds cannot make this arduous journey and are thereby removed from the breeding cycle. Researchers have shown that juvenile steppe eagles tend to fly the farthest, ensuring that each new generation maintains its fitness. As with most raptors, female steppe eagles are larger than males, giving them greater strength and stamina to reach their nesting grounds. Even among the young there is a ruthless pecking order. *Aquila nipalensis* lays one to three eggs. When these hatch, the eaglets immediately begin competing for food their parents bring to the nest. Often the strongest chick will kill its siblings.

Competition continues as the eagles mature. As Naoroji explains, some of their most dramatic behaviour takes the form of aerial combat. Both playfully and in earnest, young birds try to dominate their rivals in flight, gaining a superior position overhead and forcing opponents into submission. These winged tussles often end with the two birds locking talons and spinning through the air in a lethal chakra of beaks, claws and flapping wings.

In recent years, steppe eagles have played an important role in filling the gap created by the near-extinction of India's vultures, which were decimated after feeding on carcasses of animals containing anti-inflammatory medicines like Diclofenac. Commonly used to treat livestock, this veterinary drug weakens the shell of a vulture's egg and causes it to crack while the chicks are still in embryo. As a consequence, eight species of vultures in India, particularly the white-rumped vulture (*Gyps bengalensis*), have been largely wiped out. Steppe eagles and other raptors like kites do not appear to be affected by Diclofenac and have, to a certain extent, taken the place of vultures in the disposal of carcasses, which are left to rot along the roadside or in bone yards throughout rural India.

Unlike many other species of eagles, *Aquila nipalensis* is a relatively sociable bird. It is often found in groups from five to twenty and when crossing the Himalaya they fly together in streams. In the fall of 1984, Robert Fleming Jr. estimated 45,000 steppe eagles passing over the Kali

Gandaki gorge near Dhaulagiri and in the spring of 2002, Jan Willem den Besten counted 10,000 soaring above Dharamshala in Himachal Pradesh. He recorded a peak number of 294 birds passing overhead in the space of forty-five minutes. Steppe eagles also migrate to Africa and the world population could range anywhere from 100,000 to 1,000,000. It has been included in the International Union for Conservation of Nature (IUCN) red list of endangered species because of declining numbers, largely due to degraded and disappearing habitats in Tibet and Central Asia.

Mountaineers have found the frozen remains of steppe eagles in high places like the South Col of Everest, where the birds must have died in a storm or from exposure and exhaustion. A sudden drop in temperature or a shift in wind direction can be fatal for the raptors, whose migration traces a thin line between survival and death. In captivity, steppe eagles have lived up to the age of forty years though it is unlikely they would survive that long in the wild. Ultimately, the instincts that carry them over the Himalaya lead to self-destruction, when the winds they ride no longer hold them aloft or drive them into a blizzard out of which they cannot escape.

To comprehend the extreme challenges of a bird's migration across the Himalaya, we can compare human flight under similar conditions. Paragliding is the closest our earthbound species comes to experiencing an eagle's journeys. One of the most popular places for this sport is in Himachal Pradesh at a village called Bir, near Palampur. The Dhauladhar range pitches up almost vertically from Bir and resulting air currents create a perfect place to ride the thermals. Not surprisingly, it lies directly along the migratory flight path of steppe eagles. Every year, a convocation of paragliders collects at Bir. This eclectic fraternity of extreme adventurers launch themselves off cliffs with nothing but a few ounces of nylon fabric to keep them from crashing to the ground.

Ameeta, my wife, who is much braver than me, decided that she wanted to try paragliding to celebrate her sixtieth birthday. From Bir, a twelve-kilometre drive up a winding hill road brings us to the takeoff point at Billing, which is little more than a tea shop on the crest of a high meadow. The drop from here to the broad valley below is more than 1,000 metres. When we arrive at the top a dozen paragliders are preparing to take flight, including an Englishman who looks like a cross between a weather-beaten hippie and an old-fashioned aviator. Despite the warm sunshine, he is bundled up as if for a polar expedition and shows us his woollen mittens, which are equipped with battery-powered heaters. He casually explains how he got frostbite the first time he flew from Billing. For several years he has been coming here and enjoys soaring towards the snow peaks of Kulu and Spiti to the north, climbing to altitudes above 4,500 metres.

Glancing up at the vultures wheeling above us, he says that one of the dangers of paragliding is that the birds sometimes think they can land on your kite. This sparks a series of anecdotes from other fliers, who describe being trailed by vultures and eagles. One of the women in the group recalls the story of an unfortunate Russian who crash-landed after an eagle got tangled up in his lines. Despite these risks, the Englishman is philosophical and says he doesn't begrudge the birds because, 'after all, we're invading their space'.'

A short while later, with a rustle of nylon, he is airborne and we watch him swoop down over the treetops at the edge of the meadow and then circle back as he searches for air currents that eventually lift him high over our heads. Within minutes, the English flier has climbed several hundred metres and after a quarter of an hour, he is a speck in the sky.

Soon afterwards, I watch Ameeta take off in a tandem rig with an instructor. As they glide towards a rocky spur of the Dhauladar Range, two vultures appear on cue, though they keep their distance before climbing into the clouds. While paragliding uses the same medium of the wind to carry fliers aloft, even our friend with his electrified mittens cannot match the altitudes steppe eagles reach or the risks they face. The real struggle for survival begins above 6–7,000 metres as the birds enter a death zone. In 1933, the Royal Air Force (RAF) conducted the first aerial survey of Everest in a pair of Westland biplanes, one of which almost crashed because of turbulence, dropping several hundred metres out of the jet stream. A second survey was carried out twenty years later in 1953, immediately after Edmund Hillary and Tenzing Norgay scaled the summit. India's first environment secretary, Nalni Jayal, was on that flight, as a young Air Force officer. A few years earlier he had been a member of two climbing expeditions to Kamet and Trishul, along with his cousin, Nandu Jayal, founding director of the Himalayan Mountaineering Institute in Darjeeling.

When the Indian Air Force decided to photograph Everest from the air, Nalni was chosen for the mission because of his mountaineering experience. His account of this historic flight, in an old 'four engine piston driven Liberator', which had seen service in World War II and was officially retired by the US Air Force in 1945, illustrates the desperate odds against which migrating eagles make their biannual journeys.

As the plane took off from Patna, on the Gangetic plain, sweltering summer temperatures were above 45° Celsius. 'But in just over an hour, we climbed to 8,000 metres and the temperature dropped to 27 degrees below freezing,' Jayal recounts. 'Originally, we had planned to synchronize our flight with the Everest expedition, to try and get photographs of the climbers approaching the summit but this was postponed because they were afraid that the roar of the engines and wind from the propellers might trigger avalanches.'

At 4,000 metres the pilot instructed his team to don their oxygen masks and electrically heated suits. The old bomber was insulated but the roar of its engines was deafening. Jayal and the others prepared to 'shoot' Everest through the gun ports. Every time these were opened the rush of air was so cold that several of the cameras jammed. Eventually, they had to make a second sortie the following day to complete their survey. With clear skies over Everest, the pictures they produced were dramatic, including 16 mm footage with a cine-camera, as the bomber circled the summit. The photographs were used to illustrate Sir John Hunt's published account of the Everest expedition and the film clips became part of an accompanying documentary.

While Nalni Jayal and his fellow Air Force officers were protected by heated flight suits and breathed supplemental oxygen to stay alive, steppe eagles and other migratory birds enjoy none of these comforts. They overfly mountains like Everest without any protection other than their feathers, nor do they have navigational aids or weather reports. Flying under their own power, they ascend to heights at which human beings need weeks to acclimatize, whereas the birds rapidly adapt to icy temperatures and the lack of oxygen. This extreme exposure and exertion would be enough to defeat a lesser species but the eagles complete their trans-Himalayan journeys, twice a year, against all odds.

chapter 26

ORIENTAL AVIFAUNA

At 4 a.m., as we set out on foot from camp, at Eaglenest Wildlife Sanctuary in Arunachal Pradesh, the jungle is submerged in darkness. No birds are visible but their calls surround us—the piercing wail of a common hawk cuckoo, the burbling of oriental turtle doves, a mountain scops owl's chiming tempo, the piping of wren babblers, a solemn thrumming of imperial pigeons and the ardent crowing of peacock pheasants. Even as the trees gradually begin to shift from shades of grey and blue to different hues of green, most birds remain hidden from sight.

Arunachal Pradesh means 'land of the dawn-lit mountains' and this region, once known as NEFA, lies at the eastern edge of the Himalaya. Here the sun rises an hour earlier than it does in Kashmir, at the opposite end of the time zone. Sensing a new day, even before the sky brightens, the birds have already risen.

Gradually, as daylight seeps into the air a few birds begin to appear. From the top of a bare branch overlooking the valley, a golden-throated barbet is calling. This green herald is capped in crimson with a gilded beard. On another tree nearby sits an orange-bellied leaf bird that has a higher-pitched, more melodious call. In mid-air, a lesser racquet-tailed drongo chases an insect. Two long black feathers on its tail follow the drongo's aerobatics like ribbons in the breeze. Minutes later, a slow-moving bird flies up in front of us and out of sight. Creeping forward we spot it perched on a low branch—a red-headed trogon, with a scarlet breast, buff back, barred wings and a long tail edged in white.

In the moist gloom beneath a dense tunnel of leaves, a chestnut-headed tesia flits about, as if someone were trying to light a match in the humid shadows. The flash of yellow on the tesia's throat, like a spark of sulphur, is the only glimpse we get of this tiny, stub-tailed bird. Its soft chirrup is barely audible within a decaying under-realm of humus and rotting moss, where the tesia lives out its secretive purpose on earth.

Few other forms of life capture our imagination in the same way as birds do, elevating and expanding our consciousness beyond the narrow limits of human perception. Their ability to fly gives them a freedom we covet while their variegated colours illuminate the bright palette of creation. Each morning, a dawn chorus of birdsong transforms the forest into a complex soundscape of wild cacophonies.

By now, the birdcalls have reached a crescendo, from the fluting cries of scimitar babblers to a woodpecker's inharmonius squawk. The trilled whistle of a spotted laughingthrush announces its appearance on a creeper above us. The plumage on this gaudy songster has so many polka dots and bars, it looks like a generalissimo on parade, sporting insignia and medals. As we continue to wander through the jungle, mixed flocks of tiny birds swarm around us, hunting parties made up of six to a dozen species. White-tailed nuthatches and minivets congregate with fantails and leaf warblers. A sultan tit makes a dramatic appearance amidst one flock, a handsome little bird jacketed in black with an unruly tuft of yellow feathers on his head and an underbelly to match.

Juggling binoculars and camera, I try to consult my well-thumbed *Oxford Pocket Guide to the Birds of the Indian Subcontinent*. As I begin to double-check the list of species I've jotted down in a notebook, a flight of scarlet finches distracts me. The females are a dowdy brown but the single male among them is bright red as a raspberry. Leafing through my bird book, I try to find the coloured plates of finches but a flapping sound interrupts me as two large, ungainly birds pass overhead. Their awkward, syncopated flight is easy to recognize, as is the distinctive profile of their heavy beaks and long, flared tails. After the pair have alighted on a wild fig tree in the distance, my binoculars bring them into focus, confirming that these are rufous-necked hornbills. With a shock of rusty red feathers on their heads and throat, bright blue eye patches and dark lines on their beaks that look like a clown's makeup, they have an absurdly comical appearance.

Birdwatching proceeds at its own pace and rhythm, distinct from other forms of ambulation. Synchronized to the movements of avifauna, it doesn't have the steady momentum of a trek, the competitive arithmetic of golf or the leashed routines of taking a dog for a walk. Joining me on this expedition are Bhrigu Singh and Viveck Crishna, both of whom are armed with lethal-looking cameras, bearing the appropriate brand name, Canon. Though we cover 5 kilometres before breakfast, this isn't a morning constitutional. Every twenty steps or so, we pause to focus on a whiskered yuhina or a rufous-vented fulvetta. Gazing up into the trees, our group shambles along, as if we've lost our bearings. One person or another takes the lead as someone else holds back to photograph a beautiful niltava with iridescent feathers, sunning itself on a twig.

With recent advances in audio technology, many birdwatchers, guides and photographers use digital playback recordings of birdcalls to lure certain species into view. This has become a significant problem in places like Eaglenest because it agitates and confuses the birds, disturbing their normal feeding, social and breeding behavior. While skilled naturalists have always been able to whistle up the birds they are looking for, smartphones are now equipped with special apps connected to portable amplifiers that are used to mimic a wide range of calls downloaded from online sites. While the occasional use of recorded birdsongs probably has a limited effect, when a number of guides and birders in a relatively small area repeatedly use audio playback or 'tape lures', it becomes intrusive and disruptive, particularly for rare and endangered species.

Between November and April every year, when the rains cease and leeches disappear, Eaglenest attracts an annual migration of ornithologists and amateur birdwatchers. They are drawn to these forests because of the diversity of resident species as well as transients that pass through on yearly journeys between the higher Himalaya and the lowlands of Assam. A narrow dirt track that runs through the sanctuary was once the old NEFA road, the only motorable access to the mountains until the mid-1960s, when the military highway was built from Tezpur to Tawang. Fortunately, the new road follows a different route and Eaglenest was declared a wildlife sanctuary in 1989.

In 2006, a previously unknown bird was discovered here, the Bugun liocichla (*Liocichla bugunorum*). This is the first new bird to be described in India in half a century. Ramana Athreya, an astronomer by profession, first spotted it in 1995 but only found the bird again, ten years later, in 2005, when he was able to catch a couple of live specimens using mist nets.

A relatively small bird, about 20 centimetres long, with a black cap and distinctive colouration of greyish green with streaks of gold, the Bugun is easy to differentiate from other species, which makes it even more remarkable that it went unnoticed for so many years. These days, new birds are usually 'discovered' as a result of genetically 'splitting' a known species using DNA analysis. The closest relative of the Bugun is the Emei Shan liocichla from the mountains of Southeastern China. Athreya chose to name his discovery after the Bugun tribe of forest dwellers who share these jungles with the liocichla. From research done so far, this rare endemic babbler seems to inhabit a very limited range of a few square kilometres.

Amongst the Bugun and Sherdukpen communities, whose tribal territory includes parts of Eaglenest Sanctuary, birds play an important part in their mythology and folklore. During annual festivals, the Sherdukpen perform a ritual dance that re-enacts the story of two giant birds called Jachung that used to prey on human beings until the gods become worried that *Homo sapiens* might face extinction. Eventually these feathered monsters were trapped and exterminated to ensure the survival of our species. This story and other folklore from the North-eastern Himalaya were collected by Verrier Elwin, quoted earlier in this book, an English missionary who became an Indian citizen and turned his attention to tribal culture.

Another myth that Elwin recorded describes a huge bird called Jatung-Tung-Karmu that laid three eggs in a nest high up in the Himalaya. When the first egg hatched a white yak emerged and flew up to heaven. Out of the second egg came a red yak that vanished into the forest. And from the third egg a black yak was born, which was tamed by human beings, providing them with milk and wool. There is also a folk tale about Gyamu-Lala-Pipi, the most beautiful bird of all, who refuses to marry any of her suitors. Eventually, she is seduced by a bat who comes to her at night when she cannot see what he looks like. Pretending to be the king of the birds, he whispers endearments in the dark. The next day, when Gyamu-Lala-Pipi discovers the true identity of her lover, she renounces him in front of a council of birds who mock his ugly demeanour. This is why the bat always hangs his head in shame.

Our birding expedition takes us across Se La, at 4,000 metres, to Tawang, where we see pink-browed rosefinches and white-winged grosbeaks as well as a winter wren that looks like a check mark on the snow but the true diversity lies at lower altitudes. Eaglenest is a wild, unfenced aviary full of unique species, each of which has its own story to tell, from trogons to tragopans and sibias to sunbirds. Our guide, Micah, grew up in a small village on the periphery of the sanctuary and began working with ornithologists eight years ago, assisting them in setting up and monitoring mist nets for ongoing bird surveys in the sanctuary. These nets are virtually invisible and allow researchers to capture even the most elusive species without causing injury, so that specimens can be identified, weighed, measured, photographed, tagged and then released back into the wild.

Birds have become a form of livelihood for Micah and several other young men in his village. When they are not working with researchers, they get hired as guides for visitors like us. Micah's parents originally came here from Nepal. He is a confident, articulate young man who answers our questions with a look of mild amusement on his face. Having grown up in these forests, he knows every landmark, trail and water source. Though he has learned both common and Latin names from the scientists he works with, Micah was already familiar with these birds from an early age.

'As a boy, I hunted in these jungles using a catapult. We would eat whatever we shot,' he says, with a guilty smile, 'even sunbirds. We plucked the feathers and roasted them over a fire. I also used to raid sunbird nests.'

He tells us how he tried to boil the tiny eggs, the size of pomegranate seeds, but the fragile shells burst. 'After that I made an omelette.' He laughs, admitting that even a dozen sunbird eggs produced no more than a mouthful.

Micah is now a committed conservationist. During our week-long visit to Arunachal Pradesh, he shows us three different species of sunbirds—green-tailed, fire-tailed, and Mrs Gould's. Among the smallest but most intensely coloured creatures in the Himalaya, sunbirds have a jewel-like brilliance. With thin, curved beaks they feed on nectar, darting from flower to flower.

The naming of Indian birds has a colonial legacy going back to the early nineteenth century. Many of the first scientific descriptions of Himalayan species can be traced to B. H. Hodgson. The British resident in Kathmandu for ten years, from 1833 to 1844, Hodgson is considered the founding father of Himalayan ornithology. Though he was not permitted to travel outside Kathmandu, Hodgson had a team of Nepali collectors who helped him acquire more than 20,000 specimens that were skinned and shipped back to the Zoological Society in London. The taxidermist or 'bird-stuffer' at the Zoological Society museum was a man named John Gould, whose wife Elizabeth was an artist. Together they produced the *Century of Birds from the Himalaya Mountains*, a lavish folio edition with lithographs by Mrs Gould, who enjoyed the unique privilege of having a sunbird named in her honour, *Cinnyris gouldiae*. In the text that captions her illustration of a male and female of the species, Nicholas Vigors, secretary of the Zoological

Society, paid tribute to both the subject and the artist:

> This very elegant little bird—named after Mrs. Gould, by whom the
> 'Century' was delineated—was received from the highest portions of
> the Himalaya, to which it is supposed to be principally confined...The
> top of the head, ear-coverts, throat, a spot on each side of the chest
> near the shoulder, tail-coverts and the two middle tail feathers, are of
> a rich metallic blue with brilliant purple reflections; the back and sides
> of the neck, and shoulders, are deep sanguineous red; the rump and
> under surface bright yellow, the latter having a few sanguineous dashes;
> the quills and outer tail-feathers dark brown.

The accompanying lithograph is an exquisite likeness that brings the
luminous birds to life. Assisting the Goulds was a young artist in his twenties
named Edward Lear who drew a number of specimens, as well as the foliage
and foregrounds for Elizabeth's illustrations. He later collaborated with the
Goulds on *Birds of Europe* but soon gave up scientific illustrations because his
eyesight began to suffer from the intricate work. Later on, after he became
famous for his limericks and nonsense verse, Edward Lear sailed to India in
1874 and produced landscape paintings and a journal from his travels that
includes visits to the Himalayan hill stations of Mussoorie and Darjeeling.

Elizabeth Gould never saw her namesake in the wild. Her lithograph
must have been based on specimens collected by Hodgson, who also had
a number of birds named after himself, including a redstart (*Phoenicurus
hodgsoni*) and a frogmouth (*Batrachostomus hodgsoni*) as well as the Tibetan
antelope or chiru (*Pantholops hodgsonii*). Most of these names were assigned
by Edward Blyth, curator of the Royal Asiatic Society of Bengal and one
of the reigning taxonomists of his time. As the British secured their eastern
dominions they carefully catalogued the natural history of the subcontinent,
as if creating an inventory of prized acquisitions. The Himalaya were one
of the richest repositories of new species and the list of English and Latin
names became a roll call of East India Company officials.

The tradition of recognizing renowned scientists by naming species
in their honour continues today, though the discovery of new birds or
animals is now a rare event. In 2016, an international team of ornithologists,
with the help of genetic analysis, determined that the plain-backed thrush
(*Zoothera mollissima*) should be split into two species. The new bird, renamed
the Himalayan forest thrush, was dubbed *Zoothera salimalii,* in honour of
Dr Salim Ali.

While I try unsuccessfully to differentiate between a plain-backed and a

Himalayan forest thrush, Micah is determined to show us a Bugun liocichla. In recent weeks, he has sighted this new bird several times and tells us that the best place to find a Bugun is an area called Alluvali, near his village, in a degraded patch of forest covered with open scrub, particularly the medicinal weed, *Artemisia vulgaris*. Bugun often socialize with barwings, Micah tells us, and we soon find a flock of rusty-fronted barwings, a hundred metres from the motor road. For half-an-hour we scour the underbrush keeping a lookout for a small brown bird with rosy patches on the secondaries and streaks of red under its tail.

Eventually, Micah hears a Bugun's call from the slope above and immediately beckons for us to follow. Scrambling through the underbrush, we stop every couple of minutes to try and locate the call. Though I cannot hear it at first, when Micah points excitedly in the direction of a patch of nettles, a warbling medley of notes is barely audible. The chase continues across a rocky ravine and up a forested ridge. Every time we stop, out of breath, the call grows fainter and fainter until, after twenty minutes, it fades away completely.

Though we fail to add the Bugun to our bird list, Micah shows us a variety of other rare species. One of these is the fire-tailed myzornis, an emerald-green warbler with a black mask over its eyes, like a miniature bandit who has dipped his tail in red nail polish. Three of these feathery gems move nervously through tangled shrubs at the side of the road. Soon afterwards we also get a good look at a wedge-billed wren babbler. An endemic species found only in the Eastern Himalaya, it has a lilting four-note call that emanates from the damp recesses of the jungle where it hides.

Eaglenest Sanctuary contains more than just birds. Driving along the forest track, we turn a corner and come upon a male serow (*Naemorhedus sumatraensis*) in the middle of the road. With a dark brown coat, prominent ears and short spiked horns, it looks like a cross between a donkey and a goat. Usually a reclusive animal that stays hidden within the underbrush, this one seems unbothered by our presence and takes his time before climbing the hill out of sight. Belonging to the same family as goral, these goat-antelopes are found throughout the Himalaya up to Kashmir, though serow are more plentiful in the east, ranging across Southeast Asia. They are also related to takin (*Budorcus taxicolor*), the national animal of Bhutan. While birdwatching, we also spot several giant squirrels but they are more skittish than the serow, scrambling away from branch to branch. Eaglenest is home to clouded leopards and golden cats as well as red pandas. The other large mammal in these forests is the mithun, a cross-breed of wild gaur and domestic cattle that stands almost 2 metres at the shoulder. Tribal communities raise semi-feral mithun and these massive animals are considered a measure of a man's wealth. Wandering through the sanctuary, we encounter several mithun with dangerous-looking horns. They seem docile enough, browsing in the forest, but could do a lot of damage if provoked.

The biggest surprise, however, is finding elephants at 3,000 metres above sea level. This is the only place on earth where *Elephas maximus* climbs to these heights. The forest is full of bamboo and wild bananas, but the terrain seems too steep and temperatures too cold for elephants. Nevertheless, on one of our morning bird walks, we come upon recent prints in the mud as well as fresh clods of dung. Less than 200 metres away, I can hear a herd in the jungle, breaking branches. Not wanting to confront them on a narrow mountain trail, we leave the elephants alone.

A few days earlier, at Tawang Monastery, in the north-west corner of Arunachal Pradesh, we saw a large pair of tusks on display, the aged ivory stained a burnished brown. A small sign below them read: 'This pair of elephant tusks was discovered by the mother of Khandro Drowa Zangmo (the Queen of King Kala Wangpo) in the 7th Century A.D. buried deep underneath her field where she was ploughing to prepare her field for cultivation.' From the curved shape of the tusks, which resemble giant forceps, it seems possible that these might be the remains of a woolly mammoth that wandered across the Tibetan Plateau during the last ice age. Mammoth tusks are regularly dug up in Siberia and there is a growing market for Pleistocene ivory, now that the sale of elephant tusks has been banned. The provenance of the tusks in Tawang is difficult to determine, except perhaps by DNA testing. Drowa Zangmo (also spelled Sangmo), whose mother is said to have dug them out of the earth, is a popular character in Tibetan and Bhutanese folklore, a wise Dakini reborn on earth in order to spread the Buddhist Dharma. History, science and myth have a way of getting muddled, particularly when it comes to sacred relics. The other intriguing image at Tawang is a large Garuda figure with a serpent in its beak, overlooking the main courtyard of the monastery. Both in Buddhist and Hindu tradition, this divine raptor is the enemy of snakes.

◆

Though Arunachal Pradesh is now an Indian state, China claims that most of this territory was once part of Tibet. In 1962, the People's Liberation Army (PLA) crossed over Bum La and took Indian forces by surprise. During a brief border war, the Chinese penetrated as far as Bomdila, about

30 kilometres from Eaglenest Sanctuary. As the Indian Army regrouped and fought back, they positioned an artillery battery on the high point of the ridge at the centre of the sanctuary, facing Bomdila. The guns have long since been removed but Micah recalls collecting shell casings and other scrap metal from the site when he was a boy. The dense forests and rugged terrain were difficult to defend but, fortunately for India, the Chinese commanders realized that they had overextended themselves and retreated before snow fell on the high passes. Since then, this mountainous frontier has been heavily militarized and new highways have been built up to the border. Tensions continue and for many years Arunachal Pradesh was closed to tourists. Even today, both foreign and Indian visitors are required to get a 'restricted area permit'.

Military installations are everywhere, with regiments from all across India stationed here to guard the border. Though the army camps are neatly maintained and squads of soldiers pick up trash along the roadside, the environmental impact of militarization is inevitable. Aside from the fact that Indian Army aesthetics seem to dictate that every rock should be painted white, the fences and fuel depots, lines of barracks and supply sheds are impossible to ignore, even when hidden under camouflage netting. Convoys of trucks, carrying troops, equipment and rations, inch their way up the switchbacks, emitting clouds of diesel exhaust.

Thanks to the efforts of conservationists, Eaglenest has been spared from army occupation. Had the old NEFA road been widened it would have certainly destroyed the Bugun liocichla's habitat and disturbed many other rare species in these forests. Even the few short sections of the road that are being paved to provide easier access to the sanctuary are causing damage. Given the fact that no villages are located in the core zone, there would seem to be no need to improve the forest track beyond its present condition.

Though the original NEFA road leads down to the plains of Assam, only 40 kilometres away, we leave the mountains by a much longer, more circuitous route. Micah and others have warned us that Bodo insurgents still operate at the foot of the hills below Eaglenest and it is better to avoid this region and travel to Guwahati by the military highway. A few years back, a group of butterfly enthusiasts were kidnapped and held for ransom.

The extended detour offers us an opportunity to compare the forests along the highway with the protected jungles of the sanctuary. It comes as no surprise that the motor road has caused widespread destruction. Not only are there large military transit camps but also a number of temporary shanties for road crews, all of whom depend on the forest for firewood and bamboo. More than anything, erosion is the most evident result of road building and it has a devastating effect on the forests. At several points, where the slope is unstable, landslides have carried away most of the vegetation leaving huge lesions of mud and rock. While the highway linking Tezpur with Tawang was initially constructed fifty years ago by the Defence Ministry's Border Roads Organisation, it remains in a perpetual state of disrepair, with JCB power shovels clearing rubble and dumping debris into streams and rivers. Military planners, whose first priority is national security, require motorized access to border regions and they show little concern for ecology that gets in the way.

Eventually, as we descend from the mountains into the Brahmaputra Valley, temperatures rise and the foliage becomes increasingly tropical. The Arunachal Pradesh Forest Department maintains an orchid research centre at Tipi, where the highway leaves the hills. After hours of driving on winding roads it is a pleasant stop but the orchids are disappointing, only a few species in bloom.

Crossing the state border into Assam, we see a number of paramilitary camps set up to deal with Bodo insurgents. Despite years of hostility and bloodshed, however, the region seems remarkably peaceful, at least on the surface. Passing through a small roadside village, I notice a group of four women praying in front of a potted plant. Only later, in an article by folklorist Faguna Barmahalia, do I learn that the Bodo people, who are animists by tradition, consider a flowering shrub, *Euphorbia milii*, a living symbol of their supreme deity, Bathoubrai. Known locally as 'sijou' and as 'Christ thorn' or 'crown of thorns' in the West, this hardy, cactus-like spurge, with delicate pink flowers, is planted at Bodo altars and represents the resilience of life because it can grow under almost any conditions.

As we drive over a bridge spanning the Brahmaputra at Tezpur, the broad alluvial current stretches between forested hills and tea gardens. It is a striking contrast to my memories of the Tsang Po in Tibet, where the river begins as a tiny rivulet near Mount Kailas. The Himalaya are now an indistinct blur of blue ridges to the north and we have left behind the dense forests of Eaglenest with its multitude of birds. A few egrets are wading in a rice paddy and an occasional myna flies overhead. Along the highway, beyond Tezpur, I spot an Amur falcon perched on a power line. Further east of here, in the hills of Nagaland, these tiny raptors, no larger than a pigeon, migrate in swarms, their graceful silhouettes filling the sky. Several years ago this annual passage was threatened when local fishermen strung nets in the trees and caught hundreds of falcons to be sold as meat. Fortunately, conservationists intervened and the migration of Amur falcons has become a popular tourist attraction, saving the birds before they could have been wiped out.

Though we leave Arunachal Pradesh with an indelible sense of nature's rampant diversity, our trip ends on a disturbing note. Friends had recommended that we stop to see a flock of greater adjutant storks on the outskirts of Guwahati. As the sun is setting through a haze of pollution over the city, we turn off the highway and ask for directions to the garbage dump. After seven days in the pristine forests of the Eastern Himalaya, we suddenly find ourselves in a smouldering wasteland of accumulated filth with mountains of refuse ignited by spontaneous combustion.

Perched on these huge piles of burning rubbish are hundreds of storks, stooped like solemn hunchbacks with bald heads and heavy beaks. Hanging under their throats is a loose pouch of skin that looks like a deflated balloon. A few kites and crows circle through the smoke but most of the birds are *Leptopilos dubius*, their charcoal black wings folded over legs as thin as sticks of bamboo. Making hoarse, croaking noises they argue with each other and flap their wings. Like the steppe eagles outside Dehradun, these flesh-eating birds feed on scraps of carrion brought here from butcher shops and road kills all over the city. Mixed with the sour, charred odour of smoke is the putrid stench of decomposing flesh.

Worse still is the presence of ragpickers who live in hovels along the margins of the dump, scavenging whatever recyclable materials can be gleaned. Children run about barefoot through streams of sewage and glaciers of broken glass, while the grim birds look like creatures out of an apocalyptic mirage. Reminded of the giant man-eating birds of Sherdukpen folklore, I can't help feeling that this is how our world may end, a grotesque vision of a polluted land, populated by carnivorous storks, who squawk and squabble over rotting skin, entrails and bones.

V

MOUNTAIN MAMMALS
Ungulates and Others

chapter 27

FIELDS ON THE HOOF

Crossing an unnamed pass, more than 200 goats and sheep pour down the ridge, over a snowfield and onto a steep slope of loose scree. Some of them pause to crop mouthfuls of grass though they are not grazing, but descending with the combined volition of a flock, spilling down the mountainside as relentlessly as an avalanche. A protective impulse herds them in formation, a moving mass of hair and horns, as if it were one huge animal emerging out of the rock-strewn heights. Their instincts are as sure-footed as their hooves, an unerring Caprinae nature braided into their genes.

Where our trails converge, near a shallow stream spilling out from under a tongue of ice, I step aside to let them pass. The collective momentum of the herd makes it seem as if the mountain itself has come to life, sloughing off its winter pelt. Spring has just begun. The first anemones and primulas are opening their petals. Mouse hares emerge from rocky lairs. Flies are hatching in a vernal tarn.

While the goats and sheep make no sound, the herdsmen whistle through their teeth, a shrill birdlike call that keeps the flock moving, as if it were the cry of a raptor circling overhead in the hope of taking one of the straggling lambs. Two Tibetan mastiffs with matted fur and steel collars patrol behind the flock. One of the shepherds carries a newborn kid in the crook of his arm. The herdsman wears a rough, loose-fitting jacket and trousers woven from the raw, rough-spun wool of his animals, sharing their rank odour. The goats emit an overpowering stench, the foetid perfume of anal glands mixed with sour fragrances of milk, urine and dung.

We greet each other with cautious reticence brought on by the silent magnitude of the mountains and the isolation of this place. The shepherds have been travelling for a week from their village to the south of here. After another day or two, they will reach the high bugiyal meadows, where they spend four months of each year, herding their flocks above the treeline.

Most of the animals are fitted with compact saddlebags made of handspun woollen fabric. They jostle one another with their loads but seem untroubled by the extra weight. Each bag contains 2.5 kilograms of rice or flour, provisions for the summer. Though a single load is small, a hundred goats can transport as much as a tonne. Years ago, these animals would have carried coarse crystals of salt, collected from the shores of saline lakes in Tibet, several weeks' journey beyond the highest mountains. But the traditional trading routes between India and Tibet are now closed because of disputed borders.

The shepherds camp for the night beside a stand of moru oaks and firs, where a stream has cut a gash in the meadow. I pitch my tent a hundred metres above them, amidst a field of boulders dragged here by glaciers now extinct. Though the mountains appear static and frozen in time, evidence of movement is everywhere, a pulsing spring seeping down the slope, the upward thrust of tapered ridges, irises twitching in a gust of air. An accentor rises out of the grass on deft brown wings, catching a breeze and sailing down the slope. The goats and sheep fan out to graze.

From the cliffs above, wild goral watch their tame cousins, suspicious of these creatures that share the company of man. Goral (*Naemorhedus goral*) are a species of goat-antelope, with short, sharp horns and grey-brown coats. Scientists believe they are similar to the ancient ancestors of goats and sheep. As George Schaller, the eminent field zoologist, writes in his book *Mountain Monarchs*, the genealogy of these species goes back to the formation of the Himalaya and other ranges. He explains that the evolution of Caprinae coincides with periods of prehistory when mountains began rising up in different parts of Eurasia and Africa during the late Miocene and early Pliocene epochs (between twenty-three to five million years ago). Subsequently, during the late Pliocene and Pleistocene (between three to two million years ago), when another spurt of 'mountain building' occurred, the ancestors of contemporary wild goats and sheeps evolved, with larger, more elaborate horns. Schaller notes that though few fossilized remains of early Caprinae have been found to establish intermediary links they appear to have quickly developed traits ideally suited to precipitous terrain.

Higher up in the mountains, where the shepherds spend the summer, their flocks will share pastures with blue sheep or bharal (*Pseudois nayaur*) that also represent an intermediary link between goats and sheep. Bharal have adapted perfectly to harsh climates and vertical terrain, blending into the rocks. Human beings arrived long after these creatures populated the Himalaya, first as hunters who stalked goral, bharal, ibex, thar, markhor and the argali with spiral horns. The origins of domesticated goats and sheep are obscure, though early pastoralists must have tamed and bred wild *Caprinae*, rearing them for transport, milk, wool, meat and dung.

Leaving the flock to feed under the watchful eyes of their dogs, the herdsmen gather dry twigs and light a fire within a ring of rocks, the same hearth they used last year and the year before that. As nightfall approaches, I visit their camp. Smoke trails up the slope like strands of wool unravelling on the breeze. The shepherds boil a pan of water from the spring and make tea with goat's milk. It gives off a greasy, pungent aroma but these men have lived with it since birth, the odour as familiar as the resinous incense of their campfire or the musky earth thawing out after a long winter. Each smell is arranged in the air like an alphabet of odours. A lurking fox or leopard can read the different scents on the breeze.

Throughout the Himalaya, goats and sheep are a pervasive presence, moving back and forth from one meadow to the next. Shepherds follow traditional routes of migration that have been used for centuries. Years ago, trekking through the Zanskar Valley in Ladakh, Ameeta and I arrived at Shingo La in the dark. Casting about for a campsite, we finally settled on a broad ledge at the side of the path, just below the pass. To our surprise, this ended up being the most comfortable night we spent on the three-week journey. Only in the morning did we realize that our tent was pitched on a layer of dry goat dung, 15 centimetres deep and soft as a foam mattress. This luxurious bed must have accumulated over several years as herdsmen and their flocks halted here, on their way in and out of Zanskar.

Robert Ekvall, one of the first ethnographers to study Tibetan pastoralists, refers to migrating goats and sheep as 'fields on the hoof', a phrase that captures the essence of a Himalayan shepherd's life. These nomadic herdsmen cultivate their flocks just as agriculturalists work the soil. The 'sowing and reaping' of a herd follows the same patterns as farmers plowing and planting, then watering and nurturing their crops. Rather than being tied to the ownership or tenancy of terraced farms, nomadic herdsmen cover great distances, moving between lower and higher pastures. What they own and tend is a living acreage of animals that travels across the mountains, forming a drifting fleece upon the land.

chapter 28

A FERAL NATURALIST

When asked why he is drawn to high places, George Schaller smiles and shrugs.

'Because it's not so crowded,' he replies.

A tall, agile man with rumpled grey hair and a ready smile that hides a critical reticence in his eyes, he is the consummate 'outsider', preferring a life outdoors, away from cities and suburbs, conferences and classrooms. Schaller refers to himself as a 'feral naturalist'. As he writes in his book, *Tibet Wild,* his career as a wildlife biologist has had an impact on his character: 'The study of animals over the decades has defined me and, in a way, superseded me as a person.'

Though he seems more comfortable in the company of other species, Schaller gives generously of his time to individuals and institutions committed to interpreting and preserving nature. His books have inspired several generations of naturalists and his message of conservation is clear and concise. As a scientist, he sums up the essential question that drives his research: 'What facts do I need to help protect and manage a species and its habitat?' He then adds a simple mantra: 'Ignorance is no longer an excuse.'

Mountain Monarchs, his seminal study of wild sheep and goats in the Himalaya, is based on years of fieldwork at high altitudes and in remote regions from northern Pakistan to isolated valleys in Nepal. Considering his own legacy, what reassures him most is that he has motivated wildlife scientists working in their own countries. Schaller writes: 'I believe that my greatest gift to a country is to leave behind trained nationals who will continue the fight to protect nature's beauty. In this way my legacy of knowledge and spirit will flow onward long after I have ceased to be even a memory.'

Wildlife biology has evolved into a highly specialized field, in which species are now identified using DNA analysis rather than a pair of binoculars. Yet, Schaller insists that you cannot understand nature without observing it first-hand. 'Natural history remains the cornerstone of conservation…' he explains. 'Technology helps to open the world but technology can also close it unless one learns directly from nature.' He argues for a generalist approach rather than the narrow research in which a PhD student may study the enzymes in an urial's digestive tract but rarely observes this creature in the wild.

'Look, to get a job today you have to know how to use a computer,' he admits, when we meet at the Wildlife Institute of India in Dehradun, yet shakes his head in frustration. 'But they do all this computer modelling, using fancy statistics and Google Earth, without ever going into the field. The other day, somebody sent me a paper on the botany of Eastern Tibet and I told him, "It's all wrong. I've been there and seen what plants there are".'

When Schaller started his career as a researcher in Alaska, he spent months traversing the tundra on foot. Later, he got an opportunity to study mountain gorillas in Rwanda. 'Some so-called professors told me that gorillas were too dangerous to study, but having spent time with grizzly bears, they didn't bother me.' Through patience and perseverance, Schaller gained acceptance from these 250 kilogram primates, who got used to his presence and let him approach within a few metres. After Africa, he moved on to India where he conducted research for his book, *The Deer and the Tiger*. He tells a story of walking alone through Kanha National Park. 'There was a big boulder and I approached it cautiously because sloth bears often dig near these rocks. As I circled around it, I glanced up and there was a tiger dozing on top. He and I looked at each other at the same moment, a few feet apart. I backed away slowly and climbed into the closest tree. The tiger got down from the rock and came to the foot of the tree and stared up at me. I waved my hands and said, "Go away, tiger." And that's what he did, walking off into the jungle.'

Of course, Schaller recognizes the risks he's taken and explains that wild animals can be unpredictable. 'They can have a bad day, like any of us, and if you're in the way…' He holds up both hands in a gesture that suggests the inevitable. He relates a story of another PhD student, like himself, who was researching grizzlies in Alaska. 'They got used to having him around and he was able to approach them on foot, but then one night a bear came into his tent and ate him.'

Human beings are often a greater threat to his work than some of the large predators he's studied. Politics and paranoia have obstructed Schaller's research and he has had confrontations with government officials and other naturalists who have accused him of working for the CIA or exploiting his position as a foreigner. India, in particular, hasn't welcomed research by outsiders and most of his work in the Himalaya took place in Pakistan, Nepal and Tibet, where he has been able to collaborate with local wildlife researchers. The Chinese authorities, in particular, have given him access to areas where few foreigners have been admitted.

He tells me about a festival at a Tibetan monastery, where monks dedicated themselves to preserving the environment. 'I was the only foreigner allowed to watch the ceremonies,' he says. 'Everything I write gets translated into Chinese, even if they don't like what I have to say, but of course I can't read the language so I don't know what they change or leave out.' Schaller has a pragmatic approach to his work. Acknowledging that the Dalai Lama has done a lot to promote conservation, he adds: 'But I don't try to meet the Dalai Lama because I know he's got spies around him who report back to Beijing. That would cause problems for me when I work in Tibet.'

Recently, his research has focused on the Chang Tang, in northwestern Tibet, which remains one of the least developed regions of the globe and home to several endangered species particularly the chiru or Tibetan antelope. Working alongside a team of Chinese scientists, Schaller helped locate several of the chiru's calving grounds, witnessing the culmination of their annual migration. Coming upon large herds of female chiru and their young, grazing in a sheltered valley, he exclaims: 'Wonderful. Wonderful. To see all these animals leading their ancient and traditional lives, seemingly unaffected by humankind, is truly a gift of the spirit.'

But only so much time can be afforded to pure delight in this scene. 'Rapture must give way to hardheaded science in the form of a population count to give to the Tibet Forestry Department.' Altogether, he and his team counted more than 16,000 female antelope gathered together on the plain, giving birth to another generation of chiru. Despite these numbers, the animals face an uncertain future because of poaching and the illegal trade in shahtoosh, the underlayer of wool, which is smuggled into Kashmir and woven into high-priced shawls.

Schaller helped expose the ugly truth behind shahtoosh. For years the merchants who sold this precious wool maintained the fiction that it was collected from live animals, or gathered from thorn bushes high in the mountains where fleecy strands simply brushed off a passing herd. Schaller and others revealed that, in fact, the antelope were being slaughtered for their wool and the carnage would soon lead to their extinction.

Now in his eighties, George Schaller has spent much of his life on the move. Fit and full of energy, he can still outwalk many of his younger colleagues. But he admits that it has been more than simply a scientific quest. His restless nature comes from a challenging childhood, growing up in wartime Germany. As a boy he witnessed the bombing of Dresden and was homeless for much of his youth until he came to the United States as a refugee. This rootlessness may explain his urge to wander as well as his commitment to protect the planet from the ravages of man. In much of his writing, his voice carries a lonely, sometimes melancholy, sense of purpose as he seeks the solitude and 'hermetic stillness' of wild, unsettled landscapes.

More than with any other creature, Schaller has a special affinity for snow leopards. *Panthera uncia* is the highest roaming of the big cats, an animal that was hardly known outside the Himalaya and Central Asia until the twentieth century. Schaller's first encounter with one of these near-mythical creatures was in the Karakoram, when he was studying wild goats. Coming face-to-face with a snow leopard left him with a haunting sense of its elusive beauty and the way in which it seemed to dissolve into rocks and snow.

After tranquillizing a trapped snow leopard, Schaller describes touching this rare creature. Lifting the drugged animal and holding it in his arms, he admires the huge paws, one of which he massages to restore circulation cut off by a snare. Then running a hand over the snow leopard's body and tail, Schaller describes the 'sensuous' feel of its fur.

These reclusive predators exist within a narrow band of elevation that marks the upper margins of sustainable life. As the snow line descends in winter, the ghostly carnivores move lower in pursuit of their natural prey— bharal, urial and smaller mammals like marmots and hares. Domesticated sheep and goats are fair game for snow leopards, especially in the lean, cold months of winter. These high mountain cats walk a thin line between existence and extinction. For a scientist like Schaller, the basic question is understanding their distribution, behaviour and environmental needs in order to keep them from roaming off into oblivion.

In many cases the solution to the survival of an endangered species lies in the behaviour, ethics and economic pressures of human populations. In 1973, Schaller undertook an expedition to the remote Dolpo Valley in Nepal, where he conducted a study of bharal near Shey Monastery. He was accompanied by Peter Matthiessen whose book, *The Snow Leopard*, is an account of their trek. An award-winning bestseller it describes a spiritual journey through the high Himalaya, as well as an inner search for solace and transcendence.

Schaller also wrote about his travels in Dolpo in *Stones of Silence*, a naturalist's memoir that describes his research on Caprinae, as well as the pursuit of metaphysical answers. Though his narrative is grounded in empirical knowledge and describes the day-to-day routines of a zoologist on the hoof, he often strikes a spiritual note that echoes Matthiessen's ruminations. While collecting hard data on blue sheep, he is also aware of Buddhist teachings and the quest for enlightenment that his companion pursues. Schaller acknowledges the limits of his own research: 'Science still remains a dream, for it takes us no more than a few faltering steps toward understanding; graphs and charts create little more than an illusion of knowledge. There is no ultimate knowing. Beyond the facts, beyond science, is a domain of cloud, the universe of the mind, ever expanding as the universe itself.'

In October 2016, Schaller returned to Dolpo for the first time since he travelled there forty-three years earlier. Accompanying him was Matthiessen's son, Alex, whose father died in 2014. After revisiting Dolpo, Schaller describes the changes that have occurred. Instead of setting off on foot for weeks of trekking, before motor roads penetrated the Kali Gandaki Valley, they flew from Pokhara to an airstrip at Juphal. More than wild sheep, this time Schaller was interested in learning how things had changed for the human residents of Dolpo.

'I printed some pictures of people I'd photographed in 1973 and took those with me. It was interesting to watch how people reacted when they recognized friends or family, and sometimes themselves.'

The effects of increased tourism, inspired partly by Matthiessen's book, were evident in the number of trekkers they met. Some of the development was positive, Schaller explains, such as the small hydroelectric projects that provide power and light to villages. But he was disappointed by the condition of the monasteries, which were largely deserted.

'At Shey, there was only one monk,' he tells me. 'The others were off in Kathmandu, "studying", or overseas in places like New York, raising funds. The villagers had nobody to conduct rituals and prayers.'

The reason Schaller originally visited Shey was because the head lama had forbidden hunting in the valley and protected the bharal, which allowed him to observe the animals closely and witness their annual rut. He still believes that religious edicts against killing wildlife are an effective tool of conservation. Buddhist beliefs in the unity of all life and the ethics of compassion provide a compelling message for preserving and protecting wild species throughout the Himalaya and Tibet.

While his recent visit to Dolpo was relatively comfortable and not overly strenuous, the original trek in 1973 was much more challenging, crossing snowbound passes with dwindling supplies and long hours spent under harsh conditions. At one point, while following the bharal and searching for snow leopards, Schaller spent a night in a small cave. In *Stones of Silence* he describes how in the faint light of his torch, he could see the fossils of scalloped shells and tube worms embedded in the rocks around him. Before falling asleep he imagines himself lying within the depths of the Tethys Sea, surrounded by aquatic life and eventually becoming part of those ancient sediments, his skull transformed into a saligram, or fossilized ammonite.

Schaller's writing often takes on a mystical tone, expressing a sense of oneness with the land and its creatures. Though he has experienced this in many different environments from Amazon rainforests to the grasslands of the Serengeti, it is the Himalaya that truly bring his experiences into focus and make him understand that his scientific inquiry is balanced by a spiritual search. 'Sometimes, while watching bharal, my eyes unconsciously leave the animals to climb along the skyline, and my mind struggles to escape its confines, travelling, searching, seeking, until on rare occasions a brief vision of shining clarity seems to define the world.'

chapter 29

REWILDING JABARKHET

In the space of thirty seconds, a story of conservation unfolds through the omniscient eye of a camera trap. Two goral, a mother and her offspring, are standing by a waterhole. Suddenly, both creatures express alarm, lifting their heads and looking nervously about, tensed muscles preparing to make a quick escape. After a few moments the object of their attention struts into view, a male koklass pheasant approaching the waterhole with the proprietorial air of a regular customer entering his local pub. The bird's dark crest bobs up and down like a cowlick, while his white collar looks as if it were neatly buttoned around his throat. A female pheasant is foraging on the slope above. Her mate opens his beak, as if to greet the goral and, as the sequence ends, they share a drink.

This video comes from one of the camera traps at Jabarkhet Nature Reserve (JNR). Not only does this sequence show the interaction of two species but it also underscores the encouraging fact that goral are multiplying. In another photograph from JNR, a herd of fifteen goral can be seen in a single frame. Five years ago, when Dr Sejal Worah started using camera traps, most of the animals came to drink at night but now they feel secure enough to visit the waterholes at all hours of the day. The presence of koklass pheasant, not a common species, proves that JNR protects the habitat they require. Altogether, in the half-minute window of the video clip, we see wild creatures occupying a safe space without any human beings in sight.

Sejal Worah is the programme director at the World Wide Fund for Nature (WWF) in New Delhi and managing director of JNR. In collaboration with Vipul Jain, the owner of this 100-acre wood, Sejal started the reserve as a personal conservation project. Her efforts and passion for environmental action prove that private land can be converted into a viable wildlife sanctuary that sustains at least twenty species of mammals and more than a hundred different kinds of birds.

'I used to visit Mussoorie as a child,' Sejal recalls. 'These mountains and forests always inspired me. My father had a strong connection to the outdoors. While growing up, we were immersed in nature in unstructured ways.'

An energetic, intensely focused person, Sejal speaks with a blunt manner that suggests no sentimental motives for protecting animals but instead a clear-headed vision of environmental purpose. 'I believe in diversity,' she says. 'We've got to do whatever it takes to ensure that endangered species don't disappear.'

After completing her bachelor's degree in Life Sciences in Mumbai, Sejal went on to do her master's at Syracuse University in the US and a PhD at the University of Poona in conjunction with the Wildlife Institute of India. Her dissertation was on human and wildlife coexistence in the fragmented forests of southern Gujarat. While she fulfilled her dream of getting a degree in Wildlife Biology at Syracuse University, she found it frustrating. 'In the US, everything has been done already and I found myself researching the drumming behaviour of ruffed grouse, which didn't really interest me. Solving conservation problems did.'

She has worked with WWF for seventeen years, posted in the UK, Thailand and India. Returning to Mussoorie as an adult, Sejal realized that she wanted to do something to restore and protect the environment she'd experienced as a girl. The forests she remembered from childhood were now badly degraded.

'When I came back, I was astonished how hammered it was,' she says. 'Ironically I had studied fragmented forests and this is exactly what I found.'

One of the first steps in securing Jabarkhet Nature Reserve was to control access by people from nearby settlements who let their cattle graze in the jungle, lopped the trees for firewood and fodder or set snares for the little wildlife that remained. However, instead of simply building fences and locking gates, Sejal engaged with neighbouring communities. Three of the women who used to release their cows in the forest while they cut wood and collected fodder, are now caretakers of the reserve. Several young people from the villages of Kolti, Kanda and Bataghat are employed as wildlife guides. Virendra 'Viru' Panwar, in particular, has become an accomplished birder and photographer who leads visiting groups through the forest and manages the camera traps. The success of JNR rests on community involvement as much as it does on innovative and well-managed scientific approaches to conservation in the Himalaya.

Adjoining the reserve is a large tract of government forest that allows the animals to extend their range. A hundred acres may be enough for a few smaller, sedentary species but most of the wildlife, including leopards, bears, goral and barking deer, need more space to roam. Nevertheless, with its waterholes and protected jungle, JNR provides a core refuge for resident species, as well as migratory animals like sambar that come down from higher forests in winter.

'The idea is to create ecological stepping stones,' Sejal explains. 'The Himalaya are very different from forested areas on the plains. They are a connected landscape, an open rangeland for roaming wildlife. Hopefully, JNR will be replicated in other places because we've proved it can work.'

Within 3 kilometres of Mussoorie's crowded Mall Road, with its traffic jams and swarms of tourists, the sanctuary provides a haven for every major species of mammal that inhabits this altitudinal zone. In the winter of 2015, a tiger showed up on one of the camera traps. It was identified as a wandering resident of Rajaji National Park in the Dehradun Valley at the foot of the mountains, more than 50 kilometres away.

When asked about the greatest threats to Himalayan wildlife, Sejal hesitates and then replies, 'I wouldn't have said this a few years ago but climate change is a serious threat, especially in the Central Himalaya.'

The fragmentation of Himalayan forests is caused by many factors including dry winters and erratic rainfall that leads to forest fires. At the end of May 2018, a severe fire burned through JNR, charring over half the area. Fortunately, the majority of trees will survive and the monsoon helped resuscitate the forest, though a large percentage of the ground cover had gone up in smoke. While most of the larger mammals and birds were able to escape into nearby areas, a whole generation of smaller creatures, such as reptiles and insects, was wiped out. Living nearby, I have seen these jungles go up in flames at least six times, over the past fifty years. The resilience of nature is remarkable but each time it happens, walking through the ashes and breathing in the sour, acrid odours of combustion that linger for months, I keep wondering how long these forests can survive.

The cause of wildfires in the Lower Himalaya is almost always human beings and the destruction usually occurs when villagers burn grasslands, in the belief that new growth will be more abundant. Chir pines, planted by the forest department years ago along the slopes to the west and north of JNR, accelerate and disperse the conflagration, which quickly burns out of control, particularly when there has been little rain.

In addition to fires the other causes of forest fragmentation are also related to human activity, such as road-building, illegal felling and lopping of trees and overgrazing by livestock. But Sejal isn't entirely pessimistic about the future.

'Pastoralism is a dying occupation,' she says. 'It's hard work and young people aren't interested in being shepherds like their parents and grandparents.'

While the annual migrations of pastoral communities, particularly to the high meadows or bugiyals in summer months, have always put pressure on Himalayan ecosystems, Sejal feels that the solution may lie in, 'containing pressure and making sure that pastoralism isn't replaced by something worse. In remote areas many villages are emptying out and herds are no longer being taken up to the bugiyals. We have to manage this transition.'

Her work with WWF involves everything from shaping policy in Delhi and around the world to overseeing research projects in the field. 'There's a lot of interest in wildlife,' Sejal explains, 'yet very few people are doing the kind of studies that need to be undertaken. There's an obsession with large carnivores but we must look at other animals too, particularly ungulates like ibex and markhor. They need to be seen not just through the lens of snow leopard prey. For example, when was the last musk deer study done? Maybe thirty years ago. We don't really know what's going on with these Himalayan mammals.'

Camera traps and other forms of technology have made it much easier for wildlife biologists to carry out surveys and record the behaviour of certain species but there is a downside to all these innovations.

'Technology comes with a price. At WWF we probably have between three and four hundred cameras set up in North India. Recently, I had to approve Rs. 800,000 just to pay for batteries. Where is all that e-waste going? I keep saying we need to use rechargeable batteries but for some reason it doesn't happen. Here at JNR we use rechargeable batteries and they work just fine.'

The use of drones and surveillance towers for monitoring wildlife in national parks or other forest areas can be intrusive and disturbs animals, particularly when employed indiscriminately. At the same time, new technologies offer a number of tools for conservation. During her doctoral research, Sejal conducted one of the first aerial surveys of forest lands in India and she believes in the value of mapping wildlife habitat using satellite imagery. DNA analysis has proved exceptionally useful in tracking the illegal trade in skins and animal parts.

She also points to 'clear applications that have taught us so much,' like a radio collar placed on a tiger relocated from Pilibhit to Dudhwa National Park. This tiger, known as 'Chandu', set off on his own from the park and crossed the border into Nepal, walking through heavily settled farmland, up into the mountains.

'We have learned so much from that one collar,' Sejal says. 'How tigers use human-dominated landscapes and follow water courses and streams.' Information like this assists conservationists in designing and advocating the location and requirements for wildlife corridors.

While she is involved in high level national and international debates regarding wildlife policies, at JNR Sejal has an opportunity to put her experiences into practice on a much smaller and more immediate scale. The reserve is open to visitors and researchers but the objective is to try to protect the forest as much as possible from human interference. Camping or entering the sanctuary after dark is forbidden, partly for safety but also to give the animals time to themselves. The camera traps are used judiciously and have become an effective educational tool for visiting school groups. Showing students pictures and videos of animals that have walked the same paths as them, a few hours earlier, helps bring the forest to life and captures a visitor's imagination. Video clips like the two gorals at the waterhole with koklass pheasants are the kind of images that help persuade people about the importance of preserving wild creatures and their dwindling habitat.

chapter 30

IN SUNLIGHT AND SHADOW

Wildlife photography has progressed to a point where we are able to capture some of the most intimate and detailed images of forest creatures. Digital technology has turned the camera into an all-consuming eye, recording every millisecond in the jungle while instantly processing light and shadow, feathers, foliage and fur. We are fortunate to live in a time when pictures like these bring endangered species into focus. Of course, the irony is that even as wild places on our planet have shrunk we are able to observe so much more thanks to lavish coffee-table books, televised nature films and watermarked posts on social media. Perhaps the only negative consequence is that, as these close-up images of snow leopards, pangolins and red pandas become increasingly accessible and prevalent, we may forget that the animals themselves are disappearing.

In our collective quest to understand, document and preserve the natural history of the Himalaya, the camera plays a critical role. One of India's finest naturalists and writers, M. Krishnan, pioneered wildlife photography in the 1960s and 1970s. Over the past five decades, the Bedi brothers, Naresh and Rajesh, have compiled a vast archive of still and cinematic images of Indian wildlife, particularly Himalayan species. Not only are their pictures a vivid reminder of nature's beautiful allure but also a storehouse of scientific information that will be used by researchers in the future.

Today, two of the most dedicated and accomplished wildlife photographers working in the Himalaya are Sandesh Kadur and Dhritiman Mukherjee. Both of them spend most of the year in the wild, huddled in hides or trekking from one mountain habitat to another. While their remarkable portraits of clouded leopards and one-horned rhinos may appear on the covers of glossy publications like *Sanctuary Asia* or *Saevus*, as well as many journals abroad, they have made invaluable contributions to a wider body of knowledge through photographs of less celebrated species, from cicadas and lynx spiders to white-browed piculets and tiger leeches.

My only complaint with the current state of wildlife photography is that visits to national parks in India have become increasingly dangerous because of the possibility of suffering a concussion. Everybody seems to be armed with the latest Canon or Nikon attached to a large-calibre zoom lens with a pistol grip. The minute a tiger appears, or even a mongoose, amateur photographers swing into action and there's a serious risk of being bludgeoned by a 200–500 mm f/2. 8 APO EX DG. Jeeps on jungle safaris now look like anti-terrorist squads full of camouflaged, camera-wielding commandos with lenses the size of howitzers.

Yet, in all of this, there are some benefits. Human beings who would otherwise be sitting at a desk or entering data on spreadsheets are motivated to go outdoors, partly because of the gear they buy. But the pleasure of being in the forest unencumbered by the trappings of technology is lost and we often forget that our own eyes are the most sophisticated and sensitive cameras we own.

Some of the earliest wildlife photography in India was done in the 1920s by F. W. Champion, a forest officer in the United Provinces, now Uttar Pradesh and Uttarakhand. Most of his pictures were taken in the Terai and foothills of the Himalaya between Dehradun and Haldwani. Champion was ahead of his time, as most of his colleagues and fellow-colonials were far more interested in hunting tigers and other large mammals with firearms, whereas he pioneered remote flash photography. The technology was unpredictable and cumbersome, involving glass plate negatives and magnesium flash powder ignited by pressure pads and synchronized to explode in concert with the shutter. Compared to the infrared beams and multiple exposures on camera traps used today, Champion's equipment seems primitive, though he made up for its limitations by understanding his subjects and patiently using jungle craft to set up each of the shots.

His two books, *The Jungle in Sunlight and Shadow* and *With a Camera in Tiger-Land*, contain an array of black-and-white portraits of India's wildlife as well as an evocative text that describes the submontane jungles he loved and a plea for their preservation. Champion's books influenced hunters like Jim Corbett, who took up wildlife photography with a passion, heeding Champion's call:

> I would...appeal to others who do not enjoy spilling the blood of beautiful animals, many of which are rapidly being exterminated, to abandon the rifle in favour of the camera, the use of which provides all the pleasures and excitements so dear to the heart of the big-game hunter. Indeed, it provides others as well, for, in addition to giving one a far greater insight into Nature and all her marvelous ways, a camera in skillful hands produces pictures of great scientific value, which may give pleasure to many others in a way that mere horns and skins can never do, be they ever so large.

Though the photographs that Champion published, almost a century ago, may not compare with the bright colours and sharp focus of wildlife images today, they represent an important part of the legacy of conservation that needs to be remembered and reaffirmed. Most importantly, these are not just lucky shots clicked at random but carefully composed images based on hours of observation and accumulated knowledge gathered through years spent in the jungle.

chapter 31

CONFLICTED EDENS

Among the most aggressive predators in the Himalaya are yellow-throated martens (*Martes flavigula*), often called pine martens. They are about the size of an otter, measuring roughly a metre from their pointed snout to the end of their long furred tails. Colouring varies—some are almost black while others can be a light brown—though the heads and tails are always a darker shade, contrasting with a pale yellow patch under the throat and chest. Martens move with fluid agility both on the ground and through the branches of trees, constantly hunting for birds' nests, reptiles and small mammals. According to Valmik Thapar, in his book *Tiger Fire,* these lithe and graceful killers are very similar to miacids, the ancient ancestors of tigers and other big cats, which lived fifty million years ago.

In the early spring of 2014, below the false summit of Nag Tibba, one range back from Mussoorie, I watched a crested serpent-eagle (*Spilornis cheela*) chasing a pair of yellow-throated martens. Emitting a series of shrill cries, the raptor harassed them from a height of a metre or two above the ground, as the martens scrambled over a lightly wooded stretch of rocky, scrub-covered cliffs.

Despite their names, serpent-eagles eat more than just snakes and pursue the same variety of prey as martens. They are equally aggressive and opportunistic hunters. A serpent-eagle isn't likely to kill a full-grown marten but it is possible the pair may have had their young with them, though I saw only the two adults. *Martes flavigula* often scavenge for food and it is more likely they might have stolen the eagle's kill or that *Spilornis cheela* may have been intent on stealing theirs. At the same time, the fierce conflict could have been a simple case of animosity between competing species occupying the same arena of predation. For ten minutes, I was witness to a violent chase between a killer in the sky and two carnivores on the ground. At intervals the serpent-eagle screamed at the pair and dove between the trees with its talons extended, while the martens remained mostly silent, darting in and out of cover, as if they were pursuing the serpent-eagle's shadow. Once or twice, when the bird swooped down, the martens wheeled about and made threatening, chirring sounds and lunged at the eagle. This adversarial display only ended when the pair finally vanished into a dense patch of jungle where the eagle couldn't follow.

Despite the non-violent teachings of Buddhist dharma and romantic illusions about nature's 'peaceable kingdom', in which the leopard lies down with the lamb, conflict is an integral part of every animal community. Both within a herd and between different species, aggression and confrontation govern most relationships in the wild. This doesn't mean that the violence is either random or gratuitous. It is carefully calibrated through the adaptive process of natural selection. While plenty of ecological checks and balances help keep the peace, conflicts inevitably arise, not just between predators and prey, but also among creatures that seldom interact with each other. Most birds and animals are territorial and they will fight to occupy choice areas of forest, grasslands or water sources for themselves. For that matter, even plants attack each other, strangling and smothering their competitors.

Most of the time, however, in the struggle for survival, compromise is the best strategy. The majority of creatures are too busy feeding and procreating to get into fights without good reason though a few rogue individuals occasionally attack others out of hostility that we might interpret as being mean-spirited. Elephants in musth, for example, become short-tempered and have little patience for anything that gets in their way. Amongst langur monkeys, when a dominant male has been displaced, his successor often murders the youngest members of a troop in order to dominate the gene pool. Infanticide and cannibalism are part of the behaviour of other species as well, from tigers to rats. Of course, plenty of animals coexist within a healthy ecosystem and even collaborate from time to time when it suits their purposes but they will turn on each other if resources become scarce or instinctual boundaries are crossed.

Nature programmes on television often highlight conflicts in the wild by showing carefully edited confrontations between species such as crocodiles and pythons or hyenas and wild dogs. As far back as the Roman empire, human beings have staged combat between 'ferocious' creatures like lions and tigers. In India, Mughal and Rajput miniature paintings record similar events like rhinoceros fights and battles to the death between tigers and other beasts. But these are a symptom of our own savagery and brute ignorance rather than the so-called 'law of the jungle'. More often than not it is our human presence that provokes a fight.

In January 2005, I visited Corbett National Park with my son, Jayant. A glossy travel magazine was footing the bill and our hosts at a jungle lodge had arranged an exclusive elephant safari, hoping I would endorse the experience and their establishment. Early on a winter morning, we climbed onto the back of Phool Kali (flower blossom), one of the oldest and most experienced park elephants. The foothills were silhouetted against the eastern sky as we set off through long, wet grass towards the Ram Ganga River. The mahout urged Phool Kali forward while sitting astride her neck, his toes tucked behind her ears. We were perched on a simple howdah made from an upturned cot, with a lumpy quilt for padding. The wooden legs of the cot, which we straddled, were the only handholds. The first half hour of the ride was a gentle, swaying journey across a series of dry streambeds. Docile and even-tempered, Phool Kali helped herself to leaves and grass along the way. Eventually, we came to a patch of thorn bushes and tall grass, beyond which lay the river.

All at once, a langur monkey sitting on the branch of a terminalia tree gave a hoarse alarm call, as if he were clearing his throat. We knew that a tiger was nearby and I gestured for Jayant to get his camera ready. As the elephant advanced, our anticipation increased. My attention was fixed on a clearing ahead but when I happened to glance behind us, the tigress was following on Phool Kali's heels. Her stripes blended perfectly with the long grass. At the same moment, our elephant smelled the big cat and pivoted abruptly. Letting out a shrill trumpet of rage, Phool Kali charged.

Riding an elephant is a relatively secure means of moving through the jungle but when *Elephas maximus* lowers its head and rushes forward in a violent display of anger, staying in your seat isn't easy. Fortunately, none of us were unsaddled, clutching the legs of the cot as Phool Kali blundered through the underbrush like a bulldozer whose brakes have failed. The target of her hostility backed away but gave a low, gruff cough of displeasure. In a stage whisper, the mahout informed us that Phool Kali had encountered this tigress several times before and there was 'bad blood' between them.

Circling around another section of scrub jungle, a few minutes later, we came upon the tigress once more. She was standing directly in front of us, blocking our path and staring straight into our eyes. Without hesitation, Phool Kali charged again, rushing 50 metres over rough ground, as we held on for our lives. The tigress let out a snarl of annoyance before retreating into the bushes, from where we kept hearing her angry growls.

At this point, I tried to persuade the mahout that we had seen enough but ignoring my protests he urged Phool Kali to cross a sandy channel and come around from the other side. This time, the tigress burst out of the bushes and we were treated to another violent charge. The elephant bellowed, trunk raised, and tried to trample the tigress who emitted a full-throated roar. Until then, I had only heard tigers calling at a distance, a deep, resonant moan that carries for several kilometres, but from 10 metres away a tiger's roar is enough to shake anyone's nerves. Every leaf in the forest seemed to quake and I was relieved when the mahout regained control and turned his elephant aside.

A few minutes later we crossed back over the dry channels of sand and rocks, where we spotted the tigress's two cubs—both of them full grown—lounging in the sun. They seemed content to let their mother carry on her quarrel with Phool Kali by herself, while Jayant and I were happy to have simply stayed aloft. Though the experience provided an exciting story to tell, I have always been ashamed of this encounter, for the tigress and elephant would never have come face-to-face if it hadn't been for our intrusive foray in the jungle and the provocative compulsions of adventure tourism.

While *Homo sapiens* are often the cause of confrontations between creatures, no species is more adversarial than our own. Human-animal conflict in the Himalaya is a chronic problem for conservationists, especially in buffer zones and marginal settlements near national parks. Every year there are news reports of man-eating leopards and tigers. While any loss of human life is tragic, the truth is that human beings are to blame for most of these deaths because we trespass and encroach on the other species' territory, destroying their habitat and cutting off routes of migration. The simple truth is that most man-eaters are man-made. Human-animal conflict takes many forms, often with less dangerous creatures such as wild pigs, porcupines or peacocks destroying crops. There was a time when animals like these were classified as 'vermin'. More than any other mammal, however, it is monkeys with whom we clash both in rural and urban areas.

The 'monkey menace', as journalists like to call it, is a good example of human beings causing problems for themselves. In hill stations like Mussoorie, troops of rhesus macaques scavenge through garbage heaps that provide enough sustenance for them to multiply exponentially. Household waste is their principal diet though they also raid fruit and vegetable stalls, gardens and orchards. When they don't find sufficient food within easy reach, monkeys break into homes and shops. Unafraid of human beings they become aggressive, snatching grocery bags or sometimes even attacking and biting people.

In rural areas the situation is equally acrimonious, where wandering bands of marauding macaques destroy fruit trees and fields. Some villagers in Garhwal have given up farming in the face of these crop raiders, especially in areas that are difficult to protect. Closely associated with the Hindu deity Hanuman, monkeys enjoy the protection of his ardent devotees. Though Hanuman is usually associated with the larger, silver-haired langur monkeys (*Semnopithecus entellus*), the smaller rhesus macaques (*Macaca mulatta*) with brown fur, are also deified. Forest department regulations and religious injunctions make the culling or harming of monkeys illegal as well as taboo. Animal rights activists have also come to their defence. Out of desperation some communities have resorted to using monkey catchers who trap the macaques and then release them at a distance of twenty or thirty kilometres, so they become another person's problem. In many cases these displaced monkeys live by the side of the road, begging for handouts from passing motorists. Controlling and managing the proliferating monkey population in India raises legal, ethical, environmental and practical questions. Alongside concerted efforts to regulate and enforce proper methods of garbage disposal, probably the only feasible solution is oral contraceptives administered through food the monkeys scavenge.

Recently, when I visited a historic temple in Garhwal, one of the oldest and most prosperous in the region, the ironies of this situation became acutely apparent. After taking darshan at the temple, I met the head priest and manager of the religious complex. He seemed a convivial, easy-going man and we spoke about the mythology and traditions associated with the shrine. But as we were talking, I noticed an air pistol lying on the chair beside him and I asked what it was for.

'The monkeys, of course,' he replied, then rattled off a string of unpriestly abuse, cursing them and calling their parentage into question.

Just then, two macaques appeared on the roof of the temple, lurking about to try and steal fruit and other edible offerings from inside the main sanctuary. Immediately, the pundit reached for his weapon and fired several shots as he chased them off like a Bollywood gunslinger. He seemed unbothered by the fact that a larger-than-life image of Hanuman guarded the threshold of his temple.

chapter 32

ACROSS THE DEOSAI PLATEAU

At the confluence of the Indus and Gilgit rivers lies the 'Fulcrum of Asia' where the northwestern extremities of the Himalaya face off against opposing ranges of the Karakoram and the Hindu Kush. Much older than the mountains it divides, the turgid, glacier-fed current of the Indus has its source a thousand kilometres away in Tibet. All around us is crushing evidence of geological trauma, where the clash of continents has levered up some of the highest peaks in the world. Despite neat lines on survey maps, separating distinct regions, the mountains seem to merge into each other, their barren slopes scarified by erosion. Jagged blades of ridgelines, clenched gauntlets of rock and overlapping layers of rust-coloured strata rise up like dusty heaps of discarded armour, bent and broken swords, axe heads and cudgels all piled together in disarray at the end of an epic battle.

Centuries of human warfare have marked the course of the Indus, as if mirroring tectonic conflicts. Skardu, the largest town in Baltistan, has a long history of invasions by successive armies of Kushanas, Tibetans, Mughals, Afghans, Dogras and the British, all of whom established tenuous control along this strategic trade route by forging alliances with local rajas and warlords. Violent skirmishes and bloodshed accompanied chronic struggles for power. Even today, the fighting continues. Gilgit–Baltistan, as this administrative region is now known, remains disputed territory, claimed by both India and Pakistan as part of Kashmir, where a fractious 'Line of Actual Control' bifurcates the mountains like a seismic fissure.

Flying into Skardu from Islamabad, I am seated next to a young officer in the Pakistan Army. He is on his way to Siachen Glacier, the highest battlefield on earth. Out of uniform and dressed in a polo shirt, jeans and baseball cap he looks as if he should be loitering about in the Gulshan-e-Iqbal gardens of his hometown, Lahore, rather than dug into an ice trench at 5,500 metres above sea level. With an ambivalent smile, he tells me that it will take him more than a week of walking and acclimatization to reach his post on the western flank of the Saltoro Range.

From Skardu airport we drive upriver and cross a bridge over the Indus. Here the valley broadens as the river bends southward between expansive margins of sand and rubble deposited by long-forgotten floods. We head on to Shigar, one of several erstwhile kingdoms in Baltistan, situated on a large tributary of the Indus that flows down from the Baltoro Glacier, K2, Broad Peak and Gasherbrum massif. Travelling with me is Didar Ali, co-owner of Silk Route Expeditions, the tour company that has organized my itinerary. He also runs a carpet business in Hunza. A compact, energetic man, with a perpetual smile and a limitless supply of anecdotes, Didar is an authority on the history and culture of Gilgit–Baltistan. He likes to quote the Sufi poet Rumi: 'Travel leaves you speechless, then turns you into a storyteller', an aphorism also attributed to the Moroccan explorer, Ibn Battuta.

Shigar Fort was renovated and restored by the Aga Khan Cultural Service and is now run as a heritage hotel by the Serena Group, which is part of the Aga Khan Development Network. Many of the people in northern Pakistan are members of the Ismaili sect of Islam, who regard the Aga Khan as their spiritual leader or imam. Being an Ismaili himself, Didar is proud of the many philanthropic projects that the Aga Khan has initiated to provide employment, education and healthcare.

Shigar Fort is a seventeenth-century royal residence of the Amacha rulers, a feudal dynasty, whose descendants still live in the valley. Built at the foot of a vertical rock face, with a fast-flowing stream on one side, the fortified palace is surrounded by groves of poplars and willows, as well as a walled orchard full of apples, pears, mulberries, peaches, apricots and almonds. Flower beds overflow with roses, dahlias and cosmos. The fort is a rambling structure made of large boulders, half-timbered with rough-hewn beams of wood, supporting a three-storey tower at the centre. A green oasis tucked between desolate ridges, the raja's estate at Shigar is more of a pleasure garden than a defensible citadel. At the top of the cliffs overlooking the palace is a secure fortification where the Amacha ruler and his courtiers could retreat if they were attacked. A historic wooden mosque stands nearby, with arched fretwork and chiselled calligraphy, as well as a flared pagoda-style roof instead of a dome and minarets.

Though once isolated and remote, Shigar is a relatively prosperous settlement with plenty of water to irrigate fields of barley, corn and potatoes. Straddling traditional trade routes to Tibet, its rulers used to extract taxes from any shipments that passed through their territory. The mountains also yield precious gems like amethysts and other minerals, including a green, jade-like 'serpentine stone' that is carved into teacups and ornaments. These are supposed to provide protection from poisons and evil spells. Sitting under the shade of a venerable chinar tree at Shigar, it is easy to imagine the historical procession of travellers that used this route from warriors and merchants to explorers and mountaineers.

Re-crossing the Indus the next day, we are joined by Izhar Ali, the son of Didar's business partner. Having just finished his MA in economics, Izhar is spending the summer working as a tour guide and photographer. After stocking up on provisions in Skardu, our Land Cruiser climbs out of the valley towards the Deosai Plateau, one of the highest meadows in the world. Along the way, we stop to see a huge slab of rock carved with images of meditating bodhisattvas. These date to the ninth century, when this region was occupied by Tibetans. A delicate tracery of lines depicting different incarnations of the Buddha contrasts with the weathered solidity of stone.

Entering a narrow valley that funnels down from Deosai, we pass through scrubby patches of dwarf juniper and scattered stands of birches above 3,000 metres. At the beginning of autumn the colours in the trees are changing. Didar comments that the mingled hues of green and yellow remind him of dyed yarn used for carpets, which often have variations in colour, called 'abrash'. He goes on to explain how blue dye is produced from indigo and natural yellow pigments are extracted from pomegranate husks or a wild flower called milkwort. To create a green colour the yellow yarn is overdyed with indigo, which can result in unpredictable effects because of oxidization. Sometimes the yarn ends up with an uneven combination of greens and yellows, like the birches. Seeing their variegated foliage carpeting the slopes, I think of how the seasons dye the land.

At 3,800 metres we are well above the treeline now, as the winding road finally emerges from the valley and enters the Deosai Plateau. Suddenly, the vertiginous terrain opens out into a sprawling landscape of undulating hills and meadows. Only in the distance are there snow-capped peaks that ring these highland pastures. It reminds me of places in Tibet, though not as dry and barren. When we stop, I can see the remains of summer flowers now scorched by frost and going to seed—allium with its oniony smell, wild thyme that is used for herbal tea and tufts of edelweiss. Only a few hardy gentians and asters are still blooming. A herd of sheep and goats pass by below us, as well as a couple of dzos—a cross between cows and yaks.

Deosai means 'place of the gods' in the Shina language, which is spoken throughout much of this region. As Didar explains, Shina is Sanskrit-based unlike the Balti language, which is closer to Tibetan, and Burushaski, the mother tongue of Hunza that has no ties to any other linguistic heritage. Though Islam predominates throughout Pakistan and the people of Gilgit–Baltistan are mostly Shias and Ismailis, there are remnants of ancient faiths dating back to periods before Muslim conquest. Folktales of djinns and fairies, giants and animistic sprites, are woven into narratives of traditional communities like the Gujjar shepherds who bring their herds to Deosai each summer. Didar speaks about village shamans in Hunza who still dance to the beat of drums and inhale juniper smoke to induce a trance. Though mosques remain the primary place of prayer, where mullahs preach monotheistic sermons, here in the upper reaches of the Himalaya, Karakoram and Hindu Kush, wandering ghosts of ancient gods still haunt the land.

After Deosai was declared a national park in 1993, many of the shepherds were moved out and even the military surrendered this territory to conservationists. Though the Pakistan Army used to operate throughout the plateau, which extends to the Line of Actual Control, harsh conditions in winter meant that there was little strategic value in building army installations here. Though we come upon several police posts, as well as a convoy of United Nations military observers, who monitor the volatile ceasefire between Pakistan and India, there are no army vehicles or troops in sight.

The most common form of wildlife is the long-tailed marmot (*Marmota caudata*) that digs burrows under hillocks, from where it can survey the plain in all directions. Averaging 5 kilograms in weight, they are roughly the same size as Himalayan marmots (*Marmota himalayana*) that are distributed eastward. A handsome creature, the long-tailed species in Deosai are a rich, red colour with black highlights on their fur. These large rodents lounge about in the sun, often in groups of four or five, but at the first sign of danger they sit up on their hind legs and look anxiously about. If a human being or any other threat approaches, the marmots shriek loudly and disappear into their dens. During a short spring and summer they feast on the many plants that proliferate on the plain, growing fat and sleek so that they can hibernate in winter when Deosai is buried under deep snow.

No glaciers intrude on the plateau though a number of streams and wetlands thread their way through the rolling meadows. This vast area serves as an extensive aquifer with several lakes, collecting snow in winter that gradually percolates into the ground and is then released through brooks and small rivers. Unlike glacial meltwater, which is always cloudy, these clear springs are as transparent as the air. Throughout the summer, swarms of midges and other insects torment both shepherds and their flocks. Some of the rivers are stocked with trout and also contain native species of fish that attract brown-headed gulls. Migrating from the Indian Ocean, these seabirds travel 1,500 kilometres inland from their winter homes near Karachi. The meadows and wetlands support a variety of other birds like terns, wagtails, buntings and larks. Eagles, buzzards and kestrels circle overhead, though it is difficult to identify them on the wing, as they wheel across the sky keeping a sharp lookout for pikas, voles and lizards on the ground.

We have come here in search of *Ursus arctos*, brown bears that spend the summer in Deosai. Though essentially the same species as European and Siberian brown bears, as well as grizzlies in North America, the Himalayan subspecies *isabellinus* is severely endangered and this is one of the few places where they congregate in substantial numbers. Deosai National Park was created primarily as a sanctuary for bears, though it is also home to a small population of wolves, snow leopards and wild sheep. Scientists estimate that when the park was opened there were only nineteen bears in Deosai and their habitat had been badly degraded and disturbed, mostly by nomadic shepherds. Poachers also threatened the population, killing bears for their fat and other body parts that are sold as medicinal remedies. After the park was established and grazing was restricted, the numbers began to climb. In 2006, a census conducted by WWF tallied up forty-three bears. By 2008, there were fifty-six and in 2009, the total had reached sixty-two. Current estimates have risen further to between sixty-eight and seventy-five bears. Deosai National Park is one of the rare success stories of Himalayan wildlife conservation and it proves that if the land is left to its own regenerative devices, nature can replenish her bounty. Minimal intervention is required, except to limit grazing and prevent poaching.

This doesn't mean that *Ursus arctos isabellinus* is easy to find. Arriving at our camp on the riverbank at Bara Pani, we meet Sher Muhammad, a forest guard who will be our guide and tracker. With a despondent look on his face, he shakes his head and tells us that a group of Japanese wildlife enthusiasts just spent three days with him and he wasn't able to show them a single bear. They drove to every corner of the park but without success. In the official Visitors Book the Japanese have written a complaint that has hurt Sher Muhammad's pride. A tall, angular man in a camouflage uniform, with an unruly moustache and sharp, attentive eyes, he has worked at Deosai for the past twelve years.

With a generous admixture of expletives, he tells us a story about a divisional forest officer (DFO) who came to inspect the park several years ago. After two days of seeing no bears the officer began to berate the guards, accusing them of not doing their jobs. Finally, as the disgruntled DFO was preparing to depart, Sher Muhammad spotted a bear in a sheltered side valley, some distance from the road. Radioing the news he waited for the officer to arrive and then led him on foot over the rugged uplands until they had a successful sighting. On the way back to his jeep, however, the DFO stepped in a marmot hole and twisted his ankle. Sher Muhammad was then forced to carry the officer on his back for more than a kilometre. As this tale progresses, the language becomes more and more colourful and it is difficult to tell whether accusations of incest and other obscenities are being directed at the elusive bear or the officious DFO.

Though temperatures on the plateau are warm during the day, with sunlight streaming down on the grasslands, as soon as darkness settles the air grows frigid and I am reminded that we are camped almost 4 kilometres above sea level. A true test of any wilderness is the clarity of the night sky and the sequined dome of stars above us is as brilliant as I have ever seen. The burbling of the river is the only sound though there is a police outpost and a WWF team camped nearby as well as two other groups of tourists. Earlier, when we arrived at Bara Pani, Izhar, Didar, our driver and I had to wrestle with the tents to set them up in a strong wind that blew across the plateau. But now the air is still, as if crystallized by the cold. A rime of frost has already formed on the outer fly of my tent as I crawl inside.

At 5.30 the next morning, we are up again. The stars are still out though a faint glow of dawn illuminates the eastern horizon where the rolling grasslands give way to a line of white summits in Kashmir. As we wait for the sun to rise and a pan of water to boil for our tea, Sher Muhammad suddenly appears and announces that he has located a couple of bears about 2 kilometres from our camp. Grabbing binoculars and cameras, we set off immediately on foot across the open meadows on the opposite bank of the river. In the half-light, Sher Muhammad points out two specks on a low hill in the distance. Through my binoculars I can just make out the shaggy profile of one bear, and then another, though they are much too far away for us to see anything more than a shadowy blur.

Half running over uneven ground, Sher Muhammad leads us at a frantic pace despite the altitude. The plain is like tundra, with tussocks of grass underfoot. After fifteen minutes, we come to a stretch of wetlands, with pools of water and meandering streams. Clusters of delphinium are blooming here, their cupped petals a smoky blue. Missing my footing, I step into a hidden trough of mud halfway up my calf. Remembering the story of the DFO spraining his ankle I force myself to slow down. Izhar and Sher Muhammad are 30 metres ahead while Didar follows at a more cautious pace. Fortunately, bears have poor eyesight and the two specks on the ridge are still there. After another half an hour we come to a gradual rise in the grasslands where the ground is drier and we are hidden from the bears. Cutting across the slope at an angle, Sher Muhammad beckons urgently. Crouching, he creeps forward into a shallow depression on a shoulder of the ridge.

Sucking the thin air into our lungs with painful gasps, Izhar and I crawl into position, though it takes several minutes before my hands are steady enough to focus a camera. The bears are about 200 metres away, on a grass-covered knoll that is just catching the first rays of sunlight. In the tunnel vision of my binoculars I can see that they are feeding on something. By now it is possible to make out that one is an adult female and the other her large cub, only slightly smaller than its mother. The pair raise their heads and sniff the air, chewing and gazing in our direction without any sign of alarm. Though bears have an acute sense of smell there is no breeze to carry our scent at this hour.

Ursus arctos are omnivorous and their staple diet in Deosai is plants and tubers that they root up with their claws, though they also hunt for marmots and other mammals, as well as fish from time to time. Occasionally, they prey on sheep or goats and scavenge carrion. Though dangerous if confronted at close quarters, here on the open plain the bears mostly avoid contact with human beings. At our camp, however, we are shown a waste bin that one of the bears ripped open, several nights ago, searching for food.

Though they do not have the feline agility or stealth of snow leopards, bears do possess a kind of bulky grace and remarkable dexterity. When I was a child, I remember watching street performances by trained bears (mostly Himalayan black bears and their lowland cousins the sloth bear). Obediently rising up on their hind legs the animals danced to the rattle of a captor's drum, but those were cruel displays of human choreography, whereas in the wild, these giant creatures shamble and sway to the unrestrained rhythms of their ursine nature.

After twenty minutes of watching the two bears, I can feel the first gusts of air begin to stir as the plateau starts to warm up. Almost immediately, the mother and cub catch our scent, turning abruptly and shuffling out of sight, down the other side of the hill. We know there is little chance of spotting them again but decide to go across and see what they've been eating.

As we climb the knoll and come to the spot where the bears were feeding, we find the mangled remains of a marmot. All the meat and bones have been devoured and there is only a shredded strip of red fur with the head and tail still attached. It looks a bit like a fur stole that has been chewed by a disobedient dog. The dead marmot's complacent expression, with its buck teeth and squinted face, makes it seem as if the unfortunate animal isn't yet reconciled to its fate. Next to a large rock nearby, we can see the marmot's burrow, which has been dug up by the bears, though the hole is only partly excavated and they must have ambushed their prey, catching its long tail as it attempted to dive for safety underground. The stomach and entrails have been discreetly set aside. This kill probably provided the bears with no more than a kilogram of meat each, a welcome addition to their standard vegetarian diet. On the other side of the rock is a fresh turd, black as tar, containing a gummy melange of fibrous plant remains.

Half a dozen burrows lie nearby and Sher Muhammad shows us where other marmots have been dug out of the ground with greater effort, the dry, rocky soil clawed up to a depth of a metre or more. Seeing these dens reminds me of films I've watched of polar bears hunting seals in the Arctic, waiting patiently beside air holes in the ice until their victims emerge. I also recall a favourite poem of mine, Galway Kinnell's 'The Bear' in which he narrates the story of a desperate hunt in a frozen landscape and describes a dream of 'lumbering flatfooted across the tundra…' in pursuit of some, 'parabola of bear-transcendence'.

Heading back to camp, we pick our way through the marshy wetlands, jumping from one tussock to the next. Suddenly, Sher Muhammad gestures to our left and far off on the broad hump of a distant meadow, we see another bear running full tilt. With binoculars, I follow his progress up the sunlit slope. He blunders along at a rapid gait, as if chasing his own shadow uphill.

After packing up our tents and other gear, we drive westward across the plateau, scanning the open terrain for any signs of life. Except for a few raptors and gulls, the broad expanse of sky and meadows remains empty. With the end of summer, whatever flocks of sheep and goats are still permitted to graze here have left. Unlike the forests of the Eastern Himalaya, which support a wide diversity of species, these bleak grasslands contain only a limited population of creatures. Though we have been fortunate enough to see brown bears, I can't help but feel that there should be more wildlife present. At one time argali and urial sheep must have fed on these pastures and perhaps even musk deer and hangul, emerging out of the lower forests. Their presence would have attracted wolves and snow leopards, so rarely seen these days. Even though the Pakistan Army is stationed out of sight, the militarization of this region has had a significant impact. Pakistani officers, shooting for meat and sport, have wiped out argali in the Khunjerab National Park and it is likely that many of the ungulates that would have come up to Deosai in summer have suffered collateral damage in the decades-long battle over Kashmir.

As we drop down off the edge of the plateau and into the Astore Valley, the first permanent settlement we come upon is Chilam, where Pakistan's flag, with its white crescent and star, flutters above a graveyard in which soldiers are buried. The dead men were recruited from this high village to fight along the Line of Actual Control, which lies 30 kilometres to the south-east. Chilam used to be one of the halts on the traditional route from Kashmir to Gilgit, a road used by political agents, tax collectors and traders, as well as early mountaineers who came here to climb Nanga Parbat and K2. Those expeditions started from Kashmir's capital, Srinagar, now on the other side of a disputed frontier.

Descending into swathes of birches and juniper, we come upon several groups of Gujjars herding goats and sheep to lower pastures. Didar explains that one of the problems in Deosai was that large 'commercial herds' were dispatched to the plateau, alongside traditional nomadic shepherds who raise animals primarily for milk and wool. Investors from the plains hired Afghan refugees to take thousands of goats and sheep up to the high pastures to fatten them up. Upon their return these animals were slaughtered and sold as meat. Our Land Cruiser noses through the Gujjars' flock, which includes a number of dumba sheep whose bulbous tails are considered a delicacy. After a summer of grazing the accumulation of fat on their hindquarters has swollen to the size of melons. When a Gujjar woman knocks at my window, begging for money, I wonder about the economics of her occupation and how long the shepherds' nomadic way of life will survive.

Below Chilam, we pass a meadow where flowers are still blooming, including buttercups and balsam. Here we come upon two teams of beekeepers who have set up their hives along the side of the road. Didar explains that Deosai honey, produced from the nectar of wild flowers, fetches a high price. Like migrant shepherds, beekeepers truck their hives up onto the plateau in summer and spend two or three months amidst the flowering pastures. When the blooms are finished, they move downhill, collecting honey as they go.

'The only problem,' Didar says, 'is that the weather in Deosai is so unpredictable that when monsoon clouds close in and it rains all day for several weeks, the bees remain in their hives and eat up all their own honey.'

Harvesting the sugars produced by Himalayan plants through photosynthesis, beekeepers depend on the same cycles of nature as the shepherds with their flocks of sheep and goats. The chemical process, by which carbon dioxide and water is transformed into glucose and oxygen, through the energy of the sun, also sustains the marmots and bears. In this way, the abundant renewable resources of the Deosai Plateau feed insects, birds and mammals, dispersing their sweetness as nourishment for all.

After leaving Deosai we spend the night in Gorikot. The name of our hotel, the Wazeer Mahel, translates as 'palace of the chief minister', though that is something of a misnomer. The property does belong to a descendant of the former Wazir of Kashmir who settled here in 1947, at the time of Partition. However, unlike Shigar Fort, the Wazeer Mahel is hardly palatial. Didar apologizes but this is the best accommodation in town. A clutter of concrete guest rooms have been thrown together in a dry, untended garden with a few dusty apple and almond trees but there is little else in sight to relieve the desolation of this arid valley. A pair of squabbling magpies perch on coils of razor wire atop the perimeter wall. The main building has a faux Romanesque facade with strings of blinking coloured lights wrapped around gilded plaster columns.

But the most incongruous element of all is a collection of hunting trophies on display. A pair of stuffed ibex stand outside in withered flowerbeds, their arching horns and weather-beaten hides stiffly mounted like rocking horses. The taxidermy has split open at the seams and the nose of one ibex is missing while the other's glass eyes stare sadly at the pulsing electric lights of blue and pink. Under the front portico of the hotel are the mounted heads of a third ibex, a blue sheep and two Kashmir markhor. They peer down at us with the mournful demeanour of endangered Caprinae, sought after for the huge horns that surmount their skulls. The ibex has tapered, swept-back scimitars, ribbed like bamboo, while the blue sheep's horns are thicker at the base, unfurling in opposite directions like an elaborate, corrugated bouffant. Markhor possess the most impressive racks, like giant corkscrews, twisting upward in a double spiral.

These 'mountain monarchs' are crowned with regal headgear that is used for combat during their annual rut, when males compete for mating rights. As George Schaller observes, 'Often long and massive with graceful twists and flowing lines, horns are objects of symmetrical beauty, ornaments which hunters constantly endeavor to remove from the owners.'

Inside the Wazeer Mahel's main drawing room is a pair of poorly mounted snow leopards, their faces contorted in unnatural grimaces meant to show off canine teeth. The mottled pelage and long, curving tails look artificial, like cheap furry toys that have been manhandled by a temperamental child. As with the ibex, blue sheep and markhor trophies, these dead predators have a shabby, ill-gotten appearance that pervades the hotel, all of which is decorated in bad taste.

Trophy hunting is legal in parts of Pakistan. Ironically, it is touted as part of an innovative strategy for wildlife conservation and rural development. While the ethics and efficacy of the programme are debatable, those who advocate this approach seem to be convinced that allowing big-game hunters to shoot large horned sheep and goats with price tags of $50,000 to $75,000 is an effective means of protecting rare species. Silk Route Expeditions is one of the leading outfitters for trophy hunting in Gilgit–Baltistan. Didar's partner, Mohammed Shifa, Izhar's father, regularly takes foreign clients, mostly Americans, as well as wealthy Pakistanis, in pursuit of record-book heads. The hunting season corresponds with winter when the animals move down to lower elevations because of the snow. Each year, the forest department auctions a limited number of permits and 80 per cent of the proceeds are given to local village communities. The logic behind this arrangement is that instead of poaching animals for meat, the villagers will appreciate the value of protecting wildlife because it generates revenue.

On one level, it can be argued that trophy hunting in Gilgit–Baltistan gives remote communities control over the land and natural resources, which was earlier taken away from them by government agencies. Royalties they receive from hunters are used to fund village projects like water pipelines and roads. Some of the earnings are distributed directly to each family, allowing them to pay back loans or invest in property or livestock. In one instance, villagers in Shimshal have used the bounty from hunting to buy land near Islamabad where elderly villagers can escape the harsh winters and be closer to their children who work in the city.

Nevertheless, trophy hunting as a means of managing wildlife conservation is a highly controversial and divisive issue, though it has worked with some success in places like Namibia, the United States and Mongolia. Both the International Union for Conservation of Nature (IUCN) and the World Wide Fund for Nature (WWF) have cautiously endorsed this approach.

A policy statement posted online by WWF asserts that: 'Trophy hunting—where it is based on a clear scientific understanding of species population dynamics and is properly managed—has been proven to be an effective conservation tool in some countries and for certain species, including threatened species.' This statement goes on to list some of the benefits of trophy hunting such as income generation for rural communities, salaries for forest guards and compensation for damage to livestock and crops by wild animals.

In *Unasylva*, the international journal of forestry and forest industries, Dr Rosie Cooney, IUCN's chairperson, and a team of researchers and policy makers have written: 'Well-managed trophy hunting can be a positive driver of conservation because it increases the value of wildlife and the habitats it depends on, providing crucial benefits that can motivate and enable sustainable management approaches.'

The selective killing of animals removes only elderly males and allows the rest of the herd to multiply. Some of the hunting is done in Khunjerab National Park where it seems the number of ibex is increasing. On his phone, Izhar shows me a video of a Pakistani hunter shooting a world record ibex with 135-centimetre horns. The client fires his rifle at relatively close range, first wounding the ibex and then killing it with a second bullet. Izhar also plays another video of an enormous male markhor trying to mount a young female. The huge goat has an Abrahamic grey beard and looks as big as a donkey. The clip was filmed in Chitral and Izhar tells me that this markhor was later killed by a trophy hunter after the video had been circulated on social media. His phone also displays several photographs of clients posing with dead animals. Most of the hunters are middle-aged American men but there is also a blonde Norwegian woman who has bagged an ibex.

While I gave up hunting in my early twenties, I can still understand the excitement of the chase and the challenges of stalking wild animals across mountainous terrain. However, there is something contrived and perverse about these commercial shoots in which wealthy foreigners are guided within range of well-endowed trophies, simply to line up a crosshairs and pull a trigger. Most hunters pride themselves on a code of sportsmanship but in this case the odds are clearly stacked against the unfortunate ibex or markhor. Several organizations in America and Europe, such as the Safari Club and the National Shooting Sports Foundation, promote the hunting of rare animals, mostly to foster competitive bragging rights amongst their members. While they do support certain conservation initiatives, the driving motivation behind these institutions is always the preservation of the hunter rather than the hunted.

Though I try to set my scepticism aside, it is difficult to reconcile images of privileged white hunters gloating over the carcasses of endangered Himalayan mammals. Trophy hunting may generate much-needed funds for conservation in places like northern Pakistan, but this strategy seems to be a short-sighted option based on questionable compromises rather than a sustainable long-term solution. While poverty alleviation, funded through regulated culling of ageing wildlife, may seem to be a valid case of the ends justifying the means, the fundamental ethics are not so easy to balance. The core problem with this approach is that it is motivated by human arrogance and greed. If these hunters really wanted to protect rare animals they could easily donate the bounties they pay to the local communities without collecting trophies in return. And if they still felt a pressing need to end the lives of wild creatures there is nothing to stop them from shooting white-tailed deer or other plentiful species in their own backyards.

Conservation must be grounded in a moral sense of responsibility and stewardship towards nature. So long as we continue to consider ibex and markhor fair targets for commercial bloodsport and people profit from their destruction there can be no lasting solution. Pragmatism is certainly a good thing but when it comes to our relationship with other species it must be linked to compassion and cannot surrender to the convoluted calculus of persuasive dollars.

Of course, the stuffed snow leopards and other trophies on display at Wazeer Mahel were not killed as part of this project. They were probably shot years ago when fewer restrictions were placed on hunting. But, whether the trophies were legally or illegally obtained, these animal remnants symbolize a human impulse to dominate and destroy other life forms. Looking into their glass eyes, it is impossible not to recall the brown bears that we observed less than twenty-four hours earlier, wandering free and unthreatened on the Deosai Plateau. By the same logic that gives trophy hunters a licence to selectively shoot wild goats and sheep, some of those bears, and perhaps even snow leopards, could also be auctioned off for a sizeable profit, all in the name of conservation. Yet, if we simply allow these rare creatures the space and habitat they require, as well as consistent protection from guns and snares, they will endure through their own wild, inhuman compulsions.

chapter 33

BESTIARY OF A DIVINE MADMAN

Flying across Nepal and into Bhutan, we can see nine of the world's highest mountains, each of them over 8,000 metres. This aerial panorama begins with Dhaulagiri and the Annapurna massif, punctuated to the east by Manaslu's twin exclamation points. Off in the distance, beyond Nepal's border with China, stands the crumpled spire of Shishapangma, which appears much smaller than lesser peaks in the foreground. Ten minutes further on, the towering profiles of Cho Oyu, Everest, Lhotse and Makalu slip by the wingtips of our Drukair jet.

On the first day of 2019, the winter atmosphere is brilliantly clear. Stretching towards the northern horizon is the tawny expanse of Tibet. As we fly on, Kanchenjunga now appears, strands of snow unravelling from its summit. Moments later, the Chumbi Valley breaks the white chain before giving way to Jomolhari, Jichu Drake and an imposing barrier of other mountains in Bhutan, including Gangkhar Puensum (7,570 metres), the highest unclimbed summit on earth. For religious and cultural reasons, as well as security concerns, Bhutan has banned all mountaineering within its borders, leaving several major peaks inviolate. While policies like this may frustrate alpinists they provide the last best hope of protecting those few areas of Himalayan wilderness that remain.

Descending into the airport at Paro we follow the same flight path as

Guru Rinpoche, who was carried here on the wings of his consort after she turned herself into a flying tigress. As our plane skims over pine-clad ridges we spot her lair, perched on a cliff face overlooking the valley—Taktsang, popularly known as 'the Tiger's Nest'. This is where Buddhism first touched down in Bhutan when the great teacher, also known as Padmasambhava, arrived in the eighth century to dispel shamanistic and occult beliefs or practices while spreading a message of compassion and non-violence. Two centuries later, the poet-magician, Milarepa, visited Bhutan and meditated at Taktsang where he composed some of his 100,000 songs of devotion and enlightenment.

Bhutan is the last surviving Himalayan kingdom, a political relic of a feudal age when chieftans ruled from fortified dzongs, twenty of which still stand in different districts of this landlocked nation. Not only are the highest peaks in Bhutan inaccessible but also large areas of forest that cover roughly seventy per cent of country. With a remarkably small population of only 700,000 citizens, the kingdom can afford to set aside extensive tracts of land as protected sanctuaries. Approximately half of the country has been designated as national parks or wildlife corridors, covering every altitudinal zone from semi-tropical lowlands bordering Assam to areas well above the treeline. Unlike most Himalayan regions there are places in Bhutan where *Homo sapiens* have never set foot. An array of endangered species such as red pandas, musk deer, hispid hares and pygmy hogs are found here. In 2017, the Ugyen Wangchuck Institute for Conservation and Environmental Research counted 103 tigers in Bhutan. The most encouraging aspect of their presence is that camera trap images show the tigers roaming from jungles bordering the Manas River at 100 metres above sea level to points as high as 4,000 metres. Both the monarchy and parliament, as well as the religious establishment, have committed themselves to wildlife conservation as a national priority.

Nevertheless, Bhutan is developing rapidly with a spreading network of roads that thread their way across the ridges, connecting remote parts of the country. Several large hydropower projects have also been built or are under construction. Collaborating with India, Bhutan plans to export surplus electricity produced by its many rivers. While efforts have been made to reduce the environmental impact, the damage to riverine ecosystems is severe and the influx of labour from India and Nepal undoubtedly puts pressure on the forests.

After a night in Paro, where temperatures dip below freezing, Ameeta and I set off for Thimphu the next morning. Guiding us is Tandin Gyeltshen, an expert on the cultural heritage of Bhutan as well as an accomplished birdwatcher. Dressed in the official state costume, a loose, belted robe called a gho that is gathered at the waist and extends to his knees like a kilt, Tandin explains that this form of dress for men is a variation of the Tibetan chuba. It was redesigned and shortened by the founder of Bhutan, Zhabdrung Ngawang Namgyal, who consolidated his rule over the country in the 1600s.

Known as Druk Yul, land of 'the thunder dragon', Bhutan is home to many fabulous creatures both mythological and real. Our first objective is to visit the Royal Takin Preserve at Motithang, on the outskirts of Thimphu, to see Bhutan's national animal. One of the most unusual Himalayan mammals around, takin (*Budorcas taxicolor whitei*) are a species of Caprinae related to goat antelopes like the goral and serow, though in appearance they seem more akin to musk oxen or wildebeests. Several subspecies of takin are found in the mountains of southern China, Myanmar and Arunachal Pradesh. In Bhutan, the takin live in high forests above 3,000 metres, descending to lower valleys during winter. Being sociable animals, they congregate in herds of twenty or thirty.

With a heavy-set body that combines the size and musculature of a mule with the bulk of a cow, their hide is covered in coarse brown and grey fur. The head of this strange beast is attached to its shoulders by a thick, short neck that sprouts a shaggy mane. The takin's features are bovine to the point of being a caricature, with a broad, bulbous snout and relatively small eyes and ears. Its horns are compact and curl up from its forehead in two symmetrical points. Altogether it is a clumsy-looking, mismatched creature—an anatomical riddle.

M. K. Ranjitsinh in his book, *A Life With Wildlife*, describes visiting Bhutan in 1965, when 'there were very few roads, sparse population and no hunters other than the royal family. I found black musk deer nibbling away unconcernedly just 20 m from me; and a male satyr tragopan, indescribably gorgeous in its shimmering crimson coat, tilted its blue-black head and gazed at me in wonderment five paces away.' As a guest of the king, Ranjitsinh explored several of the valleys on foot. At first he found the takin elusive but eventually, in the north-eastern corner of the kingdom, at a place called Seijathang, he came upon a herd of more than sixty animals that he first mistook for yaks. When he picked up his binoculars, however, he saw that they were 'Dong khimse' (gyem tsey), the Bhutanese name for takin. The animals were 'sparring and chasing each other with their ungainly, lurching run,' as well as licking patches of wet clay for salt and other minerals.

Though the Takin Preserve above Thimphu is set amidst several acres of blue pines, it is essentially a zoo, caged in with wire mesh fences. Tandin explains that this herd of takin was originally kept on the palace grounds but the fourth king decreed that they should be released into the wild. However, the animals were so used to living in captivity that they soon found their way back to Thimphu, wandering the streets of the capital, feeding on handouts and garbage. After that, it was decided to establish the park, which now includes a number of sambar deer and a 'rescued' serow, as well as a monal pheasant and a satyr tragopan.

The captive takin in the Motithang Preserve seem relatively content in their spacious enclosure, though they appear overweight, lounging about on beds of pine needles or browsing dry winter grass. While I had hoped to see them in the wild, the Jigme Dorji National Park, where takin are found, isn't set up for casual visitors or trekkers in winter. As I was paying the required $250 a day that foreign tourists are charged in Bhutan, going in search of wild takin would have been a prohibitively expensive expedition.

A popular folk tale about the origin of the takin involves one of the patron saints of Bhutan, Drukpa Kunley, often referred to as 'the divine madman'. He is regarded as a great teacher, who promoted the sacred tenets of Buddhism through the reverse logic of irreverent and offensive behaviour. A wandering monk from Tibet, he was known for his uncouth appearance and a love of chang and beautiful women. His erect penis is an auspicious symbol in Bhutan and decorates the facades of many homes. While representing fertility, it also wards off evil. In a number of his songs he compares his phallus to a dorje, or sacred thunderbolt, while the vulvas of his many lovers become the padma or lotus. As a Buddhist 'adept' Drukpa Kunley's primary goal, beyond helping others to achieve enlightenment, was to subdue demons. Keith Dowman has translated a 'secret' biography, *The Divine Madman: The Sublime Life and Songs of Drukpa Kunley,* which is full of stories of ferocious demons with gnashing teeth and goitres bulging out of their necks, who were driven off by the lama's erections. This biography contains a number of folk tales about wild creatures including the story of how the takin was created.

One day, Drukpa Kunley arrived at a village where the people pleaded with him to perform a miracle. In turn, he demanded that the villagers feed him both a cow and a goat for his dinner. Knowing his reputation as an eccentric holy man, his hosts did as they were told and both animals were cooked together in a stew. Drukpa Kunley's appetite was insatiable and he consumed all the meat that was placed before him. Then, after finishing the food, he gathered up the bones and joined the skeletons together. Snapping his fingers he brought the two animals back to life as a single creature, which is why the takin appears to be a combination of a cow and a goat.

The divine madman devoured all kinds of flesh but whenever he finished a meal, he resurrected the bird or animal he had eaten. Most paintings of Drukpa Kunley portray him as a hunter carrying a bow and arrows, with a dog at his heels. Many of his stories symbolize the ethical paradox of a carnivorous diet. On occasion, the outcomes of his miracles were unpredictable as in the case of a chicken that was reconstituted with only one leg because the other drumstick had been left behind in a cooking pot. In another story, Drukpa Kunley was confronted by a greedy chieftain who demanded a tax of meat. The lama then gathered together 110 musk deer and herded them into the dzong. When the chieftain complained that he could not kill the deer himself, for fear of acquiring bad karma, Drukpa Kunley promptly chopped off all their heaids and skinned the carcasses. Horrified by the bloodshed, the chieftain refused to collect the tax. Having made his point, the lama then reattached the heads and hides, before releasing the deer back into the wild, though some of the larger heads got attached to smaller bodies and vice versa.

Fables like these suggest an evolutionary process and emphasize the connection between humans and other mammals, particularly the Buddhist belief that one species can be reincarnated as another. Drukpa Kunley once arrived at a monastery where the monks were scandalized when he offered prayers to a donkey:

> …most pitiful of beasts!
> Rarely finding grass or water,
> Overloaded, overburdened,
> We pray to your beaten backside
> For the blessings of your bent shoulder.

The monks protested that he should instead be offering prayers to their deceased Rinpoche, 'The Tulku of Loving Kindness'. Drukpa Kunley responded by saying that many years ago, on a journey to Tibet, their Rinpoche had overloaded his pack animals and the resulting karma caused him to be reborn as an ass.

Descending along the highway from Thimphu and entering the Punakha Valley we come to a site where Drukpa Kunley defeated a ferocious demon and trapped it under a rock. He then built a chorten here, on a low hill overlooking the river. This shrine was later expanded into the temple of

Chimi Lhakhang to commemorate the provocative wisdom of a ribald saint. Tandin explains that women who are childless often visit the temple and circumambulate the shrine carrying a large phallus to invoke fertility. Murals and carved totems of penises, many of them squirting fire or semen, decorate the walls of the sanctuary.

Driving upriver for an hour we arrive at Punakha Dzong, which was the capital of the country until 1955, when the king and his government shifted to Thimphu. It remains the headquarters of His Holiness the Je Khenpo, Bhutan's spiritual leader. At least 1,000 monks live and worship in the monastery, which has served as a venue for royal coronations and weddings.

As we come in sight of the dzong, Tandin asks Wangchuck, our driver, to stop as he points out different elements of this sacred landscape. Punakha Dzong is built at the confluence of the Mho Chhu and Pho Chhu, the former being female and the latter male. Tandin also describes how the layout of the dzong reflects the shape of an elephant. The two rivers are its tusks and the fortress is built upon its trunk, while the hills beyond are its head and body. Elephants are a divine symbol of the Buddha as well as an emblem of political power.

Situated at roughly 1,200 metres above sea level, Punakha is considerably warmer than Thimphu or Paro. Shelducks and cormorants congregate along the riverbank and a short distance upstream is one of the few places where the severely endangered white-bellied heron is found. Less than 250 of these birds exist, of which thirty live along the riverbank of the Pho Chhu above Punakha.

The grand architecture of the dzong with its huge walls of rammed earth and stone convey a sense of historic solidity while the tiered rooftops with gilded finials add elements of lightness to the structure. Ameeta and I cross a wooden, cantilevered bridge and then climb a steep staircase to pass through the main gates into a spacious, flagstone courtyard with a spreading ficus tree at one end. Bare, whitewashed walls contrast with heavily decorated balconies and windows. Monks in maroon robes pass by silently, while from an inner sanctum there is the sound of drumming and chanting, as mynas chatter in the branches of the tree.

Not only does Buddhism preach the protection of all forms of life but it also employs animals, birds, plants and trees in its proverbs and parables. Inside the main sanctuary of Punakha Dzong the walls are painted with bright murals depicting episodes from Gautama Buddha's life, including his mother's dream of a white elephant that signalled his divine conception.

Each of the four critical moments in the Buddha's earthly existence occurred beneath the sheltering branches of trees. He was born in the shade of a sal tree in Lumbini. He received enlightenment under a pipal tree in Bodh Gaya. He preached his first sermon in a forested grove at Sarnath. And, in the end, he died beneath two sal trees in Kushinagar.

One of the most popular jatakas or teaching tales that also appears in the murals at Punakha is 'the story of four friends'. As Tandin recounts this parable, four wild creatures contributed to the propagation of a fruit tree: the bird ate the seed and then dropped it on the ground; the hare dug up the soil and buried it; the monkey fertilized it with his dung; and the elephant sprayed water on the seed with his trunk and stood guard until the tree grew tall and healthy. Years later, in order to pluck the fruit from the high branches, the four friends had to collaborate once again. Illustrating this jataka is the image of an elephant with a monkey, hare and bird perched on each others' backs. As Ashi Dorji Wangmo Wangchuck, one of the queen mothers of Bhutan, elaborates in her memoir, *Treasures of the Thunder Dragon*, 'The fable underlines the virtue of cooperation, and the connections and interdependence between all creatures great and small, and all the elements, in nature's cycle.' She goes on to emphasize how these stories have promoted a conservation ethic. 'A unique aspect of Buddhism in Bhutan,' she writes, 'is that it has absorbed many practices from the earlier Bon religion and its strong animist beliefs, which imbue not just trees and forests, but also mountains, rivers, lakes, rocks, caves and other natural formations with divinity.'

Driving eastward from Punakha, we arrive in the Phobjikha Valley after dark. Snow powders the upper slopes and sections of the road are covered in ice. A new moon glistens in the sky but offers only the faintest illumination and the headlights of our vehicle reveal nothing beyond the edges of the road. The next morning, however, we wake up to find ourselves in a seemingly magical world. When I open the curtains in our hotel room, a broad alpine valley is spread out before us covered in a white mantle of frost. Ringed by forested mountains, with circuitous streams winding their way across open meadows, the landscape has an idyllic quality like visions of paradise in thangka paintings.

Every winter, black-necked cranes (*Grus nigricollis*) migrate to Phobjhika from remote water bodies in Ladakh and Tibet, flying across the Himalaya, to spend the cold season in these sheltered wetlands. Only 10,000 black-necked cranes remain and their summer breeding grounds are threatened by development, pollution, the effects of climate change and predation by feral dogs. In Phobjikha, however, they are protected and relatively secure, though the frozen marshes where they feed are also used for grazing cattle. The cranes have an eclectic diet, eating roots and plants, as well as snails, small fish, amphibians and reptiles.

As sunlight spills into the bowl of the valley and begins to melt the frost, we can see clusters of large birds scattered for several kilometres in all directions. At night they congregate in large flocks while during the day they disperse to feed in pairs or small groups. Fully grown, they stand almost a metre and a half tall, with a long black neck and a red patch on the forehead. Unlike heavy-billed storks, they have a thin, tapered beak and a well-proportioned body covered in white feathers, with a neat bustle of black plumes. Their long legs make it seem as if they are walking on stilts and when they fly these extend behind them like a rudder as they glide on outstretched wings.

A short distance from our hotel, we come upon a pair of cranes feeding in a ploughed-up field, gleaning scattered grains of barley. Males and females appear identical, though juveniles can easily be distinguished by their pale brown colouration. Monogamous by nature, the cranes are paired for life, which elicits romantic associations in folklore. Their courtship rituals are elaborate and males perform a rhythmic dance, leaping and flapping their wings to attract a female's attention before mating. The calls of black-necked cranes have a honking resonance that can be heard more than a kilometre away, like a reedy medley of notes played on a saxophone.

At the Gangtey Gompa in Phobjikha, on a hillock above the valley, an annual festival is held every November to celebrate the arrival of the cranes. Their migration is seen as an auspicious sign and the graceful birds are said to circle the gompa three times upon arrival and before departure in the spring. Dressed in black and white costumes with beaked masks, monks imitate the cranes in a ritual dance. Though Bhutan's national bird is the raven, which graces the royal crown, more than any other creature, black-necked cranes represent the country's efforts to preserve and celebrate its natural heritage.

The Royal Society for the Protection of Nature has set up a Black-Necked Crane Information Centre in Phobjikha with exhibits that detail the biology and behaviour of these birds and maps of their migratory routes. A short film titled 'Birds of Heaven', is screened at the centre and there are spotting scopes through which visitors can view the cranes without disturbing them. Next to the centre is a cage housing an injured female, who broke a wing two winters ago. Separated from her consort, she can no longer migrate to Tibet and remains in Bhutan throughout the year.

Leaving Phobjikha we pass three cranes standing in a sunlit glade by the side of the road, two parents and one of their young. Though juveniles are able to fly across the Himalaya within six months of hatching, it takes them two years to mature and pick their own mates. Ascending to the pass out of the Phobjikha Valley, we come upon several dozen yaks grazing on open meadows. The herders, Tandin tells us, have migrated to this region from summer pastures further north and their yaks, with thick black coats, are feeding on frostbitten grass and bamboo. Laughing, Tandin regales us with a folk tale about the yak and the buffalo, who were once friends and decided to enter into a business partnership. 'If you lend me your coat,' the yak said to the buffalo, 'I'll go to Tibet and bring back things to trade and sell.' The unwitting buffalo removed his coat and gave it to his friend who set off across the mountains. But instead of keeping his promise, the yak never came back, which is why he has such a thick coat and lives at high altitudes, while the buffalo has little or no hair and remains in the lowlands.' After a brief pause, Tandin adds, 'That's also why the buffalo always glances over its shoulder with a resentful expression, still looking for his deceitful friend.'

Yak herding is an arduous and, for the most part, unrewarding occupation. However, Tandin informs us that these nomadic herders have recently found a new source of income, gathering *Ophiocordyceps sinensis,* the caterpillar fungus. Sometimes called 'Himalayan Viagra', it would seem to be a creature conjured up in the divine madman's imagination. Essentially, the larvae of ghost moths are infected by a parasitic fungus that kills them and then grows out of the caterpillar's dry husk. A valuable ingredient in traditional Chinese medicine, yartsa gombu, as it is also known, is considered a powerful tonic that is credited with everything from boosting immune systems to helping Chinese athletes win gold medals at the Beijing Olympics. Whatever its attributes, most of which would seem to be exaggerated, *Ophiocordyceps* can fetch a retail price of more than $100,000 per kilogram. Though found in Tibet, yartsa gombu has been overexploited in the trans-Himalayan region. High places in Bhutan and Nepal are now the primary sources. Government regulations restrict collection of the caterpillar fungus, allowing herding communities to gather it within their traditional high altitude pastures along the snow line. According to Tandin, this windfall has made some of the yak herders suddenly wealthy.

Along the six-hour drive from Phobjikha to Trongsa, we pass the Black Mountains, which contain some of the thickest forests in Bhutan.

The dark colour of the rocks and the shadowy foliage give this region its name. The entire area lies within the Jigme Singye Wangchuck National Park. Giant hemlocks rise above a lower canopy of hoary oaks, maples and rhododendrons, as well as fast-growing alders that take over areas where landslides have occurred because of road building. When we stop for a cup of tea at a roadside restaurant, Tandin tells us that an infamous demon inhabits these forests. Her name is Neyla Dhuem and she takes the form of a beautiful woman, though anyone who sets eyes on her is doomed. 'Years ago,' he says, 'there was a mail-runner named Garbi Lungkharlo, the fastest man in Bhutan. He used to carry official messages between Trongsa and Wangdue Phodrang. To save time, Garbi followed the shortest route, across the Black Mountains. Passing through an uninhabited part of the forest, he came upon a woman kneeling beside a stream and noticed that she was washing something in the water. Entranced, the mail-runner asked her who she was and what she was doing. The woman replied, "I am Neyla Dhuem and I am washing the entrails of an ox." Unsettled by this encounter, Garbi continued on his way but the woman kept haunting his thoughts. When he reached Trongsa and lay down to rest after delivering letters to the governor, the messenger suddenly remembered that he had been born in the year of the ox. Next morning, Garbi Lungkharlo was dead.'

Both Tandin and our driver, Wangchuck, insist that nobody dares enter the forest or cut any trees in the Black Mountains because of their fear of Neyla Dhuem. Further down the valley, Tandin points out a forested ridge that tapers to a point, clad in tiered pavilions of foliage. 'That's Neyla Dhuem's palace,' we're told. With the sky overcast and the layered shadows of surrounding ridges converging on the eerie shapes of pagoda-like conifers, it seems the sort of place where a beautiful ogress might waylay unsuspecting travellers.

Trongsa is the largest dzong in the country, located at the centre of Bhutan, and this region has always been politically and economically important. Visiting the dzong in the late afternoon we come upon a group of men taking part in an archery contest in a field outside the walls. Unlike Drukpa Kunley's rustic bamboo bow, with which he shot magic arrows that guided him to waiting lovers, these men are using modern, high-tech bows with pulleys and counterweights, firing at a target 140 metres away. Those who hit the bullseye collect colourful scarves to take home to their wives. Archery is the national sport in Bhutan and dates back to a time when each dzong had to be defended against hostile invaders. A tall cypress stands outside the gate and Tandin points out dozens of arrowheads embedded in its bark. The walls of the dzong are more than a metre and a half thick, with narrow slits at strategic places, through which archers took aim. Today, the only invaders at Trongsa Dzong are troops of Assam macaques (*Macaca assamensis*), a darker, bulkier version of rhesus monkeys, with whom they share a penchant for breaking and entering to steal food. Tacked to the door of the main sanctuary at Trongsa is a sign warning visitors to keep the temple door shut while an elaborate network of electric fences have been erected on all sides of the dzong to ward off monkeys.

The next day, descending from Trongsa, we pass the 720 megawatt Mangdechhu Hydroelectric Project, one of ten giant hydropower projects that Bhutan is building. Further on, we come upon a number of settlements where the slopes have been terraced into fields and orange orchards have replaced stands of virgin jungle. Citrus is an important crop in this part of Bhutan and the harvest is underway. Trucks loaded with oranges are heading for the plains, to be exported to India and Bangladesh.

As we cross a small bridge, Tandin points out a cluster of beehives hanging from a cliff nearby. Giant Himalayan honeybees (*Apis dorsata laboriosa*), often called rock bees, are prevalent in Bhutan, though the honey they produce can be toxic because of poisonous flowers from which the nectar is gathered, particularly certain species of rhododendrons. European honeybees have been introduced for commercial apiaries in Bhutan but the collection of wild honey is strictly regulated and sold for medicinal purposes. The giant bees can be dangerous if they attack as a swarm. Along one section of the highway signs have been put up, warning motorists to keep their windows closed. Earlier, however, at Punakha Dzong, we noticed several large honeycombs hanging from the carved rafters above the main gateway, where the wild bees seem to live in harmony with the monks.

After showing us the beehives on the cliffs, Tandin identifies a yellow-rumped honeyguide, a small, active grey-green bird that feeds on bee larvae. All along our route there is plenty of bird life, particularly spotted forktails and white-capped redstarts, as well as the ubiquitous whistling thrush. We also spot a subspecies of kalij pheasant (*Lophura leucomelanos lathami*) that has much darker plumage than kalij in the Western and Central Himalaya. Further on, when we stop to photograph a waterfall, Ameeta suddenly calls out and there is a loud, thumping sound like a helicopter passing overhead. Looking up, I see two great hornbills flying out across the valley. They have been feeding on a wild fig tree beside the waterfall. Another pair remains in the branches, watching us with wary eyes. The protruding orange casque on top of their long, curved beaks gives the birds a top-heavy appearance.

Great hornbills (*Buceros bicornis*) are some of the largest birds in the Lower Himalaya with pied feathers and a wingspan of more than a metre. Their distribution extends across Southeast Asia, with an isolated population along the Malabar Coast of southern India. Great hornbills flock together in noisy groups, croaking and cackling at each other.

As we enter the buffer zone of the Royal Manas National Park, human settlements diminish and the dense forest takes over once again. The park is Bhutan's oldest wildlife sanctuary, contiguous with India's Manas Tiger Reserve. Roughly equal in size, these two parks together cover 2,000 square kilometres. At this elevation, below 1,500 metres, chir pines replace hemlocks and cedars. Stopping for lunch by a bamboo grove, we come upon our first troop of golden langurs. These agile primates live within a narrow strip of forest, between the Sankosh and Manas rivers. They are smaller and leaner than grey Himalayan langurs and have pale blonde fur that turns a russet gold during their breeding season in fall and winter. As with all langurs, they have black faces and contrasting side-whiskers. Their tails are proportionately thicker and longer than other species, dangling below them like velvet bell pulls.

In Buddhist teaching, monkeys are compared to the restless human mind that resists the stillness of contemplation. Watching the golden langurs moving from branch to branch, the metaphor seems appropriate though these gentle primates have meditative expressions on their faces. *Trachypithecus geei* (originally dubbed *Presbytis*) was identified as a separate species in 1956 and named after the man who first photographed golden langurs, the naturalist E. P. Gee. His book *The Wild Life of India* is a classic of nature writing and influenced both politicians and the public to take up the cause of conservation. Having heard uncomfirmed reports of 'white langurs' in the submontane jungles between the Sankosh and Manas rivers, Gee set off to explore this region. A tea planter by profession, he spent much of his free time pursuing wildlife with still and cine cameras. In 1953, Gee found two troops of golden langurs near the Sankosh River.

> ...when I was in the middle of filming them, a huge male swung down branch by branch till it was only a few feet away. It glared at me menacingly, before returning to the tree tops. I presumed this was a feint attack to scare me away, so I stayed perfectly still, just where I was. They seemed to be harmless and timid creatures, and I learned later that they never raid the rice crops as the common and very familiar rhesus monkeys do.

Gee reported his discovery to the Zoological Survey of India and the Zoological Society of London. A survey party was dispatched in 1956 and shot six specimens that were then skinned and examined to confirm that this was a new species. A few years later, Gee returned to the area and spent several weeks along the Manas River, where he found ten more troops of golden langurs. In his book he emphasizes the environmental significance of the Himalayan foothills, where the Duars descend into the grasslands of Manas. Gee also rhapsodizes over the beauty of this place and the tranquil current of the river as it leaves the hills. He writes: 'This spot could well be described as the answer to a fisherman's prayer and the artist's dream, and the so-far unrealized hope of the wild life conservationist.'

Unfortunately, within a few decades, this peaceful, unspoiled realm was under threat and nearly destroyed. During the 1980s and 1990s several militant groups in Assam, primarily the United Liberation Front of Assam (ULFA) and the Bodo Liberation Tiger Force, began an armed insurgency against the Government of India. Fighting a guerrilla war with state police and paramilitary forces, these militants retreated into the forests of Manas and set up camps in Bhutan, from where they launched attacks on Indian targets, carrying out kidnappings and extortion, while feeding and funding themselves by poaching wildlife.

As Prerna Bindra explains in her book, *The Vanishing*, Manas 'was emptied of its tigers and rhinos. Hundreds of elephants were slaughtered. Even "department" elephants, employed for patrolling during the heavy monsoons were shot, burnt, killed. An incredibly heroic staff stayed through this traumatic period to protect wildlife, and tragically, a few paid with their lives.' Bindra praises one of the forest guards in particular, Babulal Oraon, whom she describes as armed with a 'rusty .315 rifle slung over his shoulder. It's not an antique showpiece purely for effect. It's a weapon he has used repeatedly and brutally against the enemies of the park. In his career he has had over 100 encounters and killed 32 poachers.' Oraon received an award for his bravery from former prime minister Indira Gandhi.

In Bhutan, the presence of Indian militants was viewed with alarm. Not only did their jungle camps threaten the kingdom's sovereignty but the park had special significance for the king. A modest palace stands on a high bank overlooking the Manas River, at the point where it flows out of the hills. This has always been a favourite winter retreat for the royal family, who often spend three or four weeks in Manas.

In addition to the insurgents decimating animals in the park there were serious security threats to Bhutanese citizens living along the border.

As Tandin tells us, negotiations were carried out with the various militant groups who were repeatedly asked to leave but refused. In the winter of 2003–04, pressure was intensified and the infiltrators were warned that the Royal Bhutanese Army would take action to drive them back across the Indian border.

'Every attempt was made to reach a peaceful solution but at the same time the army was ready with a special commando force, like America's Navy Seals,' Tandin tells us. 'In order to find out how many insurgents there were, the negotiators handed out oranges in the camps and by counting how much fruit they distributed they figured out the total enemy numbers.'

The initial approach to the militants was exceedingly Buddhist in its spirit of compassionate dialogue but when the army finally struck at the insurgents they showed little mercy. The fourth king approved and commanded the assault, which was code named Operation All Clear. More than 120 militants were killed and a large number were captured and handed over to Indian authorities. Fifteen Bhutanese soldiers died in the fighting. At Dorchu La above Thimphu, 108 memorial chortens were constructed to honour those who died in the conflict, commemorating Bhutan's first modern battle.

Following the 'flushing out' of militants, the difficult task of reviving the park began. On the Indian side, several rhinos and herds of elephant were reintroduced from nearby sanctuaries in other parts of Assam. Gradually the wildlife began to regenerate and wild buffalo, deer and even tigers reappeared. As Bindra reports, some of the poachers were rehabilitated and employed as forest guards, protecting the animals they once hunted. Today, Manas has reclaimed most of its natural splendour, though anxieties remain. Permits to visit Bhutan's side of the park are difficult to obtain and we were restricted to a small area near the forest department headquarters and the palace. 'Security' was the main concern, we were told, and an army contingent is posted next to the palace. Though forbidden from entering the jungle, we were able to walk around the main compound, where several tame sambar watched us with complacent curiosity. Only 100 metres above sea level, the jungle had changed dramatically from higher up in the mountains. Huge silk cotton trees (*Bombax ceiba*) were in full bloom, with scarlet leathery blossoms that attracted hill mynas and Alexandrine parakeets.

In recent years, Tandin has brought several groups of birdwatchers to Manas but tourists are rare in this part of Bhutan. Groups of Indian visitors, crossing over from the other side of the park in jeep safaris, are permitted to drive 12 kilometres beyond the border to Panbang, the nearest town.

Along this route there is little or no wildlife to be seen and many of the tourists queued up at the park entrance to take selfies beside a concrete model of a tiger, painted bright yellow and black. The convoy of vehicles full of noisy families and picnic parties was a depressing reminder of the ever-increasing pressures of 'eco-tourism' on national parks in India. More and more, I am convinced that wildlife sanctuaries should be closed to the public, allowing animals the space to survive. Aside from forest guards, only scientists and serious naturalists conducting conservation research should be permitted entry. For everyone else, carefully maintained and regulated safari parks can be set up with caged enclosures that guarantee tiger sightings. Otherwise, the value of preserving natural habitat containing protected birds and animals will soon be destroyed by the overwhelming presence of too many human visitors, most of whom have little appreciation for conserving wild places.

While our first day in Manas is disappointing, on the second morning we decide to float down the river in an inflatable raft. Accompanying us is a local naturalist, Kunley, named after the divine madman. A cheerful, attentive guide, he explains that river rafting is part of a community development project that has been started in Panbang. Kunley also tells us that a few years ago he participated in a research project with American fisheries experts who tagged and tracked mahseer in the river using GPS equipment to study their migration and breeding.

A new motorable bridge was recently built at Panbang but the old steel footbridge remains intact, covered with prayer flags that rustle in the breeze. As Kunley tosses a handful of salted snacks into the water below us, a large school of mahseer appears and there is a brief feeding frenzy. Most of the fish seem to weigh about 5 to 6 kilograms but after several more handfuls of food are tossed in the water, an enormous 20 to 25 kilogram mahseer appears below the surface. Kunley says the river contains both 'golden' and 'chocolate' mahseer, though these are somewhat arbitrary distinctions since colours vary from gold and silver to a murky green. For a number of years fishing has been banned in Bhutan but efforts are being made to introduce 'catch and release' angling on rivers like the Manas.

Though Kunley and our boatman outfit us with helmets and life jackets this stretch of the river has virtually no rapids. Floating with the current is one of the most pleasurable ways of observing a forest. The dense tangle of creepers and wild bananas remind me of jungles in Arunachal Pradesh, to the east of here. Forest giants with buttressed roots rise up amidst the lush verdure of flowering shrubs and bamboo. In winter, the river level drops, and on either side lie margins of boulders and sand marking the upper limits of the swollen current during the monsoon.

As we slip downstream, beyond a rippled confluence, a pair of ibis bills fly past us, going in the opposite direction, their wings snipping the air like scissors. Common mergansers, a duck that winters in Manas, float in the shallows while several great hornbills pass overhead, the pulsing sound of their flight like muted applause. A sudden movement on the riverbank catches my eye as two otters scramble over the rocks and plunge into the water. Swimming away from us they look as if they are part of the current and finally dive beneath the surface and disappear. Further on, Kunley points out a monitor lizard sunning itself on a half-submerged boulder. This reptile can grow to more than a metre long, the closest species to a thunder dragon that Bhutan has to offer. When we ask about crocodiles, Kunley reassures us that there are none in these waters. The river Manas is named after a serpent goddess in Hindu mythology, the queen of the Nagas, who protects her devotees from snakebite. Though pythons and cobras inhabit the park, none of them make an appearance during our visit.

The raft eventually drifts in sight of the royal palace and we reluctantly paddle ashore. After the cool breezes accompanying the current the bright glare of sunlight off the sand and bleached rocks is blindingly hot. In the trees above us is a troop of black-capped langurs, about the same size as the golden but with darker fur and a somewhat scruffier appearance.

Our journey through Bhutan is almost over but there is one more animal to see. Kunley and two forest guards on duty, lead us down the shore and into an area of high grass. Loose sand pulls at our heels as we walk a short distance to a dry streambed that floods during the monsoon. Dead tree trunks and branches have been washed down from the forest above and in the bright sunshine they look like twisted skeletons. Ahead of us in the grass is a dark shape with humped shoulders and a sloping back. After several minutes the animal raises its huge head, crowned with a giant pair of horns.

Wild buffalo (*Bubalus arnee*) are relatively common in Manas though they have disappeared in most of the forests along the foothills in other parts of the Himalaya. Several hundred years ago these massive creatures would have been plentiful across Southeast Asia and the Indian subcontinent but now there are only about 3,000 in the wild, mostly in Assam. They have the largest horns of any mammal on earth and can weigh more than a tonne. The solitary bull that we are watching is a grand specimen though he is now past his prime. According to the forest guards this buffalo was once the dominant male in a herd but a few weeks ago he was driven away by a younger challenger. Injured and beaten, the old bull retreated across the river and now lives alone.

Wild buffaloes can be extremely dangerous and often charge unprovoked but this one seems untroubled by our presence though he watches us with sullen eyes. Having lost his coat to the yak, as the folk tale recounts, the buffalo's bare black hide is stretched taut over his spine and hipbones. A few patches of hair grow on his legs and face but his dark complexion gives him a naked, vulnerable appearance.

Buffaloes are one of the most maligned and underappreciated creatures though they have been domesticated for as long as anyone can remember. Through selective breeding, tame water buffaloes (*Bubalus bubalis*) have been reduced in size and their horns shortened, making them easier to manage. The few wild herds that remain in parks like Manas and Kaziranga have crossbred with domestic buffaloes, diluting their genes. While the cow is considered sacred by Hindus, the buffalo receives no such veneration, though they produce far more milk than other livestock and are the primary dairy cattle in South Asia. Mythology has demonized these beasts, characterizing them as evil and a symbol of brute aggression. The mother goddess, in her many manifestations, as Durga, Mahakali or Nanda Devi, battles with Mahishasura, the buffalo demon, and kills him, ridding the earth of danger and mayhem. In some parts of the Himalaya, particularly Nepal, buffalo sacrifices are a common ritual that re-enact the slaying of demons.

Through no fault of its own, this creature that stands before us has been victimized by human beings, who have taken its species captive and bred away its wild traits while projecting supernatural fears and moral judgements upon it. The lone bull in Manas, his horns spreading more than 2 metres from end to end and curving up like scimitars, has been exiled to the east bank of the river. How long he will survive it is hard to guess. Though this glowering patriarch no longer enjoys the protection of his herd, even a tiger would think twice before attacking him. As we watch the buffalo and he watches us, there is a tragic look of defiance in his demeanour, as if he were the lone survivor of his wild species.

VI

ANCESTRAL JOURNEYS
Our Human Presence

North Face of Mount Kailas at sunset

Khumbu Glacier with Mount Everest in the background

Ama Dablam at sunrise from Kala Patthar

Dhaulagiri at sunrise from Muktinath

Nanga Parbat amidst monsoon clouds

Ama Dablam from Tengboche Monastery

Machapuchere at sunset from Pokhara

Cho Oyu with one of the Gokyo lakes in the foreground and numerous small cairns along the shore

Kanchenjunga from the ridge above Thangsing

Thorung La at sunrise

Gangapurna with a lake in the foreground where the glacier used to extend less than sixty years ago

Raikot Glacier, the snout, from Fairy Meadows

A monsoon stream in Sikkim

Confluence of the Alakananda and Mandakini at Rudraprayag, before the 2013 flood. The old bridge is no longer there.

Primulas blooming near a spring on a bugiyal meadow below Darwa Pass

A seasonal waterfall flowing over foliated gneiss near Ukhimath, Garhwal

Shepherds and their flocks on the Deosai Plateau

A patch of green fields and poplars along the Zanskar River, Ladakh

Cairn, Songad Valley, Garhwal

Petroglyphs along the Khyamar Chu, Ladakh

Cairn below Goecha La, Sikkim

Rock inscriptions, Solu-Khumbu Valley, Nepal

Brahma Kamal, Garhwal

Epiphytic rhododendron, Sikkim

Rhododendron forest, Sikkim

Magnolia, Arunachal Pradesh

Himalayan griffon, Garhwal

Blood pheasant in a forest below Kanchenjunga, Sikkim

Collared owlet, Oakville

Pika or mouse hare with a bite taken out of its ear, probably the result of a raptor's attack, Songad Valley, Garhwal

Bharal or blue sheep, Songad Valley, Garhwal

Serow, Eaglenest Wildlife Sanctuary, Arunachal Pradesh

Himalayan brown bears, a mother and grown cub, Deosai Plateau

Villagers dancing to the beat of dhol, Agoda Village, Garhwal

Dhol and damaun players, performing the Panwara of Jitu Bagdwal in Chandrapuri Village, Garhwal

Father and son in the Raikot Valley below Nanga Parbat

Gujjar herdsmen migrating with their buffaloes, Garhwal

Gujjar herdsman carrying a newborn buffalo calf, Garhwal

Pandavlila performance at Pali Village, Garhwal

Taktsang Monastery (Tiger's Nest) above Paro, Bhutan

Waterspout in the shape of a cow's head, Muktinath, Nepal

Wild buffalo, Royal Manas National Park, Bhutan

Golden langur, Royal Manas National Park, Bhutan

chapter 34

EVIDENCE OF ARRIVAL

The exact origins of human settlement in the Himalaya are impossible to
determine with any certainty but it is only logical to assume that people
entered the mountains from various directions, for multiple purposes and
at different points in history. Like migrating plants and animals that moved
upward after glaciers began to recede, the earliest human nomads would
have followed the thawing ice in pursuit of prey. Petroglyphs in Ladakh and
elsewhere suggest that some of the first hunters came from the north, out of
Central Asia and across the Tibetan Plateau—areas that escaped glaciation
because of an arid climate. As passes and transverse valleys became accessible
some of these early explorers may have crossed over to the southern ranges,
where residual forests survived. These isolated tracts, tucked away at lower
elevations, contained a diverse population of birds and mammals. Instead
of choughs and ravens they found quail and pheasant. Instead of bharal and
ibex there were deer and boar. Coming down out of the frigid steppes over
ice-bound cols it must have seemed to them like paradise with plenty of
water to drink, fuel to burn and food to kill.

By all accounts we were latecomers. Our arrival in the Himalaya is
estimated to have occurred anywhere from 7,000 to 10,000 years ago, though
it is difficult to pin down a date because there are no fossil records, no
skulls in caves or communal tombs from which to test the bones for age

or origin. The only previous ancestor that has been described is *Sivapithecus*, an ancient primate who wandered through the submontane jungles of the Shivalik foothills twelve million years ago. There is no evidence to suggest that this creature ascended into the Himalaya.

Geneticist David Reich's account of early human wanderings, *Who We Are And How We Got Here*, deciphers chromosomes that map out ancient pathways radiating from Africa, Europe and East Asia. He explains how our predecessors travelled the globe with an itinerant lineage that is far more complex than previously assumed. While Africa was the birthplace of the first hominids like *Australopithecus*, other branches of the family tree extended into Europe, Central Asia and all the way across the Siberian land bridge to the Americas. Based on DNA samples from ancient skeletal remains, some as small as a single bone, Reich argues that during the Pliocene and Pleistocene eras several different species or subspecies of early humans were roaming the earth and interbreeding.

Mythology and folklore offer parallel narratives, as stories of origin hint at ancestral liaisons. The Northern Magar people of the Kali Gandaki watershed in Central Nepal recount a number of tales about their progenitors. In one story, recorded by ethnographer Michael Oppitz, an anonymous figure emerges from the mountains each night and has sex with a young woman who eventually becomes pregnant. When her mother and father demand an explanation the daughter admits that a secret lover has shared her bed though she doesn't know his identity. The next night, her parents persuade her to tie a long string to his ankle. After he departs in the morning, they follow the thread, which leads them into a narrow ravine. Beneath an overhanging rock they find the string tied to a desiccated shin bone. In this way, they determine that the lover is either a demon or a ghost, a restless soul that has not yet departed this world. Eventually, when the woman gives birth to twins, the sons of this union become the first Magar hunters who set off in pursuit of wild boar.

In a similar manner, geneticists trace our ancestry back to dry bones, following strings of DNA to find out who was sleeping with whom. The answers are never simple and the science sometimes borders on psychic readings with 'ghost populations' like the Denisovans, a hypothetical species, who are believed to be contemporaries of the Neanderthals, though the only proof of their existence lies in a single finger bone discovered in Denisova cave in the Altai Mountains. Comparing ancient DNA samples to recent data collected from different populations around the world, Reich and his colleagues have reconstructed evidence of considerable crossbreeding between early humans and other hominids.

On the Tibetan Plateau, where *Homo sapiens* first roamed as hunters and gatherers about 10 to 11,000 years ago, ultimately establishing permanent settlements more than six centuries later, Reich presents evidence to suggest that the first inhabitants brought with them a genetic adaptation to thin air. 'One of the most striking genomic discoveries of the past few years,' he writes, 'is a mutation in a gene that is active in red blood cells and that allows people who live in high altitude Tibet to thrive in their oxygen poor environment…' Tracing this evolutionary trait to the Denisovans he suggests that the mutation proliferated after people began to live in Tibet, though he admits that this prediction can only be tested directly by studying the DNA of early Himalayan inhabitants.

Oral histories and folklore confirm the migration of Tibetans from the trans-Himalayan region onto the southern flanks of the mountains. The provenance of these journeys is, again, difficult to determine though some communities, like the Sherpas of Solu-Khumbu, probably crossed over only 500 to 600 years ago. Far older movements of population to the lower ranges are likely and many indigenous people in the Himalaya trace their ancestry to Tibet. Language and cultural practices underscore this link.

Based on DNA analysis, Reich speaks of South Asia as being 'composed of a large number of small populations'. This is particularly true in the Himalaya where geographical boundaries isolate communities. Later 'population bottlenecks' were caused by social strictures like the caste system. The traditional narrative of Indian history has always suggested that waves of invaders—Aryans, Kushanas, Scythians, Greeks and others crossed over the mountains at different times and settled in North India, from the borderlands of Bactria in Afghanistan and Kashmir to the lower reaches of the Gangetic Plain.

Origin stories, whether told by Himalayan shamans or post-modern geneticists, reach back into a prehistoric age and reveal the dalliances of our foremothers and forefathers. Another version of the Magar origin story about the young woman and her secret lover, describes how she and her parents follow the string to a crevice in the mountains. Hidden inside the rocks is a god who cries out in pain every time they pull the string, which is tied to his thumb. When the parents demand that he come out of hiding and marry their daughter, the divine lover refuses but then negotiates a settlement. As compensation for the illicit pregnancy, he offers the girl's family a plough and other farm implements, which brings about the birth of agriculture.

Many mythological traditions, including Christianity, contain stories of human mothers inseminated by the gods. The idea of supernatural origins is an appealing conceit. An equally familiar narrative in Himalayan folklore, which repeats itself across different cultures, is the interbreeding of humans and animals, out of which hybrid monsters emerge. Whether consciously or unconsciously, we imagine ourselves to be the offspring of either gods or beasts, and sometimes both. Unfortunately, DNA analysis hasn't reached a point where we can establish whether our antecedents are demonic or divine.

In northern Pakistan I was told a folk tale from Hunza about an adolescent girl who became pregnant. When her parents demanded to know how this had occurred, she insisted that no man had touched her and she was still a virgin. Eventually, when a child was born it was covered with hair like the fur on a goat. Alarmed and perplexed, the parents approached a shaman in their village for an explanation. He questioned the girl and learned that she had been herding a flock of sheep high in the mountains. When she grew thirsty, the only source of water the girl could find was a stagnant pool in the shallow depression of a rock. Hearing this, the shaman concluded that this was rainwater mixed with the urine of a markhor and by drinking it the girl had ingested the wild goat's sperm.

chapter 35

PRIMATE HUNTERS

Wearing capes of cotton fabric loosely knotted over their shoulders, the hunters quietly secure nets between trees, stringing them across forested hillsides. Made of ropes woven from the strong, supple fibres of stinging nettles as well as bauhinia vines and other forest creepers, each net is roughly 2 metres long and 1 metre wide, approximately the size of a blanket with a mesh about 8 centimetres in diameter. Several of these are tied together and camouflaged with leaves. The jungle itself is a web of foliage and the nets are virtually invisible within a dense tangle of monsoon shrubs and plants. Silently, the human predators prepare their hunting grounds, where the heavily wooded slopes funnel into narrow ravines. Forest gods have already been propitiated with a sacrifice of baby chicks to ensure the success of the hunt. Women and children are left behind in camp. Only the men participate, carrying sharp axes with double blades to dispatch their quarry.

Removing capes and excess clothing, the hunters are barefoot and virtually naked, except for loincloths. Imitating the soft, hooting cries of monkeys, the hunters call out to their prey. They also communicate with each other through whistle speech so as not to alarm the monkeys they pursue. These shrill signals alert the hunters whenever prey has been sighted or monkeys are on the move. Eventually, the drive begins, when several of the beaters make loud 'Hrrr' sounds and wave their arms. The rhesus macaques, sensing danger, gather together in a protective huddle, then begin to scramble through the underbrush as the hunters chase them towards their nets, emitting piercing 'kill whistles'.

While preparations can take several hours the hunt itself is relatively brief, as the men race through bushes, over rocks and fallen trees. The element of surprise is followed by chaos and confusion that disorients the monkeys and makes them panic. Instead of seeking the safety of higher branches, they rush headlong down the hill, away from the human beings, in a desperate race to escape. But soon they find themselves trapped, held fast by the loosely woven nets—males, females, juveniles and infants—floundering in a web of braided fibres. Before they can break free, the hunters close in upon them and their axes cut them down, crushing skulls, severing limbs, delivering death with the finality of sharpened iron. The monkeys scream, baring their teeth in terror as their attackers swiftly decimate the troop.

We can only imagine this scene, for the Raute hunters do not permit outsiders to witness the killing for fear of displeasing a host of forest spirits and demigods that oversee their hunt. The spiritual aspects of the chase are as important as the bloodshed. Though the hunt is brutal and violent, it is justified through ancient narratives of survival. Rautes believe in the unity of nature and call the monkeys their 'little brothers' but they also assert that the gods created these lesser apes in order to provide their people with food.

Jana Fortier, an American anthropologist, whose book *Kings of the Forest* explores the endangered culture and traditions of these primate hunters, writes about their affinity with the natural and supernatural environment. She explains that as animists, the Rautes maintain a close subjective relationship with the natural world, viewing other species and even inanimate objects such as rocks and rivers as persons whom they relate to directly. 'About an animal, a Raute asks not "What is it?" but rather "Who is it?" and "What relationship does she or he have to me?" A bird, for example, is called not just "bird" but "elder-brother bird" (*manko bwa*)... Thus, it is only natural for Rautes to utter such statements as, "We who live in the forest are all children of God."'

When the hunt is finished, the Rautes build a fire and scorch the hair and skin from their victims before butchering the meat, which is divided into portions that are shared within the tribe. The head is given to the hunter who 'struck the first blow' and a monkey's thigh is always presented to the shaman who conducted prayers and rituals before the hunt. Nothing is wasted, from the ribs and shoulders to the liver and heart. Even the blood and entrails are eaten. Each member of the clan receives his or her share, including widows and those too old to take part in the hunt. Most of the meat is consumed the same day, though if there is any excess it is cut into strips and dried.

The first people to make their home in the Himalaya would have been nomadic hunter-gatherers like the Rautes. Today, only a few isolated communities remain in Nepal and North-eastern India. For these indigenous hunters, wild meat continues to be an important part of their diet, though a severe depletion of prey species makes it more and more difficult to find the creatures they eat. Because of strict conservation laws, hunting has become a surreptitious activity. Farmers sometimes kill wildlife to protect their crops or supplement their diet. Shotguns and muzzle-loaders, many of them unlicensed antiques, are the most common weapons, though snares and traps are still widely used.

Fortier's fieldwork among the Rautes (also spelled Rawats) was undertaken in the 1990s in the forests of Western Nepal, along the Mahakali River that separates Nepal from India, though these hunter-gatherers have little concern for borders. They are closely related to Banraji hunters who live in eastern Kumaon. Unlike the occasional village hunters who kill wild pigs and deer, the Rautes primarily prey on rhesus macaques and langurs. The killing of these species, though viewed with disapproval by most Hindus because of associations with Hanuman, is tolerated by farmers because the monkeys pose a threat to their fields.

The semi-tropical and temperate forests of the Mahabharata Lekh range are home to the wandering Rautes who migrate across the mountains according to the seasons and the availability of food. In addition to stalking monkeys, they gather roots and tubers, fruit, berries and nuts from the forest. Their favourite vegetable is tarul (*Dioscorea belophylla*), a wild yam that sustains the Rautes with its starchy roots. They also forage for more than a hundred other species of greens and wild vegetables or fungi, from the leaves of nettles to the seedpods of bauhinia vines and edible mushrooms. In addition to food, forest plants provide them with herbal medicines that can cure bleeding wounds, stomach ailments and other maladies.

The Rautes and Banrajis are also known for carving wooden vessels, which they barter for rice and millet. Despite these transactions, they remain a secretive, reclusive community spending most of their time in the forests. Traditionally, the hunter-gatherers would slip into a village at night and leave an empty wooden jar or bowl near the door of a hut. A farmer would then fill it with grain and the following night the Rautes quietly collected his payment, leaving the vessel behind. In this way, they remained aloof from agrarian communities but acquired rice and other grains to supplement their diet. The wooden jars are used for making beer, which is drunk throughout the day, as much for nutrition and sustenance as intoxication. Though the hunters have more interaction with other communities these days, they still guard their privacy and avoid contact with outsiders.

According to Dor Bahadur Bista, an anthropologist and social activist, who had a brief encounter with a group of nomadic Raute hunters in 1972, the villagers in Central and Western Nepal view these forest dwellers with suspicion and fear. They are sometimes referred to as 'van manush', men of the jungle, which is a name that is also used for Yetis. Bista writes, 'Most people in the village, and almost all I met and talked to on the way, believed that the Raute had very effective magical powers and spells which they always used in catching monkeys and would use on human beings, especially women, whenever they could be found alone or in small numbers.' He also reports that there were unconfirmed 'rumours' that the Rautes kidnapped children and conducted human sacrifices, which illustrates the paranoid manner in which these nomadic hunters are shunned by settled society.

The Raute and Banraji languages are unique and closer to Tibeto–Burman than the Sanskrit-based languages of Hindi and Nepali. This linguistic link with the trans-Himalayan region seems in concert with their ethnicity though the languages are in danger of disappearing, as are many of their cultural practices and traditions. Population estimates show how small these communities are: only 700 Rautes live in the Nepal–India border region, while there are no more than 2–3,000 Banrajis. Cultural extinction would seem a foregone conclusion yet they continue to endure with remarkable resilience, pursuing their 'little brothers' through the forest.

One of the Raute folk tales that Fortier retells is the story of how langur monkeys got black faces while rhesus macaques have red bottoms. As recounted by one of the hunters, the goddess Sita was being harassed by monkeys that were trying to steal food from her kitchen. When a langur began to pester her, she picked up a sooty tawa and threw it at him, blackening his face. Later, when a rhesus did the same, she took a hot pan from the fire and hit him on the buttocks, which seared his hindquarters bright red. The fact that this folk tale is framed within the Ramayana narrative of Rama and Sita's exile in the forest, demonstrates the way in which the hunters' stories become enmeshed with more dominant myths. Yet despite these elements of assimilation the Rautes retain a considerable degree of cultural autonomy and their own gods remain intact, like Berh, a solar deity that is neither male nor female but remains a constant presence in the sky.

As with most tribal communities in the Himalaya, the Rautes literally live on the edge, both geographically and culturally. Modern society in South Asia has little patience for hunter-gatherers or nomads of any kind and the general thrust of development tries to draw them into the mainstream, erase their gods, stop their wanderings and eliminate their language. Those who advocate for tribal culture are often accused of promoting primitivism and holding these communities back from the benefits of economic and social progress, particularly education. Yet the extinction of cultural identity, language and indigenous knowledge represents an incalculable loss that can never be retrieved.

This dilemma is clearly expressed by Dor Bahadur Bista, when he writes: 'It looks as though the Raute stand a fairly good chance of being integrated into the settled economy…' He goes on to explain that the carved wooden bowls that they produce will inevitably be replaced by mass-produced plastic and metal vessels and they will find it difficult to subsist on hunting alone. Bista predicts, 'As has happened with so many other tribal groups in Nepal, their women will be the first to marry outside. Looking at the Raute women, they will not have any difficulty in finding husbands outside. This is sad speculation, but I do not see any other possibilities under the present circumstances.'

chapter 36

THE STORYTELLER OF BOMPHU

In the smoky aura of firelight our faces are masked with shadows. Strangers who have wandered here together by chance, we share the anonymity of darkness, gathering around the meagre warmth of a smouldering log. Our camp lies 2 kilometres above sea level in the Eastern Himalaya. After sunset, in late March, it grows suddenly cold as the humidity turns to mist.

'Our people worship the mountains,' the storyteller begins, unprompted, '…and stones.'

Spirits surround us. They live in the rivers, in clouds and forests, in caves hidden away in the jungle, in the wind and rain, amongst birds and insects.

'When we collect wild honey, we always go at night, lighting a fire at the foot of the cliff where a hive hangs from the rocks. As we climb through the smoke, we sing to the bees, telling them, "We mean you no harm. We are only collecting your honey as offerings for the gods."'

Though his voice is loud and assertive, the storyteller starts speaking in a distracted tone as if he doesn't know where to begin. He is a stocky man in his early fifties with broad, open features but a narrow gaze that makes it look as if he is squinting because of the smoke. Dressed in a black windcheater over a grey tracksuit with a folded fleece hat on his head, his feet are bare. Three of his companions sit with us but he does all the talking.

Dorjee Khandu speaks in Hindi, adding an English word now and then.

'Today, everything is "climate change",' he tells me, though he means it in a broader sense, not just the weather but the world in general—politics, money, society—everything is in flux. Yet, here in the forest we could be living in the past. Collecting his thoughts, Khandu goes on to speak of origins:

'Our first ancestor was a brave hunter who understood the ways of wild creatures and possessed a complete knowledge of forest herbs and edible plants. One day he was hunting in the high mountains and shot an arrow at a wild boar. The animal was wounded and the hunter set off in pursuit, following a blood trail through the jungle. For several days, he travelled across ridges and through valleys until he eventually left the mountains and reached the plains of Assam. There he finally caught up with the boar and killed it. Our ancestor, Asu Gyaptong, butchered and cooked his prey, flavouring the meat with wild herbs and spices. He then shared his feast with the people of Assam and they found it delicious. After that, he was invited to come down from the mountains every year. In this way, our forefathers began trading with the plains dwellers, bartering salt from Tibet and medicinal plants from the high forests, for rice and other produce in Assam...'

As the stories continue, one tale leads on to the next like spirals of smoke from our campfire braided together and curling into the night. Dorjee Khandu is a spontaneous raconteur. His hands perform an expressive pantomime to enliven forest lore and mythic history. In the darkness, we can hear night sounds from the jungle around us—the measured four-note call of a collared owlet and the steady clicking of nightjars, as well as the hoarse alarm cries of barking deer.

'We are Sherdukpen tribals,' Khandu explains with pride in his voice. 'These are our mountains and forests. Our ancestor, Asu Gyaptong, was the son of a Tibetan king and an Assamese princess. Long ago, the king sent his minister across the mountains to fetch his bride from the plains and bring her to Tibet. The journey took many months and along the way, the minister and the princess succumbed to temptation. Later, soon after the royal marriage, the king realized that his new queen was already pregnant. He confronted his minister, who confessed that the loneliness of his mission had weakened his resolve. Being a compassionate ruler, the king forgave the minister along with his wife. However, when the child was born, it had the head of a dog and the horns of a goat. Immediately, this grotesque creature was cast into the forest, where it became a demon. Later, the king and queen had a second son, who was Asu Gyaptong. He grew up to be a strong and handsome hunter. But the King of Tibet had an older son, from another wife, who was heir to the throne, so the king granted Asu Gyaptong this lower range of mountains, stretching all the way down to the foothills of Assam…'

Arunachal Pradesh is home to twenty-six major tribes, each of which has its own language and customs. In addition, as many as a hundred sub-tribes occupy separate territories divided by rivers and ridgelines. The Sherdukpen live in West Kameng District, along the highway from Guwahati to Tawang. Altogether, they number only 3,500–4,000 people but the Sherdukpen are an influential clan. The first chief minister of Arunachal Pradesh, Prem Khandu Thungon, came from this tribe.

Our camp lies on the southern slopes of Eaglenest Wildlife Sanctuary, at a place called Bomphu, which is a sacred site for the Sherdukpen. This morning, when Dorjee Khandu and his companions first arrived, crowded into five vehicles, driving down a rough jeep track through the forest, I mistook them for Tibetans. They were flying Tibetan flags and performing Buddhist rituals wherever they stopped, burning pine branches as incense and tying strings of prayer flags along their route. But when we finally introduced ourselves they made it clear that they were not Tibetans but Sherdukpen from the village of Thungre.

'We only became Buddhists one or two generations ago,' Khandu explains, 'around the time the Dalai Lama left Tibet in March, 1959. This is the same road he travelled after crossing into NEFA over Bum La above Tawang. He was a young man then, in his twenties, but very sick and weak from the long journey. Most of the way he rode on a yak. Our people helped him and the other refugees. This is the sixtieth anniversary of his escape from Tibet.'

As we sit around the fire at Bomphu, the Sherdukpen tell us that they are retracing the Dalai Lama's journey into exile. For them it has become an annual pilgrimage. Here in the forest they have cleared the bamboo and creepers around a sacred mane wall, which they paint white, with verses and motifs in bright colours. Oil lamps have been lit under a makeshift windbreak of corrugated metal sheets. Tomorrow, more than 300 people are expected in Bomphu, including lamas who will offer prayers and perform rituals. Together they will travel down to Kelang, a level clearing at the foot of the mountains, to commemorate the Dalai Lama's arrival.

'At Kelang, the Dalai Lamaji planted a tree,' Khandu tells us. 'But he put the sapling in the ground upside down with its roots in the air. Dalai Lamaji said that if this tree survived it meant his people would return to Tibet…'

He pauses for a few seconds to underscore the significance of the prophecy, and then continues...

'That sapling is now a large tree. My arms won't reach around the trunk and its branches have spread in all directions as if they were rooted in the sky. Leaving here, we will spend a few days in Kelang to conduct our puja and bathe in the river. Among us there are many old people who remember the Dalai Lama's journey. When they see the tree, they have tears in their eyes.'

The Sherdukpen occupy an intermediary zone in the Himalaya, between the higher mountains inhabited by the Monpa, and the lowlands where the Bodo live along the northern bank of the Brahmaputra. The largest town in Sherdukpen territory is Rupa, which gets its name from silver rupees the British gave their ancestors in lieu of taxes the tribe once extracted from traders who passed through their lands. Sherdukpen culture represents a mingling of Buddhist faith and animistic traditions, just as their home lies between the high passes into Tibet and the tropical jungles of the plains.

For generations they practised jhum agriculture, slashing and burning the forest and planting their crops in the ashes. Today the Sherdukpen have permanent, irrigated fields and are known for the vegetables they grow, particularly tomatoes. But their roots remain in the forest and their pilgrimage, retracing the Dalai Lama's path into exile, seems an excuse to return to the wild. Over the two days we spend in their company, I watch them gathering plants and ferns in the forest and preparing feasts of wild vegetables. They seem to revel in the rampant fertility of the jungle with its tree ferns as large as beach umbrellas and flowering magnolias that cast a confetti of white blossoms amidst a green tapestry of clambering vines and shrubs. Though I do not see them hunting, our guide assures me that they are carrying guns and setting snares. Surely, they will kill a barking deer or something larger. A few years back, he tells us that they shot a mithun. When I show Dorjee Khandu the picture of a serow that I photographed the day before, he immediately wants to know where we found this animal, obviously eager to track it down despite the fact that we are in a wildlife sanctuary. Regardless of government regulations, Khandu and the others believe that this is their forest and they can do what they please.

While Arunachal Pradesh has the most forest cover of any state in India and the richest diversity of species, it also suffers from widespread human predation. Tribal hunters have decimated wildlife in many areas of the Eastern Himalaya, indiscriminately killing birds and animals, including a number of endangered species. As George Schaller writes, 'All too often in history the last of a species has disappeared into the belly of a hungry hunter, its epitaph a belch.'

Hunting has always been a way of life for the Sherdukpen long before the rest of the world closed in around them. The story of Asu Gyaptong reveals an umbilical narrative that ties them to the forest, a primal journey that follows a blood trail from the Himalaya to Assam, tracing their own migrations over the course of a mythical chase. Not only is the boar a favourite prey of tribal hunters but also a symbol of transition between foraging and agriculture, rooting about in the earth for tubers while ploughing the soil with its tusks. Wild pigs often live at the edge of a forest and raid farmers' fields at night, occupying unsettled territory between their natural habitat and human cultivation. As a creature that traverses boundaries, the wounded boar in Khandu's story leads the hunter across the mountains and brings the Sherdukpen out of isolation and into contact with lowland tribes like the Bodo. After sharing the boar's meat, seasoned with highland herbs and salt from Tibet, they create an alliance for trade, a transactional link between the uplands and the plains.

In *Myths of the North-East Frontier of India*, Verrier Elwin included a number of Sherdukpen stories. Many of their folk tales reveal the paradox between a tradition of hunting and the strict injunctions of Buddhist lamas who forbade the killing of other sentient beings. In one of these parables Elwin relates:

> There were two brothers; the elder was a Lama and the younger made his living by hunting. When the hunter brought the meat home the Lama used to eat it, even though he was not supposed to. But one day he repented and said, 'Don't go hunting any longer, for it is a sin to take the life of others.' His brother said, 'But how can I give up my only means of livelihood?' They argued for a long time and finally the Lama said, 'I shall turn into a red deer. If you can kill me you will be a great hunter and without sin. But if you cannot kill me, great sin will rest upon your head.' The hunter agreed to this.

Accompanied by his dog and carrying a bow, the hunter set off in pursuit of his brother. After several days of stalking the deer through the forest he finally caught up with his quarry.

> The hunter waited by a stream and sent his dog to chase the deer. After a time the deer came to the water and the hunter said, 'Brother, shall I shoot or not?' The Lama replied, 'Brother, you must not shoot. From today I will be a man no longer but will live in the forest as a deer.' It was from this Lama that the race of deer began.

Elwin also records the folklore of the Bugun people, who live on the northern slopes of Eaglenest Sanctuary, a smaller, less prosperous tribe. They believe that thunder and lightning are caused by a brother and sister who live in the clouds. Both are virgins but the brother lusts after his sister and the tumult of the storm is caused by their quarrels, as the girl fends off the boy's incestuous desires. Lightning flashes when her hairpin falls to earth and shatters trees.

Much of tribal folklore in Arunachal Pradesh contains sexual tensions arising out of social taboos that conflict with nature's fecundity. Women give birth to animals and demons, just as human beings emerge out of eggs or the wombs of beasts. In another Bugun story that echoes the tale of lightning and thunder, a brother and sister live together in the mountains. The boy tells the girl to bring him fruit from the jungle. When she goes out to gather it, the sister finds a bear in the tree feeding on the fruit. She asks the bear to give her some of what he is eating but he insists that she must have sex with him first. After submitting to the bear's lusty advances she eventually falls in love with him, ensuring a regular supply of fruit for her brother. 'The fruit is sweet,' the girl sings to the bear, 'it is for my brother, but you are sweet, because you are for me.' In his passion, the bear keeps tearing her clothes with his claws and the brother becomes suspicious. Finally, he follows his sister into the forest and kills her ursine lover with an arrow.

While these stories were originally told in tribal tongues, Elwin translates them into English and Dorjee Khandu speaks to us in Hindi. When I ask him how he learned the language, he shrugs and replies, 'from the army'. Tens of thousands of Indian troops are posted in Arunachal Pradesh, especially along the route from the foothills up to the border. One of the largest army encampments is situated at Tenga, just a few kilometres from Bomphu. The original road passing through this jungle was built by army engineers soon after independence and Khandu recalls how vintage Dodge Power Wagons were the first vehicles to reach Rupa.

'Before that, the local administrator had a jeep disassembled and carried up to Bomdila, so that he could ride around town.'

As we sit beside the campfire at Bomphu, Khandu digresses from his folk tales of wild boar, honey gathering and the casual infidelities of Tibetan queens. He launches into a heroic tale about Jaswant Singh, an Indian soldier in the Garhwal Rifles, who held the Chinese forces at bay for seventy-two hours, as they fought their way up to Se La during the 1962 War.

'Jaswant Singh tricked the Chinese into thinking there were many more

Indian soldiers guarding the pass. In his bunker he had sten guns set up at different places and he would go back and forth from one to the other and fire down at the Chinese. At night, he tied lanterns around the necks of sheep and let them loose on the mountainside so the invaders thought these were Indian patrols. Jaswant Singh had fallen in love with a Monpa girl, who brought him food every day. While he was eating, she kept firing the guns. But after three days of fighting, the Chinese learned that only one man was holding them back. They circled around and ambushed him from behind. After he was killed the Chinese commander was so angry, he cut off his head and sent it back to Tibet. Later, the head was returned and Jaswant Singh remains a legend.'

On the north side of Se La is a war memorial at Jaswantgarh, named in his honour. The martial lore of Jaswant Singh's bravery has become a potent myth for the people of this region as well as the Indian Army, which has bolstered its presence to repel any future Chinese attacks. All the officers and soldiers who serve in this theatre pay their respects to Jaswant Singh. He is revered as a martyr and the army maintains his outpost as a shrine. Throughout the year soldiers are assigned to bring him tea and polish his boots, just as a deity is given offerings and propitiated with acts of devotion.

'A Bollywood movie is being made about Jaswant Singh's life,' Khandu tells us with excitement, 'and a Sherdukpen girl has been chosen to play the part of his lover, the girl Sela, who is named after the pass.'

Himalayan narratives can be as convoluted as the roads that cross these mountains, full of zig-zags and hairpin bends, looping around steep contours. But for Sherdukpen storytellers their repertoire always leads back into the forest, following overgrown trails, surrounded by fauna and flora. Like the other men in his group, Dorjee Khandu carries a heavy dao at his waist, a sharp machete with which he clears away vines and underbrush near our campsite. They also cut dozens of rhododendron blossoms to decorate the mane walls at Bomphu.

Later in the evening, women begin to sing and dance, holding hands in a line and swaying to the choral rhythm of their voices. They invite us to drink 'ara', a raw liquor distilled from rice beer. 'It is medicine,' they assure me, 'made from herbs in the forest. We even give it to our children when they are three days old, just a few drops…enough to fit in a fish's mouth.'

Insisting we join in their songs and dancing, another man in the group encourages us to come back later in the year and visit Thungre Village during the Khiksabha celebrations.

'It is our most important festival. All the Sherdukpen must return home from wherever they have travelled and we call together each of the spirits, from the rivers, forests and mountains. We worship the spirits and make them happy, so they will protect our tribe throughout the rest of the year.'

chapter 37

AN OCEAN OF DRUMMING

While many Himalayan people trace their lineage to Tibet an even larger number came up into the mountains from the plains of North India. In Nepal, Uttarakhand and Himachal Pradesh most villages are populated by Hindus who are divided into innumerable clans and castes, each with their own stories of origin and migration. Even those people who have lived here for so many generations they cannot remember when or how their ancestors first arrived, acknowledge that they must have come from somewhere else.

This sense of displacement is embedded in the cultural memory of Himalayan society and emerges in the beliefs, rituals and stories that animate both everyday life and extraordinary events. Though not always apparent or overtly expressed, an underlying sense of exile punctuates many Himalayan narratives, particularly those that recall and retell the great epics of the Mahabharata and Ramayana. Both these texts contain core episodes in which the heroes are banished to the forests and hills. Hindus in the Himalaya, particularly those living within the watershed of the Ganga, identify closely with these myths of abandoned homelands. Both a real and imagined sense of separation and isolation, with all its traumatic anxieties and uprooted defiance, infuses the feudal hierarchies that govern village society.

On the road to Kedarnath, the sound of thunder farther up the valley merges with the rumbling torrent of a flooded river rattling stones in its grasp. Mandakini, once the most beautiful and alluring tributary of the Ganga, flows between bleak mounds of rubble and debris washed down four years ago by a devastating glacial lake outburst. Sections of the road have disappeared and we follow rough detours along the riverbed. On 13 June 2013, a powerful flash flood uprooted steel bridges and cast them aside like twisted coat hangers. Village homes and rest houses for pilgrims, constructed near the banks of the Mandakini, collapsed into its swollen current. Terraced fields that used to be lush with rice are now unrecognizable, trees torn from the ground, retaining walls ripped apart and the soil replaced by sand and gravel. Rain is falling in the higher mountains and the thunder has an ominous rhythm, as if warning us of more natural disasters to come.

Datta Ram Purohit insists we stop for an early lunch of fish and rice at a roadside restaurant with no sign and only a couple of benches under a rusty tin roof.

'The fish come straight from the river,' he tells me. 'When I was doing my fieldwork years ago, I ate here all the time.'

The shack looks as if it couldn't be that old, though the rafters are black with soot and the owner is a grizzled septuagenarian, who ladles our meal into dented steel thalis. Swimming belly-up in a fiery curry, the fingerlings have been gutted though the heads are still intact and I can see from their pursed mouths that they are bottom feeders, probably loaches. One or two of the larger fish have been cut in half but none of them are more than 15 centimetres long, netted in the rocky shallows of the river. As we eat with our fingers, it is difficult to have a conversation, picking the delicate but treacherous bones from between our teeth.

One of the foremost folklorists in Uttarakhand, Professor Purohit is chair of the Department of English at Hemvati Nandan Bahuguna Garhwal University in Srinagar. He quotes William Wordsworth and Northrop Frye, but his first love and passion is the folk theatre of Garhwal. Not only is he a scholar but a practitioner as well, producing and directing modern renditions of dance dramas from Uttarakhand. With a trim beard and a jaunty red hat, Purohit looks more the part of a debonair thespian than a professor. His sense of humour is infectious, whether he is telling a joke or poking fun at ruling elites. With a spontaneous array of interests and ideas, he switches subjects rapid-fire. One moment, Purohit points out the village of the celebrated poet Chandra Kunwar Bhartwal who wrote lyrical verses full of romantic images of clouds, birds and flowers—'Nature never did betray the heart that loved her!' Minutes later he recounts a folk tale from eastern Kumaon, in which four legendary heroes travel to Kathmandu and retrieve the wooden mask of a powerful deity. He then segues into a story about his own academic career.

'Originally, I planned to study geography,' he recalls, 'and one of my teachers encouraged me, but I had no money and my family persuaded me to take a government job instead, at the Post Office in Chopra, our village. At the same time, I had always been interested in theatre. Whenever a Ram Lila was performed in a village nearby, I would go every night. Later, I took on the role of Lakshmana. After two years of working for the postal department, I learned of an opportunity to get a fellowship in Hyderabad, doing my MA in English. Everyone warned me, "You come from a Hindi medium education. You'll never be able to do English." This was a challenge for me and I decided that I would prove them wrong.'

After lunch, we drive on to the village of Chandrapuri, where drums are beating. Climbing a steep path that angles up from the motor road we approach the temple square, set up as a ritual performance space for a dance drama about the heroic exploits of Jitu Bagdwal. These pawara or epic ballads are part of the oral tradition of the Central Himalaya, sponsored by village committees. This is the second day of the performance, which is scheduled to continue for two weeks.

The heroic legends are recited by village bards, who accompany their narrative with the percussive beat of a dhol and damaun. These paired drums, suspended from shoulder straps, are played by two men, while standing or walking together. The dhol is the dominant instrument, with a large, two-sided barrel made of brass and copper, and drum skins of deer hide. The right face of the dhol, which drummers often refer to as the 'male' side, is played with a wooden stick and has a slightly higher pitch. The left face is 'female' and played with the open palm of the left hand, using several different strokes from a firm slap to a gentle caress. The damaun is a smaller, one-sided kettledrum with a shallow wooden base covered in cowhide and played with a pair of sticks.

The musical tradition of drumming in Garhwal is known as Dhol Sagar— an ocean of drumming. My brother, Andrew Alter, is an ethnomusicologist who has studied Garhwali drumming and works closely with Purohit. As they have documented, the skill and lore of drumming is believed to have been handed down as a sacred manual from the earliest generation of musicians. Despite attempts at compilation and publication, Dhol Sagar is essentially an unwritten, aural text, part of the ethereal soundscape of the Himalaya. It evolved out of the first sound in the cosmos, the beating of

Lord Shiva's drum, which sets the tempo of creation. Among many rhythms and tonal variations, the Dhol Sagar records sixty-four sounds made by animals and birds that are translated into drumbeats, from the inauspicious sneezing of a goat to the rattle of a woodpecker's beak drilling a hollow pine. It reminds us of a cicada's syllabic scraping of its inner wings against the brittle chitin of its body. ('ham ram ram ram ram ram ram tam gam tam or khini khini ta ta tani tajhe jhe ta jhi gi ta...') Drummers can reproduce the rustle of dry leaves, the flutter of a partridge taking flight or the snapping of a pinecone's resinous ignition.

The ballad of Jitu Bagdwal that Purohit and I witness in Chandrapuri is a popular story amongst Panwar Rajputs. Jitu Bagdwal is a likeable protagonist but hardly a heroic character, though he comes from a lineage of powerful landowners. Carefree and reckless, he sets off to meet his sister who is married in a faraway village, across the ranges. Stopping at a bugiyal meadow along the way, Jitu takes out his flute and begins to play a lively, seductive tune. The music attracts a swarm of parris, fairies or sprites, who are malevolent spirits despite their deceptive charms and beauty. The sprites threaten to carry him off but Jitu talks his way out of the dilemma, saying that he has given his word that he will bring his sister home with him to plant rice. After that, he promises to come back and play his flute again for the fairies. However, when he fails to show up the parris arrive at Jitu's village while he is ploughing his fields. They overwhelm him and suck his blood like a ravenous swarm of mosquitoes. This legend emphasizes family loyalties as well as the separation of brother and sister but it also warns us of the dangerous mysteries of these mountains and the power of music, particularly the flute.

As the bard recites the story, accompanying himself on the dhol, a troupe of dancers from the village take on the roles of Jitu and his brothers. The costumes they wear are white cotton tunics, leggings and turbans, with bright coloured garlands and sashes around their waists. The mandan, or open square in front of the temple, is paved with flagstones and the dancers are barefoot. One of the brothers performs a whirling dance, while the rest of the players sit on the ground next to the temple, waiting their turn. The dancer is clearly possessed by the music, sweat trickling down his face, glazed eyes staring into space as he wheels about.

'The drumming induces a trance,' Purohit explains, 'but the dancer has to be receptive. It's very easy to tell when someone is simply pretending to act the part but when a character actually enters his body, it is a completely different thing.'

Spirit possession is common in Garhwal and dance is a central part of being possessed, not just by the music but by deities that can be either benevolent or malicious. Most forms of possession are considered auspicious for they carry messages from supernatural beings into our world—omens, blessings and prophecies. In all of this, the drum is the vehicle of possession, dictating the limits between measured time and eternity, through the vibrations it sets in motion.

Part of the reason for the prevalence of drums in the Himalaya is that their sound carries from one mountain to another, spanning great distances and reaching across valleys. Drums are also a processional instrument and most public events in the mountains, from weddings to pilgrimages, involve journeys up and down the valleys and ridges. Drummers lead the way, setting the pace and motivating the celebrants with festive tempos. Within the silence of the mountains, the pulse of a drum awakens the gods and invites them to dance. As my brother writes:

> Of all musical instruments used by musicians in Garhwal, the *dhol* is regarded as the most significant in terms of repertoire, function and spirituality. The *dhol* is both a physical musical instrument and a symbol of supernatural power. It produces musical sound that is deemed to be auspicious and powerful, and therefore appropriate for both natural and supernatural 'consumption.' Thus, the instrument is symbolic of the interface between the physical and the spiritual, the natural and the supernatural and the production of sound and sound itself. While all instruments in some sense invoke the same spiritual world of sound, the *dhol* carries the strongest symbolic referent of the connection between the natural world and the realm of the gods.

Drums challenge boundaries and test territorial limits. Historically, in times of war, they were used to demarcate positions on a battlefield, threatening the enemy and inciting warriors to prepare for conflict. Garhwal takes its name from the many forts, most of which are now in ruins, scattered throughout the region, where duelling drumbeats once emanated from rival fiefdoms.

For all their ritual importance and sanctified rhythms, drums evoke ambivalence as well—secret fears and unease, as well as the anxiety of pollution. Part of this comes from the materials out of which they are made, the skins of animals that are cured and stretched. Within the inequitable codes and stigmas of caste, those who skin dead animals and cure their leather lie at the lowest rungs of Hindu society, considered untouchables.

Nevertheless, as Purohit explains, while the drummers are playing and singing, they are said to be 'purified' by the music and the sacred narratives they recite. Empowered by the beat of their drums, the bards control both the dancers and the audience. Ultimately, they are the custodians of these myths, which are preserved in the safekeeping of their collective memory. Though in their daily lives these men are shunned by higher caste Hindus, during festivals, weddings and folk theatre, percussionists can command both a high price for their drumming as well as an elevated level of authority. It is also intriguing to note that the Himalayan hunters who helped Frederick 'Pahari' Wilson track down musk deer and other 'wild game' in the nineteenth century came from a community of drummers near Gangotri and their skills as shikaris obviously helped them acquire the necessary hides for drumskins.

Yet, more than the material substance of the instrument, it is the performance too that unsettles and discomfits social norms. Drumming excites unwanted desires, held in check by the rules and etiquette of civilized society. As we absorb its beat, the rhythm arouses something of our primal, primitive selves and we are often afraid that our bodies may respond with unrestrained passion.

The Jitu Bagdwal episode that we observe concludes with a sacrifice. Holding a pumpkin in one hand, a lone male dancer circles the temple square. Pumpkins and other gourds often symbolize sacrificial offerings and are cut in half to suggest the beheading of an animal. Spinning around the square as the drumbeats grow louder and more intense, the dancer finally smashes the pumpkin on the ground where it bursts into fragments in a violent pantomime of annihilation.

Drums also signal departure and arrival, whether it is a bridegroom's party or pilgrims carrying their deity home to her highland shrine. 'Processional rhythms move people up steep mountain paths and echo off distant cliffs in consonance with Garhwal's geography.' The invisible vibrations of the dhol give shape and contours to the land, as much as rocks and soil, snow and ice, but they also map out hidden worlds that lie beneath the transparent veil of reality—historic and mythological places of origin that come alive through the magical cadence of drums.

◆

From Chandrapuri, Purohit and I continue on to Ukhimath, a temple town and winter residence of the deities and priests of Kedarnath. We have been told that the Pandavas will dance tonight, at a village called Pali,

4 kilometres beyond Ukhimath. The Pandavlila is a cycle of dance dramas in which scenes from the Mahabharata are enacted through folk theatre. This ritual event is a combination of worship and entertainment, as well as a reaffirmation of caste and clan identities. When people in Garhwal speak of the Pandavlila, it is not just an ordinary play or dance performance but a divine visitation.

The landscape of the Himalaya is an integral part of the cultural and spiritual heritage of this region. Snow-covered peaks and glaciers above Kedarnath provide a geographical backdrop for mythology and lore. They infuse both the sacred and secular imagination of Himalayan people. All around us are reminders of the transcience of nature and the many-layered stories of migration, pilgrimage and exile. Driving up to Ukhimath, we pass a small waterfall along the side of the road where a seasonal spring spills over a boulder of foliated gneiss. The fluid patterns in the rock flow at right angles to the cascading stream. Every element is in motion, though each proceeds at its own pace—the stone tilting upward as the water tumbles down its surface while strands of mist circle round us on a passing breeze. A scene like this sets the stage for mythological journeys and tales of saintly sages who retreat into the forest, surrendering their fate to the providence of nature.

Darkness comes early as we arrive in Ukhimath, with a sudden thunderstorm that hides the higher mountains beneath ominous layers of clouds. Streaks of lightning flash above us and a light rain begins to fall but by the time we are ready to depart for Pali the clouds have disappeared and the November night is cold yet still. To guide us, Purohit and I have enlisted a man named Nautiyal, one of the caretakers at the rest house in Ukhimath, where we are staying. The drive seems longer than 4 kilometres, as our headlights weave around the bends on the narrow road, picking out pine trees on either side. Finally, when the lights of Ukhimath are far behind us, Nautiyal tells me to park at the side of the road across from a deserted schoolhouse, next to a pile of bricks.

A path leads down the ridge to Pali, though there is nothing else to indicate a village below. The light on Purohit's mobile phone illuminates a steep descent with dozens of uneven steps. On the slopes across from us, each scattered settlement is like a constellation of stars, gleaming with electricity. This side of the river there is nothing but darkness. I begin to wonder if our informants were mistaken about the Pandavlila until I hear the faint murmur of a drum from somewhere below us.

Purohit has never been to Pali before but fifteen minutes later, when we finally arrive at the venue, several of the villagers recognize him and welcome us enthusiastically. The performance is just starting, as the bard sings an invocation, calling the Pandavas to dance. More than a hundred women are seated on carpets along one side of the courtyard, where makeshift spotlights hang from the rafters. The men are segregated in a separate gallery where we are given front row seats. In the shadows across from us, I can see the wavering flames of a log fire, next to which the musicians are seated. The metal barrel of the dhol must remain warm to maintain the correct pitch and tone.

Within a few minutes, the Pandavas appear, emerging from a doorway to our right. The slow tempo of the dhol restrains the dancers who begin to circle the open courtyard, their movements captive to a throbbing beat. Hands rotate at the wrists with sensual gestures, while unshod feet mark out the dhol's rhythm on the flagstones. The bard sings the praises of the five noble sons of Pandu—Yudhishthira, Arjuna, Bhima, Sahadeva and Nakula. Reciting their names and attributes, his voice is full of awe and anguish, each stanza of his song leading us inevitably into battle, the final, horrific tragedy of war that lies at the heart of the Mahabharata.

In addition to the Pandavas, other characters appear, including Lord Krishna, Arjuna's immortal charioteer. He has a crown on his head and wears a dhoti, as well as a diaphanous shawl. Hanuman is also present. Though associated more often with the Ramayana epic, here in Garhwal the monkey god plays a significant part in the Pandavlila—half jester and half deity of the forest, where the Pandavas live in exile for thirteen years. Draupadi, their common wife, enters the courtyard followed by several other women, including Subhadra, Krishna's sister and Arjuna's wife.

Most Pandavlila performances in Garhwal are sponsored and performed by the Kshatriya castes, who consider themselves warriors by tradition. They believe that they are direct descendants of the Pandavas, whose feats of military valour reinforce a Kshatriya's sense of selfhood. For them, the Pandavlila is a form of ancestor worship, a ritual of devotion and remembrance. The auspicious presence of the Pandavas in the village recalls their heroic legacy and emphasizes ideals of courage, loyalty and righteousness. It is also a re-enactment of their ascent into the Himalaya, leaving behind a lost kingdom and making the mountains their home.

The lyrics sung by the bard have never been committed to paper, passed down instead from the memory of one generation of drummers to the next. The language is rustic Garhwali, everyday words and phrases that the audience comprehends. Over the twelve nights of the performance, the extracted episodes remind the villagers of the Mahabharata's larger, limitless ocean of stories. With operatic gestures, Nakula and Sahdeva, practise their martial arts in a flurry of gesticulating limbs. As they dance opposite each other, the fierce physical contest foreshadows real battles to come. Later, when the Pandavas pick up their weapons, there is no need to show the enemy. Everyone understands that they are about to wage war with their cousins, the Kauravas.

Kshatriyas, or Rajputs as they are commonly known in Garhwal, fund the performance, being landholders and political leaders, whose wealth and authority comes from the fields they inherit, as well as employment outside their village—as soldiers, building contractors, taxi drivers or hoteliers. Whatever careers or enterprises they pursue, this performance brings them back to their roots and celebrates the martial heritage of their caste. Because of poverty and unemployment large numbers of men have been forced to leave the mountains to work in cities like Dehradun and Delhi. Many have joined the army. This makes the return of their ancestors all the more poignant and meaningful, for they too have been forced into exile through a reverse migration from the mountains into the plains.

Most of the men who dance in the Pandavlila have inherited their roles from fathers and grandfathers, yet they must be capable of allowing the spirit of the Pandavas to enter their minds and bodies. Instead of simply being actors who take on a part, each player is considered an incarnation of the mythological character he represents. The performer actually becomes Arjuna or Lord Krishna and those who watch him dance regard him as such, so that his own everyday identity is erased. At several points during their dance, the Pandavas bless the audience with open palms while spectators fold their hands in obeisance.

To appreciate the layers of meaning in this ritual, it is important to understand that the Pandavas are not just mythical heroes but also supernatural beings, half-human and half-god. Because of a curse, the patriarch of their clan, Pandu, could not father a child, and the five brothers were the result of divine conception. Indra, supreme lord of sky, is the father of Arjuna. Yudhishthira is the son of Dharma, the god of virtue. Vayu, the god of wind, is the father of Bhima. While the first three Pandavas were born to Kunti, the younger two, Nakula and Sahadeva, are the sons of Pandu's second wife, Madri, and their celestial fathers were the twin Ashwins, outriders of the dawn.

As more people arrive in Pali, visitors from neighbouring villages or relatives from afar, they are greeted and ushered in. Each person attending the

Pandavlila makes a donation that helps cover the costs of the performance. One of the organizers, a village elder, enters names and amounts in a ledger. At the end of the evening, these donations are announced and acknowledged. Every audience member is welcomed with a tika. Using a marigold flower, dipped in turmeric and vermilion powder, the sacred colours are daubed in the centre of our foreheads. The yellow and red pigments of the tika, along with a few grains of rice, signify devotion and piety.

After the opening sequence, the Pandavas approach the temple and conduct an aarti in front of the deities, lighting oil lamps and incense. Throughout the performance cycle, which can range from one to three weeks, the dancers are expected to remain celibate, eat only vegetarian food and abstain from alcohol. They also pray regularly and bathe twice a day. The only vice, discreetly allowed, is tobacco, Purohit whispers with a smile. As the dancers gather before the shrine, a pundit attends to the rituals, not as a performer but in his everyday role as a priest. He gives each dancer a few drops of gaumutra, cow's urine, to drink from a small brass vessel. This sacrament ensures that in addition to their austerities any accidental pollution is absolved.

The Pandava's costumes are stylized versions of traditional Garhwali attire, which has been embellished with colourful designs and patterns. The men are dressed in white leggings and long-sleeved tunics, with red trim around the hems and cuffs. Each of them wears a compact turban. Saffron sashes are wrapped about their waists. Bhima, the strongest of the five brothers, sports a thick woollen vest that enhances his powerful physique.

Throughout the performance, Hanuman provides comic relief, dressed in a clown's costume, with a monkey's tail and make-up to give him ape-like features. Though he participates in the solemn dances, he also breaks free from time to time and snatches bananas offered to him by women in the audience. A man seated at the edge of the courtyard teases him, making hissing and chuckling noises. Hanuman bares his teeth and hisses back, grimacing like a monkey. Children and others in the audience laugh and point at this game of mischief.

Many elements in the Pandavlila are unique to Garhwal. Though the dance dramas re-enact episodes from the Mahabharata, each performance interprets the epic in regional terms. Some of the most popular episodes in Garhwal, like the rhinoceros hunt, do not appear in any other version of the Mahabharata. Others, like the Chakravyuh, a fatal maze in which Abhimanyu is killed, are common to most renditions. In this way, the drummers and village players choose and choreograph their performances according to local preferences and perceptions.

All the female parts are played by men, except for Kunti, the mother, who is represented by one of the elderly women from the village. She wears a traditional black woollen coat and skirt, with a white scarf wrapped about her head. The Pandavas solicitously lead her by the hand or carry her in their arms. Whenever her presence is not required, she retreats beneath a quilt to stay warm. The men who are dressed as women wear red saris and wool cardigans. The pallu, or loose end of the sari, covers their heads. Heavily made up with lipstick and eyeliner they wear costume jewellery, earrings, bangles and necklaces. Though each of these men is from Pali village and their families are watching, there is no embarrassment or titillation because of cross-dressing. None of the children, women or men in the audience appear at all unsettled by the ambiguities of gender. Like all the actors, these men are possessed by the characters they play, transitioning seamlessly from male to female.

Following the aarti, Draupadi and the other women circle the courtyard, moving their bodies gracefully, faces fixed with expressions of trance-like devotion. Though none of their gestures are exaggerated or caricatured, one of the young men in a female role appears more effeminate than the others and Purohit comments that he has a convincing 'lachak' or swaying motion. As the drummer quickens the tempo, Draupadi steps forward and begins to tremble, her body quaking until she breaks into a frenzied dance, arms swinging and feet leaping off the ground.

Idealized stereotypes of women play a crucial part in the narrative. While Kunti represents the perfect mother, who is chaste and loving towards her children, Draupadi is seen as an incarnation of the goddess Kali, who initiates the war between the Pandavas and Kauravas in order to avenge an insult to her modesty and slake her thirst for blood. Anthropologist William Sax, who has studied the Pandavlila, analyses how these two characters are perceived:

> The elderly, maternal Kunti is associated with motherhood, sexual modesty, nurturance and especially virtue, while the dangerous and sexually active Draupadi is explicitly identified as Kali and sometimes the recipient of dramatic blood sacrifices. Daughter-in-law and mother-in-law embody both sides of the distinction between the fierce, bloodthirsty goddess and sexually active female, on the one hand, and the benevolent, vegetarian goddess and nurturing, nonsexual mother, on the other... What they share is a concern for personal and familial honor.

A unique element of the Pandavlila in Pali is the arrival of a gardener, who distributes flowers to the heroes. Purohit cannot recall such a scene in any of the Pandavlilas he has attended before, nor in the sixteen versions of the Mahabharata he has studied. It seems to be a local improvisation. The gardener's role is played by a bespectacled man in his thirties, a member of the organizing committee. With a hastily tied turban on his head, a kurta and dhoti, and a basket of both real and artificial flowers on his back, he joins the dance, garlanding the Pandavas and presenting them with marigolds.

Several women in the audience take out mobile phones to record videos as the flower vendor provides a colourful interlude to the martial spirit of the drama. This is followed, soon afterwards, by a sorrowful scene of leave-taking as the five heroes receive Kunti's blessings before shouldering their weapons. Most of them are armed with wooden clubs, which have been sanctified by the village priests. On top of the clubs are lumps of butter, garnished with leaves and rose petals, signifying the purity of their purpose and the righteous execution of dharma. Yudhishthira, Bhima, Nakula and Hanuman each carry a mace. Arjuna brandishes his bow while Sahadeva carries a slate to suggest that his weapon is learning.

As soon as these instruments of war appear, the tempo changes once again. Marching around the village square, the heroes prepare to set off for battle, as drumbeats signal their departure at the end of tonight's performance. In this way, folk theatre animates myths and legends, bringing them to life through the percussive heartbeat of a drum. Himalayan archetypes of heroes, both ancient and contemporary, symbolize the cultural pride and traditions of various people such as musicians, warriors, herdsmen, farmers and brave mountaineers.

chapter 38

CHOMOLUNGMA'S PEOPLE

All the flights to Lukla have been delayed because of bad weather and we are warned that they might be cancelled. Nepal is cloud-bound, even at the beginning of October, because of a prolonged monsoon. But, suddenly, after I've given up hope, staff at the airline counters become animated and passengers who have been sitting on their duffel bags since dawn, with dejected expressions, are now eagerly jostling to join disorderly queues. Pushing my bag to the front of the line and reaching around a pair of recalcitrant Germans, I get a boarding pass. The security check is perfunctory though once we reach the departure gate there's another long wait and nobody is sure if our flight will actually take off. Eventually, though, we board our plane.

The twelve-seat Dornier is the workhorse of Nepal's smallest airports and shortest runways. Less than a year earlier, I flew out of Jomsom in an identical plane, an ungainly aircraft with a long, beak-like nose, that roared and shuddered as it took off into the fierce headwinds of Mustang before executing an aerobatic U-turn and skimming the lower slopes of Dhaulagiri.

As we finally depart for Lukla, our pilot aims for gaps in the clouds. Through my window, I see the Kathmandu Valley disappear beneath a quilt of mist and am reminded of the opening chapters of James Hilton's *Lost Horizon*, in which a plane full of Europeans crash-lands in Tibet. The passengers on our flight include six Spaniards and their Sherpa guide, two Germans who haven't forgiven me for bucking the line and a queasy-looking British couple clutching airsickness bags.

Our forty-five minute flight is mostly uneventful, except for a few incidents of 'gastric lurch', as Hilton describes it, when the 'plane bumped and tossed in air-pockets as uncomfortably as a rowboat in a swell'. No mountains are visible, only the dense grey monsoon clouds. While any sign of a horizon is utterly lost, I resign myself to fate, like one of the characters in the novel, believing that, 'whatever the course taken, the pilot presumably knew best'.

Eventually, the Dornier banks sharply and its engines rev a little louder. Through the cockpit's windscreen I can see that the clouds have parted. Directly ahead lies a forested slope, with waterfalls spilling down one side and terraced fields level with the plane's propellers. Moments later, the runway appears but it lies above us rather than below. A thin strip of tarmac curves down the ridge like a ski jump or the tongue of a very thirsty dog. *The pilot presumably knows best* as he targets the lower end of this asphalt ribbon. A few seconds later, when we finally touch down with a definitive thump and skidding of wheels, the steep angle of the runway helps slow the plane down.

As the only convenient point of entry for the Solu-Khumbu region, Lukla provides access for thousands of climbers and trekkers who pass through this portal every year. Originally built to receive construction materials for the Sherpa school and hospital that Edmund Hillary sponsored, the airport has now become the gateway for Everest and its base camp. But unpredictable weather and poor visibility, particularly at the end of the monsoon, mean that flights are often cancelled. As if to prove this point, for the three days following my arrival, Lukla airport remains closed, smothered in clouds.

The travel agent in Kathmandu has told me to look out for a 'tall Sherpa' when I get off the plane. He will be my guide on the 'EBC' trek. Retrieving my duffel, I scan the arrivals hall and soon spot Chuldim Dorjee Sherpa, who stands at about six feet, several inches taller than most of his compatriots. He is fifty-four years old with sobre features and no urgency to his gestures. When we shake hands I sense a quiet confidence in his manner. Fluent in English, Chuldim speaks softly but without hesitation. As it turns out, he is the perfect trekking companion. An experienced mountaineer, with plenty of stories to tell but no need to brag, Chuldim shares a generous supply of information, observations and opinions. Accompanying him is Da Lakhpa, a younger porter who carries my duffel bag.

Before setting off, we eat breakfast at the Paradise Lodge next to the airport. On the walls are photographs of Edmund Hillary with katha scarves draped over the frames. In one picture, Hillary is posing with the proprietors of the lodge, many years ago, when the airstrip at Lukla first opened. Chuldim explains that the lodge owners are originally from the village of Khunde, adjacent to his own village, Khumjung, where the Sherpa hospital and school were built.

'Have you climbed Everest?' I ask.

Chuldim shrugs and nods, 'Only twice.'

When I can't help laughing at his self-effacing answer, he smiles and adds, 'These days, everybody says they've climbed it nine times, ten times…'

In 1950, when Bill Tilman and Charlie Houston visited Solu-Khumbu they were the first Europeans to enter this valley. After trekking all the way from the outskirts of Kathmandu, rather than flying in a Dornier, Houston remarked that it was like 'entering Eden just before the fall'. Until then, these remote valleys in Eastern Nepal were off limits for foreigners. The government in Kathmandu had kept the country closed to outsiders. Sherpas, however, had already made a name for themselves. At the beginning of the twentieth century many young men migrated from Solu-Khumbu and settled in Darjeeling, beyond the borders of Nepal. Most of these Sherpas worked as day labourers, rickshaw pullers and porters. All the early expeditions to Everest, beginning with the first reconnaissance in 1921, led by Charles Howard-Bury, set off from Darjeeling and approached the mountain through Tibet. This long, roundabout route required armies of porters, recruited off the streets of Darjeeling. The hardy hillmen of Solu-Khumbu proved invaluable on those pioneering expeditions when Sherpa lore and legends were born.

Bill Tilman, a mountaineering legend himself, expressed great admiration for the Sherpas, having employed men like Ang Tharkay and Tenzing Norgay on his expeditions. His visit to Solu-Khumbu was motivated by a desire to see the Sherpas' homeland. Like many others, he praised them for their fortitude and character. 'To be their companion was a delight,' Tilman wrote, 'to lead them, an honour.'

Once Nepal opened up the southern approach to Everest, this proved an easier route, though it was still a long journey by foot, requiring hundreds of porters. For the Darjeeling-based Sherpas, it was a homecoming and they were able to visit ancestral villages after a long absence. Within three years of Tilman and Houston's first trek to the region, Tenzing and Hillary stood on the summit of Everest. The inevitable 'fall' that Houston predicted had already begun. Sixty-seven years later, as I head out of Lukla along the path towards Namche Bazaar, it is obvious that those early, exploratory days are now a distant mirage.

Today, the Everest Base Camp Trek has become one of the most popular itineraries in Nepal. During October and November, swarms of foreigners from every hemisphere on earth trudge up these trails, testing themselves against Himalayan terrain and trying to relive the adventures of the past while enjoying the relative comforts of the present. Most summit attempts are made in spring and early summer, when days are longer and temperatures higher, but the post-monsoon season is the most popular time of year for trekking, with open skies and clear views of the mountains.

The upper valleys of Solu-Khumbu are now part of Sagarmatha National Park, established in 1976. Designated as a World Heritage Site, this conservation area covers roughly 275 square kilometres, extending from just below the confluence of the Bhote Kosi and Dudh Kosi rivers up to the Mahalangur Himal range of the Himalaya, which marks the border between Nepal and Tibet. Trekkers enter the park at Monjo, four or five hours walk from Lukla. Dense forests of pine, spruce, rhododendron and birch cover the steep slopes until the treeline. Though I keep an eye out for monal and blood pheasant, the traffic on the trails makes it unlikely that we will come across these species. Higher up we see plenty of snowcocks and other birds, from golden eagles and kestrels to redstarts and accentors, as well as a few ducks on the Gokyo lakes. The only wild mammals I spot on my trek are a weasel that has made its home in a stone wall next to a lodge at Gorakshep and several herds of thar, a wild goat with dark, ruddy fur. Chuldim says that during winter the wildlife is more evident. Near Khumjung, they have snow leopards and black bears, as well as wolves. He also mentions that musk deer and red pandas live in the jungles of Sagarmatha National Park, though these are rare and seldom seen.

On the ridge above Namche, where Everest makes its first appearance, stands a bronze statue of Tenzing Norgay, erected in 2014 as a memorial by his son and other family members. In this three-dimensional representation of the famous photograph taken by Edmund Hillary on 29 May 1953, he strikes a triumphant pose raising his ice axe toward the sky. The statue is larger than life, framed by an installation of low walls with plaques that recount Tenzing's biography as well as the cultural and spiritual significance of Chomolungma. Born at a pilgrimage site called Tsa-chu, 'a day's march from Everest', Tenzing was raised in the village of Thame, three hours walk from Namche, along the trading route to Tibet. According to his autobiography, *Tiger of the Snows,* Tenzing ran away from home to Darjeeling at the age of eighteen. After working as a day labourer for a couple of years, he was selected by Eric Shipton to work on the 1935 Everest expedition. The imposing memorial at Namche, unveiled on Tenzing's 100th birth anniversary, celebrates his preeminence as a mountaineer but also the story of an anonymous Sherpa who rose from the ranks of menial labourers to become one of the most famous men on earth. A similar statue stands at the Himalayan Mountaineering Institute in Darjeeling, part of the hagiography of a Himalayan hero.

The ascent of Everest is one of the core narratives of the Solu-Khumbu region, a thread upon which many other stories are strung. While this is not the oldest tale or the most sacred myth of the Sherpa people, it is potent lore, nevertheless, despite its recent provenance. Tenzing's ascent helped shape the Sherpa identity, giving his people a sense of purpose and pride. While the essential role of Sherpas in the climbing of Everest, from the early expeditions until today, has been a complicated and controversial collaboration between foreign climbers and local mountaineers, it evokes enormous resonance both here and around the world. Chomolungma. Sagarmatha. Everest. By whatever name she is called, for the people of Solu-Khumbu this is not just the highest peak on earth. It is their goal, their goddess, and a keystone of their culture. The mountain's presence, even when hidden behind clouds or intervening ridges, is a reminder of the way in which a geographical entity can become an icon for the people who live within its embrace.

Historians believe that the Sherpa community settled in Solu-Khumbu sometime during the fifteenth or sixteenth century. They migrated here from Tibet but initially kept their ties with the trans-Himalayan region by trading and marrying across the 5,716-metre Nagpa La. Yak and sheep herding were the primary Sherpa occupations, though some villagers adopted a monastic life. The growing season at high altitudes is brief and the only crops are potatoes and buckwheat. By all accounts it was a bleak existence, with few comforts, harsh winters and no opportunities to earn anything more than a subsistence living.

Two 'autobiographies' of Sherpas exist, though neither of them was written by the subject himself. Tenzing Norgay's *Tiger of the Snows* was dictated to James Ramsey Ullman, an American writer and mountaineer. The second is Ang Tharkay's *Mémoires d'un Sherpa*, which has a more convoluted history. The book was originally published in French in 1954, after Ang Tharkay received the Légion d'honneur in recognition of his contributions to the successful French Annapurna expedition, when Maurice Herzog and Louis Lachenal became the first men to climb an 8,000-metre peak. The memoir was supposedly transcribed by an Englishman, Basil P. Norton, who lived in Darjeeling. He took down Ang Tharkay's story from the oral translation of a mutual friend named Mohan Lal Mukherjee. Ang Tharkay himself spoke neither English nor French. In 2016, this memoir was translated and published in English as part of Mountaineers Books' Legends and Lore Series. However, a number of questions remain regarding its antecedents because nobody has been able to identify Basil P. Norton, which is likely a pseudonym.

While Tenzing and Ang Tharkay's voices do come through with clarity and candour, sections of the autobiographies have obviously been heavily edited and in some cases, augmented and embellished by the interlocutors. Part of the reason for this was to give Western readers a complete picture of the context but more so to celebrate the heroics of European climbers. Nevertheless, there is a good deal of information about the Sherpa community that seems to have been transmitted first-hand. For example, we learn that both Ang Tharkay's and Tenzing's mothers came from Tibet and married men from the Khumbu region. Though Ang Tharkay was born in Khunde, he spent six years of his childhood living with an unmarried aunt on the Tibetan side of Nagpa La, over which he and his father frequently travelled to the trading town of Kyetrak. In recent years, the Chinese have sealed Nagpa La. According to Chuldim, a large military installation has been constructed on the other side of the pass and anyone who tries to cross over gets arrested. Though the border is now closed, when Ang Tharkay was growing up a century ago, the people of Khumbu felt a greater affinity to Tibet than they did to the rest of Nepal.

'We made this trip to Tibet nearly every year and sometimes more often. Our relationship with the Tibetans was one of brotherhood. They are the same ethnicity as we are, and several centuries ago we were also governed by Tibet. Many of our people settled in Tibet, and over the course of my several trips there, I went to visit many, many friends, and in their homes I always felt like family.'

Though he acknowledges his trans-Himalayan heritage, Ang Tharkay does make certain distinctions between Sherpa and Tibetan culture. While explaining that Sherpas are Buddhists, he writes, '...we also place a great deal of importance on sorcery and necromancy, and I believe that we are more intent on consulting shamans and following their instructions than on observing our lamas' or priests' dictates...' In many instances, the lamas opposed the idea of climbing itself, issuing warnings that anyone who defiled the highest, most sacred peaks by trespassing on their summits risked the wrath of mountain deities. Even as Sherpas chose to ignore these pronouncements they approached the high Himalaya with caution and did their best not to antagonize the gods.

Tenzing's perspective on Buddhist lamas is more ambivalent than Ang Tharkay's, though his maternal uncle was a Rinpoche at Rongbuk Monastery and his aunt was a nun. As one of thirteen children, Tenzing was sent to Tengboche as an acolyte when he was a young boy but he found the strict discipline and monastic life intolerable and soon ran away. After that he always had a suspicion of the lamas. He writes, 'Some of our lamas are true holy men. Some are great scholars and mystics. But there are others about whom you wonder if they could take care of a herd of yaks, let alone human souls, and you are pretty sure they are monks only because it gives them the best living with the least work.'

Several academic studies on the Sherpas have been published. Sherry Ortner's book, *Life and Death on Mt. Everest: Sherpas and Himalayan Mountaineering*, confirms Ang Tharkay's comments about shamanism. Until the beginning of the twentieth century, when Tengboche was established in 1916, Sherpas had no monasteries or resident lamas, relying on lay priests and shamans to perform whatever rituals were required at festivals, weddings and funerals. After several monasteries opened, the lamas from Tibet immediately set out to purge the animistic and occult practices prevalent in Solu-Khumbu, and provide a 'purer' level of religious instruction. As Ortner suggests, the influx of more orthodox Tibetan beliefs and practices probably reflected a desire amongst Sherpas to elevate their cultural status in keeping with their economic aspirations. It also asserted independence from the predominantly Hindu culture of Nepal.

Even today, villages like Khumjung rely on married or lay priests, though they invite lamas from Tengboche to preside over annual festivals. Ironically, despite the prosperity of the region, local support from Solu-Khumbu is insufficient to sustain the monks. Tengboche, the largest monastery, where every Everest expedition seeks the blessings of the lamas, depends heavily on foreign donations.

The Sherpas' sometimes cynical views of lamas comes through in a Khumbu folk tale that Ortner recounts:

Once there was a very high and holy lama who was approached by a *dirnmu,* a demoness. The dirnmu appeared in the guise of a beautiful woman, carrying a container of chang and leading a goat. She forced the lama to choose—kill the goat, drink the chang, or have intercourse with her. The lama chose the chang as seemingly the least of the evils, but then he got drunk and in his drunken state he killed the goat and had intercourse with the woman.

Tenzing's autobiography also contains a satirical story in which two lamas arrive at the home of a woman who is cooking sausages. While they are chanting and praying, she steps out of the kitchen for a minute and one of the lamas immediately helps himself to the sausages. But before he can eat them, the woman returns and the lama quickly hides them under his hat. As they continue praying and chanting, the sausages start to slide out from beneath the monk's hat. His companion tries to warn him but the greedy lama begins praying with even greater intensity and starts dancing wildly about, not out of religious fervour but because the hot sausages are burning his shaved scalp.

An observant Buddhist, Chuldim walked with a string of beads wrapped around one wrist and chanted his prayers as we went along. He also made sure that I always kept the chortens and mane walls on my right when we passed. In Khumjung, I stayed at the Mandala Lodge owned and run by Chuldim and his wife, Kinju. Standing outside the entrance, he directed my attention to a rocky mountain above the village.

'That is Khumbila,' he explained, pointing out the barren, jagged summit, 'our mountain god. Nobody is permitted to climb this peak. Whenever we have pujas, we always make offerings to Khumbila first, then to Padmasambhava and the others.' It is surprising that here in a region full of enormous, snow-covered peaks like Ama Dablam, which towers over the Khumbu valley, Sherpas give precedence to their nearest mountain, a dark and forbidding summit that looms above Khumjung, inspiring fear and devotion. Though the lamas purged many shamanistic beliefs, Khumbila, as a local deity, has been incorporated into masked dances and rituals, particularly during the Dumje festival, which takes place in June.

Chuldim emphasized on several occasions that it is taboo for Buddhists, like himself, to take the life of other sentient beings. At the same time, he and his family regularly eat meat. When I told him that I had recently witnessed the Dashain festival in Kathmandu, where hundreds of buffaloes, goats and sheep are slaughtered as offerings, his face took on a pained expression of disgust and remorse. During the course of our two-week trek, he often reminded me that killing animals is a sin. Several times, he repeated the story of how, a few years back, Hindu butchers had herded buffaloes up to Namche. A short distance below the town, they set up a makeshift abattoir to supply fresh meat to the lodges and restaurants, all of which advertise steak sizzlers and buff burgers on their menus.

'After they started cutting the buffaloes a number of bad things happened and we chased them away,' Chuldim told me. 'Now they kill the animals somewhere below Lukla and the meat is carried up from there.'

As in Tibet and Bhutan, the paradox of Buddhist non-violence and a non-vegetarian diet requires certain ethical contortions. Chuldim explained that every winter each family in Khumjung used to have a yak slaughtered by members of the Tibetan butcher caste, who accept the stigma of blood on their hands. The meat was then hung inside the house. 'Because of the cold it doesn't spoil or smell. Whenever we wanted to cook meat, we would cut off a piece and it lasted most of the winter.' Chuldim also told me that his favourite food is sausages made from yak's blood mixed with potato flour and spices. In earlier days, for people living in an extreme climate with scarce resources, these compromises between compassion and survival would have been logical, but today Sherpa traditions face new challenges.

'Unfortunately, we have no Tibetan butchers left anymore,' Chuldim said with regret. 'But then again, we hardly have any yaks.'

Some years ago, he explained, before the Nagpa La was closed, a group of Tibetan traders crossed over and purchased most of the yaks in Khumjung to take back to Tibet. The villagers were only too ready to sell their animals, which were no longer an essential part of their economy because the government had imposed grazing restrictions within the boundaries of Sagarmatha National Park.

'These days people keep yaks mostly for show,' said Chuldim, 'and a few of the females are used for transport.'

♦

More than any other deity, Chomolungma has brought prosperity to Solu-Khumbu. Nowhere is this more evident than in Namche Bazaar. What was once a remote market town, where yaks were bought and sold, as well as salt and wool from the far side of the Himalaya, is now a hub for trekkers and mountaineers. The North Face Company has a showroom here that looks as if it could be straight out of an American mall. Dozens of other outfitters sell gas stoves, mountaineering boots, climbing rope, karabiners, water-purifying pills and mummy bags rated to 20 degrees below zero. Another company, with an outlet in Namche, is Sherpa Adventure Gear. Its slogan is, 'A Modern Brand, An Ancient Wisdom' and as its website explains:

Sherpa Adventure Gear was founded in May of 2003 by Tashi Sherpa, as a living memorial to the unsung heroes of Mt. Everest. For decades, climbers have always been grateful for having a Sherpa companion on the treacherous slopes of the Himalaya. It is the Sherpa who makes the route, carries the load and sets the ropes to the top and back.

In this spirit, Sherpa Adventure Gear seeks to honor the legendary high-altitude climbers by creating adventure gear that earns their praises.

The merchandizing of Sherpa identity is only natural, for trading has always been in their blood and Namche Bazaar has served for centuries as a centre of Himalayan commerce. While some might argue that the people of Solu-Khumbu have sold out to Western demands, this was the most obvious route leading from poverty and deprivation to self-sustaining sources of income.

Nonetheless, Namche's hustle and hype can be disorienting. Chuldim had warned me, 'It's just like Thamel, in Kathmandu. You can buy anything here.' Aside from trekking gear shops, art galleries sell oil paintings of Everest, baristas offer mocha cappuccinos, and an Irish pub serves Khumbu Kolsch, Sherpa Breweries' craft beer as well as Khukri Rum. Street vendors display Tibetan handicrafts and cheap souvenirs, while everything from a Thai foot massage to herbal smoothies is available for a price.

More remarkable than the array of products on sale in Namche is the fact that virtually all these items were carried up here by porters. No motor road connects Khumbu with the rest of Nepal and except for a couple of Russian-made cargo helicopters that deliver construction materials and cooking gas cylinders, every can of Coke or Red Bull has been transported on someone's back. Trains of mules and yaks haul supplies, including bags of rice and lentils, but the predominant mode of transport remains manpower.

Porters engaged by trekking companies shoulder a maximum of 30 kilograms each, which usually amounts to two clients' duffel bags. Yaks and mules are loaded with no more than 60 kilograms. But the strongest porters often carry triple loads, up to 90-100 kilograms, at least 30 per cent more than their own body weight. To secure and balance these impossible loads, they use triangular bamboo frames, to which they lash crates of beer and boxes of mango juice, bags of sugar and powdered milk, or whatever else must be delivered. Steel girders for building new lodges and even refrigerators travel on the backs of these men.

'Porters are paid by weight,' Chuldim explains. 'The current rate, from Lukla to Namche, is sixty rupees per kilo.'

This means that for a gruelling 14-kilometre walk uphill, which takes at least a day, a porter can earn as much as 5,400 rupees. In the abstract, that is a considerable amount, given low wages in Nepal, but anyone who has watched these men struggling up the steep switchbacks to Namche will realize it is an inhuman effort. Tendons and muscles in the porters' necks and shoulders strain to hold the load steady on slippery, uneven ground. Every few bends in the path, they stop to rest their burden on crude wooden supports. Manual labour throughout the Himalaya is a harsh, inequitable reality, but nowhere else do human beings force their bodies to such backbreaking extremes.

Originally, Sherpas made their reputations hauling loads up mountains like Everest and earned acclaim for their feats of endurance at high altitudes. But part of the change that has overtaken this region and the people of Solu-Khumbu is that those who bear the heaviest burdens are no longer Sherpas but poorer men, from lower elevations and other districts, particularly the less privileged Tamangs.

While some of the early European mountaineers entertained a self-serving impression that Sherpas chose to climb for the sheer pleasure of alpine adventure and they would happily carry loads for no wages at all, Ortner makes it clear that this absurd, idealized misconception was anything but the truth. As hierarchies within expeditions became established, Sherpa Sirdars contracted other porters and the first thing the men from Solu-Khumbu did was lighten their loads, except when climbing at high altitudes. This should come as no surprise. In virtually every occupation there is a tendency to pass off the most onerous tasks to younger, poorly paid workers. The Sherpas are no different from university professors, whose responsibilities get successively lighter with seniority while untenured, junior instructors are assigned the heaviest teaching loads.

Despite their obvious and desperate need for work, both Tenzing and Ang Tharkay make it clear in their memoirs that they were looking for something more in their relationships with foreign climbers than simply wages or letters of recommendation. Like anyone else, they also wanted equality and respect. On early expeditions there were 'sahibs' and 'coolies', colonial terms that became common usage in most of the early published accounts of mountaineering. Yet, from the beginning, Sherpas negotiated a rise in rank, elevating themselves to a position that was certainly lower than a 'sahib' but considerably higher than a 'coolie'. As consciously and as skilfully as they cut steps in the ice and fixed ropes to ascend the mountains, Sherpas also ensured their own incremental elevation from the ranks of menial day labourers to trusted companions and mountain guides. By the

1970s, according to Ortner, expedition terminology gradually changed so that the foreign 'sahibs' were being referred to as 'members' of an expedition while virtually nobody was using the derogatory expression, 'coolie'.

Both Ang Tharkay and Tenzing Norgay were conscious of their ambiguous rank within European expeditions, even as they became 'sirdars' or Sherpa leaders. They appreciated the acceptance and bonhomie of the French and Swiss mountaineers who were not as class-conscious as the British. Tenzing explains:

> With the Swiss and the French I had been treated as a comrade, an equal, in a way that is not possible for the British. They are kind men; they are brave, they are fair and just, always. But always, too, there is a line between them and the outsider, between sahib and employee, and to such Easterners as we Sherpas, who have experienced the world of no-line, this can be a difficulty and a problem.

Plenty of disagreements arose between Sherpas and sahibs, even on early expeditions, when strikes occurred and discord erupted at base camp or above. Most mountaineering books gloss over these disputes with the moderation of hindsight but the Sherpas themselves seldom forgot the slights and disrespect. The successful 1953 Everest expedition, in particular, began on an acrimonious note when Sherpas were housed in an empty garage in Kathmandu, without a toilet. Their response was to urinate on the British embassy walls. Colonel John Hunt, an infantry officer who led this expedition, stuck to protocol and didn't fraternize with the Sherpas. After returning to Kathmandu, following his triumphant climb to the summit of Everest, Tenzing refused to attend a celebratory function at the embassy because the staff had earlier turned him away and treated him with disdain.

Chuldim's career reflects a fairly typical trajectory. Born in 1961, his first employment, at the age of twenty-four, was on the 1985 Norwegian Everest expedition. He began as a porter then gradually worked his way up the ladder until he was providing high altitude support for summit parties. Most of his climbing has been on Everest. While he summited 'only twice' Chuldim ascended at least a dozen times from every side, including multiple attempts from the North Col and Kangshung Face. He worked for British, American, Chilean and Japanese teams. Towards the end of his career, he was employed on a couple of commercial expeditions. In addition to Everest, Chuldim has climbed on Makalu, Annapurna III and Hungchchi. When I asked him what his most difficult expedition had been, he said, 'the Kangshung Face, which is very exposed and vulnerable to avalanches'.

In 2005, after twenty years of climbing, he finally quit because his wife didn't want him to continue. Over the years, he has known a number of Sherpas who lost their lives on the mountains and acknowledges that he is fortunate to be among the survivors. For a while, he worked for Nepal's first trekking agency, Mountain Travels, as a guide before setting up his own lodge.

Unlike many other Sherpas, who have moved to Kathmandu and opened their own trekking and climbing companies, Chuldim has chosen to remain in Khumjung. However, his eldest son now lives and works in Mumbai, where he has a corporate job. After his first wife died, Chuldim remarried and he now has a second son, who is six years old. He emphasized that, though a number of the younger Sherpas have taken up climbing and earn good money with commercial expeditions, many more have left the Solu-Khumbu region to work in India or other countries abroad. A repeated refrain in our conversations was Chuldim's complaint that aside from mountaineering and trekking, there are few employment opportunities in the region and even the adventure tourism business had been taken over by 'Chhetris and Bahuns' (Kshatriyas and Brahmins), Nepal's moneyed, influential castes.

'Many times, when someone books a trek, they are told that a Sherpa will be leading their group,' Chuldim says with a cynical smile. 'Foreigners ask for Sherpa guides and tour companies promise them. But then, a week before the trek, the travel agent writes to say that the Sherpa is sick or has been called away for family reasons. Sometimes, even Chhetris and Bahuns just call themselves Sherpas and the foreigners can't tell the difference.'

Another complaint that Chuldim repeated more than once was the lack of government support for the people of Khumjung and Khunde. 'The politicians come by helicopter and promise a lot, but nothing happens,' he said. 'In 2015, the earthquake did a lot of damage and there were huge cracks in our walls. We were even afraid to sleep indoors and asked the government for help but they gave us nothing. We had to rebuild our houses ourselves.'

Though Namche has several government offices, there remains a sense of isolation from the rest of the country. On the other hand, compared to many places in Nepal, Solu-Khumbu appears to be thriving and probably needs fewer handouts of development funds than poorer regions, where tourism does not provide jobs or investment.

The walk from Namche to Khumjung takes less than two hours but the contrasts between the two settlements are much greater than the distance that separates them. Khunde and Khumjung have several lodges but the two villages remain agrarian communities, where potatoes and buckwheat are the main crops grown in a single, short season. Yaks were once an important part of the economy but today the most valuable product is their dung, which is used for fuel. All over the hills surrounding the village young children and older people scour the hillside for yak droppings, which are then flattened and dried into disc-shaped cakes. Wood is scarce because of the creation of Sagarmatha National Park. Villagers are only allowed to gather firewood for ten days of the year and each household is restricted to two loads a day. Park authorities also rotate the areas of forest where they are allowed to cut dead branches and trees, so they often have to haul the wood from 8 or 10 kilometres away.

On my first day in Khumjung, Chuldim took me to see the monastery, which was being restored following damage in the 2015 earthquake. Two painters were at work on murals but the building was otherwise deserted, for no lamas stay here and they have to be invited from Tengboche during festivals. The prized possession at the monastery is the famous Yeti scalp. For the price of a Rs. 250 ticket, the caretaker of the monastery unlocked a steel cupboard and took out a dusty glass box for me to see this relic, which has travelled around the world.

When it was first photographed in the 1950s, the Yeti scalp excited a lot of attention. It has a reddish tint, as if dyed with henna, and the bristly hairs are neatly parted in the middle. The conical shape has inspired a number of fanciful artistic impressions of Abominable Snowmen. Following his triumph on Everest, Edmund Hillary mounted an expedition to search for the Yeti. By some accounts the villagers of Khumjung extracted a promise that he would build a school and hospital for the Sherpas, in exchange for letting him take the scalp abroad to have it tested. Scientists at the Field Museum of Natural History in Chicago determined that the Yeti's scalp was actually made from the hide of a serow.

Pertemba Sherpa, who climbed the southwest face of Everest with Peter Boardman, Doug Scott and Dougal Haston in 1975, has set up a Sherpa Heritage House Museum in his ancestral home in Khumjung, not far from Chuldim's lodge. Collecting antique household and farming implements, such as wooden jars for making chang and butter churns, Pertemba recreated the interior of a traditional Sherpa dwelling that would have existed before Solu-Khumbu became a highway to Everest. Unfortunately, the 2015 earthquake destroyed the museum when its walls collapsed and it remains closed until more funds can be raised for renovations.

On a bright October morning, Chuldim's wife, Kinju, and an elderly neighbour sit in the sun outdoors peeling new potatoes. Da Lakhpa, our porter, joins them, sitting beside a large plastic tub that is full to the brim. The potatoes have been recently dug up from a field next to the lodge. Most are the size of golf balls. The peels are carefully kept and dried to feed yaks, particularly during winter when fodder is scarce. As soon as temperatures begin to drop, potatoes and other vegetables like carrots are placed in an underground pit to keep them from freezing.

The potatoes that Kinju is peeling will be grated and dried, then turned into flour. More than barley and buckwheat, potato flour is used in Sherpa cooking. At lunch, when I am served a meal of thukpa soup with noodles and vegetables, Chuldim eats 'mash'. A combination of potato, buckwheat and millet, it is the colour and consistency of chocolate pudding, though the flavour is something like salty porridge, with a slightly bitter aftertaste. Scooping up the mash with his fingers, Chuldim mixes it with a chicken curry. This hearty meal isn't easy to eat politely but there is no question that it provides plenty of fuel for hard work in the hills.

'Eat one plate of mash,' Kinju jokes, 'and you'll go to the top of Everest.'

Though she lets her husband do most of the talking, Kinju speaks enough English to manage the lodge when Chuldim is away. Their son, Tsering Tashi, is on holiday from school and spends most of his time watching cartoons on TV in the main dining room of the lodge. Along with SpongeBob SquarePants and other Western cartoons, he watches a lot of children's shows from India and Chuldim says he has learned Hindi from these programmes.

Later in the afternoon, Kinju sends Tsering Tashi off for private tuition.

'To make sure he doesn't forget what he learned at school,' says Chuldim. 'My elder son, in Mumbai, has a daughter the same age. He keeps trying to get me to send Tsering Tashi to live with them, but we don't want him to go right now. He needs to stay in Khumjung for a while and understand that this is home.'

'Do you think he will become a climber like you?' I ask.

Chuldim shakes his head and glances at Kinju, suggesting that his mother would prefer he followed a safer, more secure occupation. There seems little doubt in either parents' minds that for Tsering Tashi, a successful future lies somewhere outside the Khumbu Valley. On the walls of the lodge are pictures of Chuldim standing on the summit of Everest and other images of the high Himalaya but these seem part of a past existence, a proud but precarious legacy that is unlikely to be passed down to the next generation.

◆

In the upper reaches of Khumbu, where for centuries yaks, goats and sheep were taken to high pastures during summer, thousands of tourists are now herded by Sherpas. The paths they follow are the same and at each meadow, where the animals once grazed, trekking lodges have been built to accommodate flocks of foreign visitors. From Khumjung, Chuldim and I set off for Phortse, another large Sherpa village on the other side of the Dudh Kosi River.

The lodge where we stay in Phortse belongs to an Everest summiteer, who has a display case in the dining room full of old climbing equipment from expeditions thirty or forty years ago, including helmets and crampons, snow anchors and empty oxygen cylinders, as well as a metal jerry can for fuel, stamped with the date 1981. Decades of climbing in the region have generated a cargo cult, with salvaged clothing and equipment left behind by expeditions. The detritus of mountaineering is scattered throughout these valleys but especially around the high camps on Everest, where recent efforts to clean up some of the garbage have retrieved tonnes of waste off the mountain.

On a field behind our lodge at Phortse, the Alex Lowe Charitable Foundation is constructing a new facility to train young Sherpas in the fundamentals of mountaineering. A sign outside the half-finished building reads: 'Founded in 2003, the Khumbu Climbing Centre's mission is to increase the safety margin of Nepali climbers and high altitude workers by encouraging responsible climbing practices in a supportive community-based program.' Eventually the centre will have a training wall and classrooms where visiting instructors can conduct courses in ice-climbing, search and rescue, and wilderness medicine. Initiatives like this are part of a more collaborative approach to mountaineering. Unlike the early days on Everest, when Sherpas were given little training and expected to fend for themselves, efforts like the Khumbu Climbing Centre introduce more professionalism to the sport.

Instead of trekking up the shorter, standard route to Everest Base Camp, Chuldim, Lakhpa and I follow the Dudh Kosi River to the Gokyo lakes. This detour is less crowded and because of the recent cancellation of flights into Lukla, we have much of the route to ourselves, with clear views of Cho Oyu. Though the trails are relatively empty, dozens of helicopters pass back and forth overhead, ferrying tourists on a round-trip from Lukla to give them aerial views of Everest and other mountains. Helicopters are also used to rescue trekkers suffering from exhaustion or altitude sickness but mostly these are joy rides. After a while the persistent throbbing of their engines grows irritating and intrusive.

As we climb on from Phortse, we stop for lunch at a small lodge in Luza where Chuldim's sister is the proprietor. She serves us dal bhat as we sit in the warmth of the dining room, with the midday sun pouring through the windows. Chuldim seems to know everyone along this route. Before the Sagarmatha National Park was established, families in Khunde, Khumjung and Phortse had exclusive pasturage rights to different areas of this valley and stone walls still mark out each family's corral. Below Machermo, we leave behind the last of the trees, though the slopes are covered with stunted barberry bushes. *Rhododendron anthopogon*, most of its flowers faded and its foliage a rusty orange, fills the air with a sickly sweet perfume. Each of the lodges has an altar in the courtyard, where juniper and rhododendron twigs smoulder, the smoky incense drifting on the breeze.

A few minutes after we arrive at Machermo, a helicopter lands in a yak pasture behind our lodge. We are told that the chopper was supposed to go down to Lukla but clouds have sealed off the valley and the pilot has decided to stay the night in Machermo. His passengers are three young Japanese in their twenties who blunder into the dining room, order Cokes and buy Everest Link Wi-fi scratch cards, so they can share photographs on Instagram and Facebook. Most of the lodges in the Solu-Khumbu region have Internet access. While the Japanese are typing on their iPhones, the chopper pilot suffers a sudden anxiety attack, growing pale and breathless. Chuldim and the lodge owner prescribe garlic soup then pack him off to bed. Their treatment seems effective, for the next morning, when I wake up, the sky is clear and I hear the helicopter depart at dawn.

In these high valleys, a strange combination of isolation and connectivity prevails, where the twenty-first century intrudes, though the mountains themselves remain ancient and remote. The Dudh Kosi, with its frothy current, flows out of the Ngozumba Glacier. Several trekking routes converge at Gokyo and at least a dozen lodges are clustered at the northern end of the largest lake. Most of the accommodation is basic—four walls, a window, two beds and a light bulb on the ceiling. Electricity is generated by solar power. The shared toilets are squalid and the plumbing is makeshift but the lodges provide adequate shelter and their menus offer everything from pancakes to muesli for breakfast and momos, fried potatoes and dal bhat for lunch or dinner.

A day and a half walk beyond Gokyo we cross the Cho La where fresh snow has fallen the previous night. Though only a few centimetres, it makes for treacherous walking on the rough moraine, as we work our way up to the notch of the pass. If any more snow had accumulated, the pass would have been closed because porters refuse to cross over until lodge owners break the trail. Fortunately, Chuldim and Lakhpa are familiar with the route and we are the first group to cross over onto the Cho La Glacier, which extends down the other side of the pass.

Descending to Lobuche, we join the main trail to Everest Base Camp with spectacular views of Pumori and Nuptse, as well as brief glimpses of Everest, wedged between the ridges. The following morning, we carry on to Gorakshep, the highest settlement in Khumbu at 5,164 metres. Gorakshep is usually translated as 'graveyard of the crows' though Chuldim corrects me and says that 'gorak' is actually a raven. The most common birds at this altitude are yellow-beaked choughs, which have black feathers like crows but are more agile, flocks of them sailing on the wind. Choughs go up as high as the South Col of Everest, at 7,900 metres and feed off scraps at Camp IV.

'Sometimes, if you don't keep watch, they'll tear open bags of supplies,' Chuldim says, then makes a face. 'I don't like these birds. They say that if a climber dies on the mountain, they will peck out his eyes.'

Leaving our backpacks at Gorakshep, we carry on to Base Camp in the afternoon, an easy hour's scramble. Though Everest itself disappears from view, the Khumbu Icefall is clearly visible, a frozen escalator of seracs that tumble onto the lower part of the glacier, where pinnacles of ice are spread out like rows of bleached white tents. Base Camp itself is deserted when we get there for the climbing season ended months ago and the glacier has rearranged its contours so that the tent platforms have broken up and been displaced. Each year, the camp must be re-excavated and often moved to different locations. Chuldim laughs when he tells me, 'Sometimes you set up camp, then you go up the mountain and when you come back down your tent is six feet higher or six feet lower than where you left it,' for the glacier is always shifting.

◆

Stepping out of the lodge at 5 a.m. the following morning, it takes me a moment to realize that the surrounding mountains are lit up with moonlight rather than the first aura of dawn. Sunrise is still an hour away. Though the moon is only half-full, it is bright enough to illuminate the entire valley, decanting its milky luminescence over the encircling ring of peaks. Immediately in front of us rises the frosted profile of Pumori, its snow-plastered summit reflecting a lunar glow. Below this frozen tower, where converging ridgelines fold into shadows, I can see the dark pyramid of Kala Patthar, our destination. A straggling procession of headlamps is already moving up the steep slope ahead of us, as groups of trekkers set off to get a daybreak view of Everest.

The dry lakebed at Gorakshep looks like a salt flat in the moonlight, so bright I switch off my headlamp as Chuldim and I head across. The temperature is well below freezing and the rocks are rimed with frost. Thankfully, the sky is perfectly clear and the persistent clouds that stalked us all week have finally vanished.

As we begin to climb the winding track towards Kala Patthar, my breathing grows strained. After nine days of trekking together, Chuldim and I quickly fall into step, pacing ourselves with the slow, monotonous rhythm of an uphill slog. Pausing every ten steps to rest, we catch our breath for a moment or two before moving on without losing momentum. The altitude at Kala Patthar is 5,643 metres above sea level, high enough for me to feel the lack of oxygen in the air, though I remind myself that the top of Everest is still another 3,205 metres above us. As we continue to ascend towards Kala Patthar, the summit and South-West Face gradually come into view. Stark white streaks of snow crease the mountain's brow while the exposed rocks are much darker than the sky. No stars are visible though Venus punctuates the night with a single laser-like bead. More than any of the other mountains, including Everest, Nuptse dominates the scene, caked with glaciers on its lower slopes and rising to a sharp, uneven cone that hides Lhotse from view.

Time seems to have stopped, arrested in this early hour as fading moonlight seeps into a brightening dawn. For a while it is hard to tell whether night has ended or day has begun. When we finally reach the top of Kala Patthar, thirty or more people are clambering about on a heap of rocks along the crest of the ridge, trying to get the best seats in the house. Instead of competing for the highest perch, I move across to a narrow ledge, where tilted slabs of rock form an exposed balcony facing east. My fingers are cold but the rest of me is still warm from the climb and I have come prepared, wearing several layers. Chuldim, however, has only a light jacket and no gloves. When I suggest he return to the lodge, he seems relieved and gladly heads back down the trail.

Making myself as comfortable as I can on an uneven cushion of granite, I take a few photographs before setting my camera aside. On another rock nearby, one of my fellow trekkers has assumed a lotus posture. Stray wisps of windblown snow, like strands of lint on the upper slopes of Everest, catch the first light along the mountain's rim. Faint streaks of sunbeams angle off the ridges, forming a pale chevron in the rarified atmosphere. Wondering where the sun will come up, I hug myself to retain what little body heat remains. Over my right shoulder I can see the opaque moon, like a misshapen pearl, disappearing in the west. Waiting, as if for some sort of epiphany from the goddess Chomolungma, I huddle on the rocks and feel my pulse and breathing ease, after the exertion of the climb.

Minutes later, Pumori catches fire, its icy crown turning gold. Changtse, which stands beyond the border in Tibet and connects with the North Col of Everest, is the next peak to ignite, its eastern slopes kindled by the rising sun, still hidden behind the Mahalangur Range. Soon afterwards, off to the south, Ama Dablam is aflame, its tapered summit like the burning wick on a butter lamp. Reaching for my camera, I try to capture each moment, before realizing that the sky behind Everest is noticeably brighter.

Until now, the sun has kept us in suspense but as I watch it emerge directly above the South Col it ascends rapidly in a blinding sphere that seems to obliterate everything in its path. Within seconds, all of us at the top of Kala Patthar are bathed in the sun's radiance, shielding our eyes and feeling its welcome warmth against our skin. The crowd of trekkers has swelled to more than fifty and many others are still clambering towards the top. Yet, in this transcendent moment, I feel completely alone, absorbed into the omniscient eye of creation.

◆

Later that morning, leaving Gorakshep, we retrace our route to Leboche and then drop down to Thok La, just below the snout of the Khumbu Glacier. This rocky meadow rimmed with glacial debris has become a memorial site for Sherpas and foreign climbers killed on Everest.

The first chortens constructed here were built for six porters who died in an avalanche on the Khumbu Icefall during the 1970 Japanese ski expedition. Since then, dozens of cairns and chortens have been erected to honour Everest's dead. Most of the corpses are entombed in ice, high on the mountain. Some were brought down and cremated; others carried home for burial. Many different nationalities are represented here and the memorials range from simple piles of rock to elaborate structures, with brass plaques and inscriptions. One of the largest is for Scott Fischer, the American Mountain Madness guide whose death on Everest in 1996 is described in Jon Krakauer's bestseller, *Into Thin Air*.

The memorials at Thok La have a melancholy quality, partly because of the number of cairns as well as the empty, windswept landscape. Most of the dead are men from these mountains who gave their lives in support of foreign adventurers. Their sacrifices underscore the dangers of mountaineering but also serve as a testimony to their community, whose ancestors had no quarrels with these peaks and no ambitions to reach their summits. Yet, the fatal motives of European and other climbers sealed their destiny as Sherpas sought to make a living out of scaling forbidden heights. Each winter, the harsh winds and weather eat away at the cairns, just as they do with the mountains, eroding the memory of men who dared to risk their lives for lonely, tragic quests.

VII

AT THE EDGE OF BEYOND
In Pursuit of the Unknown

chapter 39

THE PUNDIT

1874. Somewhere on the Tibetan Plateau, the Pundit walks alone though he can see the ragged line of his caravan two furlongs on ahead. A flock of thirty sheep is strung out across the steppes, bearing his equipment and supplies. Four yaks accompany them and a couple of ponies on which his Ladakhi retainers ride, slumped forward in their saddles, dozing.

Though the air is cold, the sun is at its zenith, warming the Pundit's face and hands. He squints as he surveys the undulating horizon. There is no need to check his compass. They are heading east, towards Lhasa. In the distance, he sees a herd of kiang, wild asses, their dusty brown shapes blending into the arid plain. Further off he spots a pair of long-legged Marco Polo sheep with broad, curling horns. A kestrel circles overhead, its tremulous wings holding it aloft as it scans the ground for rodents and reptiles. Suddenly, the bird surrenders to gravity and plummets from the sky, talons poised to pluck a vole or lizard from the grass.

Walking with an even stride, the Pundit fingers a string of prayer beads, though he is not invoking the names of gods but simply counting each slow step. At the beginning of his journey, near one of the monasteries on the outskirts of Leh, he passed two pilgrims prostrating themselves in the dust. Progressing by lengths of their bodies, like inchworms, they measured themselves against the earth in an act of extreme devotion. When asked where they were going, the pilgrims replied 'Kang Rinpoche' the sacred Mount Kailas, 300 miles to the east. The Pundit calculated that the pilgrims could cover no more than a mile between sunrise and sunset, while he and his small caravan proceeded in stages of eight to ten miles a day.

Forty-three years old, the Pundit is a short, wiry man with weathered features and rheumy eyes. His build and stature convey endurance. Despite his humble appearance, he is the greatest spy-explorer of his day, a secret agent of the British Raj, whose clandestine journeys across the Himalaya have been compared to the explorations of Livingstone and Stanley. An account of his exploits has been read out to sensational acclaim in the lecture hall of London's Royal Geographical Society. Identified only as 'the Pundit' his full name remains an official secret. No more than a handful of men know his true identity.

The Scottish orientalist, Sir Henry Yule, Vice-President of the Royal Geographical Society, praised the Pundit as a geographer in search of unknown truths. 'He is not a topographical automaton,' Yule declared, 'or merely one of a great multitude of native employees with an average qualification. His observations have added a larger amount of important knowledge to the map of Asia than any other living man, and his journals form an exceedingly interesting book of travel.'

As a young man, the Pundit first left home and travelled to Kashmir and Ladakh, when he accompanied the Schlagintweit brothers. Their initial survey of that region was conducted in 1856–57, when the rest of India was embroiled in the Sepoy Rebellion. The Schlagintweits published their *Report of a Scientific Mission to India and High Asia* as well as *An Atlas of Panoramas, Views and Maps*, which were some of the first images of the Himalaya to reach Europe. Decades earlier, the Pundit's uncles had joined William Moorcroft on his explorations of the Kailas–Manasarovar region in 1812. Their family, of Shauka or Tibetan ancestry, had been engaged in trans-Himalayan trade for generations. Long journeys are in the Pundit's blood, a restless impulse of migration along with inherited instincts for survival.

The title 'Pundit' means learned man, an epithet usually reserved for Brahmin priests, though this Pundit is not defined by caste. For several years he worked in the Education Department of Kumaon and was appointed headmaster of a vernacular school in Milam. Soon enough, his reputation as an explorer attracted the attention of the Survey of India, which was intent on mapping Tibet. As his handler, Captain T. G. Montgomerie, explained, the authorities in Lhasa had forbidden entry to white explorers:

A European, even if disguised, attracts attention when travelling among Asiatics, and his presence, if detected, is now-a-days often apt to lead to outrage. The difficulty of redressing such outrages, and various other causes, has, for the present, all but put a stop to exploration by Europeans. On the other hand, Asiatics, the subjects of the British Government, are known to travel freely without molestation in countries far beyond the British frontier; they constantly pass to and fro between India and Central Asia, and also between India and Tibet, for trading and other purposes, without exciting any suspicion.

Along with his brother and a cousin, the Pundit was recruited by Colonel J. T. Walker, surveyor general and superintendent of the Great Trigonometrical Survey of India. The three hillmen were taken to Dehradun and Mussoorie where they received instruction in the dual arts of surveying and espionage, learning how to operate a sextant and make precise measurements of latitude and longitude, as well as calculating altitude. Using a pace-stick, the Pundit's stride was measured over and over again, until he could mark out a mile with precision, his two legs serving as instruments of cartography. To help keep count, his handlers provided him with a simple, surreptitious device. The string of prayer beads he was given had exactly a hundred beads, unlike Buddhist and Hindu rosaries, which have 108. Most of the beads were made of polished pebbles but every tenth bead was a sacred rudraksha seed, slightly larger and rougher in texture. This allowed the Pundit to accurately and discreetly measure the distances he traversed.

At the same time, he was instructed to observe whatever he encountered with a geographer's eye—the course of streams and rivers, the customs of men he met, the authority and dictates of local governors, what crops were planted and profits gleaned, means and methods of taxation, forms of official and private communication. This kind of intelligence gathering required a shrewd, attentive nature and an ability to listen in on the conversations of fellow travellers. Whenever necessary, the Pundit could be a master of disguise, whether he shaved his head and put on a lama's robes to pass himself off as a Buddhist monk, or wore a false pigtail in the fashion of a Ladakhi trader. Wherever he travelled the Pundit had an innate ability to win the trust of strangers. Even on those rare occasions when the mask slipped, he was able to escape detection. More than once, he was detained by Tibetan authorities, his identity challenged, but each time the Pundit extricated himself from the threat of imprisonment or execution.

After hours of tedious walking, the Pundit arrives on the saddle of a broad ridge from where he can see the distant summits of the Himalaya to the south, like a line of white tents pitched along the horizon. On ahead is a lake, the first water they have come upon in the past two days. A small cluster of chortens are built near the shore, sacred reliquaries, along with a wall of mane stones inscribed with Buddhist verses. Taking out his prayer wheel, the Pundit snaps open the top and removes his compass from its hiding place inside the copper cap. After getting his bearings, he jots down locations and distances on a scroll of paper hidden inside the barrel of the prayer wheel.

By the time the sheep have reached the lakeshore, the Pundit catches up with them. He and the Ladakhis remove the saddlebags and unpack their belongings near the chortens. Their tents are made of woven yak hair with braided ropes of the same material. The struts are willow boughs. For tent pegs, they use the horns of antelope collected along their route. One of the men goes off to the lake, carrying a waterskin made from the stomach of a sheep. A short while later, he returns with discouraging news. The lake is brackish, its water undrinkable. They have only one skin left between them and it will have to last until they reach the next source of fresh water.

Fortunately, there is enough grass for the animals to graze on and plenty of dung to fuel their fire. The Pundit collects the droppings of yaks, kiang and antelope in a gunny sack, while one of the Ladakhis uses his tinderpouch to get the fire started, kindling it with brittle stems of dry grass. The sour-sweet scent of burning dung wafts over them as the smoke drifts out across the lake. There is no sign of anyone else along this route, though they have been warned about bandits. The last human beings they met, three days ago, were a group of Changpa nomads tending their flocks north-east of Pangong Lake.

While his retainers brew a kettle of tea, the Pundit discreetly unpacks his instruments, hidden under the false bottom of a compact wooden chest. Leaving these inside his tent, he joins his companions by the fire. Their evening meal is parched barley flour or tsampa mixed with butter tea, a lumpy gruel that staves off hunger. The Pundit has noticed that one of the sheep is lame. If it does not recover soon, they will slaughter it, which will give them meat for several days. Of the original flock, purchased in Ladakh, only three of these sheep will ultimately reach Lhasa. The rest are eaten or traded for others along the way. A pair of dogs have attached themselves to the caravan and lurk near the campfire, though there are no scraps to feed them. Firelight glimmers in their watchful, hungry eyes.

After the Ladakhis have bedded down for the night, the Pundit takes out his sextant and gazes up at the sky, littered with stars. The night breeze is cold and the tents rustle against their moorings. He adds more dung to the fire and blows on it, before setting a pan of water to boil. Digging a shallow hole in the ground, the Pundit positions a wooden bowl, like those they use to drink their tea. The depression shelters it from the breeze. After this, he takes several cowrie shells from his bag and peels off scabs of wax. Each shell contains a secret store of mercury, which the Pundit pours into the bowl. The only illumination, other than the stars, is the furtive glimmer of the dung fire. At the beginning of this journey, the Pundit was equipped with a bull's eye lantern, which gave off a bright light and did not blow out in the wind. But at the last settlement they passed through, in a flea-infested serai, the lantern caught the eye of a Tibetan official, who insisted on buying it. Reluctantly, the Pundit was forced to sell the lantern to avoid suspicion.

In the flickering firelight, he opens his Eliot sextant, with a six-inch radius. He aligns it to the brightest star on Orion's belt, Epsilon Orionis, also known as Alnilam. The intense blue colour of the star is magnified in the sextant's lens, as the Pundit takes a sighting, using the quicksilver in the wooden bowl as an artificial horizon. He checks the time on his pocket watch, then jots down details on a slip of paper from the prayer wheel. It is slow, painstaking work, especially in the dark, but the Pundit has mastered this crude technology. After he finishes, he dribbles the mercury back into the cowrie shells before sealing them again with wax.

By now the pan of water is simmering and the Pundit carefully removes a thermometer from its case. He checks the temperature of the air, which is three degrees below freezing. Slipping the thermometer into the steaming pan of water, he waits for it to boil, shivering inside his coat as he holds his hands to the feeble flames. Finally, after an interminable wait, he records the boiling point at 186 degrees and calculates the altitude of their camp, 14,100 feet above sea level.

Earlier, just after dusk, the dogs had begun to bark, catching the scent of a wolf on the breeze, but now they are silent. Huddled together as a woolly mass, the sheep and yaks have settled down nearby. In the starlight the chortens are silhouetted against the glossy smear of the lake. For a few moments, before he retreats to his tent, the Pundit scans the sky where the stars are scattered like crystals of salt. He listens but hears nothing except for the wind strumming the guy ropes on his tent. Instinctively, the Pundit faces south where the Himalaya are buried in darkness beyond the edge of the plain. He feels a tug of emotion drawing him back, an impulsive reflex, calling him home.

As a raven flies, the Pundit's birthplace is less than a hundred miles south-east of here, though the Himalaya stand as a barrier that would make the journey much longer. In his mind, he can trace the graceful profile of Panchachuli, the line of five snow peaks he looked out upon as a boy every morning from Munsiari. The memory of that scene washes over him in a wave of homesickness and nostalgia. Despite the urge to turn aside from his destination and return to Kumaon, the Pundit knows he must continue on to Lhasa. From there, he will follow the course of the Tsang Po into eastern Tibet and then cross back over the Himalaya at Tawang. The entire journey will take almost a year. His assignment is to survey the northerly route from Leh to Lhasa, through the high deserts of the Aksai Chin and on across the lake region that divides the southern plateau from the northern tablelands of the Chang Tang, one of the largest 'blanks on the map', a vacant expanse of rolling steppes and frozen marshland.

Shuddering with cold the Pundit crouches by the last embers of the fire and checks his pocket watch again: 4.30 p.m. His timepiece is set to Greenwich Mean Time though here in Tibet the hours pass by unmeasured. He winds his watch with frozen fingers after crawling into his tent. Kicking off his boots, before drawing the blankets and quilts around him, he feels his age. His body has survived the rigours of long journeys but his joints have begun to ache and the cold afflicts him more severely than before. The ground beneath his bed is hard and unyielding. These days it takes him longer to fall asleep and as he lies awake in the darkness, his thoughts range back to other journeys, his earliest forays into Tibet. On his first covert survey, he was supposed to cross over the Kingri Bingri Pass above Milam but it was covered in snow and ice. After that, he made his way to Nepal and finally breached the Himalaya at Kirong, reaching Shigatse and Lhasa before doubling back along the road to Mount Kailas. In those days, he was in his early thirties with much more stamina and a reckless sense of adventure. On that journey, he pretended to be a Nepali trader. As he wrote in his journal, 'I was frequently asked who I was by the inhabitants, and I always said that I was a Bisahari merchant, called *Khumu* in these parts, and had purchased a quantity of Nirbisi root at Pati Nubri and Muktinath, which I had sent on to Mansarowar by another route, and had come here merely to worship.'

Because of his Bhotia ethnicity, the Pundit was generally mistaken for a Tibetan, and spoke the language fluently, along with Hindustani, Urdu and Nepali, as well as a smattering of English. He made friends easily, whether they were armed Khampas from eastern Tibet who hunted antelope and kiang, or Muslim traders from Yarkhand and Khotan. When questioned by provincial governors or curious abbots, revenue officials and soldiers, he lied convincingly, spinning out stories of fictitious origins and itineraries. A number of other spies were employed by the Survey of India towards the end of the nineteenth century, including the Pundit's brother and cousin, as well as Abdul Hamid, code named 'The Munshi'. There was also Mirza Shuja, who was trained in Dehradun at the same time as the Pundit and later travelled throughout the Hindu Kush and Karakoram. Meanwhile, in Darjeeling, Sarat Chandra Das (known as 'the Babu'), a Bengali schoolmaster who travelled to Lhasa twice, recruited and trained a coterie of spies in the 1870s. This included Kinthup, a Lepcha man who was one of the first to connect the Tsang Po to the Brahmaputra by floating marked logs down the river, though he was enslaved by the Tibetans before his discovery could be confirmed.

Each of these men risked their lives for the Great Game—a futile, paranoid contest between the British and Russian empires, competing for power and influence on the roof of the world. Unlike the other men, however, the Pundit was not just a spy but a consummate geographer. He travelled where few others had gone before and sought to understand the places and people he encountered. Though employed as a secret agent who crossed forbidden frontiers, the Pundit pursued much more than ordinary intelligence, seeking to unlock the secrets of the Himalaya and beyond. He had sworn loyalty to the British, who would ultimately reward his services with a generous pension and land grants, or jagirs. But his motives were as fluid as his aliases and he had a persistent sense of curiosity for whatever he discovered along the way, extending the boundaries of knowledge.

In their book, *Asia ke Peeth Par* (*On the Shoulders of Asia*), Shekar Pathak and Uma Bhatt have pieced together an authoritative biography of the Pundit and have republished the Royal Geographical Society's reports on his exploration. These include extracts from his journals, which are full of descriptive passages that prove the Pundit was an astute observer and compelling storyteller. Aside from distances and altitudes, he remarks on the habits and appearance of fellow travellers, such as official messengers from Lhasa, whom he meets along his route:

> ...these men always looked haggard and worn. They have to ride the whole distance continuously, without stopping either by night or day, except to eat food and change horses. In order to make sure that they never take off their clothes, the breast fastening of the overcoat is sealed, and no one is allowed to break the seal, except the official to

whom the messenger is sent... (I) saw several of the messengers arrive at the end of their 800 mile ride. Their faces were cracked, their eyes blood-shot and sunken, and their bodies eaten by lice into large raws, the latter they attributed to not being allowed to take off their clothes.

The Pundit also comments on the weather:

> During my stay at Lhasa, Shigatze, and in the Lhasa territory, I do not recollect either having seen lightning or heard thunder, and on making inquiries I was informed that during the winter season there is neither one nor the other, though there is a little during the rains...
>
> The inhabitants regard snow as an evil, and attribute the slight fall during the winter to the goodness of their chief divinities and head Lamas. Should the fall ever exceed a foot, it is looked on as an evil sign, expressing the displeasure of their gods, and to propitiate them large sums of money are expended on the priests, &c. They call snow 'kha,' after the word kha, meaning nothing.

All of this was written in Hindustani using the Devanagari script in a legible, fastidious hand that suggests a devotion to precise observation and unembellished detail. The journals were translated by Montgomerie and other Survey of India officials. Recording the myths, lore and customs of those he met, the Pundit describes funeral rites of Tibetans and methods of mining gold. He also relates several dangerous encounters.

> Marching along the bank of Yamdokcho Lake we came upon a band of robbers. One of them took hold of my horse's bridle and told me to dismount. Through fear, I was on the point of resigning my horse to him, when a Mohammedan who accompanied me raised his whip; whereupon the robber drew a long sabre and rushed on the Mohammedan. Taking advantage of this favourable moment I whipped my own horse forward, and as the robbers could not catch us they fired on us, but without effect and we arrived at Demalung village all safe.

After reaching Lhasa, the Pundit happened to recognize a provincial official he had met on an earlier journey and took cover before he was discovered.

> I was at about this time very much alarmed by seeing the Kirong Jongpon on the streets of Lhasa one day; and I was still more alarmed on seeing the summary manner in which treachery in these parts was dealt with, in the person of a Chinaman, who had seditiously raised

a quarrel between the priests of the Sara and Debang monasteries. He was (on the receipt of an order from Pekin to kill him) brought out before the whole of the people, and beheaded with very little hesitation. Owing to my alarm, I changed my residence, and seldom appeared in public again.

In numerous passages from his journals, the character and personality of the Pundit comes through in his words, along with descriptions of the landscapes he traversed. His own story and tales of the high Himalaya merge together as if the geographical details were part of his own biography. He is both the subject and the narrator, who becomes synonymous with the mountains he explores.

Now, lying here in his tent, enveloped by darkness, the Pundit knows this will be his final journey. If he survives, his colonial handlers will allow him to retire with honour and dignity. They will also release him from the anonymity of his service, giving him back his name and his identity.

Pundit Nain Singh Rawat, son of Amar Singh Rawat, was born in 1830 in Johar–Bhattkura, in a remote corner of northeastern Kumaon. His parents were shepherds and traders from the Johar Valley. As a child, Nain Singh had no formal education because there was no school in the region though he taught himself to read and write and ultimately became a teacher and headmaster. He was employed by the Survey of India from 1863 to 1877. In recognition of his travels and surveys, he received the Patron's Medal, the highest award of the Royal Geographical Society in London. They also presented him with a gold chronometer. Queen Victoria bestowed on him the Order of Companion of the Indian Empire and the Society of Geographers of Paris honoured him as well. Nain Singh's last trans-Himalayan expedition ended on 17 February 1875, when he reentered British territory near Udalguri, Assam, after having walked 1,319 miles across Tibet.

chapter 40

EVEREST HOUSE

The ruins lie on a saddle of the ridge carpeted with grass that has been grazed to its roots by goats and cattle. Like so many neglected hill station bungalows this crumbling structure has succumbed to the elements, caving in upon itself after more than a century and a half of monsoon storms. Masonry walls and limestone plaster have eroded like the cliffs and crags on either side, much older formations hewn from the fossilized remains of molluscs and corals. The building's beams and rafters have been removed to use as firewood and timber. Door and window frames have also been scavenged. Only the bare bones of the building remain like the skull of a giant sea creature, full of hollow cavities and crevices through which the wind and mist flow as easily as ancient tides.

Written on the walls are dozens of names: Nisha, Mohan, Renu, Lalit, Wasim. Lovers and loners have left their signatures on discoloured whitewash. Some have used charcoal from dead campfires left behind by shepherds and picnic parties, others have wielded felt pens or simply scratched their names in the plaster. The graffiti covers every surface, mostly first names or initials, occasionally a date to commemorate a visit. Munna. Bobby. Tinku. Pet names only allow us to guess at their identities. What purpose do these signatures serve, other than a momentary claim to having been here? Yet, the hundreds of names seem oddly appropriate on this abandoned house at Park Estate where Sir George Everest once lived—a man whose own name is scrawled on the highest Himalayan peak.

Everest was Surveyor General of India from 1830 to 1843. He began his career with the East India Company at the age of sixteen and soon joined the Great Trigonometrical Survey, started by William Lambton in 1802. Following Lambton's death in 1823, Everest took over as superintendent and carried on measuring and mapping the Great Arc that extended like triangulated vertebrae along the spine of India from Cape Comorin to the Himalayan foothills. Between 1833 and 1843, George Everest lived at Park Estate in Mussoorie. Also known as Hathi Paon (elephant's foot) the area around Everest House is a forested estate to the west of the main town. Rumour and folklore have promoted whispers that Everest built an adjacent structure called the 'bibighar' where he kept his 'native concubines' but this story seems unlikely for the surveyor general seems to have spent all his waking hours either working with his theodolites or sick in bed with malaria and other diseases. In the backyard of the house is a plaque that marks the original benchmark, over which a barberry bush has grown. Five kilometres to the north-west, below the nearby summit of Benog Tibba, lie the remains of an observatory Everest built, overlooking the snow peaks of Garhwal.

Towards the end of his career, Everest was forced to shift his office and residence 30 kilometres downhill to Dehradun where the Survey of India headquarters still stand. John Keay's *The Great Arc* chronicles the exploits of British surveyors and recounts how Everest joined the survey as a young lieutenant. He was passionate about his duties but a difficult man, even at a young age, prickly and particular about everything from the precise length of a baseline to the pronunciation of his name. As Keay explains his surname was not pronounced '"Everest" (like "cleverest") but "Eve-rest" (like "cleave-rest").' George Everest was a stickler for details and had little time for informality. When one of his fellow officers casually referred to him as a 'compass-wallah', Anglo-Indian slang for a surveryor, Everest became irate and insisted on an apology.

The Doon School's former headmaster and mountaineer, John Martyn, wrote a short account of Everest's career for the *Himalayan Journal* in which he quotes Henry Lawrence as saying that Everest, 'completed one of the most stupendous works in the whole history of science…a measurement exceeding all others as much in accuracy as in length'. Though acknowledging his volatile temperament, Martyn paints a sympathetic portrait of the man, who was seriously ill during most of his time in India and once complained of having been 'bled to fainting' by more than a thousand leeches, the favourite therapy of the day. Yet, on occasion, Everest forgot his ailments and aggravations and could even wax poetic about the hills and valleys he surveyed: 'My station of Hathipaon, where my office stood, looks down on this lovely valley of Dehra, and it was a really beautiful and interesting sight to watch the cultivation growing as if by enchantment. When I left Hathipaon on 1st October 1843 the whole was a rich and glowing mass of fields and orchards—fortunately my base line had already been measured.'

Bill Aitken, a writer and wandering sage who has made his home in Mussoorie, is less charitable, when it comes to Everest, the man: 'While the high praise for his work is beyond dispute, his deficiencies as a person were so glaring that instead of having his name elevated to the highest peak it could just as well have been reviled for the ugly impression he left on people.'

In October 2013, during one of the Mussoorie Writers Mountain Festivals, I had an opportunity to visit Everest House in the company of historian Shekhar Pathak, co-author of Pundit Nain Singh Rawat's biography. Also with us was Loveraj Singh Dharamshaktu, a mountaineer from Kumaon, who has climbed to the summit of Everest seven times. Though I've been to Park Estate on a number of occasions, it was illuminating to see these colonial ruins through the eyes of two contemporary Himalayan explorers, one of whom has researched and written about the mountains throughout his academic career and the other who has ascended the highest peak on earth by various routes.

Shekhar immediately recognized the significance of the site, pointing out: 'This building should be restored and renovated. Anywhere else in the world it would be a historic monument that crowds of tourists would visit, not just because of George Everest himself but because of the Survey of India's heritage.'

He admits the Great Arc was an overtly colonial enterprise that employed oppressive means, such as forced labour, to survey the length and breadth of the subcontinent. Nevertheless, Shekhar argues, 'The Survey of India ultimately contributed to the greater body of human knowledge and our understanding of geography. It was started in 1767, only ten years after the battle of Plassey,' in which the British East India Company's army defeated the Nawab of Bengal and his French allies, to become the dominant colonial power in India. The fact that one of the first major projects of the British Raj was to map its future dominions shows how scientific exploration and cartography served as a driving force of empire.

A tall, lanky man who speaks with expressive gestures and draws upon an irrepressible wealth of information, Shekhar Pathak founded the People's Association for Himalaya Area Research (PAHAR)—an acronym that means mountains in Hindi. Some of his early research was on the Coolie–Begar Movement, in which activists during the early twentieth century led a non-violent struggle against the institution of forced labour in the hills. Men from villages in Kumaon were coerced into serving as unpaid porters for the British authorities. Every ten years, over the past four decades, Shekhar has led a padyatra (foot pilgrimage) across the state of Uttarakhand from Askot to Arakot, to assess the conditions and concerns of rural communities, particularly related to environmental issues, and to build awareness about the heritage of the Himalaya. Though he received a Padma Shri in 2007, Shekhar returned the award in 2015 to protest the 'looting' of Himalayan resources and the government's indifference to bigoted attacks on writers and intellectuals. As a professor at Kumaon University and a Nehru Fellow, he has studied early Himalayan explorers like William Moorcroft whose journeys he retraced across Tibet, where he also followed in the Pundit's footsteps.

'A range of mountains in Tibet, stretching from the east of Pangong Lake across to Mount Kailas, used to be called the "Nain Singh Range" and his name appeared on maps until 1961,' Shekhar tells me, 'after which it was removed because the International Geographers Union felt that mountains shouldn't be named after individuals.'

Nevertheless, Everest's name persists. When I ask Shekhar if he thinks it will ever be replaced by Chomolungma, he hesitates for a moment and then muses, 'Probably not, but there's nothing wrong with having several names, is there? That's a more democratic approach. We also call it Sagarmatha in Nepali.'

From his build and demeanour it's easy to recognize that Loveraj Singh Dharmshaktu is a climber for he conveys the quiet assurance of someone who has been in difficult and dangerous places. After listening to our conversation he agrees with Shekhar that Everest House should be restored as a heritage site, 'so future generations will learn about the man whose name is attached to the mountain'.

He explains how, as a young boy, growing up in Bona Village near Munsiari, 'I didn't hear about Everest until I was in 8th Class,' he says, 'when Bachendri Pal became the first Indian woman to reach the summit. It was only much later that I discovered that this mountain was named after an Englishman.'

Pointing to all the litter strewn about the ruins at Park Estate, as well as the vandalism that scars the old building, Loveraj shakes his head, 'Look at this rubbish. It's like all the garbage on Everest that needs to be cleaned up.'

In 2012, Loveraj was part of an international 'eco-expedition' that climbed Everest with the objective of removing garbage off the mountain.

Later, in 2017, he led an Oil and Natural Gas Corporation (ONGC) expedition to Everest. 'While we were acclimatizing above the Khumbu Icefall at Camp II, we collected 1,500 kilos of garbage and hired helicopters to carry it out to Kathmandu.' He feels that climbers need to take responsibility for the waste that's been left on the mountain. Working with Dawa Steven Sherpa of Asian Trekking, Loveraj is committed to preserving the mountain.

'Now, when we climb we use special bags for human waste. They have a double zip, tissue paper and chemicals inside. Each climber's name is written on the bag and when we go to the toilet we keep the waste and carry it back with us.'

Loveraj has climbed Everest from several directions including the North Face, above the Rongbuk Glacier, and the Kangshung Face, where he was injured in a rockfall. He has also summited other major peaks like Nanda Kot and Kanchenjunga, though he still feels that Everest is the 'toughest challenge, especially the risks on the Khumbu Icefall and Lhotse Face'.

Being one of India's most successful mountaineers, Loveraj is an officer in the Border Security Force (BSF) and has received numerous awards including the Tenzing Norgay Award and a Padma Shri. His wife, Reena Kaushal Dharamshaktu, is also a mountaineer and the first Indian woman to ski to the South Pole.

Coming from the same area of the Himalaya as Pundit Nain Singh Rawat, Loveraj has carried on a tradition of exploration and adventure. He laughs, however, when I ask him which man he heard about first—Nain Singh or George Everest.

'Definitely, Everest,' he admits. 'When I was growing up, nobody spoke about Pundit Nain Singh, though he was a famous surveyor from our region. It was only much later, when he received recognition that we learned about all he had done.' A statue of the Pundit now stands inside the gates of the Survey of India Headquarters in Dehradun, alongside a bust of Sir George Everest.

Shekhar Pathak's research and writing has contributed to correcting this gap in history books. He explains: 'Nain Singh worked for the Survey of India long after George Everest had retired. He never saw Chomolungma because he travelled east from Lhasa by a northerly route, along the Tsang Po.

But Nain Singh contributed as much as anyone to mapping the Himalaya. Everest's name is on the mountain but it's important to recognize the contributions of others, even though many have been forgotten.'

Looking at the empty shell of the old bungalow, Shekhar adds, 'With Google Maps and satellite imagery, there isn't much left for the Survey of India to do today. They should focus on preserving and promoting their legacy. After all, as an institution, it's even older than the Royal Geographical Society and they have a khazana, a treasure house of documents, old maps and historical equipment.'

Meanwhile, Mussoorie's municipality struggles to decide how to preserve Park Estate as a historic site and tourist destination. More than seventy years after independence, we still debate whether to condemn or commemorate the colonial period, even if it is an important part of Indian and Himalayan history.

Half-hearted attempts have been made to restore the building, including a disastrous decision, several years ago, to build toilets inside the main structure, so that tourists—Gents and Ladies—would not foul the surrounding landscape. Unfortunately, there was no running water and, for a while, Everest House became a stinking latrine. Around the same time, the ruins of the observatory on Benog Tibba were dismantled to build a temple nearby.

Earlier, during the 1970s and 1980s, the hills and ridges in the vicinity of Everest House were devastated by mining, as limestone from the Krol Belt deposits was extracted. Over aeons, these prehistoric remains of Tethys clams and corals had been compressed into calcium carbonate, a valuable geological resource. Fortunately, a group of civic-minded citizens protested the strip mining that was turning Hathipaon into a wasteland and the Supreme Court of India stopped all mining in the Mussoorie Hills. Gradually the grass and shrubs have returned, though terraced scars remain. Perhaps geological relics deserve more preservation than nineteenth century bungalows where cantankerous old men drew triangles on maps. In the end, Everest House, along with its graffiti, may simply crumble and dissolve into the ground out of which it was built. However, at least for the foreseeable future, thanks to a mountain in Nepal, the compass-wallah's name will endure, albeit mispronounced.

chapter 41

DEMONS OF THE DEATH ZONE

A lone figure ascends a wind-whetted ridge, sinking into the deep snow up to his knees. He gains only a few inches with each step. All the other summits are beneath him now and the slow struggle to the top seems almost futile against the vast scale of the landscape, which is cast in bronze by a setting sun. This solitary mountaineer is the only sign of life crawling up the frozen, precipitous slope.

'I walked and walked, climbed and climbed, for hours and hours. My earlier climbs had taught me not to give up before I reached the top; and I had never given up… But this was quite different; this was an incredible irresistible urge that drove my exhausted body onward.'

The final push up a mountain is always a lonely challenge, especially in the 'death zone' above 8,000 metres. A human body deteriorates rapidly at altitudes like this and the solo climber seems ready to collapse. The dark lenses on his glacier goggles reflect the serrated profile of the summit. His skin is blistered and raw. His breath freezes on his beard though his mouth is dry. He has left everything behind. His climbing partner has turned back. He has no bottled oxygen, no food or water. Memories have been erased and only the present exists. He has even forgotten the war, his capture and internment. For him there is only this unclimbed peak.

My thoughts, my dreams, my whole life were nothing but the Mountains!... I climbed down a gully, crossed some boulders to the left, but soon found myself facing a vertical rock face, to climb which seemed to me a sheer impossibility. I was finding great difficulty now in keeping myself upright. I kept on sitting down on the rocks, wanting to go to sleep, overcome by a terrible feeling of lassitude. But I had to push on; the final prize glittered before me and some secret urge drove me on, its daemonic energy planting one foot ahead of the other, endlessly.

Hermann Buhl's ascent of Nanga Parbat in 1953 remains one of the most remarkable achievements in Himalayan mountaineering. Defying the conventional wisdom and siege tactics of the day, he set out from Camp 5 by himself to reach the summit and survived a forty-one hour ordeal that included standing overnight on a snow ledge. At a time when medical science still didn't have a clear understanding of the effects of oxygen deprivation and extreme cold, he swallowed amphetamines called Pervitin, to keep himself going, and another drug, Padutin, which was supposed to increase circulation and protect him from frostbite. The pills made him hallucinate, adding to the disorientation caused by altitude, so that his descent from Nanga Parbat became a delusional nightmare out of which he only emerged after reaching Base Camp. Despite the Padutin, his feet were badly frostbitten and he had to be carried off the mountain. But Buhl's photograph of his ice axe with a Tyrolese pennant, planted on the summit, proved that he'd been there.

◆

Aside from standing atop Nanga Parbat, the only way to get a complete sense of the enormous dimensions and complex structure of this mountain is to see it from the air. As our PIA flight from Islamabad to Skardu follows the course of the Indus, circling to the west of the mountain, each of the three main faces come into view. To the south is the terrifying 4,600-metre wall of the Rupal Face bounded by the Mazeno Ridge, a crenellated rampart of ice and rock. On the other side of this barrier, along the western flank of the mountain, lies the Diamir Face, a huge trough of snow scored with aretes and glaciers. Turning north-east, the aircraft banks sharply as it crosses another buttress beyond which rises the North or Raikot Face (often misspelled Rakhiot) directly beneath the airplane's wing. The main peak of Nanga Parbat (8,126 metres) sits atop the southern end of a summit ridge, trending roughly north to south, with broad snowfields to the east. This aerial view reveals both the tremendous scale and tortured features of the ninth highest mountain on earth, situated at the north-western extreme of the Himalayan arc.

While flights to Skardu take forty-five minutes or less, driving back by road to Islamabad involves a journey of almost twenty hours because of the rugged terrain and twisting course of the Indus. The Karakoram Highway, built for Pakistan by the Chinese, is a breathtaking feat of engineering and provides a relatively smooth, two-lane surface even as it coils its way through gorges and across high passes. At Raikot Bridge, however, we turn off the well-graded asphalt onto a rough, unpaved track. For this section of the trip we must abandon our Land Cruiser and climb aboard a smaller, more manoeuvrable jeep. The two-hour drive to the village of Tato traces a terrifying route, along the vertical face of a precipice that falls 1,000 metres into the chasm below. Most of this narrow, badly rutted road ascends a steep gradient that makes it feel as if the jeep is about to tip over backward. And when our vehicle meets another, coming in the opposite direction around a blind corner, the driver casually reverses to within a few centimetres of the edge, where a crumbling wall of loose rocks is the only thing that keeps us from sliding off the side of the ridge.

After a drive like this, trekking can only be a pleasure and from the roadhead at Tato we gladly set off on foot up a winding trail through a forest of pines and juniper. Didar Ali, with whom I've just travelled over the Deosai Plateau, tells me that the treacherous jeep road was constructed almost thirty years ago by an army officer, Brigadier Aslam Khan, who built it to extract timber from the Raikot Valley. Nobody is sure what strings were pulled or how many bribes were paid to secure this lucrative forest contract but the entrepreneurial officer made a fortune cutting down trees and carting them away by the jeepload. He is remembered in Gilgit–Baltistan as a rapacious timber baron who pillaged the Raikot Valley of its greenery and robbed forest resources from local villagers. Fortunately, after his death, the clear felling of trees finally ended at the insistence of regional leaders, and many of the pines, spruces and firs have now grown back.

Didar and I are headed for Fairy Meadows or 'Marchenwiese' as the early German climbers called it. These high pastures, ringed with conifer forests, lie at the foot of Nanga Parbat, the naked mountain. A peaceful, idyllic landscape with tumbling brooks and wooded glades, it is a verdant contrast to the dry wasteland of the Indus gorge below and the ice-encrusted cliffs overhead.

When we arrive at the Raikot Serai, our lodgings at Fairy Meadows, most of Nanga Parbat is covered by a dense curtain of monsoon clouds and only a narrow band along the lowest slopes is visible. Flowing down from these eroded foundations is the Raikot Glacier, a broad current of ice covered with a layer of rocks and gravel. It looks more like an ash heap, or a lava flow that has burned itself out and cooled into tumultuous shapes. The mouth of the glacier is close enough for us to see a fast-running stream of meltwater coursing out of a frozen cavern, its sources buried within a maze of hidden crevasses. On either side of the valley are shelves of moraine, where the glacier topped out centuries ago when this ancient river of ice extended much further down the valley. Though considerably reduced from its earlier dimensions, Raikot is one of the few Himalayan glaciers that are currently advancing while most, at lower latitudes, are receding as temperatures rise.

Dark evergreen forests extend up the valley on either side until birches take over below the treeline. Under a gloomy drapery of clouds most of the scene is submerged in shadows. A few donkeys and goats are grazing on the lawns in front of our lodge and a scattered assortment of wooden huts fills the alpine pastures on all sides. Fairy Meadows has become a popular tourist destination for visitors from Pakistan and abroad. What was once a remote, unspoiled sanctuary is now a bustling summer resort.

◆

In 1895, A. F. Mummery, one of the pioneers of mountaineering, who popularized 'guideless ascents', set out for Nanga Parbat, because he found the Alps 'overcrowded'. Accompanying him was Norman Collie, whose book *From the Himalaya to Skye* (originally titled *Climbing on the Himalaya and Other Mountain Ranges*) recounts the events of this expedition that ended with the death of Mummery and two Gurkha soldiers, Ragobir and Goman Singh. In Mummery's journal, which Collie quotes, he seems to have anticipated tragedy in an ominous and prophetic note: 'This dark mountain realm with all its hidden threats lies at the end of the source of all that is living.' Before it was finally climbed in 1953, Nanga Parbat claimed thirty-one lives and became widely known as 'the killer mountain' or 'the man-eater'.

Starting from Srinagar, Mummery and Collie undertook a relatively lightweight, alpine-style approach. Supported by Kashmiri, Balti and Chilas porters, they were venturing into unknown, uncertain territory. From the perspective of today's mountaineers, they were under-equipped and poorly informed. Most of the prominent features and many of the lesser peaks were still unnamed and unmapped. The remote terrain with sparse habitation was cut off from the rest of the world. Yet Mummery and Collie seemed to revel in the isolation and unpredictable nature of their exploration.

'During our wild nocturnal wanderings, first down the Mazeno, and then down the Rupal glacier, where in the dim candle-light and in a semi-conscious condition we slipped, tumbled and fell, but always with one dominant idea—namely, we must go on!'

The legendary mountain leader, George Granville Bruce, then a young Gurkha officer who had already made a name for himself climbing with Martin Conway, joined them for a month while on leave from his regiment in Abbotabad.

> Over our dinner we forgot the weary tramping of the last forty hours, celebrating the occasion by drinking all the bottles of Bass's pale ale—a priceless treasure in these parts—that we had brought from Kashmir. Then afterwards, when we turned into our sleeping-bags before the roaring camp-fire, and the twilight slowly passed into the azure night... it was agreed unanimously that it was worth coming many thousand miles to enjoy climbing in the Himalaya, and that those who lived at home ingloriously at their ease knew not the joys that were to be found amidst the ice and snows of the greatest of mountain ranges.

Collie's record of the 1895 expedition is punctuated by romantic poetry and he quotes Shelley's strangely prescient lines:

> And this, the naked countenance of earth,
> On which I gaze, even these primaeval mountains,
> Power dwells apart in their tranquility,
> Remote, serene, and inaccessible.

At the end of the nineteenth century the effects of altitude were still a mystery and they kept wondering what would happen to them higher up. At one point Collie remarks, half-facetiously, that, 'Probably mountain-sickness was a disease which lurked in the higher mountains and was ready at any moment to rush in and seize its prey. Lucky for us the particular bacillus was not just then in the surrounding atmosphere, consequently we had not been inoculated...'

Mummery and Collie never got above 6,500 metres or even came close to climbing Nanga Parbat though they did reach the summits of several lower peaks. But the object of their expedition seems more an excuse, rather than a goal, to simply revel in the lonely physicality of high altitudes, crossing back and forth over passes to reconnoitre possible routes that others might follow.

For Ragobir and Goman Singh, the two Gurkhas that Bruce assigned to the expedition and who stayed on after his departure, it must have been a puzzling change from the disciplined routines of their regiment. Rather than doing route marches and military drills, they set off aimlessly up steep slopes following men whose language they hardly understood and whose purpose in the mountains must have seemed as frivolous as it was dangerous. Yet, they took to mountaineering with an ease and enthusiasm that Collie applauded.

> Ragobir was sent to the front. He led us down the most precipitous places with tremendous rapidity and immense enjoyment. It was all 'good' according to him, and his cheery face down below made me feel that there could be no difficulty, till I found myself hanging down a slab of rock with but the barest of handholds, or came to a bulging mass of ice overhanging a steep gully, which insisted on protruding into the middle of my stomach, with direful result to my state of equilibrium.

One of the men recruited from the Chilas region near Nanga Parbat was also singled out for equal praise:

> Lor Khan, who came behind me on the rope, seemed to be enjoying himself immensely; of course he had never been in such a position before but these Chilas tribesmen are famous fellows. What Swiss peasant, whilst making his first trial of the big snow peaks and the ice, would have dared to follow in such a place, and that, too, with only skins soaked through by the melting snow wrapped round his feet? Lor Khan never hesitated for a moment; when I turned and pointed downwards he only grinned, and looked as if he were in the habit of walking on ice slopes every day of his life.

Shortly after this moment, Lor Khan slips and falls, dragging Ragobir after him. Collie saves them by driving his ice axe into the frozen slope. Throughout his book, danger is described but underplayed, as if it were something to be shoved to the back of the mind. Death on the mountain was a real possibility, every day, but the climbers speak of it with a cavalier air of invincibility. And in the end, when Mummery and the two Gurkhas disappear beneath an avalanche, Collie's elegiac lines strike a stoic yet sentimental chord.

...although Mummery is no longer with us, though to those who knew him the loss is irreparable, though he never can lead and cheer us on up the 'gaunt, bare slabs, the square, precipitous steps in the ridge, and the bulging ice of the gully,' yet his memory will remain— he will not be forgotten. The pitiless mountains have claimed him— and amongst the snow-laden glaciers of the mighty hills he rests. 'The curves of the wind-moulded cornice, the delicate undulations of the fissured snow,' cover him, whilst the 'grim precipices, the great brown rocks bending down into immeasurable space,' and the snow-peaks he loved so well, keep watch, and guard over the spot where he lies.

◆

On our first morning at Fairy Meadows, I wake up early, hoping for clear skies but Nanga Parbat is still hidden from view and a murky dawn seeps through porous layers of monsoon clouds. Gradually, though, as the air begins to warm and winds circulate on the upper slopes of the naked mountain, swirling clouds perform a dance of seven veils. In a way, it is more dramatic and suspenseful to observe the mountain through these drifting shoals of moisture, with shifts of light and shadow, rather than having Nanga Parbat appear as it does on tourism posters and websites, a towering, unclouded mass of snow and rock framed by a seemingly photoshopped foreground that looks like a fairway on a golf course.

Nanga Parbat's name, 'the naked mountain', applies more to the exposed aspects of the Raikot Face, which isn't shielded by foothills, and less to its bare rocks and denuded profile. Seeing the mountain wrapped in clouds and glaciers, I can appreciate the poet Muhammad Iqbal's lines in his ode to the Himalaya, when he describes them as 'turbaned with snow'. Many writers have tried to capture the fearsome grandeur of this massif but, for the most part, ordinary metaphors fail to convey its awesome presence and a sublime paradox of beauty and horror that emanates from its looming, tortured features.

The dramatic contrast between idyllic alpine meadows fringed with shapely conifers and the stark, disfigured visage of the mountain scarred by avalanches and scabbed with ice both captures and repels our imagination. Most fairy tales contain dangerous beasts and threatening villains that stand in opposition to more timid, nurturing spirits. German alpinists dubbed these meadows 'marchenwiese' because they present a gentle, enchanting counterpoint to the monstrous face of the peak they hoped to climb. For them, the green charms of the Raikot meadows would have reminded them of Grindelwald and Chamonix while Nanga Parbat must have looked like the Eiger, Jungfrau and Mont Blanc all piled together into one enormous, daunting summit.

In Himalayan folklore, fairies are not the benign or benevolent sprites that we usually associate with European fables. According to one folk tale from Gilgit, a tree laden with pearls grows on the summit of Nanga Parbat. These riches are the property of fairies and giants who haunt the peak. One day, a brave mountaineer sets off to climb the naked summit. When he reaches the top, he fills his pockets with pearls but as soon as he begins to descend, the climber sees a hoard of fairies and giants chasing after him. Terrified, he throws away the pearls and escapes. Returning to his village, however, he notices that one of the fairies is still pursuing him. Only when he finally gets home and removes his boots does he find a lone pearl inside. Snatching it away from the mountaineer, the malevolent sprite disappears.

After breakfast, we prepare to head off for a day's trek up the valley. Answering a knock at the door of my hut, I am confronted by a tall, bearded man, dressed all in black, carrying an AK-47. When I greet him cautiously in Urdu, he explains that he is my police escort. Any foreigners that go trekking above Fairy Meadows must be accompanied by an armed guard. This security precaution was put in place after a terrorist attack at the Diamir Base Camp in 2013. Ten foreign mountaineers and one local guide were shot dead in what seems to have been a botched kidnapping attempt. Their attackers, disguised in military uniforms, were recruited from local villages by Taliban extremists.

Didar reassures me that there is no reason to be concerned about terrorists at Fairy Meadows, though I still find it unnerving to be walking through the dappled shadows of a pine forest with a heavily armed bodyguard at my heels. His name is Halimullah and he comes from a small village on the outskirts of Gilgit. Despite his lethal weaponry and fierce demeanour, Halimullah is a quiet, easy-going man. Both he and Didar explain that the people of this region, often referred to as 'Yaghistan', are known to be wild and unpredictable. 'But everyone benefits from tourism, so they won't cause any trouble.' Also accompanying us is a young man, whose family are local shepherds. Along the way, we meet his father coming down from a higher camp. He greets us with a reserved but friendly smile and a welcoming handshake. Though herding remains their primary occupation, the people of Raikot have tapped into the tourist trade, taking visitors on horseback or operating tea stalls and seasonal hotels.

'Yaghis have a reputation for being violent and temperamental,' Didar tells me with a grin, as we head on, 'but when they dance, they perform the most delicate, restrained movements. The people of Hunza are the opposite. We are peaceful and soft-spoken, but when we dance, we leap about wildly, out of control.'

Each valley in Gilgit–Baltistan has its own culture and traditions. As we trek towards the upper end of the Raikot Glacier, Didar tells me several jokes about a village called Bagrot, whose inhabitants are known for their naivete. In one story, a group of Bagrotis are trying to cross a swollen river and they determine that the only way to reach the other side is to wait until nightfall, when the river goes to sleep. Of course, in the darkness, as they step into the swift current, the Bagrotis are immediately swept away and drown. This is followed by another anecdote that takes place many years ago, when loads of salt were carried across the high passes out of Tibet. A group of Bagrotis grew tired of the arduous trek back and forth. So, they came up with the ingenious idea of planting their fields with rock salt, believing the coarse crystals would sprout like seeds. However, instead of producing a plentiful harvest, their fields were reduced to a saline wasteland.

Stories like these convey a rustic sense of humour that provides some respite from the harsh conditions of life in the mountains. Though roads and other forms of development have relieved some of the isolation that existed in earlier days, people still live close to the land and their narratives are linked to rugged, unyielding terrain. Many stories also reflect an affinity with animals, which are an integral part of their pastoral culture.

The legend of Sri Badat, a tribal chief who became a man-eater, is a popular but gruesome fable from Gilgit. As the folklorist Ghulam Muhammad recounts, this fierce warlord, 'was in the habit of obtaining a sheep daily from his subjects. One day, when eating his dinner, he was much surprised to find that the meat was more tasty than before.' When he demanded to know where the animal had come from, his retainers fetched the woman who had raised the sheep. At Sri Badat's insistence, she explained: 'The mother of this sheep had died a few days after its birth, and the lamb being very beautiful was very much admired by me. Thinking it a hardship to lose the lamb as well as the ewe, I fed it with my own milk until it was old enough to graze.' Believing that the 'tastiness of the meat' was a result of the lamb having suckled at a woman's breast, Sri Badat decided that human flesh must be equally flavourful. 'Coming to this conclusion, he gave orders that a tax of human children should be levied in future instead of sheep, and that their meat should always be served at his dinner.'

Flocks of sheep and goats are scattered over the meadows and herdsmen's log huts add to the picturesque scenery. The further up the valley we go, the larger Nanga Parbat appears, looming above us out of the clouds. By now, I can see the uppermost ridges and a broad snowfield between the main summit and Raikot Peak. Eventually, we leave the pines and firs behind, entering a narrow band of birch trees. Our path finally ends at an eroded lip of moraine overlooking the upper end of the Raikot Glacier. A huge icefall, more than 3 kilometres in breadth, descends from the north face of Nanga Parbat. The Base Camp from which Hermann Buhl and others set off for the summit is situated on a protruding ridge above us and I can just make out the route he followed, avoiding bergschrunds along the upper rim of the glacier.

Retracing our steps, we return to a shepherd camp at the edge of the meadow. A few birds appear, including a brown dipper that plunges into the stream and a hoopoe with a flared crest that flies off on pulsing wings. Aside from goats and sheep, there are no other mammals in sight, not even marmots. Perhaps on the surrounding cliffs and in the dense forests away from the path, there may be some wildlife. Two days ago, we stopped at the estate of a wealthy landowner near Askote, on the other side of Nanga Parbat. He had his own private menagerie that included a rhesus macaque in a miniature sentry box by the main gate and an ibex and markhor, both females, confined to a wire mesh cage. Though they nibbled at stems of grass and leaves from our hands there was a limpid wildness in their eyes, as if they were constantly looking to escape. The owner said he hopes to cross-breed them with domestic goats but he spends most of the year outside Pakistan and hasn't been able to find the right mate. He also complained that in his absence the caretakers of his estate did a poor job of looking after the animals. Only a few months back, while he was in Switzerland, a pet musk deer had died. Each of these creatures had been caught in the wild, at a young age, and reared in captivity. Trekking through the high meadows and forests below Nanga Parbat, I can't help but imagine those caged animals running free in this open, unfettered habitat.

Along the path, Didar has collected a kind of lichen that grows on dead branches of juniper and pine. He says it is used for making tea. When we stop for lunch at a shepherd's hut, where the owner caters to tourists, Didar takes over in the kitchen and produces a meal of fresh chapattis with lentils and a kind of spinach that grows at this altitude. Recalling the carnivorous stories of Sri Badat, and after eight days of eating nothing but mutton and chicken, it is a relief to enjoy a vegetarian meal. We wash it down with mugs of lichen tea that Didar calls 'juniper blood', because of its red colour. The mild flavour is slightly acidic, not unlike a weak but nuanced Darjeeling.

◆

In the evening, after we return to Fairy Meadows, the clouds finally drift apart enough for us to get a complete view of the mountain, its summit tinted saffron by the setting sun. At this hour Nanga Parbat seems almost benign despite its ravaged countenance. To call it a 'killer mountain' seems unfair despite its fatal legacy. This natural citadel that guards the north-western limits of the Himalaya is no more to blame for the deaths of those who perished on its slopes than a besieged fortress would be guilty of the casualties within its walls. Mountains don't bestow victory or defeat. They are what they are: giant protrusions of the earth's crust surmounted with layers of frozen moisture, wreathed in clouds. The men and women who climb these peaks contest their fate, employing the skills, instincts and endurance that mountaineering demands. And in the end, whatever 'horrific' or 'monstrous' events occur, these are nothing more than the results of human choices, courage, arrogance and desire.

Tacked on the walls of the dining room at Raikot Sarai are photographs of Hermann Buhl and other climbers, including Amir Mehdi, a porter from Hunza who assisted Buhl on his successful climb of Nanga Parbat. Mehdi later lost all his toes after spending a night at 8,100 metres in a bivouac on K2 with Walter Bonatti. He was presented the *Al Valor Civile* medal by the Italian government and lived until the age of eighty-six. There is also a black-and-white portrait of Karl Maria Herrligkoffer and a colour photograph of Reinhold Messner. Hanging from a nail nearby is a rusty pair of crampons that look like a bear trap with a scribbled note indicating that these were recovered from the Raikot Glacier and were probably left behind by the 1932 expedition.

During the years between the two world wars, Nanga Parbat became the primary objective for German and Austrian climbers, their 'mountain of destiny' as it was called. Kenneth Mason, whose *Abode of Snow* is the most comprehensive history of Himalayan mountaineering up until the ascent of Everest, devotes several chapters to the German expeditions on Nanga Parbat between 1932–39. He writes with admiration of their efforts, particularly the leadership of Paul Bauer. Mason, who was superintendent of the Survey of India, founding president of the Himalayan Club, and a professor of geography at Oxford, adds a rare personal aside to what is mostly a dry but reliable catalogue of climbs. 'By a curious coincidence,

Bauer and I had fought each other in the trenches a hundred yards apart in France in 1915. The mountains have drawn us together since and we remain close friends.' Bauer and some of the other German climbers visited and stayed with Mason at his home in Oxford. As vice-president of the Royal Geographical Society in London, their host helped them obtain permissions in British India.

The parallels between war and mountaineering make for a complex and enduring story. Most of the German climbers had survived the trenches and carried with them a burden of anguish and guilt for having survived a conflict that claimed so many lives. The Himalaya, in their remote and unexplored sanctity, offered escape and absolution. At the same time, large expeditions of this period replicated the martial spirit and command structure of an army campaign. For the men who took up the challenge, climbing offered a form of redemption and recovery from the horrors of battle, as well as a return to the familiar discipline and camaraderie of military service. This was particularly true for the Germans. Mason observes that many young men who had believed in Germany's invincibility struggled to come to terms with the traumas of war and their defeat. Mountains, first the Alps and then the Himalaya, provided some solace. He quotes Paul Bauer: 'Years passed in which we spent every free day among them and in many a night watch we probed nature's deepest secrets.' Seeking release from their inner demons, they pitted themselves against the highest peaks on earth.

In group photographs of these expeditions, cheerful young men in thick sweaters and stout boots gaze earnestly at the camera, but one can hardly imagine the wounds they bore and the urgency with which they sought to put the devastation behind them. Though the Himalaya harboured pristine and inspiring beauty, these mountains were as dangerous as the battlefields of Europe.

The first German 'reconnaissance in force' led by Paul Bauer actually began in the east on Kanchenjunga, in the summer of 1929. Working their way up the mountain with methodical determination, they established ten camps and reached a high point of roughly 7,400 metres. The next year, in 1930, Professor G. O. Dyhrenfurth led an enormous expedition to Kanchenjunga with 500 porters carrying several tonnes of equipment, including cine cameras to film the climb. They abandoned this campaign after one of the most experienced Sherpas, Chettan, died in an ice avalanche. In 1931, Bauer and five other members of Akademischer Alpenverein München, returned to Sikkim for another unsuccessful attempt. By this time, the

Himalayan Club had established a system of recruiting and registering porters and Sherpas in Darjeeling, many of whom were seconded to the German expedition.

1932 marks the beginning of the campaign to conquer Nanga Parbat. The initial effort was led by Willy Merkl and did not include any of the veterans of Kanchenjunga. Mason tells us that the expedition suffered from theft by Kashmiri porters and ended in disarray, without identifying a practicable route up the mountain. Two years later Merkl returned, in 1934. This time, with the help of the Himalayan Club and its Sherpas, he was able to mount a more credible assault. They also happened to be funded by the Nazi regime, which had taken power in Berlin. Inevitably, Hitler's grotesque fantasies of Aryan supermen became enmeshed with German mountaineering.

Yet all the systematic planning, Deutsche Mark and experience could not restrain Nanga Parbat, which 'struck back' with a vengeance. Early into the climb, one of the team, Alfred Drexel, was hit with altitude sickness and died of pulmonary edema. His companions buried him on the mountain beneath a cairn marked with the Nazi swastika, then carried on. But the worst was still to come.

A month later, five German climbers and eleven Sherpas were high on the mountains atop the 'silver plateau', a three-kilometre snowfield above 7,000 metres that extends across the nape of the summit ridge. Without warning a fierce blizzard blew in, destroying tents and scattering the group. Over eight brutal days of the storm, the climbers tried desperately to descend, without shelter, food or liquids. Suffering from exhaustion, altitude sickness, frostbite and snow blindness, the Germans and Sherpas floundered about in white-out conditions and gale-force winds, fighting to get off the mountain.

Mason describes it as the 'greatest mountain disaster of our time'. Over the years, similar storms have killed numerous climbers on Himalayan peaks, but it was the first time this generation of mountaineers had witnessed the apocalyptic consequences of the monsoon. During the storm, three Germans, including Willy Merkl and six Sherpas died on Nanga Parbat. With Drexel's earlier death the final toll in 1934 was ten fatalities.

Fritz Bechtold, one of the climbers who remained below, records the remarkable story of survival by Ang Tsering, who received a Medal of Honour from the German Red Cross for his efforts to save his companions:

> From below in Camp IV a man was seen pressing forward along the level saddle. Now and again the storm bore down a cry for help. The lone figure reached and came down over the Rakhiot (Raikot)

Peak. It was Ang Tsering, Willy Merkl's second orderly, who at length, completely exhausted and suffering from terrible frostbite, found refuge in Camp IV. With almost superhuman endurance he had fought his way down through storm and snow, a hero at every step. Since he brought no letter from Merkl or Gaylay, his simple tale was the last news of the heroic struggle of our comrades and their faithful porters high on the ridge above.

Under Nazi rule, the Deutsche Himalaja Stiftung was established in an effort to regroup after the 1934 disaster. The veteran Paul Bauer was appointed to lead a concerted effort to conquer Nanga Parbat. He recruited a few survivors from the Merkl expedition and other seasoned climbers. In 1936, Bauer took his team back to Kanchenjunga on a training expedition to help prepare them for the rigours of the Himalaya. Then, in May 1937, they set off for Kashmir with the full assistance of the British government in India. After almost a month on the mountain, the Germans established Camp IV above 6,000 metres.

Bauer and some of the climbers descended and began to ferry loads from below. But when they returned the next day, Camp IV had disappeared. In its place was the debris from a huge avalanche, 150 metres wide and 400 metres long. Beneath this frozen shroud lay seven German climbers and nine Sherpas. Runners carried a desperate call for help to the nearest colonial outpost in Gilgit but by the time rescue efforts were set in motion, there was no hope. Trenches were dug in the hardened snow and the victims were found buried in their tents and sleeping bags. 'Diaries had been written up on the evening of 14 June. Watches had stopped soon after 12 o'clock; the avalanche fell just after midnight. Sixteen men were overwhelmed in their sleep,' as Mason described it, 'Nanga Parbat is pitiless.'

One of the diaries retrieved was Hans Hartmann's, which detailed his research on the physiological effects of altitude. It began with an opening epigraph:

Though frost be fierce and pain be dire,
My oath shall be my burning fire.

For Paul Bauer, who had struggled so hard to capture a major Himalayan summit, and lost so many of his countrymen in this quest, it must have been a terrible defeat, as traumatic as his military service in World War I. But he was determined to carry on and returned to Nanga Parbat in 1938, following the same route to the 'Silver Saddle' between Raikot Peak and the main summit. On the way up they discovered the bodies of Sherpas Pintso

Nurbu and Gaylay, as well as Willy Merkl's frozen corpse, which had lain on the mountain since 1934. From the pocket of Merkl's coat they retrieved a final, desperate letter written to his teammates below.

Though Bauer reached higher than others had gone before, he was mindful of the earlier disasters and when it became clear that his team would not reach the summit, he ordered a retreat, ending his last climb in the Himalaya. He later published a book titled *The Siege of Nanga Parbat*, which recounts with patriotic fervour the German struggle against this mountain. Nationalism was now securely roped to mountaineering and the ascent of unsummited peaks, literally and symbolically, fulfilled a desire for territorial conquest.

In 1939, one of the younger members of Bauer's team, Peter Aufschaiter returned once more to Nanga Parbat, exploring a different route on the Diamir Face. Among this team was Heinrich Harrer, who had earned a reputation for daring and skill on the Eiger. They ascended to just over 6,000 metres, on a spur dubbed 'the pulpit', after which they turned back and retreated to Gilgit, only to discover that England and Germany were now at war. The climbers were soon arrested by British authorities and this chapter of German exploration came to an end. Harrer went on to escape from a British POW camp in Dehradun and, after two failed attempts, made his way through the mountains to Lhasa, a story that he relates in his bestseller, *Seven Years in Tibet*.

Between the two world wars, the German obsession with Nanga Parbat had become a patriotic crusade, aligned with Hitler's ambitions. Lee Wallace Holt, an American historian, outlines the cultural implications of this modern mythology: 'The 1934 expedition to Nanga Parbat…became a key event in German mountaineering history, elevating Nanga Parbat to the "*Schicksalsberg der Deutschen*", the German mountain of fate.'

As Holt explains, Bauer and others traced a link to Nanga Parbat through the story of Adolf Schlagintweit, the German geographer hired by the East India Company, who was the first European to stand in front of the massive Rupal Face on 14 September 1856. As they told the story, Schlagintweit 'discovered' the naked mountain that lured so many brave German youth to their death on her fatal slopes. During the 1930s, Nanga Parbat became a symbol of national aspirations and an object of imperial conquest. The fact that this mountain lay within British India added to the motivation, even as the British helped them attempt to achieve their goal. Through books, films and journalistic fervour, alpine achievement was equated with Germany's national destiny and mountaineers were seen as heroes battling abroad for the fatherland.

Holt also reveals a darker, more damning side of Paul Bauer. In addition to being a well-organized and skilled mountain leader, whom Kenneth Mason praises, Bauer was clearly part of the Nazi regime and helped shape and steer German legends of mountaineering to promote the Third Reich. Hitler's propaganda machine used sport and film as part of its efforts to justify anti-Semitic and other racist doctrines. Movies made about the Himalaya during the 1930s clearly underscored this theme like *Nanga Parbat: Ein Kampfbericht der Deutschen Himalaja-Expedition 1934* (A Frontline Report on the German Himalaya Expedition of 1934). Under Hitler, the German Mountaineering Association was an instrument of the state and Bauer faithfully carried out Nazi orders.

The censorship of G. O. Dyhrenfurth's film *Der Dämon des Himalaya* (Demon of the Himalaya) illustrates this point. Following his 1930 expedition to Kanchenjunga, Dyhrenfurth had made a successful documentary, *Himatschal: Der Thron der Götter*, released in 1931. Inspired by the 1934 catastrophe, Dyhrenfurth conflated the mythology of Kanchenjunga, its deities and demonic creatures, with the dangerous terrain and monsoon storms on Nanga Parbat. *Der Dämon des Himalaya* was a feature film, starring Gustav Diessl, which dramatized the horrors and heroics of mountaineering. It was also littered with racist stereotypes, including a Yeti-like Sherpa who repeatedly ogles the German heroine played by Erika Dannhoff. The rest of the Sherpas are depicted as childish elves who touch the Europeans' feet before setting off up the mountain.

Der Dämon des Himalaya was not well received. Reviewers complained it was too melodramatic, though they praised the cinematography. Within the German mountaineering fraternity, Dyhrenfurth's fictional account of the Nanga Parbat expeditions elicited scorn and derision. They saw it as a cheap, perverse exploitation of a noble, national crusade. Of course, it didn't help that Dyhrenfurth was Jewish.

As an example of the kind of liberties the director took, there is a climactic scene in which the hero, Dr Wille (an obvious nod to Willy Merkl), confronts the demon, high on the mountain. In a surreal sequence with shadowy special effects he is hurled off the ridge and tumbles headlong down the glacier into a Tibetan monastery full of chanting monks, where he finally breathes his last.

Scenes like this offended Bauer's sense of authentic alpine adventure but also outraged his conviction in the national cause. Under the Nazis, Paul Bauer had been promoted head of the Mountaineering Department in the German Association for Sports. In this capacity he petitioned the Reich Film Office to ban Dyhrenfurth's film. His reasoning: 'At this point in time in the Third Reich, when the fundamental law of nations clearly identifies the Jews, and international Jewry, as the opponents of Nazi Germany, we should have no patience for Jewish business people who try to bring their shady deals into the Reich; these Jewish businessmen are clearly exploiting the current interest in faraway mountains.'

◆

When Hermann Buhl ultimately fulfilled the German–Austrian dream of conquering Nanga Parbat in 1953, it was a victory carved out of defeat. During World War II he had served in a Mountain Division of the German Army and was taken prisoner by American troops. After the war he worked as a guide near his home in Innsbruck, climbing throughout the Tyrolean Alps and Dolomites. The German–Austrian expedition of 1953 was mounted by Karl Herrligkoffer, Willy Merkl's half-brother, and led by Peter Aschenbrenner, a survivor of the 1932 and 1934 expeditions. Just as Paul Bauer and his compatriots had sought to put their demons to rest after World War I, this expedition continued the struggle and sought redemption from the horrors of battle following World War II.

In Buhl's memoir, *Nanga Parbat Pilgrimage: The Lonely Challenge*, he writes about his awareness of those who went before him and the inspiration of their sacrifice. 'Those men, of similar spirit, whom the mountain had struck down, were still alive as we saw them in our memories. They accompanied us not as messengers from the dead but as guides for the living—guides to take us to the top.'

Though they understood the tragic history of the mountain and the fears and obsessions that motivated Herrligkoffer and Aschenbrenner, Buhl and several younger climbers chafed under the cautious yet domineering leadership of their elders. After reaching the East Ridge, they were ordered to come down off the mountain because a storm was forecast, but Buhl insisted that they be permitted to attempt the summit. A protracted argument ensued, full of 'strong Bavarian words' after which they defiantly carried on up the mountain. This was a decisive moment. Buhl and the other young climbers were finally able to shed the weight of historic defeats and move beyond a legacy of unquestioning discipline and failure.

Of course, 1953 was a crucial year for mountaineering. While the German–Austrian expedition was retracing its destiny up the Raikot Face and onto the Silver Saddle, the British were pitching their tents high on the South Col of Everest. A few days before Buhl set off for the summit of Nanga Parbat, he was waiting out a storm at Camp III and was surprised to see four teammates arrive in the midst of a blizzard. At first he thought they had come to rescue him but they had brought news that Hillary and Tenzing had just summited the highest mountain on earth. 'Everest had been climbed! I was immensely impressed by the information, for I had never thought it possible that giant peak would be conquered for another year or two. It was certainly a great spur to our own endeavours.'

Ultimately, Buhl was the only member of the team to reach the top of Nanga Parbat, by taking risks that others were unwilling to accept and pushing his body beyond any known limits of endurance. While so much of the narrative until now had been a story of selfless teamwork, martial discipline and dedication to patriotic ideals, as well as a sense of historic destiny that placed national pride above individual goals, Hermann Buhl's solo ascent, though it certainly depended on the support of others, finally came down to one man, alone on the mountain.

Buhl's success was marred by accusations of insubordination. In particular, Aschenbrenner was furious because his order to retreat had been ignored. Offended and irate, the leader of the expedition did not wait to congratulate Buhl and left Base Camp as soon as he got word that Nanga Parbat had been climbed.

In the epilogue of his book, Buhl writes: 'The storm has died away. It was a storm raised by men, to whirl up a hideous cloud of dust, which for a time obscured even the shining magic of the Mountain.' He then goes on to justify his solitary quest for the summit.

> You cannot climb a great mountain, least of all a 26,000 foot peak like Nanga Parbat, without personal risk. The leaders of the 1953 Expedition would not face this truth or the responsibility underlying it. They were entitled to take the line they took—from their point of view, which was influenced by well-founded caution and erroneous weather reports. The summit party shouldered the risk involved. They were entitled to do so, for they were in a position to interpret the conditions and the weather correctly. There was nothing wild or rash about our decision; it was governed by deliberate judgment. We, moreover, were moved by our oath to do justice to the Mountain and those who had given their lives for it.

With personal conviction and individual skill, Hermann Buhl set an example for generations of climbers who followed in his footsteps. Despite the acrimonious conclusion to the expedition, he was hailed as a hero in Austria and Germany, as well as in Britain and around the world.

Four years later, in 1957, Buhl stood atop another 8,000-metre summit, completing the first ascent of Broad Peak (8,051 metres) with Kurt Diemberger, Fritz Wintersteller and Marcus Schmuck. A few weeks later, he and Diemberger attempted Chogolisa, also known as Bride Peak (7,668 metres), once again climbing alpine style without supplemental oxygen. During a storm, Buhl fell to his death after an ice cornice collapsed beneath him.

◆

As a twelve-year old boy, Reinhold Messner burst into tears when he heard of Hermann Buhl's death. Buhl was his idol and Messner later co-authored a biography, *Hermann Buhl: Climbing Without Compromise*. Both men were born in the Tyrolean Alps and Messner grew up to challenge Buhl's reputation as the world's greatest mountaineer. Ultimately, he became the first man to summit all fourteen peaks over 8,000 metres and Nanga Parbat was his first 'eight-thousander'. It remains the most important yet contentious summit on Messner's formidable list of ascents. The mountain nearly defeated him and claimed the life of his brother, Günther, but it also cast a stain of controversy over his career. In 1970, Reinhold and Günther were part of a German–Austrian expedition led by the indefatigable Karl Maria Herrligkoffer, who had organized the 1953 expedition and was now fifty-four. Reinhold was twenty-five and Günther twenty-four, two of the youngest climbers in the team. This was their first Himalayan expedition. Neither of the brothers was even born when German climbers were struck down on Nanga Parbat between the two world wars, yet they were fully aware of its knotted and tangled history.

As Reinhold explains in his book, *The Naked Mountain*, he and Günther shared a close bond from childhood, which he traces to a particular moment when he found his younger brother cowering in a dog kennel after having been beaten by their abusive father. As they grew into their teens, climbing became a form of escape, a shared passion that lifted them out of the traumas of early life.

In the summer of 1970, the Messner brothers climbed a new route up the Rupal Face. By the time they reached the top of this forbidding wall, Günther was suffering from altitude sickness. With great difficulty, they continued on to the summit but realized it would be suicidal for them to attempt a descent by the same route. They bivouacked on the upper slopes of the Mazeno Ridge, shouting and signalling for help but received no response from a second summit team and the others below. Because the Messners had no radio, Herrligkoffer had arranged to fire a flare to give them news of the weather forecast. A blue rocket meant good weather and a red rocket indicated an approaching storm. When they saw a red flare rise from below, they believed the weather was turning against them.

This led them to cross over to the Diamir Face on the western flank of the mountain, which they believed might offer a safer descent. As they worked their way down, with no idea of what lay ahead, the Messners got separated and Günther disappeared. Reinhold began to search for his brother, desperately calling out his name, again and again. Finally, he realized that an avalanche must have swept him down onto the glacier. Tormented by grief and guilt, Reinhold finally had to descend the Diamir Face alone, thereby completing the first traverse of Nanga Parbat. As a result of the ordeal he lost seven toes to frostbite and the tips of several fingers.

Soon after the expedition returned to Europe, recriminations began. Messner accused Herrligkoffer of having abandoned them on the mountain and failing to mount a rescue for Günther. The team leader dragged him to court for libel while Messner countersued for manslaughter. Both men had lost a brother on Nanga Parbat but rather than sharing their grief, they attacked each other. Greg Child, an authority on mountaineering, writing in *Outdoor* magazine, described the entire affair as, 'The most extraordinary fight in modern-day climbing history—a blood feud that has spawned more than a dozen lawsuits, countless attacks and counter-attacks.' The controversy festered for years and erupted again in 2002, with the publication of Messner's *The Naked Mountain*, in which he castigated the other members of the expedition for betraying their teammates. Outraged by these accusations, the surviving members of the expedition (Herrligkoffer had died by then), including Hans Saler and Baron Max von Kienlin, finally broke their silence to defend the honour of 'comrades who can no longer defend themselves'. They published books and articles blaming Messner for his brother's death and saying that he had lied about the circumstances of the accident. According to Saler and von Kienlin, Messner had boasted at Base Camp about planning the traverse even before starting up the Rupal Face. They also produced a scribbled confession that Messner had given Herrligkoffer, accepting responsibility for Günther's death. Reinhold had abandoned his brother on the summit ridge, they argued, and recklessly gone down alone, out of blind ambition and a desire for self-glorification.

Since Günther's body had not been located, these counter-accusations could neither be confirmed nor denied. Meanwhile, the battle of words grew as hostile as the storms that batter Nanga Parbat. Added to this were snarled jealousies and bitterness, for Messner had run off with von Kienlin's wife, Ursula Demeter, whom he married in 1972 and later divorced in 1977.

In 1978, still distraught and eager to redeem himself, Messner returned to Nanga Parbat and climbed the mountain once again, in a daring solo ascent up the Diamir Face. Whether this was an extreme act of penance for losing his brother or a futile search for Günther's remains it is difficult to judge. Messner writes about the events in a highly emotional stream-of-consciousness style. In the intervening years he made several attempts to find Günther's body, partly out of filial duty but also to absolve himself. Messner is still judged by many to be the finest climber of all time, though the tragedy of his first encounter with the Himalaya will always cast a shadow over his remarkable accomplishments. Attempting to justify his actions, Messner has written: 'For years I have had to defend myself against all the persecution and accusations that this Nanga Parbat traverse brought in its wake... For the decision to climb down the Diamir Face, I alone bear the responsibility. Whether it was the right decision, or not, nobody can know. Although many have passed judgment, the truth is we had no other choice.'

As Greg Child reports in 2005, thirty-five years after Günther was lost, a group of Pakistani and Spanish climbers came upon the headless, desiccated remains of a mountaineer on the Diamir Glacier. That year, the summer had been unusually warm and the surface had melted, revealing the gruesome remains. This anonymous victim could have been any one of dozens of climbers who had died on the 'killer' mountain. Though most of the corpse had been reduced to bones and shreds of frozen flesh, one of the boots was intact, along with scraps of his clothes. From what the climbers reported, the leather Lowa boots were the same brand the Messners wore in 1970.

Child goes on to recount that Reinhold immediately set out for Pakistan and trekked up onto the glacier, where he identified his brother's remains. DNA samples later confirmed, beyond any reasonable doubt, that the dead climber was Günther. The position of the corpse, allowing for the steady progress of the glacier, validated Reinhold's version of events, though it did not completely silence his accusers.

'Es ist mein Bruder!' Reinhold declared before cremating the remains with Buddhist rituals and constructing a memorial chorten at the base of Nanga Parbat. He also carried back with him the boot that encased his brother's mummified foot and buried it in the Tyrolean Alps, finally laying his anguish to rest.

chapter 42

AN ALPINIST'S DISCONTENT

Unlike other sports, climbing a mountain takes place without an audience. Only after a summiteer returns home is he or she is greeted with applause and, perhaps, cheering crowds. Whatever motives may drive a mountaineer to ascend beyond the limits of life, alpinism is an extreme form of ascetic abnegation. Yet, paradoxically, many mountaineers claim to feel the 'most alive' when they are far above it all. Death may be their constant companion but the exhilaration of testing its limits and achieving survival seems to drive so many to take such risks despite unforgiving odds.

Regardless of its primal appeal, mountaineering is an entirely modern pursuit. Until roughly 200 years ago, nobody thought of climbing a mountain simply to reach the top. Early hunters may have scaled cliffs in search of prey and graziers herded flocks to high pastures but there was no purpose seen in going beyond the snow line, except to cross into another valley. Though sometimes portrayed as a contest between man and nature, mountaineering is more often the struggle of an individual against the physical limitations of the human body and the onerous constraints of society. Climbing is, essentially, a byproduct of the industrial age, not only because the sport depends on steel implements, nylon ropes, synthetic fabrics and bottled oxygen, but also because it is largely driven by a subliminal sense of discontentment. More often than not, those who climb seek to break free of the oppressive conventions and routines of the mechanized, digitized world we have created for ourselves. Mountaineering promises a release from existential malaise through the physicality of climbing and its rejection of social norms and responsibilities. Though often justified as a form of exploration and a quest for knowledge, it is essentially an act of defiance and repudiation of manufactured experiences, from motorized transport to central heating.

Wade Davis in his monumental book, *Into the Silence,* has shown in convincing detail how the early Everest expeditions were a quest for healing and redemption following the horrors of World War I—the first modern Armageddon. As he writes, 'One of the peculiar and unexpected outcomes of peace was the desire of many veterans to go anywhere but home.' The trauma of the trenches and the residual anxiety of bombs, machine guns and poison gas haunted this 'lost generation' and the Himalaya, which were as far away as they could get from mechanized warfare, offered a kind of catharsis for men like Charles Howard-Bury, George Finch, Edward Norton and George Leigh Mallory. All of them were survivors of the 'Great War' and bore the anguish and suffering of industrialized conflict, as if it were shrapnel in their souls. The same held true for German climbers who sought their destiny in the Himalaya.

The British, more than any other people, found a need to explore vertical terrain, first at home and in the Scottish Highlands, then in the Alps and ultimately the Himalaya. Perhaps they were obsessed with mountaineering because they were the first truly industrialized nation on earth, with their furnaces and factories, rail lines, steam engines and iron ships riveted and welded together in the name of progress. It was out of the anonymity of modern society that Kenneth Mason and his compatriots formed the Himalayan Club with its goal of creating 'a solid core of men who have done something'. Whether it was Mummery scrambling about on Nanga Parbat, Shipton and Tilman breaching the Nanda Devi sanctuary, or the counterculture climbers of the seventies and eighties like Doug Scott grappling with the Ogre, British alpinists wandered away from the assembly lines and managerial flow charts of conventional careers in search of some sort of higher purpose.

Excavating our earliest preoccupations with alpine adventure, Robert Macfarlane's *Mountains of the Mind* reaches back into the European imagination of high places, including scientific, romantic and spiritual conceptions of mountainous terrain. Macfarlane also reflects on how the upper reaches of the earth became both a modern problem and an enduring passion. He writes: 'Mountains seem to answer an increasing imaginative need in the West. More and more people are discovering a desire for them, and a powerful solace in them.' Mcfarlane then goes on to say that wild and remote places like the Himalaya remind us, 'that there are environments which do not respond to the flick of a switch or the twist of a dial, and which have their own rhythms and order of existence. Mountains correct this amnesia.'

Following two world wars in the twentieth century, an uneasy sense of disillusionment and alienation with modernity extended across the developed world and found particular resonance in the countries of Eastern Europe ruled by communist regimes. Bernadette McDonald's books on Polish and Yugoslavian mountaineers show how a disenchantment with industrialized development and socialist autocracies led a large number of climbers from Soviet Bloc countries to project their aspirations and ideals onto Himalayan landscapes. In particular, McDonald's descriptions of Polish climbers roping up to earn a living by painting factory smokestacks, in order to save enough money to finance expeditions in Nepal, show how they exploited limited resources and opportunities to realize their dreams. Unlike well-funded climbers from countries like Britain, America or Japan, East European mountaineers had to rely on subversive, entrepreneurial means of support. Because of a shortage of foreign currency, Polish climbers smuggled sausages, Bohemian crystal, chewing gum and alcohol overland to South Asia, in order to garner enough funds once they reached Kathmandu to pay for climbing permits, porters and other expenses. As repressive regimes in Poland and elsewhere began to lose power, McDonald argues that mountaineering was at the forefront of resistance. 'Success in the mountains and the resulting optimism amongst Polish climbers reflected the growing popularity and influence of the Solidarity movement. Nothing seemed impossible as individual citizens rediscovered their potential; Polish climbers were ample proof of that.'

While the history and culture of mountaineering demonstrates how climbers have always rebelled against the dehumanizing conditions of modern society, there is often a personal discontentment too. Psychologically, a mountain can represent many different things, from an overpowering obstacle to a great white hope, but as many mountaineers have observed, inner landscapes offer the greatest challenge. Nature in all its ferocity and benevolence is not only an external phenomenon, separated from the human body and mind, but an integral element of our psyches.

The question continues to be asked: why do mountaineers choose to climb? There are multiple answers, of course, but for many climbers it becomes an addiction. Maria Coffey's *Where the Mountain Casts its Shadow* explores the motives behind mountaineering and the way in which a climber's death can devastate family and friends. She also details the manic-depressive quality of climbing in which the mountain provides a 'high' while returning home often leads to severe depression. Coffey quotes Reinhold Messner: 'Endurance, fear, suffering, cold and the state between survival and death are such strong experiences that we want them again and again. We become addicted. Strangely, we strive to come back safely, and being back, we seek to return, once more, to danger.'

A large part of modern discontentment comes out of our alienation from the natural world. Aside from seeking adventure, many climbers are naturalists too, in the broadest sense of that word. Edward 'Teddy' Norton, who was a member of both the 1922 and 1924 Everest expeditions, and took over as leader in 1924 after General Bruce fell ill, spent most of the long approach march to the Rongbuk Glacier collecting specimens of birds, mammals and plants. He was so diligent in this scientific pursuit that Tibetan lamas strongly objected to his killing of living creatures. Later on, climbing to 8,500 metres, a record height on Everest, Norton carried a paintbox and sketchbook to record the scenery. His watercolours are some of the most beautiful images of the high Himalaya, with a discerning eye for light and texture. Even more remarkable is the fact that the water on his brush and paper kept freezing every time his shadow fell upon the painting.

Published accounts of expeditions almost always acknowledge the environment they pass through, whether it be swarms of midges or flocks of rosefinches, fields of anemones, sentinel pines or circling hawks. Generally, these wild species are observed and commented upon as a flourishing contrast to the lifeless conditions further up the mountain where colourful blossoms and greenery are replaced by black rocks and white snow. At the highest altitudes, nature often becomes an abstraction, sometimes capitalized to suggest an invisible presence greater than ourselves—Nature as a synonym for God.

Despite their hard-bitten rhetoric and single-minded resolve, many mountaineers are philosophers and poets, with a romantic appreciation for nature. In *Alpine Warriors,* Bernadette McDonald quotes Nejc Zaplotnik, whose book *Pot* (The Path) is a cult manifesto of Slovenian mountaineering that describes a mystical connection with high places:

> You are slowly overcome by the eternal restlessness of high mountains,
> by the natural current of life that we have almost forgotten…when

you sense that you were given birth by Mother Earth, that you are just a part of desolate valleys, green meadows, broken glaciers, that you are part of the rushing river and the black, silver-strewn sky. This is when you become aware that these lonely paths keep drawing you back to the highest peaks, where the sky and Earth meet amidst the howling wind.

Of all the British mountaineers, Frank Smythe successfully combined a climbing career with the avocation of a naturalist. Though he trained to be an electrical engineer, Smythe quickly gave it up for a peripatetic life of climbing and writing. On his first Himalayan expedition to Kanchenjunga, he was struck not only by the ethereal splendour of the great mountain they sought but also the semi-tropical abundance of the jungles en route to Base Camp. Later, after summiting Kamet in 1931, Smythe and his party crossed over a high pass and entered the Bhyundar Valley in Garhwal, a place he made famous in his book *The Valley of Flowers*:

> As we descended, the flora became more and more luscious, until we were wading knee deep through an ocean of flowers, ranging in colour from the sky blue of the poppies to the deep wine red of the potentillas. We filled our buttonholes and adorned our hats. A stranger had he seen us might have mistaken us—at a distance—for a bevy of sylphs and nymphs. But had he taken a closer look he would have seen, beneath a canopy of flowers, beards sprouting from countenances browned, scorched and cracked by glacier suns. Nor are tricouni-nailed climbing boots an appropriate footwear for sylphs and nymphs.

The Bhyundar Valley left a lasting impression on Smythe and in 1937 he returned to spend a month amidst its alpine flowers while ascending several nearby summits. His son, Tony Smythe, has written an insightful biography, *My Father, Frank*, in which he recounts the circumstances surrounding this interlude between major expeditions. At home in England, Smythe had become an avid gardener and on two earlier trips to Everest, he had attempted to collect seeds and tubers. After visiting the Botanical Gardens in Edinburgh, Smythe became acquainted with the curators, who encouraged him to bring back seeds and plants from the Himalaya and provided him with the equipment he required. He was driven, in part, by a commercial motive, for there was a ready market for exotic seeds, corms and bulbs. Smythe hoped to defray the costs of his expedition by selling these to horticulturalists.

Despite the lucid transparency of his prose, Frank Smythe was a complicated, conflicted man. During his lifetime, he became a celebrity and his mountaineering books were bestsellers. He was an accomplished photographer too and made a name for himself as a popular fixture on the lecture circuit. The success of his publications—both large format photographic books like *The Mountain Scene* and his accounts of adventure travel, *Kamet Conquered* and *Camp Six*—led to resentment amongst fellow climbers and accusations of opportunism and self-promotion. Not being independently wealthy, Smythe had to hustle to support his family. This entrepreneurial spirit was frowned upon by other members of the Alpine Club, like Tom Longstaff, one of the first Englishmen to explore Garhwal and the Bhyundar Valley. Just as it did in all walks of life, the British class system cast its layered shadows over the mountaineering community. Those who had to make ends meet, through writing and lecturing, were scorned by others who could afford to indulge in the sport because of inherited wealth.

In much of Smythe's writing there is a note of sadness, even when he celebrates the beauty of Himalayan landscapes. As his son and biographer explains, he was a troubled and often unhappy man. Long absences from home took a toll on his first marriage and his wife, Kathleen, raised their three boys mostly on her own, while he was off in the mountains or away on speaking tours. Whenever he did come home, Smythe's mother was a demanding presence who tormented her son and daughter-in-law. His extended ramble in the Bhyundar Valley, seems to have been an escape from domestic tensions and the guilt of neglecting his family. Smythe's third son was born while he was away in Garhwal. Unlike on earlier expeditions, he travelled to the Valley of Flowers without European companions, hiring four Sherpas from Darjeeling to assist him in collecting plants and scaling the surrounding peaks. The solitude of the Bhyundar Valley seems to have given him the space to reflect on his relationships as well as bigger questions that troubled his mind. 'For the first time in my life I was able to think,' he wrote, and later elaborated:

> All about me was the great peacefulness of the hills, a peacefulness so perfect that something within me seemed to strain upwards as though to catch the notes of an immortal harmony... So, we go to seek beauty on a hill, the beauty of a larger freedom, the beauty that lifts us to a high window of our fleshy prison whence we may see a little further over the dry and dusty plains to the blue ranges and eternal snows. So we climb the hills, pitting our strength against difficulty, enduring hardship, discomfort and danger that through a subjugation of body we may perceive beauty and discover a contentment of spirit

beyond all earthly imaginings. And through beauty and contentment we gain peace.

At the end of his time in Garhwal, Smythe was joined by a friend, Peter Oliver, with whom he made two significant ascents, of Nilkantha and Mana peaks. When he returned to England that fall, Smythe's marriage collapsed. The happy sojourn in Garhwal was replaced by external and inner strife and he reached a psychological turning point. In a letter to Sir Francis Younghusband, his mentor at the Royal Geographical Society and the Alpine Club, he complained of a tortured upbringing after his father died when he was two. 'My mother unhappily ought never to have had a child— she is a religionist in the wrathful and vindictive God sense. She possessed me body and soul and I was always struggling against this.' Bullied at school and at home, Smythe grew up within the unyielding embrace of Christian intolerance. 'I had a nurse who used to lock me in a dark cupboard and tell me the devil was coming for me. And then when I grew older I was made to believe that sex was utterly degrading and beastly, a mistake on the part of the Almighty.'

Younghusband himself had struggled with the demons of puritanical Christianity and a caustic marriage but by the time Frank wrote this letter, the grand old man of Himalayan exploration had undergone a mystical transformation and became an advocate of Eastern philosophy and free love. Younghusband's biographer, Patrick French, describes how the great explorer coached visitors on the benefits of sexual liberation. In addition to Smythe, one of his converts was Verrier Elwin who had been severely admonished by Mahatma Gandhi to remain celibate, though after he visited Younghusband the missionary turned folklorist returned to India and promptly married a young tribal woman named Kosi.

It was at Currant Hill, Younghusband's home in Westerham, that Frank Smythe first met Nona Miller, a nurse from New Zealand who was employed as a caregiver for Lady Younghusband. Nona was married to a businessman named Guthrie but that didn't stop her from falling in love with Frank. Subsequently, they travelled together by ship to Bombay in 1938, as Smythe set off for Everest. Nona went on to New Zealand and visited her family, then sailed back to Bombay and the two of them were reunited for the return journey to England.

More than any of his celebrated summits, Smythe's idyll in the Bhyundar Valley seems to have been a watershed in his life as he botanized amidst the moraine of ancient glaciers, colonized by a myriad species of flowering plants. Collecting wild clematis, columbine, larkspur, St. John's wort and balsam, he seems to have experienced a transformative epiphany. As he writes:

> The West assumes its superiority over the East primarily because it is
> further advanced in mechanical matters, but woe betide it should it
> continue to associate mechanisms with spiritual progress. In Garhwal I
> met a true civilization, for I found contentment and happiness. I saw a
> life that is not enslaved by the time-factor, that is not obsessed by the
> idéa that happiness is dependent on money and materials. I had never
> before realized until I camped in the Valley of Flowers how much
> happiness there is in simple living and simple things... Happiness is best
> achieved by adapting ourselves to the standards of our environment.

A large part of Smythe's feelings of contentment came from the company of
the four Sherpas with whom he spent those weeks in Garhwal. 'Such were
my companions—I cannot think of them as porters—and I could scarcely
have wished for better. They contributed generously and in full measure to
the pleasure and success of the happiest holiday of my life.'

In passages like this and many others there is a distinct change from
some of Smythe's earlier writings, when he often expressed patronizing
and racist views. On his first Himalayan expedition to Kanchenjunga, he
parroted the prejudices of tea planters and other British colonials. *Kamet
Conquered* contains derogatory remarks about Indians in general and some
of the porters in particular, despite their sacrifices on the mountain. His
Sherpa Sirdar, Lewa, who accompanied him to the summit nearly died and
was badly frostbitten. Another porter, Kesar Singh from Garhwal, ascended
with the second summit party and instead of wearing boots, he wrapped
his feet in layers of burlap. Though Smythe commended both men for
their loyalty and service, he also put them down as being weak-spirited
and disingenuous. Reading these early books it is hard to forgive Smythe's
opinions, which are offensive by any standards, but a change occurs after
he returns to the Bhyundar Valley in 1937.

Of all the Sherpas who climbed with Smythe, the man he admired
most was Wangdi Norbu. They were together on almost every Himalayan
expedition that Smythe undertook, beginning with Kanchenjunga in 1930.
During that climb, Wangdi fell into a crevasse and was stuck for three hours,
before being rescued. Later, on Everest, in 1933, Wangdi nearly died of
pneumonia but after recovering, he quickly returned to carrying loads up
to the North Col. Hugh Ruttledge, the leader of the expedition, referred
to Wangdi as 'a real "stilt"... Very strong' and Tilman commented in his chit
book that he was, '...a first class man and able to take charge of a party'.

One of the revealing moments in *The Valley of Flowers* is when they first pitched camp. 'Wangdi came to me with a happy grin on his hard face. He swept his arm in a single comprehensive gesture over the birches and across the valley, past the glowing snows of Rataban. "Ramro, sahib!" He was right; it was beautiful.' Later on, Smythe describes how Wangdi often broke into song as they collected flowers or sat around the campfire. He even provides a few bars of musical notation, as well as a translation of the lyrics: 'In immeasurable contentment I sat by the fire.'

Among the many photographs that Smythe took in the Bhyundar Valley, is a group shot of himself and his Sherpa companions. Seated in the middle, with Wangdi and Pasang on his left and the younger Tewang and Norbu on his right, Smythe stares into the camera with a look of calm satisfaction in his eyes. The Sherpas are sober-faced, perhaps out of self-conscious formality, though they all seem at ease. Wangdi's face bears the most serious expression, which his employer described as 'the hardest countenance I have seen', though he goes on to say that it did not reflect his character. Unlike so many other group photographs of expeditions there is no hierarchical pose; the five men are all seated cross-legged on the ground. One can easily imagine Smythe setting up this shot, his camera on a tripod, arranging the men in the viewfinder, then pressing the timer, removing his hat and quickly taking a seat in the middle.

Contentment is a word that gets repeated again and again in *The Valley of Flowers* and it is hard not to imagine that both Smythe and the Sherpas were genuinely enjoying themselves. Though they climbed Rataban and several other unnamed peaks there was none of the slog and tension of a major expedition. The few dangers they confronted posed little risk compared to avalanches and crevasses on Everest or Kamet. Though the privileged separation between 'Ishmay Sahib' as he was called, and the porters remained, there is a sense that Smythe and Wangdi shared a genuine bond of friendship.

Wangdi Norbu was one of the first ten recipients of the Tiger Medal presented by the Himalayan Club to Sherpas who demonstrated exceptional skill and commitment at high altitude. Nandini Purandare and Deepa Balsaver have chronicled his life in an article, 'The Story of Wangdi Norbu'. A veteran of many significant expeditions, starting on Kanchenjunga with Paul Bauer in 1929, he was also on the fateful 1934 Nanga Parbat campaign in which four German mountaineers and six Sherpas died during a storm high up on the mountain.

The pleasurable interlude that Wangdi and the others enjoyed in Garhwal was soon followed by tragedy. Pasang Bhotia, who did the cooking for Smythe and his team, was hired the next year for the 1938 Everest expedition. He suffered a stroke on the North Col. Many of the other team members and porters were prepared to abandon him for he was semi-comatose and partially paralysed. They were also disgusted because he had lost control over his bowels and his clothes were badly soiled. As they departed for Base Camp, one of the porters covered Pasang's face with a cloth as a final gesture but a young Sherpa came to his rescue. As Ang Tharkay writes in his memoir, 'The only thing I could do was to tie his hands and feet together to hoist him on my back…' Finally two other Sherpas agreed to help when they saw Ang Tharkay struggling through deep snow. Pasang was then tethered to a long rope, 'leaving enough slack for the descent. Two of us held the upper end of the rope, and the third slid alongside Pasang until he reached a flat spot, then the other two slid down.' Though they got him to Base Camp and back to Darjeeling, Pasang remained paralysed and died soon afterwards.

A year later, World War II brought a cessation to climbing, and it was a lean time for all the Sherpas. Wangdi continued to work as a porter in Darjeeling and eventually, in 1947, he was hired as Sirdar for the Swiss Garhwal expedition to Kedarnath, led by André Roch. In a horrific accident, Wangdi became entangled in his climbing rope and fell 200 metres down an ice slope. He broke his leg, fractured his skull and gouged his knee with the point of a crampon. After giving him morphine, the other climbers dragged Wangdi to a sheltered crevasse where they left him to go and bring help. However, when the rescue party returned they were unable to find him. Thinking he had been abandoned, tormented by thirst and unwilling to prolong the pain and suffering, Wangdi tried to kill himself with a knife, first stabbing his chest and then cutting his throat. Meanwhile, Tenzing Norgay, who was also on this expedition, raced back up the mountain with two other Sherpas. They found Wangdi covered in blood with his neck slashed. Fortunately, he had not cut a major artery. Soon afterwards, Roch joined Tenzing, along with several other team members, and he describes how, 'We harnessed ourselves to the wounded man like dogs to an Eskimo sled, three of us in front, two at the side for traversing, and four behind to hold him back.' In this way Wangdi was transported down to Base Camp and ultimately survived the ordeal. He was taken to a hospital in Mussoorie for treatment before returning to Darjeeling. Disabled and distraught from the experience, he never climbed again and died in 1952.

Frank Smythe returned to India in 1949 and visited Darjeeling, awaiting permission to climb again in Garhwal. India was now independent and the new government was less forthcoming about issuing mountaineering permits. Smythe had spent the last few years climbing in the Alps and Canadian Rockies but he was closing in on fifty and not as fit as he had been a decade earlier. Following a prolonged separation, Kathleen had reluctantly granted him a divorce so that he and Nona were finally able to marry.

Smythe's last trip to the Himalaya, at the age of forty-eight, ended in tragedy when he fell ill with cerebral malaria, which caused a swelling of the brain, not unlike the cerebral edema brought on by altitude sickness. There is no record of whether he visited his old friend Wangdi Norbu, though the two of them must have met in Darjeeling. He was also reunited with Tenzing Norgay, whom he'd known on the 1938 Everest expedition. In *Tiger of the Snows*, Tenzing recalls Smythe's illness. 'Almost at once…it was clear to people that he was not the same as before—and this was not only a matter of age.' Visiting the studio of M. Sain, an artist in Darjeeling, Smythe forgot his own name when he was asked to sign the guestbook and put down the date as December, though it was the middle of May.

A short while later, when he and Tenzing were walking on Chowrasta, the promenade in Darjeeling, Smythe began behaving strangely and demanded his ice axe. At first Tenzing thought it was a joke. 'But he kept on demanding his ax, very seriously; he thought we were up in the mountains somewhere; and I realized that things were badly wrong with him. Soon after, he was taken to the hospital, and when I visited him there he did not recognize me, but simply lay in his bed with staring eyes, talking about climbs on great mountains.'

When news of Frank's illness reached Nona, she immediately chartered an airplane and flew to India, where she found Smythe disoriented and delusional. They returned to England by air and he was admitted to hospital but the malaria had progressed too far and Frank died a few days later, still hallucinating that he was climbing in the high Himalaya.

For a man who had struggled with discontentment all his life, the mountains were where he found true happiness. On his first visit to Darjeeling, sitting on the lawns of a planter's bungalow at Rangli Rangliot estate, in April 1930, Smythe described his feelings: 'Up there in the evening stillness of the tea gardens I experienced for the first time in my life that subtle feeling of joy and sorrow intermixed which comes to all who are born with the love for mountains, joy for the vision and hope, for the unknown and sorrow in realizing how many adventures there are to seek, and how pitifully short is the life in which to seek them.'

chapter 43

NANDA'S DAUGHTER

Compared to the main highway through Uttarkashi, which is jammed with pilgrim buses and taxis, the inner lanes of this temple town are quiet and clean. A red cow grazes on tufts of grass growing out of cracks in the walls on either side. As Chandraprabha Aitwal leads the way to her home, neighbours greet her respectfully with folded hands. Known to many as 'Didi', elder sister, she is recognized as one of India's most distinguished mountaineers. Though now retired at the age of seventy-seven, Chandraprabha was an instructor at the Nehru Institute of Mountaineering (NIM) in Uttarkashi for several decades. Deputy leader and a member of the successful summit team on the first joint expedition of women and men to Nanda Devi in 1981, she has climbed many of the major peaks in Garhwal, including Kamet, Abi Gamin, Kedar Dome, Rataban and Bhrigupanth.

Passing through a low gateway, Chandraprabha enters her home, which she shares with her nephew and his family. The drawing room is decorated with framed photographs from expeditions, pictures of her posing for the camera with other climbers, wearing alpine gear and glacier glasses or receiving honours from former prime minister Indira Gandhi. Her awards and certificates are also on display, including the Tenzing Norgay Lifetime Achievement Award, an Arjuna Award and a Padma Shri from the Government of India. Within the comfort and security of her home in

Uttarkashi, it is difficult to imagine the remote, extreme conditions of the climbs that earned her these accolades, though Chandraprabha's confident voice and gentle but resolute features convey the strength and endurance that carried her to the top of some of the wildest, most inaccessible places on earth.

'Until the age of thirty, I had no interest in mountaineering,' she says. 'I didn't even know what it was. I had done my degree in physical education and was employed as a teacher at a government girl's school in Dharchula when I was invited to take part in a basic mountaineering course at NIM in 1972.'

Three years earlier, she had been persuaded to submit her name for the course but had almost forgotten about her application. In the end, Chandraprabha enjoyed the experience and excelled at climbing. She went on to complete an advanced course at NIM in 1975 and succeeded in reaching her first major summit, Bandarpunch (6,316 metres), though the training expedition was marred by the death of one of the students who drowned in the Songad River below Base Camp.

Mountaineering came naturally to Chandraprabha for she was born and raised in the borderlands between Nepal, India and Tibet. As a young girl she was used to scrambling over rough, exposed cliffs while herding her family's goats, and carrying heavy loads of firewood or fodder. Though the thin air and steep slopes near her home were something she took for granted at that age, it would never have occurred to her that she might be able to scale the surrounding peaks.

Her memories from childhood are of simple, rustic pleasures despite the hardships of living in the Himalaya. Her family came from the same region and community as the nineteenth century explorer, Pundit Nain Singh Rawat. Chandraprabha's parents belonged to the Byansi Shauka tribe, pastoralists who spent the summers in their high village of Chhangru on the Nepal side of the Kali River and then moved down each year to their winter home in Dharchula, which lies across the river in India.

'In those days, nobody thought about Nepal or India. We didn't even know there was a border and crossed back and forth without thinking,' she says.

Her father, Dorjee Singh Aitwal, used to travel to Tibet, taking his flocks of sheep and goats across the high passes to the trading town of Taklakot on the route to Mount Kailas. He carried grain for barter and brought back salt. Chandraprabha remembers accompanying him on these journeys from Chhangru, walking three days in each direction. She remembers on one of their trips, a goat carrying saddlebags of sattu or barley flour, slipped and fell down the side of the hill. The load burst open in a cloud of flour as the animal died on the rocks below.

The word for migration in the Shauka language is 'kuncha'. Chandraprabha speaks of the rigours of those journeys and the closeness she felt for the animals. 'My parents had more than a hundred sheep and goats, as well as yaks but my elder sister knew all their names,' she recalls. Each animal was identified by its colour, size or temperament and they had a whole vocabulary of commands, whistles and exclamations with which they directed their animals along the trails—'khiyal, khiyal...hyun, hyun...tee, tee!'

'Though our family ate meat, we never slaughtered our own animals. Palle hue janwar ko nahin khaate,' Chandraprabha explains, with a wry smile. 'Besides, the Tibetan goats and sheep always taste better because they eat more salt.'

She makes a clear distinction between Shaukas and Bhotias. 'Our people are not Buddhists. We are Hindus,' she insists, though they speak a Tibeto-Burman dialect and share the same ethnicity as the people of Taklakot.

Like many tribal communities throughout the Himalayan highlands, the Byansi Shaukas inhabit ambiguous terrain where boundaries are not always clearly defined. While a nomadic existence suggests a rootless way of life, the Shaukas are tied to the paths they follow as much as the seasonal settlements they occupy at either end of their journeys. The passage from one elevation to another carries them through a transitional homeland that maps out itinerant identities. The cairns they build, known as kshyatam, are trail markers but these carefully stacked piles of rock also punctuate the Shauka's domain and commemorate their migration.

Chandraprabha has written an autobiography in Hindi, *Pahar ki Pukar,* translated into English as *Mountains Calling.* She writes with nostalgia about the slate-roofed homes of her birthplace Chhangru as well as the paths leading to and from her village. She grew up playing in the central courtyard at Chhangru known as the rauthaton where the elders sat on a circle of wooden benches, sharing stories and news.

One of the chapters in her autobiography describes her father's conservative prejudices though she narrates the incident without bitterness. Chandraprabha writes that when her eldest sister was born Dorjee Aitwal was disappointed for he wanted a son, despite the fact that daughters are considered 'as goddesses incarnate'. After his wife gave birth to a second daughter, he became so depressed he refused to eat for four days. Finally, when Chandraprabha, the third daughter, was born, her father disappeared for a whole week. Though she recalls being told this story by her mother, Padidevi Aitwal, Chandraprabha remembers her father as a loving and generous man.

The fact that there were no sons in the family allowed Chandraprabha more freedom and she was encouraged to attend school and complete her education. She began studying at a primary school in the village of Garbyang. At the age of seven, she walked back and forth, 5 kilometres each way, but then moved to a hostel in Pangu to complete her higher secondary classes. Returning home during the holidays meant long treks but as she writes, 'Walking on foot is a true educator.' Aside from schoolwork, the students in the hostel had to cook their own meals and wash their laundry in a stream nearby. After this, Chandraprabha moved to Nainital where she enrolled in the Government Girl's Inter College. Whenever she returned home, however, she went back to the chores and responsibilities of pastoral life—cutting and carrying fodder, spinning and weaving wool for making the karpanch sacks that the goats carried, taking grain to the watermill for grinding and collecting rasaa, dead leaves and humus to use as mulch and fertilizer.

The tragedies of migrant life gave Chandraprabha the determination and resilience that made her a successful mountaineer. When her eldest sister died in childbirth, Chandraprabha was still studying in class seven at the age of fourteen. After receiving a postcard with the news, she set out on foot alone from Pangu to walk the 70 kilometres to her sister's village. The struggle and sorrow of that journey resonates in her accounts of mountaineering ascents when she felt pangs of loneliness and the overpowering presence of death.

'A person may or may not select a mountain but a mountain selects a person,' she writes of her first climbing experience. 'Words cannot describe the zeal and energy I felt in those days. I would run to help everyone with a happy heart; my shoulders, too, were always full of energy and joy to lift the rucksacks of tired companions.' Even today, when she recalls the sense of accomplishment she experienced atop a mountain she says, 'A feeling of shanti (peace and fulfilment) comes over me.'

As her reputation increased, Chandraprabha was recruited to join international expeditions like the 1976 joint Indo–Japanese women's attempt on Kamet (7,756 metres). Remembering this climb she says, 'Himalayan climbers are better at acclimatization while foreign climbers are better at technical climbing.' After reaching Camp VI at 7,000 metres, they had to turn back from the main summit because of high winds. The next day a group of them, including Chandraprabha, scaled the adjacent summit of Abi Gamin (7,355 metres). On many of these climbs, Chandraprabha was appointed quartermaster, which made her responsible for all the meals and other supplies, including the distribution of cigarettes to climbers and porters. In 1977 Chandraprabha returned to Kamet with an all-Indian 'ladies' expedition and reached the summit.

One of her most memorable climbs was Rataban (6,166 metres), which stands at the head of the Bhyundar Valley in Garhwal. In 1979, Chandraprabha was invited to join an Indo–New Zealand expedition led by Colonel Balwant Sandhu. The natural beauty of the valley left a lasting impression on her. She remembers, in particular, the Brahma Kamal flowers (*Saussurea obvallata*) sometimes called the Himalayan lotus. Though she joined the expedition a week late, because she had to complete an exam for her master's degree in Economics, Chandraprabha caught up with the team as they were setting up Camp 1. Despite the fact that she hadn't fully acclimatized, she was able to be part of the summit team and reached the top of Rataban with two New Zealanders. Chandraprabha admired their skills and cooperative behaviour, in contrast to some of her fellow Indian climbers.

Throughout her autobiography, Chandraprabha is critical of those she feels play politics on expeditions, steal the limelight and quarrel or shirk responsibilities. Asked whether she always speaks her mind, she says, 'Not always, but yes, when something is in my heart I say it. Even with Colonel Sandhu, I would argue with him and voice my opinions.'

On two occasions, Chandraprabha attempted Everest in 1991 and 1993 but she didn't reach the summit, which is one of her lingering regrets. The ascent of Nanda Devi (7,819 metres) was the high point of her climbing career and the greatest challenge she faced. Recounting her experiences on the mountain, she always refers to the peak as Maa Nanda Devi, the maternal goddess who is both dangerous and nurturing. During the three weeks she was above Base Camp, Chandraprabha was sick with stomach cramps and vomitting. Though advised to turn back several times, she struggled to get fit. In the end, on 19 September 1981, Chandraprabha Aitwal, Rekha Sharma and Harshwanti Bisht, became the first women to stand atop Nanda Devi, accompanied by their climbing companions Dorjee Lahtoo, Sonam Paljor and Ratan Singh. The team was fortunate to succeed and even more fortunate to survive. An Indian Army parachute regiment expedition that followed immediately after them suffered multiple casualties.

Mountaineering in India, like so many other sports at the state and national level, has been plagued with cronyism, bureaucracy and corruption.

Military expeditions dominate and civilian alpinists face a tangle of red tape and regulations. Foreign expeditions, which are well funded and accompanied by liaison officers, sometimes include Indian climbers but there is often tension between the better equipped and trained mountaineers from abroad and local climbers who seldom get the support and recognition they deserve.

Despite having stopped climbing more than a decade ago, Chandraprabha is still active in the mountaineering community. She is an honorary life member of the Indian Mountaineering Foundation, attending its annual meetings in Delhi. Chandraprabha's last expedition was in 2010 as the leader of an IMF joint women's and men's attempt on Jaonli (6,632 metres). The climb was unsuccessful because of bad weather but she has been asked by the Nainital Mountaineering Club to lead another team to Jaonli in 2018. Laughing, she says, 'I don't even know if I will make it to Base Camp, but I'm willing to try.'

For a Shauka woman whose life could easily have settled into the predictable and mundane routines of an early marriage, housework, child-rearing and herding livestock, mountaineering provided adventure and escape. Chandraprabha was never content to accept the destiny her parents imagined for her. She approached her education and teaching career with a dream of travelling beyond the fixed routes of Shauka migration. Breaking free of her ancestral journeys, she has travelled throughout India and even to Japan and New Zealand. Connecting with the Himalaya at a higher level, Chandraprabha remains a daughter of the mountains, proud of her roots but equally determined to push beyond conventional thresholds.

VIII

IN A THOUSAND AGES OF THE GODS
Himalayan Mindscapes

chapter 44

REMEMBRANCE AND IMAGINATION

Even when I am away from the mountains, I can still see them in the distance, rising up like waves of light and shadow in my mind, profiled against a pale grey sky, as if at dusk. Receding colours stain their slopes— slate blue where snowfields fold in upon themselves, a blush of pink on glacial ice that quickly fades to ash. Green forests in the valleys turn as dark as exposed cliffs above, each tree converging into shades of black.

An artist friend, Tobit Roche, visits the Himalaya from time to time and does oil sketches en plein air, trekking with his box of paints and collapsible easel packed into a rucksack. Over the years he's done a series of pictures of Nanda Devi from different angles and at different times of day. His wanderings have taken him to Chaukori, Binsar, Kausani, Gwaldam and Auli. Each vantage point provides a unique perspective. In one painting, the twin summits glow at sunset amidst a flurry of purple brushstrokes. Another image frames the mountain within a panorama of surrounding peaks, bleached white by a midday sun. Elsewhere, looking eastward, Nanda Devi stands alone at daybreak, a solitary silhouette.

Returning to his studio in London, Tobit paints the mountains once again, but this time from memory. These are much larger canvases on which he projects a remembered vision of the Himalaya that does not depend on the accuracy of immediate observation. Imagination has often been described as 'imperfect memories' and a dreamlike abstraction emerges in Tobit's mountain mindscapes, range upon range of fretted ridgelines held together by clouds and valleys. Each coat of paint adds another layer of pigment and texture. Rather than the swift, deft lines of his plein air sketches, Tobit's studio paintings evolve slowly, one day at a time, over weeks and months, until they accumulate the polished depth of lacquer so that the light upon the mountains looks like varnished gold.

Another artist, whose watercolour miniatures capture the essence of the Himalaya, is Bireswar Sen (1897–1974). Ameeta and I are fortunate to have a dozen of his paintings on our walls at Oakville. These were collected separately by the two of us, almost fifty years ago, when we were in high school, long before we had any interest in getting married. My parents also bought several of Sen's paintings, which our art teacher, Frank Wesley, sold on behalf of the artist, who was his guru and friend. Most of Sen's paintings are Himalayan mindscapes, slightly larger than a visiting card. We were told that the artist painted one miniature every morning as a form of meditation.

These tiny images are simple yet subtle scenes emerging out of his imagination. An imposing peak is rendered with a single stroke of the brush. Blank areas of the paper suggest clouds and snow. The less he paints the more we see. Almost as an afterthought, the artist includes a delicate tracery of moraine or the shape of a ruined monastery silhouetted against the horizon. Occasionally, human figures stand out like exclamation points in the foreground, pilgrims or mendicants, transfixed by the view. Unlike photographs that trap and filter light through a camera lens, processing it by mechanical and chemical means, Sen's miniatures are keyholes on reality that reveal his appreciation for the totality of nature. Though I have admired and studied these paintings for decades, each time I look at them I keep finding something new within those few square centimetres of paint.

Bireswar Sen wrote an essay titled, 'Essentials of Art' in which he asks the rhetorical question: 'What does a Poet or Artist really see? Is his vision the same as ours, a matter of fact optical impression of the fleeting moment, or something deeper and different?' His paintings provide the answer in luminous, contemplative detail, like mantras of colour. A student of Abanindranath Tagore and Nandalal Bose, Sen taught at the School of Arts and Crafts in Lucknow, where Frank Wesley was his student. In 1932, he met Nicholas Roerich, the Russian artist and émigré, who settled in the mountains of Kullu where he built a Himalayan home and studio. Sen was inspired by the charismatic personality of the expatriate artist whose work was praised by Tolstoy. In addition to his paintings, Roerich designed sets for Russian ballets, including the premiere of Stravinsky's *The Rite of Spring* in 1913. Today his art survives in several collections, a few in his Kullu home, as well as in the Nicholas Roerich Museum in New York City, where his paintings fill several rooms of a gallery in Upper Manhattan.

In later life Roerich created some of his most memorable mindscapes of the Himalaya, many of which are based on allegorical imagery from his own mystical wanderings, which he describes in his travel memoir, *Heart of Asia*. Fascinated by the mythology of Shambala and fuelled by theosophist philosophy, he transformed the mountains into a symbolic realm of ancient wisdom, hidden truths and lost traditions. Even his most realistic paintings, such as the spectacular vision of Kanchenjunga seen from Darjeeling in 1924, rising out of the clouds, contains a metaphysical dimension. Other paintings like 'Arjuna' or 'The Master's Command', his final work of art, completed shortly before his death in 1947, depict mountain landscapes with Hindu and Buddhist figures arranged in bold relief with the vivid colours of a Russian icon.

As Roerich wrote in a letter to his wife Helena, who shared her husband's fascination for spiritual quests:

> Himalaya! Here is the Abode of Rishis. Here resounded the sacred Flute of Krishna. Here thundered the Blessed Gautama Buddha. Here originated all Vedas. Here lived Pandavas. Here—Gesar Khan. Here—Aryavarta. Here is Shambhala. Himalayas—Jewel of India. Himalayas—Treasure of the World. Himalayas—the sacred Symbol of Ascent.

chapter 45

THE HOUSE OF HOURS

On 29 October 2006, the waters of the Bhagirathi began to rise and fill the reservoir of the Tehri Dam, submerging a historic town as well as villages and fields that lay upriver. The huge structure, 260 metres high and roughly a kilometre across, is one of the largest dams in the world. It took more than thirty years to construct. Controversies and protests raged for decades but in the end this giant hydroelectric project was completed, blocking a major tributary of the Ganga.

During the first few weeks, swirling water gradually inundated the bathing ghats and temple complex near Ganesh Prayag, the confluence of the Bhagirathi and Bhilangana rivers. A few weeks later the stalled current washed over the steel girders of the old bridge that once linked Tehri with the motor road between Rishikesh and Gangotri. By the end of November the water level had reached the bus stand and main bazaar. Virtually all the houses and shops were empty, vacated a year ahead of time. Those residents who resisted had been forcibly removed. Anything of value was carried off—doors and windows, hinges, light bulbs, brass faucets, books and ledgers, corrugated metal sheets, calendars that still had a few months to spare, bathroom mirrors and lamp posts sold as scrap.

By the start of the New Year, 2007, the Purana Durbar of the royal palace was finally under water. Built by Sudershan Shah, the Maharaja of Tehri Garhwal, who founded the city as his new capital in 1815, the masonry walls and crumbling grandeur of the palace were swallowed up by the lake, which now extended several kilometres upstream consuming the abandoned villages of Sonadevi, Bhagavatpur, Malideval and Siroin. Had the tunnel been closed during the monsoon, the reservoir would have filled more rapidly but in winter the Bhagirathi drops to its lowest ebb and the water crept slowly, almost imperceptibly, upward.

The final landmark of the town to be submerged was the clock tower, which stood higher than any other structure in Tehri. It was built by Maharaja Kirti Shah to commemorate Queen Victoria's diamond jubilee in 1897. The pale yellow tower, designed in florid colonial style with columned arches and four clocks facing north, south, east and west, had been a symbol of the town for more than a century. As February came and went, only the upper portion of the ghantaghar (the house of hours) stood above the still, green waters of the lake, the last relic of the capital city to defy this man-made flood.

The clocks themselves had been removed, looted in the final rush to dismantle Tehri. Empty circles that once framed their faces looked like vacant eyes keeping watch over the dam with a timeless gaze, until they too were drowned. On 19 March 2007, the surface of the lake finally closed over the clock tower and erased all evidence of the submerged town.

Activists like Sunderlal and Vimla Bahuguna, who protested the dam for years, had been warning about the environmental consequences, as well as the human costs. The Bhagirathi Valley lies in an unstable seismic zone and Garhwal has experienced severe earthquakes in the past. If another occurs, the dam might burst and the water will destroy all settlements downstream, including the holy cities of Rishikesh and Hardwar. Aside from the inundation of several hundred square kilometres of farmland and forest, the ridges on either side have suffered severe erosion and villages far above the high water mark are endangered because of subsidence and landslides.

But the most severe environmental damage caused by the dam is its impact on the river itself. The Bhagirathi remains a lifeline for a variety of aquatic creatures as well as plants, trees, insects, reptiles, birds and mammals that live along its banks. The free movement of the river and its tributaries sustains a diverse community of species. With the creation of the dam, migratory fish like the mahseer have been blocked from moving upstream in the monsoon for their annual spawning. Even as the reservoir extended its reach above the dam, the effects downstream were immediately noticeable. The level of the Ganga now fluctuates significantly, rising and falling two or three metres within the space of several hours, as hydraulic engineers hold back or release the water according to their calculated needs.

Most of the inhabitants of Tehri were resettled in a new town built on a high ridge above the reservoir. Christened 'New Tehri' it boasts a replica of the old clock tower. Instead of the chaotic sprawl of houses that once filled the valley below, anonymous ranks of multi-storey flats are built along the steep contours of the mountain, reshaped by a phalanx of retaining walls. Other residents and farmers from outlying villages have been relocated to vacant forest and agricultural land in the Dehradun Valley near Hardwar.

During the protests leading up to the inundation of Tehri, a number of posters appeared on walls around the doomed town. Many of these were poems expressing sadness, anger, frustration and disbelief. Some of the verses were by well-known writers and others by ordinary people who felt a need to put their feelings into words. The majority were written in Hindi but many in Garhwali too. Hemchandra Saklani, a writer and editor, collected these posters and, in 2006, he published an anthology titled *Doobti Tehri ki Aakhri Kavitain* (Submerged Tehri: The Last Poems). Sunderlal Bahuguna contributed a foreword for the book in which he writes: 'The grief and pain has made the poets weep. Their tears were not shed in vain for they will provide a historical perspective to a new generation and other generations to come by leaving a clear, unequivocal message.'

A remarkable collection of sixty-five poems full of nostalgia and sorrow, the anthology is also an archival document and a literary memorial to a lost town.

A tribute to memory and metaphor, the book is much more than just voices of protest. It is a reflection on loss and evokes the sense of a place that no longer exists. While many of the poets employed familiar clichés of 'watery graves', 'floods of tears' and 'drowned hopes', others made references to ancient myths like the story of King Bhagirath, after whom the river is named. His extreme austerities and penance persuaded the goddess Ganga to descend from heaven. Now, the poets wondered whether the sacred river might retreat back into the clouds. The names of ascetic saints like Swami Ram Tirtha and martyrs like Sridev Suman were invoked, echoing the sacrifices of Tehri's people, who gave up everything for their nation's progress. Among the more subtle poets, Mangalesh Dabral tells the story of Gunanand Pathak, a Marxist folk singer who used to perform on the streets of Tehri, singing to the accompaniment of his harmonium and distributing revolutionary tracts and pamphlets. At the end of his life, unappreciated and ignored, Gunanand abandons his music. Dabral uses the simile of a forgotten folk song to suggest that like Gunanand's verses, even the town of Tehri will eventually fade from memory.

Narendra Singh Negi, one of Uttarakhand's most popular balladeers, wrote a plaintive lament about the dam, with lyrics such as, 'Let the eyes of aged people close so they may die in peace/ before they witness the devastation caused by the dam.' There was cynicism too, in Rajan Todariya's lines, 'The jackals cry at night/ In the day the intellectuals offer condolences.' He also wrote a poem titled 'The Benefits of Drowning' in which bureaucrats, 'dancing to the melody of coins', justify the dam.

Most of the verses echo a repeated refrain of sadness and loss. In Surendra Pundeer's 'A Town', he lists what will vanish, including the familiar profile of the clock tower, 'the dome of the royal durbar,' temple bells, kirtan from the gurudwara and the call to prayer from the mosque. Like several other poets in the anthology, Pundeer celebrates Tehri's famous singori, a popular sweet made of khoya (evaporated milk and sugar) wrapped in a bauhinia leaf cone. He also reminisces about Badho ki Magri, a well-known eating place, serving fish and rice, near the confluence of the Bhagirathi and Bhilangana. Each of these memories, repeated in multiple poems, elicits a nostalgic response from anyone who ever lived in Tehri or passed through its streets. But the most powerful poem in the collection is also one of the simplest because it distils memory into metaphor in an effortless few lines that capture the sense of helplessness the townspeople felt. The poem is titled, 'An Effort' by Navendu, the pen name for an unknown poet displaced by the dam.

> Lying in the current of the river
> I am a stone.
> My intention
> is not to stop
> the river from flowing.
> I am only trying
> to stop myself
> from floating away.

chapter 46

PARADISE DIVIDED

My father was born in Kashmir, where my grandparents spent their summers escaping the heat of the plains. Every year, Emmet and Martha Alter would camp with their four sons in Nasim Bagh, beneath the chinar trees of Srinagar, or on meadows above Pahalgam. For my father, Kashmir represented idyllic memories of his childhood that drew him back, not only because it was his birthplace but out of a sense of irretrievable loss.

Writing to her parents in Mansfield, Ohio, during the Great Depression, my grandmother exclaimed over the charms of Pahalgam:

> Our camp here is in a beautiful pine grove high above the river. Wood is lying around in such abundance that we have a huge bonfire every night. To be so rich in any one thing is quite a novel and not altogether unpleasant experience... How I wish that you all could be here with us in this beautiful spot. The scenery is wild and grand with the mountains all about us—the nearer ones covered with pines, the higher lined with glaciers.

I first visited Kashmir at the age of fourteen. Driving from Mussoorie, three days' journey by road, our family crossed the sunburnt plains of the Punjab to Jammu in an old Willys Jeep that my father had bought as 'army disposal', then wound our way up into the Pir Panjal. The old route to Srinagar that my grandparents used to take was now closed because of the border with Pakistan. Passing through the Banihal Tunnel, we got our first view of the green mosaic of the Kashmir valley with its orchards and lush fields, waterways and floating gardens. After a few days in a houseboat in Srinagar, we moved on up to Pahalgam, where we camped for a couple of weeks, just as my father had done when he was a boy. We ate cherry pie made from fresh-picked fruit, an all American dessert baked in a portable oven over a kerosene stove.

I could see that my father was reliving his childhood, revelling in his early memories of Kashmir. He had not been back for almost thirty years. Until then, I had never thought of my father as a romantic but Kashmir brought out another side of his personality. My mother was the poet in our family while Dad was practical and pragmatic, good at fixing jeeps. The trip to Kashmir was a family reunion. My Uncle Jim and Aunt Barry were with us too, and our cousins, John and Tom. My brothers, Joe, Andy, and I rode ponies and fished for trout in the Lidder River, surrounded by the picture postcard scenery of Kashmir, alpine meadows and snow-creased ridges.

During that summer, we took a trek up the valley to the Kolahoi Glacier. Along the way, I remember passing flocks of sheep and goats heading to higher pastures. We camped near the snout of the glacier, where the Lidder narrowed into a thin trickle, flowing out of ice. At the head of the valley we could see Kolahoi peak, an impressive spire of rock and snow, burnished by the setting sun.

Sitting around our campfire that night, we listened as Dad told us how my grandfather and his brother, my great uncle Joe, attempted to climb Kolahoi peak. This was in 1927, the year after my father was born. Of course, he had no memory of the event though the story was part of our family lore. Emmet and Joseph Alter were missionaries not mountaineers but they had been inspired to try and climb Kolahoi after reading accounts of the first ascent in 1912 by Dr Ernest Neve, a British surgeon who lived in Kashmir. Setting off from the family camp in Aru, above Pahalgam, my grandfather and his brother hoped to conquer the summit, carrying crampons, ice axes and ropes. Somewhere high up on those slopes that stood in the moonlight before us, great uncle Joe slipped on the rocks and gashed his palm and leg. A short while later my grandfather fell headfirst into a crevasse. Fortunately, the heels of his boots were within reach and his brother was able to haul him to safety.

Emmet was conscious but dazed and his scalp had split open. Somehow the two injured men got back down off the glacier, though both of them lost a fair amount of blood. The next day they walked 20 kilometers to reach the camp in Aru, where my grandmother rushed out of the tent to see her husband staggering towards her covered in blood. 'They were a gory sight when they came in,' she wrote. No doctor was stationed in Pahalgam and these were the days before penicillin. Fortunately, a veterinarian happened to be visiting the area and he stitched my grandfather's scalp back together and dosed him with enough sulfa drugs to cure a horse.

Summers in Kashmir continued to be a family tradition. My grandmother painted watercolours of Dal Lake and wild flowers that grew on the meadows. We still have many of those paintings, as well as some of the carpets and Kashmiri artifacts they collected over the years. Their last visit to Kashmir was in 1938, after which they moved to Mussoorie where my grandfather became principal of Woodstock School. In 1943, my father graduated from Woodstock and left India for college in America, but he was miserably homesick for the mountains.

After getting his bachelor's degree in 1947, Dad returned to India, just as Independence arrived and the British were leaving. Partition had occurred and my grandparents were back in Rawalpindi, which was now part of Pakistan. They witnessed the riots and killings that accompanied one of the largest mass migrations in history. As a foreigner, my father was able to move back and forth across the new border. In December 1947, he volunteered with the American Friends Service Committee (AFSC), who were doing relief work among Kashmiri refugees. The situation was still volatile. In his diary, my father recalls Pathan raiders being trucked through Rawalpindi to fight in Kashmir, 'whole convoys of them armed to the teeth with bandoliers and rifles, shooting their guns in the air in a wild show of exuberance. At night, we could hear their guns all over the city, going off like an irregular barrage of fireworks. Even power lines went down and lights went out, when trigger-happy Pathans shot, as targets, the porcelain insulators on lamp posts.'

AFSC had learned of a group of 3,000 Hindu and Sikh refugees trapped inside the area of Kashmir controlled by Pakistan. They hoped to persuade the newly appointed Pakistan authorities to allow them to be exchanged for Muslims on the other side. Much of the work involved chasing down government officials and politicians to try and broker their release. Lines of authority were ambiguous and chaos prevailed in the region. My father was particularly useful to AFSC because he spoke Urdu but as he writes: 'I have taken to playing dumb, that is I don't use any Urdu and I let it pass that I don't understand it, and as a result have heard things that weren't meant for my ears.'

Eventually, they were permitted to visit the refugee camp in a gurudwara at Ali Beg, along the road to Srinagar. The AFSC team arrived at night and entered through the main gate, carrying flashlights. '…I still picture in my mind,' my father recalled, 'a mass of bodies sprawled and packed on the floor with an opening here and there for an open fire. The smell of wood smoke and human bodies saturated the warm air with a nauseating potency. Most of them had been asleep and a few of the men stood up and greeted us but were asked to sit again by the guards.'

Back in Mirpur, the district headquarters, they met the deputy commissioner and tried to persuade him of their plan. He seemed sympathetic but insisted that he wanted to exchange the refugees for 500 'abducted girls,' who he claimed were being held on the Indian side. Discouraged but hoping to use this as leverage, Dad travelled down to Lahore and borrowed an old Jeep from an American missionary, driving across the border and heading up to Pathankot and Jammu to meet AFSC colleagues in India, who were in contact with a group of 300 Muslims in Jammu 'desiring evacuation.' But on the Indian side there was a strong sense of denial and the Home Minister of Kashmir insisted, 'We have no Muslim refugees on our side that we can exchange.'

Returning to Pakistan, they met one of the newly appointed cabinet ministers, Mr Sunna Ullah. 'The poor man must have worked himself into an emotional frenzy at least three times while we were there, and repeated the performance when we met him the next afternoon,' my father recounts. 'What would start him off would be the slightest intimation on our part that there might not be as many Muslims wanting to be evacuated from Jammu as he believed, and he would start on a long spree about their wives, children, virgins, men, boys, community leaders, and so on, who were being held brutally by the Dogra monsters.'

Eventually, after months of wrangling, an exchange took place but the experience left my father with a sense of disillusionment about motives on either side. The Kashmir he had known as a boy, a Himalayan paradise, was now a combat zone, with a UN ceasefire line established in 1948. This eventually became known as the Line of Actual Control (LAC), though neither India nor Pakistan has ever accepted it as a legitimate border. Part of my father's nostalgia for Kashmir came out of this sense of loss, the division of land and violent reprisals that continue until today. In 2009, two years before his death, he began writing about Partition and Kashmir. To spark his memory, he found his old diary, 'recorded in a small, green, hard-backed notebook I bought in a stationer's shop in Rawalpindi. It remained untouched, hidden in desks and office drawers, for over sixty years.'

In the midst of detailed accounts of negotiations with officials and the journeys back and forth between Pakistan and India, there are moments where my father, as a twenty-one-year-old, lapses into lyrical descriptions of the mountains.

> Soon after leaving Amritsar, on the way to Pathankot, we saw what we first thought were clouds but as we went on we realized they were snow-topped ridges. All afternoon we seemed to creep up on them with a sensation much the same as when you approach land at sea. First they were only faint white clouds low on the horizon. They then crystallized into a definite hazy outline. As we grew closer they rose higher and the outline grew sharper, and broad shadows outlined nearer ridges and valleys... As we travelled along, the sun set and the last rays slid up the wall and lingered for a moment on the snow, before it disappeared. The wall changed rapidly from a pale white to blue and finally to gray which seeped into black and all we could see was what came in the way of our head lamps, and we could only smell the pines and firs that were around us, and hear the streams we crossed.

chapter 47

UNSPINNING THE YARN

Separating fable from fact in Himalayan narratives can be a challenge, as
fraught with uncertainty as crossing a snow-covered glacier full of hidden
crevasses. But in a curious way, the lore and legends of these high places
tend to erase whatever lines exist between truth and fiction, memory and
imagination, or even dictatorial proof and egalitarian invention. Science can
sometimes be as enigmatic as poetry, while lyric verses often contain more
clear-sighted observations than rational interpolation. There is probably no
better example of the ambiguous intersection of reality and perception or
logic and make-believe, than various quests for the 'Abominable Snowman'.

Toward the end of their stay in the Valley of Flowers, Frank Smythe
and Wangdi Norbu set off to reconnoitre a route to Nilgiri Parbat. While
crossing a high pass into a parallel valley, they came upon a set of footprints
in the snow. Freshly made and not yet melted by the sun, the tracks appeared
to be impressions of exceptionally large, unshod human feet.

Wangdi immediately insisted that these were the prints of a 'Ban Manshi'
or 'Mirka', as he called it. Trying to make Smythe understand, he also
used a combination of Tibetan and Hindustani, calling it a 'Kang Admi'
or snow-mountain man.

Sceptical but intrigued, Smythe drew outlines of the prints on pages
of a *Spectator* magazine he was carrying in his rucksack and took several

photographs. The Sherpas, whom he described as terrified, claimed that these were tracks of a ferocious beast that fed on yaks and men. According to the lore of Solu-Khumbu, the creature's toes pointed backward. When Smythe insisted on trying to discover where it had come from, Wangdi refused to accompany him, saying that they would be walking into a trap. According to Sherpa beliefs, simply setting eyes on a Mirka caused death and for that reason no man alive had ever seen one.

Going on alone, Smythe followed the spoor in the snow to a small cave beyond which the tracks disappeared into the rocks. To the relief of Wangdi, the sahib returned safely and then followed the tracks in the opposite direction until they descended a steep rock face 300 metres to the glacier below. Using a monocular, Smythe traced the route.

> I was much impressed by the difficulties overcome and the intelligence displayed in overcoming them. In order to descend the face, the beast had made a series of intricate traverses and had zig-zagged down a series of ridges and gullies. His track down the glacier was masterly, and from our perch I could see every detail and how cunningly he had avoided concealed snow covered crevasses. An expert mountaineer could not have made a better route and to have accomplished it without an ice-axe would have been both difficult and dangerous, whilst the unroped descent of a crevassed snow-covered glacier must be accounted as unjustifiable. Obviously the 'Snowman' was well qualified for membership of the Himalayan Club.

Later, when his photographs were developed, Smythe sent copies to the Zoological Society and Natural History Museum in London, where scientists reached a consensus that these were the prints of a brown bear, *Ursus arctos* (uncertainty remained over which subspecies—*isabellinus* or *pruinosus*). The fact that the tracks seemed to have been made by a biped was explained through a less-than-convincing theory that the bear's hind feet were placed directly on the prints of the forefeet. The resulting irregularities supposedly led to the Sherpa belief that this creature walked with its feet pointing backward.

None of this, of course, would have reassured Wangdi and the others who were convinced that they had found evidence of a superhuman carnivore, half-beast and half-man. According to their legends, the Mirka was covered with fur, varying in colour from white to brown or black. The female of this strange species was slightly smaller and had 'exceptionally large pendulous breasts, which she must perforce sling over her shoulders when walking or running.'

Stories like this from different parts of the Himalaya have generated widespread fascination for the 'Yeti', another Sherpa name for the creature. When Smythe published an article in *The Times* detailing his observations and emphasizing that it must have been a bear, the story provoked an eager, excited response from English readers, some of whom insisted that an expedition should be mounted immediately by the Royal Geographical Society to track down this exotic and mysterious beast.

While there is no empirical evidence to support belief in the Yeti, it is equally impossible to completely discount or disprove its existence, simply because it hasn't been found. Whatever our convictions, most of us want to believe in something as yet undiscovered. Smythe, himself, admitted tongue-in-cheek, that he hoped his rational conclusions might be disproved. 'In this murky age of materialism,' he wrote, 'human beings have to struggle to find the romantic, and what could be more romantic than an Abominable Snowman, together with an Abominable Snow-woman, and, not least of all, an Abominable Snow-baby?'

Even with the cold and critical gaze of modern science upon us, our human imagination conjures up a host of unknown creatures that embody our deepest fears. Mythology is full of monsters that are composites of ourselves and other animals, just as we imagine there may be angels and heroic giants, born of men and gods. This represents a core anxiety of our species, that somehow we can cross-breed with other life forms, either demonic or divine. In the Himalaya, where life exists on the edge, these fears and fantasies become acutely amplified.

More than 150 kilometres to the east of Solu-Khumbu, in Sikkim, the Lepcha people tell stories similar to Sherpa accounts of the Yeti, though they call their creature Jyamphi Moong. Folklorist Lyangsong Tamsang describes a fierce monster with long hair and feet turned backward. The Lepchas believe that these beasts live near the snow line and communicate through whistles. Males and females live alone for most of the year except during the mating season when they seek each other's company.

Once upon a time, a shepherd named Atek, who was camped in the high mountains with his flock of goats and sheep, picked up his flute at dusk and began to play 'a haunting melancholy tune'. Soon, he was alarmed to see a female Jyamphi Moong emerge out of the shadows. Though the creature looked ferocious, she was obviously attracted to the music and Atek continued playing as she listened. Whenever he set aside his flute, the Jyamphi

Moong immediately picked it up and put the instrument to his lips again so that he was forced to play all night. Only in the morning, when the sun rose, did the creature disappear. Night after night, the monster returned, insisting that Atek play his flute until dawn. Exhausted and desperate, the shepherd finally came up with a plan. The next night, when the Jyamphi Moong arrived, she found Atek standing by a blazing bonfire, slathering his body with butter. As he began to play his flute, the creature imitated him by rubbing butter all over herself, until her hair was sleek and glossy. Atek then drew a burning log from the fire and pretended to warm himself. The hairy beast did the same but, in a flash, her well-greased fur caught fire. Enveloped in flames, she ran away into the snow-covered mountains, never to return. Because of this story, Lepchas believe it is bad luck to play a flute or even whistle after dark.

Stories of fearsome and fabulous creatures that inhabit the Himalaya have percolated down through the centuries, beginning with accounts of early Hellenic explorers. Pliny's *Historia Naturalis* contains a passage that quotes Megasthenes, Alexander the Great's ambassador, who travelled through India around 300 BCE.

> According to Megasthenes, on a mountain called Nulo there live men whose feet are turned backward, and who have eight toes on each foot; while on many of the mountains there live a race of men who have heads like those of dogs, who are clothed with skins of wild beasts and whose speech is barking, and who, being armed with claws, live by hunting and fowling.

Much later, as Victorian England struggled to come to terms with Darwin's *On the Origin of Species,* the search for a 'missing link' began and rumours of shaggy primates haunting the Himalaya surfaced in accounts of explorers like Major L. A. Waddell, a British army doctor and big-game hunter who found 'hominoid-like footprints' high on a glacier. As Daniel Taylor, in his book *Yeti: The Ecology of a Mystery* writes, 'New truths were being articulated about relationships with nature. "New peoples" were being brought to the "civilized" world. Fantastic postulates of the hypothesized were being proven. Indeed, science fiction was gaining respectability as a literary form.'

More recent legends and lore of the Yeti are entwined with tales of Himalayan mountaineering, thanks in large part to Frank Smythe but also two other British climbers who dominated this sport between the world wars. Eric Shipton and Bill Tilman were the most successful climbing duo of their generation and both men were exceptional writers. Their books, along with Smythe's, form the canon of alpine literature from what is often referred to as 'the golden age of Himalayan mountaineering'. Each of these men, and the Sherpas who accompanied them, accomplished remarkable feats from the ascent of Kamet and Nanda Devi to a reconnaissance of Everest, as well as extended high altitude exploration ranging across the Himalaya. But it was the tales they told and the manner in which they recounted their exploits that made these adventures compelling and memorable.

Every storyteller, from a campfire raconteur to a Nobel Prize-winning novelist, knows how to use suspense, embellishment, humour and felicitous language to capture the imagination of his or her audience. Jim Perrin, in his double-barrelled biography, *Shipton & Tilman: The Great Decade of Himalayan Exploration*, uses the myth of the Yeti to illustrate how his two protagonists exchanged winks, nudged ribs and pulled legs within the mountaineering establishment, even as they carved out their own formidable reputations. Like Smythe, they heard stories from Sherpas, particularly Sen Tenzing, a former lama who was a colourful character with a mischievous sense of humour. Tilman gave him the nickname 'The Foreign Sportsman' on account of his eccentric wardrobe that included a waistcoat and knee socks. At the same time, Sen Tenzing and the other porters called Tilman 'Bhalu' (the bear) because of his facial hair and compact yet rugged physique.

After Smythe's account of the Yeti appeared in *The Times* in 1937, along with a protracted and animated response in letters from its readers, Shipton and Tilman began to spin this Himalayan yarn into a long-standing joke that continued over the next fifteen years. Though most of the humour went into abeyance during World War II, the Yeti story surfaced again most prominently in Shipton's 1951 reconnaissance of the southern approaches to Everest during which he photographed a set of footprints that were captioned:

> Footprint of the 'Yeti' found on a glacier of the Menlung basin. In general the tracks were distorted and obviously enlarged by melting; but where, as in this case, the snow overlying the glacier was thin, the imprint was very well preserved and the form of the foot could be seen in detail. When the tracks crossed a crevasse we could see clearly how the creature, in jumping across, had dug its toes in to prevent itself slipping back.

Perrin sifts through the various accounts of Abominable Snowmen, which Tilman in mock-naturalist style spoofed in a 1955 piece in the *Alpine Journal*, titled 'Himalayan Apery', predicting the future discovery of a giant 'anthropoid' in the Himalaya. In a fictitious letter to *The Times*, Tilman even quotes 'the Foreign Sportsman' and pokes fun at Smythe as well as others who stalked the Yeti.

In Perrin's book the final word is given to Sir Edmund Hillary, who was part of the 1951 Everest expedition. Later on, Hillary himself used Yeti folklore to help raise funds for expeditions and took the famous Khumjung scalp to America, where, as we've seen, it was identified as a scrap of serow hide. Nevertheless, when asked about Shipton's photographs, Hillary set the record straight in a 1984 interview with Perrin:

> What you've got to understand is that Eric (Shipton) was a joker. He was forever pulling practical jokes, fooling around in his quiet way. This footprint, see, he's gone round it with his knuckles, shaping the toe, pressed in the middle. There's no animal that could walk with a foot like that! He made it up, and of course he was with Sen Tenzing who was as big a joker as Eric was. They pulled the trick, and Mike Ward had to keep quiet and go along with it. We all knew, apart from Bill Murray maybe, but none of us could say, and Eric let it run and run. He just loved to wind people up that way.

This light-hearted hoax inspired numerous other stories as well as expeditions in search of the snowman. The most persistent and well-organized Yeti-hunter was a Texas millionaire named Tom Slick, who travelled to Nepal three years in succession from 1957 to 1959. Slick focused on the Arun Valley south-east of Everest. '(His) first expedition found three sets of Yeti footprints, hair, and excrement,' Daniel Taylor writes. 'The second used blue tick bloodhounds, trained in Arizona on mountain lions and bears…this second expedition found another set of Yeti tracks and visited four remote monasteries to study two Yeti scalps and a mummified Yeti hand.' Though Slick predicted a 'major discovery' his third expedition ended inconclusively and the Texan died soon afterwards in an air crash. The craze to find the Abominable Snowman prompted the Nepal government to impose regulations and royalties on Yeti hunting. Taylor, himself, has mounted several expeditions in the remote Barun Valley but most of the evidence still points to bears, even as the elusive, enigmatic Yeti continues to prowl our Himalayan imaginations.

◆

Another element of mountain lore that gained currency during the 1930s goes back to Shackleton's epic struggle for survival in Antarctica between

1914–17. The apparition of a 'third man' is a guiding spirit or benevolent presence that appears in times of extreme stress, loneliness and danger. This 'guardian angel,' as it is sometimes called, is the antithesis of the Abominable Snowman. Rather than being a grotesque man-eater it is a gentle, comforting companion that emerges from the climber's mind to help resolve a crisis.

John Geiger's *The Third Man Factor* is the most comprehensive analysis of this phenomenon, which many mountaineers have described. Once again, Frank Smythe and Eric Shipton play an important part in the story, with a famous incident on Everest in 1938. This was one of the few times they climbed together, the year after Smythe's visit to the Valley of Flowers. Ultimately, the expedition, which also included Tilman, was unsuccessful and a declaration of war soon afterwards postponed British ambitions on Everest.

After being trapped in a storm at Camp VI, above the North Col, Shipton and Smythe set off for the summit as soon as the weather cleared, though both of them were in poor condition. In his account, Smythe notes that they should have been hospitalized rather than scrambling about above 8,000 metres. Nevertheless, they struggled upward, aware that they were following in the fatal footsteps of Mallory and Irvine. Shipton eventually collapsed and could go no further. Smythe, however, carried on and continued up to within 300 metres of the summit, higher than any other man had climbed. As he ascended through the death zone, Smythe became aware of an enigmatic presence on the mountain. 'All the time I was climbing alone I had a strong feeling that I was accompanied by a second person. This feeling was so strong that it completely eliminated all loneliness I might otherwise have felt. It even seemed that I was tied to my "companion" by a rope, and that if I slipped "he" would hold me.' Reaching the limits of endurance and realizing that Everest lay beyond his grasp, Smythe sat down to rest on a rocky ledge. He later recalled, 'When I reached the ledge I felt I ought to eat something in order to keep up my strength. All I had brought with me was a slab of Kendal Mint Cake. This I took out of my pocket and, carefully dividing it into two halves, turned round with one half in my hand to offer to my "companion".'

Conscious of the sensational speculation this paranormal experience would generate, Smythe was reluctant to reveal what happened, though the leader of the expedition, Hugh Ruttledge, encouraged him to include the incident in his published account. Shipton, who dragged himself back to camp, makes no mention of a 'third man' though he had earlier experienced a similar encounter while climbing with Tilman on Mount Kenya. Unlike stories of the Yeti, this phenomenon is confined to the experiences of foreign climbers and there don't seem to be any reports of Sherpas encountering a 'third man'.

Again, the instincts of a storyteller, writing up an account of recent adventures in the comfort of a cabin on the sea voyage home would allow for some poetic licence. But unlike the Yeti, for which we demand some sort of 'proof', the third man phenomenon is a semi-mystical experience that cannot be corroborated through scientific evidence. Nevertheless, a convincing number of other climbers from Hermann Buhl to Stephen Venables, have reported identical experiences and emotions. While frantically searching for his lost brother on Nanga Parbat, Reinhold Messner was acutely aware of a 'third man's' presence, assisting him in this desperate quest.

In 1994, Steve Swenson, a respected mountaineer from Seattle and former president of the American Alpine Club, had a strangely similar experience on the same route on Everest as Smythe. Leaving an exhausted climbing partner at Camp VI, Swenson set off on his own for the summit, which he successfully climbed without supplemental oxygen. In Swenson's account he recalls, 'Alone in this intensely beautiful and potentially dangerous place, I talked to myself to support the life and death decisions I was making.' But later, on his return to Camp VI, he began hallucinating: 'The head of an elderly Asian woman appeared just over my left shoulder, and in a slow, gentle voice she gave me step-by-step instructions on how to start the stove, fill the pot with snow, and brew a cup of tea.' The next morning, after the woman helped him stay awake throughout the night, 'I looked up and noticed the head of a Sikh man floating off to the left in front of me. He had a full beard and wore a light blue turban. With a heavy Indian accent he greeted me in a loud and cheery voice: "Good morning, sir! It is time to start moving."'

Whether it is oxygen deprivation or fatigue and fear that lead to these persistent illusions, some believe that we are not alone in the mountains. Explanations like this tend to patch together physiological and psychological theories but provide no definitive answers. Yet, questioning the authenticity of either the third man or the Abominable Snowman is like trying to interpret a dream. Searching for a being that doesn't exist may seem a futile exercise but, at the same time, in the process of hunting for a chimera we can discover so much else.

Himalayan lore, for the most part, comes out of an oral tradition in which a raconteur tells the tale again and again, amidst a circle of friends or strangers. In this way, stories migrate just like birds or people, trees or insects, following shared itineraries, to be heard in different contexts, embellished here and there, refashioned and restructured according to the circumstances under which they are told. The truth rests as much in the imagination of the listener as it does in the storyteller's voice. Whether it is myth or science, we speak to each other through metaphors, which are the bedrock of language. Just as a mountain is made up of different layers of rock so is a folk tale or legend that celebrates or interprets a wild creature, or hints at supernatural companions. The words and phrases rest upon each other like tiers of slate, granite, limestone and other strata that shift over time. As much as stories, poetry too relies on disassembled facts and distilled dreams.

T. S. Eliot's hymn to modernity, *The Wasteland,* contains multiple references to Hindu and Buddhist texts as well as a passage inspired by the 'third man', possibly a ghost or a figment of postwar delirium. Published in 1922, on the eve of the first Everest expedition, Eliot's verses refer to Shackleton's Antarctic ordeal but could just as easily speak of the Himalaya.

> Who is the third who walks always beside you?
> When I count, there are only you and I together
> But when I look ahead up the white road
> There is always another one walking beside you.

chapter 48

BLOOD HARVEST

Kathmandu is a mandala of streets and squares, narrow lanes and gullies marked out by temples and shrines to one deity or another. This urban landscape incorporates Himalayan cosmology, laid out like a mystical diagram of hidden realms—both natural and supernatural. As a modern yet ancient city, Kathmandu is far removed from the high mountains of Nepal, though in the minds of its residents the Himalaya remain a constant presence within its sacred precincts. Today, my guide is Vishnu, a middle-aged Hindu from the lowlands of Nepal, with a bored but accommodating manner. He would rather be at home with his family, celebrating the ninth day of Dashain, which is the most important festival on Kathmandu's religious calendar. Instead, he has agreed to show me a buffalo sacrifice.

As we walk through Thamel, the city's tourist quarter, shortly after 8 a.m., the souvenir shops and restaurants are closed, but plenty of residents are out on the streets. The Newar merchants of Kathmandu, who own most of the property in Thamel and have conducted trade across the Himalaya for generations, operate businesses on the ground floor and live in apartments upstairs. Hundreds of Newar women in red saris with gilded borders and streaks of vermilion in the parting of their hair, are carrying small bowls made of dry leaves, containing offerings of nine different grains—barley, corn, wheat, millet, buckwheat, rice, black lentils, etc., as well as sliced fruit and flowers.

At this hour of the morning most people are moving about on foot, though an occasional car or motorcycle noses through the procession of supplicants. When we arrive at a busy crossroads, Vishnu points out a three-tiered temple with a pagoda-style roof, dedicated to Annapurna Devi, the goddess of plenty. The word 'anna' translates as grain or cereal and 'purna' means fulfilment. Dashain begins with a ritual planting of seeds on the first night of the new moon. These grains sprout during the course of the celebrations and the fresh green shoots are offered to the goddess to ensure fertility. Dashain is essentially the same as Dussehra or Navratri, which is celebrated throughout the Hindu world and takes on regional variations such as Durga Puja in Bengal. In North India, Dussehra is mostly connected to the re-enactment of the Ramayana, or Ramlila performances, but in Nepal, Dashain is a celebration of Shakti, or divine feminine power.

The offering of nine different seeds is associated with nine manifestations of the goddess, Vishnu explains. During Dashain they germinate together and become Mahakali, the supreme goddess, who is often depicted with ten heads and ten arms, each of which bear her weapons and ritual implements. In contrast to the nurturing, maternal deities like Annapurna, Mahakali is the violent, bloodthirsty form of Shakti, a dangerous, all-powerful goddess who demands sacrifices of her devotees. Often depicted with her bloodied tongue hanging out and garlanded with a necklace of severed human heads she crushes the buffalo demon beneath her feet. Dashain commemorates the final victory of the goddess over Mahishasura, the embodiment of evil who takes the form of a rampaging buffalo.

Turning down a side street to avoid the crowds, we pass a row of dental clinics. Though all the shopfronts are shuttered, lines of false teeth with bright pink gums grin at us from display windows. At the corner of a secluded square, with cobwebs of electric wires and telephone cables overhead, Vishnu pauses at a small shrine that protrudes onto the street from a brick wall. Hundreds of coins have been hammered into its surface, like dusty armour plating. Twisted nails and dented rupees overlap in an uneven pattern of scales. The bulbous shape of the shrine is hardly recognizable but Vishnu tells me it is a ram's head and points out the curling wrought-iron horns.

'If somebody has a toothache,' he says, 'they nail a coin here, and it helps ease the pain.' Of course, if that doesn't work, any of a dozen dentists nearby will obligingly extract the rotten molar.

Beyond this shrine to pain, we come upon gouts of blood coagulating on the flagstones, where an animal has recently been killed. A sprinkling of marigold and rose petals decorates the gore. Vishnu explains that on the ninth day of Dashain, some people perform a 'panchbali', sacrificing five different animals—a buffalo, goat, ram, rooster and drake. Ahead of us, men are carrying live ducks for sale, holding four or five of them together upside down by their webbed feet, as the birds' necks twist and turn pathetically. Most of these vendors have come from Bihar in India, especially for Dashain. The atmosphere in the streets is like a country fair. Hawkers are selling flowers and vermilion powder, as well as balloons and cheap plastic toys. Families greet each other and children run about with excitement. Yet, the bright colours and joyous celebrations are tempered by the spectacle of death. While everyone seems to be going about his or her rituals with joyous devotion, the bloodletting is happening all around us.

Entering Durbar Square, we come face to face with the dark stone idol of Kal Bhairava, freshly painted in gaudy enamel hues. He stands alone, without a sheltering temple, exposed to the October sun. Bhairava is associated with the violent, destructive aspects of Lord Shiva but some scholars suggest he is originally a Tibetan deity, exported across the Himalaya. The large statue in Durbar Square is similar to fierce Jambala figures or sentinel deities, with snarling features and bulging eyes, that stand guard at Buddhist shrines. In one hand Bhairava brandishes a large sword while the crown on his head is decorated with skulls. Like the goddess Mahakali, he is a destroyer of demons who demands sacrifices in return. A throng of devotees press in upon each other, offering prayers and penance to Kal Bhairava. Supplicants have brought black goats as offerings. One man thrusts his animal forward, into an alcove to the right of the idol, where a ready executioner, arms and legs bathed in blood, promptly severs its head with a kukri. The decapitated body struggles for a moment in the devotee's grasp and then goes limp, pumping blood into a stone trough at Kal Bhairava's feet. The ritual is repeated every few minutes as more goats are led forward and killed.

Blood sacrifice is the most extreme expression of religious zeal and devotion. It is also the antithesis of compassion and in this brutal ritual we can see how our own species asserts dominance over other forms of life through a conscious act of violence. Both the person who makes the offering and the priests who prescribe it, conceive of the animal's death as a necessary propitiation of divine entities for whom we, as human beings, are as expendable as a goat. By ending another creature's life we recognize our own mortality, while myth and metaphor create surrounding narratives, tranforming the sacrifice into a theatrical performance that slakes our thirst for tragedy. Both the participants and the audience share in this cruel paradox, a ritual demanded by gods in order to fulfil our human desires. As Barry Lopez has written in *Arctic Dreams*, 'No culture has yet solved the dilemma each has faced with the growth of a conscious mind: how to live a moral and compassionate existence when one is fully aware of the blood, the horror inherent in all life, when one finds darkness not only in one's own culture but within oneself.'

Beyond the Kal Bhairava shrine, dozens of buffaloes are being herded through a narrow lane into a gateway of the Hanuman Dhoka Palace. When I begin to follow them, an armed soldier at the entrance turns me back with a threatening gesture. Though there was a time when the mass sacrifice of these animals was open to public viewing and Kathmandu's fire department would have to hose down Durbar Square to wash away the blood, protests by animal rights activists and other reformers have now forced the army to keep most of the slaughter out of sight. Seeing the dusty procession of docile animals disappearing into the inner courtyard of the palace I can imagine the slate-lined gutters of Hanuman Dokha overflowing with blood just as they did in 1846, after fifty-five courtiers were killed in a massacre instigated by the Regent Queen Rajaylakshmi Shah.

For the past three centuries, under both the Shah dynasty and the Rana regime, succession to power in Nepal occurred almost exclusively through fratricide even though the king was considered an incarnation of Vishnu and ruled by divine right. Nepal has often been described as a peaceable kingdom and compared to Shangri La in tourist brochures, though the country has a violent, caste-ridden heritage of feudal politics. The final blood-soaked chapter occured in 2001 after crown prince Dipendra gunned down seven members of his family, including his parents, King Birendra and Queen Aishwarya. Though Dipendra shot himself in the head he survived on life support long enough to be crowned a comatose king. After his death, desperate efforts were made to resuscitate the Shah dynasty by placing Birendra's unpopular brother, Gyanendra, on the throne, but the slaughter of the royal family, combined with an ongoing Maoist insurgency, brought Nepal's monarchy to an end and erased any illusions about Shangri La.

Today, on the ninth day of Dashain, the primary focus of devotion is the Taleju Bhawani temple, located in Durbar Square, next to the Hanuman Dhoka Palace. Taleju Bhawani is the personal deity of the royal families of Nepal, going back to the Malla rulers who built this multi-tiered sanctuary for their goddess in the sixteenth century. Once a year, the temple is thrown open to the public. An orderly queue of penitents stretches out into the square and around one side of the temple, which rises several storeys above, with encircling balconies. In 2015, this historic structure was damaged by an earthquake and metal scaffolding has been erected to keep it from collapsing under the weight of the crowds.

Several historic buildings in Durbar Square were completely destroyed in the earthquake, including the ancient Kasthamandap pavilion, which gave Kathmandu its name. Believed to have been made out of timber from a single sal tree, this wooden structure was originally a shelter and rest house for pilgrims and other travellers. According to my guide, Vishnu, when the earthquake struck, on a Saturday morning in April, a charitable blood drive was underway inside Kasthamandap and a large number of donors were killed. When the victims were dug out of the rubble some of them still had intravenous needles in their arms.

Virtually all the heritage buildings in Durbar Square were damaged by the earthquake (which measured 7.9 on the Richter Scale), including the famous 'hippie temple' that stood beside the Kasthamandap, where global nomads in the 1970s gathered to share chillums of hashish on the front steps. The grandiose, colonial style Gaddi Baithak, an audience hall built by the Ranas, is still intact but has huge cracks in the walls.

Across the way stands the temple of the living goddess, which survived the earthquake, though wooden supports, wedged under ornate rafters, have been installed to shore up this structure. Kumari Devi, the resident deity, is a pre-pubescent Newar girl, who is worshipped as a virginal goddess. She resides in the temple for several years until she begins menstruating, after which the living goddess is replaced by another, younger virgin. Her sacred residence is made of bricks and intricately carved wood, with a narrow doorway that opens onto an inner courtyard, where the Devi occasionally makes an appearance in one of the upstairs windows. Vishnu explains that only a few days ago a new Kumari was installed, at the beginning of the Dashain festival. Her predecessor had reached an age when her attendants and priests noticed, 'certain physical changes, so it was decided that the Kumari should be replaced before she shed blood'.

In conservative Hindu tradition, a menstruating woman is often isolated and considered polluted, though the blood from her womb is symbolic of fertility. The significance of animal sacrifices in Nepal and other parts of the Himalaya can be linked to the uterine blood of the goddess. Through myth and metaphor, menstruation arouses sexual awe and anxiety amongst the male population who dominate religious and public life but recognize the monthly cycle of a woman's body as the wellspring of creation.

Suddenly, a volley of gunfire echoes through Durbar Square, as if a firing squad were carrying out an execution. Vishnu quickly escorts me across to the far side of the Kumari Devi temple. Here in the open, a regimental sacrifice is underway, performed by Nepali army officers and soldiers. Immediately behind the virgin's sanctuary, a temporary shrine has been erected, at the centre of which is a tall pole draped with flags and topped with tassels of fresh green leaves. Piled at the base are offerings of fruit and vegetables as well as pots of sprouted grain. Lined up in front of the flagpole are the severed heads of four black goats and a buffalo, their sightless eyes gazing at the crowd of spectators. After making sure that I have a clear view, Vishnu excuses himself with a pained expression, saying that he prefers not to watch the beheadings. Being from the lowlands of the Terai, he finds the violent rituals of his highland compatriots distasteful and disturbing.

Though the Rig Veda and other early Brahmanic scriptures celebrate the idea of sacrifice, contemporary Hinduism throughout most of South Asia, rejects the killing of animals, as do Buddhists, Jains and Sikhs. In the Himalaya, however, particularly Nepal, animal sacrifice remains an important part of Hindu rituals. Though frowned upon by urbanized plains-dwellers, the beheading of goats, sheep and buffaloes is more than just a religious rite. It could be argued that sacrifice is a convenient means of culling male animals, increasing the efficiency and manageability of a herd. Only one or two males are required to inseminate a much larger number of females, who produce offspring and milk. For Himalayan pastoralists it becomes a practical, cost-effective equation in which religious practice justifies the elimination of male livestock, satisfying both spiritual and economic demands.

A Brahmin priest in scarlet vestments directs the commanding officer, as they conduct a brief puja. Both men are seated on the ground, which is paved with bricks. Instead of wearing his military uniform, the officer is dressed in traditional Nepali attire, known as daura suruwal, a grey wraparound tunic tied at the shoulder and waist, with matching leggings and a Dhaka topi, or conical hat with a dent at the centre. Both the officer and the priest are barefoot. So are two Gurkha soldiers assigned to carry out the sacrifice. They are wearing white T-shirts and gym shorts. Surrounding them is a ceremonial honour guard of Gurkhas in camouflage and campaign hats, with automatic rifles in their hands. A broad smear of blood encircles the open shrine, where the carcasses of the sacrificed animals have been dragged before being placed discreetly in one corner of the square, under a white tarpaulin that shields them from flies and the curious stares of onlookers. Later, a military vehicle will take the dead animals away to be butchered and cooked for a regimental feast.

A live goat and buffalo stand calmly nearby, waiting their turn. As incense is lit and prayers are offered, one of the two soldiers picks up a large kukri and examines its sharp steel blade. The goat is then led forward but becomes uncooperative, butting its captors, until one of them placates it with a handful of straw. As the priest and commanding officer get to their feet, another soldier grabs the animal by its horns, lowering its neck. At the last moment, however, the goat buys itself a brief reprieve by urinating on the bricks. Everyone stands still and watches as a stream of urine flows out from between its splayed legs. Then, as soon as the goat has relieved itself, the kukri descends with a swift, chopping motion and the animal's head comes away in the soldier's hands, while its body falls to the ground. At the same moment, the riflemen fire into the air. Blood flows over the dusty bricks and mixes with the goat's urine, as the carcass is dragged around the shrine and then stowed beneath the tarpaulin.

Moments later, the second man in gym shorts takes up his position and hefts an even larger kukri, with a broader, heavier blade, nearly a metre long. He looks anxiously over his shoulder for a moment and then composes himself, concentrating on the task at hand. To lop off the head of a male buffalo in a single stroke cannot be easy, even for a Gurkha soldier. In preparation for this ritual, a green petha gourd, the size and shape of a rugby ball, is chosen from the heap of fruit and vegetables. It is placed on a wadding of fresh leaves and the soldier neatly chops it in half, revealing the white flesh of the gourd. One of his companions quickly steps forward and smears the sliced face of the gourd with vermilion powder, symbolic of blood.

Wiping the blade of his kukri with a fresh leaf, the Gurkha now turns his attention towards the buffalo, which has been brought forward into the sacrificial square. A large log, wrapped with rope, is positioned between its forelegs and under its throat, so that the blade of the kukri will not strike the bricks after cutting through the animal's neck. The young buffalo has grown increasingly nervous, even more so than the goat and seems to know its end is near. For a minute or two, the soldiers make reassuring noises and one of them scratches the buffalo's back trying to calm it down. From their gestures it is obvious that these men have grown up with animals, tending buffaloes and goats in their villages. Though they are gentle with the animals their impassive faces express neither pity nor remorse. By now, the crowd has grown and the team of riflemen reload their weapons.

The buffalo is anything but demonic, with short, stubby horns and an anxious look in its eyes. The broad snout and nostrils give it a sullen, stupid appearance. Its ill-fitting hide is a dull black colour, stretched taut over the prominent bones of its hips and shoulders but sagging along its flanks. Compared to the few wild buffaloes that still roam Nepal's Koshi Tappu Wildlife Reserve or sanctuaries in Bhutan and Assam, this is a tame and sedentary creature. The nape of the animal's neck has a scruff of hair, which also grows in patches on the back of its legs and under its belly. The limp tail hangs between its hindquarters like a frayed length of rope.

The sucking sound of the kukri, chopping off the buffalo's head, is like a valve opening and air entering a vacuum. Instantly, the rifles crackle and I hear the heavy thump of the animal falling to the ground. All this happens within a couple of seconds and there is no reaction from the crowd. We stand transfixed by the banal violence of the moment, as if it were an everyday occurrence. Whatever suspense there was is over now. The steel blade has sliced through skin, muscle, veins, fat, tendon and bone, cutting the invisible thread between life and death. The blood that sprays from the arteries is darker than vermilion, spattering the white gym shorts with flecks of red. Two other soldiers take hold of the carcass by its hooves and drag it around the shrine while a third places the severed head neatly in line with the others. One of the celebrants blows into a conch and the regimental band strikes up a martial tune. As the ceremonies end, one of the buffalo's hind legs is still kicking under the tarpaulin, nerves twitching in a futile reflex of escape.

chapter 49

THE OWLET'S CURSE

In *Biophilia*, a treatise on our affinity to other forms of life, E. O. Wilson writes: 'We are essentially what we remember, or can remember at some time in the future.' As he goes on to explain, the human mind accumulates memories—visual images, stories, bird calls, the cold current of a river flowing between our legs, the bitter taste of walnut bark, the fragrances of different flowers—and we link these disparate fragments to whatever we already know, and go on connecting them to new pieces of information absorbed throughout a lifetime. In this way, Wilson compares our minds to the accretions of a coral reef anchored to the seabed that is constantly expanding and building upon itself.

Here in the Himalaya we might, instead, compare our memories, both personal and collective, to a glacier that contains a myriad crystals of ice and rock, minerals and moisture that have been carried down off the mountain, as well as the remains of frozen creatures, the bones of a bear that fell into a crevasse or an equally unfortunate mountaineer. Unlike coral reefs, of course, glaciers are not alive though they move forward inexorably and this momentum serves as an appropriate analogy of science or art furthering our understanding of the world.

As Wilson emphasizes, the process by which we assimilate meaning—including language, reason and ethics—is constructed entirely out of metaphors like the coral reef or the glacier. On a basic cognitive level, we constantly compare and contrast our voluminous store of recollections in order to define and classify knowledge by creating patterns of association. Linnaean taxonomy, which attaches Latin names to biological species, is actually a chain of metaphors that assembles and organizes our understanding of the natural world. For example, ammonites, the extinct molluscs whose fossils are found in the Himalaya, take their name from the Egyptian god Ammon, symbolized by a ram's horn, which reflects the curled shape of the ammonite's shell. As often happens, when we cannot comprehend an object, sensation or idea, we search for something similar that creates a sympathetic resonance in our brain. Metaphors lie at the core of subjective reality and our quest for truth. Many scientists and artists spend their entire careers in pursuit of the ideal metaphor with which to illuminate a particular problem or discovery.

'The innovator searches for comparisons that no one else has made,' Wilson explains. 'He scrambles to tighten his extension by argument, example, and experiment. Important science is not just any similarity glimpsed for the first time. It offers analogies that map the gateways of unexplored terrain.' In this way, the accumulation of human memories or knowledge becomes both an ethical and a biological imperative. Metaphors organize the synaptic impulses in our brains but also illuminate our souls.

Being one of the most eminent Darwinists of our time, E. O. Wilson raises the essential question of whether the motives behind scientific inquiry and environmental conservation could be a result of our genetic makeup operating through the innate logic of natural selection. He argues that preserving our species as well as others and maintaining the diversity of life on our planet is both a moral and a genetic choice.

An evolutionary scientist's definition of compassion would probably differ from that of a Buddhist teacher. Yet, Wilson's words sound very much like the message of conservation contained in the Dalai Lama's 'Policy of Kindness'.

> Just as we should cultivate more gentle and peaceful relations with our fellow human beings, we should also extend that same kind of attitude toward the natural environment. Morally speaking, we should be concerned for our whole environment. This, however, is not just a question of morality or ethics, but a question of our own survival.

◆

Metaphors have consequences, not just for sacrificial buffaloes but for all living creatures and plants, as well as rivers, rocks and mountains too. Whether we are willing to admit it or not—and despite the Dalai Lama's compassionate pronouncement—an inherent conflict exists between most religious narratives and natural history. The symbols, rituals, beliefs and social norms of different faiths that have evolved over time, as human beings settled into a sedentary, systematic way of life, are, at heart, a means of denying and repressing our wild origins. Being the dominant species on this planet and placing ourselves at the centre of a web of man-made meaning, we have consciously and unconsciously separated ourselves from the wilderness out of which our ancestors emerged. Nevertheless, from time to time, most of us still experience an inexplicable longing for the lost memories and mysteries of our primal habitat.

The impulsive urge to observe, recall, document, classify and preserve the earth's threatened biomes is a strategy of survival but also the cry of a lost creature separated from its past. Despite our exile from the wilderness, many of us seek out the remnants of a natural world untouched by man's intrusive achievements. Yet, to our inevitable dismay and discontentment, every Eden evokes a history that excludes us.

Being a naturalist is a rational pursuit, even if it sometimes verges on mysticism. Instead of placing our confidence and convictions in the intelligent designs of an immortal creator, we attempt to track down the forgotten and forsworn connections between all forms of life, celebrating nature's near-infinite diversity as well as our own finite existence. A naturalist's compassion comes not from a god-given sense of morality and ethics or the teachings of philosophers and saints but out of an innate appreciation for our kinship with other species, both a genetic and an existential bond. Awareness of this 'oneness of being' leads us outside the boundaries of conventional religion, beyond the pale of sanctified culture and society.

◆

One morning, a few weeks before the festival of Diwali, I woke up to hear a commotion in the tree outside my bedroom window. When I went to investigate, I found a collared owlet being mobbed by a whistling thrush and two yellow-breasted greenfinches. The birds were agitated because owlets often raid nests to prey on hatchlings as well as fully-fledged adults. A collared owlet's four-note whistle—toot-to-toot-toot—elicits an instinctual response from other birds that immediately come forward to chase away this feathered predator. Coincidently, birdwatchers have discovered that by imitating an owlet's call, they are able to lure elusive species out of hiding to be more easily identified and observed. Bob Fleming Jr., who initiated me into the pleasures of ornithology, first showed me this trick when we were trying to spot a couple of birds in a thicket of indigo bushes. Because of the dense foliage it was impossible to tell what species they were but the minute Bob mimicked an owlet's call, a whiskered yuhina and a bar-throated minla emerged from cover, ready to pick a fight.

Collared owlets (*Glaucidium brodiei*), also called pygmy owlets, are crepuscular hunters, most active at dawn and dusk. No more than 15 centimetres tall, their brown plumage has a barred pattern like the rough weave on a tweed jacket that complements a professorial gaze. In the west, owls are considered wise while in India they are thought of as foolish and bad luck. Unfortunately, human associations and superstitions have fatal implications for collared owlets. In the weeks leading up to Diwali, villagers near Mussoorie catch different species of owls and surreptitiously sell them for sacrifice. In Hindu mythology, owls are the sacred vehicle, or vahana, of Lakshmi, the goddess of wealth, who is worshipped on Diwali. By killing an owl, some devotees believe they can ensure that the goddess, and any prosperity she bestows, remains in their home. A second version of the myth recounts that Lakshmi has an inauspicious twin sister, Alakshmi, who takes the form of an owl and deprives us of riches. By killing these birds, a small, misguided minority of ardent believers is convinced that they can hold onto their wealth.

From its perch in the tree, the collared owlet looked down at me accusingly as if I were responsible for this cruel and unjust curse. While the story of a goddess borne aloft on the wings of an owl may have an innocent, beguiling quality, it has been perverted from an allegory of benevolence into a tale of greed. In this way, natural history is often misinterpreted and distorted, through myths and fables that reach back thousands of years. As these stories are retold and re-enacted, the relationship between human beings and other species often becomes increasingly divisive and fraught with sanctified antipathies.

Forty kilometres from Mussoorie, near the historic village of Jagatgram, the Yamuna flows out of the Himalaya. On the eastern bank of the river lies the site of an Ashwamedha yagna, or horse sacrifice, by which the rulers of ancient India established their dominion over the land. Releasing a stallion and allowing it to wander at will, a king named Silavarman, who ruled during the third century CE, claimed all the territory his unsaddled steed traversed. Remains of brick altars where the horse was ultimately slaughtered and grilled are preserved by the Archeological Survey of India, amidst mango and litchi orchards, which have replaced the original jungles and grasslands that once grew here.

Across the river, less than 5 kilometres to the west, stands the Ashokan edict at Kalsi carved on the face of a granite boulder. In Brahmi script the Mauryan emperor, also known as Devanampiya Piyadasi (He who loves all beings), proclaimed the Buddhist doctrine of non-violence and forbade the killing of animals. This edict was inscribed in 250 BCE and also includes the carving of an elephant. The antiquity and proximity of these two sites with their contradictory messages represents a long-standing tension between ritual sacrifice and compassion.

◆

The prevailing idea that the Himalaya represent a sacred landscape may seem an appealing vision of environmental and spiritual harmony. Unfortunately, by investing mountains with mythical significance and scattering their slopes with religious symbols and stories, human beings have set in motion a cycle of ecological destruction. Natural phenomena like hot springs, caves or unusual rock formations, as well as the sources and confluences of rivers, become popular pilgrimage destinations that are often cluttered with rest houses, food stalls and parking lots, obscuring the beauty and isolation of these sites.

Religious tourism is one of the fastest growing and least regulated industries in the Himalaya. The circumambulation of Mount Kailas in Tibet is the most sacred itinerary for Buddhist and Hindu pilgrims but much of the route is littered with rubbish—discarded juice packets, biscuit wrappers, aerosol tins, sanitary pads, cigarette butts and plastic Pepsi bottles. Remote shrines at the headwaters of the Ganga attract countless busloads of devotees from the plains. These pilgrims pay obeisance to highland gods and goddesses who embody ideals of purity, beauty and immortality. Mountains and rivers are revered and worshipped as maternal deities yet the same streams of holy water are defiled with untreated sewage from 'Vedic Resorts' while many temple towns along the Ganga are no better than garbage dumps. Poorly constructed, multi-storey hotels with sanctimonious names encroach along the riverside in defiance of regulations governing 'eco-sensitive zones'. Himalayan vistas that once inspired the faithful to give up material pursuits are now hidden behind garish hoardings announcing the chauvinistic discourses of self-aggrandizing holy men, while the eternal silence of the Himalaya echoes with digitized hymns set to a Bollywood beat.

Piety and pollution seem to go hand in hand while godliness has become inherently grubby. Pilgrims who travel to the mountains, along with those who enable these spiritual journeys, believe that Himalayan destinations will cleanse their sins. In return, the mountains receive nothing but offerings of filth. This depressing litany of devastation is the direct result of religious metaphors projected onto the landscape. It also reflects human indifference, wastefulness and greed as well as the wilful exploitation of nature's generous yet limited bounty. Bad planning, poor management and a lack of spiritual and political integrity have depleted natural resources and reduced many areas of the mountains to a desperate, untenable state.

Of course, religion alone is not responsible for environmental degradation. Science and technology are also to blame by having generated fables of eternal growth and progress. These justify the construction of giant dams and contribute to the design and manufacture of engines that burn carbon fuels and expel pollutants into the atmosphere, increasing greenhouse gases that hasten the melting of glaciers. Just as organized religion fosters a mythology that justifies the violation of nature so do the narratives of science often lead from discovery to desecration.

◆

Metaphors reshape our consciousness, often to the point of confounding our sense of identity and place. One of the consequences of modernity is a pervasive sense of geographical uncertainty. The world seems to be shrinking even as it appears to be falling apart. As each of us is cut loose from a secure knowledge of where we belong, something as definitive as the location and physical presence of mountains can be transposed through stories and symbols, leaving us wondering where we came from and where we are going. The great Hindu epics contain accounts of Hanuman, the simian deity, uprooting a Himalayan peak and carrying it through the air. Similarly, the demon king Ravana persuades Lord Shiva to let him remove Mount Kailas from Tibet and transport it to Lanka, though his plan is forestalled by other gods. These ancient auguries of displacement seem ominously close to the global realities of our twentieth and twenty-first century world.

Just over fifty years ago, in a tragic episode of Himalayan irony, an Air India Boeing 707 named 'Kanchenjunga' descending towards Geneva en route to New York, crashed into Mont Blanc on 26 January 1966. Fifteen years earlier, at virtually the same spot, another Air India plane, 'The Malabar Princess', also collided with the Alps. There were no survivors in either crash. The aircraft, 'Kanchenjunga', was carrying India's renowned nuclear scientist, Homi Bhabha, along with a cargo of rhesus macaques that Bill Aitken, in his book *The Nanda Devi Affair*, tells us were destined for vivisection in American laboratories.

Wreckage from the crash of Air India Flight 101 was strewn across glaciers. Even today, half a century later, fragments of the doomed jet, as well as human body parts, are still emerging out of the ice. The untimely death of Homi Bhabha, a distinguished physicist who initiated India's nuclear programme, generated paranoid Cold War conspiracy theories though it seems the cause of the accident was a combination of faulty instruments and miscommunication between the pilots and air traffic controllers in Geneva. In all this, perhaps the most perplexing element were the rhesus macaques that must have been captured somewhere in northern India, possibly in the foothills of the Himalaya, to be airfreighted halfway around the world for lab experiments. Like the collared owlet that is killed to keep the goddess from flying away, these monkeys, if they had survived, would have been sacrificed at the altar of science.

On the other side of the Swiss Alps, less than a hundred kilometres from the crash site on Mont Blanc, lies the historic village of Gruyères, famous for its cheeses. The medieval town also contains one of the most beautiful museums of Himalayan art. Housed in the thirteenth century Chapel of St. Joseph, this treasure house of Tibetan iconography is displayed within a desanctified church where Tara, the green goddess, occupies a niche instead of a Madonna. The silver chalice for serving holy sacrament has been replaced by a cup made from a human skull. Tantric symbols like sacred thunderbolts and copulating deities are juxtaposed against crucifixes and stained glass windows depicting images of Christ and his apostles. The objects in this museum were acquired by a Swiss property developer named Alain Bordier, whose foundation set up the museum to display his personal collection. The recorded chanting of Tibetan monks reverberates inside the sanctuary and in the sepulchral shadows of the main gallery the exiled deities seem almost at home.

As a Himalayan mindscape the Tibet Museum in Gruyères invokes a haunting sense of dislocation. All these objects seem to have arrived here by accident yet each of them has a story and their significance extends beyond the carefully labelled names and identities of gods and goddesses. Both Christianity and Buddhism are obsessed with suffering and this is a tale of violence and absolution. A horned Garuda figure—the sacred raptor—made of gold and inlaid with turquoise spreads his wings while holding a snake in his beak. The seated image of Padmasambhava is carved out of a rhinoceros horn. Buddha Sakyamuni peacefully meditates inside the unfolding petals of a lotus across from another statue that depicts Mahavajrabhairava, the protector of religion, with the head of a ferocious-looking yak and garlands of decapitated human skulls. Also on display are several Phurba daggers, sometimes called kilas, which are symbolic instruments of sacrifice with which we seek to eliminate the evil in our souls.

chapter 50

LOST IN THE WILD

Coming down off the high meadows we take a wrong turn, cutting into a side valley and descending a steep, wooded ridge. There is no path though Bir Bahadur, our guide, claims this is a route he used three years ago. Well before we reach the bottom it is obvious that the main valley lies further west. Heavily forested slopes converge in a narrow gorge. Along the lower end of the opposite ridge is a near-vertical cliff with overhanging rocks. Upstream lies the debris of a flash flood, huge boulders and uprooted trees tossed one upon the other. Downstream, where a clear spring-fed current spills over a ledge and collects in a series of shallow pools, we make our way cautiously to the lip of a waterfall that drops a hundred metres or more into a leafy chasm below. Even if we had ropes and the right equipment, it wouldn't make sense to try and go on.

Climbing back up through a tangle of trees, clutching at the roots of rhododendrons and moss-covered rocks, it takes us more than an hour to regain the top of the ridge. Casting about for any sign of a path, we finally locate indistinct traces of an unused trail that seems to zigzag down the slope. Without acknowledging his mistake, Bir Bahadur agrees that this might be the best way to reach the streambed of the Assi Ganga. Our trek is supposed to take us from Dayara Bugiyal to Dodital and over the Darwa Pass, traversing from the Bhagirathi into the Yamuna Valley. An

established route lies higher up, clearly marked on our maps, though at
this time of year sections of that path are blocked by snow. Lower down
is a mule track to the village of Agora but that means circling around an
extra 15 kilometres and then facing a much longer climb, which we want
to avoid. So, once again, we begin to scramble down an overgrown ridge,
hoping that this time we'll be able to find our way to the valley floor
and up the other side.

Earlier in the morning, we stopped at a Gujjar camp on the crest of
a meadow, where nomadic herdsmen have brought their buffaloes to graze.
An elderly Gujjar with an embroidered cap and hennaed beard offered
us buttermilk to drink and chatted for a while. He spoke about how
last year's floods along the Assi Ganga had washed away sections of their
traditional migration routes and how they had to cut new trails for their
buffaloes this spring. Gujjar is a generic term for herdsmen in northern
India but here in Uttarakhand the name identifies a unique community of
Muslim nomads who migrate from the lowland forests of the Shivalik Hills
to bugiyal meadows, 3,000 metres higher up, beneath the snow peaks of
Garhwal. Their journeys, in spring and autumn, take two or three weeks
in either direction and are synchronized to the seasons. Often called Van
Gujjars, or forest herders, they trace their ancestry to Kashmir. According
to tribal lore, the Gujjars came to Uttarakhand many centuries ago, at the
invitation of local rulers whom they supplied with milk and butter. Though
Gujjars have been using forest resources in the Himalaya for generations,
today they face an uncertain and rapidly changing future, caught between
a variety of ecological and developmental pressures as well as bureaucratic
restrictions and harassment by forest officials.

As the old man spoke about his concerns that the government might
block access to the bugiyals and force his family to settle in the plains,
several dozen buffaloes were grazing nearby. Despite myths of buffalo demons,
there is nothing dangerous or malevolent about these docile creatures. The
Gujjars, who are vegetarians, treat their livestock with care and compassion.
Milk is their only source of livelihood. Michael Benanav, a photographer
and journalist, who has followed the Gujjar migration and wrote a book
about them, *Himalaya Bound*, tells the moving story of a young buffalo that
broke its leg and was carried over the Darwa Pass by four herdsmen in an
effort to save its life. Having spent months in their company, Benanav is
convinced that the Gujjars do not pose a serious threat to the Himalayan
environment. 'Put simply, if the idea is to encourage economic growth
without harming the planet,' he writes, 'it's looking more and more as

though traditional and indigenous herding communities are already part of the solution.'

The forests that extend from Dayara Bugiyal westward across the watershed of the Assi Ganga are some of the wildest and least disturbed regions in Uttarakhand. These deep, unsettled valleys contain a diverse population of wildlife including musk deer and bears, as well as a significant number of sambar deer, which are rare at this altitude. Their presence, as potential prey, means that even tigers may venture up to these heights. Dodital, a small lake at 3,085 metres, tucked into a hollow between two ridges, has become an increasingly popular destination for trekkers though it suffers from poorly planned development as an 'eco-tourism' campsite. Fortunately, because of the steep terrain, few people wander off the main path. The entire Assi Ganga watershed urgently needs to be preserved and protected. Because these forests aren't part of a national park, with prescribed regulations, this offers a unique opportunity for testing new approaches to conservation, involving local and migrant communities.

Making our way down into the valley we cross several ravines and gullies. Assi Ganga means 'eighty Gangas' and this river, which ultimately flows into the Bhagirathi above Uttarkashi, has multiple tributaries streaming in from all sides. A series of flash floods over the past few years have gouged out large sections of the main valley while forest fires have devastated virgin stands of fir trees that tower above the cliffs and grass-covered slopes below Dodital. The further we descend, the thicker the jungle becomes, a mixed growth of deciduous species, mostly oaks, and a variety of conifers, including Himalayan yews, which have all but disappeared in other parts of Uttarakhand. While no true wilderness areas remain in the Central Himalaya, this valley comes as close to being a relict of primeval forests that took root in these mountains 7–8,000 years ago, when the Pleistocene glaciers retreated.

Our path is more of a game trail than a man-made passage and I can see the hoofprints of sambar and other spoor as we descend. It seems no human beings have gone this way for at least a year, possibly longer. We wade through ferns and brambles. Several trees have fallen and block our route but, eventually, I can hear the sound of a running stream as shadows close in around us. The sky is a ragged pennant of blue, high overhead. At this time of year, direct sunlight only penetrates the inner recesses of the Assi Ganga for an hour or less each day. The extended twilight has a dull green aura, as if the dense foliage emits a faint glow.

By the time we reach the valley, it is too late to go on and none of

us is sure where to cross the stream, which flows swiftly between a jumble
of flood-polished boulders. We decide to set up camp on a natural terrace
overlooking the Assi Ganga though the ground is uneven and covered
with rocks. Despite having lost our way, there is no cause for concern.
This valley is not as narrow as the gorge we descended earlier and there is
likely to be some sort of exit through a labyrinth of trees across the river.

After pitching my tent, I set off to explore while there is still some
light. The rocky terrace extends along the lower end of the ridge that we
descended and falls away in series of broad ledges to the riverbed below.
As I scramble down onto a lower level, a flash of bright colours amidst
the weeds catches my eye—the scattered feathers of a monal pheasant,
iridescent blues and greens as well as a ruddy copper. The way these are
strewn about, it looks as if the monal was killed by an eagle but I soon
discover that the predator was not a bird. In a clutch of rocks and grass
nearby, lies the hoof of a goral with the shin bone attached, though it has
been snapped in two and the meat stripped away. The kill is recent and
has no smell. Further on, I find a second hoof and a scrap of skin.

Suddenly, this place, which seemed so deserted, takes on a different
character and atmosphere. The poacher, who killed the pheasant and goral,
must have been here only two or three days ago. He did not take the path
we descended but probably climbed up the valley from one of the villages
downstream. To my right, I notice a steep gully between a cleft in the
rocks, which are covered with creepers. Going closer, I can see the prints
of a goral in the loose dirt. Gradually, a picture of the hunt emerges. The
poacher knows this place well and he hid himself amongst the rocks on the
ledge, probably around this hour of dusk, waiting for his prey to descend
and drink from the river. In the shadowy half-light, I can imagine him
listening to the sounds of an animal coming down out of the forest. He
holds an old muzzle-loader in his hands, the single steel barrel blemished
with rust, its hammer cocked and the well-worn stock resting against his
side. As the goral makes its way down the gully, he raises the gun and
waits until it comes into view, at a range of 20 metres. When he fires, the
explosion reverberates within the valley.

After gutting and skinning the goral, the hunter must have spent the
night here, on this ledge. The pale ash of his campfire nestles between
two rocks but there is no other evidence of a human presence, aside from
the feathers, skin and bones left behind. The poacher has disappeared into
the forest and the echo of his gunshot has been swallowed up by the
constant murmur of the stream. Dropping down onto the sand, I come

upon a sambar's three-pronged antler, as long as my forearm. These animal remnants endow this place with a sense of mystery, as if they were ancestral totems or fetish objects gleaned from the forest. Holding the monal's feather between my fingers, I twirl it about, watching the colours change from metallic blue to emerald green. Even in death the pheasant's plumage has an animated brightness.

Later in the night, once the darkness is complete, I sit by myself and listen to the droning whisper of the Assi Ganga. Though I have no idea what path will lead us out of this valley tomorrow, the forest that surrounds me is reassuring and I feel both solitude and solace in this hidden place. Three thousand years ago an anonymous poet experienced a similar moment and composed verses in praise of a forgotten goddess we no longer worship. One of the ancient hymns compiled in the Rig Veda is addressed to a forest deity, possibly the protector of naturalists.

Aranyani...
  Aranyani...

> Timorous spirit of the forest, elusive goddess
> who vanishes amidst the leaves. You do not ask: Where is
> the nearest village?
> Lost in the wilderness, I hear a chichika bird echoing the
> crickets,
> the alarm cries of animals. Could it be a hunter? Do I see
> a hut?
> At twilight your presence fills the forest. I listen in vain
> for cow bells.
> Insects creak like the unoiled wheels on a cart laden with
> firewood.
> Afraid of the shadows, I hear imaginary voices, graziers
> calling,
> the sound of an axe. Silence. I am alone in the forest at
> night.
> Aranyani, gentle spirit who threatens no one. Unlike the
> tiger you
> feed on fruit. You do not lie in ambush like the bandit.
> Mother of wild creatures, your untilled forests are full of
> food,
> fragrant incense and sweet herbs—Aranyani, accept my
> prayers,
> sheltering goddess of the trees.

ACKNOWLEDGEMENTS

I am indebted to many people who have helped me along the way, as I travelled to various parts of the Himalaya and researched the natural history and lore of these mountains. Special thanks, alphabetically, to: Bill Aitken, Chandraprabha Aitwal, Andrew Alter, Joseph Alter, Didar Ali, Izhar Ali, Deborah Baker, Prerna Bindra, Raanu Bisht, Greg Chen, Karma Choden, Viveck Crishna, Tsering Dekey, Loveraj Singh Dharmshaktu, Chitaranjan Datt, Bob Fleming Jr., Tandin Gyeltshen, A. J. T. Johnsingh, Harish Kapadia, Dorjee Khandu, Lalitha Krishnan, Krishnan Kutty, Justin Lepcha, Dorjee Lhatoo, Bernadette McDonald, Viraf Mehta, Renu Oberoi, Maharaj Pandit, Bengia Mirnal, Shekhar Pathak, Suman Panwar, Virendra Panwar, Sudhir Prakash, Surendra Pundeer, Nandini Purandare, Datta Ram Purohit, Anantha Rai, Micah Rai, Govind Ram, M. K. Ranjitsinh, Steve Rasmussen, Gopal Rawat, Tsewang Rigzen, Tobit Roche, Ganesh Saili, George Schaller, Akshay Shah, Dawa Sherpa, Chuldim Dorjee Sherpa, Lakhpa Sherpa, Mingma Tshering Sherpa, Pertemba Sherpa, Ajeet Singh, Brighu Singh, Digambar 'Titu' Singh, Peter Smetacek, Rabi Thapa, Sejal Worah. Many thanks too to my publisher and editor at Aleph: David Davidar and Aienla Ozukum. And to my family: Ameeta, Jayant, Kristen and Shibani.

A version of the chapter 'A Scholar of Stones' appeared in the *Himalayan Journal*, Vol. 73, 2018.

My rendition of the hymn to Aranyani, at the end of the book, is based on several earlier versions, particularly Ralph T. H. Griffith's translation of the *Rig Veda* and Wendy Doniger's 'Lost in the Forest'.

SELECT BIBLIOGRAPHY

Aitken, William McKay, 'An Inquiry into the Real Name of Mount Everest', *Himalayan Journal,* Vol. 59.

———, *The Nanda Devi Affair,* Delhi: Penguin Books, 1994.

Aitwal, Chandraprabha, *Mountains Calling,* Dehradun: Saraswati Press, 2012.

Albinia, Alice, *Empires of the Indus,* New York: Norton, 2008.

Ali, Salim, *The Fall of a Sparrow,* Delhi: Oxford University Press, 1985.

———, *Field Guide to the Birds of the Eastern Himalaya,* Mumbai: Oxford University Press, 1977.

———, 'The Himalaya in Indian Ornithology', *A Bird's Eye View,* edited by Tara Gandhi, Delhi: Permanent Black, 1981, pp. 156–76.

Alter, Andrew, *Dancing with Devtas: Drums, Power and Possession in the Music of Garhwal,* London: Ashgate Publishing, 2008.

———, *Mountainous Sound Spaces: Listening to History and Music in the Uttarakhand Himalayas,* Delhi: Foundation (Cambridge), 2014.

Alter, Joseph, *Knowing Dil Das: Stories of a Himalayan Hunter,* Philadelphia: University of Pennsylvania Press, 2000.

Alter, Martha Payne, *Letters from India to America 1916-1951,* Ellen and Bob Alter, eds., Dehradun: Vikalp Printers, 2006.

Alter, Robert, *Early Memories,* an unpublished memoir, 2010.

Alter, Stephen, *Becoming a Mountain,* New Delhi: Aleph Book Company 2014.

———, *Sacred Waters.* Delhi: Penguin Books, 2001.

Art Sacre du Tibet. Collection Alain Bordier, Suilly-la-Tour: Editions Findakly, 2013.

Atkinson, Edwin T., *The Himalayan Gazetteer,* Allahabad, 1886.

Auden, J. B., 'Traverses in Nepal', *Himalayan Journal,* Vol. 7, 1935.

———, 'An Excursion to Gangotri', *Himalayan Journal.* Vol. 8, 1936.

———, 'A Season's Work in the Central Himalaya', *Himalayan Journal,* Vol. 12, 1940.

Auden, W. H., 'Autumn Song', *Look Stranger,* London: Faber & Faber, 1935.

Auden, Rita, 'Obituary for Dr. J. B. Auden', *Himalayan Journal*, Vol. 47, 1991.

Aurobindo, *The Secret of the Veda, The Complete Works of Sri Aurobindo*, Vol. 15, Pondicherry: Sri Aurobindo Trust, 1998.

Baker, Deborah, 'From the Summits of Empire', *The Caravan*, January 2013. pp. 43–51.

———, *The Last Englishmen: Love, War and the End of Empire*, New Delhi: Penguin Random House India, 2018.

Balsavar, Deepa and Nandini Purandare, 'The Story of Wangdi Norbu', *Indian Quarterly*, Vol. 5, No. 3, April–June 2017, pp. 68–74.

Barmahalia, Faguna, 'Revivalism of Bathouism Among the Bodos', *IOSR Journal of Humanities and Social Science* (IOSRJHSS), ISSN: 2279-0845, Vol. 1, No. 5 (Sep–Oct 2012), pp. 42–45, available at <www. iosrjournals.org>.

Bawa, Kamal and Sandesh Kadur, *Himalaya: Mountains of Life*, Bangalore: Ashoka Trust for Research in Education and the Environment, 2013.

Benanav, Michael, *Himalaya Bound: An American's Journey with Nomads in North India*, New Delhi: HarperCollins Publishers, 2015.

Bhatt, Uma and Shekhar Pathak, *Asia ke Peeth Par: Pandit Nain Singh Rawat*, Nainital: Pahar Publications, 2006.

Bindra, Prerna, *The Vanishing*, New Delhi: Viking, 2017.

———, *The King and I: Travels in* Tigerland, New Delhi: Rupa Publications, 2005.

Bista, Dor Bahadur, 'Encounter with the Raute: The Last Hunting Nomads of Nepal', available at <http://www.dspace.cam.ac.uk/handle/1810/227426>.

Buhl, Hermann, *Nanga Parbat Pilgrimage: The Lonely Challenge*, Hugh Merrick, trans., Seattle: Mountaineers, 2001 (first English edition, 1956).

Champion, F. W., *The Jungle In Sunlight and Shadow*, London: Chatto & Windus, 1933.

———, *With a Camera in Tiger-Land*, London: Chatto & Windus, 1927.

Chatak, Govind, *The Folk Tales of Uttarakhand*, Arun Pant, trans., Delhi: Jaykay Enterprises. 2015.

Child, Greg, 'Es Ist Mein Bruder!', *Outside*, 1 January 2006.

Chopra, Jaskiran, 'Watery Grave for Tehri's Historic Ghantaghar', *Times of India*, 20 March 2006.

Coffey, Maria, *Where the Mountain Casts its Shadow*, New York: St Martin's Griffin, 2003.

Collie, Norman, *From the Himalaya to Skye*, Findon, Aberdeenshire: Rockbuy Ltd. 2003. (Original title *Climbing on the Himalaya and Other Mountain Ranges* published in 1902 by David Douglas, Edinburgh.)

Cooney, Rosie et al., 'The Baby and the Bathwater: Trophy Hunting, Conservation and Rural Livelihoods', available at <https://www.iucn.org/sites/dev/files/trophy_ hunting_conservation_and_rural_livelihoods. pdf>.

Corbett, Jim, *Man-eaters of Kumaon*, New Delhi: Aleph Book Company, 2017 (first edition, Oxford University Press, 1944).

Curran, Jim, *K2: Tragedy and Triumph*, Boston: Houghton Mifflin, 1987.

Dabral, Mangalesh, 'A Fire Still Burns' in *Submerged Tehri: The Last Poems*, Hemchandra Saklani, ed., Dehradun: Samaya Sakshaya, 2017, p. 25.

Dang, Rupin, *Flowers of the Western Himalayas*, Delhi: Wilderness Films India, 1998.

Darwin, Charles, *Insectivorous Plants*, London: John Murray, 1875.

———, *The Power of Movement in Plants*, London: John Murray, 1880.

Davis, Wade, *Into the Silence*, London: Vintage Books, 2012.

Decter, Jacqueline, *Nicholas Roerich: The Life and Art of a Russian Master*, Rochester: Park

Street Press, 1989.

Den Besten, Jan Willem, 'Migration of Steppe Eagles *Aquila nipalensis* and Other Raptors along the Himalaya past Dharamsala, India, in autumn 2001 and spring 2002', *Forktail* 20, 2004, pp. 9–13.

'Deosai National Park Gilgit-Baltistan' pamphlet published by Parks & Wildlife Department, Gilgit, Baltistan, ND.

Dhendup, Tashi, 'High Hopes for Mountain Tigers of Bhutan', available at <https: www. iucn. org/news/species/201707/high-hopes-mountain-tigers-bhutan>.

Diemberger, Kurt, *The Diemberger Omnibus*, London: Baton Wicks, 1999.

Dowman, Keith, *The Divine Madman: The Sublime Life and Songs of Drukpa Kunley*, Varanasi: Pilgrim's Publishing, 2000.

Dowson, John, *A Classical Dictionary of Hindu Mythology and Religion, Geography, History and Literature*, London: Routledge & Kegan Paul, 1950.

Dyrenfurth, Gunter, *Der Damon Des Himalaya*, Tobis Film, 1935.

Ekvall, Robert, *Fields on the Hoof: Nexus of Tibetan Nomadic Pastoralism*, New York: Holt, Rinehart & Winston, 1968.

Eliot, T. S., *The Wasteland,* London: Faber & Faber, 2015 (first edition, 1922).

Elwin, Verrier, *Myths of the North-East Frontier of India*, Delhi: Munshiram Manoharlal, 1999 (first edition, 1958).

Fleming, Robert L. Sr., R. L. Fleming Jr., and Lain Singh Bangdel, *Birds of Nepal*, New Delhi: Adarsh, 2000.

Fortier, Jana, *Kings of the Forest: The Cultural Resilience of Himalayan Hunter-Gatherers*, Honolulu: University of Hawaii Press, 2009.

French, Patrick, *Younghusband,* London: Penguin, 2011.

Gadgil, Madhav and Ramachandra Guha, *This Fissured Land: An Ecological History of India*, Delhi: Oxford University Press, 1992.

Gee, E. P., *The Wild Life of* India, London: Fontana, 1969.

Geiger, John. *The Third Man Factor*, New York: Weinstein, 2009.

Gorer, Geoffrey, *Himalayan Village: An Account of the Lepchas of Sikkim*, Varanasi: Pilgrim's Publishing, 2005 (first edition, 1938).

Gould, Stephen J., *Ever Since Darwin*, New York: Norton, 1977.

Gould, John, *Century of Birds from the Himalayan Mountains*, London, 1831 available at <https://archive. org/stream/centurybirdsfro00Goul#page/n5/mode/2up>.

Griffith, Ralph T. H., *The Hymns of the Rg Veda*, Delhi: Motilal Banarsidass, 1999 (first edition, 1896).

Grimmett, Richard, Carol Inskipp and Tom Inskipp, *Oxford Pocket Guide to the Birds of the Indian Subcontinent*, Delhi: Oxford University Press, 1999.

———, *Birds of Nepal*, Helm Field Guides, New Delhi: Bloomsbury, 2015.

Guha, Ramachandra, *Savaging the Civilized*, New Delhi: Penguin, 2016.

Hagen, Toni photographs 'Adapting in the shadow of Annapurna: A Climate Tipping Point', available at <https://www.researchgate.net/figure/227620514_fig4_Figure-2-Retreat-of-Gangapurna-glacier-Manang-Valley-Nepal-Left-1850>.

Harrer, Heinrich, *Seven Years in Tibet*, Richard Graves, trans., London: Harper Perennial, 2005 (first edition, 1953).

Hilton, James, *Lost Horizon*, New York: Pocket Books, 1933.

Himalayan Journal, Special Volume, February 2017.

Holt, Lee Wallace, *Mountains, Mountaineering and Modernity: A Cultural History of German and Austrian Mountaineering, 1900-1945*, Dissertation, Doctor of Philosophy, University of Texas at Austin, May 2008.

Hooker, Joseph Dalton, *Himalayan Journals*, Dehradun: Natraj, 1999 (first edition 1854).

————, *The Rhododendrons of Sikkim-Himalaya*, London: Reeve, Benham and Reeve, 1849, Peter H. Raven Library, Missouri Botanical Garden/ Biodiversity Heritage Library, available at <http://www.biodiversitylibrary.org/item/42878#page/32/mode/1up>.

Jayal, N. D., 'Indian Air Force Flights Over Everest, 1953', *Himalayan Journal*, Vol. 18, 1954.

Jha, Vanya and Ajeya Jha, *Ethno-Ornithology of Lepchas of Sikkim*, New Delhi: Readworthy, 2012.

Johnson, Michael and Simon Harley, *Orogenesis: The Making of Mountains*, Cambridge: Cambridge University Press, 2016.

Kala, D. C., *Frederick Wilson: "Hulson Sahib" of Garhwal*, Delhi: Ravi Dayal, 2006.

Kalidasa, *Kumarasambhavam*, Hank Heifetz, trans., New York: Penguin Books, 2015.

Kapadia, Harish, *Exploring the Highlands of Himalaya*, Delhi: Indus, 2006.

————, and Soli Mehta, *Exploring the Hidden Himalaya*, London: Hodder & Stoughton, 1990.

————, *Into the Untravelled Himalaya*, Delhi: Indus, 2008.

————, *Legendary Maps from the Himalayan Club*, Delhi: Roli Books, 2018.

Keay, John, *The Great Arc*, London: HarperCollins, 2000.

————, *The Gilgit Game*, London: John Murray, 1979.

Khatri, Prabodh Chander, 'Winter Migration of Steppe Eagles (*Aquila nipalensis*) at Jorbeer, Bikaner, *International Journal of Innovative Research and Review* ISSN: 2347—4424, Vol. 3, No. 1, January–March 2015, pp. 1–5, available at <http://www. cibtech. org/jirr. htm>.

Koehler, Jeff, *Darjeeling: A History of the World's Greatest Tea*, New Delhi: Bloomsbury, 2015.

Lopez, Barry, *Arctic Dreams*, New York: Scribner, 1986.

Macfarlane, Robert, *Mountains of the Mind*, London: Granta, 2003.

Mayhew, Bradley and Lindsay Brown, *Bhutan*, London: Lonely Planet, 2017.

Mason, Kenneth, *Abode of Snow*, London: Diadem Books, 1987.

Martyn, John, 'What George Everest Did', *Himalayan Journal*, Vol. 33, 1975.

Mathiessen, Peter, *The Snow Leopard*, New York: Viking, 1978.

McCrindle, J. W., *Ancient India as Described by Megasthenes and Arrian*, Calcutta: Chuckervertty, Chatterjee & Co. 1960.

McDonald, Bernadette, *Alpine Warriors*, Victoria: Rocky Mountain Books, 2015.

————, *Freedom Climbers*, Victoria: Rocky Mountain Books, 2011.

————, *Tomaž Humar*, London: Hutchinson, 2008.

McPhee, John, *Annals of the Former World*, New York: Farrar, Straus and Giroux, 1981.

Mehta, Viraf, 'Rock of Ages', *Indian Quarterly*, Vol. 5 Issue 3, April–June 2017, pp. 110-15.

Menon, Vivek, *Indian Animals: A Field Guide*, New Delhi: Hachette, 2014.

Messner, Reinhold, *The Naked Mountain*, Tim Carruthers, trans., Seattle: Mountaineers Books, 2003.

Miehe, Georg and Colin Pendry, *Nepal: An Introduction to the Natural History, Ecology and Human Environment of the Himalaya*, Edinburgh: Royal Botanic Gardens, 2015.

Montgomerie, Capt. T. J., 'Report of a Route Survey made by Pundit "_____" from Nepal to Lhasa, and thence through the Upper Valley of the Brahmaputra to its Source.' *Journal of the Royal Geographical Society*, London, Vol. 38. 1868, pp. 129–219.

————, 'Report of the Trans-Himalayan Explorations during 1867', *Journal of the Royal Geographical Society*, London, Vol. 39, 1869, pp. 146–87.

Moore, Thomas, *Lalla Rookh,* 1817, available at <http://www.columbia.edu/itc/mealac/pritchett/00generallinks/lallarookh/>.

Moorcroft, William, *Travels in the Himalayan Provinces of Hindustan and the Panjab*, Karachi: Oxford, 1979 (first edition published by John Murray, London, 1841).

Moulton, Sam and Grayson Schaffer, 'Why did so Many People Die in Nepal?' *Outside Online*, 16 October 2014, available at <https://www.outsideonline.com/1926921/why-did-so-many-people-die-nepal>.

Muhammad, Ghulam, 'Festivals and Folklore of Gilgit', Calcutta: *Journal of the Asiatic Society of Bengal*, Vol. 1, No. 7, 1905, pp. 93–127.

Naoroji, Rishad, *Birds of Prey of the Indian Subcontinent*, London: Christopher Helm, 2006.

Norgay, Tenzing with James Ramsey Ullman, *Tiger of the Snows*, New York: Putnam, 1955.

Norton, Hugh, *Norton of Everest*, Sheffield: Vertebrate, 2017.

Oakley, E. S. and Tara Dutt Gairola, *Himalayan Folklore: Kumaon and West Nepal*, Kathmandu: Bibliotheca Himalayica, 1935.

O' Flaherty, Wendy Doniger, *The Rig Veda*, London: Penguin Books, 1981.

Oosthoek, K. Jan, 'The Colonial Origins of Scientific Forestry in Britian', *Environmental History Resources*, 25 June 2007, available at <https://www. eh-resources. org/colonial-origins-scientific-forestry/>.

Oppitz, Michael, 'The Wild Boar and the Plough: Origin Stories of the Northern Magar', *Kailas* 10 (3-4) pp. 187-226.

Ortner, Sherry, *Life and Death on Mt. Everest: Sherpas and Himalayan Mountaineering*, Princeton: Princeton University Press, 1999.

Pandit, Maharaj, *Life in the Himalaya*, Cambridge: Harvard University Press, 2017.

Perrin, Jim, *Shipton & Tilman: The Great Decade of Himalayan Exploration*, London: Arrow, 2014.

Phuntsho, Karma, *The History of Bhutan*, Delhi: Random House India, 2013.

Pollock, John, *Way to Glory: The Life of Havelock of Lucknow*, London: John Murray, 1957.

Polunin, Oleg and Adam Stainton, *Flowers of the Himalaya*, Delhi: Oxford University Press, 2006.

Pranavananda, Swami, *Kailas-Manasarovar*, New Delhi: Pranavananda, 1983.

Ranjitsinh, M. K., *A Life with Wildlife*, New Delhi: HarperCollins Publishers, 2017.

Rawat, G. S., *Alpine Meadows of Uttaranchal*, Dehradun: Bishen Singh Mahendra Pal Singh, 2005.

Rawat, Indra Singh, *Indian Explorers of the 19th Century*, Delhi: Publications Division, Ministry of Information and Broadcasting, 2002.

Reich, David, *Who We Are And How We Got Here*, New York: Oxford University Press, 2018.

Roehrich, Nicholas, *Light of Asia*, New York: Nicholas Roehrich Museum, 2018 (first edition, 1928).

Roch, Andre et al., 'The Swiss Garhwal Expedition of 1947', *Himalayan Journal*, 1949.

Saklani, Hemchandra, *Submerged Tehri: The Last Poems*, Dehradun: Samaya Sakshya, 2017.

Santayana, George, 'The Philosophy of Travel', *The Birth of Reason and Other Essays*, New York: Columbia University Press, 1968.

Sax, William, *Dancing the Self: Personhood and Performance in the Pandav Lila*, Oxford: Oxford University Press, 2002.

Schaller, *George, Mountain Monarchs*, Chicago: University of Chicago Press, 1977.

———, *Stones of Silence*, Chicago: University of Chicago Press, 1979.

———, *Tibet Wild*, Washington: Island Press, 2012.

Sehgal, K. L., 'Coldwater Fish and Fisheries in the Indian Himalayas Rivers and Streams', available at <http://www.fao.org/docrep/003/x2614e/x2614e04.htm>.

Sen, Bireswar, 'The Essentials of Art', available at <https://www.bireswarsenart.com/artists-writings/essentials-of-art-bireswar-sen>.

Seth, Vikram, *From Heaven Lake*, New Delhi: Penguin Books, 1983.

Sherpa adventure gear website, available at <www.sherpaadventuregear.com>.

Smetacek, Peter, *A Naturalist's Guide to the Butterflies of India*. Delhi: Prakash, 2017.

———, *Butterflies on the Roof of the World*, New Delhi: Aleph Book Company, 2012.

Smythe, Frank S, *Kamet Conquered*, London: Gollancz, 1932.

———, *The Kanchenjunga Adventure* anthologized in *The Six Alpine/Himalayan Climbing Books*, Seattle: Mountaineers Books, 2000 (first edition, 1930).

———, *The Valley of Flowers*, Dehradun: Natraj, ND, (first edition, 1938).

Smythe, Tony, *My Father, Frank*, Sheffield: Baton Wicks, 2013.

Snelling, John, *The Sacred Mountain: The Complete Guide to Tibet's Mount Kailas*, Delhi: Motilal Banarsidass, 2006.

Swenson, Steve, *Karakoram*, Seattle: Mountaineers Books, 2017.

Tamsang, Lyangsong, *Lepcha Folklore and Folk Songs*, Delhi: Sahitya Akademi, 2008.

Taylor, Daniel, *Yeti: The Ecology of a Mystery*, Delhi: Oxford University Press, 2017.

Thapa, Manjushree, *A Boy From Siklis: The Life and Times of Chandra Gurung*, New Delhi: Penguin Books, 2009.

———, *Forget Kathmandu: An Elegy for Democracy*. New Delhi: Aleph Book Company, 2013.

Thapar, Valmik, *Tiger Fire: 500 Years of the Tiger in India*, New Delhi: Aleph Book Company, 2013.

Tharkay, Ang with Basil P. Norton, *Sherpa: The Memoir of Ang Tharkay,* Corinne Mckay, trans., Seattle: Mountaineers Books, 2016 (first edition titled *Memoires d'un Sherpa*. Paris: Amiot-Dumont, 1954).

Thomas, Henry Sullivan, *The Rod in India*, London: W. Thacker & Co., 1897.

Tilman, H. W., 'Himalayan Apery', *Alpine Journal*, Vol. 60, No. 291, pp. 296–301.

Trotter, Capt. H., 'Account of the Pundit's Journey in Great Tibet from Leh in Ladakh to Lhasa, and of his Return to India via Assam', *Journal of the Royal Geographical Society*, London, Vol. 47, 1877, pp. 86–136.

Wadia, D. N., *The Geology of India*, London: Macmillan, 1937.

———, 'The Trend-Line of the Himalaya: North-west and South-east Limits', *Himalayan Journal*. Vol. 08, 1936.

Wangchuck, Ashi Dorji Wangmo, *Treasures of the Thunder Dragon: A Portrait of Bhutan*, New Delhi: Viking, 2012.

Ward, Frank Kingdon, *The Land of the Blue Poppies,* Tom Christopher, ed., New York: The Modern Library, 2003.

Watt, Jeff, 'An Introduction to Bon Art', *Bon: The Magic Word*, Samten G. Karmay and Jeff Watt, eds., New York: Rubin Museum of Art, 2007, pp. 35–36.

Wilson, Edward O., *Biophilia*, Cambridge: Harvard University Press, 1984.

———, *Half-Earth*, New York: Norton, 2016.

Wilson, W., *A Summer Ramble in the Himalaya*, London: Hurst and Blackett, 1860.

Wohlleben, Peter, *The Hidden Life of Trees*, New Delhi: Penguin Books, 2015.

'WWF Policy and Considerations on Trophy Hunting', available at <https://d2ouvy59p0dg6k.cloudfront.net/downloads/wwf_policy_and_considerations_re_trophy_hunting_1.pdf>.

Sources for Black & White Images

Blanford, W. T., *The Fauna of British India*, Calcutta: Thacker, Spink & Co., 1888.

Collett, H. *Flora Simlensis*, Miss M. Smith, illustr., Calcutta: Thacker, Spink & Co., 1921.

Maxwell-Lefroy, H., *Indian Insect Life*, Calcutta: Thacker, Spink & Co., 1909.

Sterndale, Robert A., *Natural History of the Mammals of India and Ceylon*, London: W. Thacker & Co., 1884.

Whistler, H., *Popular Handbook of Indian Birds*, London: Gurney and Jackson, 1935.

INDEX